PRENTICE HALL LITERATURE

COPPER

BRONZE

SILVER

GOLD

PLATINUM

THE AMERICAN EXPERIENCE

THE BRITISH TRADITION

WORLD MASTERPIECES

PRENTICE HALL

LITERATURE
COPPER

PARAMOUNT EDITION

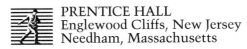

RED GATE, 1983
Elena Borstein
Collection of Glenn C. Janss

PRENTICE HALL
Englewood Cliffs, New Jersey
Needham, Massachusetts

ISBN 0-13-722398-6

4 5 6 7 8 9 10   97 96 95

Art credits begin on page 801.

PRENTICE HALL
A Division of Simon & Schuster
Englewood Cliffs, New Jersey 07632

STAFF CREDITS FOR PRENTICE HALL LITERATURE

Publisher: Eileen Thompson

Editorial: Ellen Bowler, Douglas McCollum, Philip Fried, Kelly Ackley, Eric Hausmann, Lauren Weidenman, Megan Mahoney

Multicultural/ESL: Marina Liapunov, Barbara T. Stone

Marketing: Mollie Ledwith, Belinda Loh

National Language Arts Consultants: Ellen Lees Backstrom, Ed.D., Craig A. McGhee, Karen Massey Riley, Vennisa Travers, Gail Witt

Permissions: Doris Robinson

Design: Susan Walrath, Carmela Pereira, Leslie Osher, AnnMarie Roselli

Visual Research: Libby Forsyth, Emily Rose, Martha Conway

Production: Suse Bell, Joan McCulley, Elizabeth Torjussen, Amy E. Fleming, Lynn Contrucci, Garret Schenck, Lorraine Moffa

Publishing Technology: Andrew Black, Deborah J. Jones, Monduane Harris, Cleasta Wilburn, Greg Myers

Pre-Press Production: Laura Sanderson, Natalia Bilash, Denise Herckenrath

Print and Bind: Rhett Conklin, Gertrude Szyferblatt

ACKNOWLEDGMENTS

Grateful acknowledgment is made to the following for permission to reprint copyrighted material:

Atheneum Publishers, an imprint of Macmillan Publishing Company

"If I Were in Charge of the World" from *If I Were in Charge of the World and Other Worries* by Judith Viorst. Copyright © 1981 by Judith Viorst. Reprinted by permission.

The Belknap Press of Harvard University Press and the Trustees of Amherst College
"How soft a Caterpillar steps–" by Emily Dickinson from *The Poems of Emily Dickinson,* Thomas H. Johnson, Editor, Cambridge, Massachusetts: The Belknap Press of Harvard University Press. Copyright 1951, © 1955, 1979, 1983 by the President and Fellows of Harvard College. Reprinted by permission.

(Continued on page 798.)

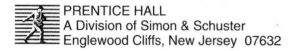

CONTENTS

SHORT STORIES

DRAMA

NONFICTION

READING ARTICLES FROM THE MEDIA

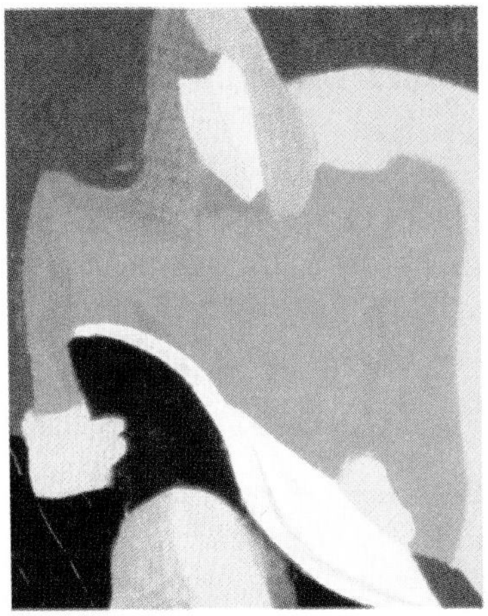

POETRY

THE ORAL TRADITION

THE NOVEL

ADDITIONAL FEATURES

BAREBACK RIDERS
W. H. Brown
National Gallery, Washington, D.C.

SHORT STORIES

Everyone loves a story. Stories invite us into another world, where we meet new people, places, events, and ideas. Stories can be about anybody or anything—young people who have exciting adventures or who face problems and learn to deal with them, or creatures and places that are completely imaginary. Whatever they are about, they entertain us, and at the same time, they help us to understand how people live their lives.

The short story, as a form of literature, is fiction. That means it is made up. The writer invents the plot, characters, setting, and theme. The plot is what happens—the events in the story. The characters are the people—or animals—who are involved. The setting is the time and place of the story. The theme is the underlying idea or insight into life that the story suggests.

As you read these stories, you will see how plot, character, and setting work together to develop a theme. You will meet and live briefly with interesting characters. And you will respond to them and their situations, just as if you knew them in real life.

HOW TO READ A SHORT STORY

A short story is fiction—a work of literature in which the characters and events are imagined by the author. When you read fiction, you can explore new worlds, share feelings and experiences of characters, and learn how people live in the world.

Reading short stories is an active process. When you read actively, you imagine what is happening in the story and you derive meaning from the picture you are seeing. You do this through the following active-reading strategies:

QUESTION What questions come to mind as you are reading? For example, why do characters act as they do? What causes events to happen? Why does the writer include certain information? Look for answers to your questions as you read on.

VISUALIZE Use details from the story to create a picture in your mind. As you read along, change your picture as the story unfolds and your understanding grows. Use your visualization to clarify whatever may not at first seem clear to you.

PREDICT What do you think will happen? Look for hints in the story that seem to lead to a certain outcome. As you read on, you will see if your predictions are correct.

CONNECT Bring your own experience and knowledge to the story. Make connections with what you know about similar situations or people in your own life.

Also, make connections between one event and another in the story. Try to summarize how all the pieces of the story fit together.

RESPOND Think about what the story means. What does it say to you? What feelings does it evoke in you as you read? What has the story added to your understanding of people and events?

Use these strategies as you read the stories in this unit. They will help you increase your enjoyment and understanding of literature.

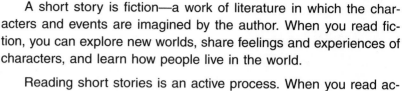

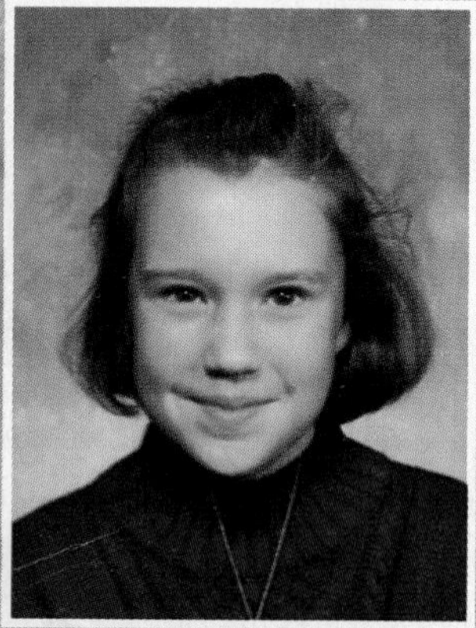

On pages 3–11 you can see an example of active reading by Elizabeth Thompson of The Edgar School in Metuchen, New Jersey. The notes in the side columns include Elizabeth's thoughts and comments on "Zlateh the Goat." Your own thoughts as you read may be different—each reader brings something different to a story and takes away something different.

MODEL

Zlateh the Goat

Isaac Bashevis Singer

"Aaron . . . knew that if they did not find shelter they would freeze to death."

Predict: *Since the name of the story is "Zlateh the Goat," then Zlateh, who is the goat, is the main character, and something will happen to it.*

At Hanukkah[1] time the road from the village to the town is usually covered with snow, but this year the winter had been a mild one. Hanukkah had almost come, yet little snow had fallen. The sun shone most of the time. The peasants complained that because of the dry weather there would be a poor harvest of winter grain. New grass sprouted, and the peasants sent their cattle out to pasture.

For Reuven the furrier it was a bad year, and after long hesitation he decided to sell Zlateh the goat. She was old and gave little milk. Feivel the town butcher had offered eight gulden[2] for her. Such a sum would buy Hanukkah candles, potatoes and oil for pancakes, gifts for the children, and other holiday necessaries for the house. Reuven told his oldest boy Aaron to take the goat to town.

Connect: *Guldens must be worth a lot of money to buy so much with 8 of them.*

Aaron understood what taking the goat to Feivel meant, but had to obey his father. Leah, his mother, wiped the tears from her eyes when she heard the news. Aaron's younger sisters, Anna and Miriam, cried loudly. Aaron put on his quilted jacket and a cap with earmuffs, bound a rope around Zlateh's neck, and took along two slices of bread with cheese to eat on the road. Aaron was supposed to deliver the goat by evening, spend the night at the butcher's, and return the next day with the money.

Question: *Does Aaron's family always cry when giving away these animals, or just for Zlateh?*

---

1. Hanukkah (khä′ n$\overline{\text{oo}}$ kä) *n.*: A Jewish festival celebrated for eight days in early winter. Hanukkah is also called the "festival of lights," and a candle is lit on each of the eight days.

2. gulden (g$\overline{\text{oo}}$l′ dən) *n.*: A unit of money.

"When Aaron brought her out on the road to town, she seemed somewhat astonished."

Illustration from ZLATEH THE GOAT
Maurice Sendak

Question: *Does Zlateh know what is happening?*

While the family said goodbye to the goat, and Aaron placed the rope around her neck, Zlateh stood as patiently and good-naturedly as ever. She licked Reuven's hand. She shook her small white beard. Zlateh trusted human beings. She knew that they always fed her and never did her any harm.

When Aaron brought her out on the road to town, she seemed somewhat astonished. She'd never been led in that direction before. She looked back at him questioningly, as if to say, "Where are you taking me?" But after a while she seemed to come to the conclusion that a goat shouldn't ask questions. Still, the road was different. They passed new fields, pastures, and huts with thatched roofs. Here and there a dog barked and came running after them, but Aaron chased it away with his stick.

The sun was shining when Aaron left the village. Suddenly the weather changed. A large black cloud with a bluish center appeared in the east and spread itself rapidly over the sky. A cold wind blew in with it. The crows flew low, croaking. At first it looked as if it would rain, but instead it began to hail as in summer. It was early in the day, but it became dark as dusk. After a while the hail turned to snow.

Predict: *This sudden change in weather may be the key to survival for Zlateh or the toll of death for both of them.*

In his twelve years Aaron had seen all kinds of weather, but he had never experienced a snow like this one. It was so dense it shut out the light of the day. In a short time their path was completely covered. The wind became as cold as ice. The road to town was narrow and winding. Aaron no longer knew where he was. He could not see through the snow. The cold soon penetrated his quilted jacket.

At first Zlateh didn't seem to mind the change in weather. She, too, was twelve years old and knew what winter meant. But when her legs sank deeper and deeper into the snow, she began to turn her head and look at Aaron in wonderment. Her mild eyes seemed to ask, "Why are we out in such a storm?" Aaron hoped that a peasant would come along with his cart, but no one passed by.

Question: *Why aren't Aaron's parents looking for them?*

The snow grew thicker, falling to the ground in large, whirling flakes. Beneath it Aaron's boots touched the softness of a plowed field. He realized that he was no longer on the road. He had gone astray. He could no longer figure out which was east or west, which way was the village, the town. The wind whistled, howled, whirled the snow about in eddies.[3] It looked as if white imps were playing tag on the fields. A white

---

3. eddies (ed′ ēz) *n.*: Currents of air moving in circular motions; little whirlwinds.

Question: *How are they going to survive?*

dust rose above the ground. Zlateh stopped. She could walk no longer. Stubbornly she anchored her cleft hooves in the earth and bleated as if pleading to be taken home. Icicles hung from her white beard, and her horns were glazed with frost.

Aaron did not want to admit the danger, but he knew just the same that if they did not find shelter they would freeze to

"Suddenly he made out the shape of a hill."

Illustration from ZLATEH THE GOAT
Maurice Sendak

death. This was no ordinary storm. It was a mighty blizzard. The snow had reached his knees. His hands were numb, and he could no longer feel his toes. He choked when he breathed. His nose felt like wood, and he rubbed it with snow. Zlateh's bleating began to sound like crying. Those humans in whom she had so much confidence had dragged her into a trap. Aaron began to pray to God for himself and for the innocent animal.

Visualize: *Aaron is beginning to feel guilty now.*

Suddenly he made out the shape of a hill. He wondered what it could be. Who had piled snow into such a huge heap? He moved toward it, dragging Zlateh after him. When he came near it, he realized that it was a large haystack which the snow had blanketed.

Question: *Is this going to be the shelter that takes Zlateh and Aaron in from the cold?*

Aaron realized immediately that they were saved. With great effort he dug his way through the snow. He was a village boy and knew what to do. When he reached the hay, he hollowed out a nest for himself and the goat. No matter how cold it may be outside, in the hay it is always warm. And hay was food for Zlateh. The moment she smelled it she became contented and began to eat. Outside, the snow continued to fall. It quickly covered the passageway Aaron had dug. But a boy and an animal need to breathe, and there was hardly any air in their hideout. Aaron bored a kind of a window through the hay and snow and carefully kept the passage clear.

Connect: *If the snow keeps coming down, then they aren't saved.*

Zlateh, having eaten her fill, sat down on her hind legs and seemed to have regained her confidence in man. Aaron ate his two slices of bread and cheese, but after the difficult journey he was still hungry. He looked at Zlateh and noticed her udders were full. He lay down next to her, placing himself so that when he milked her he could squirt the milk into his mouth. It was rich and sweet. Zlateh was not accustomed to being milked that way, but she did not resist. On the contrary, she seemed eager to reward Aaron for bringing her to a shelter whose very walls, floor, and ceiling were made of food.

Connect: *There is a special friendship growing between them.*

Through the window Aaron could catch a glimpse of the chaos outside. The wind carried before it whole drifts of snow. It was completely dark, and he did not know whether night had already come or whether it was the darkness of the storm. Thank God that in the hay it was not cold. The dried hay, grass, and field flowers exuded the warmth of the summer sun. Zlateh ate frequently; she nibbled from above, below, from the left and right. Her body gave forth an animal warmth, and Aaron cuddled up to her. He had always loved Zlateh, but now she was like a sister. He was alone, cut off from his family, and wanted to talk. He began to talk to Zlateh. "Zlateh, what do you think about what has happened to us?" he asked.

Visualize: *Right now Aaron is the only person that Zlateh has, and Zlateh is all that Aaron has.*

"Maaaa," Zlateh answered.

"If we hadn't found this stack of hay, we would both be frozen stiff by now," Aaron said.

"Maaaa," was the goat's reply.

"If the snow keeps on falling like this, we may have to stay here for days," Aaron explained.

"Maaaa," Zlateh bleated.

"What does 'maaaa' mean?" Aaron asked. "You'd better speak up clearly."

"Maaaa, maaaa," Zlateh tried.

"Well, let it be 'maaaa' then," Aaron said patiently. "You can't speak, but I know you understand. I need you and you need me. Isn't that right?"

"Maaaa."

Aaron became sleepy. He made a pillow out of some hay, leaned his head on it, and dozed off. Zlateh, too, fell asleep.

Visualize: *The snow must have gone on for a long time because Aaron's arm couldn't fit through.*

When Aaron opened his eyes, he didn't know whether it was morning or night. The snow had blocked up his window. He tried to clear it, but when he had bored through to the length of his arm, he still hadn't reached the outside. Luckily he had his stick with him and was able to break through to the open air. It was still dark outside. The snow continued to fall and the wind wailed, first with one voice and then with many. Sometimes it had the sound of devilish laughter. Zlateh, too, awoke, and when Aaron greeted her, she answered, "Maaa." Yes, Zlateh's language consisted of only one word, but it meant many things. Now she was saying, "We must accept all that God gives us—heat, cold, hunger, satisfaction, light, and darkness."

Aaron had awakened hungry. He had eaten up his food, but Zlateh had plenty of milk.

"For three days Aaron and Zlateh stayed in the haystack."

Illustration from ZLATEH THE GOAT
Maurice Sendak

For three days Aaron and Zlateh stayed in the haystack. Aaron had always loved Zlateh, but in these three days he loved her more and more. She fed him with her milk and

Connect: *Since both Aaron and Zlateh are snow children, they may have a special bond.*

Question: *What will Aaron's parents say?*

helped him keep warm. She comforted him with her patience. He told her many stories, and she always cocked her ears and listened. When he patted her, she licked his hand and his face. Then she said, "Maaaa," and he knew it meant, I love you, too.

The snow fell for three days, though after the first day it was not as thick and the wind quieted down. Sometimes Aaron felt that there could never have been a summer, that the snow had always fallen, ever since he could remember. He, Aaron, never had a father or mother or sisters. He was a snow child, born of the snow, and so was Zlateh. It was so quiet in the hay that his ears rang in the stillness. Aaron and Zlateh slept all night and a good part of the day. As for Aaron's dreams, they were all about warm weather. He dreamed of green fields, trees covered with blossoms, clear brooks, and singing birds. By the third night the snow had stopped, but Aaron did not dare to find his way home in the darkness. The sky became clear and the moon shone, casting silvery nets on the snow. Aaron dug his way out and looked at the world. It was all white, quiet, dreaming dreams of heavenly splendor. The stars were large and close. The moon swam in the sky as in a sea.

On the morning of the fourth day Aaron heard the ringing of sleigh bells. The haystack was not far from the road. The peasant who drove the sleigh pointed out the way to him—not to the town and Feivel the butcher, but home to the village. Aaron had decided in the haystack that he would never part with Zlateh.

Aaron's family and their neighbors had searched for the boy and the goat but had found no trace of them during the storm. They feared they were lost. Aaron's mother and sisters cried for him; his father remained silent and gloomy. Suddenly one of the neighbors came running to their house with the news that Aaron and Zlateh were coming up the road.

There was great joy in the family. Aaron told them how he had found the stack of hay and how Zlateh had fed him with her milk. Aaron's sisters kissed and hugged Zlateh and gave her a special treat of chopped carrots and potato peels, which Zlateh gobbled up hungrily.

Nobody ever again thought of selling Zlateh, and now that the cold weather had finally set in, the villagers needed the services of Reuven the furrier once more. When Hanukkah came, Aaron's mother was able to fry pancakes every evening, and Zlateh got her portion, too. Even though Zlateh had her own pen, she often came to the kitchen, knocking on the door with her horns to indicate that she was ready to visit, and she was always admitted. In the evening Aaron, Miriam, and Anna played dreidel.[4] Zlateh sat near the stove watching the children and the flickering of the Hanukkah candles.

Visualize: *You never know how inportant something is until you've lost it.*

Once in a while Aaron would ask her, "Zlateh, do you remember the three days we spent together?"

And Zlateh would scratch her neck with a horn, shake her white bearded head, and come out with the single sound which expressed all her thoughts, and all her love.

Reader's Response

If you were Aaron, what decision would you have made about Zlateh? Why?

Respond: *I would have made the same decision because Zlateh was so good to him. I don't think I could bring any goat to a butcher.*

4. **dreidel** (drā′ d'l) *n.*: A small top with Hebrew letters on each of four sides, spun in a game played by children.

Isaac Bashevis Singer (1904–1991) was born in Radzymin, Poland, and came to the United States in 1935. Mr. Singer has written many stories, both for children and adults. Many of his novels and stories, like "Zlateh the Goat," are set in simple villages suggesting Singer's birthplace in Eastern Europe. For the totality of his work, he received the Nobel Prize for Literature in 1978. He liked writing for children because, he said, "The young reader demands a real story with a beginning, a middle, and an end, the way stories have been told for thousands of years."

Responding to the Selection

Your Response

1. Do you agree with Aaron's decision? Explain.

Recalling

2. How do Aaron and Zlateh work together to survive the storm?

Interpreting

3. Explain how the storm both causes a problem and solves a problem.
4. Contrast Aaron's feelings when he and Zlateh take shelter in the haystack with the way he feels when the snow finally stops.
5. What kind of person is Aaron? Base your answer on the way he handles the situations in the story.
6. What has Aaron learned from this experience? Give evidence from the story.

Applying

7. Aaron comes to believe that we must accept all that we are given in life, "—heat, cold, hunger, satisfaction, light, and darkness." Do you feel it is important to accept the difficulties in life as well as the joys, or should we fight against the hard times? Explain.

Analyzing Literature

Reading a Short Story

A short story like "Zlateh the Goat" is a work of fiction. Even though the characters and events are made up by the author, you can learn something about life and living through what happens. In reading short stories, you can share the joys and sorrows of characters and learn from their experiences.

1. Although this story is fiction, in what ways is it also real?
2. What do you learn about life from Aaron's experience?

Critical Thinking and Reading

Evaluating Judgments

A **judgment** is a statement of opinion about the quality or value of something. A sound judgment is based on sound reasons—facts, observations, or experience. Aaron makes a judgment about Zlateh's worth when, after the storm, he takes Zlateh home rather than to the butcher.

1. On what does Aaron base this judgment?
2. What does this judgment show about Aaron?
3. What judgment does Aaron's family make after Aaron returns home?

Thinking and Writing

Writing About an Animal

Many of us have pets or know of animals that seem to have some humanlike qualities. Write about such an animal—a pet if you like. First describe the animal's major qualities. Then tell of an instance in which the animal showed these qualities. With your writing partner, check your draft for specific examples of the animal's behavior that prove the point you are making. Revise your draft and make a final copy.

Learning Options

1. **Multicultural Activity.** Aaron and his family celebrate Hanukkah, a festival of lights. Find out about this holiday or another festival of lights, such as Santa Lucia's Day—which is celebrated in Sweden, Norway, and Italy—or Las Posadas, which is celebrated in Mexico. In a report to your class, explain the origin of the festival and how it is celebrated. You can demonstrate the customs and present the food.
2. **Speaking and Listening.** Imagine that you are Aaron arriving home with Zlateh. Tell the story of your three days in the storm and haystack, filling in additional details.

Reading for Plot

NUPTIAL DANCE
Yaponi Araujo

GUIDE FOR READING

John Gardner

(1933–1982) first achieved fame for a novel based on the old English poem, *Beowulf,* which tells about the struggle between a hero named Beowulf and a monster called Grendel. Gardner's novel, entitled *Grendel,* gives this traditional story a special twist, telling it from the monster's point of view. Although Gardner is best known for his novels, he also wrote stories for young people. In "Dragon, Dragon," he includes elements found in fairy tales, but he adds a bit of humor and a few modern details.

Dragon, Dragon

Plot

The **plot** of a story is the sequence of events that occur in the story. These events usually follow a certain pattern: The story begins with a problem. As characters attempt to solve the problem, the action builds to a climax, or turning point. At this point, the problem is solved and the story comes to a conclusion.

Focus

In "Dragon, Dragon," you will read about the value of advice. Imagine that one of your friends was about to fight a dragon. What advice would you give him or her? What would you tell him or her to wear or to bring? In a group with three or four classmates, write down at least four pieces of advice for your friend. Then explain how each piece of advice would help fight a dragon. Share your ideas with the rest of the class. As you read this story, try to guess the meaning of the advice the cobbler gives his sons as they prepare to fight a dragon.

Vocabulary

Knowing the following words will help you read "Dragon, Dragon."

plagued (plāg'd) *v.*: Tormented (p. 15)

lair (ler) *n.*: The resting or dwelling place of a wild or imaginary animal (p. 15)

ravaged (rav′ ig'd) *v.*: Violently destroyed; ruined (p. 15)

tyrant (tī′ rənt) *n.*: A cruel, unjust ruler (p. 16)

reflecting (ri flekt′ iŋ) *v.*: Thinking seriously about something (p. 20)

craned (krānd) *v.*: Stretched the neck for a better view (p. 20)

flabbergasted (flab′ ər gast′ ′d) *adj.*: Speechless; surprised or astonished (p. 21)

Spelling Tip

Do not confuse the spelling of *lair* with that of *liar,* a person who tells lies.

Dragon, Dragon

John Gardner

" 'Dragon, Dragon, how do you do? I've come from the king to murder you.' "

There was once a king whose kingdom was plagued by a dragon. The king did not know which way to turn. The king's knights were all cowards who hid under their beds whenever the dragon came in sight, so they were of no use to the king at all. And the king's wizard could not help either because, being old, he had forgotten his magic spells. Nor could the wizard look up the spells that had slipped his mind, for he had unfortunately misplaced his wizard's book many years before. The king was at his wit's end.

Every time there was a full moon the dragon came out of his lair and ravaged the countryside. He frightened maidens and stopped up chimneys and broke store windows and set people's clocks back and made dogs bark until no one could hear himself think.

He tipped over fences and robbed graves and put frogs in people's drinking water and tore the last chapters out of novels and changed house numbers around so that people crawled into bed with their neighbors.

He stole spark plugs out of people's cars and put firecrackers in people's cigars and stole the clappers from all the church bells and sprung every bear trap for miles around so the bears could wander wherever they pleased.

And to top it all off, he changed around all the roads in the kingdom so that people could not get anywhere except by starting out in the wrong direction.

"That," said the king in a fury, "is enough!" And he called a meeting of everyone in the kingdom.

Now it happened that there lived in the kingdom a wise old cobbler who had a wife and three sons. The cobbler and his family came to the king's meeting and stood way in back by the door, for the cobbler had a feeling that since he was nobody important there had probably been some mistake, and no doubt the king had intended the meeting for everyone in the kingdom except his family and him.

"Ladies and gentlemen," said the king when everyone was present, "I've put up with that dragon as long as I can. He has got to be stopped."

All the people whispered amongst themselves, and the king smiled, pleased with the impression he had made.

But the wise cobbler said gloomily, "It's all very well to talk about it—but how are you going to do it?"

And now all the people smiled and winked as if to say, "Well, King, he's got you there!"

The king frowned.

"It's not that His Majesty hasn't tried," the queen spoke up loyally.

"Yes," said the king, "I've told my knights again and again that they ought to slay that dragon. But I can't *force* them to go. I'm not a tyrant."

"Why doesn't the wizard say a magic spell?" asked the cobbler.

"He's done the best he can," said the king.

The wizard blushed and everyone looked embarrassed. "I used to do all sorts of spells and chants when I was younger," the wizard explained. "But I've lost my spell book, and I begin to fear I'm losing my memory too. For instance,

I've been trying for days to recall one spell I used to do. I forget, just now, what the deuce it was for. It went something like—

Bimble,
Wimble,
Cha, Cha
CHOOMPF!

Suddenly, to everyone's surprise, the queen turned into a rosebush.

"Oh dear," said the wizard.

"Now you've done it," groaned the king.

"Poor Mother," said the princess.

"I don't know what can have happened," the wizard said nervously, "but don't worry, I'll have her changed back in a jiffy." He shut his eyes and racked his brain for a spell that would change her back.

But the king said quickly, "You'd better leave well enough alone. If you change her into a rattlesnake we'll have to chop off her head."

Meanwhile the cobbler stood with his hands in his pockets, sighing at the waste of time. "About the dragon . . ." he began.

"Oh yes," said the king. "I'll tell you what I'll do. I'll give the princess' hand in marriage

to anyone who can make the dragon stop."

"It's not enough," said the cobbler. "She's a nice enough girl, you understand. But how would an ordinary person support her? Also, what about those of us that are already married?"

"In that case," said the king, "I'll offer the princess' hand or half the kingdom or both—whichever is most convenient."

The cobbler scratched his chin and considered it. "It's not enough," he said at last. "It's a good enough kingdom, you understand, but it's too much responsibility."

"Take it or leave it," the king said.

"I'll leave it," said the cobbler. And he shrugged and went home.

But the cobbler's eldest son thought the bargain was a good one, for the princess was very beautiful and he liked the idea of having half the kingdom to run as he pleased. So he said to the king, "I'll accept those terms, Your Majesty. By tomorrow morning the dragon will be slain."

"Bless you!" cried the king.

"Hooray, hooray, hooray!" cried all the people, throwing their hats in the air.

The cobbler's eldest son beamed with pride, and the second eldest looked at him enviously. The youngest son said timidly, "Excuse me, Your Majesty, but don't you think the queen looks a little unwell? If I were you I think I'd water her."

"Good heavens," cried the king, glancing at the queen who had been changed into a rosebush, "I'm glad you mentioned it!"

Now the cobbler's eldest son was very clever and was known far and wide for how quickly he could multiply fractions in his head. He was perfectly sure he could slay the dragon by somehow or other playing a trick on him, and he didn't feel that he needed his wise old father's advice. But he thought it was only polite to ask, and so he went to his father, who was working as usual at his cobbler's bench, and said, "Well, Father, I'm off to slay the dragon. Have you any advice to give me?"

The cobbler thought a moment and replied, "When and if you come to the dragon's lair, recite the following poem.

Dragon, dragon, how do you do?
I've come from the king to murder you.

Say it very loudly and firmly and the dragon will fall, God willing, at your feet."

"How curious!" said the eldest son. And he thought to himself, "The old man is not as wise as I thought. If I say something like that to the dragon, he will eat me up in an instant. The way to kill a dragon is to out-fox him." And keeping his opinion to himself, the eldest son set forth on his quest.

When he came at last to the dragon's lair, which was a cave, the eldest son slyly disguised himself as a peddler and knocked on the door and called out, "Hello there!"

"There's nobody home!" roared a voice.

The voice was as loud as an earthquake, and the eldest son's knees knocked together in terror.

"I don't come to trouble you," the eldest son said meekly. "I merely thought you might be interested in looking at some of our brushes. Or if you'd prefer," he added quickly, "I could leave our catalogue with you and I could drop by again, say, early next week."

"I don't want any brushes," the voice roared, "and I especially don't want any brushes next week."

"Oh," said the eldest son. By now his knees were knocking together so badly that he had to sit down.

Suddenly a great shadow fell over him, and the eldest son looked up. It was the dragon. The eldest son drew his sword, but the dragon lunged and swallowed him in a single gulp, sword and all, and the eldest son found himself in the dark of the dragon's belly. "What a fool I was not to listen to my wise old father!" thought the eldest son. And he began to weep bitterly.

"Well," sighed the king the next morning, "I see the dragon has not been slain yet."

"I'm just as glad, personally," said the princess, sprinkling the queen. "I would have had to marry that eldest son, and he had warts."

Now the cobbler's middle son decided it was his turn to try. The middle son was very strong and he was known far and wide for being able to lift up the corner of a church. He felt perfectly sure he could slay the dragon by simply laying into him, but he thought it would be only polite to ask his father's advice. So he went to his father and said to him, "Well, Father, I'm off to slay the dragon. Have you any advice for me?"

The cobbler told the middle son exactly what he'd told the eldest.

"When and if you come to the dragon's lair, recite the following poem.

Dragon, dragon, how do you do?
I've come from the king to murder you.

Say it very loudly and firmly, and the dragon will fall, God willing, at your feet."

"What an odd thing to say," thought the middle son. "The old man is not as wise as I thought. You have to take these dragons by surprise." But he kept his opinion to himself and set forth.

When he came in sight of the dragon's lair, the middle son spurred his horse to a gallop and thundered into the entrance swinging his sword with all his might.

But the dragon had seen him while he was still a long way off, and being very clever, the dragon had crawled up on top of the door so that when the son came charging in he went under the dragon and on to the back of the cave and slammed into the wall. Then the dragon chuckled and got down off the door, taking his time, and strolled back to where the man and the horse lay unconscious from the terrific blow. Opening his mouth as if for a yawn, the dragon swallowed the middle son in a single gulp and put the horse in the freezer to eat another day.

"What a fool I was not to listen to my wise old father," thought the middle son when he came to in the dragon's belly. And he too began to weep bitterly.

That night there was a full moon, and the dragon ravaged the countryside so terribly that several families moved to another kingdom.

"Well," sighed the king in the morning, "still no luck in this dragon business, I see."

"I'm just as glad, myself," said the princess, moving her mother, pot and all, to the window where the sun could get at her. "The cobbler's middle son was a kind of humpback."

Now the cobbler's youngest son saw that his turn had come. He was very upset and nervous, and he wished he had never been born. He was not clever, like his eldest brother, and he was not strong, like his second-eldest brother. He was a decent, honest boy who always minded his elders.

He borrowed a suit of armor from a friend of his who was a knight, and when the youngest son put the armor on it was so heavy he could hardly walk. From another knight he borrowed a sword, and that was so heavy that the only way the youngest son could get it to the dragon's lair was to drag it along behind his horse like a plow.

When everything was in readiness, the youngest son went for a last conversation with his father.

"Father, have you any advice to give me?" he asked.

"Only this," said the cobbler. "When and if you come to the dragon's lair, recite the following poem.

Dragon, dragon, how do you do?
I've come from the king to murder you.

Say it very loudly and firmly, and the dragon will fall, God willing, at your feet."

"Are you certain?" asked the youngest son uneasily.

"As certain as one can ever be in these matters," said the wise old cobbler.

And so the youngest son set forth on his quest. He traveled over hill and dale and at last came to the dragon's cave.

The dragon, who had seen the cobbler's youngest son while he was still a long way off, was seated up above the door, inside the cave, waiting and smiling to himself. But minutes passed and no one came thundering in. The dragon frowned, puzzled, and was tempted to peek out. However, reflecting that patience seldom goes unrewarded, the dragon kept his head up out of sight and went on waiting. At last, when he could stand it no longer, the dragon craned his neck and looked. There at the entrance of the cave stood a trembling young man in a suit of armor twice his size, struggling with a sword so heavy he could lift only one end of it at a time.

At sight of the dragon, the cobbler's youngest son began to tremble so violently that his armor rattled like a house caving in. He heaved with all his might at the sword and got the handle up level with his chest, but even now the point was down in the dirt. As loudly and firmly as he could manage, the youngest son cried—

Dragon, dragon, how do you do?
I've come from the king to murder you.

"What?" cried the dragon, flabbergasted. "You? *You?* Murder *Me???*" All at once he began to laugh, pointing at the little cobbler's son. *"He he he ho ha!"* he roared, shaking all over, and tears filled his eyes.

"He he he ho ho ho ha ha!" laughed the dragon. He was laughing so hard he had to hang onto his sides, and he fell off the door and landed on his back, still laughing, kicking his legs helplessly, rolling from side to side, laughing and laughing and laughing.

The cobbler's son was annoyed, "I *do* come from the king to murder you," he said. "A person doesn't like to be laughed at for a thing like that."

"He he he!" wailed the dragon, almost sobbing, gasping for breath. "Of course not, poor dear boy! But really, *he he,* the *idea* of it, *ha, ha, ha!* And that simply ri*dic*ulous *poem!"* Tears streamed from the dragon's eyes and he lay on his back perfectly helpless with laughter.

"It's a good poem," said the cobbler's youngest son loyally. "My father made it up." And growing angrier he shouted, "I want you to stop that laughing, or I'll—I'll—" But the dragon could not stop for the life of him. And suddenly, in a terrific rage, the cobbler's son began flopping the sword end over end in the direction of the dragon. Sweat ran off the youngest son's forehead, but he labored on, blistering mad, and at last, with one supreme heave, he had the sword standing on its handle a foot from the dragon's throat. Of its own weight the sword fell, slicing the dragon's head off.

"He he ho huk," went the dragon—and then he lay dead.

The two older brothers crawled out and thanked their younger brother for saving their lives. "We have learned our lesson," they said.

Then the three brothers gathered all the treasures from the dragon's cave and tied them to the back end of the youngest brother's horse, and tied the dragon's head on behind the treasures, and started home. "I'm glad I listened to my father," the youngest son thought. "Now I'll be the richest man in the kingdom."

There were hand-carved picture frames and silver spoons and boxes of jewels and chests of money and silver compasses and maps telling where there were more treasures buried when these ran out. There was also a curious old book with a picture of an owl on the cover, and inside, poems and odd sentences and recipes that seemed to make no sense.

When they reached the king's castle the people all leaped for joy to see that the dragon was dead, and the princess ran out and kissed the youngest brother on the forehead, for secretly she had hoped it would be him.

"Well," said the king, "which half of the kingdom do you want?"

"My wizard's book!" exclaimed the wizard. "He's found my wizard's book!" He opened the book and ran his finger along under the words and then said in a loud voice, "Glmuzk, shkzmlp, blam!"

Instantly the queen stood before them in her natural shape, except she was soaking wet from being sprinkled too often. She glared at the king.

"Oh dear," said the king, hurrying toward the door.

Reader's Response

Humor is very personal. What makes one person laugh may not affect another person at all. Did you find this story funny? If so, tell why. If not, what would have made the story funny for you?

Responding to the Selection

Your Response

1. The father is described as wise. Do you think he is wise? Explain your answer.
2. Which of the cobbler's three sons are you most like? Explain.

Recalling

3. Why are both the king's knights and his wizard unable to get rid of the dragon?
4. How does the father's advice actually help the youngest son to kill the dragon?

Interpreting

5. The storyteller describes the dragon as ravaging the countryside. How are the things the dragon does different from what you would expect based on the word *ravage*?
6. How is the king different from the type of kings you usually find in fairy tales?
7. How do you think the king expected people of his kingdom to react to his proposal? How is the cobbler's reaction different?
8. What characteristics of the two older brothers result in their getting eaten?
9. How is the youngest son different from his brothers? What did you predict would happen when he went to slay the dragon?

Applying

10. You could argue that the dragon is slain by the power of laughter. In what other ways can laughter help solve problems?

Analyzing Literature

Understanding Plot

The **plot** is the pattern of related events in a story. You can trace these events on a chart like the following:

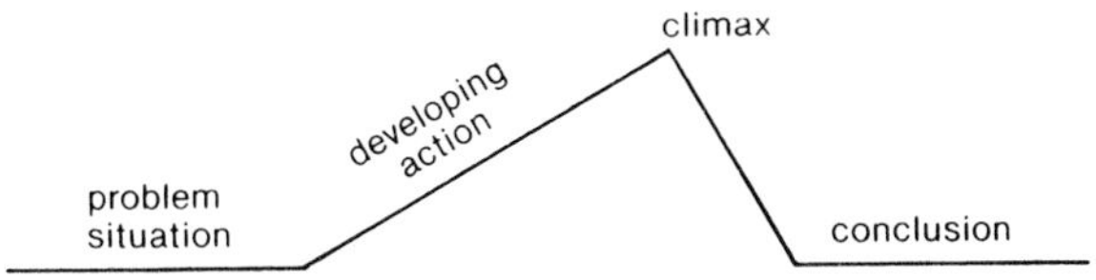

As you answer the following questions, trace the events on a plot chart.

1. What is the problem facing the characters at the beginning of "Dragon, Dragon"?
2. What actions do the characters take to try to solve the problem?
3. What event or action is the climax, or turning point, in "Dragon, Dragon"?
4. What remaining details are explained as the story concludes?

Critical Thinking and Reading

Recognizing Chronological Order

The events in "Dragon, Dragon" take place in **chronological order**. This means that they follow one another as time moves forward. Writers help you to recognize when events occur by using certain words or phrases. For example, Gardner writes "Meanwhile" and "When he came at last to the dragon's lair . . ." to indicate time.

Find three other words or phrases that Gardner uses to show the chronological order of events in "Dragon, Dragon."

Thinking and Writing

Extending the Plot

Think about what might happen after the story "Dragon, Dragon" ends. How does the queen feel about having been turned into a rosebush? How are the lives of the cobbler and his two older sons changed after the youngest son marries the princess? Brainstorm with your classmates on all these possibilities. Then write a continuation of the story, putting the events in chronological order. After you have finished a draft, let a classmate read it to see if you have made the events exciting and interesting. When your draft is revised, read it to your classmates.

GUIDE FOR READING

Jack London

(1876–1916) is best known for his tales of the Alaskan gold rush. He experienced the gold rush firsthand, traveling in the 1890's to the Yukon in search of a fortune. Instead of gold, however, London found many subjects for his writing. His most popular novel, *The Call of the Wild,* describes the people who came to the frozen North and the bonds they established with their sled dogs. "The King of Mazy May" tells of a fourteen-year-old boy's adventure with claim jumpers in the Yukon.

The King of Mazy May

Conflict

Stories develop around a **conflict,** a struggle between opposing sides or forces. In a story, a conflict can occur between characters or between a character and a force of nature. Another kind of conflict may occur between opposing ideas or feelings within a character. In "The King of Mazy May," the main character finds himself in conflict with a group of older men with bad intentions.

Focus

Walt Masters, the main character in "The King of Mazy May," performs a heroic act to protect a friend. In a small group, make a cluster map that shows the characteristics you think heroes have. To make a cluster map, put the word "HERO" in the center of a piece of paper. Around the word, write all the words and phrases that you associate with the word "hero." As you read the story, think about how the characteristics of Jack London's hero compare to the characteristics in your diagram.

Vocabulary

Knowing the following words will help you as you read "The King of Mazy May."

toil (toil) *n.*: Hard, exhausting work and effort (p. 25)
endured (in door'd′) *v.*: Held up under (p. 25)
prospectors (präs′ pek tərz) *n.*: People who search for valuable ores, such as gold (p. 26)
liable (lī′ ə b'l) *adj.*: Likely (p. 27)
poising (poiz′ iŋ) *v.*: Balancing (p. 28)
declined (di klīn'd′) *v.*: Refused (p. 29)
summit (sum′ it) *n.*: Highest part (p. 31)

Spelling Tip

The endings *-er* and *-or* both indicate someone who performs an action, as in *prospector.* Notice that in *prospector,* the final syllable is spelled *or.*

The King of Mazy May

Jack London

"He did not dare to think what would happen if they caught him; he just clung to the sled, his heart beating wildly. . . ."

Walt Masters is not a very large boy, but there is manliness in his make-up, and he himself, although he does not know a great deal that most boys know, knows much that other boys do not know. He has never seen a train of cars nor an elevator in his life, and for that matter he has never once looked upon a cornfield, a plow, a cow, or even a chicken. He has never had a pair of shoes on his feet, nor gone to a picnic or a party, nor talked to a girl. But he has seen the sun at midnight, watched the ice jams on one of the mightiest of rivers, and played beneath the northern lights,[1] the one white child in thousands of square miles of frozen wilderness.

Walt has walked all the fourteen years of his life in suntanned, moose-hide moccasins, and he can go to the Indian camps and "talk big" with the men, and trade calico and beads with them for their precious furs. He can make bread without baking powder, yeast, or hops, shoot a moose at three hundred yards, and drive the wild wolf dogs fifty miles a day on the packed trail.

Last of all, he has a good heart, and is not afraid of the darkness and loneliness, of man or beast or thing. His father is a good man, strong and brave, and Walt is growing up like him.

Walt was born a thousand miles or so down the Yukon,[2] in a trading post below the Ramparts. After his mother died, his father and he came up on the river, step by step, from camp to camp, till now they are settled down on the Mazy May Creek in the Klondike[3] country. Last year they and several others had spent much toil and time on the Mazy May, and endured great hardships; the creek, in turn, was just beginning to show up its richness and to reward them for their heavy labor. But with the news of their discoveries, strange men began to come and go through the short days and long nights, and many unjust things they did to the men who had worked so long upon the creek.

Si Hartman had gone away on a moose hunt, to return and find new stakes driven

1. northern lights: Glowing bands or streamers of light sometimes appearing in the night sky of the Northern Hemisphere.

2. Yukon (yo͞o′ kän): A river flowing through the Yukon Territory of northwest Canada.

3. Klondike (klän′ dīk): A gold-mining region along a tributary of the Yukon River.

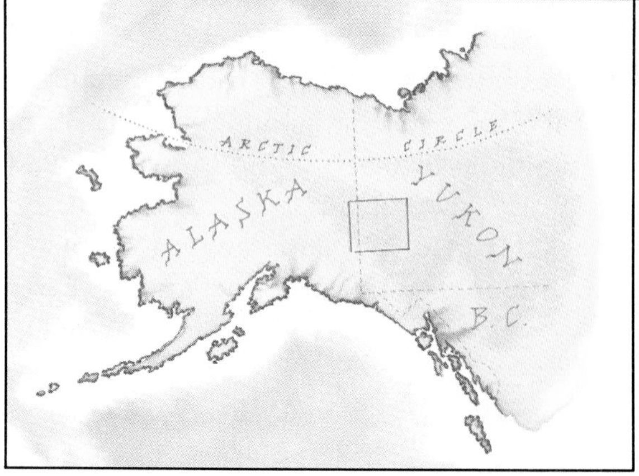

and his claim jumped.[4] George Lukens and his brother had lost their claims in a like manner, having delayed too long on the way to Dawson to record them. In short, it was the old story, and quite a number of the earnest, industrious prospectors had suffered similar losses.

---

4. claim jumped: A claim is a piece of land staked out by a miner. A claim that is jumped is stolen by someone else.

But Walt Masters's father had recorded his claim at the start, so Walt had nothing to fear now that his father had gone on a short trip up the White River prospecting for quartz. Walt was well able to stay by himself in the cabin, cook his three meals a day, and look after things. Not only did he look after his father's claim, but he had agreed to keep an eye on the adjoining one of Loren Hall, who had started for Dawson to record it.

Loren Hall was an old man, and he had no dogs, so he had to travel very slowly. After he had been gone some time, word came up the river that he had broken through the ice at Rosebud Creek and frozen his feet so badly that he would not be able to travel for a couple of weeks. Then Walt Masters received the news that old Loren was nearly all right again, and about to move on afoot for Dawson as fast as a weakened man could.

Walt was worried, however; the claim was liable to be jumped at any moment because of this delay, and a fresh stampede had started in on the Mazy May. He did not like the looks of the newcomers, and one day, when five of them came by with crack dog teams and the lightest of camping outfits, he could see that they were prepared to make speed, and resolved to keep an eye on them. So he locked up the cabin and followed them, being at the same time careful to remain hidden.

He had not watched them long before he was sure that they were professional stampeders, bent on jumping all the claims in sight. Walt crept along the snow at the rim of the creek and saw them change many stakes, destroy old ones, and set up new ones.

In the afternoon, with Walt always trailing on their heels, they came back down the creek, unharnessed their dogs, and went into camp within two claims of his cabin. When he saw them make preparations to cook, he hurried home to get something to eat himself, and then hurried back. He crept so close that he could hear them talking quite plainly, and by pushing the underbrush aside he could catch occasional glimpses of them. They had finished eating and were smoking around the fire.

"The creek is all right, boys," a large, black-bearded man, evidently the leader, said, "and I think the best thing we can do is to pull out tonight. The dogs can follow the trail; besides, it's going to be moonlight. What say you?"

"But it's going to be beastly cold," objected one of the party. "It's forty below zero now."

"An' sure, can't ye keep warm by jumpin' off the sleds an' runnin' after the dogs?" cried an Irishman. "An' who wouldn't? The creek's as rich as a United States mint! Faith, it's an ilegant chanst to be gettin' a run fer yer money! An' if ye don't run, it's mebbe you'll not get the money at all, at all."

"That's it," said the leader. "If we can get to Dawson and record, we're rich men; and there's no telling who's been sneaking along in our tracks, watching us, and perhaps now off to give the alarm. The thing for us to do is to rest the dogs a bit, and then hit the trail as hard as we can. What do you say?"

Evidently the men had agreed with their leader, for Walt Masters could hear nothing but the rattle of the tin dishes which were being washed. Peering out cautiously, he could see the leader studying a piece of paper. Walt knew what it was at a glance—a list of all the unrecorded claims on Mazy May. Any man could get these lists by applying to the gold commissioner at Dawson.

"Thirty-two," the leader said, lifting his face to the men. "Thirty-two isn't recorded, and this is thirty-three. Come on; let's take a look at it. I saw somebody had been working on it when we came up this morning."

Three of the men went with him, leaving one to remain in camp. Walt crept carefully after them till they came to Loren Hall's shaft. One of the men went down and built a fire on the bottom to thaw out the frozen gravel, while the others built another fire on the dump and melted water in a couple of gold pans. This they poured into a piece of canvas stretched between two logs, used by Loren Hall in which to wash his gold.

In a short time a couple of buckets of dirt were sent up by the man in the shaft, and Walt could see the others grouped anxiously about their leader as he proceeded to wash it. When this was finished, they stared at the broad streak of black sand and yellow gold grains on the bottom of the pan, and one of them called excitedly for the man who had remained in camp to come. Loren Hall had struck it rich and his claim was not yet recorded. It was plain that they were going to jump it.

Walt lay in the snow, thinking rapidly. He was only a boy, but in the face of the threatened injustice to old lame Loren Hall he felt that he must do something. He waited and watched, with his mind made up, till he saw the men begin to square up new stakes. Then he crawled away till out of hearing, and broke into a run for the camp of the stampeders. Walt's father had taken their own dogs with him prospecting, and the boy knew how impossible it was for him to undertake the seventy miles to Dawson without the aid of dogs.

Gaining the camp, he picked out, with an experienced eye, the easiest running sled and started to harness up the stampeders' dogs. There were three teams of six each, and from these he chose ten of the best. Realizing how necessary it was to have a good head dog, he strove to discover a leader amongst them; but he had little time in which to do it, for he could hear the voices of the returning men. By the time the team was in shape and everything ready, the claim-jumpers came into sight in an open place not more than a hundred yards from the trail, which ran down the bed of the creek. They cried out to Walt, but instead of giving heed to them he grabbed up one of their fur sleeping robes, which lay loosely in the snow, and leaped upon the sled.

"Mush! Hi! Mush on!" he cried to the animals, snapping the keen-lashed whip among them.

The dogs sprang against the yoke straps, and the sled jerked under way so suddenly as to almost throw him off. Then it curved into the creek, poising perilously on the runner. He was almost breathless with suspense, when it finally righted with a bound and sprang ahead again. The creek bank was high and he could not see the men, although he could hear their cries and knew they were running to cut him off. He did not dare to think what would happen if they caught him; he just clung to the sled, his heart beating wildly, and watched the snow rim of the bank above him.

Suddenly, over this snow rim came the flying body of the Irishman, who had leaped straight for the sled in a desperate attempt to capture it; but he was an instant too late. Striking on the very rear of it, he was thrown from his feet, backward, into the snow. Yet, with the quickness of a cat, he had clutched the end of the sled with one hand, turned over, and was dragging behind on his breast, swearing at the boy and threatening all kinds of terrible things if he did not stop the dogs; but Walt cracked him sharply across the knuckles with the butt of the dog whip till he let go.

It was eight miles from Walt's claim to the Yukon—eight very crooked miles, for the creek wound back and forth like a snake, "tying knots in itself," as George Lukens said. And because it was so crooked the dogs could not get up their best speed, while the sled ground heavily on its side against the curves, now to the right, now to the left.

Travelers who had come up and down the Mazy May on foot, with packs on their backs, had declined to go round all the bends, and instead had made shortcuts across the narrow necks of creek bottom. Two of his pursuers had gone back to harness the remaining dogs, but the others took advantage of these shortcuts, running on foot, and before he knew it they had almost overtaken him.

"Halt!" they cried after him. "Stop, or we'll shoot!"

But Walt only yelled the harder at the dogs, and dashed around the bend with a

BACK TRAIL (detail)
Jon Van Zyle

couple of revolver bullets singing after him. At the next bend they had drawn up closer still, and the bullets struck uncomfortably near him but at this point the Mazy May straightened out and ran for half a mile as the crow flies. Here the dogs stretched out in their long wolf swing, and the stampeders, quickly winded, slowed down and waited for their own sled to come up.

Looking over his shoulder, Walt reasoned that they had not given up the chase for good, and that they would soon be after him again. So he wrapped the fur robe about him to shut out the stinging air, and lay flat on the empty sled, encouraging the dogs, as he well knew how.

At last, twisting abruptly between two river islands, he came upon the mighty Yukon sweeping grandly to the north. He could not see from bank to bank, and in the quick-falling twilight it loomed a great white sea of frozen stillness. There was not a sound, save the breathing of the dogs, and the churn of the steel-shod sled.

No snow had fallen for several weeks, and the traffic had packed the main river trail till it was hard and glassy as glare ice. Over this the sled flew along, and the dogs kept the trail fairly well, although Walt quickly discovered that he had made a mistake in choosing the leader. As they were driven in single file, without reins, he had to guide them by his voice, and it was evident the head dog had never learned the meaning of "gee" and "haw."[5] He hugged the inside of the curves too closely, often forcing his comrades behind him into the soft snow, while several times he thus capsized the sled.

There was no wind, but the speed at which he traveled created a bitter blast, and with the thermometer down to forty below, this bit through fur and flesh to the very bones. Aware that if he remained constantly upon the sled he would freeze to death, and knowing the practice of Arctic travelers, Walt shortened up one of the lashing thongs, and whenever he felt chilled, seized hold of it, jumped off, and ran behind till warmth was restored. Then he would climb on and rest till the process had to be repeated.

Looking back he could see the sled of his pursuers, drawn by eight dogs, rising and falling over the ice hummocks like a boat in a seaway. The Irishman and the black-bearded leader were with it, taking turns in running and riding.

Night fell, and in the blackness of the first hour or so Walt toiled desperately with his dogs. On account of the poor lead dog, they were continually floundering off the beaten track into the soft snow, and the sled was as often riding on its side or top as it was in the proper way. This work and strain tried his strength sorely. Had he not been in such haste he could have avoided much of it, but he feared the stampeders would creep up in the darkness and overtake him. However, he could hear them yelling to their dogs, and knew from the sounds they were coming up very slowly.

When the moon rose he was off Sixty Mile, and Dawson was only fifty miles away. He was almost exhausted, and breathed a sigh of relief as he climbed on the sled again. Looking back, he saw his enemies had crawled up within four hundred yards. At this space they remained, a black speck of motion on the white river breast. Strive as they would, they could not shorten this distance, and strive as he would, he could not increase it.

5. "gee" and "haw" (jē) and (hô)): Commands used to tell an animal to turn to the right or the left.

Walt had now discovered the proper lead dog, and he knew he could easily run away from them if he could only change the bad leader for the good one. But this was impossible, for a moment's delay, at the speed they were running, would bring the men behind upon him.

TOMMY (detail)
Bryan Moon

When he was off the mouth of Rosebud Creek, just as he was topping a rise, the report of a gun and the ping of a bullet on the ice beside him told him that they were this time shooting at him with a rifle. And from then on, as he cleared the summit of each ice jam, he stretched flat on the leaping sled till the rifle shot from the rear warned him that he was safe till the next ice jam was reached.

Now it is very hard to lie on a moving sled, jumping and plunging and yawing like a boat before the wind, and to shoot through the deceiving moonlight at an object four hundred yards away on another moving sled performing equally wild antics. So it is not to be wondered at that the black-bearded leader did not hit him.

After several hours of this, during which, perhaps, a score of bullets had struck about him, their ammunition began to give out and their fire slackened. They took greater care, and shot at him at the most favorable opportunities. He was also leaving them behind, the distance slowly increasing to six hundred yards.

Lifting clear on the crest of a great jam off Indian River, Walt Masters met with his first accident. A bullet sang past his ears, and struck the bad lead dog.

The poor brute plunged in a heap, with the rest of the team on top of him.

Like a flash Walt was by the leader. Cutting the traces with his hunting knife, he dragged the dying animal to one side and straightened out the team.

He glanced back. The other sled was coming up like an express train. With half the dogs still over their traces, he cried "Mush on!" and leaped upon the sled just as the pursuers dashed abreast of him.

The Irishman was preparing to spring for him—they were so sure they had him that they did not shoot—when Walt turned fiercely upon them with his whip.

He struck at their faces, and men must save their faces with their hands. So there was no shooting just then. Before they could recover from the hot rain of blows, Walt reached out from his sled, catching their wheel dog by the forelegs in midspring, and throwing him heavily. This snarled the team, capsizing the sled and tangling his enemies up beautifully.

Away Walt flew, the runners of his sled fairly screaming as they bounded over the frozen surface. And what had seemed an accident proved to be a blessing in disguise. The proper lead dog was now to the fore, and he stretched low and whined with joy as he jerked his comrades along.

By the time he reached Ainslie's Creek, seventeen miles from Dawson, Walt had left his pursuers, a tiny speck, far behind. At Monte Cristo Island he could no longer see them. And at Swede Creek, just as daylight was silvering the pines, he ran plump into the camp of old Loren Hall.

Almost as quick as it takes to tell it, Loren had his sleeping furs rolled up, and had joined Walt on the sled. They permitted the dogs to travel more slowly, as there was no sign of the chase in the rear, and just as they pulled up at the gold commissioner's office in Dawson, Walt, who had kept his eyes open to the last, fell asleep.

And because of what Walt Masters did on this night, the men of the Yukon have become proud of him, and speak of him now as the King of Mazy May.

Reader's Response

Would you like to live as Walt lives? Why or why not?

The Alaskan Gold Rush

"MINERS LOADED WITH GOLD RETURN FROM KLONDIKE!" screamed newspaper headlines in 1897. Two steamers loaded with miners and their gold had arrived in California from the Klondike region. The news they brought triggered the "Klondike stampede," a rush of about 100,000 people who headed for Alaska and the Yukon Territory of Canada in hopes of striking it rich. Most of them never even reached the gold fields.

Look at the map on page 26 and you'll see why. Even today, with automobiles and airplanes, "Klondike country" is remote. At the turn of the century, reaching the area was challenging and dangerous. The most popular route involved sailing north from California to the Alaskan panhandle, crossing the Alaskan Coastal Range by foot, and drifting about 550 miles down the Yukon River to Dawson City on a raft constructed by hand.

This journey took almost a year. Those who completed it arrived to find harsh, primitive living conditions, sub-zero temperatures, heavy snowfall, and little gold. The miners who had been in the area all along, "sourdoughs" like Walt and his father, had already made the best claims. As a result, most of the stampeders returned home empty handed.

What are some of the things people do today to try to "strike it rich" quickly and easily?

Responding to the Selection

Your Response

1. Describe your feelings at the end of the story.
2. Do you have anything in common with Walt? Is he someone you would want to become friends with? Explain.

Recalling

3. What are Walt's responsibilities while his father is away?
4. How does Walt manage to get away from and stay ahead of the men?
5. Why is the shooting of the first lead dog a "blessing in disguise"?

Interpreting

6. List three incidents in which Walt displays good judgment and quick thinking. What other positive qualities does Walt display?
7. What makes the men's pursuit of Walt especially exciting?
8. Why is Walt's title, the "King of Mazy May," appropriate?

Applying

9. At fourteen, Walt has handled a great responsibility and proven himself to others. What responsibilities must young people face today?

Analyzing Literature

Understanding Conflict

A **conflict** is a struggle between opposing forces. In "The King of Mazy May," the conflict occurs between characters with different goals or purposes—between Walt and the men.

1. Why is the gang on the Mazy May?
2. What is Walt's purpose while his father and Loren Hall are away?
3. Explain how these opposing purposes cause a conflict.
4. How is the conflict resolved?
5. Did this conflict seem realistic? In other words, is it one that is likely to have developed in this time and place? Explain.

Critical Thinking and Reading

Recognizing Cause and Effect

A **cause** is an action that brings about a result, or **effect.** For example, Loren Hall's feet freeze, delaying his filing a claim. Freezing his feet is a cause. Being delayed is the effect.

For each of the following pairs of incidents, tell which is the cause and which is the effect.

1. a. Gold is discovered in Alaska.
   b. Thousands of men and women go north to seek their fortunes.
2. a. Walt chooses the wrong lead dog.
   b. Walt must quickly harness a team before the men return to camp.

Thinking and Writing

Writing a News Article

Imagine that you are a reporter sent by your hometown paper to cover the gold rush. Write a news article about Walt's adventure. In your prewriting, jot down information that answers the questions *who, what, where, when, why,* and *how.* After you have written a first draft, think of an appropriate headline for the article. Exchange your article with a classmate and discuss how it might be made more clear or interesting. Write your final draft and share it with your classmates.

Learning Options

1. **Speaking and Listening.** Imagine the conversation Walt might have had with his father, after his father returned. With a classmate, create a dialogue between Walt and his father in which Walt explains how he protected Loren Hall's property.
2. **Cross-curricular Connection.** Use encyclopedias and other books to find out about one of the following: (a) how gold is mined; (b) the geography and climate of the Yukon; (c) sled dogs. Present your findings to the class in an oral report.

GUIDE FOR READING

Jane Yolen

(1939–   ) has written more than eighty books for children and young people. In 1974 *The Girl Who Cried Flowers and Other Tales* was a finalist for the National Book Award. Yolen is particularly interested in the oral tradition, stories that were not written down but told, retold, and passed along by storytellers for hundreds of years. To make her own work retain features of the oral tradition, Yolen reads aloud every sentence she writes. The results of this attention are apparent in the story "Greyling."

Greyling

Conflict

A **conflict** is a struggle between opposing forces or sides. Sometimes in a story the conflict may be within a person. Sometimes the conflict occurs when a character must choose between right and wrong. Not all conflicts are so clearly defined. Sometimes, as in "Greyling," the conflict is between what the character tries to be and his true nature.

Focus

In this story, a couple get something that they wished for. However, the consequences are not what they had expected. With a small group, think of a wish you would like to have fulfilled. Then use the model below to make a flowchart of the possible consequences or results of having your wish come true. In addition, write down at least two possible effects of each consequence. As you read "Greyling," look for the consequences of the couple's wish.

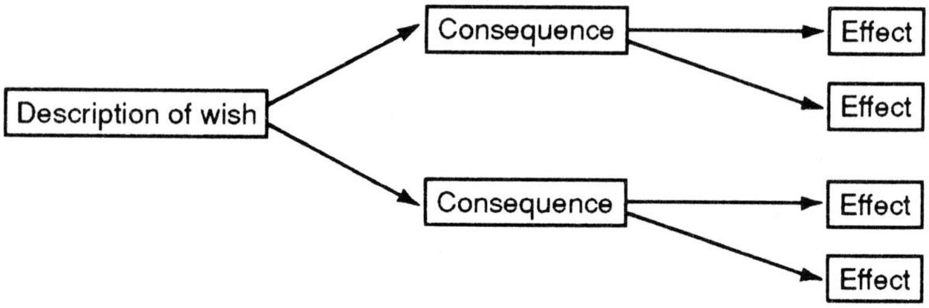

Vocabulary

Knowing the following words will help you as you read "Greyling."

sheared (shird) *v.*: Cut off sharply (p. 35)

kin (kin) *n.*: Relatives, family (p. 35)

roiling (roil′ iŋ) *adj.*: Unsettled, agitated (p. 36)

slough (sluf) *v.*: To come off (p. 38)

wallowed (wäl′ ōd) *v.*: Rolled and pitched (p. 38)

Spelling Tip

Remember that *slough* rhymes with and is spelled like *rough*.

Greyling

Jane Yolen

"Instead of a seal lying in the folds, there was a strange child with great grey eyes and silvery grey hair, smiling up at him."

Once on a time when wishes were aplenty, a fisherman and his wife lived by the side of the sea. All that they ate came out of the sea. Their hut was covered with the finest mosses that kept them cool in the summer and warm in the winter. And there was nothing they needed or wanted except a child.

Each morning, when the moon touched down behind the water and the sun rose up behind the plains, the wife would say to the fisherman, "You have your boat and your nets and your lines. But I have no baby to hold in my arms." And again, in the evening, it was the same. She would weep and wail and rock the cradle that stood by the hearth. But year in and year out the cradle stayed empty.

Now the fisherman was also sad that they had no child. But he kept his sorrow to himself so that his wife would not know his grief and thus double her own. Indeed, he would leave the hut each morning with a breath of song and return each night with a whistle on his lips. His nets were full but his heart was empty, yet he never told his wife.

One sunny day, when the beach was a tan thread spun between sea and plain, the fisherman as usual went down to his boat. But this day he found a small grey seal stranded on the sandbar, crying for its own.

The fisherman looked up the beach and down. He looked in front of him and behind. And he looked to the town on the great grey cliffs that sheared off into the sea. But there were no other seals in sight.

So he shrugged his shoulders and took off his shirt. Then he dipped it into the water and wrapped the seal pup carefully in its folds.

"You have no father and you have no mother," he said. "And I have no child. So you shall come home with me."

And the fisherman did no fishing that day but brought the seal pup, wrapped in his shirt, straight home to his wife.

When she saw him coming home early with no shirt on, the fisherman's wife ran out of the hut, fear riding in her heart. Then she looked wonderingly at the bundle which he held in his arms.

"It's nothing," he said, "but a seal pup I found stranded in the shallows and longing for its own. I thought we could give it love and care until it is old enough to seek its kin."

The fisherman's wife nodded and took the bundle. Then she uncovered the wrapping and gave a loud cry. "Nothing!" she said. "You call this nothing?"

The fisherman looked. Instead of a seal lying in the folds, there was a strange child with great grey eyes and silvery grey hair, smiling up at him.

The fisherman wrung his hands. "It is a selchie," he cried. "I have heard of them. They are men upon the land and seals in the sea. I thought it was but a tale."

"Then he shall remain a man upon the land," said the fisherman's wife, clasping the child in her arms, "for I shall never let him return to the sea."

"Never," agreed the fisherman, for he knew how his wife had wanted a child. And in his secret heart, he wanted one, too. Yet he felt, somehow, it was wrong.

"We shall call him Greyling," said the fisherman's wife, "for his eyes and hair are the color of a storm-coming sky. Greyling, though he has brought sunlight into our home."

And though they still lived by the side of the water in a hut covered with mosses that kept them warm in the winter and cool in the summer, the boy Greyling was never allowed into the sea.

He grew from a child to a lad. He grew from a lad to a young man. He gathered driftwood for his mother's hearth and searched the tide pools for shells for her mantel. He mended his father's nets and tended his father's boat. But though he often stood by the shore or high in the town on the great grey cliffs, looking and longing and grieving his heart for what he did not really know, he never went into the sea.

Then one wind-wailing morning just fifteen years from the day that Greyling had been found, a great storm blew up suddenly in the North. It was such a storm as had never been seen before: the sky turned nearly black and even the fish had trouble swimming. The wind pushed huge waves onto the shore. The waters gobbled up the little hut on the beach. And Greyling and the fisherman's wife were forced to flee to the town high on the great grey cliffs. There they looked down at the roiling, boiling, sea. Far from shore they spied the fisherman's boat, its sails flapping like the wings of a wounded gull. And clinging to the broken mast was the fisherman himself, sinking deeper with every wave.

The fisherman's wife gave a terrible cry. "Will no one save him?" she called to the people of the town who had gathered on the edge of the cliff. "Will no one save my own dear husband who is all of life to me?"

But the townsmen looked away. There was no man there who dared risk his life in that sea, even to save a drowning soul.

"Will no one at all save him?" she cried out again.

"Let the boy go," said one old man, pointing at Greyling with his stick. "He looks strong enough."

But the fisherman's wife clasped Greyling in her arms and held his ears with her hands. She did not want him to go into the sea. She was afraid he would never return.

"Will no one save my own dear heart?" cried the fisherman's wife for a third and last time.

But shaking their heads, the people of the town edged to their houses and shut their doors and locked their windows and set

their backs to the ocean and their faces to the fires that glowed in every hearth.

"I will save him, Mother," cried Greyling, "or die as I try."

And before she could tell him no, he broke from her grasp and dived from the top of the great cliffs, down, down, down into the tumbling sea.

"He will surely sink," whispered the women as they ran from their warm fires to watch.

"He will certainly drown," called the men as they took down their spyglasses from the shelves.

They gathered on the cliffs and watched the boy dive down into the sea.

As Greyling disappeared beneath the waves, little fingers of foam tore at his clothes. They snatched his shirt and his pants and his shoes and sent them bubbling away to the shore. And as Greyling went deeper beneath the waves, even his skin seemed to slough off till he swam, free at last, in the sleek grey coat of a great grey seal.

The selchie had returned to the sea.

But the people of the town did not see this. All they saw was the diving boy disappearing under the waves and then, farther out, a large seal swimming toward the boat that wallowed in the sea. The sleek grey seal, with no effort at all, eased the fisherman to the shore though the waves were wild and bright with foam. And then, with a final salute, it turned its back on the land and headed joyously out to sea.

The fisherman's wife hurried down to the sand. And behind her followed the people of the town. They searched up the beach and down, but they did not find the boy.

"A brave son," said the men when they found his shirt, for they thought he was certainly drowned.

"A very brave son," said the women when they found his shoes, for they thought him lost for sure.

"Has he really gone?" asked the fisherman's wife of her husband when at last they were alone.

"Yes, quite gone," the fisherman said to her. "Gone where his heart calls, gone to the great wide sea. And though my heart grieves at his leaving, it tells me this way is best."

The fisherman's wife sighed. And then she cried. But at last she agreed that, perhaps, it was best. "For he is both man and seal," she said. "And though we cared for him for a while, now he must care for himself." And she never cried again.

So once more they lived alone by the side of the sea in a new little hut which was covered with mosses to keep them warm in the winter and cool in the summer.

Yet, once a year, a great grey seal is seen at night near the fisherman's home. And the people in town talk of it, and wonder. But seals do come to the shore and men do go to the sea; and so the townfolk do not dwell upon it very long.

But it is no ordinary seal. It is Greyling himself come home—come to tell his parents tales of the lands that lie far beyond the waters, and to sing them songs of the wonders that lie far beneath the sea.

Reader's Response

Do you think this ending is happy? Explain your answer.

Responding to the Selection

Your Response

1. Which character in the story would you like to know more about? What would you like to know about him or her?
2. Do you think the fisherman and his wife were right to keep the selchie? Explain.

Recalling

3. Explain how the fisherman and his wife come to have a son.
4. Why is the son called Greyling?
5. Describe what happens when Greyling rescues his father.

Interpreting

6. Why does the fisherman feel "somehow, it was wrong" never to let Greyling return to the sea?
7. As Greyling grows up, his heart "longs and grieves" for something he cannot name. What might this be?
8. Does Greyling know what will happen when he dives into the sea to save his father? Support your answer.

Applying

9. Do you agree with the couple's attitude at the end of the story? Explain your answer.
10. How does being true to one's nature affect one's life?

Analyzing Literature

Understanding Conflict

A **conflict** is a struggle between opposing forces. In "Greyling" the conflict occurs between a character and nature. Greyling struggles with his inner nature—he is a seal in the sea and a human on land—even though he is not consciously aware of his animal side.

1. What clue is given in Greyling's behavior that hints at his struggle with his inner nature?
2. Near the end of the story, the fisherman says, "And though my heart grieves at his leaving, it tells me this way is best." Why does the fisherman feel this way? Do you agree with him? Why or why not?
3. At the end of the story, do you think that Greyling has set his inner struggle to rest? Why or why not?

Critical Thinking and Reading

Recognizing the Turning Point

The **turning point,** or climax, of a story is the point in the plot when the tension is the greatest and when one of the opposing forces wins the struggle.

1. At what point in this story does the turning point, or climax, occur?
2. Which force wins the struggle at the climax?
3. What is the resolution of the conflict?

Thinking and Writing

Writing as a Story Character

Imagine that you are Greyling on one of your yearly visits to your parents. Make notes about an adventure that you would like to tell them. Arrange the events of your adventure in a logical order and write the first draft. Read your first draft aloud to a partner and make any changes to improve the descriptions. Try to add figurative expressions to make your descriptions vivid. Proofread your story and prepare a final draft.

Learning Options

1. **Community Connections.** Imagine that the people of the town have decided to dedicate a monument to Greyling. In a group of two or three classmates, design a monument to honor the boy who saved his father. Write a brief inscription for the monument and a paragraph that explains how your design honors Greyling's action.
2. **Speaking and Listening.** If you could change yourself into an animal, which animal would you choose to be? Explain your choice to the class in an oral presentation.

GUIDE FOR READING

Isaac Asimov

(1920–1992) wrote about the wonders of robots, computers, and space travel long before they became a part of everyday life. Born in Russia and raised in Brooklyn, New York, Asimov wrote his first story at age eleven. Now he is considered one of the foremost writers of science fiction. Asimov was equally skilled as an essayist, explaining complicated scientific and mathematical theories in a way that readers can understand. In "Sarah Tops" Asimov examines how people think and how they solve problems.

Sarah Tops

Narrator

The **narrator** is the person who tells the story. A narrator may be either a character in the story or a speaker who is outside it. In "Sarah Tops" a character in the story is the narrator. He tells you the events as he sees them and takes part in them.

Focus

In "Sarah Tops," a clever teenager solves a crime while listening to his father describe the case. Think about stories you have read or movies you have seen about crimes and mysteries. Copy the chart below onto a sheet of paper. With two or three classmates, list all the characters you can think of in literature, movies, and television who solve mysteries. Then describe the techniques each character uses and why the character is interesting.

Name of Character	Technique Used to Solve Crime	Why Character Is Interesting
Sherlock Holmes	*Deduction/logic*	*Holmes is clever and the cases he solves often have an unusual twist.*

Vocabulary

Knowing the following words will help you read "Sarah Tops."

soothingly (sōōth′ iŋ lē) *adv.*: In a calming manner (p. 42)

hysterical (his ter′ i k'l) *adj.*: Emotionally uncontrolled; wild (p. 42)

conscience (kän′ shəns) *n.*: Knowledge of right and wrong (p. 42)

Spelling Tip

Notice that the word *conscience* is an exception to the spelling rule, "*i* before *e* except after *c*." This exception applies to any word in which the *ie* follows a *c* with an *sh* or *ch* sound.

Sarah Tops

Isaac Asimov

"She said he said three words to her, very slowly, 'Try . . . Sarah . . . Tops.' Then he died."

I came out of the Museum of Natural History[1] and was crossing the street on my way to the subway, when I saw the crowd about halfway down the block; and the police cars, too. I could hear the whine of an approaching ambulance.

For a minute I hesitated, but then I walked on. The crowds of the curious just get in the way of officials trying to save lives. My Dad, who's a detective on the force, com-

1. **Museum of Natural History:** The American Museum of Natural History, located in New York City. It has exhibitions promoting the study of the history of plants, animals, humans, and the physical makeup of the earth.

plains about that all the time, and I wasn't going to add to the difficulty myself.

I just kept my mind on the term paper I was going to have to write on air-pollution for my 7th-grade class and mentally arranged the notes I had taken on the Museum program on the subject.

Of course, I knew I would read about it in the afternoon papers. Besides, I would ask Dad about it after dinner. Sometimes he talked about cases without giving too much of the real security details. And Mom and I never talk about what we hear, anyway.

After I asked, Mom looked kind of funny and said, "He was in the museum at the very time."

I said, "I was working on my term paper. I was there first thing in the morning."

Mom looked worried. "There might have been shooting in the museum."

"Well, there wasn't," said Dad soothingly. "This man tried to lose himself in the museum and he didn't succeed."

"I would have," I said. "I know the museum, every inch."

Dad doesn't like me boasting, so he frowned at me. "The thugs who were after him didn't let him get away entirely. They caught up with him outside, knifed him, and got away. We'll catch them, though. We know who they are.

He nodded his head. "They're what's left of the gang that broke into that jewelry store two weeks ago. We managed to get the jewels back, but we didn't grab all the men. And not all the jewels either. One diamond was left. A big one—worth thirty thousand dollars."

"Maybe that's what the killers were after," I said.

"Very likely. The dead man was probably trying to cross the other two and get off with that one stone for himself. They turned out his pockets, practically ripped off his clothes, after they knifed him."

"Did they get the diamond?" I asked.

"How can we tell? The woman who reported the killing came on him when he was just barely able to breathe. She said he said three words to her, very slowly. 'Try . . . Sarah . . . Tops.' Then he died."

"Who is Sarah Tops?" asked Mom.

Dad shrugged. "I don't know. I don't even know if that's really what he said. The woman was pretty hysterical. If she's right and that's what he said, then maybe the killers didn't get the diamond. Maybe the dead man left it with Sarah Tops, whoever she is. Maybe he knew he was dying and wanted to give it back and have it off his conscience."

"Is there a Sarah Tops in the phone book, Dad?" I asked.

Dad said, "Did you think we didn't look? No Sarah Tops, either one P or two P's. Nothing in the city directory. Nothing in our files. Nothing in the FBI files."

Mom said, "Maybe it's not a person. Maybe it's a firm. Sarah Tops Cakes or something."

"Could be," said Dad. "There's no Sarah Tops firm, but there are other kinds of Tops and they'll be checked out for anyone working there named Sarah. It'll take days of dull routine."

I got an idea suddenly and bubbled over. "Listen, Dad, maybe it isn't a firm either. Maybe it's a *thing*. Maybe the woman didn't hear 'Sarah Tops' but 'Sarah's top'; you know, a *top* that you spin. If the dead guy has a daughter named Sarah, maybe he gouged a bit out of her top and stashed the diamond inside and . . ."

Dad pointed his finger at me and grinned, "Very good, Larry," he said, "A nice idea. But he doesn't have a daughter named Sarah. Or any relative by that name as far as we know. We've searched where he lived and there's nothing reported there that can be called a top."

"Well," I said, sort of let down and disappointed, "I suppose that's not such a good idea anyway, because why should he say we ought to try it? He either hid it in Sarah's top or he didn't. He would know which. Why should he say we should *try* it?"

And then it hit me. What if . . .

Dad was just getting up, as if he were going to turn on television, and I said, "Dad,

can you get into the museum this time of evening?"

"On police business? Sure."

"Dad," I said, kind of breathless, "I think we better go look. *Now*. Before the people start coming in again."

"Why?"

"I've got a silly idea. I . . . I . . ."

Dad didn't push me. He likes me to have my own ideas. He thinks maybe I'll be a detective, too, some day. He said, "All right. Let's follow up your lead whatever it is."

He called the museum, then we took a taxi and got there just when the last purple bit of twilight was turning to black. We were let in by a guard.

I'd never been in the museum when it was dark. It looked like a huge, underground cave, with the guard's flashlight seeming to make things even darker and more mysterious.

We took the elevator up to the fourth floor where the big shapes loomed in the bit of light that shone this way and that as the guard moved his flash.

"Do you want me to put on the light in this room?" he asked.

"Yes, please," I said.

There they all were. Some in glass cases; but the big ones in the middle of the large room. Bones and teeth and spines of giants that ruled the earth hundreds of millions of years ago.

"I want to look close at that one," I said. "Is it all right if I climb over the railing?"

"Go ahead," said the guard. He helped me.

I leaned against the platform, looking at the grayish plaster material the skeleton was standing on.

"What's this?" I said. It didn't look much different in color from the plaster on which it was lying.

"Chewing gum," said the guard, frowning. "Those darn kids . . ."

"The guy was trying to get away and he saw his chance to throw this . . . keep it away from *them*. . . ." Before I could finish my sentence Dad took the gum from me. He squeezed it, then pulled it apart. Something inside caught the light and flashed. Dad put it in an envelope. "How did you know?" he asked me.

"Well, look at it," I said.

It was a magnificent skeleton. It had a large skull with bone stretching back over the neck vertebrae. It had two horns over the eyes, and a third one, just a bump, on the snout. The nameplate said *Triceratops*.

Reader's Response

Have you ever solved a problem in a way similar to the way Larry and his family figured out the meaning of the clue? Explain.

Responding to Literature

Your Response

1. Were you able to solve this mystery? What were some of your guesses?
2. What is your opinion of Larry's father? If you were in his father's place, would you have followed up on Larry's idea? Explain.

Recalling

3. How does Larry know that a crime has occurred at the museum that day?
4. What were the thugs trying to get from the dead man?
5. List three ideas that the family discuss about the clue before Larry thinks of the solution.
6. Where does Larry find the missing jewel?

Interpreting

7. Explain the misunderstanding that results in people hearing the clue "Try . . . Sarah . . . Tops."
8. What personal qualities and experience does Larry have that help him to figure out the true meaning of the clue?

Applying

9. Larry's father likes Larry to think for himself. Why is it important for people to learn to think for themselves?

Analyzing Literature

Recognizing the Role of the Narrator

The **narrator** is the person who tells the story. A narrator may be a character in the story or a speaker outside it.

1. Who is the narrator in "Sarah Tops"?
2. What is his role in the story?
3. How does his telling the story affect what you learn about the events?
4. How might this story be different if it were told by the father?

Critical Thinking and Reading

Reasoning to a Conclusion

Reasoning is thinking logically. Larry and his family use reasoning to solve the mystery. They try out each possible solution to the problem. They question it, discard it when it does not work out, and discuss another possible solution. This process leads Larry to arrive at the valid, or reasonable, conclusion.

1. What helps Larry come up with the idea that perhaps Sarah Tops is not the name of a person?
2. How does Larry decide that the man could not have said "Sarah's top"?
3. How do you think Larry arrives at the correct conclusion?

Thinking and Writing

Supporting an Opinion

Would the story of how Larry and his father solve crimes make a good television series? Your answer should be based on what qualities you think a crime series should have—what aspects of a crime series attract you. First, decide whether you would recommend Larry and his father as main characters of a television series. Write the first draft of a letter to a television network, stating your view and giving reasons to back it up. Read your first draft to a small group of classmates and discuss how you can make your letter more persuasive. Use the suggestions to help you revise.

Learning Option

Speaking and Listening. Choose one of your classmates as a partner. One of you will pretend to be Larry and the other will pretend to be a reporter. As the reporter, prepare a list of questions and conduct an interview with Larry. Record your interview on a sheet of paper or on a tape recorder.

GUIDE FOR READING

James Berry

(1925–) was born in Jamaica, West Indies, and the lilting rhythms of West Indian speech flavor his writing. Berry, who is a well-known poet and literary critic, lives in England, but he has never forgotten Jamaica. His fiction for young people includes a novel called *Ajeemah and His Son,* the story of an African man and his son who are snatched by slave traders and taken to Jamaica, and *A Thief in the Village,* a collection of short stories about life in Jamaica, from which this story comes.

Becky and the Wheels-and-Brake Boys

Surprise Ending

A **surprise ending** in a story occurs when the conflict is resolved in a way other than the way the reader expects. In a well-written story, a surprise ending grows naturally from the events in the plot. The surprise ending must be believable and must fit with what the reader knows about the characters and setting.

Focus

"Becky and the Wheels-and-Brake Boys" is about a girl who wants a bicycle that her mother cannot afford to buy for her. What would you do if you had a similar problem? On a separate sheet of paper, draw the bicycle wheel shown below. In the center of the wheel, write the word *bicycle.* In between the spokes of the wheel, write all the ways you can think of to earn money for a bicycle. After you have read the story, review your wheel to compare your ideas to Becky's solution.

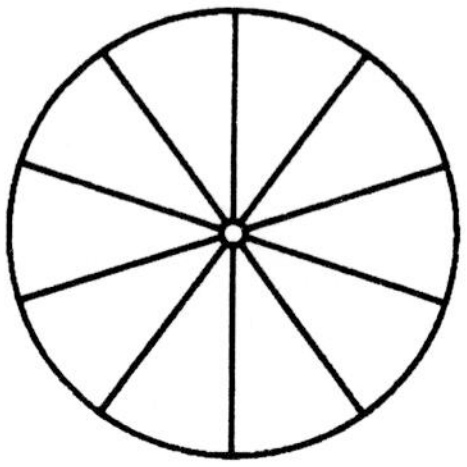

Vocabulary

Knowing the following words will help you read "Becky and the Wheels-and-Brake Boys."

veranda (və ran′ də) *n.*: An open porch, usually with a roof, along the outside of a building (p. 48)

menace (men′ əs) *n.*: A threat; a troublesome or annoying person (p. 48)

Spelling Tip

To help you spell *menace,* remember the little word *ace* that comes in the ending.

Becky and the Wheels-and-Brake Boys

James Berry

"Over and over I told my mum I wanted a bike. Over and over she looked at me as if I was crazy."

Even my own cousin Ben was there—riding away, in the ringing of bicycle bells down the road. Every time I came to watch them—see them riding round and round enjoying themselves—they scooted off like crazy on their bikes.

They can't keep doing that. They'll see!

I only want to be with Nat, Aldo, Jimmy, and Ben. It's no fair reason they don't want to be with me. Anybody could go off their head for that. Anybody! A girl can not, not, let boys get away with it all the time.

Bother! I have to walk back home, alone.

I know total-total that if I had my own bike, the Wheels-and-Brake Boys wouldn't treat me like that. I'd just ride away with them, wouldn't I?

Over and over I told my mum I wanted a bike. Over and over she looked at me as if I was crazy. "Becky, d'you think you're a boy? Eh? D'you think you're a boy? In any case, where's the money to come from? Eh?"

Of course I know I'm not a boy. Of course I know I'm not crazy. Of course I know all

that's no reason why I can't have a bike. No reason! As soon as I get indoors I'll just have to ask again—ask Mum once more.

At home, indoors, I didn't ask my mum.

It was evening time, but sunshine was still big patches in yards and on housetops. My two younger brothers, Lenny and Vin, played marbles in the road. Mum was taking measurements of a boy I knew, for his new trousers and shirt. Mum made clothes for people. Meggie, my sister two years younger than me, was helping Mum on the veranda. Nobody would be pleased with me not helping. I began to help.

Granny-Liz would always stop fanning herself to drink up a glass of ice water. I gave my granny a glass of ice water, there in her rocking chair. I looked in the kitchen to find shelled coconut pieces to cut into small cubes for the fowls' morning feed. But Granny-Liz had done it. I came and started tidying up bits and pieces of cut-off material around my mum on the floor. My sister got nasty, saying she was already helping Mum. Not a single good thing was happening for me.

With me even being all so thoughtful of Granny's need of a cool drink, she started up some botheration[1] against me.

Listen to Granny-Liz: "Becky, with you moving about me here on the veranda, I hope you dohn have any centipedes or scorpions[2] in a jam jar in your pocket."

"No, mam," I said sighing, trying to be calm. "Granny-Liz," I went on, "you forgot. My centipede and scorpion died." All the same, storm broke against me.

"Becky," my mum said. "You know I don't like you wandering off after dinner. Haven't I told you I don't want you keeping company with those awful riding-about bicycle boys? Eh?"

"Yes, mam."

"Those boys are a menace. Riding bicycles on sidewalks and narrow paths together, ringing bicycle bells and braking at people's feet like wild bulls charging anybody, they're heading for trouble."

"They're the Wheels-and-Brake Boys, mam."

"The what?"

"The Wheels-and-Brake Boys."

"Oh! Given themselves a name as well, have they? Well, Becky, answer this. How d'you always manage to look like you just escaped from a hair-pulling battle? Eh? And don't I tell you not to break the backs down and wear your canvas shoes like slippers? Don't you ever hear what I say?"

"Yes, mam."

"D'you want to end up a field laborer? Like where your father used to be overseer?"[3]

"No, mam."

"Well, Becky, will you please go off and do your homework?"

Everybody did everything to stop me. I was allowed no chance whatsoever. No chance to talk to Mum about the bike I dream of day and night! And I knew exactly the bike I wanted. I wanted a bike like Ben's bike. Oh, I wished I still had even my scorpion on a string to run up and down somebody's back!

I answered my mum. "Yes, mam." I went off into Meg's and my bedroom.

---

1. botheration (bäth′ ər ā′ shən) *n.*: Trouble.

2. scorpions (skôr′ pē ənz) *n.*: Close relatives of spiders, with a poisonous stinger at the end of their tails; found in warm regions.

3. overseer (o′ vər sē′ ər) *n.*: A supervisor of laborers.

BIKING FOR FUN, 1992
Carlton Murrell
Courtesy of the Artist

I sat down at the little table, as well as I might. Could homework stay in anybody's head in broad daylight outside? No. Could I keep a bike like Ben's out of my head? Not one bit. That bike took me all over the place. My beautiful bike jumped every log, every rock, every fence. My beautiful bike did everything cleverer than a clever cowboy's horse, with me in the saddle. And the bell, the bell was such a glorious gong of a ring!

If Dad was alive, I could talk to him. If Dad was alive, he'd give me money for the bike like a shot.

I sighed. It was amazing what a sigh could do. I sighed and tumbled on a great idea. Tomorrow evening I'd get Shirnette to come with me. Both of us together would be sure to get the boys interested to teach us to ride. Wow! With Shirnette they can't just ride away!

Next day at school, everything went sour. For the first time, Shirnette and me had a real fight, because of what I hated most.

Shirnette brought a cockroach to school in a shoe-polish tin. At playtime she opened the tin and let the cockroach fly into my blouse. Pure panic and disgust nearly killed me. I crushed up the cockroach in my clothes and practically ripped my blouse off, there in open sunlight. Oh, the smell of a cockroach is the nastiest ever to block your nose! I started running with my blouse to go and wash it. Twice I had to stop and be sick.

I washed away the crushed cockroach stain from my blouse. Then the stupid Shirnette had to come into the toilet, falling about laughing. All right, I knew the cockroach treatment was for the time when I made my centipede on a string crawl up Shirnette's back. But you put fair-is-fair aside. I just barged into Shirnette.

When it was all over, I had on a wet blouse, but Shirnette had one on, too.

DADDY'S GIRL, 1992
Carlton Murrell
Courtesy of the Artist

Then, going home with the noisy flock of children from school, I had such a new, new idea. If Mum thought I was scruffy, Nat, Aldo, Jimmy, and Ben might think so, too. I didn't like that.

After dinner I combed my hair in the bedroom. Mum did her machining[4] on the veranda. Meggie helped Mum. Granny sat there, wishing she could take on any job, as usual.

I told Mum I was going to make up a quarrel with Shirnette. I went, but my friend wouldn't speak to me, let alone come out to keep my company. I stood alone and watched the Wheels-and-Brake Boys again.

This time the boys didn't race away past me. I stood leaning against the tall coconut palm tree. People passed up and down. The nearby main road was busy with traffic. But I didn't mind. I watched the boys. Riding round and round the big flame tree, Nat, Aldo, Jimmy, and Ben looked marvelous.

At first each boy rode round the tree alone. Then each boy raced each other round the tree, going round three times. As he won, the winner rang his bell on and on, till he stopped panting and could laugh and talk properly. Next, most reckless and fierce, all the boys raced against each other. And, leaning against their bicycles, talking and joking, the boys popped soft drinks open, drank, and ate chipped bananas.

I walked up to Nat, Aldo, Jimmy, and Ben and said, "Can somebody teach me to ride?"

"Why don't you stay indoors and learn to cook and sew and wash clothes?" Jimmy said.

---

4. machining (mə shēn′ iŋ) *v.*: Sewing.

I grinned. "I know all that already," I said. "And one day perhaps I'll even be mum to a boy child, like all of you. Can you cook and sew and wash clothes, Jimmy? All I want is to learn to ride. I want you to teach me."

I didn't know why I said what I said. But everybody went silent and serious.

One after the other, Nat, Aldo, Jimmy, and Ben got on their bikes and rode off. I wasn't at all cross with them. I only wanted to be riding out of the playground with them. I knew they'd be heading into the town to have ice cream and things and talk and laugh.

Mum was sitting alone on the veranda. She sewed buttons onto a white shirt she'd made. I sat down next to Mum. Straightaway, "Mum," I said, "I still want to have a bike badly."

"Oh, Becky, you still have that foolishness in your head? What am I going to do?"

Mum talked with some sympathy. Mum knew I was honest. "I can't get rid of it, mam," I said.

Mum stopped sewing. "Becky," she said, staring in my face, "how many girls around here do you see with bicycles?"

"Janice Gordon has a bike," I reminded her.

"Janice Gordon's dad has acres and acres of coconuts and bananas, with a business in the town as well."

I knew Mum was just about to give in. Then my granny had to come out onto the veranda and interfere. Listen to that Granny-Liz. "Becky, I heard your mother tell you over and over she cahn[5] afford to buy you a bike. Yet you keep on and on. Child, you're a girl."

"But I don't want a bike because I'm a girl."

"D'you want it because you feel like a bwoy?" Granny said.

"No. I only want a bike because I want it and want it and want it."

Granny just carried on. "A tomboy's like a whistling woman and a crowing hen, who can only come to a bad end. D'you understand?"

I didn't want to understand. I knew Granny's speech was an awful speech. I went and sat down with Lenny and Vin, who were making a kite.

By Saturday morning I felt real sorry for Mum. I could see Mum really had it hard for money. I had to try and help. I knew anything of Dad's—anything—would be worth a great mighty hundred dollars.

I found myself in the center of town, going through the busy Saturday crowd. I hoped Mum wouldn't be too cross. I went into the fire station. With lots of luck I came face to face with a round-faced man in uniform. He talked to me. "Little miss, can I help you?"

I told him I'd like to talk to the head man. He took me into the office and gave me a chair. I sat down. I opened out my brown paper parcel. I showed him my dad's sun helmet. I told him I thought it would make a good fireman's hat. I wanted to sell the helmet for some money toward a bike, I told him.

The fireman laughed a lot. I began to laugh, too. The fireman put me in a car and drove me back home.

Mum's eyes popped to see me bringing home the fireman. The round-faced fireman

5. cahn: Can't.

laughed at my adventure. Mum laughed, too, which was really good. The fireman gave Mum my dad's hat back. Then—mystery, mystery—Mum sent me outside while they talked.

My mum was only a little cross with me. Then—mystery and more mystery—my mum took me with the fireman in his car to his house.

The fireman brought out what? A bicycle! A beautiful, shining bicycle! His nephew's bike. His nephew had been taken away, all the way to America. The bike had been left with the fireman-uncle for him to sell it. And the good, kind fireman-uncle decided we could have the bike—on small payments. My mum looked uncertain. But in a big, big way, the fireman knew it was all right. And Mum smiled a little. My mum had good sense to know it was all right. My mum took the bike from the fireman Mr. Dean.

And guess what? Seeing my bike much, much newer than his, my cousin Ben's eyes popped with envy. But he took on the big job. He taught me to ride. Then he taught Shirnette.

I ride into town with the Wheels-and-Brake Boys now. When she can borrow a bike, Shirnette comes too. We all sit together. We have patties and ice cream and drink drinks together. We talk and joke. We ride about, all over the place.

And, again, guess what? Fireman Mr. Dean became our best friend, and Mum's especially. He started coming around almost every day.

MOTHER I LOVE TO RIDE, 1992
Carlton Murrell
Courtesy of the Artist

MULTICULTURAL CONNECTION

Dialects

As you read James Berry's story, you must have noticed a few words and phrases that you never heard anyone say before. Some, like "total-total," were easy enough to figure out. Others were confusing enough that you probably had to look at the footnotes to find out what they meant.

You know that not everyone speaks English the same way. People have different accents and, very often, quite a few different words. They may even have different ways of using the same words.

What is a dialect? When people speak in a way that is very different from others who use the same language, their speech is called a dialect. You can find dialects not only in different countries, but in different regions of the same country. We are not surprised to hear someone from Texas speak differently from someone who grew up in Massachusetts—or California or Georgia.

Dialects around the world. Dialects are created when one group of people has little or no contact with other groups. Two thousand years ago, when the Romans ruled much of Europe, they were able to force everyone to learn Latin. Although Latin was spoken in some areas long after the Roman Empire collapsed, each one developed its own dialect. Within a few hundred years, these had become separate languages. In Spain alone, there were three new languages, Castillian, Catalán, and Galician, all of which are spoken by millions of people today.

How many dialects are there in the United States? American English is usually considered to consist of three major dialects: eastern, southern, and midwestern, but in fact there are many smaller ones.

Because Britain is so much older, its dialects are far more numerous and divergent than those of the United States. Pronunciation and vocabulary may vary so much that people from different regions cannot understand each other. For example, in Sussex, an apple is called a "scrump."

The dialects of every language show great diversity. French has dialects like Picard, spoken in northern France, and Walloon, spoken in Belgium. There are also forms of French found in Quebec, Haiti, Louisiana, and Tahiti. Some dialects of Chinese, Mandarin, Cantonese, Wu, and Min, have more speakers than many of the national languages of other countries.

American English. Very few people in the United States speak strictly standard American English. For one thing, local variations continue to exist—sometimes even within the same city. For another, language is constantly changing as everyone, from rap singers to poets to students to scientists continue to invent new ideas, new names for objects, and new reasons for communicating.

Brainstorming

With classmates, try to think of words and expressions that vary from one region to another. For example, *soda, pop,* and *tonic* are used in different parts of the country to describe the same thing. Make a list.

Reader's Response

Would you like to know Becky? Would you like her as a friend?

Responding to the Selection

Your Response

1. Should Becky have taken her father's sun helmet to sell? Why or why not?

Recalling

2. What do the Wheels-and-Brake Boys do that makes Becky's mother disapprove of them?
3. Explain how Becky gets a bicycle.

Interpreting

4. Why does Granny-Liz think that Becky would come to a bad end?
5. What does Jimmy think about girls who want to ride bicycles? Do you think that he and Granny-Liz agree with each other about Becky's dream? Explain.
6. Why does Becky think that anything that had belonged to her father would be worth a lot of money?

Applying

7. Becky's unfailing determination helped her reach her goal. Describe other situations in which a person's determination brought about effective results.

Analyzing Literature

Appreciating the Surprise Ending

A **surprise ending** is an ending that is different from what you expected. In "Becky and the Wheels-and-Brake Boys," the writer reveals enough about Becky's character to let you know that Becky will find an unusual way to get what she wants.

1. What events in the story reveal Becky's personality?
2. At what point in the story do you suspect that Becky is about to take action to get a bicycle herself?
3. What is the surprise at the end of the story? Why was Mum "only a little cross" with Becky?

Critical Thinking and Reading

Understanding Dialect

Dialect is a form of language spoken by people of a certain region or group. The people in the story you have just read speak a West Indian dialect. Explain the meaning of each of the following words and phrases:

1. total-total
2. a great mighty
3. dohn
4. bwoy

Thinking and Writing

Extending the Story

Becky's life will be different now that she has her bicycle. Write a story telling what happens next in the lives of the characters. You may want to tell the readers what Granny-Liz said about the new bicycle or to tell more about Mr. Dean. Share your draft with a writing partner; then incorporate your partner's suggestions.

Learning Options

1. **Writing.** A proverb is a short saying that contains a bit of wisdom. Granny-Liz quotes a proverb when she says, "A tomboy's like a whistling woman and a crowing hen, who can only come to a bad end." Write your own proverbs about things you have observed in your daily life.
2. **Art.** In her imagination, Becky sees all the wonderful capabilities of her bicycle. Design a bicycle that does all the things you'd like. Share your design with the class, explaining the bike's special features.

ONE WRITER'S PROCESS

James Berry and "Becky"

PREWRITING

Finding a Good Idea Did you ever wonder how writers get ideas for stories? Do they sit back in their chairs and daydream? Do they remember fascinating characters they have met or exciting stories that people have told them?

Some writers, like James Berry, use a memory as the starting point and add their own ideas about events and outcomes. "Becky and the Wheels-and-Brakes Boys" is not a true story, but it was inspired by real people and settings from Berry's childhood. In other words, Berry is not telling a story that *did* happen, he is telling a story that *could have* happened. "My first impetus to write 'Becky,'" he recalls, "was the excitement of a determined girl among boys, that came into my head. The idea for the story didn't come out of actual incidents, but my own boyhood experience reminded me of boys I have known who would behave to a girl in the same way as the boys were to do in the story. Also, when I was growing up in my Jamaican village, we—myself and some other boys—did sometimes actually play with a girl like Becky."

Planning a Story Before they begin a story, many writers plan it out in their minds or on paper. They ask themselves questions about the story and then try to answer them before they begin writing.

Who? James Berry asked himself *who* would tell his story. Would it be someone involved in the story's events or someone who observed those events from the outside?

The answer was clear to him "from the start." He says, "a strong excitement for me was the telling of the story by Becky herself. I wanted her stubborn character to come through at first hand, out of her thinking and scheming and planning and then the carrying out of her actions."

What? Berry also had to ask himself *what* would happen in the story: "Before I start the actual writing of a story," he says, "I first think it through. I have to agree with myself what I want the story to say. Although sometimes that gets changed, it is never changed much. At the planning stage I write down a very very brief outline of the story's scenes and happenings."

With this preparation, he was ready to begin actually writing his story.

DRAFTING

Working from a Blueprint When builders create a house, they use a blueprint to show them where the different rooms should go. In a similar way, Berry uses an outline to help himself decide on a structure for the story, but it is only a guide. He may refer to it to make sure he is describing the events of the story in the right order, but "It is the characters," he says, "who develop in their given situations. When I write I merely let the drama develop."

What do you think Berry means when he credits the characters with helping to develop the plot? How can an imaginary character make decisions? Like Berry, you can use someone you know or used to know as the basis for a character in a story. Asking yourself questions about how that person would react in different situations will help you decide what will happen at various points in the story.

When Berry was finished drafting his story, he liked the way it sounded, but he wanted to see what someone else would think of it.

REVISING

Getting Another Opinion You are often asked to show your written work to peer editors, classmates who will help you make it better.

Professional writers like James Berry also ask others to read and comment on their work. Berry says, "Two people read the story for me; their positive reactions made me keep the story as it was." If Berry's two readers had not liked parts of the story, however, he was prepared to revise it.

The next step was to get his story published.

PUBLISHING

Finding an Audience The real life of a story begins when it is published. Writers are always eager to hear what readers will make of their work. Will they enjoy it? Will they understand it? Will readers find something in it that connects with their own lives?

"Becky and the Wheels-and-Brake Boys" first appeared in 1987 in a book of James Berry's short stories called *A Thief in the Village*. Has Berry heard from readers about his story?

"I have had some very good feedback about 'Becky,'" he says. One reason for its success might be that, while the story takes place in the Caribbean, it really could happen anywhere.

THINKING ABOUT THE PROCESS

1. How would the story have been different if Berry had chosen someone other than Becky to tell it?
2. Why was it helpful for Berry to show the finished story to two people before he sent it out for publication?
3. **Outlining a Story** Becky's story consists of five separate scenes. Get together with several classmates and make a list of these scenes, using a few words to describe where the scene takes place and what happens in it. (You might want to make your list a part of a story map like the one on page 247.) For example, you might describe the first scene by writing, "The veranda: Becky asks for a bike." Your completed list will probably look like the outline James Berry used to write the story.

YOUR WRITING PROCESS

Writing a Narrative

Since humans first spoke, they have told stories. A piece of writing that tells a story is a **narrative**. Narratives can be entirely make-believe, such as "Dragon, Dragon," or, like "The King of Mazy May," they can be similar to real life, with just a splash of the imaginary.

Your Turn

Write a narrative about an experience that has meant something to you: the time you broke your ankle, the day your grandfather died, the time you set a videogame scoring record. The only requirements are that you can remember the experience in detail and that it made you *feel* a strong emotion: happiness, fear, pride. Your goal is to make your readers feel this emotion, too.

Prewriting

1. Brainstorm for possible topics. You can use sentence completions like these to get ideas:

1. When I ______, I took a huge step toward independence.
2. I never laughed so hard as when ______.
3. ______ was the most frightening thing I've ever seen.

2. Choose a topic. Which experience made you feel the strongest emotion? Which one would you most like to share with your readers? Select one.

3. Make a time line. A story can take place over years, months, days, or hours. For example, "Sarah Tops" occurs in about six hours, but "Greyling" takes more than fifteen years. Once you've chosen a narrative topic, make a time line and divide it into years, months, days, or hours. Arrange the actions of your story into chronological order, that is, in the order that they occurred through time.

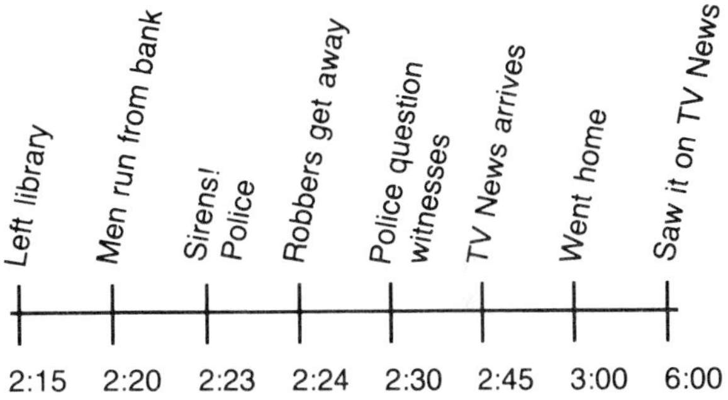

Drafting

Using your time line, write a first draft of your narrative by putting your notes into full sentences. Begin new paragraphs when you begin a new idea or when your story takes a big jump in time. Make sure that each event is clearly connected to the one before it and the one after it.

One student used the last sentence completion to write a narrative about witnessing a robbery. Here is the beginning.

> My mother and I walked out of the public library where she was doing some research for her class. It was a hot July afternoon. The sun was glaring off the windows of the tall buildings. Suddenly, we heard commotion and people screaming.
>
> My mother pulled me close to her and we saw two men come out of a bank across the street. The men had ski masks over their faces and one of them held a package in his hand. People on the street backed away quickly as the men headed for a parked car.
>
> Then we heard sirens. . . .

Notice how one event leads to the next. Words such as *suddenly* and *then* help guide the reader through the chain of events. These words, called transitions, show the order of events in time. Other time transitions include *first, soon, after, before, meanwhile*, and *at last*. As you draft your narrative, use transitions to connect events.

Notice, too, how the writer tries to make you feel the emotion of the scene by showing the events in detail. You can picture the glaring sun and the ski masks. You can hear screams and tires squealing. These details make the narrative come to life in your mind.

As you draft, just get your story onto the page. Later, you can go back and smooth out the rough spots.

Revising

Step 1: Use the revising checklist on page 749 to evaluate and revise your draft.

Step 2: Ask a writing partner or someone you trust to read your draft and answer two or three questions such as these:

- Were there any places where you were confused about what was happening?
- Were there any places where you wanted more information than you were given?
- What emotions did my narrative make you feel as you were reading?

Step 3: Pay special attention to the beginning of your narrative. Will your first sentence make your readers want to read the rest of your story? For example, the student writing about the robbery revised his first sentences like this:

> It seemed like a typical boring July afternoon. As we stepped out of the Public Library, I never suspected that I would witness something I would never forget.

This opening creates a question—What did he witness?—that pulls the reader into the narrative. There are hundreds of ways to begin stories. Find the one that fits your topic and your personality as a storyteller.

Step 4: Similarly, concentrate on your ending. It's best to end with a strong detail such as a sight or a sound. Do *not* end by telling your readers what your narrative means. Let them figure it out for themselves.

Proofreading

Use the proofreading guidelines on page 753. If you have used quotations, be sure to proofread them carefully for punctuation.

Reading for Character

WOMEN REACHING FOR THE MOON
Rufino Tamayo
Cleveland Museum of Art

GUIDE FOR READING

Auntie

Philippa Pearce

(1920–), who lives in England, has been writing children's literature for over forty years. She worked first as a children's book editor, then began to write books herself, and now devotes most of her time to her writing. She has also worked for the British Broadcasting Corporation, producing programs for educational television. Philippa Pearce was awarded England's Carnegie Medal in 1959 for *Tom's Midnight Garden* and the Whitebread Award in 1978 for *The Battle of Bubble and Squeak.*

Character Traits

Character traits are the qualities that make a person an individual. For example, one person may have a sunny disposition, another a violent temper; one person may be a talented athlete, another a gifted painter. One of a writer's jobs is to make the characters he or she creates seem like flesh and blood people. Writers do this by giving characters traits that make them stand out as individuals. These traits then determine how the character behaves and interacts with others.

Focus

"Auntie" is about a woman with foresight. Read the two definitions of foresight in the vocabulary below. In a small group, discuss the two meanings and write two sentences for each definition. Then, create a Venn diagram by drawing two overlapping circles. Under one circle write the first definition. Under the second circle write the second definition. Write words or ideas that the two definitions have in common in the area where the circles intersect. Write words that express the differences between the two definitions in their respective circles. As you read the story, look for examples of each definition of foresight.

Vocabulary

Knowing the following words will help you read "Auntie."

discontented (dis′ kən tent′ id) *adj.*: Wanting something more or different (p. 61)

expeditions (eks′ pə dish′ ənz) *n.*: Trips (p. 61)

doted (dōt′ id) *v.*: Was excessively fond of (p. 61)

foresight (fôr′ sīt′) *n.*: The power to look forward; seeing into the future (p. 61)

stupefied (sto͞o′ pə fī′d′) *adj.*: Stunned; astounded (p. 67)

Spelling Tip

Remember the silent *e* when spelling *foresight.*

Auntie

Philippa Pearce

"I'm just telling you what happens. *I see things far away, and they're coming close."*

Up to the day she died, Auntie could thread the finest needle at one go. She did so on that last rainy day of her life. And, by the end of her life, her long sight had grown longer than anyone could possibly have expected.

Auntie's exceptional eyesight had been no particular help to her in her job: She was a file clerk in a block of offices, forever sorting other people's dull letters and dull memoranda. Boring; but Auntie was not ambitious, nor was she ever discontented.

Auntie's real interest—all her care—was for her family. She never married; but, by the time of her retirement from work, she was a great-aunt—although she was never called that—and she liked being one. She baby-sat and took children to school and helped with family expeditions. She knitted and crocheted and sewed—above all, she sewed. She mended and patched and made clothes. She sewed by hand when necessary; otherwise, she whirred the handle of an ancient sewing machine that had been a wedding present to her mother long before.

Unfortunately, she was not particularly good at making clothes. Little Billy, her youngest great-nephew, was her last victim. "Do I *have* to wear this blazer-thing?" he whispered to his mother, Auntie's niece. (He whispered because—even in his bitterness—he did not want Auntie to overhear.) "Honestly, Mum, no one at school ever wears anything looking like this."

"Hush!" said his mother. Then: "Auntie's very kind to take all that trouble and to save us money, too. You should be grateful."

"I'm not!" said little Billy; and he determined, when he was old enough, he wouldn't be at Auntie's mercy any more. Meanwhile, Auntie, who doted on Billy as the last child of his generation, was perplexed by the feeling that something she had done was not quite right.

Auntie was not a thinker, but she had common sense and—more and more—foresight. She knew, for instance, that nobody can live forever. One day she said, "I wonder when I shall die? And how? Heart, probably. My old dad, your granddad, died of that."

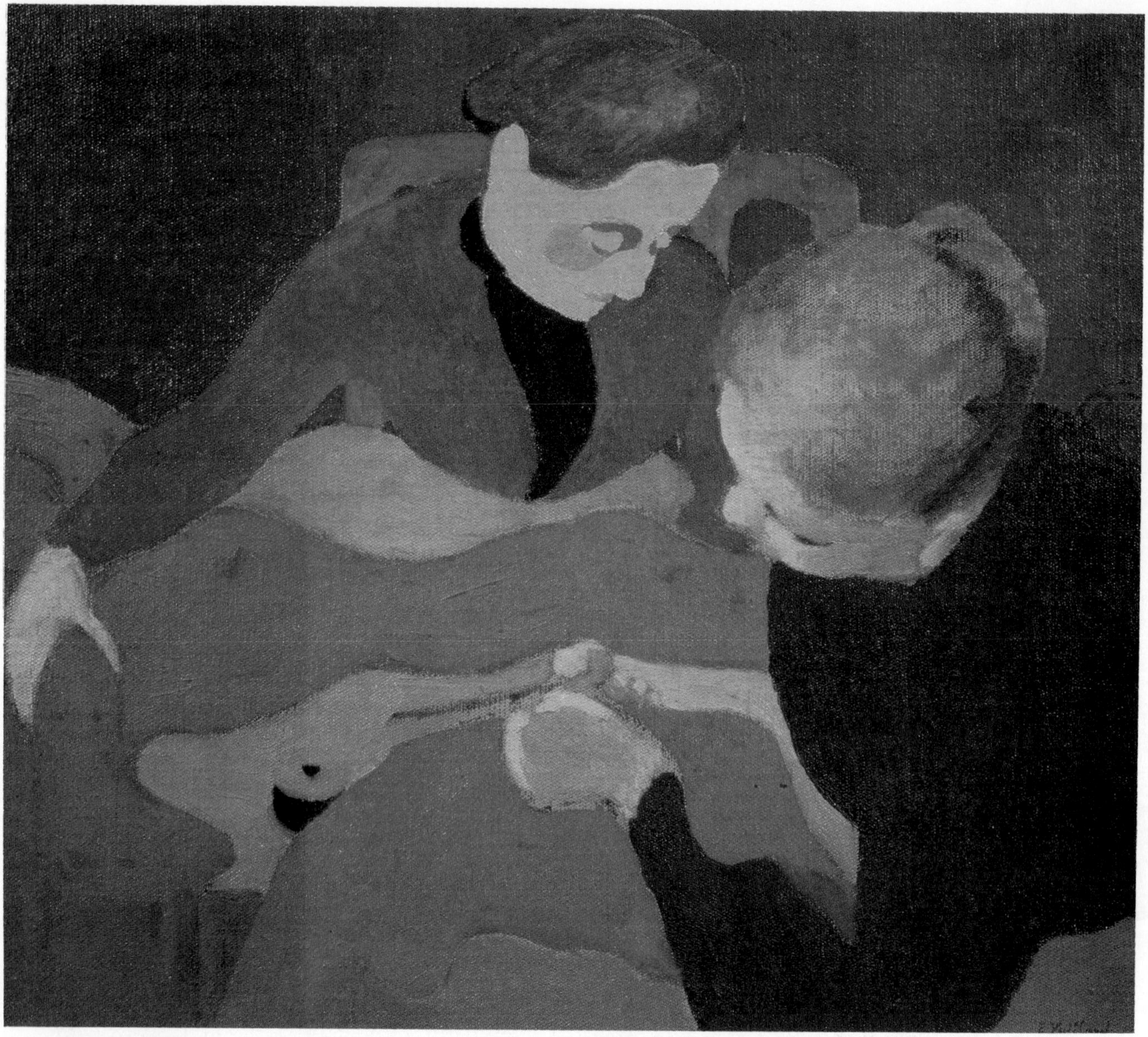

THE DRESSMAKERS
Édouard Vuillard
Josefowitz Collection

She was talking to the niece, Billy's mother, with whom Auntie now lived. The niece said, "Oh, Auntie, don't *talk* so!"

Auntie said, "My eyesight's as good as ever—well, better, really—but my hands aren't so much use." She looked at her hands, knobbling with rheumatism.[1] "I can't use 'em as I once did."

"Never *mind!*" said the niece.

"And the children are growing up. Even Billy." Auntie sighed. "Growing too old for me."

"The children *love* their auntie!" said the niece angrily. This was true, in its way; but that did not prevent great-nephews and great-nieces from becoming irritated when Auntie babied them and fussed over their clothing or whatever they happened to be doing.

Auntie did not continue the argument with her niece. She was no good at discussion or argument, anyway. That wasn't her strong point.

Her eyesight was her strong point and, yet, also her worry. In old age she sat for long periods by her bedroom window, looking out over rooftops to distant church spires and tower blocks. "I don't like seeing so far," she said once. "What's the use to me? Or to anyone else?"

"You're lucky," said her nephew-in-law, Billy's father. "Some people would give their eyes to—well, they'd give a lot to have your eyesight at your age."

"It's—it's *wrong,*" said Auntie, trying to explain something.

"If it happens that way, then it's natural," said her nephew.

---

1. rheumatism (ro͞o′ mə tiz′m) *n.*: A condition of swollen and stiff joints.

"Natural!" said Auntie; and she took to sitting at her bedroom window with her eyes closed.

One day: "Asleep?" her niece asked softly.

"No." Auntie's eyes opened at once. "Just resting my eyes. Trying to get them not to go on with all this looking and looking, seeing and seeing. . . ." Here Auntie paused, again attempting to sort out some ideas. But the ideas and what lay behind them could not be as easily sorted and filed into place as those documents in the office where she had worked years ago.

"Ah," said the niece, preparing to leave it at that.

But Auntie had something more to say. "When I'm in bed and asleep, I dream, and I know dreams are rubbish, so I needn't pay attention to them. But when I sit here, wide awake, with my eyes open or even with my eyes closed, then—"

The niece waited.

Auntie said carefully. "Then I think, and thinking must be like seeing: I see things."

"What things?"

"Things a long way off."

"That's because you're long-sighted, Auntie."

"I wouldn't mind that. But the things a long way off are coming nearer."

"Whatever do you mean?"

"How should I know what I mean? I'm just telling you what *happens*. I see things far away, and they're coming close. I don't understand it. I don't like it."

"Perhaps you're just having daydreams, Auntie."

"You mean, it's all rubbish?"

"Well, is it?"

Auntie moved restlessly in her chair. She hated to be made to think in this way; but there were some things you had to think of with your mind, when you couldn't straightforwardly see them with your eyes and then straightforwardly grasp them with your hands, to deal with them then and there.

There were these other things.

"No," said Auntie crossly. "They're not rubbish. All the same, I don't want to think about them. I don't want to talk about them."

So there was no more talk about the far things that were coming nearer; but as for thinking—well, Auntie couldn't help doing that, in her way. Her life was uneventful, so that what she thought about naturally was what she saw with her eyes or in her mind's eye.

One day the married niece asked if she could use Auntie's old sewing machine to run up some curtains—her own machine had broken down.

"So has mine," said Auntie. "The needle's broken."

"You have several spare needles, Auntie," said the niece. "I think I could put one in."

The niece went downstairs to where the ancient sewing machine was kept. When she had unlocked and taken off the wooden lid, she found that the needle was not broken, after all. It did not need replacing. She sighed to herself and smiled to herself at Auntie's mistake; and then she set to work with Auntie's sewing machine.

She threaded up the machine with the right cotton for her curtains, arranged the material in the right position under the needle, and began to turn the handle of the machine. The stitching began; but the curtain material was very thick, and the needle penetrated it with difficulty. . . .

With more difficulty at every stitch . . .

The needle broke.

So, after all, the niece had to change the needle, to finish sewing her curtains. Later on, she said to Auntie, "Your machine's all right now, but the needle broke."

"I told you so," said Auntie.

"No, Auntie. You said the needle *had* broken; you ought to have said, 'The needle *will* break.' " The niece laughed jollily.

"I don't want to say things like that," said Auntie. She spoke sharply, and her niece saw that she was upset for some reason.

So she said, "Never mind, Auntie. It was just a funny thing to have happened, after what you said. A coincidence. Think no more of it."

The niece thought no more of it; but Auntie did. She brooded over the strangeness of her long sight—over the seeing of faraway things that came nearer. She now kept that strangeness private to herself—secret; but sometimes something popped into a conversation before she could prevent it.

One family teatime, when Auntie had been sitting silent for some time, she said, "It's lucky there's never anyone left in those offices at night."

"Which offices?"

"Where I used to work, of course."

"Oh—" Nobody was interested, except for little Billy. He was always curious. "Why is it lucky, Auntie?"

But already Auntie regretted having spoken; one could see that. "No reason—" she said. "Nothing . . . I was just thinking, that's all. . . ."

The next morning, with Auntie's early cup of tea, the niece brought news.

"You'll never guess, Auntie!"

"Those old offices are burned out."

"Why, you *have* guessed! Yes, it was last night after you'd gone to bed early. An electrical short started the fire, they think. Nobody's fault; and nobody hurt—nobody in the building."

"No," said Auntie. "Nobody at all. . . ."

"But you should have seen the blaze! You were asleep, so we didn't wake you, but we took little Billy to see. My goodness, Auntie! The smoke there was!"

"Yes," said Auntie. "The smoke . . ."

"And the flames—huge flames towering up!"

"Yes," said Auntie. "The whole place quite gutted. . . ."

"And all the fire engines wailing up!"

"Yes," said Auntie, "Five fire engines . . ."

Her niece stared at her. "There *were* five fire engines, but how did you know?"

Auntie was flustered; and the niece went on staring. Auntie said, "Well, a big blaze like that would *need* five fire engines, wouldn't it?"

Her niece said nothing more; but, later, she reported the conversation to her husband. He was not impressed. "Oh, I daresay she woke up and saw the fire through her bedroom window. With her long sight she saw the size of the fire, and—well, she realized it would need at least five fire engines. As she said, more or less."

"That's *just* possible as an explanation," said his wife, "if it weren't for one thing."

"What thing?"

"Auntie's bedroom window doesn't look in that direction at all. Her old office block is on the other side of the house."

"Oh!" said Auntie's nephew-in-law.

In the time that followed, Auntie was very careful indeed not to talk about her sight, long sight, or foresight. Even so, her niece sometimes watched her intently and oddly, as she sat by her bedroom window. And once her nephew-in-law sought her out to ask whether she would like to discuss with him the forthcoming Derby and which horse was likely to win the race. Auntie said she had never been interested in horse racing and disapproved of it because of the betting. So that was that.

One afternoon in early spring—not cold, but dreary and very overcast—Auntie was restless. She went downstairs to her sewing machine and fiddled with it. She did a little hand sewing on a pair of Billy's trousers, where a seam had come undone. (That was the last time that she threaded a needle.)

Then she went upstairs and came down again in her coat and hat.

"You're not thinking of going out, Auntie?" cried her niece. "Today of all days? It's just beginning to rain!"

"A breath of fresh air, all the same," said Auntie.

"It's not suitable for you, Auntie. So slippery underfoot on the pavements."

Auntie said, "I thought I'd go and meet Billy off the school bus."

"Oh, Auntie! Billy's too old to need meeting off the bus nowadays. He doesn't need it, and he wouldn't like it. He'd hate it."

Auntie sighed, hesitated, then slowly climbed up the stairs to her bedroom again.

Five minutes later she was coming downstairs again, almost hurriedly, still hatted and coated. She made for the stand where her umbrella was kept.

"Auntie!" protested the niece.

Auntie patted the handbag she was carrying. "An important letter I've written—and must get into the post."

Her niece gaped at her. Auntie never wrote important letters; she never wrote letters at all.

"About my pension,"[2] Auntie explained. "Private," she added, as she saw that her niece was about to speak.

Her niece did speak, however. She had quite a lot to say. "Auntie, your letter *can't* be all that urgent. And if it is, Billy will be home soon, and he'll pop to the letter box for you. It's really ridiculous—*ridiculous*—of you to think of going out in this wet, gray, slippery, miserable weather!"

Suddenly Auntie was different. She was resolved, stern in some strange determination. *"I must go,"* she said, in such a way that her niece shrank back and let her pass.

So Auntie, her umbrella in one hand and her handbag in the other, set out.

The weather had worsened during the short delay. She had put up her umbrella at once against the rain. She hurried along toward the letter box—hurried, but with care, because the pavement and road surfaces were slippery, just as her niece had said.

The letter box lay a very little way beyond the bus stop where Billy's school bus would arrive. There was a constant to-and-fro of traffic, but no bus was in sight. Instead of going on to the letter box, Auntie hesitated a moment, then took shelter from the rain in the doorway of a gent's outfitter's, just by the bus stop. From inside the shop, an assistant, as he said later, observed the old lady taking shelter and observed all that happened afterward.

Auntie let down her umbrella, furled[3] it properly, and held it in her right hand, her handbag in her left.

The shop assistant, staring idly through his shop window, saw the school bus approaching its stop, through almost blinding rain.

The old lady remained in the doorway.

The school bus stopped. The children began to get off. The traffic swirled by on the splashing road.

The old lady remained in the doorway.

The shop assistant's attention was suddenly caught by something happening out on the road, in the passing traffic. A car had gone out of control on the slippery road. It was swerving violently; it narrowly missed another car and began skidding across the road, across the back of the school bus. Nearly all the children were away from the bus by now—except for one, slower than the rest. In a moment of horror, the shop assistant saw him, unforgettably; a little boy, wearing a badly made blazer, who was going to be run over and killed.

The assistant gave a cry and ran to the door, although he knew he would be too late.

But someone else was ahead of him, from that same doorway. The old lady darted—no, flung herself—*flew*—forward toward the child.

There were two—perhaps three?—seconds for action before the car would hit the child. The old lady wouldn't reach him in that time; but the assistant saw her swing her right arm forward, the hand clutching a furled umbrella by its ferrule.[4] The crook of the umbrella hooked inside the front of the little boy's blazer and hooked him like a fish from water out of the path of the skidding

---

2. pension (pen′ shən) *n.*: A regular payment to one who has retired after working a certain number of years at the same company.

3. furled (fʉrld) *v.*: Rolled up and fastened.

4. ferrule (fer′ ool) *n.*: A metal ring or cap around the end of the umbrella.

GRANDMOTHER READING TO THE CHILDREN
Mary Cassatt

car. The old lady fell over backward on the pavement with the child on top of her, and the car skidded past them, crashed into the bus stop itself, and stopped. The driver sat stupefied inside, white-faced, shocked, but otherwise uninjured.

Nobody was injured, except Auntie. She died in the ambulance, on her way to the hospital. Heart, the doctors said. No wonder, at her age, and in such extraordinary circumstances.

Much later, after the funeral, Billy's mother looked for the letter that Auntie had written to the pension people. "It should have been in her handbag, because the shopman said she didn't go on to the letter box to post anything. But it wasn't in her handbag."

"She must have left it behind by mistake," said Billy's father. "She was getting odd in old age. It'll be somewhere in her bedroom."

"No, I've searched. It isn't there."

"Why on earth do you want it, anyway?" said Billy's father. "All that pension business ceases with her death."

"I don't want the letter," said his wife. "I just want to know whether there ever was one."

"What are you driving at?"

"Don't you see? The letter was an excuse."

"An excuse?"

"She wanted an excuse to be at that bus stop when Billy got off, because she knew what was going to happen. She foresaw."

They stared at each other. Then the nephew said, "Second sight—that's what you mean, isn't it? But it's one thing to foresee, say, which horse is going to win the Derby. And it's quite another thing to foresee what's going to happen and then deliberately to prevent its happening. That's altering the course of things. . . . That's altering everything. . . ."

The niece said, "But you don't understand. She foresaw that Billy would be in danger of being killed, so she went to save him. But she also foresaw that very thing—I mean, she foresaw that she would go to save him. That she *would* save him. Although it killed her."

The nephew liked a logical argument, even about illogical things. He said, "She could still have altered that last part of what she foresaw. She could have decided *not* to go to the bus stop, because she foresaw that it would all end in her death. After all, nobody wants to die."

"You still don't understand," his wife said. "You don't understand Auntie. She knew she would save Billy, even if she had to die for it. She had to do it, because it was her nature to do it. Because she was Auntie. Don't you *see*?"

The nephew, seeing something about Auntie he had never properly perceived before, said quite humbly, "Yes, I see. . . ."

And the niece, leaning on his shoulder, wept again for Auntie, whom she had known so well since she had been a very little girl. Known so well, perhaps, that she had not known Auntie truly for what she really was, until then.

As for Billy, he never said much about that rainy day, the last of Auntie's life. He hadn't gone to Auntie's funeral—children often don't. But he wore his horrible, homemade blazer until he grew out of it. And he never, never forgot Auntie.

Reader's Response

Would you like to have an aunt like Auntie? Explain your answer.

RESPONDING TO THE SELECTION

Your Response

1. Do you believe in foresight? Explain.
2. Would you have changed the end of this story in any way? Why or why not?

Recalling

3. What was Auntie's main interest in life?
4. Give two examples of Auntie's foresight.
5. Why does Auntie insist on going to the bus stop?

Interpreting

6. How does the way in which Auntie's family reacts to her foresight change from the beginning to the end of the story?
7. Why does Auntie keep to herself her reasons for wanting to meet Billy at the bus stop?
8. Why does Billy continue to wear the blazer after Auntie's death?
9. After Auntie's death, you learn that her niece probably never knew her for "what she really was." Does this realization refer to Auntie's foresight or to something else? Explain.
10. Does Auntie fit your definition of a hero? Explain your answer.

Applying

11. Do you believe people who have a special gift like Auntie's foresight exist in real life? Explain.

ANALYZING LITERATURE

Understanding Character Traits

Character traits are those qualities that make a person a unique individual. Auntie has many traits, which you discover as you read about her. For example, you learn that Auntie is a loving person, and that she likes to sew.

1. Name three other character traits that make Auntie a unique or special person.
2. How does her family react to Auntie's ability to foresee events? How do they react to her other qualities?
3. What do you learn about Auntie from their reactions?
4. Did Auntie come alive for you as a character? Explain your answer.

CRITICAL THINKING AND READING

Identifying Significant Details

Sometimes writers supply significant, or meaningful, details that hint at or prepare for the outcome of a story. For example, the first paragraph of "Auntie" contains several hints about the importance of Auntie's foresight to the story.

1. Reread the passage in which Billy complains about having to wear the blazer (page 61). What does he promise himself?
2. Given what happens later in the story, explain the significance of this promise.
3. List two other significant details and explain why each is an important element.

THINKING AND WRITING

Writing a Personal Letter

Pretend you are Billy ten years after Auntie's death. Write a letter telling her the things you've wished you could tell her since she died. Give your paper to a writing partner for comments and corrections. Make any necessary revisions. Write a final draft.

LEARNING OPTIONS

1. **Performance.** You and your classmates have been selected to make "Auntie" into a television program. With a small group, think of two or three plot ideas. Then, give detailed descriptions of the characters, sets, and props for each idea. Present your ideas to the class.
2. **Language.** As you read "Auntie," you probably noticed several British terms. For example, in the United States we would call a "gent's outfitter's" a men's clothing store. With two or three classmates, create a dictionary of British terms used in this story. Next to each British word, write the word used in the United States.

GUIDE FOR READING

Kristin Hunter

(1931–), who was born in Philadelphia, has been a writer since she was a teenager. She began her writing career as a columnist and feature writer for the Pittsburgh *Courier.* Since then she has written several novels and magazine articles for both children and adults. Her novel, *The Landlord,* was made into a movie. Many of her stories, like "The Scribe," are set in city neighborhoods. Her work is characterized by her realistic portrayal of her settings and characters.

The Scribe

Characterization

Characterization is the art of making people in a story seem lifelike, or real. One method a writer can use to develop a character is to describe the character's appearance and actions. Another method is to develop a character through what he or she says and does. In "The Scribe," Hunter uses both methods.

Focus

In this story, the main character observes a situation in his neighborhood that needs to be changed, and he tries to change it. What problems or situations have you observed in your neighborhood that need to be changed? In a small group, make a list of problems. From your list, choose the five most serious problems. Then, brainstorm solutions. When your group has finished, create a chart of problems and solutions. As you read "The Scribe," think about how James tries to solve problems in his neighborhood.

Vocabulary

Knowing the following words will help you as you read "The Scribe."

loitering (loit′ ər iŋ) *v.*: Lingering or hanging around (p. 71)
dignified (dig′ nə fīd′) *adj.*: Noble (p. 71)
scribes (skrībz) *n.*: People employed to write letters, fill in documents and applications, and so on (p. 72)
rabbis (rab′ īz) *n.*: Scholars and teachers of Jewish law (p. 72)
substantiate (səb stan′ shē āt′) *v.*: Show to be true; prove (p. 73)
immunization (im′ yə nīz ā′ shən) *n.*: Protection from disease by getting a vaccine, or shot (p. 73)

Spelling Tip

Remember that the *sh* sound in *substantiate* and *immunization* are spelled with *ti.*

The Scribe

Kristin Hunter

"No one could read or write except. . . scribes"

We been living in the apartment over the Silver Dollar Check Cashing Service five years. But I never had any reason to go in there till two days ago, when Mom had to go to the Wash-a-Mat and asked me to get some change.

And man! Are those people who come in there in some bad shape.

Old man Silver and old man Dollar, who own the place, have signs tacked up everywhere:

NO LOUNGING, NO LOITERING

THIS IS NOT A WAITING ROOM

and

MINIMUM CHECK CASHING FEE, 50¢

and

LETTERS ADDRESSED, 50¢

and

LETTERS READ, 75¢

and

LETTERS WRITTEN, ONE DOLLAR

And everybody who comes in there to cash a check gets their picture taken like they're some kind of criminal.

After I got my change, I stood around for a while digging the action. First comes an old lady with some kind of long form to fill out. The mean old man behind the counter points to the "One Dollar" sign. She nods. So he starts to fill it out for her.

"Name?"

"Muskogee Marie Lawson."

"SPELL it!" he hollers.

"M, m, u, s—well, I don't exactly know, sir."

"I'll put down 'Marie,' then. Age?"

"Sixty-three my last birthday."

"Date of birth?"

"March twenty-third"—a pause—"I think, 1900."

"Look, Marie," he says, which makes me mad, hearing him first-name a dignified old gray-haired lady like that, "if you'd been born in 1900, you'd be seventy-two. Either I put that down, or I put 1910."

"Whatever you think best, sir," she says timidly.

He sighs, rolls his eyes to the ceiling, and bangs his fist on the form angrily. Then he fills out the rest.

"One dollar," he says when he's finished. She pays like she's grateful to him for taking the trouble.

Next is a man with a cane, a veteran who has to let the government know he moved. He wants old man Silver to do this for him, but he doesn't want him to know he can't do it himself.

"My eyes are kind of bad, sir, will you fill this thing out for me? Tell them I moved from 121 South 15th Street to 203 North Decatur Street."

Old man Silver doesn't blink an eye. Just fills out the form, and charges the crippled man a dollar.

And it goes on like that. People who can't read or write or count their change. People who don't know how to pay their gas bills, don't know how to fill out forms, don't know how to address envelopes. And old man Silver and old man Dollar cleaning up on all of them. It's pitiful. It's disgusting. Makes me so mad I want to yell.

And I do, but mostly at Mom. "Mom, did you know there are hundreds of people in this city who can't read and write?"

Mom isn't upset. She's a wise woman. "Of course, James," she says. "A lot of older people around here haven't had your advantages. They came from down South, and they had to quit school very young to go to work.

"In the old days, nobody cared whether our people got an education. They were only interested in getting the crops in." She sighed. "Sometimes I think they *still* don't care. If we hadn't gotten you into that good school, you might not be able to read so well either. A lot of boys and girls your age can't, you know."

"But that's awful!" I say. "How do they expect us to make it in a big city? You can't even cross the streets if you can't read the WALK and DON'T WALK signs."

"It's hard," Mom says, "but the important thing to remember is it's no disgrace. There was a time in history when nobody could read or write except a special class of people."

And Mom takes down her Bible. She has three Bible study certificates and is always giving me lessons from Bible history. I don't exactly go for all the stuff she believes in, but sometimes it *is* interesting.

"In ancient times," she says, "no one could read or write except a special class of people known as *scribes*. It was their job to write down the laws given by the rabbis and the judges. No one else could do it.

"Jesus criticized the scribes," she goes on, "because they were so proud of themselves. But he needed them to write down his teachings."

"Man," I said when she finished, "that's something."

My mind was working double-time. I'm the best reader and writer in our class. Also it was summertime. I had nothing much to do except go to the park or hang around the library and read till my eyeballs were ready to fall out, and I was tired of doing both.

So the next morning, after my parents went to work, I took Mom's card table and a folding chair down to the sidewalk. I lettered a sign with a Magic Marker, and I was in business. My sign said:

PUBLIC SCRIBE—ALL SERVICES FREE

I set my table up in front of the Silver Dollar and waited for business. Only one thing bothered me. If the people couldn't read, how would they know what I was there for?

But five minutes had hardly passed when an old lady stopped and asked me to read her grandson's letter. She explained that she had just broken her glasses. I knew she was fibbing, but I kept quiet.

I read the grandson's letter. It said he was having a fine time in California, but was a little short. He would send her some money as soon as he made another payday. I handed the letter back to her.

"Thank you, son," she said, and gave me a quarter.

I handed that back to her too.

The word got around. By noontime I had a whole crowd of customers around my table. I was kept busy writing letters, addressing envelopes, filling out forms, and explaining official-looking letters that scared people half to death.

I didn't blame them. The language in some of those letters—"Establish whether your disability is one-fourth, one-third, one-half, or total, and substantiate in paragraph 3 (b) below"—would upset anybody. I mean, why can't the government write English like everybody else?

Most of my customers were old, but there were a few young ones too. Like the girl who had gotten a letter about her baby from the Health Service and didn't know what "immunization" meant.

At noontime one old lady brought me some iced tea and a peach, and another gave me some fried chicken wings. I was really having a good time, when the shade of all the people standing around me suddenly vanished. The sun hit me like a ton of hot bricks.

Only one long shadow fell across my table. The shadow of a tall, heavy, blue-eyed cop. In our neighborhood, when they see a cop, people scatter. That was why the back of my neck was burning.

"What are you trying to do here, sonny?" the cop asks.

"Help people out," I tell him calmly, though my knees are knocking together under the table.

"Well, you know," he says, "Mr. Silver and Mr. Dollar have been in business a long time on this corner. They are very respected men in this neighborhood. Are you trying to run them out of business?"

"I'm not charging anybody," I pointed out.

"That," the cop says, "is exactly what they don't like. Mr. Silver says he is glad to have some help with the letter-writing. Mr. Dollar says it's only a nuisance to them anyway and takes up too much time. But if you don't charge for your services, it's unfair competition."

Well, why not? I thought. After all, I could use a little profit.

"All right," I tell him. "I'll charge a quarter."

"Then it is my duty to warn you," the cop says, "that it's against the law to conduct a business without a license. The first time you accept a fee, I'll close you up and run you off this corner."

He really had me there. What did I know about licenses? I'm only thirteen, after all. Suddenly I didn't feel like the big black businessman anymore. I felt like a little kid who wanted to holler for his mother. But she was at work, and so was Daddy.

"I'll leave," I said, and did, with all the cool I could muster. But inside I was burning up, and not from the sun.

One little old lady hollered "You big bully!" and shook her umbrella at the cop. But the rest of those people were so beaten-down they didn't say anything. Just shuffled back on inside to give Mr. Silver and Mr. Dollar their hard-earned money like they always did.

I was so mad I didn't know what to do with myself that afternoon. I couldn't watch TV. It was all soap operas anyway, and they seemed dumber than ever. The library didn't appeal to me either. It's not air-conditioned, and the day was hot and muggy.

Finally I went to the park and threw stones at the swans in the lake. I was careful not to hit them, but they made good targets because they were so fat and white. Then after a while the sun got lower. I kind of cooled off and came to my senses. They were just big, dumb, beautiful birds, and not my enemies. I threw them some crumbs from my sandwich and went home.

"Daddy," I asked that night, "how come you and Mom never cash checks downstairs in the Silver Dollar?"

"Because," he said, "we have an account

at the bank, where they cash our checks free."

"Well, why doesn't everybody do that?" I wanted to know.

"Because some people want all their money right away," he said. "The bank insists that you leave them a minimum balance."

"How much?" I asked him.

"Only five dollars."

"But that five dollars still belongs to you after you leave it there?"

"Sure," he says. "And if it's in a savings account, it earns interest."

"So why can't people see they lose money when they *pay* to have their checks cashed?"

"A lot of *our* people," Mom said, "are scared of banks, period. Some of them remember the Depression, when all the banks closed and the people couldn't get their money out. And others think banks are only for white people. They think they'll be insulted, or maybe even arrested, if they go in there."

Wow. The more I learned, the more pitiful it was. "Are there any black people working at our bank?"

"There didn't used to be," Mom said, "but now they have Mr. Lovejoy and Mrs. Adams. You know Mrs. Adams, she's nice. She has a daughter your age."

"Hmmm," I said, and shut up before my folks started to wonder why I was asking all those questions.

The next morning, when the Silver Dollar opened, I was right there. I hung around near the door, pretending to read a copy of *Jet* magazine.

"Psst," I said to each person who came in. "I know where you can cash checks *free*."

It wasn't easy convincing them. A man with a wine bottle in a paper bag blinked his red eyes at me like he didn't believe he had heard right. A carpenter with tools hanging all around his belt said he was on his lunch hour and didn't have time. And a big fat lady with two shopping bags pushed past me and almost knocked me down, she was in such a hurry to give Mr. Silver and Mr. Dollar her money.

But finally I had a little group who were interested. It wasn't much. Just three people. Two men—one young, one old—and the little old lady who'd asked me to read her the letter from California. Seemed the grandson had made his payday and sent her a money order.

"How far is this place?" asked the young man.

"Not far. Just six blocks," I told him.

"Aw shoot. I ain't walking all the way just to save fifty cents."

So then I only had two. I was careful not to tell them where we were going. When we finally got to the Establishment Trust National Bank, I said, "This is the place."

"I ain't goin' in there," said the old man. "No sir, Not me. You ain't gettin' me in *there*." And he walked away quickly, going back in the direction we had come.

To tell the truth, the bank did look kind of scary. It was a big building with tall white marble pillars. A lot of Brink's armored trucks and Cadillacs were parked out front. Uniformed guards walked back and forth inside with guns. It might as well have had a "Colored Keep Out" sign.

Whereas the Silver Dollar is small and dark and funky and dirty. It has trash on the floors and tape across the broken windows. People going in there feel right at home.

I looked at the little old lady. She smiled back bravely.

"Well, we've come this far, son," she said. "Let's not turn back now."

So I took her inside. Fortunately Mrs. Adams' window was near the front.

"Hi, James," she said.

"I've brought you a customer," I told her.

Mrs. Adams took the old lady to a desk to fill out some forms. They were gone a long time, but finally they came back.

"Now, when you have more business with the bank, Mrs. Franklin, just bring it to me," Mrs. Adams said.

"I'll do that," the old lady said. She held out her shiny new bankbook. "Son, do me a favor and read that to me."

"Mrs. Minnie Franklin," I read aloud. "July 9, 1972. Thirty-seven dollars."

"That sounds real nice," Mrs. Franklin said. "I guess now I have a bankbook, I'll have to get me some glasses."

Mrs. Adams winked at me over the old lady's head, and I winked back.

"Do you want me to walk you home?" I asked Mrs. Franklin.

"No thank you, son," she said. "I can cross streets by myself all right. I know red from green."

And then she winked at both of us, letting us know she knew what was happening.

"Son," she went on, "don't ever be afraid to try a thing just because you've never done it before. I took a bus up here from Alabama by myself forty-four years ago. I ain't thought once about going back. But I've stayed too long in one neighborhood since I've been in this city. Now I think I'll go out and take a look at *this* part of town."

Then she was gone. But she had really started me thinking. If an old lady like that wasn't afraid to go in a bank and open an account for the first time in her life, why should *I* be afraid to go up to City Hall and apply for a license?

Wonder how much they charge you to be a scribe?

Responding to the Selection

Your Response

1. How do you feel about what James did? Would you be willing to do something similar? Why or why not?

Recalling

2. What services do Silver and Dollar provide?

Interpreting

3. What are James's feelings about Silver and Dollar?
4. Explain how James applies new information to solve problems. Give two examples of information he learned and his applications.
5. What do you think James will do next?

Applying

6. Mrs. Franklin tells James never to be afraid to try something new. What new things have you tried recently?

Analyzing Literature

Appreciating Characterization

Characterization is the art of making characters in a story seem real. Writers develop characters by describing them or by revealing information through their thoughts and actions.

1. What are two characteristics of James that he tells you directly?
2. What are two of his traits that you learn from his actions? What actions reveal these traits?

GUIDE FOR READING

Sandra Cisneros

(1954–), whose last name means "keeper of swans," was born in Chicago. She attended college in her hometown. She then moved to Iowa where she received her master's degree at the University of Iowa's Writer's Workshop. It was here she began to write about the subjects she knew best—her life, family, Mexican heritage, and her feelings, including her feelings about not being or acting her age. In "Eleven" you will see that Cisneros and the main character, Rachel, share many of the same feelings.

Eleven

Character

A **character** is a person in a story. Sometimes what a character experiences or feels is more important than what the character does. In such stories you share the character's experiences or thoughts. The story "Eleven," for example, is an expression of Rachel's thoughts and feelings as she reviews the events of one day. The story consists of what takes place inside Rachel's head.

Focus

"Eleven" is the story of a young girl whose birthday turns out to be anything but the happy day the girl had imagined. With three or four classmates, create a word web using the words "eleventh birthday." Use the web below as a model. After you read "Eleven," create another web for "eleventh birthday," based on the story.

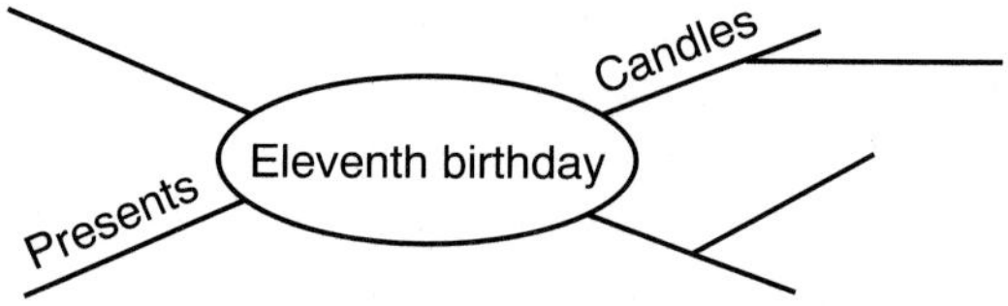

Vocabulary

Knowing the following word will help you read "Eleven."

raggedy (rag′ i dē) *adj.*: Tattered; old and worn (p. 78)

Eleven

Sandra Cisneros

"Because the way you grow old is kind of like an onion . . . each year inside the next one. That's how being eleven years old is."

What they don't understand about birthdays and what they never tell you is that when you're eleven, you're also ten, and nine, and eight, and seven, and six, and five, and four, and three, and two, and one. And when you wake up on your eleventh birthday you expect to feel eleven, but you don't. You open your eyes and everything's just like yesterday, only it's today. And you don't feel eleven at all. You feel like you're still ten. And you are—underneath the year that makes you eleven.

Like some days you might say something stupid, and that's the part of you that's still ten. Or maybe some days you might need to sit on your mama's lap because you're scared, and that's the part of you that's five. And one day when you're all grown up maybe you will need to cry like if you're three, and that's okay. That's what I tell Mama when she's sad and needs to cry. Maybe she's feeling three.

Because the way you grow old is kind of like an onion or like the rings inside a tree trunk or like my little wooden dolls that fit one inside the other, each year inside the next one. That's how being eleven years old is.

You don't feel eleven. Not right away. It takes a few days, weeks even, sometimes even months before you say eleven when they ask you. And you don't feel smart eleven, not until you're almost twelve. That's the way it is.

Only today I wish I didn't have just eleven years rattling inside me like pennies in a tin Band-Aid box. Today I wish I was one-hundred-and-two instead of eleven because if I was one-hundred-and-two I'd have known what to say when Mrs. Price put the red sweater on my desk. I would've known how to tell her it wasn't mine instead of just sitting there with that look on my face and nothing coming out of my mouth.

"Whose is this?" Mrs. Price says, and she holds the red sweater up in the air for all the class to see. "Whose? It's been sitting in the coatroom for a month."

PORTRAIT
From the estate of Eloy Blanco
Collection of El Museo del Barrio, New York City

"Not mine," says everybody. "Not me."

"It has to belong to somebody," Mrs. Price keeps saying, but nobody can remember. It's an ugly sweater with red plastic buttons and a collar and sleeves all stretched out like you could use it for a jump rope. It's maybe a thousand years old and even if it belonged to me I wouldn't say so.

Maybe because I'm skinny, maybe because she doesn't like me, that stupid Felice Garcia says, "I think it belongs to Rachel." An ugly sweater like that, all raggedy and old, but Mrs. Price believes her. Mrs. Price takes the sweater and puts it right on my desk, but when I open my mouth nothing comes out.

"That's not, I don't, you're not . . . not mine," I finally say in a little voice that was maybe me when I was four.

"Of course it's yours," Mrs. Price says, "I remember you wearing it once." Because she's older and the teacher, she's right and I'm not.

Not mine, not mine, not mine, but Mrs. Price is already turning to page 32, and math problem number four. I don't know why but all of a sudden I'm feeling sick inside, like the part of me that's three wants to come out of my eyes, only I squeeze them shut tight and bite down on my teeth real hard and try to remember today I am eleven, eleven. Mama is making a cake for me for tonight, and when Papa comes home everybody will sing happy birthday, happy birthday to you.

But when the sick feeling goes away and I open my eyes, the red sweater's still sitting there like a big red mountain. I move the red sweater to the corner of my desk with my ruler. I move my pencil and books and eraser as far from it as possible. I even move my chair a little to the right. Not mine, not mine, not mine.

In my head I'm thinking how long till lunch time, how long till I can take the red sweater and throw it over the schoolyard fence, or leave it hanging on a parking meter, or bunch it up into a little ball and toss it in the alley. Except when math period ends Mrs. Price says loud and in front of everybody, "Now, Rachel, that's enough," because she sees I've shoved the red sweater to the tippy-tip corner of my desk and it's hanging all over the edge like a waterfall, but I don't care.

"Rachel," Mrs. Price says. She says it like she's getting mad. "You put that sweater on right now and no more nonsense."

"But it's not . . ."

"Now!" Mrs. Price says.

This is when I wish I wasn't eleven, because all the years inside of me—ten, nine, eight, seven, six, five, four, three, two, and one—are all pushing at the back of my eyes when I put one arm through one sleeve of the sweater that smells like cottage cheese, and then the other arm through the other and stand there with my arms apart as if the sweater hurts me and it does, all itchy and full of germs that aren't even mine.

That's when everything I've been holding in since this morning, since when Mrs. Price put the sweater on my desk, finally lets go, and all of a sudden I'm crying in front of everybody. I wish I was invisible but I'm not. I'm eleven and it's my birthday today and I'm crying like I'm three in front of everybody. I put my head down on the desk and bury my face in my stupid clown sweater arms. My face all hot and spit coming out of my mouth because I can't stop the little animal noises from coming out of me, until there aren't any more tears left in my eyes, and it's just my body shaking like when you have the hiccups, and my whole head hurts like when you drink milk too fast.

But the worst part is right before the bell rings for lunch. That stupid Phyllis Lopez, who is even dumber than Felice Garcia, says she remembers the red sweater is hers! I take it off right away and give it to her, only Mrs. Price pretends like everything's okay.

Today I'm eleven. There's a cake Mama's making for tonight, and when Papa comes home from work we'll eat it. There'll be candles and presents and everybody will sing happy birthday, happy birthday to you, Rachel, only it's too late.

I'm eleven today. I'm eleven, ten, nine, eight, seven, six, five, four, three, two, and one, but I wish I was one-hundred-and-two. I wish I was anything but eleven, because I want today to be far away already, far away like a tiny kite in the sky, so tiny-tiny you have to close your eyes to see it.

Reader's Response

How are Rachel's thoughts about being eleven similar to or different from your thoughts about being or turning eleven?

On Being Eleven

Why does Sandra Cisneros feel eleven at times? In the following excerpt from her essay "Straw of Gold," she tells us a little about her childhood and why, even as an adult, she sometimes feels eleven again.

"What would my teachers say if they knew I was a writer? Who would've guessed it? I wasn't a very bright student. I didn't much like school because we moved so much and I was always new and funny-looking. In my fifth-grade report card, I have nothing but an avalanche of C's and D's, but I don't remember being that stupid. I was good at art and I read plenty of library books and [my girlfriend] Kiki laughed at all my jokes. At home I was fine, but at school I never opened my mouth except when the teacher called on me, the first time I'd speak all day.

When I think how I see myself, I would have to be at age eleven. I know I'm thirty-two on the outside, but inside I'm eleven. I'm the girl in the picture with skinny arms and a crumpled shirt and crooked hair. I didn't like school because all they saw was the outside me. School was lots of rules and sitting with your hands folded and being very afraid all the time. I liked looking out the window and thinking. I liked staring at the girl across the way writing her name over and over again in red ink. I wondered why the boy with the dirty collar in front of me didn't have a mama who took better care of him.

I think my mama and papa did the best they could to keep us warm and clean and never hungry. We had birthday and graduation parties and things like that, but there was another hunger that had to be fed. There was a hunger I didn't even have a name for. Was this when I began writing? . . ."

Even as an adult, Cisneros still feels shy and out of place. In several of her books, like *The House on Mango Street*, and short stories, like "Eleven," Cisneros explores her feelings about being out of place.

At what times do you feel a younger age than you are or feel out of place?

Responding to the Selection

Your Response

1. Have you ever wished to be older? Why? Have you ever wished to be younger? Why?
2. If you had been in Rachel's class, what might you have done to comfort her?

Recalling

3. According to Rachel, how old are you when you are eleven? Why?
4. Describe how Mrs. Price reacts when she learns that the sweater belongs to Phyllis.

Interpreting

5. Explain how Rachel can be eleven but also ten, nine, eight, and so on.
6. Why does Rachel react so strongly to being given the sweater?
7. What does Rachel mean when she says that her family will sing "Happy Birthday," but it will be too late?
8. Why does Rachel wish she is "one-hundred-and-two instead of eleven" at the end of the story?
9. Mrs. Price does not believe Rachel when Rachel says the sweater is not hers. By not believing her what conclusions might Mrs. Price be making about Rachel?

Applying

10. In what ways do people change over the years? How do they remain the same?

Analyzing Literature

Understanding Character

"Eleven" is about one character, Rachel. The story consists of her thoughts about one day, her birthday. Through her thoughts, you learn her problems and share her feelings. This means that you identify with her; that is, you put yourself in her place and sympathize with her.

1. Summarize Rachel's feelings.
2. How does knowing Rachel's thoughts and feelings make you feel about her?
3. Explain whether you think her thoughts and feelings are typical of eleven-year-olds.
4. When we buy presents for people, we try to choose gifts that fit their personality. Imagine you are Rachel's friend. What gift would you give her for her birthday? Explain your answer.

Critical Thinking and Reading

Making Inferences

An **inference** is a conclusion you draw from information the author gives you about a character and the way others treat that character. For example, in "Eleven" you can infer that Rachel lacks self-assurance. You draw this inference from the following information: Rachel does not stand up for herself in front of Mrs. Price, and when she finally does say something, it is "in a little voice that was maybe [hers] when [she] was four."

What inferences can you draw about Rachel from the following details?

1. Rachel puts on the sweater even though it is not hers and it is dirty and itchy.
2. Rachel tells her mother that it is okay to cry as though she were three years old.
3. Rachel does not publicly say anything bad about Felice Garcia.

Thinking and Writing

Writing About an Experience in School

Write an account of something that has happened to you in school. Although Rachel's experience was upsetting, don't limit your choice; your account might be about something amusing. Include your thoughts and feelings about the incident that will reveal more about yourself. Give your paper to a partner to read. Your partner should check that you have included thoughts and feelings, not just actions. Revise your work and write a final draft.

GUIDE FOR READING

Myron Levoy

who was born in New York, writes poetry, plays, and stories for both young people and adults. In his writing he shows a special interest for "the 'outsider,' the loner . . . who must come to terms with and face his or her own uniqueness." "Aaron's Gift" deals with a certain kind of outsider—the immigrant, like Aaron's grandmother, who came to the Upper East Side in New York City in the 1920's. Aaron himself faces a challenge alone and learns something about himself as a result.

Aaron's Gift

Major and Minor Characters

A **major character** is the one on whom a story focuses. This character is the one who plays the most important role and the one readers know the most about. A **minor character** plays a less important role, and readers usually know less about that character. The interaction of the major and minor characters produces the action in a story.

Focus

In this story, a boy is faced with peer pressure to join a gang his mother disapproves of. Explain what the term *peer pressure* means. Can you think of a time when you or a friend faced peer pressure? What did you or your friend want? How did you or your friend feel? Create a cluster map about what happened. Write a short phrase summarizing the event in the center of a sheet of paper. Circle the phrase and begin writing phrases to explain what happened and how you or your friend felt. Circle each phrase and connect related ideas with a line.

Vocabulary

Knowing the following words will help you read "Aaron's Gift."

frenzied (fren′ zēd) *adj.*: Wild; frantic (p. 83)

thrashing (thrash′ iŋ) *v.*: Moving violently (p. 83)

plunged (plunjd) *v.*: Dived or rushed (p. 83)

mascot (mas′ kät) *n.*: Any person, animal, or thing adopted by a group that is meant to bring good luck (p. 86)

coaxed (kōkst) *v.*: Tried to persuade (p. 86)

assassinated (ə sas′ ′n āt′ id) *v.*: Murdered by surprise attack (p. 86)

consoled (kən sōld′) *v.*: Comforted (p. 87)

Spelling Tip

Remember to change the final *y* to *i* when you add endings to a word. For example, to form the word *frenzied,* change the *y* in *frenzy* to *i.*

Aaron's Gift

Myron Levoy

"A group of older boys from down the block had a club . . . and Aaron had longed to join as he had never longed for anything else."

Aaron Kandel had come to Tompkins Square Park to roller-skate, for the streets near Second Avenue were always too crowded with children and peddlers and old ladies and baby buggies. Though few children had bicycles in those days, almost every child owned a pair of roller skates. And Aaron was, it must be said, a Class A, triple-fantastic roller skater.

Aaron skated back and forth on the wide walkway of the park, pretending he was an aviator in an air race zooming around pylons, which were actually two lampposts. During his third lap around the racecourse, he noticed a pigeon on the grass, behaving very strangely. Aaron skated to the line of benches, then climbed over onto the lawn.

The pigeon was trying to fly, but all it could manage was to flutter and turn round and round in a large circle, as if it were performing a frenzied dance. The left wing was only half open and was beating in a clumsy, jerking fashion; it was clearly broken.

Luckily, Aaron hadn't eaten the cookies he'd stuffed into his pocket before he'd gone clacking down the three flights of stairs from his apartment, his skates already on. He broke a cookie into small crumbs and tossed some toward the pigeon. "Here pidge, here pidge," he called. The pigeon spotted the cookie crumbs and, after a moment, stopped thrashing about. It folded its wings as best it could, but the broken wing still stuck half out. Then it strutted over to the crumbs, its head bobbing forth-back, forth-back, as if it were marching a little in front of the rest of the body—perfectly normal, except for that half-open wing which seemed to make the bird stagger sideways every so often.

The pigeon began eating the crumbs as Aaron quickly unbuttoned his shirt and pulled it off. Very slowly, he edged toward the bird, making little kissing sounds like the ones he heard his grandmother make when she fed the sparrows on the back fire escape.

Then suddenly Aaron plunged. The shirt, in both hands, came down like a torn parachute. The pigeon beat its wings, but Aaron held the shirt to the ground, and the bird couldn't escape. Aaron felt under the shirt, gently, and gently took hold of the wounded pigeon.

"Yes, yes, pidge," he said, very softly. "There's a good boy. Good pigeon, good."

The pigeon struggled in his hands, but little by little Aaron managed to soothe it. "Good boy, pidge. That's your new name. Pidge. I'm gonna take you home, Pidge. Yes, yes, *ssh.* Good boy. I'm gonna fix you up. Easy, Pidge, easy does it. Easy, boy."

Aaron squeezed through an opening between the row of benches and skated slowly out of the park, while holding the pigeon carefully with both hands as if it were one of his mother's rare, precious cups from the old country. How fast the pigeon's heart was beating! Was he afraid? Or did all pigeons' hearts beat fast?

It was fortunate that Aaron was an excellent skater, for he had to skate six blocks to his apartment, over broken pavement and sudden gratings and curbs and cobblestones. But when he reached home, he asked Noreen Callahan, who was playing on the stoop, to take off his skates for him. He would not chance going up three flights on roller skates this time.

"Is he sick?" asked Noreen.

"Broken wing," said Aaron. "I'm gonna fix him up and make him into a carrier pigeon or something."

"Can I watch?" asked Noreen.

"Watch what?"

"The operation. I'm gonna be a nurse when I grow up."

"OK," said Aaron. "You can even help. You can help hold him while I fix him up."

Aaron wasn't quite certain what his mother would say about his new-found pet, but he was pretty sure he knew what his grandmother would think. His grandmother had lived with them ever since his grandfather had died three years ago. And she fed the sparrows and jays and crows and robins on the back fire escape with every spare crumb she could find. In fact, Aaron noticed that she sometimes created crumbs where they didn't exist, by squeezing and tearing pieces of her breakfast roll when his mother wasn't looking.

Aaron didn't really understand his grandmother, for he often saw her by the window having long conversations with the birds, telling them about her days as a little girl in the Ukraine.[1] And once he saw her take her mirror from her handbag and hold it out toward the birds. She told Aaron that she wanted them to see how beautiful they were. Very strange. But Aaron did know that she would love Pidge, because she loved everything.

To his surprise, his mother said he could keep the pigeon, temporarily, because it was sick, and we were all strangers in the land of Egypt,[2] and it might not be bad for Aaron to have a pet. *Temporarily.*

The wing was surprisingly easy to fix, for the break showed clearly and Pidge was remarkably patient and still, as if he knew he was being helped. Or perhaps he was just exhausted from all the thrashing about he had done. Two Popsicle sticks served as splints, and strips from an old undershirt were used to tie them in place. Another strip held the wing to the bird's body.

Aaron's father arrived home and stared at the pigeon. Aaron waited for the expected storm. But instead, Mr. Kandel asked, "Who *did* this?"

---

1. Ukraine (yo͞o krān′): A country located in southwest Europe. From 1924 to 1991, Ukraine was part of the Soviet Union.

2. we were all . . . land of Egypt: A reference to the Biblical story of the enslavement of the Hebrew people in Egypt. Around 1300 B.C., they were led out of Egypt by Moses.

"Me," said Aaron. "And Noreen Callahan."

"Sophie!" he called to his wife. "Did you see this! Ten years old and it's better than Dr. Belasco could do. He's a genius!"

As the days passed, Aaron began training Pidge to be a carrier pigeon. He tied a little cardboard tube to Pidge's left leg and stuck tiny rolled-up sheets of paper with secret messages into it: THE ENEMY IS ATTACKING AT DAWN. Or: THE GUNS ARE HIDDEN IN THE TRUNK OF THE CAR. Or: VINCENT DEMARCO IS A BRITISH SPY. Then Aaron would set Pidge down at one end of the living room and put some popcorn at the other end. And Pidge would waddle slowly across the room, cooing softly, while the ends of his bandages trailed along the floor.

At the other end of the room, one of Aaron's friends would take out the message, stick a new one in, turn Pidge around, and aim him at the popcorn that Aaron put down on his side of the room.

And Pidge grew fat and contented on all the popcorn and crumbs and corn and crackers and Aaron's grandmother's breakfast rolls.

Aaron had told all the children about Pidge, but he only let his very best friends

PIGEONS
John Sloan
Museum of Fine Arts, Boston

come up and play carrier-pigeon with him. But telling everyone had been a mistake. A group of older boys from down the block had a club—Aaron's mother called it a gang—and Aaron had longed to join as he had never longed for anything else. To be with them and share their secrets, the secrets of older boys. To be able to enter their clubhouse shack on the empty lot on the next street. To know the password and swear the secret oath. To belong.

About a month after Aaron had brought the pigeon home, Carl, the gang leader, walked over to Aaron in the street and told him he could be a member if he'd bring the pigeon down to be the club mascot. Aaron couldn't believe it; he immediately raced home to get Pidge. But his mother told Aaron to stay away from those boys, or else. And Aaron, miserable, argued with his mother and pleaded and cried and coaxed. It was no use. Not with those boys. No.

Aaron's mother tried to change the subject. She told him that it would soon be his grandmother's sixtieth birthday, a very special birthday indeed, and all the family from Brooklyn and the East Side would be coming to their apartment for a dinner and celebration. Would Aaron try to build something or make something for Grandma? A present made with his own hands would be nice. A decorated box for her hairpins or a crayon picture for her room or anything he liked.

In a flash Aaron knew what to give her: Pidge! Pidge would be her present! Pidge with his wing healed, who might be able to carry messages for her to the doctor or his Aunt Rachel or other people his grandmother seemed to go to a lot. It would be a surprise for everyone. And Pidge would make up for what had happened to Grandma when she'd been a little girl in the Ukraine, wherever that was.

Often, in the evening, Aaron's grandmother would talk about the old days long ago in the Ukraine, in the same way that she talked to the birds on the back fire escape. She had lived in a village near a place called Kishinev with hundreds of other poor peasant families like her own. Things hadn't been too bad under someone called Czar Alexander the Second,[3] whom Aaron always pictured as a tall handsome man in a gold uniform. But Alexander the Second was assassinated, and Alexander the Third, whom Aaron pictured as an ugly man in a black cape, became the Czar. And the Jewish people of the Ukraine had no peace anymore.

One day, a thundering of horses was heard coming toward the village from the direction of Kishinev. *The Cossacks! The Cossacks!* someone had shouted. The Czar's horsemen! Quickly, quickly, everyone in Aaron's grandmother's family had climbed down to the cellar through a little trapdoor hidden under a mat in the big central room of their shack. But his grandmother's pet goat, whom she'd loved as much as Aaron loved Pidge and more, had to be left above, because if it had made a sound in the cellar, they would never have lived to see the next morning. They all hid under the wood in the woodbin and waited, hardly breathing.

Suddenly, from above, they heard shouts and calls and screams at a distance. And then the noise was in their house. Boots pounding on the floor, and everything breaking and crashing overhead. The smell of smoke and the shouts of a dozen men.

---

3. Czar Alexander the Second: The leader of Russia from 1855 to 1881.

THE ICE EATER
Kathleen Cook

The terror went on for an hour and then the sound of horses' hooves faded into the distance. They waited another hour to make sure, and then the father went up out of the cellar and the rest of the family followed. The door to the house had been torn from its hinges and every piece of furniture was broken. Every window, every dish, every stitch of clothing was totally destroyed, and one wall had been completely bashed in. And on the floor was the goat, lying quietly. Aaron's grandmother, who was just a little girl of eight at the time, had wept over the goat all day and all night and could not be consoled.

But they had been lucky. For other houses had been burned to the ground. And everywhere, not goats alone, nor sheep, but men and women and children lay quietly on the ground. The word for this sort of massacre, Aaron had learned, was *pogrom*. It had been a pogrom. And the men on the horses were Cossacks. Hated word. Cossacks.

And so Pidge would replace that goat of long ago. A pigeon on Second Avenue where no one needed trapdoors or secret escape passages or woodpiles to hide under. A pigeon for his grandmother's sixtieth birthday. *Oh wing, heal quickly so my grandmother can send you flying to everywhere she wants!*

But a few days later, Aaron met Carl in the street again. And Carl told Aaron that there was going to be a meeting that afternoon in which a map was going to be drawn up to show where a secret treasure lay buried on the empty lot. "Bring the pigeon and you can come into the shack. We got a badge for you. A new kinda membership badge with a secret code on the back."

Aaron ran home, his heart pounding almost as fast as the pigeon's. He took Pidge in his hands and carried him out the door while his mother was busy in the kitchen making stuffed cabbage, his father's favorite dish. And by the time he reached the street, Aaron had decided to take the bandages off. Pidge would look like a real pigeon again, and none of the older boys would laugh or call him a bundle of rags.

Gently, gently he removed the bandages and the splints and put them in his pocket in case he should need them again. But Pidge seemed to hold his wing properly in place.

When he reached the empty lot, Aaron walked up to the shack, then hesitated. Four bigger boys were there. After a moment, Carl came out and commanded Aaron to hand Pidge over.

"Be careful," said Aaron. "I just took the bandages off."

"Oh sure, don't worry," said Carl. By now Pidge was used to people holding him, and he remained calm in Carl's hands.

"OK," said Carl. "Give him the badge." And one of the older boys handed Aaron his badge with the code on the back. "Now light the fire," said Carl.

"What . . . what fire?" asked Aaron.

"The fire. You'll see," Carl answered.

"You didn't say nothing about a fire," said Aaron. "You didn't say nothing to—"

"Hey!" said Carl. "I'm the leader here. And you don't talk unless I tell you that you have p'mission. Light the fire, Al."

The boy named Al went out to the side of the shack, where some wood and cardboard and old newspapers had been piled into a huge mound. He struck a match and held it to the newspapers.

"OK," said Carl. "Let's get 'er good and hot. Blow on it. Everybody blow."

Aaron's eyes stung from the smoke, but he blew alongside the others, going from side to side as the smoke shifted toward them and away.

"Let's fan it," said Al.

In a few minutes, the fire was crackling and glowing with a bright yellow-orange flame.

"Get me the rope," said Carl.

One of the boys brought Carl some cord and Carl, without a word, wound it twice around the pigeon, so that its wings were tight against its body.

"What . . . what are you *doing*!" shouted Aaron. "You're hurting his wing!"

"Don't worry about his wing," said Carl. "We're gonna throw him into the fire. And when we do, we're gonna swear an oath of loyalty to—"

"No! *No*!" shouted Aaron, moving toward Carl.

"Grab him!" called Carl. "Don't let him get the pigeon!"

But Aaron had leaped right across the fire at Carl, taking him completely by surprise. He threw Carl back against the shack and hit out at his face with both fists. Carl slid down to the ground and the pigeon rolled out of his hands. Aaron scooped up the pigeon and ran, pretending he was on roller skates so that he would go faster and faster. And as he ran across the lot he pulled the cord off Pidge and tried to find a place, *any* place, to hide him. But the boys were on top of him, and the pigeon slipped from Aaron's hands.

"Get him!" shouted Carl.

Aaron thought of the worst, the most horrible thing he could shout at the boys. "Cossacks!" he screamed. "You're all Cossacks!"

Two boys held Aaron back while the others tried to catch the pigeon. Pidge fluttered along the ground just out of reach, skittering one way and then the other. Then the boys came at him from two directions. But suddenly Pidge beat his wings in rhythm, and rose up, up over the roof of the nearest tenement, up over Second Avenue toward the park.

With the pigeon gone, the boys turned toward Aaron and tackled him to the ground and punched him and tore his clothes and punched him some more. Aaron twisted and turned and kicked and punched back, shouting "Cossacks! Cossacks!" And somehow the word gave him the strength to tear away from them.

When Aaron reached home, he tried to go past the kitchen quickly so his mother wouldn't see his bloody face and torn clothing. But it was no use; his father was home from work early that night and was seated in the living room. In a moment Aaron was surrounded by his mother, father, and grandmother, and in another moment he had told them everything that had happened, the words tumbling out between his broken sobs. Told them of the present he had planned, of the pigeon for a goat, of the gang, of the badge with the secret code on the back, of the shack, and the fire, and the pigeon's flight over the tenement roof.

And Aaron's grandmother kissed him and thanked him for his present which was even better than the pigeon.

"What present?" asked Aaron, trying to stop the series of sobs.

And his grandmother opened her pocketbook and handed Aaron her mirror and asked him to look. But all Aaron saw was his dirty, bruised face and his torn shirt.

Aaron thought he understood and then, again, he thought he didn't. How could she be so happy when there really was no present? And why pretend that there was?

Later that night, just before he fell asleep, Aaron tried to imagine what his grandmother might have done with the pigeon. She would have fed it, and she certainly would have talked to it, as she did to all the birds, and . . . and then she would have let it go free. Yes, of course. Pidge's flight to freedom must have been the gift that had made his grandmother so happy. Her goat has escaped from the Cossacks at last, Aaron thought, half dreaming. And he fell asleep with a smile.

Reader's Response

Describe your feelings as you read the part in which Aaron fights to save Pidge. Would you have reacted the same way as Aaron? Explain.

The Carrier Pigeon

Once Aaron brings Pidge home, he begins training it to be a carrier. Carrier pigeons are also called homing pigeons because of their unusual ability to find their way back to their home base from distant places.

"Homers," as they are sometimes called, carry messages tied to their legs. They have been used to carry messages as early as 3,000 years ago in Egypt and Persia.

No one knows for sure how pigeons find their way across unknown territory to reach their home base. Some people think pigeons have a mysterious link with the earth's magnetic field; others believe they are guided by the position of the sun.

Although pigeons are no longer used for carrying messages to the extent they were years ago, many people still train and race homing pigeons.

How might carrier pigeons still be useful today?

Responding to the Selection

Your Response

1. Which character do you like the most? Which do you like the least? Why?
2. What would you have done if Carl had asked you to join his club? Explain.

Recalling

3. Describe how Aaron finds Pidge.
4. Why does Aaron decide to give Pidge to his grandmother for her birthday?

Interpreting

5. In what way are Aaron and his family "strangers in the land of Egypt"?
6. Other than wanting Pidge, why do you think Carl invited Aaron into his club?
7. Compare Aaron's experience with the gang to his grandmother's experience with the Cossacks. What does Aaron learn?
8. Why is it so important to Aaron's grandmother that Pidge be set free?
9. Why is the title of this story appropriate?

Applying

10. Both Aaron and his grandmother are the victims of the cruelty of which people are capable. How might you do your part in stopping cruelty against others?

Analyzing Literature

Recognizing Major and Minor Characters

A **major character** plays the most important part in a story. **Minor characters** play less important roles, but they may still influence the outcome of a story.

1. Describe the character traits of Aaron, the major character in this story.
2. List three characteristics of at least three minor characters.
3. Which minor character has the greatest effect on the outcome of the story? Why?

Critical Thinking and Reading

Summarizing

To **summarize** is to restate something briefly in different words. A good summary includes all the important details in the order in which they occurred.

1. Summarize Aaron's grandmother's story about her life in the Ukraine.
2. Summarize the part of the story in which Aaron fights to save Pidge from the boys in the gang.

Thinking and Writing

Summarizing a Story in a Letter

Like Aaron's grandmother, many parents, relatives, and friends have stories about their childhood that can help you to understand yourself or a situation better. Ask someone you know well to tell you a story about a significant event in his or her life. Then, in a letter to a friend, summarize the story related to you and briefly explain how the story helps you better understand yourself or your situation in life. When you revise, check that your summary contains all the important points. Add more details if necessary. Then write a final draft.

Learning Options

1. **Writing.** Reread Aaron's grandmother's description of the pogrom on pages 86–87. Imagine that you are Aaron's grandmother. Write a diary entry for that day from her point of view.
2. **Performance.** Perform a section of "Aaron's Gift" with several classmates. First, review the part of the story when Aaron brings Pidge to the club's shack (pages 88–89). Then, have each classmate choose a character and practice his or her part. When you are ready, act out this part of the story for the class.

YOUR WRITING PROCESS

Developing Characters Through Dialogue

What makes the action of a story occur? What makes you feel as if you're inside a story, experiencing every moment? The characters, that's who!

Where do characters come from? Sometimes characters are like real people the writer has known. For example, Philippa Pearce may actually have had a beloved aunt who loved to sew. At other times characters spring from their writers' imaginations. For example, Myron Levoy may have never known someone who escaped from the Cossacks in Russia, but if he knew how the Cossacks acted, he could create a character such as the grandmother in "Aaron's Gift."

Your Turn

You too can develop characters. You can base them on someone you have known: a relative, a teacher, a friend, or someone in the news; or you can make someone up: a mythical giant, a being from another world, or a queen from a magical land. When you have created two characters, place them in a situation and write a conversation between them that will bring both to life.

Prewriting

1. Brainstorm for possible characters. List ten people, not by name but by short descriptions. For example:

1. a teenage lifeguard
2. a telephone operator
3. a science teacher
4. a five-year-old boy

Then, create pairs by drawing arrows connecting different people. As you draw lines, imagine situations or conflicts that could develop between these two people. What could they talk about? Choose two characters and place them in a situation that seems interesting, dramatic, and believable.

2. Cluster to explore your characters. Give your two characters names and use these names as centers of two cluster diagrams. In each cluster, explore as many of the following topics as you can: age; physical appearance; occupation; parents' names and occupations; place of residence; favorite foods, music, places; strongest dislikes; wishes; important experiences; fears.

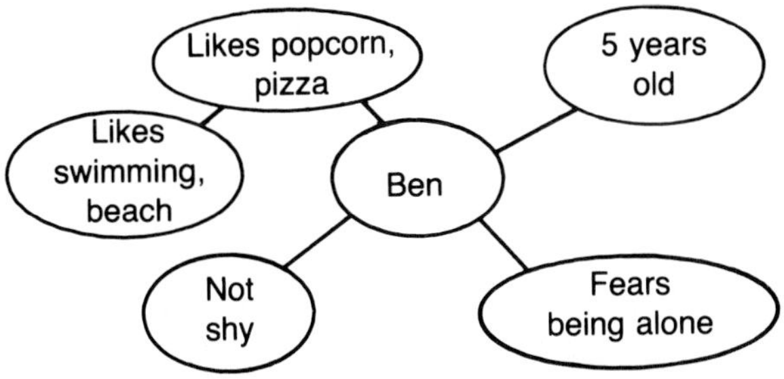

Drafting

Keeping your situation in mind, draft dialogue for your characters. Begin with a sentence or two that describe the situation of the two characters. Begin a new paragraph each time the speaker changes.

1. Getting started. It may help to begin by having one character ask a question to begin the dialogue.

2. Include gestures and actions. Gestures, such as a wink or a frown, can show your characters' emotions. Actions, such as standing, pacing, or turning away can show how your characters' physical relationship changes. Don't overdo these, but include them when they are important.

3. Include thoughts and feelings of the characters. Ask yourself, "What is this character thinking? How does he or she feel?" Sentences that show feelings and thoughts can make your readers understand your characters even more.

One student chose a lifeguard named Leslie and a five-year-old boy named Ben.

> It's a hot summer day and the beach is very crowded. A small boy toddles up to the tall, orange lifeguard chair and says to the person sitting at the top, "Miss Lifeguard, can you help me?"
>
> She takes off her sunglasses and answers, "What do you need?"
>
> The little boy rubs his eyes and responds, "My mommy."
>
> The lifeguard climbs down from her chair and kneels in front of the boy. "Is she here somewhere?"
>
> "She's gone," he cries.
>
> The girl reaches for the boy's hand, but he pulls away. "What's your name, honey?"
>
> "Benjamin Alexander Driscoll the Third."
>
> She laughs, "Well, that's quite a name! Now, let's find your mother, Benjamin."

Notice how the words here say more than the actions. The personalities of the two characters are shown by what they say and what they do. In other words the writer is *showing*, not *telling* about the characters.

For example, we learn that Leslie is kind when she reaches for Ben's hand. We learn that she is friendly when she says things like, "That's quite a name!"

Revising

Step 1: Use the revising checklist on page 749 to evaluate and revise your draft.

Step 2: In addition ask someone you trust to read your draft aloud with you. Listen for any rough spots. Afterward, ask questions such as these:

- How would you describe each character? What words show these qualities?
- Do the words seem natural for both characters? Are there any lines that seem forced, awkward, or inconsistent?

Step 3: Ask yourself, "What can I add that will show this character even more clearly?" Add gestures, actions, and words that will strengthen your dialogue.

Proofreading

Use the proofreading guidelines on page 753. Be especially careful when punctuating quotations.

Reading for Setting

THE WATER LILY POND
Claude Monet
National Gallery, London

GUIDE FOR READING

Rudyard Kipling

(1865–1936) was born in India, where his English parents lived and worked. At that time India was a colony of the British Empire. When Kipling was five, he was sent to school in England. At seventeen, he returned to India to work as a reporter and to write poems, stories, and novels. From his Indian nurses, Kipling had heard folk tales, many of which featured talking animals. Kipling wrote several collections of tales featuring talking animals, including *The Jungle Book,* in which "Mowgli's Brothers" appears.

Mowgli's Brothers

Setting

Setting refers to the time and place in which a story occurs. Authors create setting by including details that help readers see the time and place in their imaginations. Sometimes setting merely provides background for a story that might take place almost anywhere, but at other times, as in "Mowgli's Brothers," setting is of central importance to a story.

Focus

"Mowgli's Brothers" is about a boy who is raised in the jungle. Create a Venn diagram by drawing two intersecting circles. In one circle, write words and ideas about the jungle. In the other circle, write words and ideas about home. In the area where the circles intersect, write any words or ideas that "home" and "the jungle" have in common. As you read the story, compare what Mowgli thinks about home and the jungle to what you think about them.

Vocabulary

Knowing the following words will help you read "Mowgli's Brothers."

scuttled (skut′ ′ld) *v.*: Scurried; scampered (p. 96)
quarry (kwôr′ ē) *n.*: Prey; anything being hunted or pursued (p. 98)
fostering (fôs′ tər iŋ) *n.*: Taking care of; rearing (p. 98)
veterans (vet′ ər enz) *v.*: Those having experience (p. 99)
monotonous (mə nät′′n əs) *adj.*: Tiresome because it does not vary (p. 99)
dispute (di spyo͞ot′) *n.*: An argument; debate; quarrel (p. 100)
clamor (klam′ ər) *n.*: A loud demand or complaint (p. 100)
maimed (mām′d) *v.*: Crippled; disabled (p. 105)
betray (bē trā′) *v.*: Be a traitor to; give over to the enemy (p. 107)

Spelling Tip

You can remember the spelling of the word *monotonous* by noticing that all the *o*'s in the word make the spelling of it monotonous.

Mowgli's Brothers

Rudyard Kipling

" 'Now was there ever a wolf that could boast of a man's cub among her children?' "

Now Chil the Kite[1] brings home the night
That Mang the Bat sets free—
The herds are shut in byre[2] and hut
For loosed till dawn are we.
This is the hour of pride and power,
Talon and tush[3] and claw.
Oh hear the call!—Good hunting all
That keep the Jungle Law!
Night-Song in the Jungle

It was seven o'clock of a very warm evening in the Seeonee hills[4] when Father Wolf woke up from his day's rest, scratched himself, yawned, and spread out his paws one after the other to get rid of the sleepy feeling in their tips. Mother Wolf lay with her big gray nose dropped across her four tumbling, squealing cubs, and the moon shone into the mouth of the cave where they all lived. "Augrh!" said Father Wolf, "it is time to hunt again"; and he was going to spring downhill when a little shadow with a bushy tail crossed the threshold and whined: "Good luck go with you, O Chief of the Wolves; and good luck and strong white teeth go with the noble children, that they may never forget the hungry in this world."

It was the jackal[5]—Tabaqui, the Dish-licker—and the wolves of India despise Tabaqui because he runs about making mischief, and telling tales, and eating rags and

1. **kite** (kīt) *n.*: A bird of the hawk family.
2. **byre** (bīr) *n.*: A cow barn.
3. **tush** (tush) *n.*: A tusk.
4. **Seeonee** (sē ō′ nē) **hills:** Hills in central India.

5. **jackal** (jak′ əl) *n.*: A wild dog, smaller than a wolf, found in Asia and Northern Africa.

MATES
Al Agnew
Courtesy of the Artist

"It was seven o'clock of a very warm evening in the Seeonee Hills. . . ."

pieces of leather from the village rubbish-heaps. But they are afraid of him too, because Tabaqui, more than anyone else in the jungle, is apt to go mad, and then he forgets that he was ever afraid of anyone, and runs through the forest biting everything in his way. Even the tiger runs and hides when little Tabaqui goes mad, for madness is the most disgraceful thing that can overtake a wild creature. We call it hydrophobia, but they call it *dewanee*—the madness—and run.

"Enter, then, and look," said Father Wolf, stiffly; "but there is no food here."

"For a wolf, no," said Tabaqui; "but for so mean a person as myself a dry bone is a good feast. Who are we, the Gidur-log [the jackal-people], to pick and choose?" He scuttled to the back of the cave, where he found the bone of a buck with some meat on it, and sat cracking the end merrily.

"All thanks for this good meal," he said, licking his lips. "How beautiful are the noble children! How large are their eyes! And so young too! Indeed, indeed, I might have remembered that the children of Kings are men from the beginning."

Now, Tabaqui knew as well as anyone else that there is nothing so unlucky as to compliment children to their faces; and it pleased him to see Mother and Father Wolf look uncomfortable.

Tabaqui sat still, rejoicing in the mischief that he had made: then he said spitefully:

"Shere Khan, the Big One, has shifted his hunting-grounds. He will hunt among these hills for the next moon, so he has told me."

Shere Khan was the tiger who lived near the Waingunga River, twenty miles away.

"He has no right!" Father Wolf began angrily—"By the Law of the Jungle he has no right to change his quarters without due warning. He will frighten every head of game within ten miles, and I—I have to kill for two, these days."

"His mother did not call him Lungri [the Lame One] for nothing," said Mother Wolf, quietly. "He has been lame in one foot from his birth. That is why he has only killed cattle. Now the villagers of the Waingunga are angry with him, and he has come here to make *our* villagers angry. They will scour the Jungle for him when he is far away, and we and our children must run when the grass is set alight. Indeed, we are very grateful to Shere Khan!"

"Shall I tell him of your gratitude?" said Tabaqui.

"Out!" snapped Father Wolf. "Out and hunt with thy master. Thou hast done harm enough for one night."

"I go," said Tabaqui, quietly. "Ye can hear Shere Khan below in the thickets. I might have saved myself the message."

Father Wolf listened, and below in the valley that ran down to a little river, he heard the dry, angry, snarly, singsong whine of a tiger who has caught nothing and does not care if all the Jungle knows it.

"The fool!" said Father Wolf. "To begin a night's work with that noise! Does he think that our buck are like his fat Waingunga bullocks?"[6]

"H'sh! It is neither bullock nor buck he hunts tonight," said Mother Wolf. "It is Man." The whine had changed to a sort of humming purr that seemed to come from every quarter of the compass. It was the noise that bewilders woodcutters and gypsies sleeping in the open, and makes them run sometimes into the very mouth of the tiger.

---

6. bullocks (bo͝ol′ əks) *n.*: Steers.

"Man!" said Father Wolf, showing all his white teeth. "Faugh! Are there not enough beetles and frogs in the tanks that he must eat Man and on our ground too!"

The Law of the Jungle, which never orders anything without a reason, forbids every beast to eat Man except when he is killing to show his children how to kill, and then he must hunt outside the hunting-grounds of his pack or tribe. The real reason for this is that man-killing means, sooner or later, the arrival of white men on elephants, with guns, and hundreds of brown men with gongs and rockets and torches. Then everybody in the jungle suffers. The reason the beasts give among themselves is that Man is the weakest and most defenseless of all living things, and it is unsportsmanlike to touch him. They say too—and it is true—that man-eaters become mangy,[7] and lose their teeth.

The purr grew louder, and ended in the full-throated "Aaarh!" of the tiger's charge.

Then there was a howl—an untigerish howl—from Shere Khan. "He has missed," said Mother Wolf. "What is it?"

Father Wolf ran out a few paces and heard Shere Khan muttering and mumbling savagely, as he tumbled about in the scrub.

"The fool has had no more sense than to jump at a woodcutter's campfire, and has burned his feet," said Father Wolf, with a grunt. "Tabaqui is with him."

"Something is coming up hill," said Mother Wolf, twitching one ear. "Get ready."

The bushes rustled a little in the thicket, and Father Wolf dropped with his haunches under him, ready for his leap. Then, if you had been watching, you would have seen the most wonderful thing in the world—the wolf checked in mid-spring. He made his bound before he saw what it was he was jumping at, and then he tried to stop himself. The result was that he shot up straight into the air for four or five feet, landing almost where he left ground.

"Man!" he snapped. "A man's cub. Look!"

Directly in front of him, holding on by a low branch, stood a naked brown baby who could just walk—as soft and as dimpled a little atom[8] as ever came to a wolf's cave at night. He looked up into Father Wolf's face, and laughed.

"Is that a man's cub?" said Mother Wolf. "I have never seen one. Bring it here."

A wolf accustomed to moving his own cubs can, if necessary, mouth an egg without breaking it, and though Father Wolf's jaws closed right on the child's back not a tooth even scratched the skin, as he laid it down among the cubs.

"How little! How naked, and—how bold!" said Mother Wolf, softly. The baby was pushing his way between the cubs to get close to the warm hide. "Ahai! He is taking his meal with the others. And so this is a man's cub. Now, was there ever a wolf that could boast of a man's cub among her children?"

"I have heard now and again of such a thing, but never in our Pack or in my time," said Father Wolf. "He is altogether without hair, and I could kill him with a touch of my foot. But see, he looks up and is not afraid."

The moonlight was blocked out of the mouth of the cave, for Shere Khan's great square head and shoulders were thrust into the entrance. Tabaqui, behind him, was squeaking: "My lord, my lord, it went in here!"

---

7. mangy (mān′ jē) *adj.*: Having the mange, a skin disease of mammals that causes sores and loss of hair.

8. atom (at′ əm) *n.*: A tiny piece of matter.

"Shere Khan does us great honor," said Father Wolf, but his eyes were very angry. "What does Shere Khan need?"

"My quarry. A man's cub went this way," said Shere Khan. "Its parents have run off. Give it to me."

Shere Khan had jumped at a woodcutter's campfire, as Father Wolf had said, and was furious from the pain of his burned feet. But Father Wolf knew that the mouth of the cave was too narrow for a tiger to come in by. Even where he was, Shere Khan's shoulders and forepaws were cramped for want of room, as a man's would be if he tried to fight in a barrel.

"The Wolves are a free people," said Father Wolf. "They take orders from the Head of the Pack, and not from any striped cattle-killer. The man's cub is ours—to kill if we choose."

"Ye choose and ye do not choose! What talk is this of choosing? By the bull that I killed, am I to stand nosing into your dog's den for my fair dues? It is I, Shere Khan, who speak!"

The tiger's roar filled the cave with thunder. Mother Wolf shook herself clear of the cubs and sprang forward, her eyes, like two green moons in the darkness, facing the blazing eyes of Shere Khan.

"And it is I, Raksha [The Demon], who answer. The man's cub is mine, Lungri—mine to me! He shall not be killed. He shall live to run with the Pack and to hunt with the Pack; and in the end, look you, hunter of little naked cubs—frog-eater—fish-killer—he shall hunt *thee*! Now get hence, or by the Sambhur that I killed (*I* eat no starved cattle), back thou goest to thy mother, burned beast of the Jungle, lamer than ever thou camest into the world! Go!"

Father Wolf looked on amazed. He had almost forgotten the days when he won Mother Wolf in fair fight from five other wolves, when she ran in the Pack and was not called The Demon for compliment's sake. Shere Khan might have faced Father Wolf, but he could not stand up against Mother Wolf, for he knew that where he was she had all the advantage of the ground, and would fight to the death. So he backed out of the cave-mouth growling, and when he was clear he shouted:

"Each dog barks in his own yard! We will see what the Pack will say to this fostering of man-cubs. The cub is mine, and to my teeth he will come in the end, O bush-tailed thieves!"

Mother Wolf threw herself down panting among the cubs, and Father Wolf said to her gravely:

"Shere Khan speaks this much truth. The cub must be shown to the Pack. Wilt thou still keep him, Mother?"

"Keep him!" she gasped. "He came naked, by night, alone and very hungry; yet he was not afraid! Look, he has pushed one of my babies to one side already. And that lame butcher would have killed him and would have run off to the Waingunga while the villagers here hunted through all our lairs in revenge! Keep him? Assuredly I will keep him. Lie still, little frog. O thou Mowgli—for Mowgli the Frog I will call thee—the time will come when thou wilt hunt Shere Khan as he has hunted thee."

"But what will our Pack say?" said Father Wolf. The Law of the Jungle lays down very clearly that any wolf may, when he marries, withdraw from the Pack he belongs to; but as soon as his cubs are old enough to stand on their feet he must bring them to the Pack Council, which is generally held once a month at full moon, in order that the other wolves may identify them. After that inspection the cubs are free to run where they please, and until they have killed their first buck no excuse is accepted if a grown wolf of the Pack kills one of them. The punishment is death where the murderer can be found; and if you think for a minute you will see that this must be so.

Father Wolf waited till his cubs could run a little, and then on the night of the Pack Meeting took them and Mowgli and Mother Wolf to the Council Rock—a hilltop covered with stones and boulders where a hundred wolves could hide. Akela, the great gray Lone Wolf, who led all the Pack by strength and cunning, lay out at full length on his rock, and below him sat forty or more wolves of every size and color, from badger-colored veterans who could handle a buck alone, to young black three-year-olds who thought they could. The Lone Wolf had led them for a year now. He had fallen twice into a wolf-trap in his youth, and once he had been beaten and left for dead; so he knew the manners and customs of men. There was very little talking at the Rock. The cubs tumbled over each other in the center of the circle where their mothers and fathers sat, and now and again a senior wolf would go quietly up to a cub, look a him carefully, and return to his place on noiseless feet. Sometimes a mother would push her cub far out into the moonlight, to be sure that he had not been overlooked. Akela from his rock would cry: "Ye know the Law—ye know the Law. Look well, O Wolves!" and the anxious mothers would take up the call: "Look—look well, O Wolves!"

At last—and Mother Wolf's neck-bristles lifted as the time came—Father Wolf pushed

"The Lone Wolf had led them for a year now."

AKELA THE LONE WOLF from THE JUNGLE BOOK
Maurice and Edward Detmold
Donnell Library Center, New York Public Library

"Mowgli the Frog," as they called him, into the center, where he sat laughing and playing with some pebbles that glistened in the moonlight.

Akela never raised his head from his paws, but went on with the monotonous cry: "Look well!" A muffled roar came up from behind the rocks—the voice of Shere Khan crying: "The cub is mine. Give him to me. What have the Free People to do with a man's cub?" Akela never even twitched his ears: all he said was: "Look well, O Wolves! What have the Free People to do with the orders of any save the Free People? Look well!"

There was a chorus of deep growls, and a young wolf in his fourth year flung back

Shere Khan's question to Akela: "What have the Free People to do with the man's cub?" Now the Law of the Jungle lays down that if there is any dispute as to the right of a cub to be accepted by the Pack, he must be spoken for by at least two members of the Pack who are not his father and mother.

"Who speaks for this cub?" said Akela. "Among the Free People who speaks?" There was no answer, and Mother Wolf got ready for what she knew would be her last fight, if things came to fighting.

Then the only other creature who is allowed at the Pack Council—Baloo, the sleepy brown bear who teaches the wolf cubs the Law of the Jungle: old Baloo, who can come and go where he pleases because he eats only nuts and roots and honey—rose up on his hind quarters and grunted.

"The man's cub—the man's cub?" he said. "*I* speak for the man's cub. There is no harm in a man's cub. I have no gift of words, but I speak the truth. Let him run with the Pack, and be entered with the others. I myself will teach him."

THE COUNCIL ROCK from THE JUNGLE BOOK
Maurice and Edward Detmold
Donnell Library Center, New York Public Library

"A black shadow dropped down into the circle."

"We need yet another," said Akela. "Baloo has spoken, and he is our teacher for the young cubs. Who speaks besides Baloo?"

A black shadow dropped down into the circle. It was Bagheera the Black Panther, inky black all over, but with the panther marking showing up in certain lights like the pattern of watered silk. Everybody knew Bagheera, and nobody cared to cross his path; for he was as cunning as Tabaqui, as bold as the wild buffalo, and as reckless as the wounded elephant. But he had a voice as soft as wild honey dripping from a tree, and a skin softer than down.

"O Akela, and ye the Free People," he purred, "I have no right in your assembly; but the Law of the Jungle says that if there is a doubt which is not a killing matter in regard to a new cub, the life of that cub may be bought at a price. And the Law does not say who may or may not pay that price. Am I right?"

"Good! good!" said the young wolves, who are always hungry. "Listen to Bagheera. The cub can be bought for a price. It is the Law."

"Knowing that I have no right to speak here, I ask your leave."

"Speak then," cried twenty voices.

"To kill a naked cub is shame. Besides, he may make better sport for you when he is grown. Baloo has spoken in his behalf. Now to Baloo's word I will add one bull, and a fat one, newly killed, not half a mile from here, if ye will accept the man's cub according to the Law. Is it difficult?"

There was a clamor of scores of voices, saying: "What matter? He will die in the winter rains. He will scorch in the sun. What harm can a naked frog do us? Let him run with the Pack. Where is the bull, Bagheera? Let him be accepted." And then came Akela's deep bay, crying: "Look well—look well, O Wolves!"

Mowgli was still deeply interested in the pebbles, and he did not notice when the wolves came and looked at him one by one. At last they all went down the hill for the dead bull, and only Akela, Bagheera, Baloo, and Mowgli's own wolves were left. Shere Khan roared still in the night, for he was very angry that Mowgli had not been handed over to him.

"Ay, roar well," said Bagheera, under his whiskers; "for the time comes when this naked thing will make thee roar to another tune, or I know nothing of man."

"It was well done," said Akela. "Men and their cubs are very wise. He may be a help in time."

"Truly, a help in time of need; for none can hope to lead the Pack forever," said Bagheera.

Akela said nothing. He was thinking of the time that comes to every leader of every pack when his strength goes from him and he gets feebler and feebler till at last he is killed by the wolves and a new leader comes up—to be killed in his turn.

"Take him away," he said to Father Wolf, "and train him as befits one of the Free People."

And that is how Mowgli was entered into the Seeonee wolf-pack at the price of a bull and on Baloo's good word.

Now you must be content to skip ten or eleven whole years, and only guess at all the wonderful life that Mowgli led among the wolves, because if it were written out it would fill ever so many books. He grew up with the cubs, though they, of course, were grown wolves almost before he was a child, and Father Wolf taught him his business, and the meaning of things in the Jungle, till every rustle in the grass, every breath of the warm night air, every note of the owls above his head, every scratch of a bat's claws as it roosted for a while in a tree, and every splash of every little fish jumping in a pool, meant just as much to him as the work of his office means to a businessman. When he was not learning, he sat out in the sun and slept, and ate and went to sleep again; when he felt dirty or hot he swam in the forest pools; and when he wanted honey (Baloo told him that honey and nuts were just as pleasant to eat as raw meat) he climbed up for it, and that Bagheera showed him how to do. Bagheera would lie out on a branch and call, "Come along, Little Brother," and at first Mowgli would cling like the sloth,[9] but afterward he would fling himself through the branches almost as boldly as the gray ape. He took his place at the Council Rock, too, when the Pack met, and there he discovered that if he stared hard at any wolf, the wolf would be forced to drop his eyes, and so he used to stare for fun. At other times he would pick the long thorns out of the pads of his friends, for wolves suffer terribly from thorns and burs in their coats. He would go down the hillside into the cultivated lands by night, and look very curiously at the villagers in their huts, but he had a mistrust of men because Bagheera showed him a square box with a drop-gate so cunningly hidden in the jungle that he nearly walked into it, and told him that it was a trap. He loved better than

9. sloth (slôth) *n.*: A slow-moving mammal that lives in trees.

anything else to go with Bagheera into the dark warm heart of the forest, to sleep all through the drowsy day, and at night to see how Bagheera did his killing. Bagheera killed right and left as he felt hungry, and so did Mowgli—with one exception. As soon as he was old enough to understand things, Bagheera told him that he must never touch cattle because he had been bought into the Pack at the price of a bull's life. "All the Jungle is thine," said Bagheera, "and thou canst kill everything that thou art strong enough to kill; but for the sake of the bull that bought thee thou must never kill or eat any cattle young or old. That is the Law of the Jungle." Mowgli obeyed faithfully.

And he grew and grew strong as a boy must grow who does not know that he is learning any lessons, and who has nothing in the world to think of except things to eat.

Mother Wolf told him once or twice that Shere Khan was not a creature to be trusted, and that some day he must kill Shere Khan; but though a young wolf would have remembered that advice every hour, Mowgli forgot it because he was only a boy—though he would have called himself a wolf if he had been able to speak in any human tongue.

Shere Khan was always crossing his path in the Jungle, for as Akela grew older and feebler the lame tiger had come to be great friends with the younger wolves of the Pack, who followed him for scraps, a thing that Akela would never have allowed if he had dared to push his authority to the proper bounds. Then Shere Khan would flatter them and wonder that such fine young hunters were content to be led by a dying wolf and a man's cub. "They tell me," Shere Khan would say, "that at Council ye dare not look him between the eyes"; and the young wolves would growl and bristle.

Bagheera, who had eyes and ears everywhere, knew something of this, and once or twice he told Mowgli in so many words that Shere Khan would kill him some day; and Mowgli would laugh and answer: "I have the Pack and I have thee; and Baloo, though he is so lazy, might strike a blow or two for my sake. Why should I be afraid?"

It was one very warm day that a new notion came to Bagheera—born of something that he had heard. Perhaps Ikki the Porcupine had told him; but he said to Mowgli when they were deep in the Jungle, as the boy lay with his head on Bagheera's beautiful black skin: "Little Brother, how often have I told thee that Shere Khan is thy enemy?"

"As many times as there are nuts on that palm," said Mowgli, who, naturally, could not count. "What of it? I am sleepy, Bagheera, and Shere Khan is all long tail and loud talk—like Mao, the Peacock."

"But this is no time for sleeping. Baloo knows it; I know it; the Pack know it; and even the foolish, foolish deer know. Tabaqui has told thee, too."

"Ho! ho!" said Mowgli. "Tabaqui came to me not long ago with some rude talk that I was a naked man's cub and not fit to dig pig-nuts; but I caught Tabaqui by the tail and swung him twice against a palm tree to teach him better manners."

"That was foolishness; for though Tabaqui is a mischief-maker, he would have told thee of something that concerned thee closely. Open those eyes, Little Brother. Shere Khan dare not kill thee in the Jungle; but remember, Akela is very old, and soon the day comes when he cannot kill his buck, and then he will be leader no more. Many of the wolves that looked thee over when thou wast brought to the Council first are old too, and the young wolves believe, as Shere Khan has taught them, that a man-cub has no place with the Pack. In a little time thou wilt be a man."

"And what is a man that he should not run with his brothers?" said Mowgli. "I was born in the Jungle. I have obeyed the Law of the Jungle, and there is no wolf of ours from whose paws I have not pulled a thorn. Surely they are my brothers!"

Bagheera stretched himself at full length and half shut his eyes. "Little Brother," said he, "feel under my jaw."

Mowgli put up his strong brown hand, and just under Bagheera's silky chin, where the giant rolling muscles were all hid by the glossy hair, he came upon a little bald spot.

"There is no one in the Jungle that knows that I, Bagheera, carry that mark—the mark of the collar; and yet, little Brother, I was born among men, and it was among men that my mother died—in the cages of the King's Palace at Oodeypore. It was because of this that I paid the price for thee at the Council when thou wast a little naked cub. Yes, I too was born among men. I had never seen the Jungle. They fed me behind bars from an iron pan till one night I felt that I was Bagheera—the Panther—and no man's plaything, and I broke the silly lock with one blow of my paw and came away; and because I had learned the ways of men, I became more terrible in the Jungle than Shere Khan. Is it not so?"

"Yes," said Mowgli; "all the Jungle fear Bagheera—all except Mowgli."

"Oh, *thou* art a man's cub," said the Black Panther, very tenderly; "and even as I returned to my Jungle, so thou must go back to men at last,—to the men who are thy brothers,—if thou art not killed in the Council."

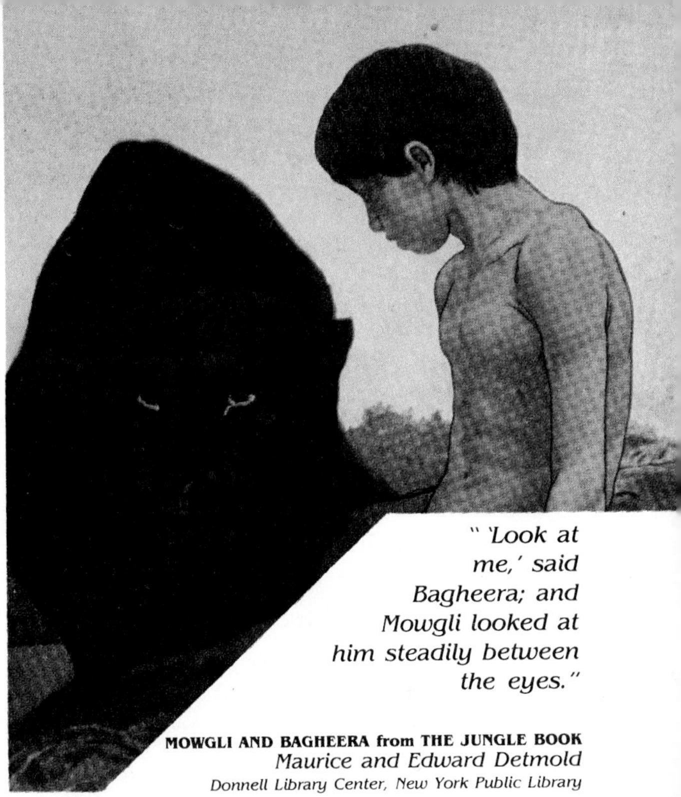

" 'Look at me,' said Bagheera; and Mowgli looked at him steadily between the eyes."

MOWGLI AND BAGHEERA from THE JUNGLE BOOK
Maurice and Edward Detmold
Donnell Library Center, New York Public Library

"But why—but why should any wish to kill me?" said Mowgli.

"Look at me," said Bagheera; and Mowgli looked at him steadily between the eyes. The big panther turned his head away in half a minute.

"*That* is why," he said, shifting his paw on the leaves. "Not even I can look thee between the eyes, and I was born among men, and I love thee, Little Brother. The others they hate thee because their eyes cannot meet thine—because thou art wise—because thou hast pulled out thorns from their feet—because thou art a man."

"I did not know these things," said Mowgli, sullenly; and he frowned under his heavy black eyebrows.

"What is the Law of the Jungle? Strike first and then give tongue. By thy very carelessness they know that thou art a man. But be wise. It is in my heart that when Akela misses his next kill,—and at each hunt it costs him more to pin the buck,—the Pack will turn against him and against thee. They will hold a jungle Council at the Rock, and then—and then—I have it!" said Bagheera, leaping up. "Go thou down quickly to the men's huts in the valley, and take some of the Red Flower which they grow there, so that when the time comes thou mayest have even a stronger friend than I or Baloo or those of the Pack that love thee. Get the Red Flower."

By Red Flower Bagheera meant fire, only no creature in the Jungle will call fire by its proper name. Every beast lives in deadly fear of it, and invents a hundred ways of describing it.

"The Red Flower?" said Mowgli. "That grows outside their huts in the twilight. I will get some."

"There speaks the man's cub," said Bagheera, proudly. "Remember that it grows in little pots. Get one swiftly, keep it by thee for time of need."

"Good!" said Mowgli. "I go. But art thou sure, O my Bagheera"—he slipped his arm round the splendid neck, and looked deep into the big eyes—"art thou sure that all this is Shere Khan's doing?"

"By the Broken Lock that freed me, I am sure, Little Brother."

"Then, by the bull that bought me, I will pay Shere Khan full tale for this, and it may be a little over," said Mowgli; and he bounded away.

"That is a man. That is all a man," said Bagheera to himself, lying down again. "Oh, Shere Khan, never was a blacker hunting than that frog-hunt of thine ten years ago!"

Mowgli was far and far through the forest, running hard, and his heart was hot in him. He came to the cave as the evening mist rose, and drew breath, and looked down the valley. The cubs were out, but Mother Wolf, at the back of the cave, knew by his breathing that something was troubling her frog.

"What is it, Son?" she said.

"Some bat's chatter of Shere Khan," he called back. "I hunt among the plowed fields tonight," and he plunged downward through the bushes, to the stream at the bottom of the valley. There he checked, for he heard the yell of the Pack hunting, heard the bellow of a hunted Sambhur, and the snort as the buck turned at bay. Then there were wicked, bitter howls from the young wolves: "Akela! Akela! Let the Lone Wolf show his strength. Room for the leader of the Pack! Spring, Akela!"

The Lone Wolf must have sprung and missed his hold, for Mowgli heard the snap of his teeth and then a yelp as the Sambhur knocked him over with his forefoot.

He did not wait for anything more, but dashed on; and the yells grew fainter behind him as he ran into the croplands where the villagers lived.

"Bagheera spoke truth," he panted, as he nestled down in some cattle fodder by the window of a hut. "Tomorrow is one day both for Akela and for me."

Then he pressed his face close to the window and watched the fire on the hearth. He saw the husbandman's wife get up and feed it in the night with black lumps; and when the morning came and the mists were all white and cold, he saw the man's child pick up a wicker pot plastered inside with earth, fill it with lumps of red-hot charcoal, put it under his blanket, and go out to tend the cows in the byre.

"Is that all?" said Mowgli. "If a cub can do it, there is nothing to fear"; so he strode round the corner and met the boy, took the pot from his hand, and disappeared into the mist while the boy howled with fear.

"They are very like me," said Mowgli, blowing into the pot, as he had seen the woman do. "This thing will die if I do not give it things to eat"; and he dropped twigs and dried bark on the red stuff. Half-way up the hill he met Bagheera with the morning dew shining like moonstones on his coat.

"Akela has missed," said the Panther. "They would have killed him last night, but they needed thee also. They were looking for thee on the hill."

"I was among the plowed lands. I am ready. See!" Mowgli held up the fire-pot.

"Good! Now, I have seen men thrust a dry branch into that stuff, and presently the Red Flower blossomed at the end of it. Art thou not afraid?"

"No. Why should I fear? I remember now—if it is not a dream—how, before I was a Wolf, I lay beside the Red Flower, and it was warm and pleasant."

All that day Mowgli sat in the cave tending his fire-pot and dipping dry branches into it to see how they looked. He found a branch that satisfied him, and in the evening when Tabaqui came to the cave and told him rudely enough that he was wanted at the Council Rock, he laughed till Tabaqui ran away. Then Mowgli went to the Council, still laughing.

Akela the Lone Wolf lay by the side of his rock as a sign that the leadership of the Pack was open, and Shere Khan with his following of scrap-fed wolves walked to and fro openly, being flattered. Bagheera lay close to Mowgli, and the fire-pot was between Mowgli's knees. When they were all gathered together, Shere Khan began to speak—a thing he would never have dared to do when Akela was in his prime.

"He has no right," whispered Bagheera. "Say so. He is a dog's son. He will be frightened."

Mowgli sprang to his feet. "Free People," he cried, "does Shere Khan lead the Pack? What has a tiger to do with our leadership?"

"Seeing that the leadership is yet open, and being asked to speak—" Shere Khan began.

"By whom?" said Mowgli. "Are we *all* jackals, to fawn on this cattle-butcher? The leadership of the Pack is with the Pack alone."

There were yells of "Silence, thou man's cub!" "Let him speak. He has kept our Law"; and at last the seniors of the Pack thundered: "Let the Dead Wolf speak." When a leader of the Pack has missed his kill, he is called the Dead Wolf as long as he lives, which is not long, as a rule.

Akela raised his old head wearily:—

"Free People, and ye too, jackals of Shere Khan, for many seasons I have led ye to and from the kill, and in all my time not one has been trapped or maimed. Now I have missed my kill. Ye know how that plot was made. Ye know how ye brought me up to an untried buck to make my weakness known. It was cleverly done. Your right is to kill me here on the Council Rock now. Therefore, I ask, who comes to make an end of the Lone Wolf? For it is my right, by the Law of the Jungle, that ye come one by one."

There was a long hush, for no single wolf cared to fight Akela to the death. Then Shere Khan roared: "Bah! what have we to do with this toothless fool? He is doomed to die! It is the man-cub who has lived too long. Free People, he was my meat from the first. Give him to me. I am weary of this man-wolf folly. He has troubled the Jungle for ten seasons. Give me the man-cub, or I will hunt here always, and not give you one bone. He is a man, a man's child, and from the marrow of my bones I hate him!"

Then more than half the Pack yelled: "A man! a man! What has a man to do with us? Let him go to his own place."

"And turn all the people of the villages against us?" clamored Shere Khan. "No; give him to me. He is a man, and none of us can look him between the eyes."

Akela lifted his head again, and said: "He has eaten our food. He has slept with us. He has driven game for us. He has broken no word of the Law of the Jungle."

"Also, I paid for him with a bull when he was accepted. The worth of a bull is little, but Bagheera's honor is something that he will perhaps fight for," said Bagheera, in his gentlest voice.

"A bull paid ten years ago!" the Pack snarled. "What do we care for bones ten years old?"

"Or for a pledge?" said Bagheera, his white teeth bared under his lip. "Well are ye called the Free People!"

"No man's cub can run with the people of the jungle," howled Shere Khan. "Give him to me!"

"He is our brother in all but blood," Akela went on; "and ye would kill him here! In truth, I have lived too long. Some of ye are eaters of cattle, and of others I have heard that, under Shere Khan's teaching, ye go by dark night and snatch children from the villager's doorstep. Therefore I know ye to be cowards, and it is to cowards I speak. It is certain that I must die, and my life is of no worth, or I would offer that in the man-cub's place. But for the sake of the Honor of the Pack,—a little matter that by being without a leader ye have forgotten,—I promise that if ye let the man-cub go to his own place, I will not, when my time comes to die, bare one tooth against ye. I will die without fighting. That will at least save the Pack three lives. More I cannot do; but if ye will, I can save ye the shame that comes of killing a brother against whom there is no fault,—a brother spoken for and brought into the Pack according to the Law of the Jungle."

"He is a man—a man—a man!" snarled the Pack; and most of the wolves began to gather around Shere Khan, whose tail was beginning to switch.

"Then Shere Khan roared: . . ."

TIGER SEARCHING FOR HIS PREY
Antoine Louis Barye
Cabinets des Dessins, Louvre

"Now the business is in thy hands," said Bagheera to Mowgli. "*We* can do no more except fight."

Mowgli stood upright—the fire-pot in his hands. Then he stretched out his arms, and yawned in the face of the Council; but he was furious with rage and sorrow, for, wolf-like, the wolves had never told him how they hated him. "Listen, you!" he cried. "There is no need for this dog's jabber. Ye have told me so often tonight that I am a man (and indeed I would have been a wolf with you to my life's end), that I feel your words are true. So I do not call ye my brothers any more, but *sag* [dogs], as a man should. What ye will do, and what ye will not do, is not yours to say. That matter is with *me*; and that we may see the matter more plainly, I, the man, have brought here a little of the Red Flower which ye, dogs, fear."

He flung the fire-pot on the ground, and some of the red coals lit a tuft of dried moss that flared up, as all the Council drew back in terror before the leaping flames.

Mowgli thrust his dead branch into the fire till the twigs lit and crackled, and whirled it above his head among the cowering wolves.

"Thou art the master," said Bagheera, in an undertone. "Save Akela from the death. He was ever thy friend."

Akela, the grim old wolf who had never asked for mercy in his life, gave one piteous look at Mowgli as the boy stood all naked, his long black hair tossing over his shoulders in the light of the blazing branch that made the shadows jump and quiver.

"Good!" said Mowgli, staring round slowly. "I see that ye are dogs. I go from you to my own people—if they be my own people. The Jungle is shut to me, and I must forget your talk and your companionship; but I will be more merciful than ye are. Because I was all but your brother in blood, I promise that when I am a man among men I will not betray ye to men as ye have betrayed me." He kicked the fire with his foot, and the sparks flew up. "There shall be no war between any of us and the Pack. But here is a debt to pay before I go." He strode forward to where Shere Khan sat blinking stupidly at the flames, and caught him by the tuft of his chin. Bagheera followed in case of accidents. "Up, dog!" Mowgli cried. "Up, when a man speaks, or I will set that coat ablaze!"

Shere Khan's ears lay flat back on his head, and he shut his eyes, for the blazing branch was very near.

"This cattle-killer said he would kill me in the Council because he had not killed me when I was a cub. Thus and thus, then, do we beat dogs when we are men. Stir a whisker, Lungri, and I ram the Red Flower down thy gullet!" He beat Shere Khan over the head with the branch, and the tiger whimpered and whined in an agony of fear.

"Pah! Singed Jungle-cat—go now! But remember when next I come to the Council Rock, as a man should come, it will be with Shere Khan's hide on my head. For the rest, Akela goes free to live as he pleases. Ye will *not* kill him, because that is not my will. Nor do I think that ye will sit here any longer, lolling out your tongues as though ye were somebodies, instead of dogs whom I drive out—thus! Go!" The fire was burning furiously at the end of the branch, and Mowgli struck right and left round the circle, and the wolves ran howling with the sparks burning their fur. At last there were only Akela, Bagheera, and perhaps ten wolves that had taken Mowgli's part. Then something began to hurt Mowgli inside him, as he had never been hurt in his life before, and he caught his breath and sobbed, and the tears ran down his face.

"What is it? What is it?" he said. "I do not wish to leave the Jungle, and I do not know what this is. Am I dying, Bagheera?"

"No, Little Brother. Those are only tears such as men use," said Bagheera. "Now I know thou art a man, and a man's cub no longer. The Jungle is shut indeed to thee henceforward. Let them fall, Mowgli. They are only tears." So Mowgli sat and cried as though his heart would break; and he had never cried in all his life before.

"Now," he said, "I will go to men. But first I must say farewell to my mother"; and he went to the cave where she lived with Father Wolf, and he cried on her coat, while the four cubs howled miserably.

"Ye will not forget me?" said Mowgli.

"Never while we can follow a trail," said the cubs. "Come to the foot of the hill when thou art a man, and we will talk to thee; and we will come into the croplands to play with thee by night."

"Come soon!" said Father Wolf. "Oh, wise little frog, come again soon; for we be old, thy mother and I."

"Come soon," said Mother Wolf, "little naked son of mine; for, listen, child of man, I loved thee more than ever I loved my cubs."

"I will surely come," said Mowgli, "and when I come it will be to lay out Shere Khan's hide upon the Council Rock. Do not forget me! Tell them in the jungle never to forget me!"

The dawn was beginning to break when Mowgli went down the hillside alone, to meet those mysterious things that are called men.

Hunting-Song of the Seeonee Pack

As the dawn was breaking the Sambhur belled—
Once, twice and again!
And a doe leaped up, and a doe leaped up
From the pond in the wood where the wild deer sup.
This I, scouting alone, beheld,
Once, twice and again!

As the dawn was breaking the Sambhur belled—
Once, twice and again!
And a wolf stole back, and a wolf stole back
To carry the word to the waiting pack,
And we sought and we found and we bayed on his track
Once, twice and again!

As the dawn was breaking the Wolf Pack yelled
Once, twice and again!
Feet in the jungle that leave no mark!
Eyes that can see in the dark—the dark!
Tongue—give tongue to it! Hark! O hark!
Once, twice and again!

Reader's Response
If you had been Mowgli at the last Council, would you have done anything differently? Explain.

Responding to the Selection

Your Response

1. How do you think Mowgli felt before and after the last Council meeting?
2. If you had been a member of the Council, would you have wanted Mowgli in the Pack? Why or why not?

Recalling

3. Why is Mowgli allowed to run with the Pack?
4. What are the issues at the last Council that Mowgli attends? Who wins? Why?

Interpreting

5. Why do many of the younger wolves turn against Akela? Why do many turn against Mowgli?
6. How is Mowgli different from the wolves? How do his differences help Mowgli?
7. Who are Mowgli's brothers? Explain.

Applying

8. Bagheera says, "Strike first and then give tongue [speak, or talk]." Are there any places or times in the world today in which this law applies? Explain.

Analyzing Literature

Appreciating Setting

Setting is the time and place in which a story occurs. In "Mowgli's Brothers," for example, Kipling mentions the time of day, the temperature, and the hills in the very first sentence.

1. Review the story to find three details that describe Council Rock.
2. Find three details that help you envision the hunting grounds.
3. Could this story have taken place in any other setting? If so, what details would have to change? Which would remain the same?

Critical Thinking and Reading

Appreciating Animal Characters

Kipling used many of the qualities of folk tales in his stories. In *The Jungle Book,* animals act like human beings. For example, in "Mowgli's Brothers" the animals talk.

1. In addition to being able to talk, what other human traits do the animals have?
2. Suppose you were creating a story like Kipling's. One character is cunning, another is brave, and the third is foolish. What animal would you use for each character? Explain your answer.

Thinking and Writing

Writing as a Character

Imagine that you are Shere Khan. Rewrite the scene in which Mowgli beats you. Before you write, work with a partner to discuss how the scene would be different when viewed through Shere Khan's eyes. When you have written a draft, read it aloud to yourself. Does it sound as if the tiger were speaking? How might it be improved? Make revisions and write your final draft. Share this with your classmates.

Learning Option

Speaking and Listening. Dialogue refers to the words in a story that the characters speak to each other. In a small group, write additional dialogue for a scene from "Mowgli's Brothers." After your group has decided what scene to write, brainstorm about the traits of the characters. Compare them to people you know so you can make each character sound authentic. Practice your dialogue within your group. Then perform the dialogue for the class.

GUIDE FOR READING

Louis Untermeyer

(1885–1977) was born in New York City. After designing jewelry in a family company for many years, he resigned in 1923 to become a full-time writer. Untermeyer wrote poetry and criticism for adults and several volumes of poems and stories for younger readers, including *The Fat of the Cat,* a retelling of favorite Swiss fairy tales, *The Donkey of God,* and *The Last Pirate.* He is probably best known as the editor of several major collections of English and American poems.

The Dog of Pompeii

Historical Setting

The time and place in which a story occurs make up its **setting.** A story may be set anywhere at any time in history. When a story centers on an important event in history, it usually contains details that reflect the historical time. "The Dog of Pompeii" is set in the ancient Roman city of Pompeii. Most of the action takes place in A.D. 79, just before and during destruction of the city by volcanic eruption and earthquake. Untermeyer considered one of the archaeological finds from Pompeii and imagined the story behind it.

Focus

"The Dog of Pompeii" is a story of friendship between a homeless boy and a dog. Have you or someone you know ever had a pet? What feelings did you or your friend have toward the pet? What feelings did the pet seem to have toward you or your friend? In a small group, discuss the answers to these questions. Then work together to create a cluster map about the qualities an ideal pet would have. As you read this story, decide whether the dog in this story would make an ideal pet.

Vocabulary

Knowing the following words will help you read "The Dog of Pompeii."

sham (sham) *adj.*: Make-believe; pretended (p. 111)
villa (vil′ ə) *n.*: A large estate (p. 112)
barometer (bə räm′ ət ər) *n.*: An instrument used to forecast changes in weather (p. 115)
proverb (präv′ ʉrb) *n.*: A short saying that expresses an obvious truth or familiar experience (p. 115)
pondering (pän′ dər iŋ) *n.*: Deep thought; careful consideration (p. 115)
vapors (vā′ pərz) *n.*: Fumes (p. 117)

Spelling Tip

You might remember that *vapors* is spelled with an *o,* not an *e,* by thinking of the sentence: *Vapors, fog,* and *smoke all have o's.*

The Dog of Pompeii[1]

Louis Untermeyer

"He was not only dog, but nurse, pillow, playmate, mother and father to Tito."

Tito and his dog Bimbo lived (if you could call it living) under the wall where it joined the inner gate. They really didn't live there; they just slept there. They lived anywhere. Pompeii was one of the gayest of the old Latin towns, but although Tito was never an unhappy boy, he was not exactly a merry one. The streets were always lively with shining chariots and bright red trappings;[2] the open-air theaters rocked with laughing crowds; sham battles and athletic sports were free for the asking in the great stadium. Once a year the Caesar[3] visited the pleasure city and the fireworks lasted for days; the sacrifices in the Forum were better than a show. But Tito saw none of these things. He was blind—had been blind from birth. He was known to everyone in the poorer quarters. But no one could say how old he was, no one remembered his parents, no one could tell where he came from. Bimbo was another mystery. As long as people could

1. Pompeii (päm pā′) *n.*: An ancient city on the southern coast of Italy.

2. trappings (trap′ iŋz) *n.*: Ornamental coverings.

3. Caesar (sē′ zər): The Roman emperor Titus. From the time of Julius Caesar until Hadrian (49 B.C.–138 A.D.), all Roman emperors were called *Caesar*.

remember seeing Tito—about twelve or thirteen years—they had seen Bimbo. Bimbo had never left his side. He was not only dog, but nurse, pillow, playmate, mother and father to Tito.

Did I say Bimbo never left his master? (Perhaps I had better say comrade, for if any one was the master, it was Bimbo.) I was wrong. Bimbo did trust Tito alone exactly three times a day. It was a fixed routine, a custom understood between boy and dog since the beginning of their friendship, and the way it worked was this: Early in the morning, shortly after dawn, while Tito was still dreaming, Bimbo would disappear. When Tito woke, Bimbo would be sitting quietly at his side, his ears cocked, his stump of a tail tapping the ground, and a fresh-baked bread—more like a large round roll—at his feet. Tito would stretch himself; Bimbo would yawn; then they would breakfast. At noon, no matter where they happened to be, Bimbo would put his paw on Tito's knee and the two of them would return to the inner gate. Tito would curl up in the corner (almost like a dog) and go to sleep, while Bimbo, looking quite important (almost like a boy) would disappear again. In half an hour he'd be back with their lunch. Sometimes it would be a piece of fruit or a scrap of meat, often it was nothing but a dry crust. But sometimes there would be one of those flat rich cakes, sprinkled with raisins and sugar, that Tito liked so much. At supper time the same thing happened, although there was a little less of everything, for things were hard to snatch in the evening with the streets full of people. Besides, Bimbo didn't approve of too much food before going to sleep. A heavy supper made boys too restless and dogs too stodgy—and it was the business of a dog to sleep lightly with one ear open and muscles ready for action.

But, whether there was much or little, hot or cold, fresh or dry, food was always there. Tito never asked where it came from and Bimbo never told him. There was plenty of rainwater in the hollows of soft stones; the old egg-woman at the corner sometimes gave him a cupful of strong goat's milk; in the grape season the fat winemaker let him have drippings of the mild juice. So there was no danger of going hungry or thirsty. There was plenty of everything in Pompeii, if you knew where to find it—and if you had a dog like Bimbo.

As I said before, Tito was not the merriest boy in Pompeii. He could not romp with the other youngsters and play Hare-and-Hounds and I-spy and Follow-your-Master and Ball-against-the-Building and Jackstones and Kings-and-Robbers with them. But that did not make him sorry for himself. If he could not see the sights that delighted the lads of Pompeii he could hear and smell things they never noticed. He could really see more with his ears and nose than they could with their eyes. When he and Bimbo went out walking he knew just where they were going and exactly what was happening.

"Ah," he'd sniff and say, as they passed a handsome villa, "Glaucus Pansa is giving a grand dinner tonight. They're going to have three kinds of bread, and roast pigling, and stuffed goose, and a great stew—I think bear stew—and a fig pie." And Bimbo would note that this would be a good place to visit tomorrow.

Or, "H'm," Tito would murmur, half through his lips, half through his nostrils. "The wife of Marcus Lucretius is expecting her mother. She's shaking out every piece of goods in the house; she's going to use the best clothes—the ones she's been keeping in pine-needles and camphor[4]—and there's an extra girl in the kitchen. Come, Bimbo, let's get out of the dust!"

Or, as they passed a small but elegant dwelling opposite the public baths, "Too bad! The tragic poet is ill again. It must be a bad fever this time, for they're trying smoke fumes instead of medicine. Whew! I'm glad I'm not a tragic poet!"

Or, as they neared the Forum, "Mm-m! What good things they have in the Macellum today!" (It really was a sort of butcher-grocer-market-place, but Tito didn't know any better. He called it the Macellum.) "Dates from Africa, and salt oysters from sea caves, and cuttlefish, and new honey, and sweet onions, and—ugh!—water-buffalo steaks. Come, let's see what's what in the Forum." And Bimbo, just as curious as his comrade, hurried on. Being a dog, he trusted his ears and nose (like Tito) more than his eyes. And so the two of them entered the center of Pompeii.

The Forum was the part of the town to which everybody came at least once during each day. It was the Central Square and everything happened here. There were no private houses; all was public—the chief temples, the gold and red bazaars,[5] the silk shops, the town hall, the booths belonging to the weavers and jewel merchants, the wealthy woolen market, the Shrine of the Household Gods.[6] Everything glittered here. The buildings looked as if they were new—

4. camphor (kam′ fər) *n.*: A hard, clear substance with a strong smell. Used as a moth repellent.

5. bazaars (bə zärz′) *n.*: Streets where people sell things.

6. Household Gods: Gods that protected the hearth, the crops, the livestock, and so on.

View of houses along a street

which, in a sense, they were. The earthquake of twelve years ago had brought down all the old structures and, since the citizens of Pompeii were ambitious to rival Naples and even Rome, they had seized the opportunity to rebuild the whole town. And they had done it all within a dozen years. There was scarcely a building that was older than Tito.

Tito had heard a great deal about the earthquake though, being about a year old at the time, he could scarcely remember it. This particular quake had been a light one—as earthquakes go. The weaker houses had been shaken down, parts of the outworn wall had been wrecked; but there was little loss of life, and the brilliant new Pompeii had taken the place of the old. No one knew what caused these earthquakes. Records showed they had happened in the neighborhood since the beginning of time. Sailors said that it was to teach the lazy city folk a lesson and make them appreciate those who risked the dangers of the sea to bring them luxuries and protect their town from invaders. The priests said that the gods took this way of showing their anger to those who refused to worship properly and who failed to bring enough sacrifices to the altars and (though they didn't say it in so many words) presents to the priests. The tradesmen said that the foreign merchants had corrupted the ground and it was no longer safe to traffic in imported goods that came from strange places and carried a curse with them. Everyone had a different explanation—and everyone's explanation was louder and sillier than his neighbor's.

They were talking about it this afternoon as Tito and Bimbo came out of the side street into the public square. The Forum was the favorite promenade for rich and poor. What with the priests arguing with the politicians, servants doing the day's shopping, tradesmen crying their wares, women displaying the latest fashions from Greece and Egypt, children playing hide-and-seek among the marble columns, knots of soldiers, sailors, peasants from the provinces—to say nothing of those who merely came to lounge and look on—the square was crowded to its last inch. His ears even more than his nose guided Tito to the place where the talk was loudest. It was in front of the Shrine of the Household Gods that, naturally enough, the householders were arguing.

"I tell you," rumbled a voice which Tito recognized as bathmaster Rufus's, "there won't be another earthquake in my lifetime or yours. There may be a tremble or two, but earthquakes, like lightnings, never strike twice in the same place."

"Do they not?" asked a thin voice Tito had never heard. It had a high, sharp ring to it and Tito knew it as the accent of a stranger. "How about the two towns of Sicily[7] that have been ruined three times within fifteen years by the eruptions of Mount Etna?[8] And were they not warned? And does that column of smoke above Vesuvius[9] mean nothing?"

"That?" Tito could hear the grunt with which one question answered another. "That's always there. We use it for our weather guide. When the smoke stands up straight we know we'll have fair weather; when it flattens out it's sure to be foggy; when it drifts to the east—"

---

7. Sicily (sis′əl ē): An island off the southern coast of Italy in the Mediterranean Sea.

8. Mount Etna (et′ nə): A volcano in eastern Sicily.

9. Vesuvius (və so͞o′ vē əs): A volcano in southern Italy.

"Yes, yes," cut in the edged voice. "I've heard about your mountain barometer. But the column of smoke seems hundreds of feet higher than usual and it's thickening and spreading like a shadowy tree. They say in Naples—"

"Oh, Naples!" Tito knew this voice by the little squeak that went with it. It was Attilio, the cameo-cutter.[10] "*They* talk while we suffer. Little help we got from them last time. Naples commits the crimes and Pompeii pays the price. It's become a proverb with us. Let them mind their own business."

"Yes," grumbled Rufus, "and others, too."

"Very well, my confident friends," responded the thin voice which now sounded curiously flat. "We also have a proverb—and it is this: Those who will listen to men must be taught by the gods. I say no more. But I leave a last warning. Remember the holy ones. Look to your temples. And when the smoke tree above Vesuvius grows to the shape of an umbrella pine, look to your lives."

Tito could hear the air whistle as the speaker drew his toga[11] about him and the quick shuffle of feet told him the stranger had gone.

"Now what," said the cameo-cutter, "did he mean by that?"

"I wonder," grunted Rufus, "I wonder."

Tito wondered, too. And Bimbo, his head at a thoughtful angle, looked as if he had been doing a heavy piece of pondering. By nightfall the argument had been forgotten. If the smoke had increased no one saw it in the dark. Besides, it was Caesar's birthday and the town was in holiday mood. Tito and Bimbo were among the merry-makers, dodging the charioteers who shouted at them. A dozen times they almost upset baskets of sweets and jars of Vesuvian wine, said to be as fiery as the streams inside the volcano, and a dozen times they were cursed and cuffed. But Tito never missed his footing. He was thankful for his keen ears and quick instinct—most thankful of all for Bimbo.

They visited the uncovered theater and, though Tito could not see the faces of the actors, he could follow the play better than most of the audience, for their attention wandered—they were distracted by the scenery, the costumes, the byplay, even by themselves—while Tito's whole attention was centered in what he heard. Then to the city walls, where the people of Pompeii watched a mock naval battle in which the city was attacked by the sea and saved after thousands of flaming arrows had been exchanged and countless colored torches had been burned. Though the thrill of flaring ships and lighted skies was lost to Tito, the shouts and cheers excited him as much as any and he cried out with the loudest of them.

The next morning there were *two* of the beloved raisin and sugar cakes for his breakfast. Bimbo was unusually active and thumped his bit of a tail until Tito was afraid he would wear it out. The boy could not imagine whether Bimbo was urging him to some sort of game or was trying to tell something. After a while, he ceased to notice Bimbo. He felt drowsy. Last night's late hours had tired him. Besides, there was a heavy mist in the air—no, a thick fog rather than a mist—a fog that got into his throat and scraped it and made him cough. He

10. cameo-cutter (kam' ē ō) *n.*: A person who makes cameos, carvings on gems or shells that form raised designs, usually of heads in profile.

11. toga (tō' gə) *n.*: A one-piece outer garment worn by people of ancient Rome.

Pompeii bakery

walked as far as the marine gate to get a breath of the sea. But the blanket of haze had spread all over the bay and even the salt air seemed smoky.

He went to bed before dusk and slept. But he did not sleep well. He had too many dreams—dreams of ships lurching in the Forum, of losing his way in a screaming crowd, of armies marching across his chest, of being pulled over every rough pavement of Pompeii.

He woke early. Or, rather, he was pulled awake. Bimbo was doing the pulling. The dog had dragged Tito to his feet and was urging the boy along. Somewhere. Where, Tito did not know. His feet stumbled uncertainly; he was still half asleep. For a while he noticed nothing except the fact that it was hard to breathe. The air was hot. And heavy. So heavy that he could taste it. The air, it seemed, had turned to powder, a warm powder that stung his nostrils and burned his sightless eyes.

Then he began to hear sounds. Peculiar sounds. Like animals under the earth. Hissings and groanings and muffled cries that a dying creature might make dislodging the stones of his underground cave. There was no doubt of it now. The noises came from underneath. He not only heard them—he could feel them. The earth twitched; the twitching changed to an uneven shrugging of the soil. Then, as Bimbo half pulled, half coaxed him across, the ground jerked away from his feet and he was thrown against a stone fountain.

The water—hot water—splashing in his face revived him. He got to his feet, Bimbo steadying him, helping him on again. The noises grew louder; they came closer. The cries were even more animal-like than before, but now they came from human throats. A few people, quicker of foot and more hurried by fear, began to rush by. A family or two—then a section—then, it seemed, an army broken out of bounds. Tito, bewildered though he was, could recognize Rufus as he bellowed past him, like a water buffalo gone mad. Time was lost in a nightmare.

It was then the crashing began. First a sharp crackling, like a monstrous snapping of twigs; then a roar like the fall of a whole forest of trees; then an explosion that tore earth and sky. The heavens, though Tito could not see them, were shot through with continual flickerings of fire. Lightnings above were answered by thunders beneath. A house fell. Then another. By a miracle the two companions had escaped the dangerous side streets and were in a more open space.

It was the Forum. They rested here awhile—how long he did not know.

Tito had no idea of the time of day. He could *feel* it was black—an unnatural blackness. Something inside—perhaps the lack of breakfast and lunch—told him it was past noon. But it didn't matter. Nothing seemed to matter. He was getting drowsy, too drowsy to walk. But walk he must. He knew it. And Bimbo knew it; the sharp tugs told him so. Nor was it a moment too soon. The sacred ground of the Forum was safe no longer. It was beginning to rock, then to pitch, then to split. As they stumbled out of the square, the earth wriggled like a caught snake and all the columns of the temple of Jupiter[12] came down. It was the end of the world—or so it seemed.

To walk was not enough now. They must run. Tito was too frightened to know what to do or where to go. He had lost all sense of direction. He started to go back to the inner gate; but Bimbo, straining his back to the last inch, almost pulled his clothes from him. What did the creature want? Had the dog gone mad?

Then, suddenly, he understood. Bimbo was telling him the way out—urging him there. The sea gate of course. The sea gate—and then the sea. Far from falling buildings, heaving ground. He turned, Bimbo guiding him across open pits and dangerous pools of bubbling mud, away from buildings that had caught fire and were dropping their burning beams. Tito could no longer tell whether the noises were made by the shrieking sky or the agonized people. He and Bimbo ran on—the only silent beings in a howling world.

New dangers threatened. All Pompeii seemed to be thronging toward the marine gate and, squeezing among the crowds, there was the chance of being trampled to death. But the chance had to be taken. It was growing harder and harder to breathe. What air there was choked him. It was all dust now—dust and pebbles, pebbles as large as beans. They fell on his head, his hands—pumice[13] stones from the black heart of Vesuvius. The mountain was turning itself inside out. Tito remembered a phrase that the stranger had said in the Forum two days ago: "Those who will not listen to men must be taught by the gods." The people of Pompeii had refused to heed the warnings; they were being taught now—if it was not too late.

Suddenly it seemed too late for Tito. The red hot ashes blistered his skin, the stinging vapors tore his throat. He could not go on. He staggered toward a small tree at the side of the road and fell. In a moment Bimbo was beside him. He coaxed. But there was no answer. He licked Tito's hands, his feet, his face. The boy did not stir. Then Bimbo did the last thing he could—the last thing he wanted to do. He bit his comrade, bit him deep in the arm. With a cry of pain, Tito jumped to his feet, Bimbo after him. Tito was in despair, but Bimbo was determined. He drove the boy on, snapping at his heels, worrying his way through the crowd; barking, baring his teeth, heedless of kicks or falling stones. Sick with hunger, half dead with fear and sulfur[14] fumes, Tito pounded on, pursued by Bimbo. How long he never knew. At last he staggered through the marine gate and felt soft sand under him. Then Tito fainted. . . .

---

12. Jupiter (jo͞o′ pit ər): The chief Roman god, known as Zeus in Greece.

13. pumice (pum′ is) *n.*: A spongy, light rock formed from the lava of a volcano.

14. sulfur (sul′ fər) **fumes:** Choking fumes caused by the volcanic eruption.

Someone was dashing sea water over him. Someone was carrying him toward a boat.

"Bimbo," he called. And then louder, "Bimbo!" But Bimbo had disappeared.

Voices jarred against each other. "Hurry—hurry!" "To the boats!" "Can't you see the child's frightened and starving!" "He keeps calling for someone!" "Poor boy, he's out of his mind." "Here, child—take this!"

They tucked him in among them. The oarlocks creaked; the oars splashed; the boat rode over toppling waves. Tito was safe. But he wept continually.

"Bimbo!" he wailed. "Bimbo! Bimbo!"

He could not be comforted.

MOSAIC OF DOG, NAPLES
National Museum, Pompeii, Italy

Eighteen hundred years passed. Scientists were restoring the ancient city; excavators were working their way through the stones and trash that had buried the entire town. Much had already been brought to light—statues, bronze instruments, bright mosaics,[15] household articles; even delicate paintings had been preserved by the fall of ashes that had taken over two thousand lives. Columns were dug up and the Forum was beginning to emerge.

It was at a place where the ruins lay deepest that the Director paused.

"Come here," he called to his assistant. "I think we've discovered the remains of a building in good shape. Here are four huge millstones that were most likely turned by slaves or mules—and here is a whole wall standing with shelves inside it. Why! It must have been a bakery. And here's a curious thing. What do you think I found under this heap where the ashes were thickest? The skeleton of a dog!"

"Amazing!" gasped his assistant. "You'd think a dog would have had sense enough to run away at the time. And what is that flat thing he's holding between his teeth? It can't be a stone."

"No. It must have come from this bakery. You know it looks to me like some sort of cake hardened with the years. And, bless me, if those little black pebbles aren't raisins. A raisin cake almost two thousand years old! I wonder what made him want it at such a moment?"

"I wonder," murmured the assistant.

15. mosaics (mō zā′ iks) *n.*: Pictures or designs made by inlaying small bits of colored stone in mortar.

Reader's Response
How did you feel when you read the last part of the story?

Responding to the Selection

Your Response

1. Do you think pets like Bimbo only exist in stories? Do you know of a pet like Bimbo?
2. How did you feel when you realized what the fate of the city would be? Explain.

Recalling

3. Describe what Tito and Bimbo do on a typical day in the city.
4. What rumors and warnings does Tito hear as he roams about Pompeii?
5. How does Bimbo get Tito out of the city?

Interpreting

6. How did Tito see "with his ears and nose"?
7. Explain how their last day in the city is different from all the other days Tito and Bimbo have spent there.
8. Why does Bimbo return to the city after getting Tito safely to the marine gate?

Applying

9. What situations do you know of in which animals have saved the lives of humans?

Analyzing Literature

Appreciating Historical Setting

"The Dog of Pompeii" has a **historical setting.** The story contains details describing an actual time and place in history.

1. Find six details in the story that help you envision the time and place.
2. Why are most buildings in the Forum only about twelve years old?
3. Describe what happens to the city Tito knows so well on the last day he spends there.
4. Near the end of the story, how does the setting change?
5. History is not only a record of facts and events but the story of how human beings lived. Even though "The Dog of Pompeii" is fiction, how does it help you understand this meaning of history?

Critical Thinking and Reading

Recognizing Superstition

A **superstition** is a belief held in spite of evidence that disproves it. Many superstitions grew out of human inability to explain events in nature, such as the earthquake that had occurred in Pompeii twelve years before the events in "The Dog of Pompeii."

1. How do the various citizens explain the earthquake of twelve years before?
2. What do all these beliefs have in common?
3. Describe one superstition you know of and tell how it might have been started.

Thinking and Writing

Writing About an Object in Time

Imagine that an object from your classroom or your home is discovered among some ruins by archaeologists 2,000 years in the future. What might they think it is? What was it used for? How did it get where it is? Write an account in which you describe the finding of the object and the archaeologists' conclusions about it. When you have written a draft, exchange papers with a partner and discuss how to improve the details of setting. Revise your account and write your final draft. Illustrate it with a drawing or a picture of the object.

Learning Options

1. **Cross-curricular Connection.** Use an encyclopedia and other books to find out about one of the following topics: (1) ancient artifacts that have been found at Pompeii, (2) how and why volcanoes erupt, (3) facts about Mt. Vesuvius. Present your findings to the class in an oral report.
2. **Art.** Archaeologists often sketch pictures or diagrams of what they find. Make a sketch of what the archaeologists find at the end of the story, based on their description. Write a caption to explain your illustration.

GUIDE FOR READING

Virginia Driving Hawk Sneve

(1933–), writer and teacher, devotes herself to telling about Native American life as she herself has experienced it. She also works "to interpret history from the viewpoint of the American Indian," who she feels has been misrepresented by historians who are not themselves Native Americans. In 1971 the Interracial Council for Minority Books for Children honored Sneve for her novel, *Jimmy Yellow Hawk.* "Thunder Butte" reflects conflicts that many Native Americans experience today.

Thunder Butte

Atmosphere

Atmosphere, or mood, is the feeling a particular setting conveys to the reader. For example, you might describe atmosphere as gloomy, or peaceful, or mysterious. Writers create and build up atmosphere through descriptive details. In "Thunder Butte," phrases such as "the ledge of the butte loomed over him" and "capped with dark, low-hanging clouds," help build the mood of the story.

Focus

In "Thunder Butte," Norman learns about the traditions of his people from his grandfather. He then must decide what place these traditions have in his life. In a small group, make a list of cultural traditions you have learned from family members or friends. Describe how each tradition is practiced and what role each plays in your life. As you read the story, decide whether Norman's attitude toward tradition changes throughout the story.

Vocabulary

Knowing the following words will help you read "Thunder Butte."

butte (byo͞ot) *n.*: A steep hill standing alone in a plain (p. 121)
meanderings (mē an′ dər iŋz) *n.*: Aimless wanderings (p. 121)
agates (ag′ its) *n.*: Hard, semiprecious stones with striped or clouded coloring (p. 121)
diminutive (də min′ yo͞o tiv) *adj.*: Very small (p. 123)
variegated (ver′ ē ə gāt′ id) *adj.*: Marked with different colors in spots, streaks, and so forth (p. 124)
heathen (hē′*th*ən) *adj.*: Uncivilized (p. 127)
adamant (ad′ ə mənt) *adj.*: Not giving in (p. 128)
relic (rel′ ik) *n.*: An object, custom, and so on that has survived from the past (p. 129)

Spelling Tip

There are five syllables in *variegated.* Pronouncing all the syllables carefully will help you spell the word correctly.

Thunder Butte

from *When Thunders Spoke*

Virginia Driving Hawk Sneve

"He remembered that this was a sacred place to the old ones and his uneasiness increased."

The sun was just beginning to rise when John woke Norman the next morning.

"You must get an early start if you are going to go to the west side of the butte and return by supper," John said to the sleepy boy. "If you are not home by the time I get back from work, I'll come looking for you."

Norman reluctantly rose. Last night he had accepted his grandfather's command to go to the Thunder Butte without too many doubts. Yet now in the morning's chill light the boy wondered if his grandfather's dreams were the meaningless meanderings of an old mind, or if his grandfather was really worthy of the tribe's respect as one of the few remaining wise elders who understood the ancient ways.

Norman dressed in his oldest clothes and pulled on worn and scuffed boots to protect his feet from the rocks and snakes of the butte. He heard his parents talking in the other room and knew his father was telling his mother where Norman was going.

As the boy entered the room, which was kitchen and living room as well as his parents' bedroom, he heard his mother say, "What if there is a rock slide and Norman is hurt or buried on the butte? We won't know anything until you get home from work, John. I don't want Norman to go."

"The boy is old enough to have learned to be careful on the butte. He'll be all right," John answered as he tried to reassure Sarah. "Besides," he added, "my father dreamed of this happening."

Sarah grunted scornfully, "No one believes in dreams or in any of those old superstitious ways anymore."

"I'll be okay, Mom," Norman said as he sat down at the table. "I should be able to find lots of agates on the west side where there is all that loose rock. Maybe I can talk the trader into giving me money for them after all." He spoke bravely despite his own inner misgivings about going to the butte.

Sarah protested no more. Norman looked at her, but she lowered her head as she set a plate of pancakes in front of him. He knew she was hiding the worry she felt for him.

John put on his hat and went to the

door. "Don't forget to take the willow branch with you," he said to Norman, "and be careful."

Norman nodded and ate his breakfast. When he was finished he stood up. "Guess I'll go," he said to his mother, who was pouring hot water from the tea kettle into her dish pan. When she didn't speak Norman took the willow cane from where he had propped it by the door and his hat from the nail above it.

"Wait," Sarah called and handed him a paper bag. "Here is a lunch for you. You'll need something to eat since you'll be gone all day." She gave him an affectionate shove. "Oh, go on. I know you'll be all right. Like your dad said, you're old enough to be careful."

Norman smiled at his mother. "Thanks," he said as he tucked the lunch into his shirt. He checked his back pocket to see if he'd remembered the salt bag to put the agates in.

He walked briskly across the open prairie and turned to wave at his mother, who had come outside to watch him leave. She waved back and Norman quickened his pace. He whistled, trying to echo the meadowlarks who were greeting the day with their happy song. He swiped the willow cane at the bushy sage and practiced spearing the pear cactus that dotted his path. The early morning air was cool, but the sun soon warmed the back of his neck and he knew it would be a hot day.

He crossed the creek south of where Matt Two Bull's tent was pitched and then he was climbing the gentle beginning slope of the butte. He stopped and studied the way before him and wondered if it wouldn't be easier to reach the west side by walking around the base of the butte even though it would be longer. Then Norman smiled as he remembered his grandfather's command to climb the south trail that wound to the top. He decided to do what the old man wanted.

The ascent sharply steepened and the sun rose with him as Norman climbed. What looked like a smooth path from the prairie floor was rough rocky terrain. The trail spiraled up a sharp incline and Norman had to detour around fallen rocks. He paused to rest about half way up and then saw how sharply the overhanging ledge of the butte protruded. Getting to the top of it was going to be a difficult struggle. He climbed on. His foot slipped and his ankle twisted painfully. Small pebbles bounced down the slope and he saw a rattlesnake slither out of the way. He tightly clutched the willow branch and leaned panting against the butte. He sighed with relief as the snake crawled out of sight. He wiggled his foot until the pain left his ankle. Then he started to trudge up the incline again.

At last only the ledge of the butte loomed over him. There appeared to be no way up. Disgusted that his laborious climb seemed dead-ended he stubbornly tried to reach the top. Remembering the courage of the ancient young men who had struggled in this same place to gain the summit and seek their visions, he was determined not to go back. His fingers found tiny cracks to hold on to. The cane was cumbersome and in the way. He was tempted to drop it, but he thought of the snake he'd seen and struggled on with it awkwardly under his arm.

Finally Norman spied a narrow opening in the ledge which tapered down to only a few feet from where he clung. He inched his way up until he reached the base of the opening and then he found a use for the

cane. He jammed the stout branch high into the boulders above him. Cautiously he pulled to see if it would hold his weight. It held. Using the cane as a lever he pulled himself to the top.

This final exertion winded the boy and he lay exhausted on the summit, boots hanging over the edge. Cautiously he pulled his feet under him, stood and looked around.

He gazed at a new world. The sun bathed the eastern valley in pale yellow which was spotted with dark clumps of sage. The creek was a green and silver serpent winding its way to the southeast. His grandfather's tent was a white shoe box in its clearing, and beside it stood a diminutive form waving a red flag. It was Matt Two Bull signaling with his shirt, and Norman knew that his grandfather had been watching him climb. He waved his hat in reply and then walked to the outer edge of the butte.

The summit was not as smoothly flat as it looked from below. Norman stepped warily over the many cracks and holes that pitted the surface. He was elated that he had successfully made the difficult ascent, but now as he surveyed the butte top he had a sense of discomfort.

There were burn scars on the rough summit, and Norman wondered if these spots were where the lightning had struck, or were they evidence of ancient man-made fires? He remembered that this was a sacred place to the old ones and his uneasiness increased. He longed to be back on the secure level of the plains.

On the west edge he saw that the butte cast a sharp shadow below because the rim protruded as sharply as it had on the slope he'd climbed. Two flat rocks jutted up on either side of a narrow opening, and Norman saw shallow steps hewn into the space between. This must be the trail of which his grandfather had spoken.

Norman stepped down and then quickly turned to hug the butte face as the steps ended abruptly in space. The rest of the rocky staircase lay broken and crumbled below. The only way down was to jump.

He cautiously let go of the willow branch and watched how it landed and bounced against the rocks. He took a deep breath as if to draw courage from the air. He lowered himself so that he was hanging by his fingertips to the last rough step, closed his eyes and dropped.

The impact of his landing stung the soles of his feet. He stumbled and felt the cut of the sharp rocks against one knee as he struggled to retain his balance. He did not fall and finally stood upright breathing deeply until the wild pounding of his heart slowed. "Wow," he said softly as he looked back up at the ledge, "that must have been at least a twenty foot drop."

He picked up the willow branch and started walking slowly down the steep slope. The trail Matt Two Bull had told him about had been obliterated by years of falling rock. Loose shale and gravel shifted under Norman's feet, and he probed cautiously ahead with the cane to test the firmness of each step.

He soon found stones which he thought were agates. He identified them by spitting on each rock and rubbing the wet spot with his finger. The dull rock seemed to come alive! Variegated hues of brown and gray glowed as if polished. They were agates all right. Quickly he had his salt bag half full.

It was almost noon and his stomach growled. He stopped to rest against a large boulder and pulled out his lunch from his shirt. But his mouth was too dry to chew the cheese sandwich. He couldn't swallow without water.

Thirsty and hungry, Norman decided to go straight down the butte and head for home.

Walking more confidently as the slope leveled out he thrust the pointed cane carelessly into the ground. He suddenly fell as the cane went deep into the soft shale.

Norman slid several feet. Loose rocks rolled around him as he came to rest against a boulder. He lay still for a long time fearing that his tumble might cause a rock fall. But no thundering slide came, so he cautiously climbed back to where the tip of the willow branch protruded from the ground.

He was afraid that the cane may have plunged into a rattlesnake den. Carefully he pulled at the stout branch, wiggling it this way and that with one hand while he dug with the other. It came loose, sending a shower of rocks down the hill, and Norman saw that something else was sticking up in the hole he had uncovered.

Curious, and seeing no sign of snakes, he kept digging and soon found the tip of a leather-covered stick. Bits of leather and wood fell off in his hand as he gently pulled. The stick, almost as long as he was tall and curved on one end, emerged as he tugged. Holding it before him, his heart pounding with excitement, he realized that he had found a thing that once belonged to the old ones.

Norman shivered at the thought that he may have disturbed a grave, which was *teȟinda*,[1] forbidden. He cleared more dirt away but saw no bones nor other sign that this was a burial place. Quickly he picked up the stick and his willow cane and hurried down the hill. When he reached the bottom he discovered that in his fall the salt bag of agates had pulled loose from his belt. But he did not return to search for it. It would take most of the afternoon to travel around the base of the butte to the east side.

The creek was in the deep shade of the butte when he reached it and thirstily flopped down and drank. He crossed the shallow stream and walked to his grandfather's tent.

"You have been gone a long time," Matt Two Bull greeted as Norman walked into the clearing where the old man was seated.

"I have come from the west side of the butte, Grandpa," Norman said wearily. He sat down on the ground and examined a tear in his jeans and the bruise on his knee.

"Was it difficult?" the old man asked.

"Yes," Norman nodded. He told of the rough climb up the south slope, the jump down and finally of his fall which led him to discover the long leather-covered stick. He held the stick out to his grandfather who took it and examined it carefully.

"Are you sure there was no body in the place where you found this?"

Norman shook his head. "No, I found nothing else but the stick. Do you know what it is, Grandpa?"

"You have found a *coup*[2] stick which belonged to the old ones."

"I know that it is old because the wood is brittle and the leather is peeling, but what is—was a *coup* stick?" Norman asked.

"In the days when the old ones roamed all of the plains," the old man swept his hand in a circle, "a courageous act of valor was thought to be more important than killing an enemy. When a warrior rode or ran up to his enemy, close enough to touch the man with a stick, without killing or being killed, the action was called *coup*.

"The French, the first white men in this part of the land, named this brave deed *coup*. In their language the word meant 'hit' or 'strike.' The special stick which was used to strike with came to be known as a *coup* stick.

"Some sticks were long like this one," Matt Two Bull held the stick upright. "Some were straight, and others had a curve on the end like the sheep herder's crook," he pointed to the curving end of the stick.

"The sticks were decorated with fur or

---

1. ***teȟinda*** (tā kȟin′ dä)

2. ***coup*** (ko͞o)

painted leather strips. A warrior kept count of his *coups* by tying an eagle feather to the crook for each brave deed. See," he pointed to the staff end, "here is a remnant of a tie thong which must have once held a feather."

The old man and boy closely examined the *coup* stick. Matt Two Bull traced with his finger the faint zig zag design painted on the stick. "See," he said, "it is the thunderbolt."

"What does that mean?" Norman asked.

"The Thunders favored a certain few of the young men who sought their vision on the butte. The thunderbolt may have been part of a sacred dream sent as a token of the Thunders' favor. If this was so, the young man could use the thunderbolt symbol on his possessions."

"How do you suppose the stick came to be on the butte?" Norman asked.

His grandfather shook his head. "No one can say. Usually such a thing was buried with a dead warrior as were his weapons and other prized belongings."

"Is the *coup* stick what you dreamed about, Grandpa?"

"No. In my dream I only knew that you were to find a *Wakan*,[3] a holy thing. But I did not know what it would be."

Norman laughed nervously. "What do you mean, *Wakan*? Is this stick haunted?"

Matt Two Bull smiled, "No, not like you mean in a fearful way. But in a sacred man-

3. ***Wakan*** (wä′ kän)

ner because it once had great meaning to the old ones."

"But why should I have been the one to find it?" Norman questioned.

His grandfather shrugged, "Perhaps to help you understand the ways—the values of the old ones."

"But nobody believes in that kind of thing anymore," Norman scoffed. "And even if people did, I couldn't run out and hit my enemy with the stick and get away with it." He smiled thinking of Mr. Brannon. "No one would think I was brave. I'd probably just get thrown in jail."

Suddenly Norman felt compelled to stop talking. In the distance he heard a gentle rumble which seemed to come from the butte. He glanced up at the hill looming high above and saw that it was capped with dark, low-hanging clouds.

Matt Two Bull looked too and smiled. "The Thunders are displeased with your thoughts," he said to Norman. "Listen to their message."

A sharp streak of lightning split the clouds and the thunder cracked and echoed over the plains.

Norman was frightened but he answered with bravado, "The message I get is that a storm is coming," but his voice betrayed him by quavering. "Maybe you'd better come home with me, Grandpa. Your tent will get soaked through if it rains hard."

"No," murmured Matt Two Bull, "no rain will come. It is just the Thunders speaking." There was another spark of lightning, and an explosive reverberation sounded as if in agreement with the old man.

Norman jumped to his feet. "Well, I'm going home. Mom will be worried because I'm late now." He turned to leave.

"Wait!" Matt Two Bull commanded. "Take the *coup* stick with you."

Norman backed away, "No, I don't want it. You can have it."

The old man rose swiftly despite the stiffness of his years and sternly held out the stick to the boy. "You found it. It belongs to you. Take it!"

Norman slowly reached out his hands and took the stick.

"Even if you think the old ways are only superstition and the stick no longer has meaning, it is all that remains of an old life and must be treated with respect." Matt Two Bull smiled at the boy. "Take it," he repeated gently, "and hang it in the house where it will not be handled."

Norman hurried home as fast as he could carrying the long stick in one hand and the willow cane in the other. He felt vaguely uneasy and somehow a little frightened. It was only when he reached the security of his home that he realized the thunder had stopped and there had been no storm.

"Mom," he called as he went into the house, "I'm home."

His mother was standing at the stove. "Oh, Norman," she greeted him smiling. "I'm glad you're back. I was beginning to worry." Her welcoming smile turned to a frown as she saw the *coup* stick in Norman's hand. "What is that?"

"Grandpa says it's a *coup* stick. Here," Norman handed it to her, "take a look at it. It's interesting the way it is made and decor—"

"No," Sarah interrupted and backed away from him. "I won't touch that heathen thing no matter what it is! Get it out of the house!"

"What?" Norman asked, surprised and

puzzled. "There is nothing wrong with it. It's just an old stick I found up on the butte."

"I don't care," Sarah insisted. "I won't have such a thing in the house!"

"But, Mom," Norman protested, "it's not like we believe in those old ways the way Grandpa does."

But Sarah was adamant. "Take it out of the house!" she ordered, pointing to the door. "We'll talk about it when your dad gets home."

Reluctantly Norman took the *coup* stick outside and gently propped it against the house and sat on the steps to wait for his father. He was confused. First by his grandfather's reverent treatment of the *coup* stick as if it were a sacred object and then by Sarah's rejection of it as a heathen symbol.

He looked at the stick where it leaned against the wall and shook his head. So much fuss over a brittle, rotten length of wood. Even though he had gone through a lot of hard, even dangerous, effort to get it he was now tempted to heave it out on the trash pile.

Norman wearily leaned his head against the house. He suddenly felt tired and his knee ached. As he sat wearily rubbing the bruise John Two Bull rode the old mare into the yard. Norman got up and walked back to the shed to help unsaddle the horse.

John climbed stiffly out of the saddle. His faded blue work shirt and jeans were stained with perspiration and dirt. His boots were worn and scuffed.

"Hard day, Dad?" Norman asked.

"Yeah," John answered, slipping the bridle over the mare's head. "Rustlers got away with twenty steers last night. I spent the day counting head and mending fences. Whoever the thief was cut the fence, drove a truck right onto the range and loaded the cattle without being seen." He began rubbing the mare down as she munched the hay in her manger.

"How did your day on the butte go?" John asked.

"Rough," Norman answered. "I'm beat too. The climb up the butte was tough and coming down was bad too." He told his father all that had happened on the butte, winding up with the climax of his falling and finding the old *coup* stick.

John listened attentively and did not interrupt until Norman told of Matt Two Bull's reaction to the stick. "I think Grandpa's mind has gotten weak," Norman said. "He really believes that the *coup* stick has some sort of mysterious power and that the Thunders were talking."

COUP STICK (probably of Sioux origin)
Shelburne Museum, Shelburne, Vermont

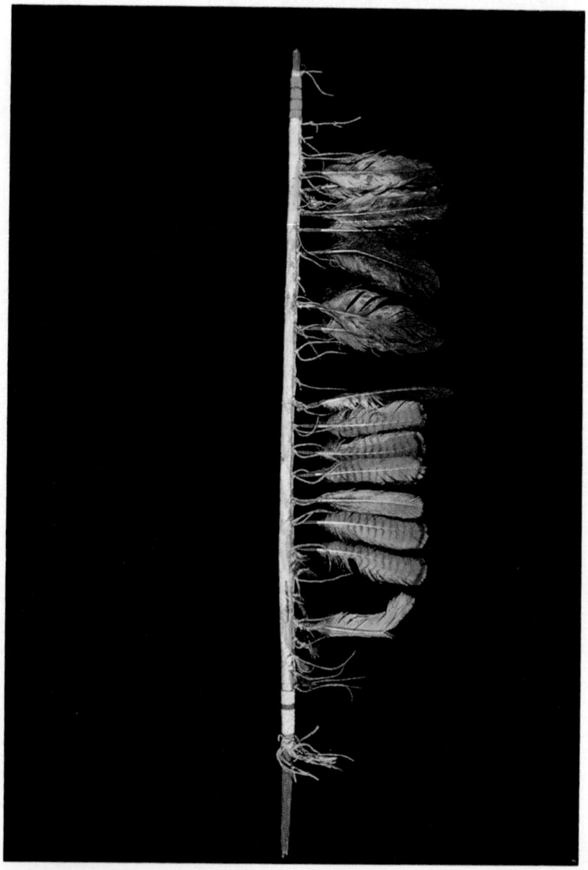

"Don't make fun of your grandfather," John reprimanded, "or of the old ways he believes in."

"Okay, okay," Norman said quickly, not wanting another scolding. "But Mom is just the opposite from Grandpa," he went on. "She doesn't want the *coup* stick in the house. Says it's heathen."

He walked to the house and handed the stick to his father. John examined it and then carried it into the house.

"John!" Sarah exclaimed as she saw her husband bring the stick into the room. "I told Norman, and I tell you, that I won't have that heathenish thing in the house!"

But John ignored her and propped the stick against the door while he pulled his tool box out from under the washstand to look for a hammer and nails.

"John," Sarah persisted, "did you hear me?"

"I heard," John answered quietly, but Norman knew his father was angry. "And I don't want to hear anymore."

Norman was surprised to hear his father speak in such a fashion. John was slow to anger, usually spoke quietly and tried to avoid conflict of any kind, but now he went on.

"This," he said holding the *coup* stick upright, "is a relic of our people's past glory when it was a good thing to be an Indian. It is a symbol of something that shall never be again."

Sarah gasped and stepped in front of her husband as he started to climb a chair to pound the nails in the wall above the window. "But that's what I mean," she said. "Those old ways were just superstition. They don't mean anything now—they can't because such a way of life can't be anymore. We don't need to have those old symbols of heathen ways hanging in the house!" She grabbed at the *coup* stick, but John jerked it out of her reach.

"Don't touch it!" he shouted and Sarah fell back against the table in shocked surprise. Norman took a step forward as if to protect his mother. The boy had never seen his father so angry.

John shook his head as if to clear it. "Sarah, I'm sorry. I didn't mean to yell. It's just that the old ones would not permit a woman to touch such a thing as this." He handed Norman the stick to hold while he hammered the nails in the wall. Then he hung the stick above the window.

"Sarah," he said as he put the tools away, "think of the stick as an object that could be in a museum, a part of history. It's not like we were going to fall down on our knees and pray to it." His voice was light and teasing as he tried to make peace.

But Sarah stood stiffly at the stove preparing supper and would not answer. Norman felt sick. His appetite was gone. When his mother set a plate of food before him he excused himself saying, "I guess I'm too tired to eat," and went to his room.

But after he had undressed and crawled into bed he couldn't sleep. His mind whirled with the angry words his parents had spoken. They had never argued in such a way before. "I wish I had never brought that old stick home," he whispered and then pulled the pillow over his head to shut out the sound of the low rumble of thunder that came from the west.

Reader's Response

With whom do you agree—Norman's mother or his father? Explain.

Responding to the Selection

Your Response

1. Do you admire Norman for accepting the challenge to climb the butte? Explain.
2. Describe how you would have reacted if you had found the *coup* stick.

Recalling

3. Why does Norman climb the butte?
4. After the rock slide, what does Norman find?

Interpreting

5. Norman and his grandfather do not agree about the cause of the thunder and lightning. Which seems less convinced of his opinion?
6. How does the conflict between the new and old ways affect the characters in this story?

Applying

7. Norman's grandfather thinks Norman should "understand the ways—the values of the old ones." How might you learn to understand the ways and the values of your ancestors? Why might this knowledge be valuable for you?

Analyzing Literature

Understanding Atmosphere

Atmosphere, or mood, is the feeling conveyed by a particular setting. The writer's choice of details helps create the atmosphere.

1. The atmosphere at the beginning of the story is one of danger. Name three details that help create this atmosphere.
2. Give three details that help create atmosphere as Norman climbs the butte.
3. What is the atmosphere like at dinner? Why?

Critical Thinking and Reading

Making Inferences About Characters

As you read you make **inferences**—judgments based on evidence. Tell what inference you can make about a character from each of the following quotations from "Thunder Butte."

1. "Sarah grunted scornfully, 'No one believes in dreams or in any of those old superstitious ways anymore.'"
2. "'This,' he [Norman's father] said holding the coup stick upright, 'is a relic of our people's past glory when it was a good thing to be an Indian. It is a symbol of something that shall never be again.'"
3. "'I wish I had never brought that old stick home,' he [Norman] whispered and then pulled the pillow over his head to shut out the sound of the low rumble of thunder that came from the west."

Thinking and Writing

Predicting Future Actions

What do you think Norman will do the next time his grandfather wants to talk with him about the ways of the old ones? Discuss this question with a partner, using what you have learned about Norman and his family to support your belief. Take notes at this meeting and use them to draft a script of a dialogue between Norman and his grandfather. Work with your partner to revise your script. Then write the final draft. With your partner, read your script aloud to your classmates and teacher.

Learning Options

1. **Multicultural Activity.** Use your school or local library to find out more about how Native Americans used *coup* sticks in battle. Then, in an oral presentation, explain why you think Native Americans admired using a *coup* stick more than killing an enemy.
2. **Performance.** In a group of three classmates, think about what might have happened when Norman woke up the next morning. Create a script that includes Norman, his parents, and his grandfather. Assign a part to each member of your group and read the script to your class.

Writing Description

Experience. You hear a lot about it. "Experience is the best teacher." "When you've had more experience. . . . " It's something we have every day, yet something we always seem to want more of.

One kind of experience is sensory: what you see, hear, touch, smell, and taste of the world we live in.

In description writers try to re-create sensory experience. They want readers to be able to imagine experiences through their words. For example, the opening paragraph of "The Dog of Pompeii" makes you see chariots, hear laughing crowds, and even smell fireworks in an ancient city.

Your Turn

You, too, can write good description. Just think—only *you* have had *your* experiences, so you are the expert. Write a good descriptive paragraph about a place that means something to you. Share an experience through sight, sound, touch, smell, and taste.

Prewriting

1. List possible places to describe. Where have you felt strong emotions? Perhaps list places from your childhood, places in which you had a good time, or places that frightened you.

2. Chart sensory details. Using a chart like the one following, explore two or three of your possible topics. It may help to imagine the place at a particular time. Include as many specific details as possible.

	An attic	The swimming hole
SIGHT	old furniture posters light bulb	
SMELL	dusty old books	
SOUND	stairs creek wind click of light chain	
TASTE	?	
TOUCH	layer of dust floor soft but steady rocking chair	

3. Choose a topic and a focus. After choosing the topic that you think you can develop best, look carefully at the details that you have charted and add more. What emotion or impression do the details create? For example, is the place peaceful, wild, threatening, or drab? This impression or idea will become the focus of your paragraph. However, you will not *tell* your audience this impression; you will *show* them with the sensory details you include.

4. Experiment with comparisons. When Kipling writes that Bagheera the Black Panther had "a voice as soft as wild honey dripping from a tree," he uses a comparison. Kipling's comparison suggests many ideas. Bagheera is wild but sweet; his voice is slow and thick; his sound is a natural part of the jungle. As you draft, experiment with one or two comparisons in your paragraph.

5. Organize your sensory details. Choose an order for your details. You might organize them according to location, time, or importance. Number your notes to indicate in what order they will appear.

Drafting

Using your prewriting notes, draft your descriptive paragraph. Always keep your focusing idea in mind.

One student chose his family's attic as the subject of his descriptive draft.

```
     As your head goes through
the trap door in the floor,
you're at eye level with the
dust. From there, the place looks
like a warehouse. Old furniture
gathers dust. Holiday trimmings
take up one corner. On the walls,
we've pinned old posters of
Mickey Mouse and the Beatles. One
single bulb hangs from a ceiling
beam. The beam is from my grand-
parents' barn. This attic is like
my family's scrapbook.
```

Notice that the writer never uses the words "saving memories" but that this idea is *shown* by the details he has included. Notice, too, that the writer has organized his details according to location—from the floor to the ceiling of the attic. How many of the five senses does this writer appeal to? Do you think the comparison in the last sentence is effective?

Revising

Step 1: Use the revising checklist on page 749 to evaluate and revise your draft.

Step 2: Good descriptive writing uses specific nouns and strong verbs. For example, the word *goes* in the first sentence of the sample draft can be strengthened, and *floor* and *dust* could be replaced by more specific nouns: As my head pokes through the trap door in the soft floorboards, I'm at eye level with a thin layer of gray dust.

Step 3: Try shifting point of view to experiment with your draft. For example, the writer of the sample began with second-person point of view ("you"), but he realizes that his last sentence shifts to first-person point of view ("my"). He decides to revise the entire paragraph to the first-person "I."

Step 4: After making your own revisions, make a clean draft of your paragraph. Ask someone you trust to read it and answer questions such as these:

- What feeling or idea do you get about my topic from my description?
- What is the strongest detail in my paragraph? The weakest?

Proofreading

Use the proofreading guidelines on page 753. You want your reader to read smoothly through your sentences, experiencing every detail, without having to pause over a misspelled word or a confusing punctuation mark.

Reading for Theme

HELIOTROPES
Marc Chagall

GUIDE FOR READING

Laurence Yep

(1948–) grew up in San Francisco, where he was born. Challenged to write by an English teacher, he sold his first science-fiction story when he was eighteen. Since then, Yep has written many books for young people. *Sweetwater* and *Dragon of the Lost Sea* reflect his interest in science fiction and fantasy. *Child of the Owl, Dragonwings,* and *Sea Glass* reflect his interest in his Chinese American heritage. The short story "Breaker's Bridge" combines his interests in both Chinese tales and strange events.

Breaker's Bridge

Theme

Theme is the underlying meaning of a work of literature. A theme is usually a comment about people or about life in general. For example, a story may reveal that "Friends are there to help when you need them" or "The events of nature are beyond the control of human beings." In some stories, theme is stated directly by the narrator or by one of the characters.

Focus

When asked to do a difficult task, people often say, "I can't do it! It's impossible!" Usually that is an exaggeration—but what if the task really is impossible? Form a group of three or four students. Brainstorm for a list of impossible tasks, such as air-conditioning the Sahara. When you have an impressive list of tasks, choose one of them to do. With the other members of the group, decide how you will go about accomplishing the impossible. Assume that you have unlimited resources, and use your imagination. As you read "Breaker's Bridge," compare your "accomplishment" with Breaker's.

Vocabulary

Knowing the following words will help you read "Breaker's Bridge."

span (span) *v.*: To reach or extend over or from one side to another (p. 135)
writhing (rīth′ iŋ) *v.*: Making twisting or turning movements (p. 135)
dismay (dis mā′) *n.*: A loss of courage when faced with trouble or danger (p. 136)
piers (pirz) *n.*: Heavy structures supporting the sections of a bridge (p. 136)
scheme (skēm) *n.*: A carefully arranged plan for doing something (p. 137)
pellets (pel′ əts) *n.*: Little balls (p. 138)
immortals (i mort′ 'lz) *n.*: Those who do not die; beings who live forever (p. 140)

Spelling Tip

When you spell *writhing,* remember that there is a silent *w* at the beginning.

Breaker's Bridge

Laurence Yep

" 'Build the bridge and you'll have your weight in gold. Fail and I'll have your head.' "

There was once a boy who was always breaking things. He didn't do it on purpose. He just had very clumsy hands. No matter how careful he tried to be, he always dropped whatever he picked up. His family soon learned not to let him set the table or send him for eggs. Everyone in the village called him Breaker.

But Breaker was as clever as he was clumsy. When he grew up, he managed to outlive his nickname. He could design a bridge to cross any obstacle. No canyon was too wide. No river was too deep. Somehow the clever man always found a way to bridge them all.

Eventually the emperor heard about this clever builder and sent for him.

"There is a river in the hills," the emperor said to him. "Everyone tells me it is too swift and deep to span. So I have to go a long way around it to get to my hunting palace. But you're famous for doing the impossible."

The kneeling man bowed his head to the floor. "So far I have been lucky. But there is always a first time when you can't do something."

The emperor frowned. "I didn't think you were lazy like my other bridge builders. You can have all the workers and all the materials you need. Build the bridge and you'll have your weight in gold. Fail and I'll have your head."

There was nothing for Breaker to do but thank the emperor and leave. He went right away to see the river. He had to take a steep road that wound upward through the hills toward the emperor's hunting palace.

It was really more than a palace, for it included a park the size of a district, and only the emperor could hunt the wildlife. The road to it had to snake through high, steep mountains. Although the road was well kept, the land became wilder and wilder. Pointed boulders thrust up like fangs, and the trees grew in twisted, writhing clumps.

Breaker became uneasy. "This is a place that doesn't like people very much."

The road twisted suddenly to the left when it came to a deep river gorge. On the other side of the gorge, the many trees of the palace looked like a dark-green sea. The yellow-tiled roofs looked like golden rafts floating on its top. Dark mountains, their tops capped with snow all year round, loomed behind the palace like monstrous guards.

Breaker carefully sidled to the edge of the gorge and looked down. Far below, he saw

THE GROTTO OF CHANG TAO-LING
Shih-T'ao
Metropolitan Museum of Art

the river. When the snow melted in the distant mountains, the water flowed together to form this river. It raced faster than a tiger and stronger than a thousand buffalo. When it splashed against a rock, it threw up sheets of white spray like an ocean wave.

Breaker shook his head in dismay. "The emperor might as well have commanded me to bridge the sea."

But his failure would mean the loss of his head, so the next day Breaker set to work. The river was too wide to span with a simple bridge. Breaker would have to construct two piers in the middle of the river. The piers would support the bridge like miniature stone islands.

From the forests of the south came huge logs that were as tough and heavy as iron. From the quarries of the west came large, heavy stones of granite. The workers braved the cold water to sink the logs in the muddy riverbed. Breaker had to change the teams of workers often. The cold numbed anyone who stayed too long in the river.

Once the logs had been pounded into the mud, he tried to set the stones on top of the logs. But the river did not want to be tamed. It bucked and fought like a herd of wild stallions. It crushed the piles of stones into pebbles. It dug up the logs and smashed them against the rocky sides until they were mounds of soggy toothpicks.

Over the next month, Breaker tried every trick he knew; and each time the river defeated him. With each new failure, Breaker suspected more and more that he had met his match. The river flowed hard and strong and fast like the lifeblood of the earth itself. Breaker might as well have tried to tame the mountains.

In desperation, he finally tried to build a dam to hold back the river while he constructed the biggest and strongest piers yet. As he was supervising the construction, an official came by from the emperor.

"This bridge has already cost a lot of

money," he announced to the wrecker. "What do you have to show for it?"

Breaker pointed to the two piers. They rose like twin towers toward the top of the gorge. "With a little luck, the emperor will have his bridge."

Suddenly, they heard a distant roar. The official looked up at the sky. "It sounds like thunder, but I don't see a cloud in the sky."

Breaker cupped his hands around his mouth to amplify his voice. "Get out," he shouted to his men. "Get out. The river must have broken our dam."

His men slipped and slid on the muddy riverbed, but they all managed to scramble out just as a wall of water rolled down the gorge. The river swept around the two piers, pulling and tugging at the stones.

Everyone held their breath. Slowly the two piers began to rock back and forth on their foundations until they toppled over with a crash into the river. Water splashed in huge sheets over everyone, and when the spray finally fell back into the river, not one sign of the piers remained.

"All this time and all this money, and you have nothing to show for it." The official took a soggy yellow envelope from his sleeve.

Breaker and the other workers recognized the imperial color of the emperor. They instantly dropped to their knees and bowed their heads.

Then, with difficulty, Breaker opened the damp envelope and unfolded the letter. "In one month," it said, "I will have a bridge or I will have your head." It was sealed in red ink with the official seal of the emperor.

Breaker returned the letter and bowed again. "I'll try," he promised.

"You will do more than try," the official snapped. "You will build that bridge for the emperor. Or the executioner will be sharpening his sword." And the official left.

Wet and cold and tired, Breaker made his way along a path toward the room he had taken in an inn. It was getting late, so the surrounding forest was black with shadows. As he walked, Breaker tried to come up with some kind of new scheme, but the dam had been his last resort. In a month's time, he would feel the "kiss" of the executioner's sword.

"Hee, hee, hee," an old man laughed in a creaky voice that sounded like feet on old, worn steps. "You never liked hats anyway. Now you'll have an excuse not to wear them."

Breaker turned and saw a crooked old man sitting by the side of the road. He was dressed in rags, and a gourd hung from a strap against his hip. One leg was shorter than the other.

"How did you know that, old man?" Breaker wondered.

"Hee, hee, hee. I know a lot of things: the softness of clouds underneath my feet, the sounds of souls inside bodies." And he shook his gourd so that it rattled as if there were beans inside. "It is the law of the universe that all things must change; and yet Nature hates change the most of all."

"The river certainly fits that description." Although he was exhausted and worried, Breaker squatted down beside the funny old man. "But you better get inside, old man. Night's coming on and it gets cold up in these mountains."

"Can't." The old man nodded to his broken crutch.

Breaker looked all around. It was growing dark, and his stomach was aching with hunger. But he couldn't leave the old man stranded in the mountains, so Breaker took out his knife. "If I make you a new crutch, can you reach your home?"

"If you make me a crutch, we'll all have what we want." It was getting so dim that Breaker could not be sure if the old man smiled.

Although it was hard to see, Breaker found a tall, straight sapling and tried to trim the branches from its sides; but being Breaker, he dropped his knife several times and lost it twice among the old leaves on the forest floor. He also cut each of his fingers. By the time he was ready to cut down the sapling, he couldn't see it. Of course, he cut his fingers even more. And just as he was trimming the last branch from the sapling, he cut the sapling right in two.

He tried to carve another sapling and broke that one. It was so dark by now that he could not see at all. He had to find the next sapling by feel. This time he managed to cut it down and began to trim it. But halfway through he dropped his knife and broke it. "He'll just have to take it as it is," Breaker said.

When he finally emerged from the forest, the moon had come out. Sucking on his cut fingers, Breaker presented the new crutch to the funny old man.

The old man looked at the branches that grew from the sides of his new crutch. "A little splintery."

Breaker angrily took his cut finger from his mouth. "Don't insult someone who's doing you a favor."

The crooked old man lifted his right arm with difficulty and managed to bring it behind his neck. "Keep that in mind yourself." He began to rub the back of his neck.

Breaker thrust the crutch at the old man. "Here, old man. This is what you wanted."

But the old man kept rubbing the back of his neck. "Rivers are like people: Every now and then, they have to be reminded that change is the law that binds us all."

"It's late. I'm tired and hungry and I have to come up with a new plan. Here's your crutch." And Breaker laid the crutch down beside the old man.

But before Breaker could straighten, the old man's left hand shot out and caught hold of Breaker's wrist. The old man's grip was as strong as iron. "Even the least word from me will remind that river of the law."

Breaker tried to pull away, but as strong as he was, he could not break the old man's hold. "Let me go."

But the crooked old man lowered his right hand so that Breaker could see that he had rubbed some of the dirt and sweat from his skin. "We are all bound together," the old man murmured, "and by the same laws." He murmured that over and over until he was almost humming like a bee. At the same time, his fingers quickly rolled the dirt and sweat into two round little pellets.

Frightened, Breaker could only stare at the old man. "Ar-ar-are you some mountain spirit?" he stammered.

The old man turned Breaker's palm upward and deposited the two little pellets on it. Then he closed Breaker's fingers over them. "Leave one of these at each spot where you want a pier. Be sure not to lose them."

"Yes, all right, of course," Breaker promised quickly.

The old man picked up the crutch and thrust himself up from the ground. "Then you'll have what you want too." And he hobbled away quickly.

Breaker kept hold of the pellets until he reached the inn. Once he was among the inn's bright lights and could smell a hot meal, he began to laugh at himself. "You've let the emperor's letter upset you so much that you let a harmless old man scare you."

Even so, Breaker didn't throw away the pellets but put them in a little pouch. And the next morning when he returned to the gorge, he took along the pouch.

The canyon widened at one point so that there was a small beach. Breaker kept his supplies of stone and logs there. Figuring that he had nothing to lose, Breaker walked down the steep path. Then he took the boat and rowed out onto the river.

As he sat in the bobbing boat, he thought of the funny old man again. "You and I," he said to the river, "are both part of the same scheme of things. And it's time you faced up to it."

Although it was difficult to row at the same time, he got out the pouch with the two pellets. "I must be even crazier than that old man." He opened the pouch and shook one of the pellets into his hand.

When he was by the spot where the first pier should be, Breaker threw the pellet in. For a moment, nothing happened. There was only the sound of his oars slapping at the water.

And suddenly the surface began to boil. Frantically, he tried to row away, but the water began to whirl and whirl around in circles. Onshore, the workers shouted and ran to higher ground as waves splashed over the logs and stones.

From beneath the river came loud thumps and thuds and the grinding of stone on stone. A rock appeared above the surface. The water rose in another wave. On top of the wave another stone floated as if it were a block of wood. The river laid the first stone by the second.

Open-mouthed, Breaker watched the river lay stone after stone. The watery arms reached higher and higher until the first pier rose to the top of the gorge.

As the waters calmed, Breaker eagerly rowed the boat over to the second spot. At the same time that he tried to row enough to keep himself in the right place, Breaker reached for the pouch and opened it.

But in his hurry, his clumsy fingers crushed part of the pellet. He threw the remainder of the pellet into the water and then shook out the contents of the pouch. But this time, the river only swirled and rippled.

Breaker leaned over the side and peered below. He could just make out the pale, murky shape of a mound, but that was all. Even so, Breaker wasn't upset. His workers

THE IMMORTAL
Chi-Fong Lei

could easily build a second pier and meet the emperor's deadline.

So Breaker finished the bridge, and that summer the emperor reached his hunting palace with ease. When the emperor finished hunting and returned to his capital, he showered Breaker with gold and promised him all the work he could ever want.

However, winter brought deep snows once again to the mountains. That spring, when the snow thawed, the river grew strong and wild again. It roared down the gorge and smashed against the first pier. But the first pier was solid as a mountain.

However, the second pier had not been built with magic. The river swept away the second pier as if it were nothing but twigs.

The bridge was repaired before the summer hunting, but the emperor angrily summoned Breaker to his hunting palace. "You were supposed to build a bridge for me," the emperor declared.

"Hee, hee, hee," laughed a creaky old voice. "He did, but you didn't say how long it was supposed to stay up."

Breaker turned around and saw it was the crooked old man. He was leaning on the crutch that Breaker had made for him. "How did you get here?" he asked the old man. But from the corner of his eye, he could see all the court officials kneeling down. And when Breaker looked back at the throne, he saw even the emperor kneeling.

"How can we serve you and the other eight immortals?" the emperor asked the crooked old man.

"We are all bound by the same laws," the old man croaked again, and then vanished.

And then Breaker knew the old man for what he truly was—a saint and a powerful magician.

So the emperor spared Breaker and sent him to build other projects all over China. And the emperor never regretted that he had let Breaker keep his head. But every year, the river washed away part of the bridge and every year it was rebuilt. And so things change and yet do not change.

Reader's Response

How would you feel if, like Breaker, you were faced with a task that seemed impossible?

The Immortals

" 'How can we serve you and the other eight immortals?' the emperor asked the crooked old man." This ninth immortal, the old man described as a "saint and a powerful magician," is a character created by Laurence Yep. Who are the other eight immortals?

The eight immortals are highly revered characters in Chinese mythology, philosophy, and literature. Often in tales, one of the eight immortals comes among the people to assist them or to test their values. In "Breaker's Bridge," the ninth immortal tests Breaker's kindness to strangers and then rewards him.

How does someone become an immortal? According to Chinese tradition, the eight immortals attained immortality through various deeds of faithfulness, kindliness, and heroism. Even in the modern world, people can be rewarded with a kind of immortality. Theirs is not a physical immortality but a lasting legacy to their culture. For example, Abraham Lincoln gained immortality by saving the Union. But even lesser people may become immortalized. Baseball players, for instance, may be elected to the Baseball Hall of Fame.

Who are other people who have gained immortality through outstanding deeds or achievements?

Responding to the Selection

Your Response

1. Would you be afraid, as Breaker was, if you were to meet the old man? Why or why not?
2. What examples do you know of "things that change and yet do not change"?

Recalling

3. How does Breaker "outlive his nickname"?
4. What help does Breaker have in building the bridge?

Interpreting

5. What kind of person does Breaker reveal himself to be in his dealings with both the emperor and the old man?
6. When Breaker meets the old man on the mountain, how does the old man suggest that he is more than he appears to be?
7. Why does the old man help Breaker? Find the statement that suggests a reason.
8. Compare and contrast the two piers, telling why each is the way it is.
9. What is important about Breaker's second meeting with the old man?

Applying

10. If the setting of this story were changed to your community at the present time, what tasks might Breaker perform?

Analyzing Literature

Recognizing a Stated Theme

The **theme,** or underlying message of a story, may be stated directly, either by the narrator or by one of the characters. In "Breaker's Bridge" the theme is directly stated by the old man—more than once.

1. According to the old man, what lesson must the river be taught?
2. What is the theme of "Breaker's Bridge" as stated by the old man?
3. What yearly event described in the story provides an illustration of the theme?

Critical Thinking and Reading

Finding Realistic and Fantastic Details

A work of fiction may contain both realistic details and fantastic details. Realistic details show life as we know it. Fantastic details show a world that is strange and unusual, one that does not obey the rules of real life. In "Breaker's Bridge," for example, the description of the dam breaking contains realistic details, while the description of the river building the pier contains fantastic ones. Find two other realistic and two other fantastic details in "Breaker's Bridge."

Thinking and Writing

Supporting an Opinion

When speaking of his work, Breaker says that part of his success depends on luck. Do you think that luck does play a part in the outcome of human efforts? Write a paragraph in which you agree or disagree. Support your opinion with examples from the story or from life. When you have written a draft, share your draft with a partner. Discuss whether your opinion would be stronger if you added more examples or used different ones. Then revise your paper and write a final draft.

Learning Options

1. **Art.** Draw Breaker's bridge. Show the details of the bridge as you imagine them, including the piers. You might also include the gorge and the river.
2. **Writing.** Write a feature story for the local newspaper in Breaker's hometown telling about the building of the bridge. Since a feature story needs human interest, you should include comments from Breaker, some of the workers, the old man, and the emperor's official representative.

GUIDE FOR READING

Francisco Jiménez

(1943–   ) was born in Mexico. He grew up in a family of migrant workers, traveling around the western part of the United States picking whatever crop was ripe. When he was in college, Jiménez was encouraged to write about his childhood, especially "the joys and disappointments of growing up in a migrant setting." "The Circuit" is based on actual events in the writer's life. It includes both the joys and disappointments of the young son of a migrant worker.

The Circuit

Theme

A **theme** in a story is a general idea or insight into life. It is the story's underlying meaning. Sometimes this meaning is stated directly; at other times it is **implied,** or suggested. When a theme is implied, you can find meaning in what happens in the story. In this story, the events of the plot suggest the theme, although the plot itself is not the theme.

Focus

In "The Circuit" a boy who seldom lives in one place for more than a few months tells about starting sixth grade. When you hear the phrase, "the first day of school," what do you think of? Copy the cluster diagram below into your notebook. Then work with a small group of classmates to fill in the diagram with words and ideas that you associate with the first day of school. Then combine your group cluster with other groups to make a class cluster. As you read this story, keep in mind the similarities and the differences between your first day of sixth grade and Panchito's first day.

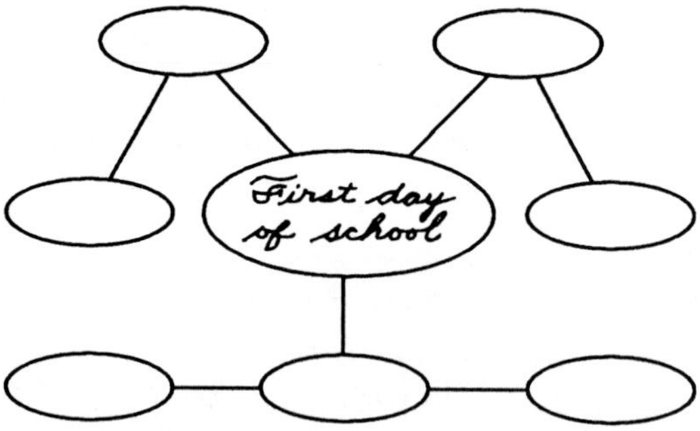

Vocabulary

Knowing the following words will help you read "The Circuit."

drone (drōn) *n.*: A continuous humming sound (p. 146)

instinctively (in stiŋk′ tiv lē) *adv.*: Done by instinct, without thinking (p. 146)

savoring (sā′ vər iŋ) *v.*: Dwelling on with delight (p. 147)

The Circuit

Francisco Jiménez

"That night I could not sleep. I lay in bed thinking about how much I hated this move."

It was that time of year again. Ito, the strawberry sharecropper, did not smile. It was natural. The peak of the strawberry season was over and the last few days the workers, most of them braceros,[1] were not picking as many boxes as they had during the months of June and July.

As the last days of August disappeared, so did the number of braceros. Sunday, only one—the best picker—came to work. I liked him. Sometimes we talked during our half-hour lunch break. That is how I found out he was from Jalisco, the same state in Mexico my family was from. That Sunday was the last time I saw him.

When the sun had tired and sunk behind the mountains, Ito signaled us that it was time to go home. "Ya esora,"[2] he yelled in his broken Spanish. Those were the words I waited for twelve hours a day, every day, seven days a week, week after week. And the thought of not hearing them again saddened me.

As we drove home Papá did not say a word. With both hands on the wheel, he stared at the dirt road. My older brother, Roberto, was also silent. He leaned his head back and closed his eyes. Once in a while he cleared from his throat the dust that blew in from outside.

Yes, it was that time of year. When I opened the front door to the shack, I stopped. Everything we owned was neatly packed in cardboard boxes. Suddenly I felt even more the weight of hours, days, weeks, and months of work. I sat down on a box. The thought of having to move to Fresno[3] and knowing what was in store for me there brought tears to my eyes.

That night I could not sleep. I lay in bed thinking about how much I hated this move.

A little before five o'clock in the morning, Papá woke everyone up. A few minutes later, the yelling and screaming of my little brothers and sisters, for whom the move was a great adventure, broke the silence of dawn. Shortly, the barking of the dogs accompanied them.

---

1. braceros (brə ser′ os) *n.*: Migrant Mexican farm laborers who harvest crops.

2. Ya esora (yä es ō′ rä): Spanish for "It's time" (Ya es hora).

3. Fresno (frez′ nō) *n.*: City in central California.

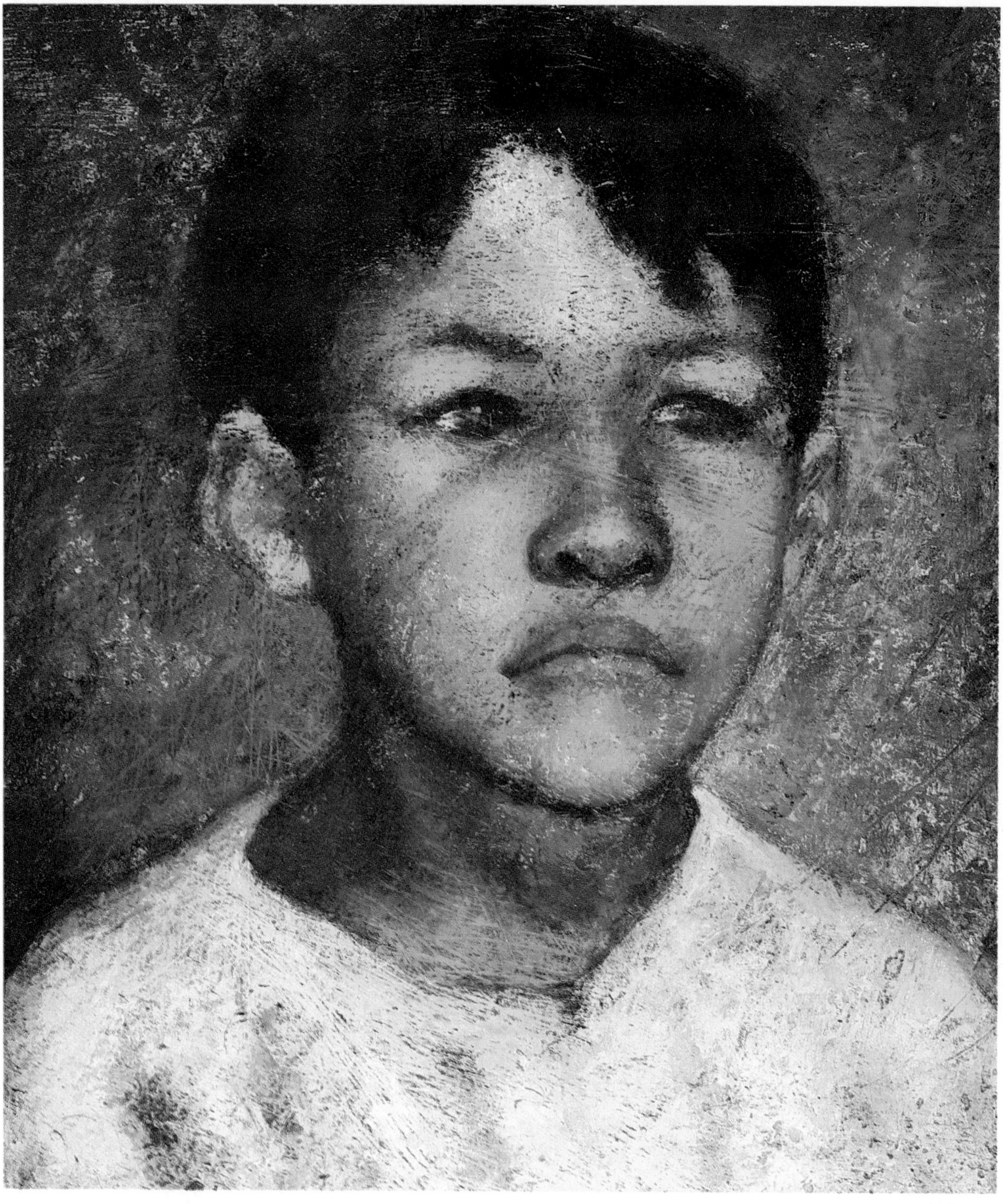

MY BROTHER
Guayasamin (Oswaldo Guayasamin Calero)
Museum of Modern Art, Inter-American Fund, New York

While we packed the breakfast dishes, Papá went outside to start the "Carcanchita."[4] That was the name Papá gave his old '38 black Plymouth. He bought it in a used-car lot in Santa Rosa in the winter of 1949. Papá was very proud of his little jalopy. He had a right to be proud of it. He spent a lot of time looking at other cars before buying this one. When he finally chose the "Carcanchita," he checked it thoroughly before driving it out of the car lot. He examined every inch of the car. He listened to the motor, tilting his head from side to side like a parrot, trying to detect any noises that spelled car trouble. After being satisfied with the looks and sounds of the car, Papá then insisted on knowing who the original owner was. He never did find out from the car salesman, but he bought the car anyway. Papá figured the original owner must have been an important man because behind the rear seat of the car he found a blue necktie.

Papá parked the car out in front and left the motor running, "Listo,"[5] he yelled. Without saying a word, Roberto and I began to carry the boxes out to the car. Roberto carried the two big boxes and I carried the two smaller ones. Papá then threw the mattress on top of the car roof and tied it with ropes to the front and rear bumpers.

Everything was packed except Mamá's pot. It was an old large galvanized[6] pot she had picked up at an army surplus store in Santa María the year I was born. The pot had many dents and nicks, and the more dents and nicks it acquired the more Mamá liked it. "Mi olla"[7] she used to say proudly.

I held the front door open as Mamá carefully carried out her pot by both handles, making sure not to spill the cooked beans. When she got to the car, Papá reached out to help her with it. Roberto opened the rear car door and Papá gently placed it on the floor behind the front seat. All of us then climbed in. Papá sighed, wiped the sweat off his forehead with his sleeve, and said wearily: "Es todo."[8]

As we drove away, I felt a lump in my throat. I turned around and looked at our little shack for the last time.

At sunset we drove into a labor camp near Fresno. Since Papá did not speak English, Mamá asked the camp foreman if he needed any more workers. "We don't need no more," said the foreman, scratching his head. "Check with Sullivan down the road. Can't miss him. He lives in a big white house with a fence around it."

When we got there, Mamá walked up to the house. She went through a white gate, past a row of rose bushes, up the stairs to the front door. She rang the doorbell. The porch light went on and a tall husky man came out. They exchanged a few words. After the man went in, Mamá clasped her hands and hurried back to the car. "We have work! Mr. Sullivan said we can stay there the whole season," she said, gasping and pointing to an old garage near the stables.

The garage was worn out by the years. It had no windows. The walls, eaten by termites, strained to support the roof full of

---

4. "Carcanchita" (kär kän chē′ tä): Affectionate name for the car.

5. Listo (lēs′ tō): Spanish for "Quick."

6. galvanized (gal′ və nīz′d′) *adj.*: Coated with zinc to prevent rusting.

7. Mi olla (mē ō′ yä): Spanish for "My pot."

8. Es todo (es tō′ thō): Spanish for "That's all."

holes. The dirt floor, populated by earthworms, looked like a gray road map.

That night, by the light of a kerosene lamp, we unpacked and cleaned our new home. Roberto swept away the loose dirt, leaving the hard ground. Papá plugged the holes in the walls with old newspapers and tin can tops. Mamá fed my little brothers and sisters. Papá and Roberto then brought in the mattress and placed it on the far corner of the garage. "Mamá, you and the little ones sleep on the mattress. Roberto, Panchito, and I will sleep outside under the trees," Papá said.

Early next morning Mr. Sullivan showed us where his crop was, and after breakfast, Papá, Roberto, and I headed for the vineyard to pick.

Around nine o'clock the temperature had risen to almost one hundred degrees. I was completely soaked in sweat and my mouth felt as if I had been chewing on a handkerchief. I walked over to the end of the row, picked up the jug of water we had brought, and began drinking. "Don't drink too much; you'll get sick," Roberto shouted. No sooner had he said that than I felt sick to my stomach. I dropped to my knees and let the jug roll off my hands. I remained motionless with my eyes glued on the hot sandy ground. All I could hear was the drone of insects. Slowly I began to recover. I poured water over my face and neck and watched the dirty water run down my arms to the ground.

I still felt a little dizzy when we took a break to eat lunch. It was past two o'clock and we sat underneath a large walnut tree that was on the side of the road. While we ate, Papá jotted down the number of boxes we had picked. Roberto drew designs on the ground with a stick. Suddenly I noticed Papá's face turn pale as he looked down the road. "Here comes the school bus," he whispered loudly in alarm. Instinctively, Roberto and I ran and hid in the vineyards. We did not want to get in trouble for not going to school. The neatly dressed boys about my age got off. They carried books under their arms. After they crossed the street, the bus drove away. Roberto and I came out from hiding and joined Papá. "Tienen que tener cuidado,"[9] he warned us.

After lunch we went back to work. The sun kept beating down. The buzzing insects, the wet sweat, and the hot dry dust made the afternoon seem to last forever. Finally the mountains around the valley reached out and swallowed the sun. Within an hour it was too dark to continue picking. The vines blanketed the grapes, making it difficult to see the bunches. "Vámonos,"[10] said Papá, signaling to us that it was time to quit work. Papá then took out a pencil and began to figure out how much we had earned our first day. He wrote down numbers, crossed some out, wrote down some more. "Quince,"[11] he murmured.

When we arrived home, we took a cold shower underneath a waterhose. We then sat down to eat dinner around some wooden crates that served as a table. Mamá had cooked a special meal for us. We had rice and tortillas with "carne con chile,"[12] my favorite dish.

---

9. Tienen que tener cuidado (tē en′ en kā ten er′ kwē t͟hä′ t͟hō): Spanish for "You have to be careful."

10. Vámonos (vä′ mō nōs): Spanish for "Let's go."

11. Quince (kēn′ sā): Spanish for "Fifteen."

12. "carne con chile" (kär′ nē kən chil′ ē): A dish of ground meat, hot peppers, beans, and tomatoes.

The next morning I could hardly move. My body ached all over. I felt little control over my arms and legs. This feeling went on every morning for days until my muscles finally got used to the work.

It was Monday, the first week of November. The grape season was over and I could now go to school. I woke up early that morning and lay in bed, looking at the stars and savoring the thought of not going to work and of starting sixth grade for the first time that year. Since I could not sleep, I decided to get up and join Papá and Roberto at breakfast. I sat at the table across from Roberto, but I kept my head down. I did not want to look up and face him. I knew he was sad. He was not going to school today. He was not going tomorrow, or next week, or next month. He would not go until the cotton season was over, and that was sometime in February. I rubbed my hands together and watched the dry, acid stained skin fall to the floor in little rolls.

When Papá and Roberto left for work, I felt relief. I walked to the top of a small grade next to the shack and watched the "Carcanchita" disappear in the distance in a cloud of dust.

Two hours later, around eight o'clock, I stood by the side of the road waiting for school bus number twenty. When it arrived I climbed in. Everyone was busy either talking or yelling. I sat in an empty seat in the back.

When the bus stopped in front of the school, I felt very nervous. I looked out the bus window and saw boys and girls carrying books under their arms. I put my hands in my pant pockets and walked to the principal's office. When I entered I heard a woman's voice say: "May I help you?" I was startled. I had not heard English for months. For a few seconds I remained speechless. I looked at the lady who waited for my answer. My first instinct was to answer her in Spanish, but I held back. Finally, after struggling for English words, I managed to tell her that I wanted to enroll in the sixth grade. After answering many questions, I was led to the classroom.

Mr. Lema, the sixth-grade teacher, greeted me and assigned me a desk. He then introduced me to the class. I was so nervous and scared at that moment when everyone's eyes were on me that I wished I were with Papá and Roberto picking cotton. After taking roll, Mr. Lema gave the class the assignment for the first hour. "The first thing we have to do this morning is finish reading the story we began yesterday," he said enthusiastically. He walked up to me, handed me an English book, and asked me to read. "We are on page 125," he said politely. When I heard this, I felt my blood rush to my head; I felt dizzy. "Would you like to read?" he asked hesitantly. I opened the book to page 125. My mouth was dry. My eyes began to water. I could not begin. "You can read later," Mr. Lema said understandingly.

For the rest of the reading period I kept getting angrier and angrier with myself. I should have read, I thought to myself.

During recess I went into the restroom and opened my English book to page 125. I began to read in a low voice, pretending I was in class. There were many words I did not know. I closed the book and headed back to the classroom.

Mr. Lema was sitting at his desk correcting papers. When I entered he looked up at me and smiled. I felt better. I walked up to him and asked if he could help me with the new words. "Gladly," he said.

The rest of the month I spent my lunch hours working on English with Mr. Lema, my best friend at school.

One Friday during lunch hour Mr. Lema asked me to take a walk with him to the music room. "Do you like music?" he asked me as we entered the building.

"Yes, I like corridos,"[13] I answered. He then picked up a trumpet, blew on it and handed it to me. The sound gave me goose bumps. I knew that sound. I had heard it in many corridos. "How would you like to learn how to play it?" he asked. He must have read my face because before I could answer, he added: "I'll teach you how to play it during our lunch hours."

That day I could hardly wait to get home to tell Papá and Mamá the great news. As I got off the bus, my little brothers and sisters ran up to meet me. They were yelling and screaming. I thought they were happy to see me, but when I opened the door to our shack, I saw that everything we owned was neatly packed in cardboard boxes.

13. **corridos** (kō rē′ t͟hōs) *n.*: Ballads.

Reader's Response

How are Panchito's hopes and dreams similar to and different from your own?

MULTICULTURAL CONNECTION

Migrant Workers

Nomadic cultures. Leaving home to find work is a practice found in cultures around the world. The Labar blacksmiths of India, for example, are nomadic artisans who travel from village to village in order to serve their customers. The Tuareg people of North Africa move, sometimes with thousands of camels in their caravans, across the Sahara desert to provide people settled at oases with a variety of essential goods. The Tibet herders follow their goats, sheep, and yaks, finding them pastures.

Moving to find work. Most migrant workers in the United States follow the seasonal demands of harvesting. It is not uncommon for a migrant family to leave California, Texas, Arizona, or New Mexico and travel as far as the Midwest each year, returning when the last crops have been harvested.

Changing schools. The entire family usually travels together, with children helping the adults to work on the farms. This may mean starting school late in the fall after the harvest season ends and leaving again early in the spring. It may also mean constantly changing schools. For Francisco Jiménez, a son of migrant workers and today a college professor, the experiences of his childhood became part of a successful writing career.

Exploring and Sharing

Find out more about the challenges faced by people who lead a nomadic lifestyle, especially migrant workers. Has your family ever moved? What are some of the advantages and disadvantages of moving, especially for a student?

Responding to the Selection

Your Response

1. How would you have reacted to Panchito if he had been introduced to your class?
2. How did you feel at the end of the story?

Recalling

3. Describe the family's living arrangements.
4. Why doesn't Panchito start school on time?

Interpreting

5. How does the narrator feel about moving from place to place?
6. How do you know that the narrator wants to make a better life for himself?
7. Describe how Mr. Lema is Panchito's "best friend at school."
8. Explain how the final paragraph in the story brings the narrator back to where he was at the beginning of the story.

Applying

9. What might be some of the difficulties of frequently moving and attending new schools?

Analyzing Literature

Recognizing Implied Theme

Theme, the underlying general idea about life in a story, is often **implied.** In "The Circuit" events of the plot suggest a theme. The theme is not a summary of the plot but an idea or message about life suggested by the plot.

1. Have the lives of the narrator and his family changed at all from the beginning of the story to the end? Explain.
2. A circuit is a regular journey around something. Explain why Jiménez might have chosen "The Circuit" for the title.
3. Which of the following ideas best states a theme in "The Circuit"? Support your answer.
   a. The narrator begins to make progress at school, but must move away again.
   b. Life is unfair.
   c. Life for migrant workers is hard.

Critical Thinking and Reading

Predicting Probable Future Events

A **prediction** is a statement about what one believes will happen in the future. Predictions are more than guesses because they are based on what you already know about a person or situation. You use this information to predict what might happen.

Predict what will happen to Panchito and his family. Give reasons for your prediction.

Thinking and Writing

Writing as a Story Character

Imagine that you are Mr. Lema. Write a letter to Panchito expressing what you hope he can achieve in the future. To begin, freewrite about your experiences in the last weeks and about your hopes for Panchito. Select the important ideas from your freewriting to organize and develop in your first draft. When you revise, check to see that your hopes are based on what you know about Panchito from your time together.

Learning Options

1. **Multicultural Activity.** Interview someone in your community who has immigrated to the United States. Make a list of questions to find out where the person is from, what work he or she did upon arrival, and the difficulties he or she encountered. Present your findings to the class.
2. **Speaking and Listening.** Prepare a speech about rights migrant workers should have. First, prepare a list of rights, for example, education for their children. Then list the rights in order of importance. Organize your speech according to your list. Read your speech to the class.

GUIDE FOR READING

Lloyd Alexander

(1924–) has created and populated an entire mythical kingdom called Prydian in his novels and short stories. In 1969 *The High King,* one of many novels set in Prydian, was awarded a Newbery medal, the highest honor for children's books. In writing his stories, Alexander found that "a writer could know and love a fantasy world as much as his real one." "The Stone" takes place in this fantasy world where magic and real-life problems exist together.

The Stone

Theme Implied Through Character

The **theme** of a story is what it tells us about life and living. In some stories, a theme is implied through what a character learns or the way a character changes. In "The Stone" theme is revealed by the actions and statements of the main character, Maibon. If you focus on the way Maibon's feelings and beliefs change, you will recognize the theme in this story.

Focus

In "The Stone" a man is given what seems to be a wonderful gift—he will never grow old. Suppose you could always stay the age you are now. In a group of two or three students, list the advantages and disadvantages of staying your age. When you finish your list, think of an answer to this question: If you could choose to be one age forever, what age would you choose? Why? List the advantages and disadvantages of that age with your group. Then as you read "The Stone," see if the man in the story experiences any of the advantages or disadvantages on your list.

Vocabulary

Knowing the following words will help you read "The Stone."

delved (delv'd) *v.*: Dug (p. 151)
plight (plīt) *n.*: An awkward, sad, or dangerous situation (p. 152)
jubilation (jo͞o′ bə lā′shən) *n.*: Great joy; triumph (p. 153)
crestfallen (krest′ fôl′ ən) *adj.*: Made sad or humble; disheartened (p. 153)
rue (ro͞o) *v.*: Regret (p. 154)
sown (sōn) *v.*: Planted for growing (p. 154)
fallow (fal′ ō) *adj.*: Inactive; unproductive; unplanted (p. 156)

Spelling Tip

Do not confuse the verb form *sown* with the verb form *sewn,* meaning "joined or fastened with stitches made with a needle and thread."

The Stone

Lloyd Alexander

" 'If a man does the Fair Folk a good turn,' cried Maibon, his excitement growing, 'it's told they must do one for him.' "

There was a cottager named Maibon, and one day he was driving down the road in his horse and cart when he saw an old man hobbling along, so frail and feeble he doubted the poor soul could go many more steps. Though Maibon offered to take him in the cart, the old man refused; and Maibon went his way home, shaking his head over such a pitiful sight, and said to his wife, Modrona:

"Ah, ah, what a sorry thing it is to have your bones creaking and cracking, and dim eyes, and dull wits. When I think this might come to me, too! A fine, strong-armed, sturdy-legged fellow like me? One day to go tottering, and have his teeth rattling in his head, and live on porridge, like a baby? There's no fate worse in all the world."

"There is," answered Modrona, "and that would be to have neither teeth nor porridge. Get on with you, Maibon, and stop borrowing trouble. Hoe your field or you'll have no crop to harvest, and no food for you, nor me, nor the little ones."

Sighing and grumbling, Maibon did as his wife bade him. Although the day was fair and cloudless, he took no pleasure in it. His ax-blade was notched, the wooden handle splintery; his saw had lost its edge; and his hoe, once shining new, had begun to rust. None of his tools, it seemed to him, cut or chopped or delved as well as they once had done.

"They're as worn out as that old codger I saw on the road," Maibon said to himself. He squinted up at the sky. "Even the sun isn't as bright as it used to be, and doesn't warm me half as well. It's gone threadbare as my cloak. And no wonder, for it's been there longer than I can remember. Come to think of it, the moon's been looking a little wilted around the edges, too.

"As for me," went on Maibon, in dismay, "I'm in even a worse state. My appetite's faded, especially after meals. Mornings, when I wake, I can hardly keep myself from yawning. And at night, when I go to bed, my eyes are so heavy I can't hold them open. If that's the way things are now, the older I grow, the worse it will be!"

In the midst of his complaining, Maibon glimpsed something bouncing and tossing back and forth beside a fallen tree in a corner of the field. Wondering if one of his piglets had squeezed out of the sty and gone rooting for acorns, Maibon hurried across the turf. Then he dropped his ax and gaped in astonishment.

There, struggling to free his leg which

WALK IN THE COUNTRY
Javran

had been caught under the log, lay a short, thickset figure: a dwarf with red hair bristling in all directions beneath his round, close-fitting leather cap. At the sight of Maibon, the dwarf squeezed shut his bright red eyes and began holding his breath. After a moment, the dwarf's face went redder than his hair; his cheeks puffed out and soon turned purple. Then he opened one eye and blinked rapidly at Maibon, who was staring at him, speechless.

"What," snapped the dwarf, "you can still see me?"

"That I can," replied Maibon, more than ever puzzled, "and I can see very well you've got yourself tight as a wedge under that log, and all your kicking only makes it worse."

At this, the dwarf blew out his breath and shook his fists. "I can't do it!" he shouted. "No matter how I try! I can't make myself invisible! Everyone in my family can disappear—Poof! Gone! Vanished! But not me! Not Doli! Believe me, if I could have done, you never would have found me in such a plight. Worse luck! Well, come on. Don't stand there goggling like an idiot. Help me get loose!"

At this sharp command, Maibon began tugging and heaving at the log. Then he stopped, wrinkled his brow, and scratched his head, saying:

"Well, now, just a moment, friend. The way you look, and all your talk about turning yourself invisible—I'm thinking you might be one of the Fair Folk."

"Oh, clever!" Doli retorted. "Oh, brilliant! Great clodhopper! Giant beanpole! Of course I am! What else! Enough gabbling. Get a move on. My leg's going to sleep."

"If a man does the Fair Folk a good turn," cried Maibon, his excitement growing, "it's told they must do one for him."

"I knew sooner or later you'd come round to that," grumbled the dwarf. "That's the way of it with you ham-handed, heavy-footed oafs. Time was, you humans got along well with us. But nowadays, you no sooner see a Fair Folk than it's grab, grab, grab! Gobble,

gobble, gobble! Grant my wish! Give me this, give me that! As if we had nothing better to do!

"Yes, I'll give you a favor," Doli went on. "That's the rule, I'm obliged to. Now, get on with it."

Hearing this, Maibon pulled and pried and chopped away at the log as fast as he could, and soon freed the dwarf.

Doli heaved a sigh of relief, rubbed his shin, and cocked a red eye at Maibon, saying:

"All right. You've done your work, you'll have your reward. What do you want? Gold, I suppose. That's the usual. Jewels? Fine clothes? Take my advice, go for something practical. A hazelwood twig to help you find water if your well ever goes dry? An ax that never needs sharpening? A cook pot always brimming with food?"

"None of those!" cried Maibon. He bent down to the dwarf and whispered eagerly, "But I've heard tell that you Fair Folk have magic stones that can keep a man young forever. That's what I want. I claim one for my reward."

Doli snorted. "I might have known you'd pick something like that. As to be expected, you humans have it all muddled. There's nothing can make a man young again. That's even beyond the best of our skills. Those stones you're babbling about? Well, yes, there are such things. But greatly overrated. All they'll do is keep you from growing any older."

"Just as good!" Maibon exclaimed. "I want no more than that!"

Doli hesitated and frowned. "Ah—between the two of us, take the cook pot. Better all around. Those stones—we'd sooner not give them away. There's a difficulty—"

"Because you'd rather keep them for yourselves," Maibon broke in. "No, no, you shan't cheat me of my due. Don't put me off with excuses. I told you what I want, and that's what I'll have. Come, hand it over and not another word."

Doli shrugged and opened a leather pouch that hung from his belt. He spilled a number of brightly colored pebbles into his palm, picked out one of the larger stones, and handed it to Maibon. The dwarf then jumped up, took to his heels, raced across the field, and disappeared into a thicket.

Laughing and crowing over his good fortune and his cleverness, Maibon hurried back to the cottage. There, he told his wife what had happened, and showed her the stone he had claimed from the Fair Folk.

"As I am now, so I'll always be!" Maibon declared, flexing his arms and thumping his chest. "A fine figure of a man! Oho, no gray beard and wrinkled brow for me!"

Instead of sharing her husband's jubilation, Modrona flung up her hands and burst out:

"Maibon, you're a greater fool than ever I supposed! And selfish into the bargain! You've turned down treasures! You didn't even ask that dwarf for so much as new jackets for the children! Nor a new apron for me! You could have had the roof mended. Or the walls plastered. No, a stone is what you ask for! A bit of rock no better than you'll dig up in the cow pasture!"

Crestfallen and sheepish, Maibon began thinking his wife was right, and the dwarf had indeed given him no more than a common field stone.

"Eh, well, it's true," he stammered, "I feel no different than I did this morning, no better nor worse, but every way the same. That redheaded little wretch! He'll rue the day if I ever find him again!"

So saying, Maibon threw the stone into the fireplace. That night he grumbled his way to bed, dreaming revenge on the dishonest dwarf.

Next morning, after a restless night, he yawned, rubbed his eyes, and scratched his chin. Then he sat bolt upright in bed, patting his cheeks in amazement.

"My beard!" he cried, tumbling out and hurrying to tell his wife. "It hasn't grown! Not by a hair! Can it be the dwarf didn't cheat me after all?"

"Don't talk to me about beards," declared his wife as Maibon went to the fireplace, picked out the stone, and clutched it safely in both hands. "There's trouble enough in the chicken roost. Those eggs should have hatched by now, but the hen is still brooding on her nest."

"Let the chickens worry about that," answered Maibon. "Wife, don't you see what a grand thing's happened to me? I'm not a minute older than I was yesterday. Bless that generous-hearted dwarf!"

"Let me lay hands on him and I'll bless him," retorted Modrona. "That's all well and good for you. But what of me? You'll stay as you are, but I'll turn old and gray, and worn and wrinkled, and go doddering into my grave! And what of our little ones? They'll grow up and have children of their own. And grandchildren, and great-grandchildren. And you, younger than any of them. What a foolish sight you'll be!"

But Maibon, gleeful over his good luck, paid his wife no heed, and only tucked the stone deeper into his pocket. Next day, however, the eggs had still not hatched.

"And the cow!" Modrona cried. "She's long past due to calve, and no sign of a young one ready to be born!"

"Don't bother me with cows and chickens," replied Maibon. "They'll all come right, in time. As for time, I've got all the time in the world!"

Having no appetite for breakfast, Maibon went out into the field. Of all the seeds he had sown there, however, he was surprised to see not one had sprouted. The field, which by now should have been covered with green shoots, lay bare and empty.

"Eh, things do seem a little late these days," Maibon said to himself. "Well, no hurry. It's that much less for me to do. The wheat isn't growing, but neither are the weeds."

Some days went by and still the eggs had not hatched, the cow had not calved, the wheat had not sprouted. And now Maibon saw that his apple tree showed no sign of even the smallest, greenest fruit.

"Maibon, it's the fault of that stone!" wailed his wife. "Get rid of the thing!"

"Nonsense," replied Maibon. "The season's slow, that's all."

Nevertheless, his wife kept at him and kept at him so much that Maibon at last, and very reluctantly, threw the stone out the cottage window. Not too far, though, for he had it in the back of his mind to go later and find it again.

Next morning he had no need to go looking for it, for there was the stone sitting on the window ledge.

"You see?" said Maibon to his wife. "Here it is back again. So, it's a gift meant for me to keep."

"Maibon!" cried his wife. "Will you get rid of it! We've had nothing but trouble since you brought it into the house. Now the baby's fretting and fuming. Teething, poor little thing. But not a tooth to be seen! Maibon, that stone's bad luck and I want no part of it!"

Protesting it was none of his doing that the stone had come back, Maibon carried it into the vegetable patch. He dug a hole, not a very deep one, and put the stone into it.

Next day, there was the stone above ground, winking and glittering.

"Maibon!" cried his wife. "Once and for all, if you care for your family, get rid of that cursed thing!"

Seeing no other way to keep peace in the household, Maibon regretfully and unwillingly took the stone and threw it down the well, where it splashed into the water and sank from sight.

But that night, while he was trying vainly to sleep, there came such a rattling and clattering that Maibon clapped his hands over his ears, jumped out of bed, and went stumbling into the yard. At the well, the bucket was jiggling back and forth and up and down at the end of the rope; and in the bottom of the bucket was the stone.

Now Maibon began to be truly distressed, not only for the toothless baby, the calfless cow, the fruitless tree, and the hen sitting desperately on her eggs, but for himself as well.

"Nothing's moving along as it should," he groaned. "I can't tell one day from another. Nothing changes, there's nothing to look forward to, nothing to show for my work. Why sow if the seeds don't sprout? Why plant if there's never a harvest? Why eat if I don't get hungry? Why go to bed at night, or get up in the morning, or do anything at all? And the way it looks, so it will stay for ever and ever! I'll shrivel from boredom if nothing else!"

"Maibon," pleaded his wife, "for all our sakes, destroy the dreadful thing!"

HARVESTING THE FRUIT CROP
Javran

Maibon tried now to pound the stone to dust with his heaviest mallet; but he could not so much as knock a chip from it. He put it against his grindstone without so much as scratching it. He set it on his anvil and belabored it with hammer and tongs, all to no avail.

At last he decided to bury the stone again, this time deeper than before. Picking up his shovel, he hurried to the field. But he suddenly halted and the shovel dropped from his hands. There, sitting cross-legged on a stump, was the dwarf.

"You!" shouted Maibon, shaking his fist. "Cheat! Villain! Trickster! I did you a good turn, and see how you've repaid it!"

The dwarf blinked at the furious Maibon. "You mortals are an ungrateful crew. I gave you what you wanted."

"You should have warned me!" burst out Maibon.

"I did," Doli snapped back. "You wouldn't listen. No, you yapped and yammered, bound to have your way. I told you we didn't like to give away those stones. When you mortals get hold of one, you stay just as you are—but so does everything around you. Before you know it, you're mired in time like a rock in the mud. You take my advice. Get rid of that stone as fast as you can."

"What do you think I've been trying to do?" blurted Maibon. "I've buried it, thrown it down the well, pounded it with a hammer—it keeps coming back to me!"

"That's because you really didn't want to give it up," Doli said. "In the back of your mind and the bottom of your heart, you didn't want to change along with the rest of the world. So long as you feel that way, the stone is yours."

"No, no!" cried Maibon. "I want no more of it. Whatever may happen, let it happen. That's better than nothing happening at all. I've had my share of being young, I'll take my share of being old. And when I come to the end of my days, at least I can say I've lived each one of them."

"If you mean that," answered Doli, "toss the stone onto the ground, right there at the stump. Then get home and be about your business."

Maibon flung down the stone, spun around, and set off as fast as he could. When he dared at last to glance back over his shoulder, fearful the stone might be bouncing along at his heels, he saw no sign of it, nor of the redheaded dwarf.

Maibon gave a joyful cry, for at that same instant the fallow field was covered with green blades of wheat, the branches of the apple tree bent to the ground, so laden they were with fruit. He ran to the cottage, threw his arms around his wife and children, and told them the good news. The hen hatched her chicks, the cow bore her calf. And Maibon laughed with glee when he saw the first tooth in the baby's mouth.

Never again did Maibon meet any of the Fair Folk, and he was just as glad of it. He and his wife and children and grandchildren lived many years, and Maibon was proud of his white hair and long beard as he had been of his sturdy arms and legs.

"Stones are all right, in their way," said Maibon. "But the trouble with them is, they don't grow."

Reader's Response

Would you have given up the stone? Explain.

Responding to the Selection

Your Response

1. What would you have asked Doli for?
2. Did this story change your opinion about the benefits of staying young forever? Explain.

Recalling

3. Describe how Maibon gets the stone.
4. Why does the stone keep coming back?
5. How does Maibon feel when he is finally rid of the stone?

Interpreting

6. Why does Maibon choose the stone over the other gifts that Doli suggests?
7. How does Maibon come to realize that it is better to grow old than to remain the same?
8. Explain what Maibon means when he says, "Stones are all right, in their way. But the trouble with them is, they don't grow."

Applying

9. At the beginning of the story, Maibon fears growing old. Do you think this feeling is true for most people? Explain.

Analyzing Literature

Understanding Theme Through Character

An **implied theme** is one that is not stated directly but is suggested through the characters and events. In "The Stone" the theme is suggested by what Maibon learns and how his attitudes change.

1. What does Maibon discover to be worse than growing old?
2. Which of the following statements do you think best states a theme for this story?
   a. Never expect rewards for good works.
   b. Change is a good and natural part of being alive.
   c. Maibon helps one of the Fair Folk and is rewarded with a magic stone.

Critical Thinking and Reading

Recognizing Attitudes

An **attitude** is the way a person thinks or feels about something. You can determine attitude from a character's speech and actions.

1. Describe Doli's attitude toward humans.
2. What speech and actions helped you determine his attitude?
3. Describe Maibon's change in attitude toward growing older. Use examples of his speech and actions to support your description.

Thinking and Writing

Responding to the Theme

Suppose that you, like Maibon, are offered the opportunity never to grow any older. Unlike Maibon's gift, however, this magic would allow other life to continue to grow around you. Decide whether you would accept the offer. List reasons that support your decision. Write the first draft of your composition, explaining your decision. Give reasons and examples in support. As you revise, evaluate whether your reasons and examples are clear and strong. Change or add support if necessary. Then prepare a final copy.

Learning Option

Performance. A readers theater is a dramatic reading of a work of literature. Work with a small group of your classmates to prepare a readers theater presentation of a scene from "The Stone." (For further information, see Your Writing Process on page 248.) First, decide who should speak the part of each character. One person can narrate the story. As you read, let your voice and gestures express the feelings and attitudes of each character.

GUIDE FOR READING

Lensey Namioka

(1929–), like the main character in this story, was born in China and moved with her family to the United States when she was a teenager. "For my writings I draw heavily on my Chinese culture," she explains. Her novel *Who's Hu?,* the story of a Chinese girl learning the ways of Americans, is among her most popular works. "The All-American Slurp" is also about a Chinese family trying to adjust to life in America.

The All-American Slurp

Theme Implied Through Characters

A story may present an important idea about life called a **theme.** Often, the way characters change in a story is a key to a theme. In "The All-American Slurp" the narrator and her family must adjust to life in the United States after moving from China. By understanding how the family changes, you can understand this theme.

Focus

The narrator of this story describes her family's efforts to learn American customs. The Lin family studies everything from the English language to how to eat American foods. What other things must immigrants learn? In a small group, make a cluster diagram of things immigrants must learn. Then give a number to each item in your cluster to indicate which things you think are most important and which least important. Note how many of the items in your diagram are mentioned in the story.

Vocabulary

Knowing the following words will help you read "The All-American Slurp."

emigrated (em′ ə grāt′ id) *v.*: Left one country to settle in another (p. 159)
mortified (môr′ tə fīd′) *adj.*: Ashamed; extremely embarrassed (p. 161)
spectacle (spek′ tə k'l) *n.*: Foolish or unusual behavior (p. 161)
smugly (smug′ lē) *adv.*: With self-satisfaction (p. 161)
systematic (sis′ tə mat′ ik) *adj.*: Orderly (p. 163)
etiquette (et′ i kət) *n.*: Acceptable social manners (p. 163)
consumption (kən sump′ shən) *n.*: Eating; drinking; using up (p. 164)

Spelling Tip

Many people confuse the words *emigrate* and *immigrate.* Remember that *emigrate,* like *exit,* begins with *e* and means "to leave."

The All-American Slurp

Lensey Namioka

"As any respectable Chinese knows, the correct way to eat your soup is to slurp."

The first time our family was invited out to dinner in America, we disgraced ourselves while eating celery. We had emigrated to this country from China, and during our early days here we had a hard time with American table manners.

In China we never ate celery raw, or any other kind of vegetable raw. We always had to disinfect the vegetables in boiling water first. When we were presented with our first relish tray, the raw celery caught us unprepared.

We had been invited to dinner by our neighbors, the Gleasons. After arriving at the house, we shook hands with our hosts and packed ourselves into a sofa. As our family of four sat stiffly in a row, my younger brother and I stole glances at our parents for a clue as to what to do next.

Mrs. Gleason offered the relish tray to Mother. The tray looked pretty, with its tiny red radishes, curly sticks of carrots, and long, slender stalks of pale green celery. "Do try some of the celery, Mrs. Lin," she said. "It's from a local farmer, and it's sweet."

Mother picked up one of the green stalks, and Father followed suit. Then I picked up a stalk, and my brother did too. So there we sat, each with a stalk of celery in our right hand.

Mrs. Gleason kept smiling. "Would you like to try some of the dip, Mrs. Lin? It's my own recipe: sour cream and onion flakes, with a dash of Tabasco sauce."

Most Chinese don't care for dairy products, and in those days I wasn't even ready to drink fresh milk. Sour cream sounded perfectly revolting. Our family shook our heads in unison.

Mrs. Gleason went off with the relish tray to the other guests, and we carefully watched to see what they did. Everyone seemed to eat the raw vegetables quite happily.

Mother took a bite of her celery. *Crunch.* "It's not bad!" she whispered.

Father took a bite of his celery. *Crunch.* "Yes, it *is* good," he said, looking surprised.

I took a bite, and then my brother. *Crunch, crunch.* It was more than good; it was delicious. Raw celery has a slight sparkle, a zingy taste that you don't get in cooked celery. When Mrs. Gleason came around with the relish tray, we each took another stalk of celery, except my brother. He took two.

There was only one problem: long strings ran through the length of the stalk, and they

got caught in my teeth. When I help my mother in the kitchen, I always pull the string out before slicing celery.

I pulled the strings out of my stalk. *Z-z-zip, z-z-zip*. My brother followed suit. *Z-z-zip, z-z-zip, z-z-zip*. To my left, my parents were taking care of their own stalks. *Z-z-zip, z-z-zip, z-z-zip*.

Suddenly I realized that there was dead silence except for our zipping. Looking up, I saw that the eyes of everyone in the room were on our family. Mr. and Mrs. Gleason, their daughter Meg, who was my friend, and their neighbors the Badels—they were all staring at us as we busily pulled the strings of our celery.

That wasn't the end of it. Mrs. Gleason announced that dinner was served and invited us to the dining table. It was lavishly covered with platters of food, but we couldn't see any chairs around the table. So we helpfully carried over some dining chairs and sat down. All the other guests just stood there.

Mrs. Gleason bent down and whispered to us, "This is a buffet dinner. You help yourselves to some food and eat it in the living room."

Our family beat a retreat back to the sofa as if chased by enemy soldiers. For the rest of the evening, too mortified to go back to the dining table, I nursed a bit of potato salad on my plate.

Next day Meg and I got on the school bus together. I wasn't sure how she would feel about me after the spectacle our family made at the party. But she was just the same as usual, and the only reference she made to the party was, "Hope you and your folks got enough to eat last night. You certainly didn't take very much. Mom never tries to figure out how much food to prepare. She just puts everything on the table and hopes for the best."

I began to relax. The Gleasons' dinner party wasn't so different from a Chinese meal after all. My mother also puts everything on the table and hopes for the best.

Meg was the first friend I had made after we came to America. I eventually got acquainted with a few other kids in school, but Meg was still the only real friend I had.

My brother didn't have any problems making friends. He spent all his time with some boys who were teaching him baseball, and in no time he could speak English much faster than I could—not better, but faster.

I worried more about making mistakes, and I spoke carefully, making sure I could say everything right before opening my mouth. At least I had a better accent than my parents, who never really got rid of their Chinese accent, even years later. My parents had both studied English in school before coming to America, but what they had studied was mostly written English, not spoken.

Father's approach to English was a scientific one. Since Chinese verbs have no tense, he was fascinated by the way English verbs changed form according to whether they were in the present, past imperfect, perfect, pluperfect,[1] future, or future perfect tense. He was always making diagrams of verbs and their inflections,[2] and he looked for opportunities to show off his mastery of the pluperfect and future perfect tenses, his two favorites. "I shall have finished my project by Monday," he would say smugly.

---

1. pluperfect (plo͞o pʉr′ fikt) *adj.*: The past perfect tense of verbs in English.

2. inflections (in flek′ shənz) *n.*: The changes in the forms of words to show different tenses.

Mother's approach was to memorize lists of polite phrases that would cover all possible social situations. She was constantly muttering things like "I'm fine, thank you. And you?" Once she accidentally stepped on someone's foot, and hurriedly blurted, "Oh, that's quite all right!" Embarrassed by her slip, she resolved to do better next time. So when someone stepped on *her* foot, she cried, "You're welcome!"

In our own different ways, we made progress in learning English. But I had another worry, and that was my appearance. My brother didn't have to worry, since Mother bought him blue jeans for school, and he dressed like all the other boys. But she insisted that girls had to wear skirts. By the time she saw that Meg and the other girls were wearing jeans, it was too late. My school clothes were bought already, and we didn't have money left to buy new outfits for me. We had too many other things to buy first, like furniture, pots, and pans.

The first time I visited Meg's house, she took me upstairs to her room, and I wound up trying on her clothes. We were pretty much the same size, since Meg was shorter and thinner than average. Maybe that's how we became friends in the first place. Wearing Meg's jeans and T-shirt, I looked at myself in the mirror. I could almost pass for an American—from the back, anyway. At least the kids in school wouldn't stop and stare at me in my white blouse and navy blue skirt that went a couple of inches below the knees.

When Meg came to my house, I invited her to try on my Chinese dresses, the ones with a high collar and slits up the sides. Meg's eyes were bright as she looked at herself in the mirror. She struck several sultry poses, and we nearly fell over laughing.

The dinner party at the Gleasons' didn't stop my growing friendship with Meg. Things were getting better for me in other ways too. Mother finally bought me some jeans at the end of the month, when Father got his paycheck. She wasn't in any hurry about buying them at first, until I worked on her. This is what I did. Since we didn't have a car in those days, I often ran down to the neighborhood store to pick up things for her. The groceries cost less at a big supermarket, but the closest one was many blocks away. One day, when she ran out of flour, I offered to borrow a bike from our neighbor's son and buy a ten-pound bag of flour at the supermarket. I mounted the boy's bike and waved to Mother. "I'll be back in five minutes!"

Before I started pedaling, I heard her voice behind me. "You can't go out in public like that! People can see all the way up to your thighs!"

"I'm sorry," I said innocently. "I thought you were in a hurry to get the flour." For dinner we were going to have pot-stickers (fried Chinese dumplings), and we needed a lot of flour.

"Couldn't you borrow a girl's bicycle?" complained Mother. "That way your skirt won't be pushed up."

"There aren't too many of those around," I said. "Almost all the girls wear jeans while riding a bike, so they don't see any point buying a girl's bike."

We didn't eat pot-stickers that evening, and Mother was thoughtful. Next day we took the bus downtown and she bought me a pair of jeans. In the same week, my brother made the baseball team of his junior high school, Father started taking driving lessons, and Mother discovered rummage sales.

We soon got all the furniture we needed, plus a dart board and a 1,000-piece jigsaw puzzle (fourteen hours later, we discovered that it was a 999-piece jigsaw puzzle). There was hope that the Lins might become a normal American family after all.

Then came our dinner at the Lakeview restaurant.

The Lakeview was an expensive restaurant, one of those places where a headwaiter dressed in tails[3] conducted you to your seat, and the only light came from candles and flaming desserts. In one corner of the room a lady harpist played tinkling melodies.

Father wanted to celebrate, because he had just been promoted. He worked for an electronics company, and after his English started improving, his superiors decided to appoint him to a position more suited to his training. The promotion not only brought a higher salary but was also a tremendous boost to his pride.

Up to then we had eaten only in Chinese restaurants. Although my brother and I were becoming fond of hamburgers, my parents didn't care much for western food, other than chow mein.[4]

But this was a special occasion, and Father asked his coworkers to recommend a really elegant restaurant. So there we were at the Lakeview, stumbling after the headwaiter in the murky dining room.

At our table we were handed our menus, and they were so big that to read mine I almost had to stand up again. But why bother? It was mostly in French, anyway.

Father, being an engineer, was always systematic. He took out a pocket French dictionary. "They told me that most of the items would be in French, so I came prepared." He even had a pocket flashlight, the size of a marking pen. While Mother held the flashlight over the menu, he looked up the items that were in French.

"Pâté en croûte,"[5] he muttered. "Let's see . . . *pâté* is paste . . . *croûte* is crust . . . hmm . . . a paste in crust."

The waiter stood looking patient. I squirmed and died at least fifty times.

At long last Father gave up. "Why don't we just order four complete dinners at random?" he suggested.

"Isn't that risky?" asked Mother. "The French eat some rather peculiar things, I've heard."

"A Chinese can eat anything a Frenchman can eat," Father declared.

The soup arrived in a plate. How do you get soup up from a plate? I glanced at the other diners, but the ones at the nearby tables were not on their soup course, while the more distant ones were invisible in the darkness.

Fortunately my parents had studied books on western etiquette before they came to America. "Tilt your plate," whispered my mother. "It's easier to spoon the soup up that way."

She was right. Tilting the plate did the trick. But the etiquette book didn't say anything about what you did after the soup

3. tails (tālz) *n.*: An informal term for a dinner coat, cutaway over the hips and hanging down in the back in a pair of tapered ends, resembling a swallow's tail.

4. chow mein (chou mān') *n.*: A thick stew of meat, celery, and other vegetables.

5. pâté en croûte (pä tā' än kro͞ot)

reached your lips. As any respectable Chinese knows, the correct way to eat your soup is to slurp. This helps to cool the liquid and prevent you from burning your lips. It also shows your appreciation.

We showed our appreciation. *Shloop*, went my father. *Shloop* went my mother. *Shloop, shloop*, went my brother, who was the hungriest.

The lady harpist stopped playing to take a rest. And in the silence, our family's consumption of soup suddenly seemed unnaturally loud. You know how it sounds on a rocky beach when the tide goes out and the water drains from all those little pools? They go *shloop, shloop, shloop*. That was the Lin family, eating soup.

At the next table a waiter was pouring wine. When a large *shloop* reached him, he froze. The bottle continued to pour, and red wine flooded the tabletop and into the lap of a customer. Even the customer didn't notice anything at first, being also hypnotized by the *shloop, shloop, shloop*.

It was too much. "I need to go to the toilet," I mumbled, jumping to my feet. A waiter, sensing my urgency, quickly directed me to the ladies' room.

I splashed cold water on my burning face, and as I dried myself with a paper towel, I stared into the mirror. In this perfumed ladies' room, with its pink-and-silver wallpaper and marbled sinks, I looked completely out of place. What was I doing here? What was our family doing in the Lakeview restaurant? In America?

The door to the ladies' room opened. A woman came in and glanced curiously at me. I retreated into one of the toilet cubicles and latched the door.

Time passed—maybe half an hour, maybe an hour. Then I heard the door open again, and my mother's voice. "Are you in there? You're not sick, are you?"

There was real concern in her voice. A girl can't leave her family just because they slurp their soup. Besides, the toilet cubicle had a few drawbacks as a permanent residence. "I'm all right," I said, undoing the latch.

Mother didn't tell me how the rest of the dinner went, and I didn't want to know. In the weeks following, I managed to push the whole thing into the back of my mind, where it jumped out at me only a few times a day. Even now, I turn hot all over when I think of the Lakeview restaurant.

But by the time we had been in this country for three months, our family was definitely making progress toward becoming Americanized. I remember my parents' first PTA meeting. Father wore a neat suit and tie, and Mother put on her first pair of high heels. She stumbled only once. They met my homeroom teacher and beamed as she told them that I would make honor roll soon at the rate I was going. Of course Chinese etiquette forced Father to say that I was a very stupid girl and Mother to protest that the teacher was showing favoritism toward me. But I could tell they were both very proud.

The day came when my parents announced that they wanted to give a dinner party. We had invited Chinese friends to eat with us before, but this dinner was going to be different. In addition to a Chinese-American family, we were going to invite the Gleasons.

"Gee, I can hardly wait to have dinner at your house," Meg said to me. "I just *love* Chinese food."

That was a relief. Mother was a good

cook, but I wasn't sure if people who ate sour cream would also eat chicken gizzards stewed in soy sauce.

Mother decided not to take a chance with chicken gizzards. Since we had western guests, she set the table with large dinner plates, which we never used in Chinese meals. In fact we didn't use individual plates at all, but picked up food from the platters in the middle of the table and brought it directly to our rice bowls. Following the practice of Chinese-American restaurants, Mother also placed large serving spoons on the platters.

MULTICULTURAL CONNECTION

Eating Customs Around the World

The Chinese have winter melon soup, the French have *bouillabaisse*, and the Mexicans have *sopa de mariscos*. In Lensey Namioka's "The All-American Slurp" we learn that it's not only food that changes from culture to culture. Like the distinctive dishes of each country, table manners and eating customs vary from one culture to the next.

Foods from other countries. Many foods eaten in other countries might come as a surprise to you. In Mexico, a sauce or *mole* made of chocolate and almonds is served with meat. In China, chicken gizzards, tripe, eel, sea slugs, and snakes are eaten. In France, you might be served such exotic items as frog's legs, snails, brains, tripe, or rabbit. In India, where food is closely tied to religious practices, many people do not eat meat, especially pork.

Foods from the United States. Likewise, many foods eaten in the United States would surprise someone from another country. As you have seen, the Chinese rarely eat raw vegetables (like celery) or products made from cow's milk.

Utensils. Although it may be hard to imagine eating without knives, forks, and spoons, many people do just that. On some occasions and in some places, some foods are still eaten with the fingers. For instance, the traditional Hawaiian poi, a paste made from taro root, is eaten by dipping one or two fingers in the bowl. The Mexican taco—a folded tortilla filled with meat, lettuce, cheese, and other ingredients—may be picked up. In the United States, we have "dips" and "finger food."

In China, chopsticks replaced knives in the fourth century B.C. (When the Chinese came in contact with Europeans many centuries later, they were shocked by the fact that Europeans "ate with swords.")

Behavior at the table. The Chinese have many rules for behavior at the table. Among them: Take equal portions of all the foods at the center, not just the ones you like best; eat more rice than other foods and try to eat at the same speed as everyone else. In Japan, children are told to talk little because talking is against good manners. In many Arabic countries the left hand is not used when taking food from communal dishes.

Sharing Your Experiences

Tell the class about restaurants where you've eaten food from another country. You may want to bring in a favorite recipe of yours and share it with the class.

The dinner started well. Mrs. Gleason exclaimed at the beautifully arranged dishes of food: the colorful candied fruit in the sweet-and-sour pork dish, the noodle-thin shreds of chicken meat stir-fried with tiny peas, and the glistening pink prawns in a ginger sauce.

At first I was too busy enjoying my food to notice how the guests were doing. But soon I remembered my duties. Sometimes guests were too polite to help themselves and you had to serve them with more food.

I glanced at Meg, to see if she needed more food, and my eyes nearly popped out at the sight of her plate. It was piled with food: the sweet-and-sour meat pushed right against the chicken shreds, and the chicken sauce ran into the prawns. She had been taking food from a second dish before she finished eating her helping from the first!

Horrified, I turned to look at Mrs. Gleason. She was dumping rice out of her bowl and putting it on her dinner plate. Then she ladled prawns and gravy on top of the rice and mixed everything together, the way you mix sand, gravel, and cement to make concrete.

I couldn't bear to look any longer, and I turned to Mr. Gleason. He was chasing a pea around his plate. Several times he got it to the edge, but when he tried to pick it up with his chopsticks, it rolled back toward the center of the plate again. Finally he put down his chopsticks and picked up the pea with his fingers. He really did! A grown man!

All of us, our family and the Chinese guests, stopped eating to watch the activities of the Gleasons. I wanted to giggle. Then I caught my mother's eyes on me. She frowned and shook her head slightly, and I understood the message: the Gleasons were not used to Chinese ways, and they were just coping the best they could. For some reason I thought of celery strings.

When the main courses were finished, Mother brought out a platter of fruit. "I hope you weren't expecting a sweet dessert," she said. "Since the Chinese don't eat dessert, I didn't think to prepare any."

"Oh, I couldn't possibly eat dessert!" cried Mrs. Gleason. "I'm simply stuffed!"

Meg had different ideas. When the table was cleared, she announced that she and I were going for a walk. "I don't know about you, but I feel like dessert," she told me, when we were outside. "Come on, there's a Dairy Queen down the street. I could use a big chocolate milkshake!"

Although I didn't really want anything more to eat, I insisted on paying for the milkshakes. After all, I was still hostess.

Meg got her large chocolate milkshake and I had a small one. Even so, she was finishing hers while I was only half done. Toward the end she pulled hard on her straws and went *shloop, shloop*.

"Do you always slurp when you eat a milkshake?" I asked, before I could stop myself.

Meg grinned. "Sure. All Americans slurp."

Reader's Response

If you were one of the narrator's new friends, what advice would you give her about adjusting to life in the United States? Why?

RESPONDING TO THE SELECTION

Your Response

1. What do you think of the narrator's behavior in the restaurant? Explain.
2. Were you surprised by the end of the story? Explain.

Recalling

3. Describe the family's experience at the Gleasons' dinner party.
4. Why does the narrator want to giggle at the way the Gleasons eat their Chinese dinner?

Interpreting

5. What does the way each family member learns English reveal about that person?
6. How are the Gleasons' actions at the Lins' dinner party similar to the Lins' actions at the Gleasons' dinner party?
7. What does the narrator learn from Meg's explanation about slurping?
8. What does the narrator's attitude indicate about how she has adjusted to American life?

Applying

9. What are the similarities and differences between the Lins' experience of moving to a new country and an American family's experience of moving to a new town?

ANALYZING LITERATURE

Recognizing Theme Through Characters

Often, the way characters change or grow is an important clue to the meaning, or **theme,** of a story. Thinking about how the Lin family changes and grows in the course of the story will help you find the theme in this story.

1. Explain why the Gleasons' eating habits remind the girl of celery strings.
2. What is the difference between American slurping and Chinese slurping?
3. How would you express the theme of this story?

CRITICAL THINKING AND READING

Using Comparison and Contrast

Comparing means looking at similarities between people or objects. **Contrasting** means looking at the differences. Comparing and contrasting different characters can help you to understand them better.

1. How is the narrator similar to Meg? How is she different from Meg?
2. How are the Gleasons and the Lins similar? How are the two families different?
3. Compare and contrast the eating customs of the Americans and the Chinese in this story.

THINKING AND WRITING

Writing a Script

Working with a group of classmates, write a script for the scene in the restaurant. In addition to writing dialogue for the characters, include directions that tell how to speak the lines and what gestures or facial expressions to use. After you have written a draft, discuss ways to improve the dialogue to match the characters and to match the mood of the scene. Then revise and write the final script.

LEARNING OPTIONS

1. **Multicultural Activity.** With a small group of classmates, brainstorm for a list of foods from at least three different cultures. Then, create a menu that lists these foods. Be sure to indicate which culture each dish comes from. Illustrate your menu with drawings that show how to eat each dish.
2. **Speaking and Listening.** Form two teams of three to debate this statement: "Immigrants to the United States should give up their traditional customs and take on the customs of their new country." One team should support the statement and the other argue against it. Have the rest of the class ask questions about the topic.

GUIDE FOR READING

Jack Cope

(1913–) lives in South Africa, the setting for much of his fiction. South Africa today is a place of conflict, as the black majority of the population and the white ruling class—descendants of early Dutch settlers—struggle for political power. While acknowledging the depth of the problems, Cope goes on to say that "Africa has a certain innocence, a certain freshness and strength." "Power" reflects these qualities as well as the quality of compassion.

Power

Symbols

A **symbol** is a thing that stands for or represents something more than itself. For example, a queen's crown could be a symbol of power and authority because she wears the crown for official occasions. In literature an object, an action, or a character can be used as a symbol. It is itself, yet it also suggests some other meaning—an idea, a belief, a value, or a group of feelings. The symbol's meaning often reflects the theme of the story.

Focus

In this story power lines and birds serve as symbols. What do power lines and birds mean to you? In a small group, make two word webs—one for power lines and the other for birds. Write all the words and ideas that you associate with these words. As you read the story, notice what is said about power lines and birds. What do they symbolize to the boy in the story? You may wish to add these ideas to your word webs.

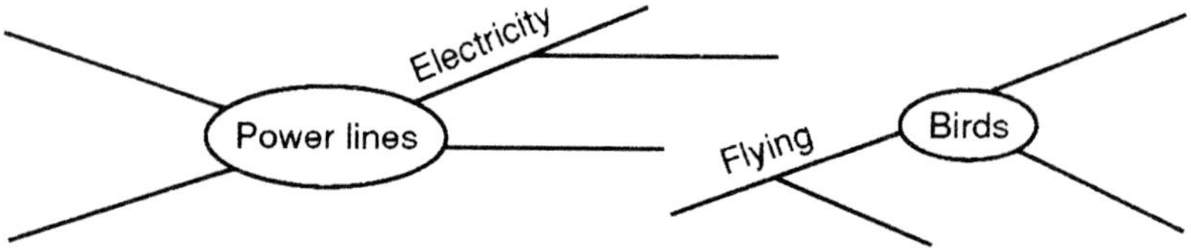

Vocabulary

Knowing the following words will help you as you read "Power."

lattice (lat′ is) *n.*: A structure of crossed strips of wood or metal, used as a support or a screen (p. 169)

pylons (pī′ läns) *n.*: Towerlike structures (p. 169)

summit (sum′ it) *n.*: The highest point; the top (p. 169)

perch (purch) *n.*: A resting place, especially a high one or insecure one (p. 171)

anxious (aŋk′ shəs) *adj.*: Uneasy in mind; worried (p. 172)

quivering (kwiv′ ər iŋ) *v.*: Shaking; trembling (p. 173)

impudently (im′ pyo͞o dənt lē) *adv.*: Shamelessly; disrespectfully (p. 174)

menacing (men′ is iŋ) *v.*: Threatening (p. 176)

Power

Jack Cope

". . . he loved the powerline dearly. It made a door through the distance for his thoughts."

From the gum tree at the corner he looked out over, well—nothing. There was nothing more after his father's place, only the veld,[1] so flat and unchanging that the single shadowy koppie[2] away off towards the skyline made it look more empty still. It was a lonely koppie like himself.

The one thing that made a difference was the powerline. High above the earth on its giant steel lattice towers, the powerline strode across the veld until it disappeared beyond the koppie. It passed close to his father's place and one of the great pylons was on their ground in a square patch fenced off with barbed wire, a forbidden place. André used to look through the wire at the pylon. Around the steelwork itself were more screens of barbed wire, and on all four sides of it enamel warning-plates with a red skull-and-crossbones said in three languages, DANGER! And there was a huge figure of volts, millions of volts.

André was ten and he knew volts were electricity and the line took power by a short cut far across country. It worked gold mines, it lit towns, and hauled trains and drove machinery somewhere out beyond. The power station was in the town ten miles on the other side of his father's place and the great line simply jumped right over them without stopping.

André filled the empty spaces in his life by imagining things. Often he was a jet plane and roared around the house and along the paths with his arms outspread. He saw an Everest film once and for a long time he was Hillary or Tensing,[3] or both, conquering a mountain. There were no mountains so he conquered the roof of the house which wasn't very high and was made of red-painted tin. But he reached the summit and planted a flag on the lightning conductor. When he got down his mother hit his legs with a quince switch for being naughty.

Another time he conquered the koppie. It took him the whole afternoon to get there

1. **veld** (velt) *n.*: Open grassy country with few bushes and almost no trees.
2. **koppie** (käp' ē) *n.*: In South Africa, a small hill.

3. **Hillary** (hil' ər ē) or **Tensing** (ten ziŋ): Sir Edmund Percival Hillary (1919–   ) and Tenzing Norgay, the first two men to climb to the top of Mt. Everest and return.

and back and it was not as exciting as he expected, being less steep than it looked from a distance, so he did not need his rope and pick. Also, he found a cow had beaten him to the summit.

He thought of conquering one of the powerline towers. It had everything, the danger especially, and studying it from all sides he guessed he could make the summit without touching a live wire.[4] But he was not as disobedient as all that, and he knew if he so much as went inside the barbed-wire fence his mother would skin him with the quince, not to mention his father. There were peaks which had to remain unconquered.

4. live wire: A wire with electricity running through it, which is potentially dangerous to touch.

He used to lie and listen to the marvelous hum of the powerline, the millions of volts flowing invisible and beyond all one's ideas along the copper wires that hung so smooth and light from ties of crinkled white china looking like chinese lanterns up against the sky. Faint cracklings and murmurs and rushes of sound would sometimes come from the powerline, and at night he was sure he saw soft blue flames lapping and trembling on the wires as if they were only half peeping out of that fierce river of volts. The flames danced and their voices chattered to him of a mystery.

In the early morning when the mist was rising and the first sun's rays were shooting underneath it, the powerline sparkled like a tremendous spiderweb. It took his thoughts away into a magical distance, far—far off among gigantic machines and busy factories. That was where the world opened up. So he loved the powerline dearly. It made a door through the distance for his thoughts. It was like him except that it never slept, and while he was dreaming it went on without stopping, crackling faintly and murmuring. Its electricity hauled up the mine skips[5] from the heart of the earth, hurtled huge green rail units along their shining lines, and thundered day and night in the factories.

Now that the veld's green was darkening and gathering black-and-gold tints from the ripe seeds and withering grass blades, now that clear warm autumn days were coming after the summer thunderstorms, the birds began gathering on the powerline. At evening he would see the wires like necklaces of blue-and-black glass beads when the swallows gathered. It took them days and days, it seemed, to make up their minds. He did not know whether the same swallows collected each evening in growing numbers or whether a batch went off each day to be replaced by others. He did not know enough about them. He loved to hear them making excited twittering sounds, he loved to see how they simply fell off the copper wire into space and their perfect curved wings lifted them on the air.

They were going not merely beyond the skyline like the power, they were flying thousands of miles over land and sea and mountains and forests to countries he had never dreamed of. They would fly over Everest, perhaps, they would see ships below them on blue seas among islands, they would build nests under bridges and on chimneys where other boys in funny clothes would watch them. The birds opened another door for him and he liked them too, very much.

He watched the swallows one morning as they took off from their perch. Suddenly, as if they had a secret signal, a whole stretch of them along a wire would start together. They dropped forward into the air and their blue-and-white wings flicked out. Flying seemed to be the easiest thing in the world. They swooped and flew up, crisscrossing in flight and chirping crazily, so pleased to be awake in the morning. Then another flight of them winged off, and another. There was standing-room only on those wires. Close to the lofty pylon and the gleaming china ties another flight took off. But one of the swallows stayed behind, quite close to the tie. André watched them fall forward, but it alone did not leave the line. It flapped its wings and he saw it was caught by its leg.

He should have been going to school but he stood watching the swallow, his cap pulled over his white hair and eyes wrinkled against the light. After a minute the swallow stopped flapping and hung there. He wondered how it could have got caught, maybe in the wire binding or at a join. Swallows had short legs and small black claws; he had caught one once in its nest and held it in his hands before it struggled free and was gone in a flash. He thought the bird on the powerline would get free soon, but looking at it there he had a tingling kind of pain in his chest and in one leg as if he too were caught by the foot. André wanted to rush back and tell his mother, only she would scold him for being late to school. So he climbed on his bike, and with one more look up at the helpless bird there against the sky and the steel

5. mine skips: Small, open carts in which miners and materials travel up and down mine shafts.

framework of the tower, he rode off to the bus.

At school he thought once or twice about the swallow, but mostly he forgot about it and that made him feel bad. Anyway, he thought, it would be free by the time he got home. Twisting and flapping a few times, it was sure to work its foot out; and there was no need for him to worry about it hanging there.

Coming back from the crossroads he felt anxious, but he did not like to look up until he was quite near. Then he shot one glance at the top of the pylon—the swallow was still there, its wings spread but not moving. It was dead, he guessed, as he stopped and put down one foot. Then he saw it flutter and fold up its wings. He felt awful to think it had hung there all day, trapped. The boy went in and called his mother and they stood off some distance below the powerline and looked at the bird. The mother shaded her eyes with her hand. It was a pity, she said, but really she was sure it would free itself somehow. Nothing could be done about it.

"Couldn't—?" he began.

"Couldn't nothing, dear," she said quite firmly so that he knew she meant business. "Now stop thinking about it, and tomorrow you'll see."

His father came home at six and had tea, and afterwards there was a little time to work in his patch of vegetables out at the back. André followed him and he soon got round to the swallow on the powerline.

"I know," his father said. "Mama told me."

"It's still there."

"Well—" his father tilted up his old working-hat and looked at him hard with his sharp blue eyes "—well, we can't do anything about it, can we, now?"

"No, Papa, but—"

"But what?"

He kicked at a stone and said nothing more. He could see his father was kind of stiff about it; that meant he did not want to hear anything more. They had been talking about it, and maybe—yes, that was it. They were afraid he would try to climb up the pylon.

At supper none of them talked about the swallow, but André felt it all right. He felt as if it was hanging above their heads and his mother and father felt it and they all had a load on them. Going to bed his mother said to him he must not worry himself about the poor bird. "Not a sparrow falls without our Good Lord knowing."

"It's not a sparrow, it's a swallow," he said. "It's going to hang there all night, by its foot." His mother sighed and put out the light. She was worried.

The next day was a Saturday and he did not have to go to school. First thing he looked out and the bird was still there. The other swallows were with it, and when they took off it fluttered and made little thin calls but could not get free.

He would rather have been at school instead of knowing all day that it was hanging up there on the cruel wire. It was strange how the electricity did nothing to it. He knew, of course, that the wires were quite safe as long as you did not touch anything else. The morning was very long, though he did forget about the swallow quite often. He was building a mud fort under the gum tree, and he had to carry water and dig up the red earth and mix it into a stiff clay. When he was coming in at midday with his khaki hat flapping round his face he had one more look and what he saw kept him standing there a long time with his mouth open. Other swallows were fluttering and hovering around the trapped bird, trying to help it. He rushed inside and dragged his mother out by her hand and she stood too, shading her eyes again and looking up.

"Yes, they're feeding it. Isn't that strange," she said.

"Sssh! Don't frighten them," he whispered.

In the afternoon he lay in the grass and twice again he saw the other swallows fluttering round the fastened bird with short quivering strokes of their wings and opening their beaks wide. Swallows had pouches in their throats where they made small mud bricks to build their nests, and that was how they brought food to it. They knew how to feed their fledglings and when the trapped bird squeaked and cried out they brought it food. André felt choked thinking how they helped it and nobody else would do anything. His parents would not even talk about it.

With his keen eyes he traced the way a climber could get up the tower. Most difficult would be to get round the barbed-wire screens about a quarter of the way up. After that there were footholds in the steel lattice supports. He had studied it before. But if you did get up, what then? How could you touch the swallow? Just putting your hand near the wire, wouldn't those millions of volts flame out and jump at you? The only thing was to get somebody to turn off the power for a minute, then he could whip up the tower like a monkey. At supper that night he suggested it, and his father was as grim and angry as he'd ever been.

"Crumbs," André said to himself. "Crumbs! They are both het up about it."

"Listen, son," his father had said. He never said "son" unless he was really mad over something. "Listen, I don't want you to get all worked up about that bird. I'll see what can be done. But you leave it alone. Don't get any ideas into your head, and don't go near that pylon."

"What ideas, Papa?" he asked, trembling inside himself.

"Any ideas at all."

"The other birds are feeding it, but it may die."

"Well, I'm sorry; try not to think about it."

When his mother came to say goodnight to him he turned his face over into his pillow and would not kiss her. It was something he had never done before and it was because he was angry with them both. They let the swallow swing there in the night and did nothing.

His mother patted his back and ruffled his white hair and said, "Goodnight, darling." But he gritted his teeth and did not answer.

Ages seemed to him to have passed. On Sunday the bird was still hanging on the lofty powerline, fluttering feebly. He could not bear to look up at it. After breakfast he went out and tried to carry on building his fort under the gum tree. The birds were chattering in the tree above him and in the wattles[6] at the back of the house. Through the corner of his eye he saw a handsome black-and-white bird fly out in swinging loops from the tree and it settled on the powerline some distance from the tower. It was a butcher-bird, a Jackey-hangman, a terrible greedy pirate of a bird. His heart fell like a stone—he just guessed what it was up to. It sat there on the wire impudently copying the calls of other birds. It could imitate a toppie or a robin or a finch as it liked. It stole their naked little kickers from their nests and spiked them on the barbed wire to eat at pleasure, as it stole their songs too. The butcher-bird flew off and settled higher up the wire near the pylon.

André rushed up the path and then took a swing from the house to come under the powerline. Stopping, he saw the other birds were making a whirl and flutter round the cannibal. Swallows darted and skimmed and made him duck his head, but he went on

6. wattles (wät′ 'lz) *n.*: Frameworks or piles of sticks, branches, etc.

BIRDS IN THE SKY
Joseph Raffael
Collection of Mrs. Glenn C. Janss

sitting there. Then some starlings came screaming out of the gum tree and flew in a menacing bunch at the butcher-bird. They all hated him. He made the mistake of losing his balance and fluttered out into the air and all the birds were round him at once, darting and pecking and screaming.

The butcher-bird pulled off one of his typical tricks: he fell plumb down and when near the ground spread his wings, sailed low over the shrubs, and came up at the house where he settled on the lightning conductor. André stood panting and felt his heart beating fast. He wanted to throw a stone at the butcher-bird but he reckoned the stone would land on the roof and get him in trouble. So he ran towards the house waving his arms and shouting. The bird cocked its head and watched him.

His mother came out. "Darling, what's the matter?"

"That Jackey, he's on the roof. He wanted to kill the swallow."

"Oh, darling!" the mother said softly.

It was Sunday night and he said to his mother, "It's only the other birds keeping him alive. They were feeding him again today."

"I saw them."

"He can't live much longer, Mama. And now the Jackey knows he's there. Why can't Papa get them to switch off the electricity?"

"They wouldn't do it for a bird, darling. Now try and go to sleep."

Leaving for school on Monday, he tried not to look up. But he couldn't help it and there was the swallow spreading and closing its wings. He quickly got on his bike and rode as fast as he could. He could not think of anything but the trapped bird on the powerline.

After school, André did not catch the bus home. Instead he took a bus the other way, into town. He got out in a busy street and threading down through the factory area he kept his bearings on the four huge smokestacks of the power station. Out of two of the smokestacks white plumes were rising calmly into the clear sky. When he got to the power station he was faced with an enormous high fence of iron staves with spiked tops and a tall steel gate, locked fast. He peered through the gate and saw some black men off duty, sitting in the sun on upturned boxes playing some kind of drafts game. He called them, and a big slow-moving man in brown overalls and a wide leather belt came over to talk.

André explained very carefully what he wanted. If they would switch off the current then he or somebody good at climbing could go up and save the swallow. The man smiled broadly and clicked his tongue. He shouted something at the others and they laughed. His name, he said, was Gas—Gas Makabeni. He was just a maintenance boy and he couldn't switch off the current. But he unlocked a steel frame-door in the gate and let André in.

"Ask them in there," he said, grinning. André liked Gas very much. He had ESCOM in big cloth letters on his back and he was friendly, opening the door like that. André went with Gas through a high arched entrance and at once he seemed to be surrounded with the vast awesome hum of the power station. It made him feel jumpy. Gas took him to a door and pushed him in. A white engineer in overalls questioned him and he smiled too.

"Well," he said. "Let's see what can be done."

He led him down a long corridor and up a short cut of steel zigzag steps. Another corridor came to an enormous paneled hall with banks of dials and glowing lights and men in long white coats sitting in raised chairs or moving about silently. André's heart was pounding good and fast. He could hear the humming sound strongly and it seemed to come from everywhere, not so much a sound as a feeling under his feet.

The engineer in overalls handed him over to one of the men at the control panels and he was so nervous by this time he took a long while trying to explain about the swallow. The man had to ask him a lot of questions and he got tongue-tied and could not give clear answers. The man did not smile at all. He went off and a minute later came and fetched André to a big office. A black-haired man with glasses was sitting at a desk. On both sides of the desk were telephones and panels of push-buttons. There was a carpet on the floor and huge leather easy chairs. The whole of one wall was a large and exciting circuit map with flickering colored lights showing where the power was going all over the country.

André did not say five words before his lip began trembling and two tears rolled out of his eyes. The man told him, "Sit down, son, and don't be scared."

Then the man tried to explain. How could they cut off the power when thousands and thousands of machines were running on electricity? He pointed with the back of his pencil at the circuit map. If there were a shutdown the power would have to be rerouted, and that meant calling in other power stations and putting a heavy load on the lines. Without current for one minute the trains would stop, hospitals would go dark in the middle of an operation, the mine skips would suddenly halt twelve thousand feet down. He knew André was worried about the swallow, only things like that just happened and that was life.

"Life?" André said, thinking it was more like death.

The big man smiled. He took down the boy's name and address, and he said, "You've done your best, André. I'm sorry I can't promise you anything."

Downstairs again, Gas Makabeni let him out at the gate. "Are they switching off the power?" Gas asked.

"No."

"Mayi babo!"[7] Gas shook his head and clicked. But he did not smile this time. He could see the boy was very unhappy.

André got home hours late and his mother was frantic. He lied to her too, saying he had been detained after school. He kept his eyes away from the powerline and did not have the stomach to look for the swallow. He felt so bad about it because they were all letting it die. Except for the other swallows that brought it food it would be dead already.

And that was life, the man said. . . .

It must have been the middle of the night when he woke up. His mother was in the room and the light was on.

"There's a man come to see you," she said. "Did you ask anyone to come here?"

"No, Mama," he said, dazed.

"Get up and come." She sounded cross and he was scared stiff. He went out on to the stoep[8] and there he saw his father in his pajamas and the back of a big man in brown

---

7. *"Mayi babo!"* (mä′ yē bä′ bō): An expression of concern.

8. stoep (sto͞op) *n.*: A stoop, a small porch or platform with steps at the entrance of a house.

overalls with ESCOM on them: a black man. It was Gas Makabeni!

"Gas!" he shouted. "Are they going to do it?"

"They're doing it," Gas said.

A linesman and a truck driver came up the steps on the stoep. The lineman explained to André's father a maintenance switch-down had been ordered at minimum-load hour. He wanted to be shown where the bird was. André glanced, frightened, at his father who nodded and said, "Show him."

He went in the maintenance truck with the man and the driver and Gas. It took them only five minutes to get the truck in position under the tower. The maintenance man checked the time and they began running up the extension ladder. Gas hooked a chain in his broad belt and pulled on his flashlight helmet. He swung out on the ladder and began running up it as if he had no weight at all. Up level with the pylon insulators, his flashlight picked out the swallow hanging on the dead wire. He leaned over and carefully worked the bird's tiny claw loose from the wire binding and then he put the swallow in the breast pocket of his overalls.

In a minute he was down again and he took the bird out and handed it to the boy. André could see even in the light of the flashlamp that the swallow had faint grey fringes round the edges of its shining blue-black feathers and that meant it was a young bird. This was its first year. He was almost speechless, holding the swallow in his hands and feeling its slight quiver.

"Thanks," he said. "Thanks, Gas. Thanks, sir."

His father took the swallow from him at the house and went off to find a box to keep it out of reach of the cats.

"Off you go to bed now," the mother said. "You've had quite enough excitement for one day."

The swallow drank thirstily but would not eat anything, so the parents thought it best to let it go as soon as it would fly. André took the box to his fort near the gum tree and looked towards the koppie and the powerline. It was early morning and dew sparkled on the overhead wires and made the whole level veld gleam like a magic inland sea. He held the swallow in his cupped hands and it lay there quiet with the tips of its wings crossed. Suddenly it took two little jumps with its tiny claws and spread its slender wings. Frantically they beat the air. The bird seemed to be dropping to the ground. Then it skimmed forward only a foot above the grass.

He remembered long afterwards how, when it really took wing and began to gain height, it gave a little shiver of happiness, as if it knew it was free.

Reader's Response

Put yourself in André's shoes. What thoughts and feelings would you have when you release the swallow?

RESPONDING TO THE SELECTION

Your Response

1. Do you think "Power" is a good title for this story? Why or why not?
2. What characters do you like? Which do you dislike? Explain.

Recalling

3. Why does André like both the power lines and the birds that gather on them?
4. How do André's mother and father react to André's concern for the trapped bird?
5. Describe the events that lead to the power company's freeing the bird.

Interpreting

6. How is André affected by his surroundings and his way of life?
7. The birds band together to protect and feed the trapped swallow. What effect do these actions have on André? How do they contrast with the actions of the people in the story?
8. At the power plant, André is told that the swallow's predicament was just "life." Why does this statement upset André?
9. The title of the story suggests several kinds of power. What are they?

Applying

10. Why do some people feel the need to help those who are unable to help themselves?

ANALYZING LITERATURE

Recognizing Symbols

A **symbol** is something that has meaning beyond itself. When a writer repeats or emphasizes an image in a story, you may suspect that it is a symbol. In this story both the power lines and the birds serve as symbols.

1. By helping André imagine a world of "gigantic machines and busy factories" and places "he had never dreamed of," both the power lines and the birds symbolize a larger world outside of André's limited world. Why are these two objects good symbols of a larger world?
2. A third symbol might be the trapped swallow, which symbolizes André. In what ways is André, like the swallow, trapped in his world? In what other ways is André like the swallow?
3. What symbol would you use for yourself? You may share your answer with your classmates or keep it private.

CRITICAL THINKING AND READING

Relating Symbols to Theme

Symbols in a story take their meaning from the context of the story. Symbols are often related to theme. You might conclude, then, that a theme in "Power" is that all creatures, no matter how young or small, deserve freedom.

1. If you were to write another story to illustrate this theme, what symbols would you use?
2. Think of a theme from another story you have read. What symbols would be appropriate to illustrate that theme?

THINKING AND WRITING

Writing About the Word *Power*

What are some of the meanings that the word power has for you? Write "power" at the top of a sheet of paper and freewrite about the kinds of power in your life. Over whom or what do you have power? Who or what has power over you? Look over your freewriting and choose one kind of power to write about. Circle the words and phrases that best describe what this kind of power means. Write the first draft of a paragraph about this particular meaning of the word. Begin with your definition of the word. Give examples of the power you describe. Revise your paragraph and prepare a final draft.

Writing About Theme

Good stories make readers think. For example, did "The Circuit" make you feel good about "belonging" to a school or a group of friends? As you finished reading "The All-American Slurp," did you wonder if people all over the world are really alike? Stories with strong themes make us think and feel.

Themes are not just "morals to the story" or advice about life. A theme is not meant to teach a lesson. However, a theme does help you reach understandings about or gain insights into life. For example, one reader might write the theme of "The Circuit" as "Moving around is difficult on children, especially once they go to school." This is not a lesson, but it is an idea about the experience of packing up and moving often. The events of the story led the reader to this idea.

The answer to the question, "What is this story's theme?" is not easy and quick, and there is never just one right answer. Different readers may see different themes in the same story. After you read, study, and discuss a short story, you can write about *your* idea of what its theme might be.

Your Turn

You've just gotten a letter from a friend who has moved to another state. The letter asks you to do a favor:

"My teacher wants us to pick out a good short story for a special project. I'm tired of reading stories that don't have anything to do with my life. I'm looking for a good story with ideas that mean something to *me*. Do you have any suggestions? Please write and suggest a story that will really make me think, one that has meant something to you."

Prewriting

1. Review the stories you've read. Jot down titles of the ones that have meant something to you. Ask yourself which stories you would recommend to a friend.

2. Choose three or four stories as possible subjects. As you think about these stories, ask yourself what they meant to you and what their themes might be.

3. Freewrite to explore your ideas about each story. It may help to answer one of the following questions: What does this story say about human nature? What idea does the writer share about a certain kind of experience? Here's an example of one student's freewriting:

> "Power" was one of the best stories I ever read about being true to yourself. I want to act independently, but sometimes I don't know what to do. I feel like André, that I have to do what adults tell me. It's hard to make decisions on my own. But this story says that you can

```
trust yourself. You don't have to
depend on others. You can make
things happen if you care and if
you want to.
```

4. Choose a topic. Read all of your freewriting. Which story do you feel most strongly about? Choose the story that you will recommend in your letter. Try to write what you think is the theme of the story in one or two sentences.

Drafting

Draft your letter. Write honestly and clearly about what this story meant to *you*.

When writing about literature, use the present tense, as if the story is happening now. For example, write "André *goes* to the power station," not "André *went* to the power station."

The student whose freewriting you saw drafted her letter as follows:

```
     I know just what you mean.
It's hard to make yourself read
stories that aren't interesting.
My recommendation is a story by
Jack Cope called "Power." It's a
story about taking risks, so I
think you will like it. You know
how a lot of stories are sweet
and have happy endings? Well,
this story makes me realize that
good stories can be about hard
choices in life, too, like acting
on what you believe, despite the
risks. In the end, it is a happy
story, and it makes me feel I'm
strong enough to do what I
believe in.
```

Notice how some of this writer's ideas came straight from her freewriting, and how other sentences build on those first, general thoughts.

Notice, too, that the student does not tell what happens in the story. Instead, she writes about the story's *meaning* and what it made her think about—it made her feel she could take risks. These ideas—that the story is really about acting on your beliefs, that risk-taking, though scary sometimes, can bring positive results—are statements about the story's theme.

Revising

Use the revising checklist on page 749 to evaluate and revise your own draft. In addition, ask someone you trust to read your letter and answer two or three questions such as these:

- Does my letter show what I think is the theme of this story?
- Does my letter make you want to read the story? Why or why not?
- Is each of my sentences clear and easy to read? If not, which need to be revised?

Proofreading

Use the proofreading guidelines on page 753 to proofread your letter. Make sure that you use quotation marks around the title of a story.

READING AND RESPONDING

The Short Story

Are you an active or a passive reader? As an active reader, you become involved with a story. You think about how the elements of plot, character, setting, and theme work together to create the story. As you read, you respond to the elements of the story. You follow the development of the plot. You feel sympathy or joy for the characters. You imagine the setting, and try to find meaning in the theme, or message of the story.

RESPONDING TO PLOT The plot is what happens in a short story. The events in the plot center on a conflict, or struggle, between opposing forces. By carefully following the plot, you will be able to make connections and predictions about the story. When you respond to the plot, you are simply telling how the story affected you.

RESPONDING TO CHARACTERS Characters are the people and sometimes the animals in a story. Like real people, characters have traits and personalities that determine the way they behave. They think and feel just as real people think and feel. Respond to the characters by letting yourself identify with them: Share their feelings and emotions, compare your own ideas with theirs, and think about what you would do in their place.

RESPONDING TO SETTING Setting is the time and the place in which the events in a story occur. The time might be in the past or in the future, and it might cover a minute or a span of years. The place might be a foreign country or someone's backyard. As you read actively, respond to the author's details about the setting. What kind of atmosphere or mood does the author create? How does the setting affect the plot and the characters? How does it affect you?

RESPONDING TO THEME Theme is the general idea about life presented in a story. It is what the story means to you. As you read, you will notice how the author has constructed the story to reveal the theme. Does the main character learn something about life? Is the theme stated or is it implied through the events and the characters? What does this story say to you?

Kristen Currise, a sixth-grader from Carmel, Indiana, actively read and responded to the story "The Sound of Summer Running," pages 183–190. The notes in the side column show Kristen's thoughts and comments while reading. Remember each reader has different responses to a story. Don't be surprised if yours are different from Kristen's.

The Sound of Summer Running
from *Dandelion Wine*
Ray Bradbury

Theme: *The title gives a clue about what the story may be about.*

"The magic was always in the new pair of shoes."

Late that night, going home from the show with his mother and father and his brother Tom, Douglas saw the tennis shoes in the bright store window. He glanced quickly away, but his ankles were seized, his feet suspended, then rushed. The earth spun; the shop awnings slammed their canvas wings overhead with the thrust of his body running. His mother and father and brother walked quietly on both sides of him. Douglas walked backward, watching the tennis shoes in the midnight window left behind.

Character: *The main character is Douglas, who seems very intrigued by the shoes.*

"It was a nice movie," said Mother.

Douglas murmured, "It was . . ."

It was June and long past time for buying the special shoes that were quiet as a summer rain falling on the walks. June and the earth full of raw power and everything everywhere in motion. The grass was still pouring in from the country, surrounding the sidewalks, stranding the houses. Any moment the town would capsize, go down and leave not a stir in the clover and weeds. And here Douglas stood, trapped on the dead cement and the red-brick streets, hardly able to move.

Setting: *June in a town.*

"Dad!" He blurted it out. "Back there in that window, those Cream-Sponge Para Litefoot Shoes . . ."

His father didn't even turn. "Suppose you tell me why you need a new pair of sneakers. Can you do that?"

"Well . . ."

Plot: *The author uses very powerful words and phrases to explain how important the shoes are to him. He paints a very clear picture.*

It was because they felt the way it feels every summer when you take off your shoes for the first time and run in the grass. They felt like it feels sticking your feet out of the hot covers in wintertime to let the cold wind from the open window blow on them suddenly and you let them stay out a long time until you pull them back in under the covers again to feel them, like packed snow. The tennis shoes felt like it always feels the first time every year wading in the slow waters of the creek and seeing your feet below, half an inch further downstream, with refraction, than the real part of you above water.

"Dad," said Douglas, "it's hard to explain."

Somehow the people who made tennis shoes knew what boys needed and wanted. They put marshmallows and coiled springs in the soles and they wove the rest out of grasses bleached and fired in the wilderness. Somewhere deep in the soft loam of the shoes the thin hard sinews of the buck deer were hidden. The people that made the shoes must have watched a lot of winds blow the trees and a lot of rivers going down to the lakes. Whatever it was, it was in the shoes, and it was summer.

Douglas tried to get all this in words.

Plot: *His dad won't buy him the shoes he desperately wants.*

"Yes," said Father, "but what's wrong with last year's sneakers? Why can't you dig *them* out of the closet?"

Well, he felt sorry for boys who lived in California where they wore tennis shoes all year and never knew what it was to get winter off your feet, peel off the iron leather shoes all full of snow and rain and run barefoot for a day and then lace on the first new tennis shoes of the season, which was better than barefoot. The magic was always in the new pair of shoes. The magic might die by the first of September, but now in late June there was still plenty of magic, and shoes like these could jump you over trees and rivers and houses. And if you wanted, they could jump you over fences and sidewalks and dogs.

"Don't you see?" said Douglas. "I just *can't* use last year's pair."

For last year's pair were dead inside. They had been fine when he started them out, last year. But by the end of summer, every year, you always found out, you always knew, you couldn't really jump over rivers and trees and houses in them, and they were dead. But this was a new year, and he felt that this time, with this new pair of shoes, he could do anything, anything at all.

They walked up on the steps to their house. "Save your money," said Dad. "In five or six weeks—"

"Summer'll be over!"

Lights out, with Tom asleep, Douglas lay watching his feet, far away down there at the end of the bed in the moonlight, free of the heavy iron shoes, the big chunks of winter fallen away from them.

"Reason. I've got to think of reasons for the shoes."

Well, as anyone knew, the hills around town were wild with friends putting cows to riot, playing barometer to the atmospheric changes, taking sun, peeling like calendars each day to take more sun. To catch those friends, you must run much faster than foxes or squirrels. As for the town, it steamed with enemies grown irritable with heat, so remembering every winter argument and insult. *Find friends, ditch enemies!* That was the Cream-Sponge Para Litefoot motto. *Does the world run too fast? Want to catch up? Want to be alert, stay alert? Litefoot, then! Litefoot!*

Character: *During this time, he's thinking of reasons he needs the shoes. This shows that Douglas is very smart and fast-thinking.*

He held his coin bank up and heard the faint small tinkling, the airy weight of money there.

Whatever you want, he thought, you got to make your own way. During the night now, let's find that path through the forest. . . .

Plot: *What is he going to do to get the shoes?*

Downtown, the store lights went out, one by one. A wind blew in the window. It was like a river going downstream and his feet wanting to go with it.

In his dreams he heard a rabbit running running running in the deep warm grass.

Character: *I think Mr. Sanderson will help make Douglas's dream come true.*

Plot: *This seems to be the climax of the story—Douglas goes into the shoe store.*

Old Mr. Sanderson moved through his shoe store as the proprietor of a pet shop must move through his shop where are kenneled animals from everywhere in the world, touching each one briefly along the way. Mr. Sanderson brushed his hands over the shoes in the window, and some of them were like cats to him and some were like dogs; he touched each pair with concern, adjusting laces, fixing tongues. Then he stood in the exact center of the carpet and looked around, nodding.

There was a sound of growing thunder.

One moment, the door to Sanderson's Shoe Emporium was empty. The next, Douglas Spaulding stood clumsily there, staring down at his leather shoes as if these heavy things could not be pulled up out of the cement. The thunder had stopped when his shoes stopped. Now, with painful slowness, daring to look only at the money in his cupped hand, Douglas moved out of the bright sunlight of Saturday noon. He made careful stacks of nickels, dimes, and quarters on the counter, like someone playing chess and worried if the next move carried him out into sun or deep into shadow.

"Don't say a word!" said Mr. Sanderson.

Douglas froze.

"First, I know just what you want to buy," said Mr. Sanderson. "Second, I see you every afternoon at my window; you think I don't see? You're wrong. Third, to give it its full name, you want the Royal Crown Cream-Sponge Para Litefoot Tennis Shoes: 'LIKE MENTHOL ON YOUR FEET!' Fourth, you want credit."

"No!" cried Douglas, breathing hard, as if he'd run all night in his dreams. "I got something better than credit to offer!" he gasped. "Before I tell, Mr. Sanderson, you got to do me one small favor. Can you remember when was the last time you yourself wore a pair of Litefoot sneakers, sir?"

Mr. Sanderson's face darkened. "Oh, ten, twenty, say, thirty years ago. Why . . . ?"

"Mr. Sanderson, don't you think you owe it to your customers, sir, to at least try the tennis shoes you sell, for just one minute, so you know how they feel? People forget if they don't keep testing things. United Cigar Store man smokes cigars, don't he? Candy-store man samples his own stuff, I should think. So . . ."

NEW SHOES FOR H
Don Eddy
The Cleveland Museum of Art

"You may have noticed," said the old man, "I'm wearing shoes."

"But not sneakers, sir! How you going to sell sneakers unless you can rave about them and how you going to rave about them unless you know them?"

Mr. Sanderson backed off a little distance from the boy's fever, one hand to his chin. "Well . . ."

"Mr. Sanderson," said Douglas, "you sell me something and I'll sell you something just as valuable."

"Is it absolutely necessary to the sale that I put on a pair of the sneakers, boy?" said the old man.

"I sure wish you could, sir!"

The old man sighed. A minute later, seated panting quietly, he laced the tennis shoes to his long narrow feet. They looked detached and alien down there next to the dark cuffs of his business suit. Mr. Sanderson stood up.

Character: *I'm not sure Mr. Sanderson likes these sneakers.*

"How do they *feel*?" asked the boy.

"How do they feel, he asks; they feel fine." He started to sit down.

"Please!" Douglas held out his hand. "Mr. Sanderson, now could you kind of rock back and forth a little, sponge around, bounce kind of, while I tell you the rest? It's this: I give you my money, you give me the shoes, I owe you a dollar. But, Mr. Sanderson, *but*—soon as I get those shoes on, you know what *happens*?"

"What?"

Theme: *Maybe the theme has to do with doing things for yourself.*

"Bang! I deliver your packages, pick up packages, bring you coffee, burn your trash, run to the post office, telegraph office, library! You'll see twelve of me in and out, in and out, every minute. Feel those shoes, Mr. Sanderson, *feel* how fast they'd take me? All those springs inside? Feel all the running inside? Feel how they kind of grab hold and can't let you alone and don't like you just *standing* there? Feel how quick I'd be doing the things you'd rather not bother with? You stay in the nice cool store while I'm jumping all around town! But it's not me really, it's the shoes. They're going like mad down alleys, cutting corners, and back! There they go!"

Mr. Sanderson stood amazed with the rush of words. When the words got going the flow carried him; he began to sink deep in the shoes, to flex his toes, limber his arches, test his ankles. He rocked softly, secretly, back and forth in a small breeze from the open door. The tennis shoes silently hushed themselves deep in the carpet, sank as in a jungle grass, in loam and resilient clay. He gave one solemn bounce of his heels in the yeasty dough, in the yielding and welcoming earth. Emotions hurried over his face as if many colored lights had been switched on and off. His mouth hung slightly open. Slowly he gentled and rocked himself to a halt, and the boy's voice faded and they stood there looking at each other in a tremendous and natural silence.

Character: *Douglas has succeeded in getting Mr. Sanderson to understand how important the shoes are to him.*

A few people drifted by on the sidewalk outside, in the hot sun.

Still the man and boy stood there, the boy glowing, the man with revelation in his face.

"Boy," said the old man at last, "in five years, how would you like a job selling shoes in this emporium?"

"Gosh, thanks, Mr. Sanderson, but I don't know what I'm going to be yet."

"Anything you want to be, son," said the old man, "you'll be. No one will ever stop you."

Theme: *You can be anything you want, if you work at it.*

The old man walked lightly across the store to the wall of ten thousand boxes, came back with some shoes for the boy, and wrote up a list on some paper while the boy was lacing the shoes on his feet and then standing there, waiting.

The old man held out his list. "A dozen things you got to do for me this afternoon. Finish them, we're even Stephen, and you're fired."

Plot: *Old Mr. Sanderson lets Douglas work to pay off the shoes.*

"Thanks, Mr. Sanderson!" Douglas bounded away.

"Stop!" cried the old man.

Douglas pulled up and turned.

Mr. Sanderson leaned forward. "How do they *feel*?"

The boy looked down at his feet deep in the rivers, in the fields of wheat, in the wind that already was rushing him out of the town. He looked up at the old man, his eyes burning, his mouth moving, but no sound came out.

"Antelopes?" said the old man, looking from the boy's face to his shoes. "Gazelles?"

The boy thought about it, hesitated, and nodded a quick nod. Almost immediately he vanished. He just spun about with a whisper and went off. The door stood empty. The sound of the tennis shoes faded in the jungle heat.

Mr. Sanderson stood in the sun-blazed door, listening. From a long time ago, when he dreamed as a boy, he remembered the sound. Beautiful creatures leaping under the sky, gone through brush, under trees, away, and only the soft echo their running left behind.

"Antelopes," said Mr. Sanderson. "Gazelles."

He bent to pick up the boy's abandoned winter shoes, heavy with forgotten rains and long-melted snows. Moving out of the blazing sun, walking softly, lightly, slowly, he headed back toward civilization. . . .

Response: *I'm impressed with Douglas. He seems to be the type of person who is willing to work for what he wants. This story made me think of all the times I've wanted things, but didn't know how to get them.*

Reader's Response

Have you ever wanted something as badly as Douglas wanted the sneakers? Describe your experience.

I would like to be on the basketball team this year. Being picked for the team is important to me, but it's hard work. The fact that Douglas was able to get his sneakers through his own hard work has made me think I can achieve my goal.

Ray Bradbury (1920–) was born in Waukegan, Illinois, and began writing at the age of twelve. His interests in circuses, magic, and the horror stories of Edgar Allan Poe influenced Bradbury's writing. These influences led Bradbury to write classic science-fiction novels such as *Fahrenheit 451* and *The Martian Chronicles.* He is now considered among the world's greatest science-fiction writers. Bradbury's highly imaginative style is evident in all his stories, including the novel *Dandelion Wine*, from which "The Sound of Summer Running" was taken.

Responding to the Selection

Your Response

1. Do you admire Doug? Why or why not?

Recalling

2. In addition to money, what does Douglas offer Mr. Sanderson for the sneakers?

Interpreting

3. Even though his old sneakers are wearable, why does Douglas feel he must have new sneakers?
4. Why does Mr. Sanderson react as he does to wearing the sneakers?
5. Why does Mr. Sanderson say that Douglas can be "anything [he] want[s] to be" when he grows up?
6. Explain the last line of the story. Where has Mr. Sanderson been? What is "civilization"?

Applying

7. Douglas thinks to himself, "Whatever you want, . . . you got to make your own way." Do you agree with this statement? Explain.

Analyzing Literature

Reviewing the Short Story

In a short story, the plot, characters, setting, and theme work together. Think of all these elements and apply them to "The Sound of Summer Running."

1. What conflicts does Douglas experience?
2. What character trait makes Douglas successful in getting the sneakers?
3. Which details of setting, especially the time, are important to the plot?
4. What do you think is the theme?

Critical Thinking and Reading

Appreciating Persuasion

Persuasion is the attempt to convince a listener to accept an opinion or take some action. Douglas uses persuasion to convince Mr. Sanderson to let him pay the final dollar for the sneakers through work.

1. What reason does Douglas give for urging Mr. Sanderson to wear a pair of sneakers?
2. Describe Mr. Sanderson's reaction to wearing the shoes.
3. Which of Douglas's statements were the most convincing to Mr. Sanderson? Support your answer.

Thinking and Writing

Describing an Emotion

In this story the author uses vivid words to paint pictures of the feelings Douglas gets when he thinks about the sneakers. Write a paragraph about an object or a situation and the feelings it brings out in you. First, think of some object or situation that arouses strong feelings in you and freewrite for several minutes about it. Look over your freewriting and circle the words and phrases that best describe your feelings. Use these words and phrases in the first draft of your descriptive paragraph. After you have written the draft, read it aloud. Are there words you might add or change that would make your description more vivid? Revise your composition and prepare a final draft.

Learning Option

Art. To get the sneakers he so desperately wanted, Douglas created a sales campaign to impress Mr. Sanderson. In a small group, invent a new and unusual product. Then, develop a television commercial to sell it. First, think of who would buy your product and why they would buy it. For example, if your product was a baby carriage with square wheels, you might want to sell it to parents who live on steep hills. Next, write a script for your advertisement. Finally, present your ad to the class.

BRIDGING FORMS

BRIDGE TO TERABITHIA
by Katherine Paterson

Meet Jesse and Leslie, two kids as believable as people sitting next to you in class. Meet them in Terabithia, their own world, in a novel that deals with realistic characters and thought-provoking themes. The novel is *Bridge to Terabithia*, by Katherine Paterson.

The two main characters in this novel, Jesse and Leslie, confront challenging questions and situations. The interaction of characters, situations, and ideas is an element that bridges the gap between one form of literature and another. Writers have characters confront challenging situations in novels, just as they do in stories. The difference between the stories and the novel is that you get to know characters in a novel so much better because a novel is longer than a short story.

The Characters

Jesse and Leslie become fast friends in this story about growing up, accepting others, and dealing with tragedy. Leslie, a quick-witted, well-read girl becomes an inspiration to Jesse, a quick-footed, artistic boy. For Leslie, Jesse becomes a partner—someone to count on, someone to listen, someone with whom to share a laugh. Paterson writes about Leslie and Jesse in a way that just might make you feel that you have met a couple of new friends.

Terabithia

Footraces during lunch are traditional at Lark Creek School, but girls winning them are not. Jesse, who wants to prove himself as the fastest runner, and Leslie, the girl courageous enough to enter and who wins the race, develop a friendship that changes both their lives. They build a secret hideout near their homes and call their imaginary kingdom Terabithia. There they share many secrets, stories, and words of wisdom. Leslie

and Jesse invent encounters with enemies, which somehow prepare them for their real encounters at school, where at times they feel they are an army of two against the world.

Eventually, Terabithia becomes a dangerous place—Jesse realizes that it represents many of his fears, and the flooding waters from torrential rains make him uncomfortable about going there. One day he takes a different excursion, into Washington, D.C., with a teacher from school. When he returns, he discovers that the danger associated with Terabithia has led to tragedy. As the novel ends, the meaning of friendship and life, of growing up and facing mysteries that we don't understand confront Jesse—and us.

Themes

When you read *Bridge to Terabithia*, you will notice several important themes, including the importance of friendship and all that it entails. Friendship is as much about accepting another person as it is about giving to another person. Jesse and Leslie both give and take as their relationship develops. They learn to be strong in their convictions, whether the situation in which they find themselves is ridiculous, threatening, or tragic. Another idea explored in this novel is that of possibility. No matter how uproarious, troubled, or miserable our lives may seem, there is always hope and promise for change. Two friends, Leslie and Jesse, give that promise to each other, to their families, and to their friends at school.

Making Connections

In *Bridge to Terabithia*, you will find those special moments when Jesse and Leslie seem to be pushing the limits of their friendship. What can get in the way of being a good friend? Of letting someone else be a good friend to you? Is it fear? Anger? Jealousy? How do Jesse and Leslie resolve these tensions, and how will you resolve them the next time you and a friend clash? Which characters in the short stories do Jesse or Leslie remind you of? Do they remind you of people you know? Through stories and novels like *Bridge to Terabithia*, we can enjoy others in ways that make us laugh, make us cry, and almost always make us think about what is important in life.

FOCUS ON READING

Comparing and Contrasting

You make comparisons and contrasts every day. When you decide what to wear to school, what flavor of ice cream to order, or which television program to watch, you compare and contrast the advantages of one choice over another. When you compare, you look at ways that things are similar. When you contrast, you note ways that things are different.

Writers often use comparisons and contrasts in their writing. These can help you gain better understanding of what you read.

Comparison

In "Mowgli's Brothers" Kipling compares Bagheera the Black Panther directly with several other animals of the jungle:

> Everybody knew Bagheera, and nobody cared to cross his path; for he was as cunning as Tabaqui [the jackal], as bold as the wild buffalo, and as reckless as the wounded elephant.

Writers often use words such as *both, as, similar, just as much,* and *like* to indicate a direct comparison.

Sometimes, however, writers only suggest a comparison. In "Eleven," for example, Rachel compares her feelings and actions indirectly with those of someone of a different age:

> . . . [S]ome days you might say something stupid, and that's the part of you that's still ten. Or maybe some days you might need to sit on your mama's lap because you're scared, and that's the part of you that's five.

Contrast

In "Mowgli's Brothers" Kipling continues his description of Bagheera by contrasting the way he really is and the way he appears:

> But he had a voice as soft as wild honey dripping from a tree, and a skin softer than down.

To show contrasting relationships, writers may use these words:

in contrast	but	although
nevertheless	yet	however
on the other hand	while	whereas

Sometimes contrasts are not stated directly. In "Thunder Butte," for example, the feelings that Norman's parents have about the old ways are contrasted indirectly in these paragraphs.

"John!" Sarah exclaimed as she saw her husband bring the stick into the room. "I told Norman, and I tell you, that I won't have that heathenish thing in the house!"

. . . "This," he [John] said holding the *coup* stick upright, "is a relic of our people's past glory when it was a good thing to be an Indian. It is a symbol of something that shall never be again."

Organizing Comparison and Contrast

You can use a diagram like the following one to organize similarities and differences. This example compares and contrasts the settings in "The King of Mazy May" and "Thunder Butte."

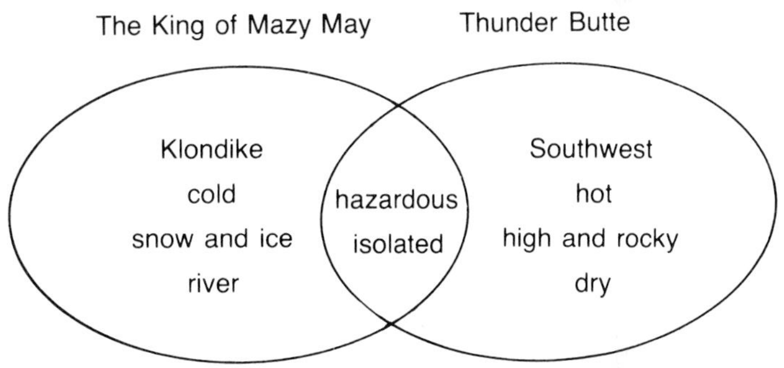

Each circle contains details for one story. The center section, where the two circles overlap, contains the details that the two have in common. These are the details that can be compared. The details in the remaining part of the circles are the details that can be contrasted.

Activity

Choose two characters from stories you have read. Make a diagram comparing and contrasting them. Include details about the characters' physical appearance, as well as traits of character, such as bravery, wickedness, curiosity, selfishness, kindness, and so on.

When you have finished your diagram, write the first draft of a paragraph. Your paragraph may compare the two characters by showing how they are alike. For this, use the details in the overlapping sections of the circles. If you prefer to contrast the characters, use the details in the outer part of the circles. Use words to indicate a comparison relationship or a contrasting relationship.

Writing a Short Story

Sometimes, the best short stories seem very simple. However, good short stories only *seem* simple. They actually take a lot of exploration, observation, planning, time, and revision. But they are worth it. When you thoughtfully and carefully write a story, you create something that no one else could ever have made—no one in the past and no one in the future.

Now you write a short story.

Prewriting

Before you draft do some planning about the following elements.

Narrative Events: What will happen in your story? How much time will pass? What will be the main conflict? Use phrases to jot notes about what will happen first, second, and so on. You may want to create a time line like the one on page 57.

Characters: How many characters will be in your story? It's best to limit the number of characters. Your story should probably have one main character who changes as a result of the action of your story. For each important character, create a cluster diagram like the one on page 91.

Setting: Where will your story take place? What year is it? What time of year, week, or day? Once you've chosen a setting, use a chart such as the one on page 131 to explore specific details.

Theme: You may know what idea your story will illustrate before you begin to write, but don't worry if you're not sure. Theme often grows out of the process of writing a story. You will probably discover meaning in your story that you didn't know was there as you planned your elements.

Stay Flexible! Just because you've made plans before you draft your story doesn't mean that you must follow them exactly. Sometimes a good story can "take off" as you write. Be open to the possibility that your well-made plans might change.

Drafting

Using your prewriting notes, draft your story. As you draft, remember these tips.

1. Use chronological order. Use transitions such as *first*, *then*, *next*, and *later* to show this order.

2. Use dialogue. Don't *tell* your readers about your characters—*show* them by writing their exact words and by describing their actions and gestures.

3. Use description to show your setting. Use sensory details throughout your story to make your reader imagine sight, sound, smell, taste, and touch. Include a comparison for a strong punch.

4. Show how your main character changes as a result of the action of your story. Include your main character's thoughts and feelings in your story so that your reader can get to know him or her well.

Here is one student's opening.

Student's opening	Notes
The snow was heavy and deep. It was	Sensory details
Saturday and Kai Chi wanted to sleep, but	Main character introduced
she had to shovel snow. She put on her boots	
and her coat. Then,	Transition
she grabbed the shovel and headed for Mr. Albright's house.	
"Don't forget your gloves!"	Dialogue
shouted her mother from under her quilt.	
Her mother was lucky; she got to sleep.	Inner thoughts of main character

Notice how this opening creates questions in the reader's mind: "Who is Mr. Albright, and why is Kai Chi shoveling the snow at his house?" Create such suspense early in your story, establish a problem, and show how the character solves the problem.

Revising

Step 1: Use the revising checklist on page 749 to evaluate and revise your draft.

Step 2: Ask someone you trust to read your draft and answer a few questions:

- At what point did my story interest you the most? Why?
- At what point did my story drag or cause you to lose interest?
- What idea did my story make you think about?

Use your reader's comments to think about your story. Can you add more detail or action to make your story more interesting or more exciting? Can you eliminate parts that don't seem to be important or others that seem to drag?

Step 3: Look at each word. Can you make your words more specific? Can you add details? The student who wrote "She put on her boots and her coat" in the sample draft revised the sentence to read "She pulled on her red boots and zipped her parka." These specific details create a more vivid picture in the reader's mind.

Step 4: What is the theme of your finished story? Write three different titles that hint at your theme. Choose the title that will appeal most to your readers' curiosity.

Proofreading

Use the proofreading guidelines on page 753 to proofread your short story.

BOOKSHELF

Here are more books to enjoy. Some of them are collections of short stories. Others are longer works—novels—some by writers of stories in this unit.

VISIONS: Nineteen Short Stories by Outstanding Writers for Young Adults edited by Donald Gallo. Dell Publishing, 1987. These stories include tales of romance, the delights of mystery and fantasy, and the struggles of growing up.

TO BREAK THE SILENCE: Thirteen Short Stories for Young Readers edited by Peter A. Barrett. Dell Publishing, 1986. This collection of short stories has been gathered especially for young readers.

SHORT TAKES: A Short Story Collection for Young Readers selected by Elizabeth Segel. Lothrop, Lee & Shepard Books, 1986. This collection of stories is about young people who learn to deal with problems in the world.

THE JUNGLE BOOK by Rudyard Kipling. Here are more stories of Mowgli and his friends in the jungle—a white seal, an elephant, and a mongoose named Rikki-tikki-tavi.

SONG OF THE TREES by Mildred Taylor. Bantam Books, 1975. This extended story, set in rural Mississippi during the Depression, is based on an incident in the author's family. Her father's description of the giant trees and the coming of the lumbermen impressed her greatly.

DRAGONWINGS by Laurence Yep. Harper & Row, 1975. This novel is the story of Moon Shadow, a young Chinese boy, and his father, Windrider, in San Francisco at the beginning of the twentieth century. Moon Shadow helps Windrider make his dream of a flying machine come true.

THE BIG WAVE by Pearl S. Buck. The John Day Company, 1947. When Jiya loses his entire family in a tidal wave, he goes to live with his friend Kino. Jiya starts life over again and learns to face danger.

UNIT ACTIVITIES

Writing

1. Select one of the stories that you read in class, perhaps one that you were not completely satisfied with. Decide how you would change the story. For instance, you may think it needs a different ending. Rewrite the story as you would like it to be. Share your story with your classmates.

Cooperative Learning

2. Working with a group of your classmates, select a story that you enjoyed, and develop it into a skit. With your group members, write a script. You might wish to use costumes and props to present your skit. Rehearse your parts and present your skit to the class.

Speaking and Listening

3. Prepare an oral report on one of the writers in this unit. Read another work by this author, and do research about the author's life and activities. You might also prepare visuals, such as a poster or pictures, to use when you present your report.

Speaking and Listening

4. Choose a story with more than one character. Put yourself in the place of one of the minor characters. Prepare a monologue retelling the main events as seen by this minor character. You might come to class dressed as that character. Present your monologue to your class. Your classmates may ask you questions, which you should answer as that character.

Cooperative Learning

5. Work with two or three classmates to write a group story. In your planning sessions, create one or more characters, develop a problem, and plan the plot (how the character or characters work out the problem). Decide if you want to emphasize the setting. While you all contribute to the story, one person will act as recorder and put the words on paper. Revise the story together so that you all agree on the final version. Present the story to your classmates.

Creative Response

6. Select a story that you enjoyed in which the setting was important. Construct a diorama of the setting in the story. A diorama is a three-dimensional, miniature scene. Display your diorama in your classroom.

EVENING AT THE MET
David Hockney

DRAMA

Did you know that when you watch television or see a movie you are seeing drama? When we think of drama, we think of stage plays and the exciting world of the theater—actors, costumes, and stage sets. But drama includes more than the theater; television plays and radio plays are drama, too. Even movies are a form of drama. In all these kinds of drama, actors make a world come alive before an audience.

This unit has one play, a play based on the book *The Phantom Tollbooth*. This play contains all the elements of drama—action on stage, characters in costume, lighting, and sound. Now take a journey with Milo and Tock in the imaginary world of *The Phantom Tollbooth*.

How to Read a Play

A play is a story written to be performed by actors before an audience. Like a story, a play has a plot, characters, and settings. The story of the drama is told mainly through dialogue, or conversation between characters. The settings are re-created on stage using scenery and props, the physical objects the characters use. Actors wear costumes to create characters. Sound effects, the planned noises that accompany the play, make action realistic. Each of these devices helps create the world of the play on the stage.

Sometimes novels are made into plays, such as this version of Norton Juster's novel *The Phantom Tollbooth.* Susan Nanus used the same characters and many of the events from Juster's book and adapted them to be performed before an audience.

Although plays are written to be performed, it is possible just to read a play. As you read, you can make the play come alive by staging it in your imagination. When you read a play, you are reading the script, which contains not only the dialogue but also the stage directions. Stage directions tell what the stage looks like, what the characters wear, and where they move.

Stage directions use a particular vocabulary: *Right, left, up, down,* and *center* refer to areas of the stage as the actors see it, not as the audience views it. To help you visualize stage directions, imagine the stage divided into these sections:

THE STAGE

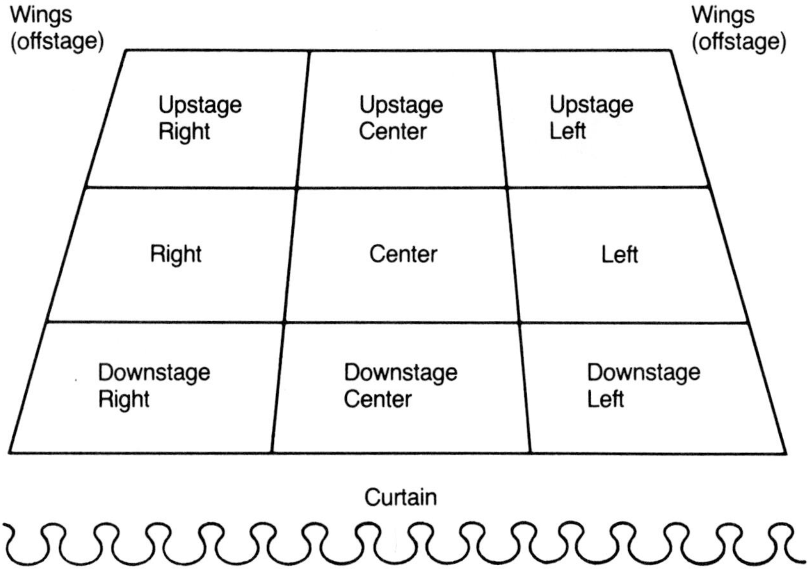

Just as you read short stories actively, you should also read drama actively. Reading actively includes envisioning the play in your mind while you continually question the meaning of what the actors are saying and doing.

Use the following strategies to help you read drama actively. These strategies will help you better understand, appreciate, and enjoy *The Phantom Tollbooth.*

VISUALIZE Use the set descriptions and stage directions to picture the stage and the characters in action. What do their voices sound like? What are they doing? Create the scene in your mind.

QUESTION What else would you like to know, or what is unclear to you? For example, as you meet the characters, ask yourself what each character is like. What situation does each character face? Why do the characters act as they do?

PREDICT Building on what you already know about the characters and events, predict what you think will happen. How will the conflict be resolved? What will become of each character? As you read on, you will see if your predictions are correct.

CLARIFY If anything is unclear to you as you read, pause and try to clarify the problem. For example, if you run into words that you are unfamiliar with, look them up. Or if a character's words or actions are not clear to you, stop and try to make sense of them.

SUMMARIZE Pause occasionally to summarize what you have read. What has happened? What ideas or actions seem important? How does one event relate to another? Try to see how all the pieces of the story fit together.

RESPOND Finally, think about what the play means. How has this play enriched you or added to your understanding of people? What is memorable about the story? What more would you like to know? Did you like the play? Why or why not?

Each active reader will have his or her own questions, predictions, problems to clarify, summaries, and responses. To become a more active reader, you might keep a notebook in which you jot down your questions, predictions, problems, and responses as you read *The Phantom Tollbooth.*

GUIDE FOR READING

Norton Juster

(1929–   ) began his career as an architect. His creative imagination found another outlet when he wrote the highly praised book *The Phantom Tollbooth,* which is the basis for this play.

Susan Nanus has earned several prizes for her writing, including the Christopher Award in 1988. She currently lives in Los Angeles, where she writes scripts for television and movies. Her skill at creating scripts is evident in this play version of *The Phantom Tollbooth.*

The Phantom Tollbooth, Act I

Staging

Staging is the art of putting a play on the stage and making it come to life for the audience. Staging includes the sets and scenery, lighting, sound effects, and special effects. When you read a play, try to stage the play in your imagination.

Focus

In *The Phantom Tollbooth,* Milo finds himself in a strange and unknown world. There, he encounters one city where words mean everything and another where numbers mean everything. Imagine a world where there were no words or numbers. What are some of the things you would not be able to do without words and numbers? In a group with three or four students, list at least four things you could not do without words and four things you could not do without numbers. As you read Act I of *The Phantom Tollbooth,* look for how the main character finds out the value of words and numbers.

Vocabulary

Knowing the following words will help you as you read Act I of *The Phantom Tollbooth.*

phantom (fan′ təm) *adj.*: Unreal, ghostlike (p. 205)
ignorance (ig′ nər əns) *n.*: Lacking knowledge, education, or experience (p. 206)
precautionary (pri kô′ shən er′ ē) *adj.*: Taking care beforehand to prevent danger (p. 207)
misapprehension (mis′ ap rə hen′ shən) *n.*: Misunderstanding (p. 214)

Spelling Tip

To help you remember that the beginning of *phantom* is spelled with *ph,* think of the statement "a PHantom is PHysically PHony."

The Phantom Tollbooth

based on the book by Norton Juster

Susan Nanus

"But then one day, the Kings had an argument to end all arguments . . ."

CAST

(in order of appearance)

The Clock
Milo, a boy
The Whether Man
Six Lethargarians
Tock, the Watchdog (same as THE CLOCK)
Azaz the Unabridged, KING OF DICTIONOPOLIS
The Mathemagician, KING OF DIGITOPOLIS
Princess Sweet Rhyme
Princess Pure Reason
Gatekeeper of Dictionopolis
Three Word Merchants
The Letterman (FOURTH WORD MERCHANT)
Spelling Bee
The Humbug
The Duke of Definition
The Minister of Meaning
The Earl of Essence
The Count of Connotation
The Undersecretary of Understanding
A Page
Kakafonous A. Dischord, DOCTOR OF DISSONANCE
The Awful Dynne
The Dodecahedron
Miners of the Numbers Mine
The Everpresent Wordsnatcher
The Terrible Trivium
The Demon of Insincerity
Senses Taker

THE SETS

1. Milo's bedroom—with shelves, pennants, pictures on the wall, as well as suggestions of the characters of the Land of Wisdom.
2. The road to the Land of Wisdom—a forest, from which the Whether Man and the Lethargarians emerge.
3. Dictionopolis—A marketplace full of open air stalls as well as little shops. Letters and signs should abound. There may be street signs and lampposts in the shapes of large letters (large O's and Q's) and windows and doors can be in the shape of H's and A's.

4. Digitopolis—a dark, glittering place without trees or greenery, but full of shining rocks and cliffs, with hundreds of numbers shining everywhere. When the scene change is made to the Mathemagician's room, set pieces are simply carried in from the wings.

5. The Land of Ignorance—a gray, gloomy place full of cliffs and caves, with frightening faces. Different levels and heights should be suggested through one or two platforms or risers, with a set of stairs that lead to the castle in the air.

Props and scenery should be two-dimensional and very colorful in order to give the effect of an imaginary place.

Act I

Scene 1

The stage is completely dark and silent. Suddenly the sound of someone winding an alarm clock is heard, and after that, the sound of loud ticking is heard.

LIGHTS UP on the CLOCK, *a huge alarm clock. The* CLOCK *reads 4:00. The lighting should make it appear that the* CLOCK *is suspended in mid-air (if possible). The* CLOCK *ticks for 30 seconds.*

CLOCK. See that! Half a minute gone by. Seems like a long time when you're waiting for something to happen, doesn't it? Funny thing is, time can pass very slowly or very fast, and sometimes even both at once. The time now? Oh, a little after four, but what that means should depend on you. Too often, we do something simply because time tells us to. Time for school, time for bed, whoops, 12:00, time to be hungry. It can get a little silly, don't you think? Time is important, but it's what you do with it that makes it so. So my advice to you is to use it. Keep your eyes open and your ears perked. Otherwise it will pass before you know it, and you'll certainly have missed something!

Things have a habit of doing that, you know.
Being here one minute and gone the next.
In the twinkling of an eye.
In a jiffy.
In a flash!

I know a girl who yawned and missed a whole summer vacation. And what about that caveman who took a nap one afternoon, and woke up to find himself completely alone. You see, while he was sleeping, someone had invented the wheel and everyone had moved to the suburbs. And then of course, there is Milo. [*LIGHTS UP to reveal* MILO'S *Bedroom. The* CLOCK *appears to be on a shelf in the room of a young boy—a room filled with books, toys, games, maps, papers, pencils, a bed, a desk. There is a dartboard with numbers and the face of the* MATHEMAGICIAN, *a bedspread made from* KING AZAZ'S *cloak, a kite looking like the* SPELLING BEE, *a punching bag with the* HUMBUG'S *face, as well as records, a television, a toy car, and a large box that is wrapped and has an envelope taped to the top. The sound of FOOTSTEPS is heard, and then enter* MILO *dejectedly. He throws down his books and coat, flops into a chair, and sighs loudly.*] Who never knows what to do with himself—not just sometimes, but always. When he's in school, he wants to be

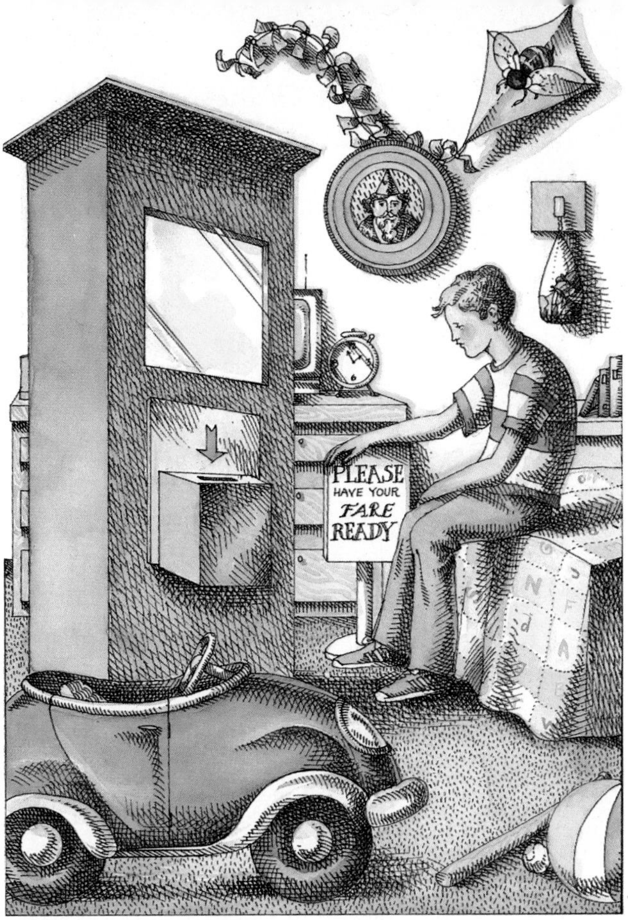

out, and when he's out, he wants to be in. [*During the following speech,* MILO *examines the various toys, tools, and other possessions in the room, trying them out and rejecting them.*] Wherever he is, he wants to be somewhere else—and when he gets there, so what. Everything is too much trouble or a waste of time. Books—he's already read them. Games—boring. T.V.—dumb. So what's left? Another long, boring afternoon. Unless he bothers to notice a very large package that happened to arrive today.

MILO. [*Suddenly notices the package. He drags himself over to it, and disinterestedly reads the label.*] "For Milo, who has plenty of time." Well, that's true. [*Sighs and looks at it.*] No. [*Walks away.*] Well . . . [*Comes back. Rips open envelope and reads.*]

A VOICE. "One genuine turnpike tollbooth, easily assembled at home for use by those who have never traveled in lands beyond."

MILO. Beyond what? [*Continues reading.*]

A VOICE. "This package contains the following items:" [MILO *pulls the items out of the box and sets them up as they are mentioned.*] "One (1) genuine turnpike tollbooth to be erected according to directions. Three (3) precautionary signs to be used in a precautionary fashion. Assorted coins for paying tolls. One (1) map, strictly up to date, showing how to get from here to there. One (1) book of rules and traffic regulations which may not be bent or broken. Warning! Results are not guaranteed. If not perfectly satisfied, your wasted time will be refunded."

MILO. [*Skeptically.*] Come off it, who do you think you're kidding? [*Walks around and examines tollbooth.*] What am I supposed to do with this? [*The ticking of the* CLOCK *grows loud and impatient.*] Well . . . what else do I have to do. [MILO *gets into his toy car and drives up to the first sign.*]

VOICE. "HAVE YOUR DESTINATION IN MIND."

MILO. [*Pulls out the map.*] Now, let's see. That's funny. I never heard of any of these places. Well, it doesn't matter anyway. Dictionopolis. That's a weird name. I might as well go there. [*Begins to move, following map. Drives off.*]

CLOCK. See what I mean? You never know how things are going to get started. But when you're bored, what you need more than anything is a rude awakening.

[*The ALARM goes off very loudly as the stage darkens. The sound of the alarm is transformed into the honking of a car horn, and is then joined by the blasts, bleeps, roars and growls of heavy highway traffic. When the lights come up,* MILO'S *bedroom is gone and we see a lonely road in the middle of nowhere.*]

Scene 2
The Road to Dictionopolis

ENTER MILO *in his car.*

MILO. This is weird! I don't recognize any of this scenery at all. [*A SIGN is held up before* MILO, *startling him.*] Huh? [*Reads.*] WELCOME TO EXPECTATIONS. INFORMATION, PREDICTIONS AND ADVICE CHEERFULLY OFFERED. PARK HERE AND BLOW HORN. [MILO *blows horn.*]

WHETHER MAN. [*A little man wearing a long coat and carrying an umbrella pops up from behind the sign that he was holding. He speaks very fast and excitedly.*] My, my, my, my, my, welcome, welcome, welcome, welcome to the Land of Expectations, Expectations, Expectations! We don't get many travelers these days; we certainly don't get many travelers. Now what can I do for you? I'm the Whether Man.

MILO. [*Referring to map.*] Uh . . . is this the right road to Dictionopolis?

WHETHER MAN. Well now, well now, well now, I don't know of any *wrong* road to Dictionopolis, so if this road goes to Dictionopolis at all, it must be the right road, and if it doesn't, it must be the right road to somewhere else, because there are no wrong roads to anywhere. Do you think it will rain?

MILO. I thought you were the Weather Man.

WHETHER MAN. Oh, no, I'm the Whether Man, not the weather man. [*Pulls out a SIGN or opens a FLAP of his coat, which reads: "WHETHER."*] After all, it's more important to know whether there will be weather than what the weather will be.

MILO. What kind of place is Expectations?

WHETHER MAN. Good question, good question! Expectations is the place you must always go to before you get to where you are going. Of course, some people never go beyond Expectations, but my job is to hurry them along whether they like it or not. Now what else can I do for you? [*Opens his umbrella.*]

MILO. I think I can find my own way.

WHETHER MAN. Splendid, splendid, splendid! Whether or not you find your own way, you're bound to find some way. If you happen to find my way, please return it. I lost it years ago. I imagine by now it must be quite rusty. You did say it was going to rain, didn't you? [*Escorts* MILO *to the car under the open umbrella.*] I'm glad you made your own decision. I do so hate to make up my mind about anything, whether it's good or bad, up or down, rain or shine. Expect everything, I always say, and the unexpected never happens. Goodbye, goodbye, goodbye, good . . . [*A loud CLAP of THUNDER is heard.*] Oh dear! [*He looks up at the sky, puts out his hand to feel for rain, and RUNS AWAY.* MILO *watches puzzledly and drives on.*]

MILO. I'd better get out of Expectations, but fast. Talking to a guy like that all day would get me nowhere for sure. [*He tries to speed up, but finds instead that he is moving slower and slower.*] Oh, oh, now what? [*He can barely move. Behind* MILO, *the* LETHARGARIANS[1] *begin to enter from all parts of*

---

1. Lethargarians (leth′ ər gar′ ē unz): A play on the word *lethargy*, which means "having a great lack of energy; a dull, sluggish state."

the stage. They are dressed to blend in with the scenery and carry small pillows that look like rocks. Whenever they fall asleep, they rest on the pillows.] Now I really am getting nowhere. I hope I didn't take a wrong turn. [*The car stops. He tries to start it. It won't move. He gets out and begins to tinker with it.*] I wonder where I am.

LETHARGARIAN 1. You're . . . in . . . the . . . Dol . . . drums . . . [MILO *looks around.*]

LETHARGARIAN 2. Yes . . . the . . . Dol . . . drums . . . [*A YAWN is heard.*]

MILO. [*Yelling.*] WHAT ARE THE DOLDRUMS?

LETHARGARIAN 3. The Doldrums, my friend, are where nothing ever happens and nothing ever changes. [*Parts of the Scenery Stand Up or Six People come out of the scenery colored in the same colors of the trees or the road. They move very slowly and as soon as they move, they stop to rest again.*] Allow me to introduce all of us. We are the Lethargarians at your service.

MILO. [*Uncertainly.*] Very pleased to meet you. I think I'm lost. Can you help me?

LETHARGARIAN 4. Don't say think. [*He yawns.*] It's against the law.

LETHARGARIAN 1. No one's allowed to think in the Doldrums. [*He falls asleep.*]

LETHARGARIAN 2. Don't you have a rule book? It's local ordinance 175389-J. [*He falls asleep.*]

MILO. [*Pulls out rule book and reads.*] Ordinance 175389-J: "It shall be unlawful, illegal and unethical to think, think of thinking, surmise, presume, reason, meditate or speculate while in the Doldrums. Anyone breaking this law shall be severely punished." That's a ridiculous law! Everybody thinks.

ALL THE LETHARGARIANS. We don't!

LETHARGARIAN 2. And the most of the time, you don't, that's why you're here. You weren't thinking and you weren't paying attention either. People who don't pay attention often get stuck in the Doldrums. Face it, most of the time, you're just like us. [*Falls, snoring, to the ground.* MILO *laughs.*]

LETHARGARIAN 5. Stop that at once. Laughing is against the law. Don't you have a rule book? It's local ordinance 574381-W.

MILO. [*Opens rule book and reads.*] "In the Doldrums, laughter is frowned upon and smiling is permitted only on alternate Thursdays." Well, if you can't laugh or think, what can you do?

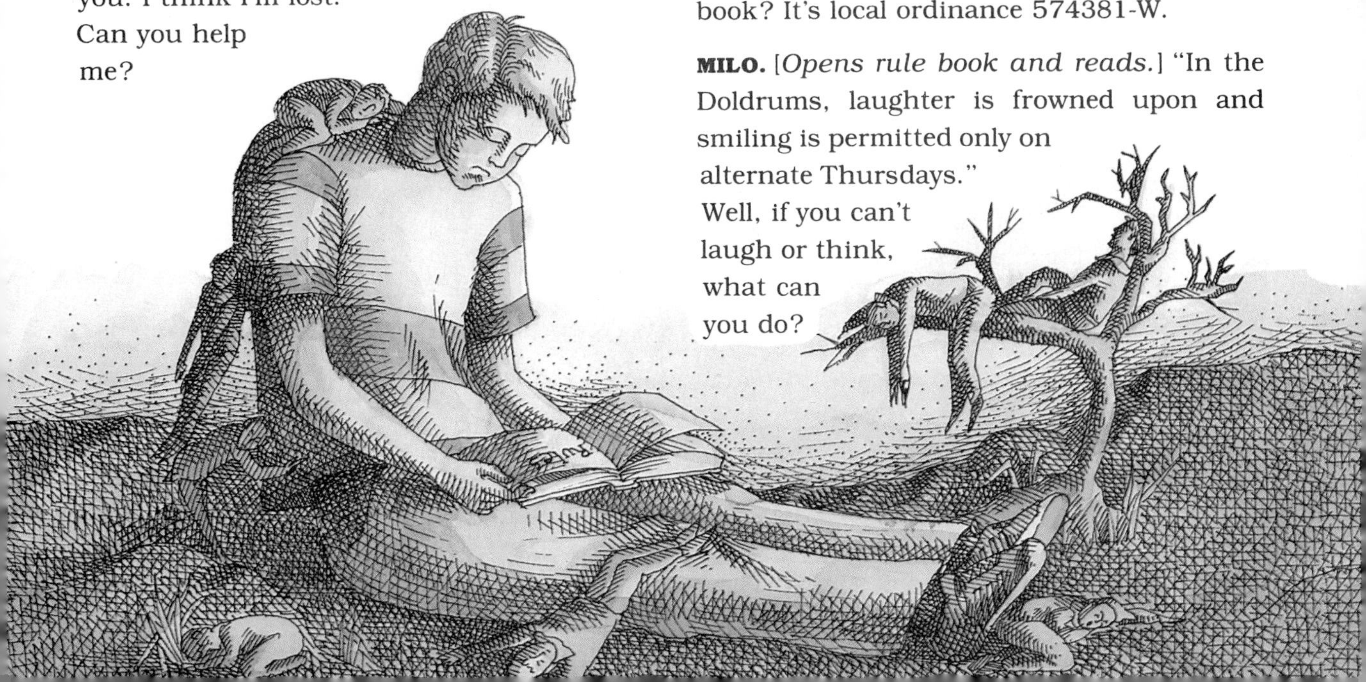

LETHARGARIAN 6. Anything as long as it's nothing, and everything as long as it isn't anything. There's lots to do. We have a very busy schedule . . .

LETHARGARIAN 1. At 8:00 we get up and then we spend from 8 to 9 daydreaming.

LETHARGARIAN 2. From 9:00 to 9:30 we take our early midmorning nap . . .

LETHARGARIAN 3. From 9:30 to 10:30 we dawdle and delay . . .

LETHARGARIAN 4. From 10:30 to 11:30 we take our late early morning nap . . .

LETHARGARIAN 5. From 11:30 to 12:00 we bide our time and then we eat our lunch.

LETHARGARIAN 6. From 1:00 to 2:00 we linger and loiter . . .

LETHARGARIAN 1. From 2:00 to 2:30 we take our early afternoon nap . . .

LETHARGARIAN 2. From 2:30 to 3:30 we put off for tomorrow what we could have done today . . .

LETHARGARIAN 3. From 3:30 to 4:00 we take our early late afternoon nap . . .

LETHARGARIAN 4. From 4:00 to 5:00 we loaf and lounge until dinner . . .

LETHARGARIAN 5. From 6:00 to 7:00 we dilly-dally . . .

LETHARGARIAN 6. From 7:00 to 8:00 we take our early evening nap and then for an hour before we go to bed, we waste time.

LETHARGARIAN 1. [*Yawning.*] You see, it's really quite strenuous doing nothing all day long, and so once a week, we take a holiday and go nowhere.

LETHARGARIAN 5. Which is just where we were going when you came along. Would you care to join us?

MILO. [*Yawning.*] That's where I seem to be going, anyway. [*Stretching.*] Tell me, does everyone here do nothing?

LETHARGARIAN 3. Everyone but the terrible watchdog. He's always sniffing around to see that nobody wastes time. A most unpleasant character.

MILO. The Watchdog?

LETHARGARIAN 6. THE WATCHDOG!

ALL THE LETHARGARIANS. [*Yelling at once.*] RUN! WAKE UP! RUN! HERE HE COMES! THE WATCHDOG! [*They all run off and ENTER a large dog with the head, feet, and tail of a dog, and the body of a clock, having the same face as the character* THE CLOCK.]

WATCHDOG. What are you doing here?

MILO. Nothing much. Just killing time. You see . . .

WATCHDOG. KILLING TIME! [*His ALARM RINGS in fury.*] It's bad enough wasting time without killing it. What are you doing in the Doldrums, anyway? Don't you have anywhere to go?

MILO. I think I was on my way to Dictionopolis when I got stuck here. Can you help me?

WATCHDOG. Help you! You've got to help yourself. I suppose you know why you got stuck.

MILO. I guess I just wasn't thinking.

WATCHDOG. Precisely. Now you're on your way.

MILO. I am?

WATCHDOG. Of course. Since you got here by not thinking, it seems reasonable that in order to get out, you must *start* thinking. Do you mind if I get in? I love automobile rides. [*He gets in. They wait.*] Well?

MILO. All right. I'll try. [*Screws up his face and thinks.*] Are we moving?

WATCHDOG. Not yet. Think harder.

MILO. I'm thinking as hard as I can.

WATCHDOG. Well, think just a little harder than that. Come on, you can do it.

MILO. All right, all right. . . . I'm thinking of all the planets in the solar system, and why water expands when it turns to ice, and all the words that begin with "q," and . . . [*The wheels begin to move.*] We're moving! We're moving!

WATCHDOG. Keep thinking.

MILO. [*Thinking.*] How a steam engine works and how to bake a pie and the difference between Fahrenheit[2] and Centigrade[3] . . .

WATCHDOG. Dictionopolis, here we come.

MILO. Hey, Watchdog, are you coming along?

TOCK. You can call me Tock, and keep your eyes on the road.

MILO. What kind of place is Dictionopolis, anyway?

TOCK. It's where all the words in the world come from. It used to be a marvelous place, but ever since Rhyme and Reason left, it hasn't been the same.

MILO. Rhyme and Reason?

TOCK. The two princesses. They used to settle all the arguments between their two brothers who rule over the Land of Wisdom. You see, Azaz is the king of Dictionopolis and the Mathemagician is the king of Digitopolis and they almost never see eye to eye on anything. It was the job of the Princesses Sweet Rhyme and Pure Reason to solve the differences between the two kings, and they always did so well that both sides usually went home feeling very satisfied. But then, one day, the kings had an argument to end all arguments. . . .

[*The LIGHTS DIM on* TOCK *and* MILO, *and come up on* KING AZAZ *of Dictionopolis on another part of the stage.* AZAZ *has a great stomach, a grey beard reaching to his waist, a small crown and a long robe with the letters of the alphabet written all over it.*]

AZAZ. Of course, I'll abide by the decision of Rhyme and Reason, though I have no doubt as to what it will be. They will choose *words,* of course. Everyone knows that words are more important than numbers any day of the week.

[*The* MATHEMAGICIAN *appears opposite* AZAZ. *The* MATHEMAGICIAN *wears a long flowing robe covered entirely with complex mathematical equations, and a tall pointed hat. He carries a long staff with a pencil point at one end and a large rubber eraser at the other.*]

MATHEMAGICIAN. That's what you think, Azaz. People wouldn't even know what day of the week it is without *numbers.* Haven't you ever looked at a calendar? Face it, Azaz. It's numbers that count.

AZAZ. Don't be ridiculous. [*To audience, as if leading a cheer.*] Let's hear it for WORDS!

MATHEMAGICIAN. [*To audience, in the same manner.*] Cast your vote for NUMBERS!

---

2. Fahrenheit (fer′ ən hīt′) *adj.*: A way to measure temperature in which 32° is the freezing point and 212° is the boiling point of water.

3. Centigrade (sen′ tə grād′) *adj.*: A way to measure temperature in which 0° is the freezing point and 100° is the boiling point of water.

AZAZ. A, B, C's!

MATHEMAGICIAN. 1, 2, 3's! [*A FANFARE*[4] *is heard.*]

AZAZ AND MATHEMAGICIAN. [*To each other.*] Quiet! Rhyme and Reason are about to announce their decision.

[RHYME *and* REASON *appear.*]

RHYME. Ladies and gentlemen, letters and numerals, fractions and punctuation marks—may we have your attention, please. After careful consideration of the problem set before us by King Azaz of Dictionopolis [AZAZ *bows.*] and the Mathemagician of Digitopolis [MATHEMAGICIAN *raises his hands in a victory salute.*] we have come to the following conclusion:

REASON. Words and numbers are of equal value, for in the cloak of knowledge, one is the warp[5] and the other is the woof.[6]

4. fanfare (fan′ fer′) *n.*: A loud blowing of trumpets.
5. warp (wôrp) *n.*: In weaving, the threads running lengthwise, crossed by the woof.
6. woof (wo͞of) *n.*: In weaving, the threads running horizontally, crossed by the warp.

RHYME. It is no more important to count the sands than it is to name the stars.

RHYME AND REASON. Therefore, let both kingdoms, Dictionopolis and Digitopolis live in peace.

[*The sound of CHEERING is heard.*]

AZAZ. Boo! is what I say. Boo and Bah and Hiss!

MATHEMAGICIAN. What good are these girls if they can't even settle an argument in anyone's favor? I think I have come to a decision of my own.

AZAZ. So have I.

AZAZ AND MATHEMAGICIAN. [*To the* PRINCESSES.] You are hereby banished from this land to the Castle-in-the-Air. [*To each other.*] And as for you, KEEP OUT OF MY WAY! [*They stalk off in opposite directions.*]

[*During this time, the set has been changed to the Market Square of Dictionopolis. LIGHTS come UP on the deserted square.*]

TOCK. And ever since then, there has been

neither Rhyme nor Reason in this kingdom. Words are misused and numbers are mismanaged. The argument between the two kings has divided everyone and the real value of both words and numbers has been forgotten. What a waste!

MILO. Why doesn't somebody rescue the Princesses and set everything straight again?

TOCK. That is easier said than done. The Castle-in-the-Air is very far from here, and the one path which leads to it is guarded by ferocious demons. But hold on, here we are. [*A Man appears, carrying a Gate and a small Tollbooth.*]

GATEKEEPER. AHHHHREMMMM! This is Dictionopolis, a happy kingdom, advantageously located in the foothills of Confusion and caressed by gentle breezes from the Sea of Knowledge. Today, by royal proclamation, is Market Day. Have you come to buy or sell?

MILO. I beg your pardon?

GATEKEEPER. Buy or sell, buy or sell. Which is it? You must have come here for a reason.

MILO. Well, I . . .

GATEKEEPER. Come now, if you don't have a reason, you must at least have an explanation or certainly an excuse.

MILO. [*Meekly.*] Uh . . . no.

GATEKEEPER. [*Shaking his head.*] Very serious. You can't get in without a reason. [*Thoughtfully.*] Wait a minute. Maybe I have an old one you can use. [*Pulls out an old suitcase from the tollbooth and rummages through it.*] No . . . no . . . no . . . this won't do . . . hmmm . . .

MILO. [*To Tock.*] What's he looking for? [*Tock shrugs.*]

GATEKEEPER. Ah! This is fine. [*Pulls out a Medallion on a chain. Engraved in the Medallion is: "WHY NOT?"*] Why not. That's a good reason for almost anything . . . a bit used, perhaps, but still quite serviceable. There you are, sir. Now I can truly say: Welcome to Dictionopolis.

[*He opens the Gate and walks off. CITIZENS and MERCHANTS appear on all levels of the stage, and* MILO *and* TOCK *find themselves in the middle of a noisy marketplace. As some people buy and sell their wares, others hang a banner which reads: WELCOME TO THE WORD MARKET.*]

MILO. Tock! Look!

MERCHANT 1. Hey-ya, hey-ya, hey-ya, step right up and take your pick. Juicy tempting words for sale. Get your fresh-picked "if's" "and's" and "but's!" Just take a look at these nice ripe "where's" and "when's."

MERCHANT 2. Step right up, step right up, fancy, best-quality words here for sale. Enrich your vocabulary and expand your speech with such elegant items as "quagmire," "flabbergast," or "upholstery."

MERCHANT 3. Words by the bag, buy them over here. Words by the bag for the more talkative customer. A pound of "happy's" at a very reasonable price . . . very useful for "Happy Birthday," "Happy New Year," "happy days," or "happy-go-lucky." Or how about a package of "good's," always handy for "good morning," "good afternoon," "good evening," and "goodbye."

MILO. I can't believe it. Did you ever see so many words?

TOCK. They're fine if you have something to say. [*They come to a Do-It-Yourself Bin.*]

MILO. [*To* MERCHANT 4 *at the bin.*] Excuse me, but what are these?

MERCHANT 4. These are for people who like to make up their own words. You can pick any assortment you like or buy a special box complete with all the letters and a book of instructions. Here, taste an "A." They're very good. [*He pops one into* MILO's *mouth.*]

MILO. [*Tastes it hesitantly.*] It's sweet! [*He eats it.*]

MERCHANT 4. I knew you'd like it. "A" is one of our best-sellers. All of them aren't that good, you know. The "Z," for instance—very dry and sawdusty. And the "X"? Tastes like a trunkful of stale air. But most of the others aren't bad at all. Here, try the "I."

MILO. [*Tasting.*] Cool! It tastes icy.

MERCHANT 4. [*To* TOCK.] How about the "C" for you? It's as crunchy as a bone. Most people are just too lazy to make their own words, but take it from me, not only is it more fun, but it's also *de*-lightful, [*Holds up a "D."*] *e*-lating, [*Holds up an "E."*] and extremely *u*seful! [*Holds up a "U."*]

MILO. But isn't it difficult? I'm not very good at making words.

[*The* SPELLING BEE, *a large colorful bee, comes up from behind.*]

SPELLING BEE. Perhaps I can be of some assistance . . . a-s-s-i-s-t-a-n-c-e. [*The Three turn around and see him.*] Don't be alarmed . . . a-l-a-r-m-e-d. I am the Spelling Bee. I can spell anything. Anything. A-n-y-t-h-i-n-g. Try me. Try me.

MILO. [*Backing off,* TOCK *on his guard.*] Can you spell goodbye?

SPELLING BEE. Perhaps you are under the misapprehension . . . m-i-s-a-p-p-r-e-h-e-n-s-i-o-n that I am dangerous. Let me assure you that I am quite peaceful. Now, think of the most difficult word you can, and I'll spell it.

MILO. Uh . . . o.k. [*At this point,* MILO *may turn to the audience and ask them to help him choose a word or he may think of one on his own.*] How about . . . "Curiosity"?

SPELLING BEE. [*Winking.*] Let's see now . . . uh . . . how much time do I have?

MILO. Just ten seconds. Count them off, Tock.

SPELLING BEE. [*As* TOCK *counts.*] Oh dear, oh dear. [*Just at the last moment, quickly.*] C-u-r-i-o-s-i-t-y.

MERCHANT 4. Correct! [ALL *Cheer.*]

MILO. Can you spell anything?

SPELLING BEE. [*Proudly.*] Just about. You see, years ago, I was an ordinary bee minding my own business, smelling flowers all day, occasionally picking up part-time work in people's bonnets. Then one day, I realized that I'd never amount to anything without an education, so I decided that . . .

HUMBUG. [*Coming up in a booming voice.*] BALDERDASH! [*He wears a lavish coat, striped pants, checked vest, spats and a derby hat.*] Let me repeat . . . BALDERDASH! [*Swings his cane and clicks his heels in the air.*] Well, well, what have we here? Isn't someone going to introduce me to the little boy?

SPELLING BEE. [*Disdainfully.*] This is the Humbug. You can't trust a word he says.

HUMBUG. NONSENSE! Everyone can trust a Humbug. As I was saying to the king just the other day . . .

SPELLING BEE. You've never met the king. [*To* MILO.] Don't believe a thing he tells you.

HUMBUG. Bosh, my boy, pure bosh. The Humbugs are an old and noble family, honorable to the core. Why, we fought in the Crusades with Richard the Lionhearted, crossed the Atlantic with Columbus, blazed trails with the pioneers. History is full of Humbugs.

SPELLING BEE. A very pretty speech . . . s-p-e-e-c-h. Now, why don't you go away? I was just advising the lad of the importance of proper spelling.

HUMBUG. BAH! As soon as you learn to spell one word, they ask you to spell another. You can never catch up, so why bother? [*Puts his arm around* MILO.] Take my advice, boy, and forget about it. As my great-great-great-grandfather George Washington Humbug used to say . . .

SPELLING BEE. You, sir, are an impostor i-m-p-o-s-t-o-r who can't even spell his own name!

HUMBUG. What? You dare to doubt my word? The word of a Humbug? The word of a Humbug who has direct access to the ear of a King? And the king shall hear of this, I promise you . . .

VOICE 1. Did someone call for the King?

VOICE 2. Did you mention the monarch?

VOICE 3. Speak of the sovereign?

VOICE 4. Entreat the Emperor?

VOICE 5. Hail his highness?

[*Five tall, thin gentlemen regally dressed in silks and satins, plumed hats and buckled shoes appear as they speak.*]

MILO. Who are they?

SPELLING BEE. The King's advisors. Or in more formal terms, his cabinet.

MINISTER 1. Greetings!

MINISTER 2. Salutations!

MINISTER 3. Welcome!

MINISTER 4. Good Afternoon!

MINISTER 5. Hello!

MILO. Uh . . . Hi.

[*All the* MINISTERS, *from here on called by their numbers, unfold their scrolls and read in order.*]

MINISTER 1. By the order of Azaz the Unabridged . . .

MINISTER 2. King of Dictionopolis . . .

MINISTER 3. Monarch of letters . . .

MINISTER 4. Emperor of phrases, sentences, and miscellaneous figures of speech . . .

MINISTER 5. We offer you the hospitality of our kingdom . . .

MINISTER 1. Country

MINISTER 2. Nation

MINISTER 3. State

MINISTER 4. Commonwealth

MINISTER 5. Realm

MINISTER 1. Empire

MINISTER 2. Palatinate

MINISTER 3. Principality.

MILO. Do all those words mean the same thing?

MINISTER 1. Of course.

MINISTER 2. Certainly.

MINISTER 3. Precisely.

MINISTER 4. Exactly.

MINISTER 5. Yes.

MILO. Then why don't you use just one? Wouldn't that make a lot more sense?

MINISTER 1. Nonsense!

MINISTER 2. Ridiculous!

MINISTER 3. Fantastic!

MINISTER 4. Absurd!

MINISTER 5. Bosh!

MINISTER 1. We're not interested in making sense. It's not our job.

MINISTER 2. Besides, one word is as good as another, so why not use them all?

MINISTER 3. Then you don't have to choose which one is right.

MINISTER 4. Besides, if one is right, then ten are ten times as right.

MINISTER 5. Obviously, you don't know who we are. [*Each presents himself and* MILO *acknowledges the introduction.*]

MINISTER 1. The Duke of Definition.

MINISTER 2. The Minister of Meaning.

MINISTER 3. The Earl of Essence.

MINISTER 4. The Count of Connotation.

MINISTER 5. The Undersecretary of Understanding.

ALL FIVE. And we have come to invite you to the Royal Banquet.

SPELLING BEE. The banquet! That's quite an honor, my boy. A real h-o-n-o-r.

HUMBUG. DON'T BE RIDICULOUS! Everybody goes to the Royal Banquet these days.

SPELLING BEE. [*To the* HUMBUG.] True, everybody does go. But some people are invited and others simply push their way in where they aren't wanted.

HUMBUG. HOW DARE YOU? You buzzing little upstart, I'll show you who's not wanted . . . [*Raises his cane threateningly.*]

SPELLING BEE. You just watch it! I'm warning w-a-r-n-i-n-g you! [*At that moment, an ear-shattering blast of TRUMPETS, entirely off-key, is heard, and a* PAGE *appears.*]

PAGE. King Azaz the Unabridged is about to begin the Royal banquet. All guests who do not appear promptly at the table will automatically lose their place. [*A huge Table is carried out with* KING AZAZ *sitting in a large chair, carried out at the head of the table.*]

AZAZ. Places. Everyone take your places. [*All the characters, including the* HUMBUG *and the* SPELLING BEE, *who forget their quarrel, rush to take their places at the table.* MILO *and* TOCK *sit near the* KING. AZAZ *looks at* MILO.] And just who is this?

MILO. Your Highness, my name is Milo and this is Tock. Thank you very much for inviting us to your banquet, and I think your palace is beautiful!

MINISTER 1. Exquisite.

MINISTER 2. Lovely.

MINISTER 3. Handsome.

MINISTER 4. Pretty.

MINISTER 5. Charming.

AZAZ. SILENCE! Now tell me, young man, what can you do to entertain us? Sing songs? Tell stories? Juggle plates? Do tumbling tricks? Which is it?

MILO. I can't do any of those things.

AZAZ. What an ordinary little boy. Can't you do anything at all?

MILO. Well . . . I can count to a thousand.

AZAZ. AARGH, numbers! Never mention numbers here. Only use them when we absolutely have to. Now, why don't we change the subject and have some dinner? Since you are the guest of honor, you may pick the menu.

MILO. Me? Well, uh . . . I'm not very hungry. Can we just have a light snack?

AZAZ. A light snack it shall be!

[AZAZ *claps his hands. Waiters rush in with covered trays. When they are uncovered, Shafts of Light pour out. The light may be created through the use of battery-operated flashlights which are secured in the trays and covered with a false bottom. The Guests help themselves.*]

HUMBUG. Not a very substantial meal. Maybe you can suggest something a little more filling.

MILO. Well, in that case, I think we ought to have a square meal . . .

AZAZ. [*Claps his hands.*] A square meal it is! [*Waiters serve trays of Colored Squares of all sizes. People serve themselves.*]

SPELLING BEE. These are awful. [HUMBUG *Coughs and all the Guests do not care for the food.*]

AZAZ. [*Claps his hands and the trays are removed.*] Time for speeches. [*To* MILO.] You first.

MILO. [*Hesitantly.*] Your Majesty, ladies and gentlemen, I would like to take this opportunity to say that . . .

AZAZ. That's quite enough. Mustn't talk all day.

MILO. But I just started to . . .

AZAZ. NEXT!

HUMBUG. [*Quickly.*] Roast turkey, mashed potatoes, vanilla ice cream.

SPELLING BEE. Hamburgers, corn on the cob, chocolate pudding p-u-d-d-i-n-g. [*Each Guest names two dishes and a dessert.*]

AZAZ. [*The last.*] Pate de fois gras, soupe a l'oignon, salade endives, fromage et fruits et demi-tasse.[7] [*He claps his hands. Waiters serve each Guest his Words.*] Dig on. [*To* MILO.] Though I can't say I think much of your choice.

MILO. I didn't know I was going to have to eat my words.

AZAZ. Of course, of course, everybody here does. Your speech should have been in better taste.

MINISTER 1. Here, try some somersault. It improves the flavor.

MINISTER 2. Have a rigamarole. [*Offers bread-basket.*]

MINISTER 3. Or a ragamuffin.

MINISTER 4. Perhaps you'd care for a synonym bun.

MINISTER 5. Why not wait for your just desserts?

AZAZ. Ah yes, the dessert. We're having a special treat today . . . freshly made at the half-bakery.

MILO. The half-bakery?

AZAZ. Of course, the half-bakery! Where do you think half-baked ideas come from? Now, please don't interrupt. By royal command, the pastry chefs have . . .

MILO. What's a half-baked idea?

[AZAZ *gives up the idea of speaking as a cart is wheeled in and the Guests help themselves.*]

---

7. Pate de fois gras, soupe a l'oignon, salade endives, fromage et fruits et demi-tasse. (Pä tā′ də fwä grä, so͞op ä lwa′ yôn, sä läd′ än dëv′, frō mäj′ ā fwēt ā də mē täs′): French for "Goose liver paste, onion soup, endive salad, cheese and fruit, and a half-cup of coffee."

HUMBUG. They're very tasty, but they don't always agree with you. Here's a good one. [HUMBUG *hands one to* MILO.]

MILO. [*Reads.*] "The earth is flat."

SPELLING BEE. People swallowed that one for years. [*Picks up one and reads.*] "The moon is made of green cheese." Now, there's a half-baked idea.

[*Everyone chooses one and eats. They include: "It Never Rains But Pours," "Night Air Is Bad Air," "Everything Happens for the Best," "Coffee Stunts Your Growth."*]

AZAZ. And now for a few closing words. Attention! Let me have your attention! [*Everyone leaps up and Exits, except for* MILO, TOCK, *and the* HUMBUG.] Loyal subjects and friends, once again on this gala occasion, we have . . .

MILO. Excuse me, but everybody left.

AZAZ. [*Sadly.*] I was hoping no one would notice. It happens every time.

HUMBUG. They're gone to dinner, and as soon as I finish this last bite, I shall join them.

MILO. That's ridiculous. How can they eat dinner right after a banquet?

AZAZ. SCANDALOUS! We'll put a stop to it at once. From now on, by royal command, everyone must eat dinner before the banquet.

MILO. But that's just as bad.

HUMBUG. Or just as good. Things which are equally bad are also equally good. Try to look at the bright side of things.

MILO. I don't know which side of anything to look at. Everything is so confusing, and all your words only make things worse.

AZAZ. How true. There must be something we can do about it.

HUMBUG. Pass a law.

AZAZ. We have almost as many laws as words.

HUMBUG. Offer a reward. [AZAZ *shakes his head and looks madder at each suggestion.*] Send for help? Drive a bargain? Pull the switch? Lower the boom? Toe the line?

[*As* AZAZ *continues to scowl, the* HUMBUG *loses confidence and finally gives up.*]

MILO. Maybe you should let Rhyme and Reason return.

AZAZ. How nice that would be. Even if they were a bother at times, things always went so well when they were here. But I'm afraid it can't be done.

HUMBUG. Certainly not. Can't be done.

MILO. Why not?

HUMBUG. [*Now siding with* MILO.] Why not, indeed?

AZAZ. Much too difficult.

HUMBUG. Of course, much too difficult.

MILO. You could, if you really wanted to.

HUMBUG. By all means, if you really wanted to, you could.

AZAZ. [*To* HUMBUG.] How?

MILO. [*Also to* HUMBUG.] Yeah, how?

HUMBUG. Why . . . uh, it's a simple task for a brave boy with a stout heart, a steadfast dog and a serviceable small automobile.

AZAZ. Go on.

HUMBUG. Well, all that he would have to do is

cross the dangerous, unknown countryside between here and Digitopolis, where he would have to persuade the Mathemagician to release the Princesses, which we know to be impossible because the Mathemagician will never agree with Azaz about anything. Once achieving that, it's a simple matter of entering the Mountains of Ignorance from where no one has ever returned alive, an effortless climb up a two thousand foot stairway without railings in a high wind at night to the Castle-in-the-Air. After a pleasant chat with the Princesses, all that remains is a leisurely ride back through those chaotic crags where the frightening fiends have sworn to tear any intruder from limb to limb and devour him down to his belt buckle. And finally after doing all that, a triumphal parade! If, of course, there is anything left to parade . . . followed by hot chocolate and cookies for everyone.

AZAZ. I never realized it would be so simple.

MILO. It sounds dangerous to me.

TOCK. And just who is supposed to make that journey?

AZAZ. A very good question. But there is one far more serious problem.

MILO. What's that?

AZAZ. I'm afraid I can't tell you that until you return.

MILO. But wait a minute, I didn't . . .

AZAZ. Dictionopolis will always be grateful to you, my boy, and your dog. [AZAZ *pats* TOCK *and* MILO.]

TOCK. Now, just one moment, sire . . .

AZAZ. You will face many dangers on your journey, but fear not, for I can give you something for your protection. [AZAZ *gives* MILO *a box.*] In this box are the letters of the alphabet. With them you can form all the words you will ever need to help you overcome the obstacles that may stand in your path. All you must do is use them well and in the right places.

MILO. [*Miserably.*] Thanks a lot.

AZAZ. You will need a guide, of course, and since he knows the obstacles so well, the Humbug has cheerfully volunteered to accompany you.

HUMBUG. Now, see here . . . !

AZAZ. You will find him dependable, brave, resourceful and loyal.

HUMBUG. [*Flattered.*] Oh, your Majesty.

MILO. I'm sure he'll be a great help. [*They approach the car.*]

TOCK. I hope so. It looks like we're going to need it.

[*The lights darken and the* KING *fades from view.*]

AZAZ. Good luck! Drive carefully! [*The three get into the car and begin to move. Suddenly a thunderously loud NOISE is heard. They slow down the car.*]

MILO. What was that?

TOCK. It came from up ahead.

HUMBUG. It's something terrible, I just know it. Oh, no. Something dreadful is going to happen to us. I can feel it in my bones. [*The NOISE is repeated. They all look at each other fearfully as the lights fade.*]

Reader's Response

Milo is faced with a perplexing question: Which are more important, words or numbers? Which are more important to you?

Responding to the Selection

Your Response

1. Have you ever been in the Doldrums? How did you get out?
2. Which of the characters do you like best? Why?

Recalling

3. Describe three characters Milo encounters. What does he learn from each?
4. Describe the places Milo and Tock visit. What are some of their experiences in these places?

Interpreting

5. What does Whether Man mean by his statement that "some people never go beyond Expectations"?
6. Why is the name Dictionopolis appropriate for the place where Milo learns expectations, information, predictions, and advice?
7. What do people mean when they say, "It was done without rhyme or reason"? Why is Dictionopolis in a state of confusion and chaos without Rhyme and Reason?

Applying

8. In Act I, Scene 1, of the play, the Clock says, "Time is important, but it's what you do with it that makes it so." Why is it important to use time wisely?

Analyzing Literature

Understanding Staging

Staging *The Phantom Tollbooth* involves sets, props, costumes, dialogue, actions, lighting, and special effects. For example, the first act of the play requires three different sets: Milo's bedroom, the road to Dictionopolis, and the city of Dictionopolis. In addition, the play requires numerous props—objects that are used by actors during the production of the play.

1. Describe the props and set of Dictionopolis.
2. How is the tollbooth important to the plot of the play?

Critical Thinking and Reading

Evaluating Generalizations

A **generalization** is an idea or statement that covers a great many specific cases. In Act I, Scene 2, a Lethargarian makes this generalization: "People who don't pay attention often get stuck in the doldrums."

When you read or hear generalizations, you need to evaluate them for their truth. What evidence makes them true? Are there exceptions? If there is evidence to support the generalization and if there are no exceptions, the generalization is true, or sound.

1. Find evidence in the play that supports the truth of the Lethargarian's generalization.
2. Evaluate this generalization: Children who are bored with their lives lack imagination.

Thinking and Writing

Writing a Persuasive Letter

In the Reader's Response, you decided whether words or numbers were more important to you. Develop your response into a letter in which you try to convince a classmate to agree with your stand on the issue. Support your opinion with facts and examples. Ask a writing partner to read your paper and suggest ways to make your ideas more forceful. Write a final draft.

Learning Option

Art. With a small group of students, create a board game based on the city of Dictionopolis. Choose a goal for the game—perhaps to get to Dictionopolis. Then decide the rules of the game. What will the players have to do to get to the goal? What obstacles will they meet along the way? (Will they get stuck in the Doldrums?) Decorate your game with scenes from the play. When you are finished, play the game with members of your class.

GUIDE FOR READING

The Phantom Tollbooth, Act II

Author's Purpose

We identify an author's purpose, or reason for writing, by answering two questions: What is the author's general intention—that is, how does the author want the reader to respond? What specific ideas does the author want to convey? General purposes might be to entertain, to inform, to persuade, or to describe. Specific purposes are tied to the theme of a piece of literature. The characters, action, and dialogue can suggest a specific purpose.

Focus

In his quest to rescue Rhyme and Reason, Milo visits Digitopolis—a world where numbers are all-important. In Digitopolis, Milo will meet a variety of interesting characters, including the Dodecahedron, the Terrible Trivium, the Demon of Insincerity, and the Senses Taker. The characters' names suggest their personalities. Choose one of these characters and try to guess what that character is like. Then, give Milo advice to deal with this character. As you read Act II, compare your description of the character with the author's. Decide whether your advice would help Milo.

Vocabulary

Knowing the following words will help you as you read Act II of *The Phantom Tollbooth.*

dissonance (dis′ ə nəns) *n.*: A harsh or disagreeable combination of sounds (p. 223)

admonishing (ad män′ ish iŋ) *adj.*: Disapproving, in a warning fashion (p. 227)

pantomimes (pan′ tə mīmz′) *v.*: Acts out silently with gestures (p. 228)

iridescent (ir′ ə des′ ′nt) *adj.*: Showing changes in color when seen from different angles (p. 228)

pessimistic (pes′ ə mis′ tik) *adj.*: Seeing the gloomy or negative side of things (p. 234)

malicious (mə lish′ əs) *adj.*: Showing evil intentions (p. 234)

hindsight (hind′ sit′) *n.*: The understanding of an event after it has already occurred (p. 237)

Spelling Tip

Remember the double *s*'s in *dissonance* and *pessimistic.*

"Milo, Tock, and Humbug have just as much chance of succeeding as they do of failing."

Act II

Scene 1

The set of Digitopolis glitters in the background, while Upstage Right near the road, a small colorful Wagon sits, looking quite deserted. On its side in large letters, a sign reads:

"KAKAFONOUS A. DISCHORD[1] Doctor of Dissonance"[2]

ENTER MILO, TOCK *and* HUMBUG, *fearfully. They look at the wagon.*

TOCK. There's no doubt about it. That's where the noise was coming from.

HUMBUG. [*To* MILO.] Well, go on.

MILO. Go on what?

HUMBUG. Go on and see who's making all that noise in there. We can't just ignore a creature like that.

MILO. Creature? What kind of creature? Do you think he's dangerous?

HUMBUG. Go on, Milo. Knock on the door. We'll be right behind you.

MILO. O.K. Maybe he can tell us how much further it is to Digitopolis.

[MILO *tiptoes up to the wagon door and KNOCKS timidly. The moment he knocks, a terrible CRASH is heard inside the wagon, and* MILO *and the others jump back in fright. At the same time, the Door Flies Open, and from the dark interior, a Hoarse* VOICE *inquires.*]

VOICE. Have you ever heard a whole set of dishes dropped from the ceiling onto a hard stone floor? [*The Others are speechless with fright.* MILO *shakes his head.* VOICE *happily.*] Have you ever heard an ant wearing fur slippers walk across a thick wool carpet? [MILO *shakes his head again.*] Have you ever heard a blindfolded octopus unwrap a cellophane-covered bathtub? [MILO *shakes his head a third time.*] Ha! I knew it. [*He hops out, a little man, wearing a white coat, with a stethoscope around his neck, and a small mirror attached to his forehead, and with very huge ears, and a mortar*[3] *and pestle*[4] *in his hands. He stares at* MILO, TOCK *and* HUMBUG.] None of you looks well at all! Tsk, tsk, not at all. [*He opens the top or side of his Wagon, revealing a dusty interior resembling an old apothecary*[5] *shop, with shelves lined with jars and boxes, a table, books, test tubes and bottles and measuring spoons.*]

MILO. [*Timidly.*] Are you a doctor?

DISCHORD. [VOICE.] I am KAKAFONOUS A. DISCHORD, DOCTOR OF DISSONANCE! [*Several small explosions and a grinding crash are heard.*]

---

1. **KAKAFONOUS A. DISCHORD** (kä kä′ fä nus ā dis′ kôrd): A playful spelling of the word *discord*, which means "a lack of harmony in tones sounded together."
2. **Dissonance** (dis′ ə nəns) *n.*: Lack of harmony or agreement. A synonym for *discord*.
3. **mortar** (môr′ tər) *n.*: A very hard bowl in which things are ground or pounded by a pestle.
4. **pestle** (pes′ 'l) *n.*: A club-shaped hand tool used to pound or grind things in a mortar.
5. **apothecary** (ə päth′ ə ker′ ē) **shop:** A druggist's or pharmacist's shop.

HUMBUG. [*Stuttering with fear.*] What does the "A" stand for?

DISCHORD. *AS LOUD AS POSSIBLE!* [*Two screeches and a bump are heard.*] Now, step a little closer and stick out your tongues. [DISCHORD *examines them.*] Just as I expected. [*He opens a large dusty book and thumbs through the pages.*] You're all suffering from a severe lack of noise. [DISCHORD *begins running around, collecting bottles, reading the labels to himself as he goes along.*] "Loud Cries." "Soft Cries." "Bangs, Bongs, Swishes, Swooshes." "Snaps and Crackles." "Whistles and Gongs." "Squeeks, Squacks, and Miscellaneous Uproar." [*As he reads them off, he pours a little of each into a large glass beaker and stirs the mixture with a wooden spoon. The concoction smokes and bubbles.*] Be ready in just a moment.

MILO. [*Suspiciously.*] Just what kind of doctor are you?

DISCHORD. Well, you might say, I'm a specialist. I specialize in noises, from the loudest to the softest, and from the slightly annoying to the terribly unpleasant. For instance, have you ever heard a square-wheeled steamroller ride over a street full of hard-boiled eggs? [*Very loud CRUNCHING SOUNDS are heard.*]

MILO. [*Holding his ears.*] But who would want all those terrible noises?

DISCHORD. [*Surprised at the question.*] Everybody does. Why, I'm so busy I can hardly fill all the orders for noise pills, racket lotion, clamor salve and hubbub tonic. That's all people seem to want these days. Years ago, everyone wanted pleasant sounds and business was terrible. But then the cities were built and there was a great need for honking horns, screeching trains, clanging bells and all the rest of those wonderfully unpleasant sounds we use so much today. I've been working overtime ever since and my medicine here is in great demand. All you have to do is take one spoonful every day, and you'll never have to hear another beautiful sound again. Here, try some.

HUMBUG. [*Backing away.*] If it's all the same to you, I'd rather not.

MILO. I don't want to be cured of beautiful sounds.

TOCK. Besides, there's no such sickness as a lack of noise.

DISCHORD. How true. That's what makes it so difficult to cure. [*Takes a large glass bottle from the shelf.*] Very well, if you want to go all through life suffering from a noise deficiency, I'll just give this to Dynne[6] for his lunch. [*Uncorks the bottle and pours the liquid into it. There is a rumbling and then a loud explosion accompanied by smoke, out of which* DYNNE, *a smog-like creature with yellow eyes and a frowning mouth, appears.*]

DYNNE. [*Smacking his lips.*] Ahhh, that was good, Master. I thought you'd never let me out. It was really cramped in there.

DISCHORD. This is my assistant, the awful Dynne. You must forgive his appearance, for he really doesn't have any.

MILO. What is a Dynne?

DISCHORD. You mean you've never heard of the awful Dynne? When you're playing in your room and making a great amount of noise, what do they tell you to stop?

MILO. That awful din.

DISCHORD. When the neighbors are playing their radio too loud late at night, what do you wish they'd turn down?

TOCK. That awful din.

DISCHORD. And when the street on your block is being repaired and the drills are working all day, what does everyone complain of?

HUMBUG. [*Brightly.*] The dreadful row.

DYNNE. The Dreadful Rauw was my grandfather. He perished in the great silence epidemic of 1712. I certainly can't understand why you don't like noise. Why, I heard an explosion last week that was so lovely, I groaned with appreciation for two days. [*He gives a loud groan at the memory.*]

DISCHORD. He's right, you know! Noise is the most valuable thing in the world.

MILO. King Azaz says words are.

DISCHORD. NONSENSE! Why, when a baby wants food, how does he ask?

DYNNE. [*Happily.*] He screams!

DISCHORD. And when a racing car wants gas?

DYNNE. [*Jumping for joy.*] It chokes!

DISCHORD. And what happens to the dawn when a new day begins?

DYNNE. [*Delighted.*] It breaks!

DISCHORD. You see how simple it is? [*To* DYNNE.] Isn't it time for us to go?

MILO. Where to? Maybe we're going the same way.

DYNNE. I doubt it. [*Picking up empty sacks from the table.*] We're going on our collection rounds. Once a day, I travel throughout the kingdom and collect all the wonderfully horrible and beautifully unpleasant sounds I can find and bring them back to the doctor to use in his medicine.

DISCHORD. Where are you going?

MILO. To Digitopolis.

DISCHORD. Oh, there are a number of ways to get to Digitopolis, if you know how to follow directions. Just take a look at the sign at the fork in the road. Though why you'd ever want to go there, I'll never know.

MILO. We want to talk to the Mathemagician.

HUMBUG. About the release of the Princesses Rhyme and Reason.

---

6. Dynne (din): A playful spelling of the word *din*, which means "a loud, continuous noise; confused clamor or uproar."

DISCHORD. Rhyme and Reason? I remember them. Very nice girls, but a little too quiet for my taste. In fact, I've been meaning to send them something that Dynne brought home by mistake and which I have absolutely no use for. [*He rummages through the wagon.*] Ah, here it is . . . or maybe you'd like it for yourself. [*Hands* MILO *a package.*]

MILO. What is it?

DISCHORD. The sounds of laughter. They're so unpleasant to hear, it's almost unbearable. All those giggles and snickers and happy shouts of joy, I don't know what Dynne was thinking of when he collected them. Here, take them to the Princesses or keep them for yourselves, I don't care. Well, time to move on. Goodbye now and good luck! [*He has shut the wagon by now and gets in. LOUD NOISES begin to erupt as* DYNNE *pulls the wagon offstage.*]

MILO. [*Calling after them.*] But wait! The fork in the road . . . you didn't tell us where it is . . .

TOCK. It's too late. He can't hear a thing.

HUMBUG. I could use a fork of my own, at the moment. And a knife and a spoon to go with it. All of a sudden, I feel very hungry.

MILO. So do I, but it's no use thinking about it. There won't be anything to eat until we reach Digitopolis. [*They get into the car.*]

HUMBUG. [*Rubbing his stomach.*] Well, the sooner the better is what I say.

[*A SIGN suddenly appears.*]

VOICE. [*A strange voice from nowhere.*] But which way will get you there sooner? That is the question.

TOCK. Did you hear something?

MILO. Look! The fork in the road and a signpost to Digitopolis! [*They read the Sign.*]

DIGITOPOLIS

5	Miles
1,600	Rods[7]
8,800	Yards
26,400	Feet
316,800	Inches
633,600	Half Inches

AND THEN SOME

HUMBUG. Let's travel by miles, it's shorter.

MILO. Let's travel by half inches. It's quicker.

TOCK. But which road should we take? It must make a difference.

MILO. Do you think so?

TOCK. Well, I'm not sure, but . . .

HUMBUG. He could be right. On the other hand, he could also be wrong. Does it make a difference or not?

VOICE. Yes, indeed, indeed it does, certainly, my yes, it does make a difference.

[*The* DODECAHEDRON[8] *Appears, a 12-sided figure with a different face on each side, and with all the edges labeled with a small letter and all the angles labeled with a large letter. He wears a beret and peers at the others with a serious face. He doffs his cap and recites:*]

DODECAHEDRON.

My angles are many.
My sides are not few.
I'm the Dodecahedron.
Who are you?

---

7. Rods (rädz) *n.*: Measures of length equal to 5.5 yards.
8. Dodecahedron (dō′ dek ə hē′ drən)

MILO. What's a Dodecahedron?

DODECAHEDRON. [*Turning around slowly.*] See for yourself. A Dodecahedron is a mathematical shape with 12 faces. [*All his faces appear as he turns, each face with a different expression. He points to them.*] I usually use one at a time. It saves wear and tear. What are you called?

MILO. Milo.

DODECAHEDRON. That's an odd name. [*Changing his smiling face to a frowning one.*] And you have only one face.

MILO. [*Making sure it is still there.*] Is that bad?

DODECAHEDRON. You'll soon wear it out using it for everything. Is everyone with one face called Milo?

MILO. Oh, no. Some are called Billy or Jeffery or Sally or Lisa or lots of other things.

DODECAHEDRON. How confusing. Here everything is called exactly what it is. The triangles are called triangles, the circles are called circles, and even the same numbers have the same name. Can you imagine what would happen if we named all the twos Billy or Jeffery or Sally or Lisa or lots of other things? You'd have to say Robert plus John equals four, and if the fours were named Albert, things would be hopeless.

MILO. I never thought of it that way.

DODECAHEDRON. [*With an admonishing face.*] Then I suggest you begin at once, for in Digitopolis, everything is quite precise.

MILO. Then perhaps you can help us decide which road we should take.

DODECAHEDRON. [*Happily.*] By all means. There's nothing to it. [*As he talks, the three others try to solve the problem on a Large Blackboard that is wheeled onstage for the occasion.*] Now, if a small car carrying three people at 30 miles an hour for 10 minutes along a road 5 miles long at 11:35 in the morning starts at the same time as 3 people who have been traveling in a little automobile at 20 miles an hour for 15 minutes on another road exactly twice as long as half the distance of the other, while a dog, a bug, and a boy travel an equal distance in the same time or the same distance in an equal time along a third road in mid-October, then which one arrives first and which is the best way to go?

HUMBUG. Seventeen!

MILO. [*Still figuring frantically.*] I'm not sure, but . . .

DODECAHEDRON. You'll have to do better than that.

MILO. I'm not very good at problems.

DODECAHEDRON. What a shame. They're so very useful. Why, did you know that if a beaver 2 feet long with a tail a foot and a half long can build a dam 12 feet high and 6 feet wide in 2 days, all you would need to build

Boulder Dam is a beaver 68 feet long with a 51 foot tail?

HUMBUG. [*Grumbling as his pencil snaps.*] Where would you find a beaver that big?

DODECAHEDRON. I don't know, but if you did, you'd certainly know what to do with him.

MILO. That's crazy.

DODECAHEDRON. That may be true, but it's completely accurate, and as long as the answer is right, who cares if the question is wrong?

TOCK. [*Who has been patiently doing the first problem.*] All three roads arrive at the same place at the same time.

DODECAHEDRON. Correct! And I'll take you there myself. [*The blackboard rolls off, and all four get into the car and drive off.*] Now you see how important problems are. If you hadn't done this one properly, you might have gone the wrong way.

MILO. But if all the roads arrive at the same place at the same time, then aren't they all the right road?

DODECAHEDRON. [*Glaring from his upset face.*] Certainly not! They're all the wrong way! Just because you have a choice, it doesn't mean that any of them *has* to be right. [*Pointing in another direction.*] That's the way to Digitopolis and we'll be there any moment. [*Suddenly the lighting grows dimmer.*] In fact, we're here. Welcome to the Land of Numbers.

HUMBUG. [*Looking around at the barren landscape.*] It doesn't look very inviting.

MILO. Is this the place where numbers are made?

DODECAHEDRON. They're not made. You have to dig for them. Don't you know anything at all about numbers?

MILO. Well, I never really thought they were very important.

DODECAHEDRON. NOT IMPORTANT! Could you have tea for two without the 2? Or three blind mice without the 3? And how would you sail the seven seas without the 7?

MILO. All I meant was . . .

DODECAHEDRON. [*Continues shouting angrily.*] If you had high hopes, how would you know how high they were? And did you know that narrow escapes come in different widths? Would you travel the whole world wide without ever knowing how wide it was? And how could you do anything at long last without knowing how long the last was? Why numbers are the most beautiful and valuable things in the world. Just follow me and I'll show you. [*He motions to them and pantomimes walking through rocky terrain with the others in tow. A Doorway similar to the Tollbooth appears and the* DODECAHEDRON *opens it and motions the others to follow him through.*] Come along, come along. I can't wait for you all day. [*They enter the doorway and the lights are dimmed very low, as to simulate the interior of a cave. The SOUNDS of scrapings and tapping, scuffling and digging are heard all around them. He hands them Helmets with flashlights attached.*] Put these on.

MILO. [*Whispering.*] Where are we going?

DODECAHEDRON. We're here. This is the numbers mine. [*LIGHTS UP A LITTLE, revealing Little Men digging and chopping, shoveling and scraping.*] Right this way and watch your step. [*His voice echoes and reverberates. Iridescent and glittery numbers seem to sparkle from everywhere.*]

MILO. [*Awed.*] Whose mine is it?

VOICE OF MATHEMAGICIAN. By the four million eight hundred and twenty-seven thousand six hundred and fifty-nine hairs on my head, it's mine, of course! [*ENTER* THE MATHEMAGICIAN, *carrying his long staff which looks like a giant pencil.*]

HUMBUG. [*Already intimidated.*] It's a lovely mine, really it is.

MATHEMAGICIAN. [*Proudly.*] The biggest number mine in the kingdom.

MILO. [*Excitedly.*] Are there any precious stones in it?

MATHEMAGICIAN. *Precious stones!* [*Then softly.*] By the eight million two hundred and forty-seven thousand three hundred and twelve threads in my robe, I'll say there are. Look here. [*Reaches in a cart pulls out a small object, polishes it vigorously and holds it to the light, where it sparkles.*]

MILO. But that's a five.

MATHEMAGICIAN. Exactly. As valuable a jewel as you'll find anywhere. Look at some of the others. [*Scoops up others and pours them into* MILO*'s arms. They include all numbers from 1 to 9 and an assortment of zeros.*]

DODECAHEDRON. We dig them and polish them right here, and then send them all over the world. Marvelous, aren't they?

TOCK. They are beautiful. [*He holds them up to compare them to the numbers on his clock body.*]

MILO. So that's where they come from. [*Looks at them and carefully hands them back, but drops a few which smash and break in half.*] Oh, I'm sorry!

MATHEMAGICIAN. [*Scooping them up.*] Oh, don't worry about that. We use the broken ones for fractions. How about some lunch? [*Takes out a little whistle and blows it. Two miners rush in carrying an immense cauldron which is bubbling and steaming. The workers put down their tools and gather around to eat.*]

HUMBUG. That looks delicious! [TOCK *and* MILO *also look hungrily at the pot.*]

MATHEMAGICIAN. Perhaps you'd care for something to eat?

MILO. Oh, yes, sir!

TOCK. Thank you.

HUMBUG. [*Already eating.*] Ummm . . . delicious! [*All finish their bowls immediately.*]

MATHEMAGICIAN. Please have another portion. [*They eat and finish.* MATHEMAGICIAN *serves them again.*] Don't stop now. [*They finish.*] Come on, no need to be bashful. [*Serves them again.*]

MILO. [*To* TOCK *and* HUMBUG *as he finishes again.*] Do you want to hear something strange? Each one I eat makes me a little hungrier than before.

MATHEMAGICIAN. Do have some more. [*He serves them again. They eat frantically, until the* MATHEMAGICIAN *blows his whistle again and the pot is removed.*]

HUMBUG. [*Holding his stomach.*] Uggghhh! I think I'm starving.

MILO. Me, too, and I ate so much.

DODECAHEDRON. [*Wiping the gravy from several of his mouths.*] Yes, it was delicious, wasn't it? It's the specialty of the kingdom . . . subtraction stew.

TOCK. [*Weak from hunger.*] I have more of an appetite than when I began.

MATHEMAGICIAN. Certainly, what did you expect? The more you eat, the hungrier you get, everyone knows that.

MILO. They do? Then how do you get enough?

MATHEMAGICIAN. Enough? Here in Digitopolis, we have our meals when we're full and eat until we're hungry. That way, when you don't have anything at all, you have more than enough. It's a very economical system. You must have been stuffed to have eaten so much.

DODECAHEDRON. It's completely logical. The more you want, the less you get, and the less you get, the more you have. Simple arithmetic, that's all. [TOCK, MILO *and* HUMBUG *look at him blankly.*] Now, look, suppose you had something and added nothing to it. What would you have?

MILO. The same.

DODECAHEDRON. Splendid! And suppose you had something and added less than nothing to it? What would you have then?

HUMBUG. Starvation! Oh, I'm so hungry.

DODECAHEDRON. Now, now, it's not as bad as all that. In a few hours, you'll be nice and full again . . . just in time for dinner.

MILO. But I only eat when I'm hungry.

MATHEMAGICIAN. [*Waving the eraser of his staff.*] What a curious idea. The next thing you'll have us believe is that you only sleep when you're tired.

[*The mine has disappeared as well as the Miners.*]

HUMBUG. Where did everyone go?

MATHEMAGICIAN. Oh, they're still in the mine. I often find that the best way to get from one place to another is to erase everything and start again. Please make yourself at home.

[*They find themselves in a unique room, in which all the walls, tables, chairs, desks, cabinets and blackboards are labeled to show their heights, widths, depths and distances to and from each other. To one side is a gigantic notepad on an artist's easel, and from hooks and strings hang a collection of rulers, measures, weights and tapes, and all other measuring devices.*]

MILO. Do you always travel that way? [*He looks around in wonder.*]

MATHEMAGICIAN. No, indeed! [*He pulls a plumb line*[9] *from a hook and walks.*] Most of the time I take the shortest distance between any two points. And of course, when I have to be in several places at once . . . [*He writes* $3 \times 1 = 3$ *on the notepad with his staff.*] I simply multiply. [THREE FIGURES *looking like the* MATHEMAGICIAN *appear on a platform above.*]

MILO. How did you do that?

MATHEMAGICIAN AND THE THREE. There's nothing to it, if you have a magic staff. [THE THREE *cancel themselves out and disappear.*]

HUMBUG. That's nothing but a big pencil.

MATHEMAGICIAN. True enough, but once you learn to use it, there's no end to what you can do.

MILO. Can you make things disappear?

MATHEMAGICIAN. Just step a little closer and watch this. [*Shows them that there is nothing up his sleeve or in his hat. He writes:*]

9. **plumb** (plum) **line** *n.*: A string with a lead weight attached to one end and used to find out how deep water is or how straight a wall is.

$4+9-2\times16+1=3\times6-67+8\times2-3+26-1-34+3-7+2-5=$ [*He looks up expectantly.*]

HUMBUG. Seventeen?

MILO. It all comes to zero.

MATHEMAGICIAN. Precisely. [*Makes a theatrical bow and rips off paper from notepad.*] Now, is there anything else you'd like to see? [*At this point, an appeal to the audience to see if anyone would like a problem solved.*]

MILO. Well . . . can you show me the biggest number there is?

MATHEMAGICIAN. Why, I'd be delighted. [*Opening a closet door.*] We keep it right here. It took four miners to dig it out. [*He shows them a huge "3" twice as high as the* MATHEMAGICIAN.]

MILO. No, that's not what I mean. Can you

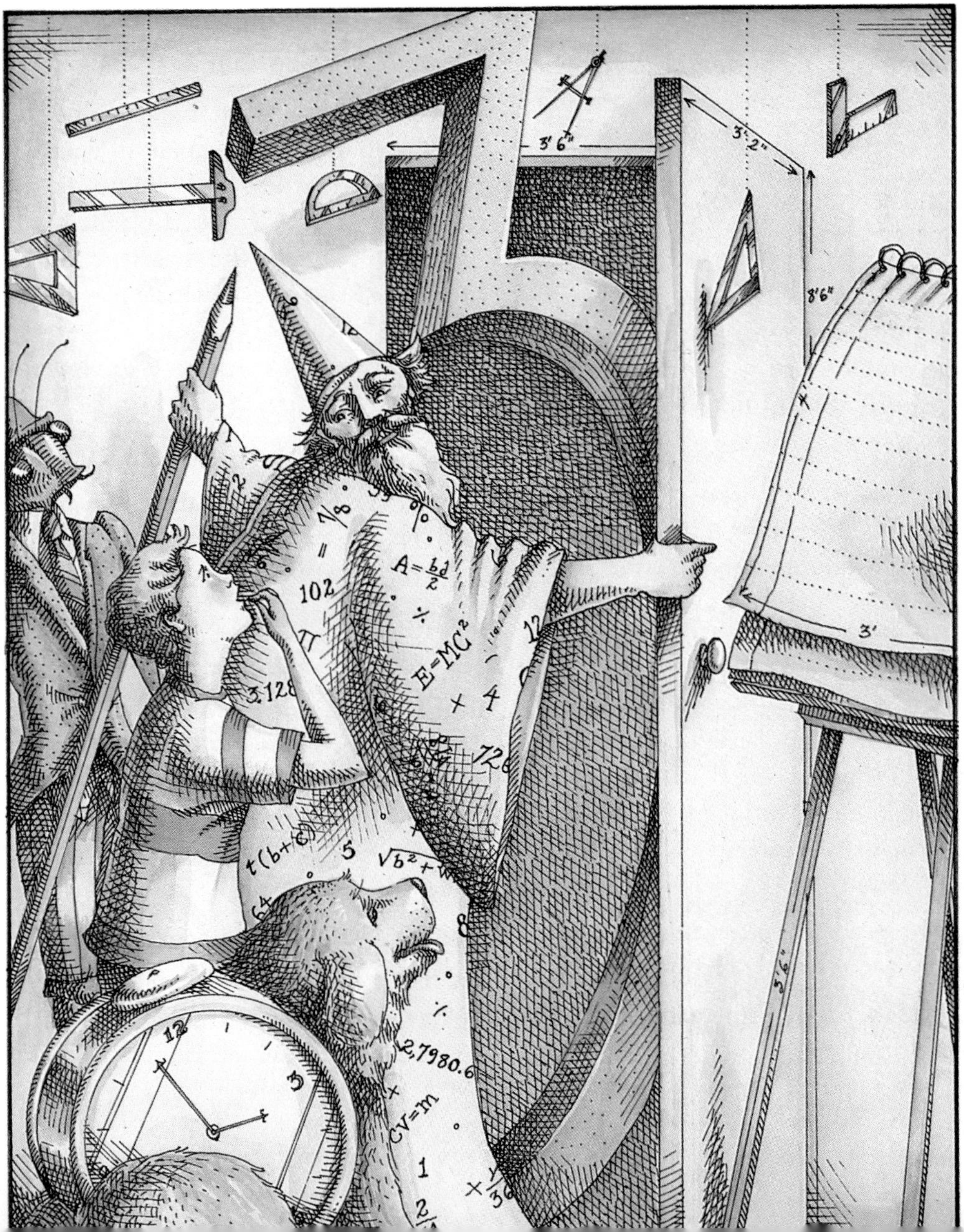

show me the longest number there is?

MATHEMAGICIAN. Sure. [*Opens another door.*] Here it is. It took three carts to carry it here. [*Door reveals an "8" that is as wide as the "3" was high.*]

MILO. No, no, that's not what I meant either. [*Looks helplessly at* TOCK.]

TOCK. I think what you would like to see is the number of the greatest possible magnitude.

MATHEMAGICIAN. Well, why didn't you say so? [*He busily measures them and all other things as he speaks, and marks it down.*] What's the greatest number you can think of? [*Here, an appeal can also be made to the audience or* MILO *may think of his own answers.*]

MILO. Uh . . . nine trillion, nine hundred and ninety-nine billion, nine hundred ninety-nine million, nine-hundred ninety-nine thousand, nine hundred and ninety-nine. [*He puffs.*]

MATHEMAGICIAN. [*Writes that on the pad.*] Very good. Now add one to it. [MILO *or audience does.*] Now add one again. [MILO *or audience does so.*] Now add one again. Now add one again. Now add . . .

MILO. But when can I stop?

MATHEMAGICIAN. Never. Because the number you want is always at least one more than the number you have, and it's so large that if you started saying it yesterday, you wouldn't finish tomorrow.

HUMBUG. Where could you ever find a number so big?

MATHEMAGICIAN. In the same place they have the smallest number there is, and you know what that is?

MILO. The smallest number . . . let's see . . . one one-millionth?

MATHEMAGICIAN. Almost. Now all you have to do is divide that in half and then divide that in half and then divide that in half and then divide that . . .

MILO. Doesn't that ever stop either?

MATHEMAGICIAN. How can it when you can always take half of what you have and divide it in half again? Look. [*Pointing offstage.*] You see that line?

MILO. You mean that long one out there?

MATHEMAGICIAN. That's it. Now, if you just follow that line forever, and when you reach the end, turn left, you will find the Land of Infinity. That's where the tallest, the shortest, the biggest, the smallest and the most and the least of everything are kept.

MILO. But how can you follow anything forever? You know, I get the feeling that everything in Digitopolis is very difficult.

MATHEMAGICIAN. But on the other hand, I think you'll find that the only thing you can do easily is be wrong, and that's hardly worth the effort.

MILO. But . . . what bothers me is . . . well, why is it that even when things are correct, they don't really seem to be right?

MATHEMAGICIAN. [*Grows sad and quiet.*] How true. It's been that way ever since Rhyme and Reason were banished. [*Sadness turns to fury.*] *And all because of that stubborn wretch Azaz!* It's all his fault.

MILO. Maybe if you discussed it with him . . .

MATHEMAGICIAN. He's just too unreasonable! Why just last month, I sent him a very friendly letter, which he never had the courtesy to answer. See for yourself. [*Puts the* *letter on the easel. The letter reads:*]

4738 1919,
667 394107 5841 62589
85371 14 39588 7190434 203
27689 57131 481206.

5864 98053,
62179875073

MILO. But maybe he doesn't understand numbers.

MATHEMAGICIAN. Nonsense! Everybody understands numbers. No matter what language you speak, they always mean the same thing. A seven is a seven everywhere in the world.

MILO. [*To* TOCK *and* HUMBUG.] Everyone is so sensitive about what he knows best.

TOCK. With your permission, sir, we'd like to rescue Rhyme and Reason.

MATHEMAGICIAN. Has Azaz agreed to it?

TOCK. Yes, sir.

MATHEMAGICIAN. THEN I DON'T! Ever since they've been banished, we've never agreed on anything, and we never will.

MILO. Never?

MATHEMAGICIAN. NEVER! And if you can prove otherwise, you have my permission to go.

MILO. Well then, with whatever Azaz agrees, you disagree.

MATHEMAGICIAN. Correct.

MILO. And with whatever Azaz disagrees, you agree.

MATHEMAGICIAN. [*Yawning, cleaning his nails.*] Also correct.

MILO. Then, each of you agrees that he will disagree with whatever each of you agrees with, and if you both disagree with the same thing, aren't you really in agreement?

MATHEMAGICIAN. I'VE BEEN TRICKED! [*Figures it over, but comes up with the same answer.*]

TOCK. And now may we go?

MATHEMAGICIAN. [*Nods weakly.*] It's a long and dangerous journey. Long before you find them, the demons will know you're there. Watch out for them, because if you ever come face to face, it will be too late. But there is one other obstacle even more serious than that.

MILO. [*Terrified.*] What is it?

MATHEMAGICIAN. I'm afraid I can't tell you until you return. But maybe I can give you something to help you out. [*Claps hands. ENTER the* DODECAHEDRON, *carrying something on a pillow. The* MATHEMAGICIAN *takes it.*] Here is your own magic staff. Use it well and there is nothing it can't do for you. [*Puts a small, gleaming pencil in* MILO'S *breast pocket.*]

HUMBUG. Are you sure you can't tell about that serious obstacle?

MATHEMAGICIAN. Only when you return. And now the Dodecahedron will escort you to the road that leads to the Castle-in-the-Air. Farewell, my friends, and good luck to you. [*They shake hands, say goodbye, and the* DODECAHEDRON *leads them off.*] Good luck to you! [*To himself.*] Because you're sure going to need it. [*He watches them through a telescope and marks down the calculations.*]

DODECAHEDRON. [*He re-enters.*] Well, they're on their way.

MATHEMAGICIAN. So I see. [DODECAHEDRON *stands waiting.*] Well, what is it?

DODECAHEDRON. I was just wondering myself, your Numbership. What actually *is* the serious obstacle you were talking about?

MATHEMAGICIAN. [*Looks at him in surprise.*] You mean you really don't know?

BLACKOUT

Scene 2
The Land of Ignorance

LIGHTS UP on RHYME *and* REASON, *in their castle, looking out two windows.*

RHYME.

I'm worried sick, I must confess
I wonder if they'll have success
All the others tried in vain,
And were never seen or heard again.

REASON. Now, Rhyme, there's no need to be so pessimistic. Milo, Tock, and Humbug have just as much chance of succeeding as they do of failing.

RHYME.

But the demons are so deadly smart
They'll stuff your brain and fill your heart
With petty thoughts and selfish dreams
And trap you with their nasty schemes.

REASON. Now, Rhyme, be reasonable, won't you? And calm down, you always talk in couplets[10] when you get nervous. Milo has learned a lot from his journey. I think he's a match for the demons and that he might soon be knocking at our door. Now come on, cheer up, won't you?

RHYME. I'll try.

---

10. couplets (kup′ lits) *n.*: Two rhyming lines of poetry that have the same rhythm and that come one after another.

[*LIGHTS FADE on the* PRINCESSES *and COME UP on the little Car, traveling slowly.*]

MILO. So this is the Land of Ignorance. It's so dark. I can hardly see a thing. Maybe we should wait until morning.

VOICE. They'll be mourning for you soon enough. [*They look up and see a large, soiled, ugly* BIRD *with a dangerous beak and a malicious expression.*]

MILO. I don't think you understand. We're looking for a place to spend the night.

BIRD. [*Shrieking.*] It's not yours to spend!

MILO. That doesn't make any sense, you see . . .

BIRD. Dollars or cents, it's still not yours to spend.

MILO. But I don't mean . . .

BIRD. Of course you're mean. Anybody who'd spend a night that doesn't belong to him is very mean.

TOCK. Must you interrupt like that?

BIRD. Naturally, it's my job. I take the words right out of your mouth. Haven't we met before? I'm the Everpresent Wordsnatcher.

MILO. Are you a demon?

BIRD. I'm afraid not. I've tried, but the best I can manage to be is a nuisance. [*Suddenly gets nervous as he looks beyond the three.*] And I don't have time to waste with you. [*Starts to leave.*]

TOCK. What is it? What's the matter?

MILO. Hey, don't leave. I wanted to ask you some questions. . . . Wait!

BIRD. Weight? Twenty-seven pounds. Bye-bye. [*Disappears.*]

MILO. Well, he was no help.

MAN. Perhaps I can be of some assistance to you? [*There appears a beautifully-dressed* MAN, *very polished and clean.*] Hello, little boy. [*Shakes* MILO'S *hand.*] And how's the faithful dog? [*Pats* TOCK.] And who is this handsome creature? [*Tips his hat to* HUMBUG.]

HUMBUG. [*To others.*] What a pleasant surprise to meet someone so nice in a place like this.

MAN. But before I help you out, I wonder if first you could spare me a little of your time, and help me with a few small jobs?

HUMBUG. Why, certainly.

TOCK. Gladly.

MILO. Sure, we'd be happy to.

MAN. Splendid, for there are just three tasks. First, I would like to move this pile of sand from here to there. [*Indicates through pantomime a large pile of sand.*] But I'm afraid that all I have is this tiny tweezers. [*Hands it to* MILO, *who begins moving the sand one grain at a time.*] Second, I would like to empty this well and fill that other, but I have no bucket, so you'll have to use this eyedropper. [*Hands it to* TOCK, *who begins to work.*] And finally, I must have a hole in this cliff, and here is a needle to dig it. [HUMBUG *eagerly begins. The* MAN *leans against a tree and stares vacantly off into space. The LIGHTS indicate the passage of time.*]

MILO. You know something? I've been working steadily for a long time, now, and I don't feel the least bit tired or hungry. I could go right on the same way forever.

MAN. Maybe you will. [*He yawns.*]

MILO. [*Whispers to* TOCK.] Well, I wish I knew how long it was going to take.

TOCK. Why don't you use your magic staff and find out?

MILO. [*Takes out pencil and calculates. To* MAN.] Pardon me, sir, but it's going to take 837 years to finish these jobs.

MAN. Is that so? What a shame. Well then you'd better get on with them.

MILO. But . . . it hardly seems worthwhile.

MAN. WORTHWHILE! Of course they're not worthwhile. I wouldn't ask you to do anything that was worthwhile.

TOCK. Then why bother?

MAN. Because, my friends, what could be more important than doing unimportant things? If you stop to do enough of them, you'll never get where you are going. [*Laughs villainously.*]

MILO. [*Gasps.*] Oh, no. You must be . . .

MAN. Quite correct! I am the Terrible Trivium, demon of petty tasks and worthless jobs, ogre of wasted effort and monster of habit. [*They start to back away from him.*] Don't try to leave, there's so much to do, and you still have 837 years to go on the first job.

MILO. But why do unimportant things?

MAN. Think of all the trouble it saves. If you spend all your time doing only the easy and useless jobs, you'll never have time to worry about the important ones which are so difficult. [*Walks toward them, whispering.*] Now do come and stay with me. We'll have such fun together. There are things to fill and things to empty, things to take away and things to bring back, things to pick up and things to put down . . . [*They are transfixed by his soothing voice. He is about to embrace them when a* VOICE *screams.*]

VOICE. Run! Run! [*They all wake up and*

run with the Trivium behind. As the VOICE *continues to call out directions, they follow until they lose the Trivium.*] RUN! RUN! This way! This way! Over here! Over here! Up here! Down there! Quick, hurry up!

TOCK. [*Panting.*] I think we lost him.

VOICE. Keep going straight! Keep going straight! Now step up! Now step up!

MILO. Look out! [*They all fall into a Trap.*] But he said "up!"

VOICE. Well, I hope you didn't expect to get anywhere by listening to me.

HUMBUG. We're in a deep pit! We'll never get out of here.

VOICE. That is quite an accurate evaluation of the situation.

MILO. [*Shouting angrily.*] Then why did you help us at all?

VOICE. Oh, I'd do as much for anybody. Bad advice is my specialty. [*A Little Furry Creature appears.*] I'm the demon of Insincerity. I don't mean what I say; I don't mean what I do; and I don't mean what I am.

MILO. Then why don't you go away and leave us alone!

INSINCERITY. [VOICE.] Now, there's no need to get angry. You're a very clever boy and I have complete confidence in you. You can certaintly climb out of that pit . . . come on, try . . .

MILO. I'm not listening to one word you say! You're just telling me what you think I'd *like* to hear, and not what is important.

INSINCERITY. Well, if that's the way you feel about it . . .

MILO. That's the way I feel about it. We will manage by ourselves without any unnecessary advice from you.

INSINCERITY. [*Stamping his foot.*] Well, all right for you! Most people listen to what I say, but if that's the way you feel, then I'll just go home. [*Exits in a huff.*]

HUMBUG. [*Who has been quivering with fright.*] And don't you ever come back! Well, I guess we showed him, didn't we?

MILO. You know something? This place is a lot more dangerous than I ever imagined.

TOCK. [*Who's been surveying the situation.*] I think I figured a way to get out. Here, hop on my back. [MILO *does so.*] Now, you, Humbug, on top of Milo. [*He does so.*] Now hook your umbrella onto that tree and hold on. [*They climb over* HUMBUG, *then pull him up.*]

HUMBUG. [*As they climb.*] Watch it! Watch it, now. Ow, be careful of my back! My back! Easy, easy . . . oh, this is so difficult. Aren't you finished yet?

TOCK. [*As he pulls up* HUMBUG.] There. Now, I'll lead for a while. Follow me, and we'll stay out of trouble. [*They walk and climb higher and higher.*]

HUMBUG. Can't we slow down a little?

TOCK. Something tells me we better reach the Castle-in-the-Air as soon as possible, and not stop to rest for a single moment. [*They speed up.*]

MILO. What is it, Tock? Did you see something?

TOCK. Just keep walking and don't look back.

MILO. You *did* see something!

HUMBUG. What is it? Another demon?

TOCK. Not just one, I'm afraid. If you want to see what I'm talking about, then turn around. [*They turn around. The stage darkens and hundreds of Yellow Gleaming Eyes can be seen.*]

HUMBUG. Good grief! Do you see how many there are? Hundreds! The Overbearing Know-it-all, the Gross Exaggeration, the Horrible Hopping Hindsight, . . . and look over there! The Triple Demons of Compromise! Let's get out of here! [*Starts to scurry.*] Hurry up, you two! Must you be so slow about everything?

MILO. Look! There it is, up ahead! The Castle-in-the-Air! [*They all run.*]

HUMBUG. They're gaining!

MILO. But there it is!

HUMBUG. I see it! I see it!

[*They reach the first step and are stopped by a little man in a frock coat, sleeping on a worn ledger. He has a long quill pen and a bottle of ink at his side. He is covered with ink stains over his clothes and wears spectacles.*]

TOCK. Shh! Be very careful. [*They try to step over him, but he wakes up.*]

SENSES TAKER. [*From sleeping position.*] Names? [*He sits up.*]

HUMBUG. Well, I . . .

SENSES TAKER. *NAMES?* [*He opens book and begins to write, splattering himself with ink.*]

HUMBUG. Uh . . . Humbug, Tock and this is Milo.

SENSES TAKER. Splendid, splendid. I haven't had an "M" in ages.

MILO. What do you want our names for? We're sort of in a hurry.

SENSES TAKER. Oh, this won't take long. I'm

the official Senses Taker and I must have some information before I can take your sense. Now if you'll just tell me: [*Handing them a form to fill. Speaking slowly and deliberately.*] When you were born, where you were born, why you were born, how old you are now, how old you were then, how old you'll be in a little while . . .

MILO. I wish he'd hurry up. At this rate, the demons will be here before we know it!

SENSES TAKER. . . . Your mother's name, your father's name, where you live, how long you've lived there, the schools you've attended, the schools you haven't attended . . .

HUMBUG. I'm getting writer's cramp.

TOCK. I smell something very evil and it's getting stronger every second. [*To* SENSES TAKER.] May we go now?

SENSES TAKER. Just as soon as you tell me your height, your weight, the number of books you've read this year . . .

MILO. We have to go!

SENSES TAKER. All right, all right, I'll give you the short form. [*Pulls out a small piece of paper.*] Destination?

MILO. But we have to . . .

SENSES TAKER. *DESTINATION?*

MILO, TOCK AND HUMBUG. The Castle-in-the-Air! [*They throw down their papers and run past him up the first few stairs.*]

SENSES TAKER. Stop! I'm sure you'd rather see what I have to show you. [*Snaps his fingers; they freeze.*] A circus of your very own. [*CIRCUS MUSIC is heard.* MILO *seems to go into a trance.*] And wouldn't you enjoy this most wonderful smell? [TOCK *sniffs and goes into a trance.*] And here's something I know you'll enjoy hearing . . . [*To* HUMBUG. *The sound of CHEERS and APPLAUSE for* HUMBUG *is heard, and he goes into a trance.*] There we are. And now, I'll just sit back and let the demons catch up with you.

[MILO *accidentally drops his package of gifts. The Package of Laughter from* DR. DISCHORD *opens and the Sounds of Laughter are heard. After a moment,* MILO, TOCK *and* HUMBUG *join in laughing and the spells are broken.*]

MILO. There was no circus.

TOCK. There were no smells.

HUMBUG. The applause is gone.

SENSES TAKER. I warned you I was the Senses Taker. I'll steal your sense of your sense of Purpose, your sense of Duty, destroy your sense of Proportion—and but for one thing, you'd be helpless yet.

MILO. What's that?

SENSES TAKER. As long as you have the sound of laughter, I cannot take your sense of Humor. Agh! That horrible sense of humor.

HUMBUG. HERE THEY COME! LET'S GET OUT OF HERE!

[*The demons appear in nasty slithering hordes, running through the audience and up onto the stage, trying to attack* TOCK, MILO *and* HUMBUG. *The three heroes run past the* SENSES TAKER *up the stairs toward the Castle-in-the-Air with the demons snarling behind them.*]

MILO. Don't look back! Just keep going! [*They reach the castle. The two* PRINCESSES *appear in the windows.*]

PRINCESSES. Hurry! Hurry! We've been expecting you.

MILO. You must be the Princesses. We've come to rescue you.

HUMBUG. And the demons are close behind!

TOCK. We should leave right away.

PRINCESSES. We're ready anytime you are.

MILO. Good, now if you'll just come out. But wait a minute—there's no door! How can we rescue you from the Castle-in-the-Air if there's no way to get in or out?

HUMBUG. Hurry, Milo! They're gaining on us.

REASON. Take your time, Milo, and think about it.

MILO. Ummmn all right . . . just give me a second or two. [*He thinks hard.*]

HUMBUG. I think I feel sick.

MILO. I've got it! Where's that package of presents? [*Opens the package of letters.*] Ah, here it is. [*Takes out the letters and sticks them on the door, spelling:*] E-N-T-R-A-N-C-E. Entrance. Now, let's see. [*Rummages through and spells in smaller letters:*] P-u-s-h. Push. [*He pushes and a door opens. The* PRINCESSES *come out of the castle. Slowly, the demons ascend the stairway.*]

HUMBUG. Oh, it's too late. They're coming up and there's no other way down!

MILO. Unless . . . [*Looks at* TOCK.] Well . . . Time flies, doesn't it?

TOCK. Quite often. Hold on, everyone, and I'll take you down.

HUMBUG. Can you carry us all?

TOCK. We'll soon find out. Ready or not, here we go!

[*His alarm begins to ring. They jump off the platform and disappear. The demons, howling with rage, reach the top and find no one there. They see the* PRINCESSES *and the heroes running across the stage and bound down the stairs after them and into the audience. There is a mad chase scene until they reach the stage again.*]

HUMBUG. I'm exhausted! I can't run another step.

MILO. We can't stop now . . .

TOCK. Milo! Look out there! [*The armies of* AZAZ *and* MATHEMAGICIAN *appear at the back of the theater, with the Kings at their heads.*]

AZAZ. [*As they march toward the stage.*] Don't worry, Milo, we'll take over now.

MATHEMAGICIAN. Those demons may not know it, but their days are numbered!

SPELLING BEE. Charge! C-H-A-R-G-E! Charge! [*They rush at the demons and battle until the demons run off howling. Everyone cheers. The* five MINISTERS *of* AZAZ *appear and shake* MILO's *hand.*]

MINISTER 1. Well done.

MINISTER 2. Fine job.

MINISTER 3. Good Work!

MINISTER 4. Congratulations!

MINISTER 5. CHEERS! [*Everyone cheers again. A fanfare interrupts. A* PAGE *steps forward and reads from a large scroll:*]

PAGE.

Henceforth, and forthwith,
Let it be known by one and all,
That Rhyme and Reason
Reign once more in Wisdom.

[*The* PRINCESSES *bow gratefully and kiss their brothers, the Kings.*]

And furthermore,
The boy named Milo,
The dog known as Tock,
And the insect hereinafter referred to as the Humbug
Are hereby declared to be
Heroes of the Realm.

[*All bow and salute the heroes.*]

MILO. But we never could have done it without a lot of help.

REASON. That may be true, but you had the courage to try, and what you can do is often a matter of what you *will* do.

AZAZ. That's why there was one very important thing about your quest we couldn't discuss until you returned.

MILO. I remember. What was it?

AZAZ. Very simple. It was impossible!

MATHEMAGICIAN. *Completely* impossible!

HUMBUG. Do you mean . . . ? [*Feeling faint.*] Oh . . . I think I need to sit down.

AZAZ. Yes, indeed, but if we'd told you then, you might not have gone.

MATHEMAGICIAN. And, as you discovered, many things are possible just as long as you don't know they're impossible.

MILO. I think I understand.

RHYME. I'm afraid it's time to go now.

REASON. And you must say goodbye.

MILO. To everyone? [*Looks around at the crowd. To* TOCK *and* HUMBUG.] Can't you two come with me?

HUMBUG. I'm afraid not, old man. I'd like to, but I've arranged for a lecture tour which will keep me occupied for years.

TOCK. And they do need a watchdog here.

MILO. Well, O.K., then. [MILO *hugs the* HUMBUG.]

HUMBUG. [*Sadly.*] Oh, bah.

MILO. [*He hugs* TOCK, *and then faces everyone.*] Well, goodbye. We all spent so much time together, I know I'm going to miss you. [*To the* PRINCESSES.] I guess we would have reached you a lot sooner if I hadn't made so many mistakes.

REASON. You must never feel badly about making mistakes, Milo, as long as you take the trouble to learn from them. Very often you learn more by being wrong for the right reasons than you do by being right for the wrong ones.

MILO. But there's so much to learn.

RHYME. That's true, but it's not just learning that's important. It's learning what to do with what you learn and learning why you learn things that matters.

MILO. I think I know what you mean, Princess. At least, I hope I do. [*The car is rolled forward and* MILO *climbs in.*] Goodbye! Goodbye! I'll be back someday! I will! Anyway, I'll try. [*As* MILO *drives, the set of the Land of Ignorance begins to move offstage.*]

AZAZ. Goodbye! Always remember. Words! Words! Words!

MATHEMAGICIAN. *And* numbers!

AZAZ. Now, don't tell me you think numbers are as important as words?

MATHEMAGICIAN. Is that so? Why I'll have you know . . . [*The set disappears, and* MILO'*s Room is seen onstage.*]

MILO. [*As he drives on.*] Oh, oh, I hope they don't start all over again. Because I don't think I'll have much time in the near future to help them out. [*The sound of loud ticking is heard.* MILO *finds himself in his room. He gets out of the car and looks around.*]

THE CLOCK. Did someone mention time?

MILO. Boy, I must have been gone for an awful long time. I wonder what time it is. [*Looks at* CLOCK.] Five o'clock. I wonder what day it is. [*Looks at calendar.*] It's still today! I've only been gone for an hour! [*He continues to look at his calendar, and then begins to look at his books and toys and maps and chemistry set with great interest.*]

CLOCK. An hour, Sixty minutes. How long it really lasts depends on what you do with it. For some people, an hour seems to last forever. For others, just a moment, and so full of things to do.

MILO. [*Looks at clock.*] Six o'clock already?

CLOCK. In an instant. In a trice. Before you have time to blink. [*The stage goes black in less than no time at all.*]

Reader's Response

Does anyone in this play remind you of anyone you know? Explain.

Copies of this play, in individual paper-covered acting editions, are available from Samuel French, Inc., 45 W. 25th St., New York, N.Y. 10010 or 7623 Sunset Blvd., Hollywood, Calif., 90046 or in Canada Samuel French, (Canada) Ltd., 80 Richmond Street East, Toronto M5C 1P1, Canada.

RESPONDING TO THE SELECTION

Your Response

1. Of all the senses that the Senses Taker wants to steal, which do you think is the most important?

Recalling

2. Describe how Tock, Milo, and Humbug rescue the two princesses.

Interpreting

3. Why is it necessary that Milo rescue the banished princesses?
4. Explain why the tollbooth is characterized as a phantom in the title of the play.
5. What does Milo learn from his adventures?

Applying

6. Do you agree with Princess Reason's comment that "often you learn more by being wrong for the right reasons than you do by being right for the wrong ones"? Explain.
7. Near the end of the play, the Mathemagician says to Milo, "And, as you discovered, many things are possible just as long as you don't know they're impossible." What examples can you share in which you or others achieved what was thought impossible?

ANALYZING LITERATURE

Identifying Author's Purpose

An author's **purpose** is his or her goal or aim in a piece of literature. A writer may have more than one purpose. For example, in *The Phantom Tollbooth,* the author's general purpose may be to entertain you. A specific purpose might be to teach about the value of knowledge and our personal responsibility in pursuing it.

1. What might be another general purpose the author had for writing this work? Explain.
2. What other specific purpose might the author have had? Explain.

CRITICAL THINKING AND READING

Analyzing Common Expressions

Common expressions are colorful, familiar phrases whose meanings are popularly understood. These expressions are not to be taken literally, and generally do not make sense when they are. Many such expressions appear in *The Phantom Tollbooth,* but the characters take the meanings literally. The result is a humorous misunderstanding. When Milo, for example, asks for a "square meal," he gets exactly that—a meal shaped like squares.

Find three more examples of common expressions that are taken literally in the play. Write down the expressions, give the literal meaning of each, and write the generally understood meaning of each expression.

THINKING AND WRITING

Writing a Script

In *The Phantom Tollbooth,* Milo and Tock meet many interesting characters and travel to strange lands. Think of another episode in which Milo and Tock travel to another strange land and meet characters that you invent. Brainstorm with classmates about possible places and characters. After you have chosen the place and the characters, write the script for the adventure. In addition to the dialogue, include a description of the scene and all the characters. If you like, use some of the same kind of word play used by the author.

LEARNING OPTION

Performance. With a small group of classmates, present a brief scene from the play. Decide on parts, discuss how each part should be played, and rehearse your parts. When you are ready, perform the scene for your classmates.

BRIDGING FORMS

A WRINKLE IN TIME by Madeleine L'Engle

What is the most evil thing that you can imagine? For Meg, the main character in Madeleine L'Engle's *A Wrinkle in Time,* IT is even more evil than she can imagine. Traveling to the imaginary world of Camazotz to face IT was the most fearful thing that she had ever had to do.

Traveling to imaginary worlds and meeting strange and fantastic characters, such as IT, can broaden our own world. In *The Phantom Tollbooth,* Milo travels to many places, including the Land of Expectations, Dictionopolis, and Digitopolis. In each place Milo meets strange, new characters, who contribute to his understanding of himself and his world. Upon Milo's return home, he learns how precious time is and why he should not waste it.

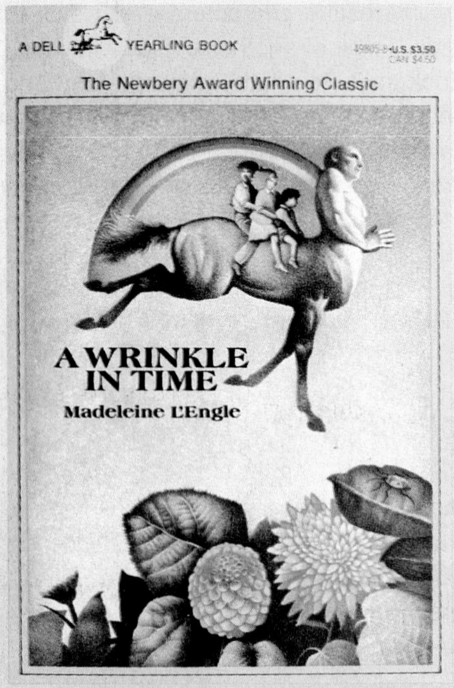

Traveling Through a Wrinkle in Time

Similarly, in the novel *A Wrinkle in Time,* Madeleine L'Engle takes Meg and Charles Wallace and a friend to Camazotz. A tesseract, or "a wrinkle in time" sends them to this mysterious place, just as Milo's tollbooth allowed his escape from boredom. In both stories Milo and Meg are up against seemingly impossible odds as they set out on their missions. In *The Phantom Tollbooth,* Milo must rescue the princesses Rhyme and Reason; in *A Wrinkle in Time,* Meg must rescue her father and then her brother from the evil IT.

Adventures like the ones Milo and Meg have take place in imaginary worlds. The imaginary world is a bridge in literature. It crosses from one form of literature to another. Whether the imaginary world is in a play, a novel, or any other form, it broadens our vision of our own world.

The Dark Thing

"Meg looked. The dark shadow was still there. It had not lessened or dispersed with the coming of night. And where the shadow was the stars were not visible.

"What could there be about a shadow that was so terrible that she knew that there had never been before or ever would be again, anything that would chill her with a fear that was beyond shuddering, beyond crying or screaming, beyond the possibility of comfort?"

This passage from *A Wrinkle in Time* describes Meg's first encounter with the evil IT. But there are to be many more encounters because what brought Meg to face IT was her search for and ultimate rescue of her father.

When Meg was younger, her father, who is a scientist, suddenly disappeared while working on a secret government project. In her quest to find her father, Meg, joined by her genius brother Charles and her friend Calvin, have to tesseract, or go through a wrinkle in time, to Camazotz. There they meet three strange ladies—Mrs. Who, Mrs. Whatsit, and Mrs. Which—who assist them in finding Meg and Charles's father.

To find out how Meg and Charles rescue their father and conquer IT and what they discover about themselves in the process, you must read the novel.

From the Unknown to the Known

Crossing bridges can move you from one place to another—from the known to the unknown, from the real to the imaginary. Once you have crossed a bridge, new experiences become probable. As you read *A Wrinkle in Time*, look for the experiences that change Meg. Does she change as a result of meeting other people? Other powers? What does she learn about herself that she doesn't know at the beginning of the novel? What can you learn about yourself from Meg?

If you would like to read more stories about traveling to imaginary worlds, look for novels, plays, short stories, and poetry in a library or bookstore. There are plenty more imaginary worlds awaiting your visit.

FOCUS ON READING

Story Mapping

One good way to help you better understand and remember any story, novel, or play that you read is to make a story map. A **story map** is an easy way of organizing information in a visual form. It is an excellent study technique that helps you to keep track of the settings, characters, conflicts, events, and solutions of a story. This study aid is especially useful when reading longer works like a play or a novel. A story map will help you to organize and remember the important information about a story. It will also show you how the parts of a story fit together.

Begin with a map outline like the one on the next page. To develop your map, you must first note who the characters are and where and when the action takes place. Next, determine what problem needs to be solved. Then, note each major event in the order it happens. These events lead from the problem to its solution. One of the events will be the climax, or turning point. Finally, state how the problem is solved.

The sample map is done for Act I of *The Phantom Tollbooth*.

Activity 1

Develop a story map for Act II. As you do your map, you will notice that some information will be stated directly. Some you have to determine yourself. Include as many events as necessary.

Activity 2

Make a map for another story you have read. Some stories may not have all the parts, and the number of events will differ.

STORY MAP

Title: The Phantom Tollbooth, Act I

Author: Norton Juster, Susan Nanus

Characters: Milo; Spelling Bee, Humbug; Whether Man, Lethargarians; King Azaz; Tock; Mathemagician

Setting:
Place Milo's bedroom, Dictionopolis
Time Late afternoon; present

Problem: Milo wastes time; doesn't seem to have a purpose.

Goal: To snap out of boredom; find something important to do.

Event 1 Milo drives through tollbooth.

Event 2 Meets Whether Man, who urges him on, and Lethargarians, who slow him down.

Event 3 Tock leads Milo to Dictionopolis.

Event 4 Milo suggests that princesses Rhyme and Reason be returned to restore order to Dictionopolis.

Climax (Turning point) Milo's suggestion that princesses be returned.

Resolution (Conclusion) The task of rescuing the princesses is given to him.

Writing a Readers Theater

Readers Theater is a dramatic reading of a piece of literature. It is like a play in that lines are read aloud from a script, but you do not need a stage or sets, lights or costumes. A Readers Theater presentation can be developed from a story, but unlike a story, which contains descriptions of people and places, Readers Theater scripts contain only dialogue and brief notes about what the characters are doing and where the action takes place.

Just as Susan Nanus made a stage play from the novel *The Phantom Tollbooth*, you can make a Readers Theater from a story.

Your Turn

Rewrite a story for Readers Theater. You will select a story and then rewrite it in script form.

Many short stories can be rewritten for Readers Theater. When selecting a piece to adapt, consider those that have been written in a style that reads easily and have several characters. You can include a narrator to provide description and additional information about the plot.

Prewriting

1. Skim several stories. Look for a story that has several good, strong characters who can tell the story mostly through their conversations. Make a list of several possibilities.

2. Select one of the stories. Read the story several times to become familiar with the characters and the plot of the story.

3. Make a list of the characters. Include a narrator to add description and to serve as a bridge between the dialogue sections.

Drafting

Using your list of characters, write the first draft of your script. You may wish to have the narrator begin with the title and author of the selection. When writing the script, write the character's name followed by a colon. Then write the exact words the character is to say. When you want a character to speak or move a certain way or to make a gesture, put that direction in parentheses within that character's part.

Following is part of one student's Readers Theater script for "Dragon, Dragon," pages 15–22.

```
KING:  Ladies and gentlemen, I've
  put up with that dragon as long
  as I can. He has got to be
  stopped.
NARRATOR:  All the people of the
  town whispered amongst them-
  selves and looked impressed
  with the king.
```

```
COBBLER:  It's all very well to
  talk about it--but how are you
  going to do it?
NARRATOR:  Now all the people of
  the town smiled and laughed at
  the king.
QUEEN:  It's not that His Majesty
  hasn't tried.
KING:  Yes, I've told my knights
  again and again that they ought
  to slay that dragon. But I
  can't force them to go. I'm not
  a tyrant.
COBBLER:  Why doesn't the wizard
  say a magic spell?
WIZARD:  (in a weak and
  embarrassed voice) I used to do
  all sorts of spells and chants
  when I was younger. But I've
  lost my spell book, and I've
  begun to fear I'm losing my
  memory, too. For instance, I've
  been trying for days to recall
  one spell I used to do. I
  forget, just now, what the
  deuce it was for. It went
  something like--
        Bimble,
        Wimble,
        Cha, Cha
        CHOOMPF!
NARRATOR:  Suddenly, to
  everyone's surprise, the queen
  turned into a rosebush.
```

Revising

When you have completed your first draft, read it aloud to make sure the story is told clearly and nothing important has been omitted. Then read the script to a partner or response group. Ask the following questions:

- What do you like best about this script?
- Is there anything about the story you don't understand?
- What suggestions can you give me to improve my script?

Now write a second draft, incorporating the changes your partner or group suggested.

Proofreading

Use the following checklist to make sure you have used the proper format for a Readers Theater script.

- Write the speaker's name in capital letters on the left side of the page.
- Use a colon after the speaker's name.
- Do not use quotation marks to indicate when a character is speaking.
- Put directions for how a character speaks or moves in parentheses.

Now use the checklist on page 753 to proofread and edit your script for spelling and mechanics.

Publishing

Ask some of your classmates to help you present your Readers Theater. Perform it for the rest of your class.

BOOKSHELF

The subject of a play can be almost anything—historical people and events, folk tales and fairy tales, imaginary situations. Here are some plays to read that will take you back in history or into imaginary worlds. All are sure to spark your imagination.

WHEN THE RATTLESNAKE SOUNDS by Alice Childress. Coward, McCann & Geoghegan, Inc., 1975. In this drama Alice Childress re-creates for you the powerful and inspiring life of Harriet Tubman, a slave and conductor on the Underground Railroad—a system that helped slaves escape to freedom.

ESCAPE TO FREEDOM: A Play About Young Frederick Douglass by Ossie Davis. The Viking Press, 1976. Ossie Davis introduces you to the people and events that helped shape Frederick Douglass into one of America's most prominent black leaders and statesmen. Davis's play so accurately captures the history and times of the South during the 1830's that you will feel as though you are living at that time.

WINTERTHING by Joan Aiken. Holt, Rinehart and Winston, 1972. In this drama Joan Aiken tells you about a mysterious legend that pervades Winter Island. Here you will meet an aunt and four children, who all reveal the secrets of their pasts and meet the spirit of winter.

CHARLIE AND THE CHOCOLATE FACTORY adapted by Richard George. Puffin Books, 1976. Adapted from Roald Dahl's novel, this play takes you into the tasty, gooey, and adventurous world of a chocolate factory. During your adventure you will meet Charlie, Willy Wonka, Augustus Gloop, Veruca Salt, and many more funny and wild characters.

THE DOOR IN THE WALL by Arthur Craig de Angeli. Doubleday and Company, Inc., 1968. In this play, adapted from the 1950 Newbery Medal–winning novel by Marguerite de Angeli, Craig de Angeli tells the adventures of Robin, the crippled son of a great lord, as he strives to become a knight in medieval times.

UNIT ACTIVITIES

Writing

1. Select one scene from *The Phantom Tollbooth* and continue the story. For example, if Milo and Tock were to have stayed in the Doldrums, what would have happened to them? Write the dialogue for your scene. Then perform it for classmates.

Writing

2. Create and write an advertising campaign for *The Phantom Tollbooth*. Your campaign can be for a newspaper, magazine, radio or television commercial, and so on. Write the script or copy for your campaign. Then either display or deliver it to classmates.

Speaking and Listening

3. Working with a partner, prepare an interview with one of the characters in the play. One of you will be the interviewer; the other will play the part of the character. The interviewer should ask the character questions that are related to the play. The character should respond to the questions as he or she imagines that character would respond. Perform your interview for classmates.

Cooperative Learning

4. Perform all or part of *The Phantom Tollbooth* for classmates and guests or for younger students. Design the costumes, stage, and programs for your production.

Creative Response

5. Theatergoers receive a playbill listing characters and giving important information about the play they are about to see. Design and create a playbill for *The Phantom Tollbooth*. Include a list and description of characters and scenes and a summary of each act. Use art to make your playbill attractive.

Creative Response

6. Create a display for the classroom or library promoting *The Phantom Tollbooth*. For example, you might make a diorama, a poster, or one character's costume. Make your drawings large and colorful. Display your project in the classroom or library.

BATHERS ON A BEACH
Walt Kuhn

NONFICTION

Nonfiction is one of the most common—and popular—types of writing. Unlike fiction, which comes from the writer's imagination, nonfiction presents information and ideas about real people and actual events, not imaginary ones. In other words nonfiction is about real life. Nonfiction includes newspaper and magazine articles, true stories about people and the events in which they took part, diaries, journals, speeches, and letters.

The people who write nonfiction are as varied as the subjects about which they write. Nonfiction writers include presidents, explorers, religious leaders, teachers, scientists—all kinds of people of all ages. They write about subjects that are important to them, sharing their information and ideas in a clear, interesting, and lively way.

In this unit you will read many types of nonfiction by a variety of writers. You will read newspaper and magazine articles, biographies and autobiographies, letters, and many types of essays. Now join those people who like to read about real life.

How to Read Nonfiction

Nonfiction is a type of literature that deals with real people, events, and ideas. When you read articles in a newspaper, when you read your textbooks or look up something in an encyclopedia, when you read information about your hobby or someone's life, you are reading nonfiction. Nonfiction instructs you, entertains you, keeps you informed about the world, and satisfies your curiosity about real people and things.

To get the most from nonfiction, you should read it actively. Reading nonfiction actively means interacting with and responding to the information the writer presents. You do this by using the following strategies.

QUESTION Preview the material before you read it. What questions come to mind? Ask yourself what the author's purpose for writing is. How does the author support the ideas presented in the selection? Do you agree with the author's ideas?

PREDICT Predict what the author will say about the topic. Check to see if your predictions match what the author says. Make new predictions as you go.

CONNECT Make connections between what you already know and what you are reading. Add the new facts and ideas presented in the selection to what you know about the topic. Then try to draw conclusions and make generalizations about the topic.

EVALUATE Evaluate the selection. What do you think of the author's conclusions? What have you learned?

RESPOND Think of what the author has said and respond personally to it. Did you find the material interesting? How do you feel about the topic? What will you do about this information?

Use these strategies as you read the selections in this unit. They will help you increase your enjoyment and understanding of nonfiction.

Nicky Dietz, from Simle Junior High School in Bismarck, North Dakota, actively read "The Drive-In Movies." The notes in the side columns on pages 255–257 include Nicky's thoughts and comments while reading. Your own thoughts as you read may be different.

MODEL

The Drive-In Movies

Gary Soto

"One Saturday I decided to be extra good."

Question: *Do they still have drive-in movies?*

Connect: *Drive-in movies must have been special.*

For our family, moviegoing was rare. But if our mom, tired from a week of candling eggs,[1] woke up happy on a Saturday morning, there was a chance we might later scramble to our blue Chevy and beat nightfall to the Starlight Drive-In. My brother and sister knew this. I knew this. So on Saturday we tried to be good. We sat in the cool shadows of the TV with the volume low and watched cartoons, a prelude of what was to come.

Question: *Will they get to go to a movie in this story?*

One Saturday I decided to be extra good. When she came out of the bedroom tying her robe, she yawned a hat-sized yawn and blinked red eyes at the weak brew of coffee I had fixed for her. I made her toast with strawberry jam spread to all the corners and set the three boxes of cereal in front of her. If she didn't care to eat cereal, she could always look at the back of the boxes as she drank her coffee.

Question: *I wonder what his mom was thinking.*

I went outside. The lawn was tall but too wet with dew to mow. I picked up a trowel and began to weed the flower bed. The weeds were really bermuda grass, long stringers that ran finger-deep in the ground. I got to work quickly and in no time crescents of earth[2] began rising under my fingernails. I was sweaty hot. My knees hurt from kneeling, and my brain was dull from making the trowel go up and down, dribbling crumbs of earth. I dug for half an hour, then stopped to play with the neighbor's dog and pop ticks from his poor snout.

Question: *Is he going to do all this work for nothing and have his mom say it was a good learning experience?*

I then mowed the lawn, which was still beaded with dew

1. candling eggs: Examining eggs for freshness by placing them in front of a candle.

2. crescents (kres′ ənts) **of earth:** Bits of earth shaped like the moon when it is only a sliver.

Connect: *He doesn't seem to be too close to his brother and sister.*

Question: *Why doesn't his dad do the yard work? Why hasn't he mentioned his dad?*

Question: *Will his mom feel sorry for him and take him to the movies because of the bee sting?*

Predict: *He's having a good time cleaning, but he'll end up being too tired to go to the movies.*

Predict: *Soon they'll have everyone out in the yard working with them.*

Predict: *They will have great memories of this one day.*

and noisy with bees hovering over clover. This job was less dull because as I pushed the mower over the shaggy lawn, I could see it looked tidier. My brother and sister watched from the window. Their faces were fat with cereal, a third helping. I made a face at them when they asked how come I was working. Rick pointed to part of the lawn. "You missed some over there." I ignored him and kept my attention on the windmill of grassy blades.

While I was emptying the catcher, a bee stung the bottom of my foot. I danced on one leg and was ready to cry when Mother showed her face at the window. I sat down on the grass and examined my foot: the stinger was pulsating. I pulled it out quickly, ran water over the sting and packed it with mud, Grandmother's remedy.

Hobbling, I returned to the flower bed where I pulled more stringers and again played with the dog. More ticks had migrated to his snout. I swept the front steps, took out the garbage, cleaned the lint filter to the dryer (easy), plucked hair from the industrial wash basin in the garage (also easy), hosed off the patio, smashed three snails sucking paint from the house (disgusting but fun), tied a bundle of newspapers, put away toys, and, finally, seeing that almost everything was done and the sun was not too high, started waxing the car.

My brother joined me with an old gym sock, and our sister watched us while sucking on a cherry Kool-Aid ice cube. The liquid wax drooled onto the sock, and we began to swirl the white slop on the chrome. My arms ached from buffing, which though less boring than weeding, was harder. But the beauty was evident. The shine, hurting our eyes and glinting like an armful of dimes, brought Mother out. She looked around the yard and said, "Pretty good." She winced[3] at the grille and returned inside the house.

We began to wax the paint. My brother applied the liquid and I followed him rubbing hard in wide circles as we moved around the car. I began to hurry because my arms were hurting and my stung foot looked like a water balloon. We were working around the trunk when Rick pounded on the bottle

3. winced (winst) *v.*: Drew back slightly, as if in pain.

of wax. He squeezed the bottle and it sneezed a few more white drops.

We looked at each other. "There's some on the sock," I said. "Let's keep going."

We polished and buffed, sweat weeping on our brows. We got scared when we noticed that the gym sock was now blue. The paint was coming off. Our sister fit ice cubes into our mouths and we worked harder, more intently, more dedicated to the car and our mother. We ran the sock over the chrome, trying to pick up extra wax. But there wasn't enough to cover the entire car. Only half got waxed, but we thought it was better than nothing and went inside for lunch. After lunch, we returned outside with tasty sandwiches.

Rick and I nearly jumped. The waxed side of the car was foggy white. We took a rag and began to polish vigorously and nearly in tears, but the fog wouldn't come off. I blamed Rick and he blamed me. Debra stood at the window, not wanting to get involved. Now, not only would we not go to the movies, but Mom would surely snap a branch from the plum tree and chase us around the yard.

Predict: *They're going to ruin something and get into trouble.*

EL AUTO CINEMA, 1985
Roberto Gil de Montes
Jan Baum Gallery, Collection of Patricia Storace

Mom came out and looked at us with hands on her aproned hips. Finally, she said, "You boys worked so hard." She turned on the garden hose and washed the car. That night we did go to the drive-in. The first feature was about nothing, and the second feature, starring Jerry Lewis,[4] was *Cinderfella*. I tried to stay awake. I kept a wad of homemade popcorn in my cheek and laughed when Jerry Lewis fit golf tees in his nose. I rubbed my watery eyes. I laughed and looked at my mom. I promised myself I would remember that scene with the golf tees and promised myself not to work so hard the coming Saturday. Twenty minutes into the movie, I fell asleep with one hand in the popcorn.

Evaluate: *I knew he was going to be too tired. This story about the author's childhood was pretty good. I am glad he got to go to the movies. It's too bad he fell asleep there.*

---

4. Jerry Lewis: A comedian who starred in many movies during the 1950's and 1960's.

Response: *I can relate to trying to convince your parents to do something you want to do. Sometimes I want to go to the movies or to the zoo and think that my parents will be too busy or too tired to take me. The author really worked hard to convince his mom to take his family to the movies.*

Reader's Response

Which details in this essay do you relate to? Explain.

Gary Soto (1952–   ), who now lives and teaches in Berkeley, California, was once a farm worker in the fields of California's San Joaquin Valley. He is a well-known poet as well as a writer of prose. Much of his work centers on his family and friends and on the large and small events of their lives. Soto's published works include *The Elements of San Joaquin*, a collection of poems, *Living Up the Street*, a book of personal recollections in prose, and *Baseball in April*, a collection of short stories about young people.

Responding to the Selection

Your Response

1. How would you have felt if, after working so hard, you had fallen asleep at the movies? Explain.

Recalling

2. Why did the boys wax only one side of the car?
3. What two things does the narrator promise to remember?

Interpreting

4. Describe the narrator's reaction to the bee sting. If it had not been Saturday, do you think he would have reacted differently? Explain.
5. Explain why the narrator's mother does not get angry with the boys for making a mess of the car.
6. Do you think the narrator is older or younger than his brother and sister? Use evidence from the story to support your answer.

Applying

7. The narrator in this story works hard to earn a reward. Do people work only when they are being rewarded? Do people ever work for other reasons? Explain.

Analyzing Literature

Understanding a Personal Narrative

A **personal narrative** is told in the first person, that is, from the viewpoint of the narrator. The narrator uses pronouns such as *I, me,* and *my* to describe the action.

A personal narrative often portrays events in the life of the writer. However, many works of fiction have been written as if they were personal narratives.

1. From whose point of view is the story written?
2. How might the story be different if it were written by a neighbor who observed the events described in the story?

Critical Thinking and Reading

Making Inferences From a Personal Narrative

Making **inferences** means drawing conclusions. In a personal narrative, the narrator expresses his or her attitudes and beliefs. To make inferences, you must pay attention to the words the narrator uses. For example, when the narrator says that the lawn was "too wet with dew to mow," you might infer that it was early morning.

1. What events in the story allow you to infer that the narrator does not give up easily when he sets out to reach a goal?
2. What inference can you make about the narrator's character based on his reaction to the dried-up wax on the car?

Thinking and Writing

Writing a Personal Narrative

Write a narrative about a special occasion in your life, such as a birthday or a vacation. Make notes about why the occasion was special, what happened, and who was there. As you write your draft, tell the story in a way that will reveal your feelings about what happened.

Read your first draft to be sure that the flow of events is clear. After you have revised and proofread your narrative, you may wish to share it with your classmates.

Learning Options

1. **Performance.** Transform "The Drive-In Movies" into a Readers Theater. With a group of classmates rewrite the selection in script form. See pages 248–249 for more details. Assign parts to members of the group. After practicing, perform your Readers Theater for the class.
2. **Art.** Choose a part of "The Drive-In Movies" that you found particularly humorous. Create a cartoon strip that illustrates this scene. Share your cartoon strip with the class.

ONE WRITER'S PROCESS

Gary Soto and "The Drive-In Movies"

PREWRITING

Kernels of Youth "The Drive-In Movies" comes from Gary Soto's collection of essays called *A Summer Life*. When Soto set out to write *A Summer Life*, he had decided to write about his boyhood in a new way. Each story, he said, centered on "one kernel of idea or memory."

Is It All True? Soto says that he remembers the bee sting, the Kool-Aid ice cubes, and the gym sock that appear in "The Drive-In Movies." "But these three things . . . ," he says, "may or may not have all shown up on the day when my brother and I were polishing our car."

Even in a personal essay, Soto believes, "you are allowed the luxury of combining experiences." The facts have to be there, but not necessarily in the order in which they happened. " . . . What matters is that you can convince the reader that everything was plausible, thus believable."

DRAFTING

A Story a Day For Soto, the hardest part of writing "The Drive-In Movies" was getting it done quickly. "When I was writing *A Summer Life*, I got it into my stubborn head that I would write one story a day." The whole book was written in less than two months.

REVISING

Tiny Changes When Soto approaches others for help with his revising, it's usually for "nit-picky details" like spelling and awkward phrasing. "Again, since I'm a swift writer," he says, "it's not unusual for me to finish a story in a day or two, which means, of course, that I will overlook some of the finer detail."

An Editor's Help It's the job of the editor at Soto's publishing house to make sure the stories are smooth, consistent, and logical. Here is a paragraph from a story Soto wrote called "Broken Chain."

> Sunday morning, Ernie and Alfonso stayed away from each other, though over breakfast they fought over the last tortilla. Their mother, sewing at the kitchen table, ~~let her eyes grow big and~~ warned them to knock it off. At church they made faces at one another when the priest, Father Jerry, wasn't looking. Ernie punched Alfonso in the arm, and Alfonso, his eyes wide with anger, punched back.

Editing Your Own Work Revising a manuscript can mean taking out words or phrases that don't belong as well as adding ones that do. Soto's editor took out the phrase "let her eyes grow big." Why? Soto also wrote "his eyes wide with anger" to describe Alfonso. Perhaps the editor felt that there were too many pairs of eyes in the same paragraph.

THINKING ABOUT THE PROCESS

1. What might be some advantages of "combining experiences" in a personal essay?
2. Why is it useful to have another person look at something you've written?

Reading Articles From the Media

LUCY HESSEL READING THE NEWSPAPER, RUE DE NAPLES
Édouard Vuillard
Kuntsmuseum, Berne

GUIDE FOR READING

Noah Webster's Dictionary (Kuralt)

Charles Kuralt

(1934–   ) is familiar to most Americans as an award-winning television news correspondent. Born in Wilmington, North Carolina, Kuralt began his career as a journalist with the *Charlotte News*. In 1957, he joined CBS News, where he has been ever since. He is the author of many books about daily life in the United States, including *Dateline America* and *On the Road with Charles Kuralt*.

Oral Commentary

A radio or television **oral commentary** is similar to a feature story in a newspaper. Like a feature story, the commentary usually begins with a "hook"—an interesting bit of information—which makes the audience want to learn more about the subject. Unlike a newspaper feature, the radio or television commentary is written to be read aloud. For this reason, the language of a commentary is often more informal than that of a newspaper feature. The commentary is also briefer than the average newspaper feature.

Focus

Charles Kuralt reveals that before Noah Webster's time, people spelled however they pleased. What if that were still the case? Translate the following letter into correctly spelled English. Then write a reply.

Dear Frend,

This mae seam stranj, butte I susspekt that sum peepul due nott ondurstanned wat I am riting uhbowt. Kleerlea, the konfuzyun ken bee traysed too ay seeryus komyounikayshen prahblum. Itte iz ay pittie that sum foex kant spel.

What due yoo thinck? Pleez repligh.

Yoors trully,
Ms. Pell

Vocabulary

Knowing the following words will help you as you read "Noah Webster's Dictionary."

atrocious (ə trō′ shəs) *adj.*: Very bad, unpleasant, inferior (p. 263)

dialects (dī′ ə lekts) *n.*: Forms of speech that are peculiar to a region or community (p. 264)

Noah Webster's Dictionary

from *Dateline America*

Charles Kuralt

". . . if it hadn't been for Noah Webster, we might never have had spelling bees or even much spelling."

West Hartford, Connecticut. I watched students of West Hartford's Bridlepath School compete in that vanishing standby of American education, the spelling bee. The spelling bee was held in Noah Webster's kitchen. That was a good place for it, because if it hadn't been for Noah Webster, we might never have had spelling bees or even much spelling. Before this Yankee schoolmaster came along, Americans spelled poorly or not at all; George Washington, to cite one atrocious example, spelled pretty much as he pleased. After Noah Webster, Americans spelled the way Noah told them to.

NOAH WEBSTER WRITING HIS DICTIONARY

The kids in the spelling bee came from all kinds of backgrounds and from all over the country. That they speak the same language—that a kid from Maine can meet a kid from Oregon and understand him right from the start—that is Noah Webster's gift to us. His little Blue-Backed Speller sold nearly 100 million copies in his lifetime. It wore out printing presses. It was read by nearly every American who could read.

And then, working for twenty-five years, alone and by hand, Noah Webster produced his dictionary—seventy thousand words, including a lot of American words that had never been in a dictionary before: *apple-sauce, bullfrog, chowder, hickory, skunk*. It was the most valuable piece of scholarship any American ever did.

Noah Webster, from this old house in West Hartford, created American style and American manners. It is not too much to say that he created American education. He was the first teacher of American history, the first influential American newspaper editor.

"What rubbed Mr. Webster's fur the wrong way," West Hartford historian Nelson Burr told me, "was that even after the Revolution, most of America's books and most of America's ideas still came from England. He wanted to put a stop to that. He wanted to create Americanism—not in the sense of jingoistic patriotism,[1] but in the sense of a new literature, a new language."

In the Italy of Noah Webster's day, there were so many dialects that many Italians couldn't talk to one another. The same thing, to a lesser degree, was true in Great Britain. America's common language, with more or less agreed-upon rules for spelling and punctuation, was the work of Noah Webster. He wanted us to be one nation, a new nation, and he showed us how.

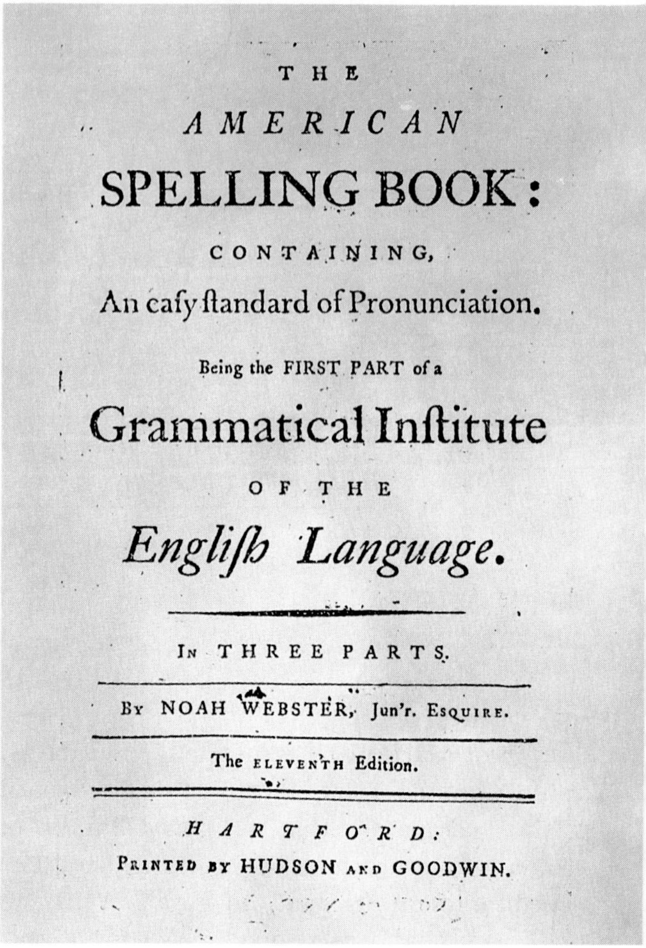
THE
AMERICAN
SPELLING BOOK:
CONTAINING,
An eaſy ſtandard of Pronunciation.
Being the FIRST PART of a
Grammatical Inſtitute
OF THE
Engliſh Language.

IN THREE PARTS.

BY NOAH WEBSTER, Jun'r. ESQUIRE.

The ELEVENTH Edition.

HARTFORD:
PRINTED BY HUDSON AND GOODWIN.

TITLE PAGE OF NOAH WEBSTER'S SPELLER

Reader's Response
What information in a dictionary do you find most useful?

1. **jingoistic** (jiŋ' gō is' tik) **patriotism** (pā' trē ə tiz' əm): Blind, uncritical love of one's country.

Responding to the Selection

Your Response

1. Do you think you would enjoy writing a dictionary? Explain.

Recalling

2. How long did it take Noah Webster to write his dictionary?
3. What bothered Noah Webster?

Interpreting

4. Why was the Blue-Backed Speller so popular?
5. What made Webster's dictionary truly American?
6. Why does the author say that Noah Webster created American education? Do you agree? Why or why not?

Applying

7. How does Noah Webster's work affect the lives of people today?

Analyzing Literature

Understanding Oral Commentaries

An **oral commentary** is a feature story that is presented aloud on radio or television. Charles Kuralt's commentary on Noah Webster presents his observations for readers' enjoyment.

1. What qualities in Charles Kuralt's essay show that it was written to be read aloud?
2. If the commentary on Noah Webster were five times as long, do you think it would have been effective as oral commentary? Explain.

Critical Thinking and Reading

Appreciating New Words

English is changing all the time. How—and when—do new words get into a dictionary? Lexicographers, the people who write dictionaries, want to include words that have truly become part of the language. They carefully evaluate new words and put them in dictionaries only after they have remained in use for a period of time.

What new words would you put into a dictionary? Work with a partner or a small group to think of five new words that you use. They may be slang words, or they may be words used only in your locality. Write dictionary entries for these words. Refer to your classroom dictionary for the format for each entry.

Thinking and Writing

Writing an Oral Commentary

Write an oral commentary about a person or event in your school or neighborhood. Brainstorm for ideas by writing down the name of the person or event on a piece of paper. Then, write down all the things you associate with that person or event.

After you have written your first draft, read your work aloud and time yourself. Your commentary should be no longer than two minutes. Listen for awkward sentences and revise them. When you complete your final draft, read your commentary to the class.

Learning Options

1. **Speaking and Listening.** Find out if your library has audiotapes of Charles Kuralt's commentaries or another media personality's commentaries. Listen to the tapes and note the way the commentator varies his or her tone of voice, speed, and volume. Then, practice reading "Noah Webster's Dictionary" aloud. When you are ready, read the commentary to the class.
2. **Writing.** Use the words listed in the Critical Thinking and Reading activity to create a class dictionary. Include your entries with those of your classmates. Arrange them in alphabetical order and prepare a final draft of your dictionary. You may wish to illustrate the entries. Prepare a cover as well.

MULTICULTURAL CONNECTION

American English Borrows From the World

Noah Webster wanted to create an American language. What is American English? It is a language that reflects the great diversity of its people. The population of the United States is made up of people from almost every nation in the world. American English contains many words borrowed from the native languages of these people.

Borrowing from Native Americans. By the 1600's, British colonists had established permanent settlements on what is now the east coast of the United States. Once the colonists made contact with the people of North America, they began using Native American words for the foods, plants, animals, and places that they saw. The names of several colonies are Native American words. For example, *Connecticut* means "place of the long river" and *Massachusetts* means "at the big hill." Other states, such as Mississippi and Michigan, have Native American names as well. The colonists also added Native American words like *skunk, hickory, canoe, tepee, moccasin,* and *wigwam* to their vocabularies.

French influence. French explorers and travelers in North America used such words as *prairie, rapids* (the fast moving part of a river), *caribou,* and *shanty* to describe what they had seen and experienced. A number of United States place names—from New Orleans, Louisiana, to Montpelier, Vermont—are French.

The Spanish contribution. From Spanish came such words as *alligator, cargo, fiesta, mosquito, potato, tornado,* and *vanilla.* Words of the West and Southwest are often Spanish in origin: *stampede, adobe, bronco, burro, canyon, corral, coyote,* and *ranch.* Even today Spanish continues to lend us words, like *cafeteria, barrio,* and *macho.* A quick look at the map of the southwestern United States shows Spanish state and city names, including Florida, Texas, New Mexico, and Arizona; San Antonio, Santa Fe, Los Angeles, Casa Grande, and Boca Raton.

Cookies are Dutch and pretzels are German. The Dutch have also contributed to American English. In the 1600's, Dutch settlers established the community of New Amsterdam—which is now New York City. Many locations in and around New York still have their original Dutch names, like Harlem (a section in Manhattan) and the Catskills (a mountainous region of New York state). The Dutch also gave us such everyday words as *cruller, coleslaw, sleigh, cookie, waffle, boss,* and *Santa Claus.*

What would a cookout be without such "American" foods as hamburgers and frankfurters? These words and foods are actually German in origin. They refer to the cities of Hamburg and Frankfurt from which they came. The words *pretzel* and *delicatessen* are also from German. Other commonly used words with German roots include *kinder-*

garten, *fresh* (meaning disrespectful), and *loafer* (one who spends time lazily).

Irish contributions. Many Irish words and expressions have found a place in American English. Although Irish immigrants already spoke English, they used many terms that were unique to Irish English. Such Irish words as *blarney* (smooth, flattering talk), *brogue* (a strong Irish accent), *galore*, *grumpy*, and *smithereens* (fragments or splintered pieces) became part of American English. Many everyday American expressions have their origins in Irishisms. For example, *give in* (in the sense of "to yield"), *mad* (in the sense of "angry"), and *quit* (meaning "to stop") come from Irish expressions.

African American contributions. Americans of African heritage contributed many words, including *gumbo* (a soup or stew thickened with okra), *goober* (from an Angolan word for peanut), and *jazz*.

Yiddish influence. Many Jewish immigrants brought Yiddish words to the United States. Such words as *kibitzer* (a meddler who offers unwanted advice), *schnook* (a stupid or easily victimized person), and *schlock* (something of obviously inferior quality) have their origins in Yiddish.

A mosaic of other languages. In addition, languages as widely varied as Finnish, Swedish, Italian, and Chinese have added words to American English. You may be familiar with Scandinavian *saunas* and *smorgasbords*. From Chinese we have *chow*, *gung-ho*, and *sampan* (a small boat). Italian is represented by food terms like *spaghetti*, *ravioli*, *cappucino*, *minestrone*, and *pizza* as well as terms related to music such as *piano*, *aria*, *adagio*, and *crescendo*. The Japanese have given us *bonsai*, *samurai*, and *kimono*. From the Turkish we have *caftan* and *kismet* (fate or destiny). Hindi, the language of the Hindus, has produced *pundit* (an authority on a particular subject) and *yoga*.

Exploring Word Origins

Below you will find a list of words of foreign origin in American English. How many do you already know? Can you guess the meanings of others? Use a dictionary to find out the meaning and origin of each word.

parachute	ukulele
gazpacho	schlep
saloon	lasagna
balalaika	banana
hominy	yen

MAP, 1961
Jasper Johns
The Museum of Modern Art

GUIDE FOR READING

Andrew A. Rooney

(1919–) has been a newspaper columnist for the *New York Herald Tribune,* but he is probably best known for his work in television. Rooney has received television's highest award, the Emmy. He appears often on the weekly program *60 Minutes,* where he presents humorous commentaries about everyday matters. Collections of his commentaries have been published in several books. In this essay from the collection *Not That You Asked . . . ,* Rooney expresses his ideas about one of the media.

How to Read a Newspaper

Newspaper Column

A **newspaper column** is a feature of many newspapers. Unlike a news story, which gives facts, a column offers a writer's opinions. Columns are as varied as the people who write them. Some columnists discuss issues of the day in a serious manner. Others focus on the human side of news—stories about individuals facing the struggles and joys of everyday life. Others write commentaries—their own ideas—about particular areas of interest, such as the environment or sports. Some take a lighter view of the news and life; these may offer advice, gossip, entertainment news, or humor.

Focus

Newspapers contain much more than news. There are sections that tell about sports, pages that give recipes, and columns that review new movies. In a small group, list all the sections of a newspaper you can think of. Then, discuss which part of the newspaper you think is most important. Which parts do you think people should read every day? Why? Which part do you like to read first? As you read this selection, compare your ideas with those of the author.

Vocabulary

Knowing the following words will help you as you read "How to Read a Newspaper."

disciplined (dis′ ə plin″d) *adj.*: Self-controlled; trained (p. 269)
columnists (käl′ əm nists) *n.*: People who write newspaper or magazine columns (p. 269)
editors (ed′ it ərz) *n.*: In this case, the heads of newspaper departments (p. 269)
stock (stäk) *n.*: Paper (p. 269)
evaporated (ē vap′ ə rāt′ əd) *v.*: Disappeared like vapor; vanished (p. 269)

Spelling Tip

Notice that in some words with an *s* sound followed by an *e* or an *i*, like *discipline,* the *s* sound is spelled *sc.*

How to Read a Newspaper

Andrew A. Rooney

"My method of reading the newspaper makes no sense at all. . . ."

Considering how much time I've spent reading newspapers in my life, it's amazing how little thought I've given to how a newspaper should be read. There's nothing I do so much of that I do so badly.

If I ate dinner the way I read the newspaper, I'd be starting with dessert; if I drove the way I read the newspaper, I'd be arrested for drunken driving because I was wandering all over the road; if I read a book the way I read a newspaper, I'd be starting near the end, working forward and then jumping to the beginning. My method of reading the newspaper makes no sense at all and yet there's no small pleasure I enjoy more. Anyone can read a newspaper any way he or she wants to. This is the great advantage of reading a newspaper over viewing television news. With television news, you take it the way they want to give it to you or not at all.

I wish I were more disciplined about the way I read the newspaper. It may be OK to start with the social notes, the gossip columns, sports pages, recipes, comic strips or the columnists, but my trouble is when I do that I often run out of reading time before I get to what I ought to read to know what's going on in the world. There is hardly a day that I don't put the newspaper down, fully intending to pick it up and finish it later. Unfortunately, there is hardly a day when I pick it up and finish it later. First thing I know, tomorrow's paper has come and the one I didn't finish reading is no longer news, it's history. I often wonder if newspaper editors read all of the things in their paper.

The reason I don't finish the paper is that there's a limit to how much time I can spend reading it before I have to get at life. I often feel guilty about that and so I save the paper. As a result, there are piles of newspapers everywhere in the house and office. They're on the floor next to my chair in the living room, on the radiator in the kitchen and on the table next to the bed. Every stack of papers reminds me that I don't get things done. Sometimes I wish that newspapers were printed on stock[1] that evaporated into thin air when it was a day old.

We're bombarded by information from every side, and it's a good thing. The hard-

1. **stock** (stäk) *n.*: A specified kind of paper.

THOMAS RAEBURN WHITE
Franklin Watkins
Collection of White and Williams, Philadelphia

ware for the distribution of intelligence is vastly better than it was even twenty years ago. Reporters, generally speaking, are not being given enough time to dig out the information they need for a complete story, but the means of spreading information around is so much better that we're getting more of it than we used to despite that sad fact. A little of that information is bound to sink in and make us better informed.

The trouble with reading novelty, gossip or sports items or reading half a news story is that we end up paying too much attention to things that have no bearing on our lives. They're dream-world stuff. They're interesting as entertainment but they have no practical value for our lives. Everything doesn't have to be important, but most of it ought to lead us somewhere, even if it's only to making a better cup of coffee or adding a tidbit of information about foreign policy that will help us vote intelligently in the next election. For all the information we have available, most of us are stupid and uninformed, and it isn't our newspaper's fault, it's our own.

It might be a good idea if schools had courses in "How to Read a Newspaper," although I don't know who is qualified to teach it. Not me.

Reader's Response
Do you agree with Rooney's claim that "most of us are stupid and uninformed"? Why or why not?

Responding to the Selection

Your Response

1. Do you think Andy Rooney has a good sense of humor? Why or why not?

Recalling

2. Describe how Rooney reads a newspaper.

Interpreting

3. How would Rooney benefit if he read the newspaper in a more disciplined way?
4. What would Rooney lose if he read the newspaper in a more disciplined way?
5. What makes Rooney think it is our own fault if we are "stupid and uninformed"?
6. Why does Rooney feel unqualified to teach a course in "How to Read a Newspaper"?

Applying

7. Do you read a newspaper regularly? What sections do you read and in what order? Why do people enjoy reading a newspaper?

Analyzing Literature

Appreciating a Newspaper Column

A **newspaper column** states a writer's opinions on a topic in the news. Some columns are serious. Others are humorous. In this column Rooney uses a personal approach, with the casual style of a conversation.

1. What personal details does Rooney reveal about himself as he discusses his topic?
2. Why does Rooney take a humorous approach rather than a serious one?

Critical Thinking and Reading

Recognizing Comparison and Contrast

A **comparison** points out similarities. A **contrast** points out differences. In the sentence that begins, "If I ate dinner the way I read the newspaper, I'd be starting with dessert," Rooney offers a string of comparisons. Each one helps us "see" the way he reads a newspaper. Rooney could have written, "I begin at the end and skip from section to section," but the comparisons make his method seem odd and personal.

1. What other comparisons does Rooney make in the second paragraph?
2. How does he contrast reading a newspaper and watching television news?

Thinking and Writing

Writing a Humorous Column

Suppose you are a columnist for your school newspaper. You want to produce a piece that looks humorously at something in the recent news. With a classmate, list current events—school, local, or national—and look for the humor in them. Every columnist needs an "angle"—a way of looking at the subject. You might try exaggerating or writing from the point of view of someone who knows nothing about our time and place. Write your column. In revising it, make sure it sounds as if you are speaking to a friend. Writing in a conversational style will help your personality show. Put your column with those of your classmates in a newspaper.

Learning Options

1. **Cross-curricular Connection.** What if you were chosen to design a course in how to read a newspaper? In a small group, decide what should be taught, who should teach it, and what materials should be used. After your group has decided about the course, present your suggestions to the class.
2. **Writing.** Create a one-page newspaper with a group of classmates. First, decide on three or four sections for your newspaper. Then, appoint editors to write a brief article for each section. Next, arrange the articles on a large sheet of paper. Finally, hang up your newspaper for the class to read.

Magazines—Something for Everyone

Scan a magazine rack. You'll find dozens of magazines on display, each beckoning you with a glossy cover and inch-high headlines. You want to reach for one. Go ahead. Pick it up, and flip through its pages. You'll find appealing pictures and photographs, short articles and stories, puzzles, games, and cartoons.

There's a magazine for everyone. You'll find magazines that contain a little of everything and those that limit their contents to what will appeal to people with specialized interests. You'll find magazines on health and beauty, sports, travel, computers, and hobbies. The articles on people and ideas will satisfy almost everyone's taste in reading.

Check What's Inside

Why read magazines? People read magazines for a variety of reasons. For one thing, the writing of some of the very best writers, both of fiction and nonfiction, appears in magazines. In addition, magazines put the reader in touch with current events. Yet they don't work on the rushed level of newspapers. A magazine article takes a broader view of its subject than an article in a newspaper, but the treatment is briefer than what you might find in books.

Probably most people turn to magazines for information, but they find much more there. Nearly all magazines include some features that are there "just for fun," and most stretch their specialized topics quite a bit. A magazine devoted to hiking and camping is likely to include recipes for dishes that can be prepared on the trail, cartoons about humorous incidents that occur around camp, and so on. Part of the appeal of magazines is that you don't feel obligated to read everything in them. You can flip through the pages, skip articles, and read only what you want.

Find One That Interests You

To get an idea of a magazine's style and decide if it might interest you, start with a look at the table of contents. There you may find photos and brief statements about the content of each article. Sometimes even a one-sentence "teaser" in the contents listing can help you decide whether the article will interest you. Browsing through the contents page and skimming an article or two will help you decide if this is a magazine you want to read.

Magazines for Young People

The following are a few of the magazines edited specifically to appeal to young people. You will find most of them in your local library or on newsstands.

Boys' Life, published by the Boy Scouts of America, focuses on sports, the outdoors, hobbies, and science. Each issue also includes cartoons, columns, and fiction.

Each issue of **Cobblestone,** the "History Magazine for Young People," is devoted to a historical theme. The theme may be taken from an event in American history, a historical figure, or a place that played a key role in history. The articles in the issue explore many aspects of the theme.

Cricket presents stories, poems, and articles that are of interest to young people. Sometimes, craft projects or riddles appear in this award-winning magazine.

Current Science features articles on the life sciences, physical sciences, and earth sciences. The longer articles explain intriguing occurrences and ideas. Shorter articles and columns keep the reader up to date on scientific developments.

National Geographic World contains articles about wild animals, pets, natural history, science, hobbies, sports, and human interest articles with an emphasis on young people. It's especially noted for its photography.

Ranger Rick is the National Wildlife Federation's magazine for young people. Hoping to further the cause of protecting wildlife, the magazine has articles and stories about zoos as well as animals in the wild. Beautiful animal photography accompanies the articles.

Sports Illustrated for Kids includes articles on both professional and amateur sports. Young athletes will find the articles, puzzles, games, and fiction lively and interesting.

Stone Soup is a young people's literary magazine. All the stories, poems, and artwork are by the readers. Readers write the book reviews, too.

GUIDE FOR READING

Neil McAleer

(1942–) lives and works in Cumberland, Pennsylvania. McAleer is interested in science and space. He shares his interest in those subjects by writing books like *The Cosmic Mind-Boggling Book, The Body Almanac,* and *The Omni Space Almanac.* McAleer's writing includes fiction, as well as nonfiction. His first book, *Earthlove,* is a fantasy novel. He also writes articles, like "Space Stations of the Mind," for magazines.

Space Stations of the Mind

Magazine Articles

Magazine articles are as varied as all of nonfiction itself. They can be about almost any subject likely to interest readers. They can be developed in any style. Some magazine articles are miniature biographies. Others explain ideas in science or the arts. Still others are narratives of travels or personal experience. "Space Stations of the Mind" contains elements of many of these, including biography, history, and explanations of ideas in science, and art.

Focus

Imagine a space station orbiting the Earth, where scientists and astronauts live and work for long periods of time. Suppose you were given the opportunity to live in a space station for one month. If you could bring one suitcase with you, what would you put in it? List the items you would select to place in one suitcase for a month-long visit in space. As you read this article, think about why people are fascinated by space travel.

Vocabulary

Knowing the following words will help you as you read "Space Stations of the Mind."

satellite (sat′ 'l īt′) *n.*: An object that orbits another, larger object; in this case, a space station that orbits the earth (p. 275)

sphere (sfir) *n.*: Ball; globe (p. 275)

physicist (fiz′ i sist) *n.*: A scientist who deals with the relationships of energy and matter (p. 275)

compound (käm′ pound) *adj.*: Made of two or more separate parts (p. 276)

monitor (män′ i tər) *v.*: Watch or check on (p. 276)

mentor (men′ tər) *n.*: Advisor; teacher or coach (p. 276)

visionary (vizh′ ən er′ ē) *adj.*: Being able to imagine the future (p. 278)

Space Stations of the Mind

Neil McAleer

"The great race to the moon was on."

The world's first space station, a 43-foot-long cylinder put in orbit by the Soviet Union, now circles the earth. The United States hopes to build its own, larger space platform by 1998.

This space station, floating 250 miles above earth, will be powered by sunlight collected on huge panels. Five times a year, men and women will be taxied to and from the station in a space shuttle.

Now that man has found ways to launch the parts of an artificial satellite and assemble them in space, he can make real a long-time dream. At last, he can build a home in space.

Ideas for space stations have been whirling through the minds of men for more than one hundred years. Some of those imaginary stations are much better known than any real satellite. Remember the Death Star from the movie *Star Wars*? How about the space-port in the *Star Trek* movies?

Space stations have appeared on the big screen for at least twenty years. People have read about them for five times that long.

Perhaps the first space station ever thought of was a large, hollow sphere made entirely of brick. Its creator was Edward Everett Hale, a Boston clergyman.

In 1869, the *Atlantic Monthly* magazine published Hale's story, "The Brick Moon." This was the first story of a manned space station to appear anywhere.

Hale's station was a hollow brick sphere two hundred feet in diameter that could be shot into space by waterpower.

Another early thinker of space stations was Konstantin Tsiolkovsky,[1] born in Russia in 1857. He dreamed up not only space stations, but also a type of rocket that would put them into orbit.

Tsiolkovsky would be remembered as a father of the space age, sharing the honor with American rocketeer Robert Goddard and the German physicist Hermann Oberth.

When Tsiolkovsky was eight years old, his mother gave him a little balloon filled with hydrogen. The balloon, which would rise to the ceiling when he released it, sparked his imagination about flight. "I dreamed," he once wrote, "there was no such thing as gravity."

Tsiolkovsky taught himself math, physics and other subjects. He applied them to the problems of flight.

---

1. **Konstantin Tsiolkovsky** (kän′ stən tēn chyol kəv′ skē)

By age twenty-one, he had worked out some basic requirements of an orbiting space station. In *Dreams of the Earth and Sky*, written in 1895, Tsiolkovsky described an earth satellite that could serve as a base for rocket travel between planets.

In his *Beyond the Planet Earth*, published in 1920, Tsiolkovsky described a "compound passenger rocket" that could change into a space station once it reached orbit. It could house twenty passengers and rotate to produce artifical gravity. The rocket also could carry parts to construct a large greenhouse. There, astronauts would grow food in the plentiful sunlight of space.

In other writings, Tsiolkovsky designed a rocket engine and described weightlessness in orbit. He even foresaw the danger of spaceships burning up as they reentered earth's atmosphere.

The imaginative ideas of Konstantin Tsiolkovsky and others inspired development of the world's first rockets.

Hermann Oberth of Germany published two important books describing technology that would become real in the space age. *The Rocket into Interplanetary Space* (1923) and *The Way to Space Travel* (1929) both suggested that orbiting rockets could be used as refueling stations or stations from which to monitor weather on earth.

Once in space, these rockets could be adapted for the purpose needed. Smaller rockets would act as ferries between the earth and the orbiting stations.

As a boy of eleven, Oberth was greatly moved by the novels of Jules Verne, especially *From the Earth to the Moon*. He read it six times. Oberth realized that Verne's method of shooting a spacecraft from a huge cannon wouldn't work. He decided to find a way that would. That kept him busy for the next sixty years.

While in his thirties, Oberth became friend and teacher to a young German boy named Wernher von Braun.[2] Von Braun would one day help design a rocket that would take men to the moon for the first time in history.

In the 1950's, von Braun brought his mentor to the United States to help our rocket program. Oberth was the only one of the three great space pioneers to actually see the huge Saturn V rockets blasting off to the moon. (Tsiolkovsky died in 1935 and Goddard died in 1945.)

In 1929, two other men added to the changing ideas of the space station. Hermann Potocnik,[3] an engineer who wrote under the pen name of Hermann Noordung, published the first book devoted almost entirely to the subject.

His *The Problem of Travel in Space* contained the first detailed diagrams of a space station. The station was shaped like a wheel. That design would remain popular for the next forty years, right up to the famous double-wheeled station in the classic 1968 movie, *2001: A Space Odyssey.*

Like a bicycle wheel, the main structure would spin around a central hub, producing artificial gravity on the outer rim. The hub would contain an air lock for entering and exiting the station. Potocnik's design included an elevator shaft as well as curved stairways connecting the hub to the rim.

Solar energy collected in a large parabolic[4] dish would support life in a cylindri-

---

2. Wernher von Braun (vər′ nər vän brôn′)
3. Hermann Potocnik (her′ mən pə tôk′ nik)
4. parabolic (par ə bal′ ik) *adj.*: Bowl-shaped.

KEN BARR

cal[5] earth observatory, the main feature of the station.

During the 1930's and 40's, space station designs were rare. The idea didn't really excite the public again until the 1950's. That decade produced several TV shows on space (*Captain Video, Space Patrol, Space Cadet,* and others).

And in 1951, Wernher von Braun, who had designed a wheel-shaped station, helped *Collier's* magazine produce a historic series on space travel.

"A Station in Space," written by space historian Willy Ley, appeared in March 1952. In words and illustrations, the article described the wheel-shaped station of von Braun. It had a diameter of 250 feet and enough room to house eighty people.

One of thousands who read the article was Ward Kimball, director of animation for Walt Disney Pictures. Kimball persuaded Disney to produce a three-part series on mankind's future in space for the new TV show *Disneyland.*

Viewers saw realistic images of Space Station 1, a von Braun design, being assembled in orbit by men in self-propelled, specially equipped "bottle suits."

Before the last program in the series was aired in 1957, something happened which changed the world: The Soviet Union launched the first artificial satellite on October 4, 1957. This marked the dawn of the space age. The great race to the moon was on.

To a generation brought up on movies like *Star Wars,* the Soviet satellite may seem crude. But Sputnik I, the first man-made object in orbit, was a beginning.

What had once been only a dream was finally becoming reality. Appropriately, that year—1957—was the 100th anniversary of Konstantin Tsiolkovsky's birth.

During the thirty-two years since Sputnik I, dozens of space station designs have come off the drawing boards at the National Aeronautics and Space Administration and off the sketch pads of Hollywood artists.

The origins of all such creations—real and fanciful—can be traced back to those visionary men of yesteryear. Their predictions about space stations are only now starting to come true.

Reader's Response

Would you like to visit or live in a space station? Explain.

Space Station Update

Now detailed designs for a real space station are ready. The United States, the European Space Agency, Japan, and Canada are cooperating to build the space station, called *Freedom.* The National Aeronautics and Space Administration (NASA) is directing the project. Teams of astronauts will stay at the station for six months at a time, living and working 200 miles above the Earth.

In the space station, scientists will develop new and improved materials. Biologists will study microorganisms, plants, and animals through several life cycles to see the long-term effects of weightlessness. *Freedom* will be a service station in space for spacecraft and satellites. Perhaps the space station will be most valuable as a place from which to launch astronauts on trips to the moon and to Mars.

---

5. cylindrical (sə lin′ dri kəl) *adj.*: Having the shape of a cylinder; shaped like a soda can.

RESPONDING TO THE SELECTION

Your Response

1. Which of these scientists and thinkers would you like to meet and why?
2. Do you think that learning how to live in space will be more important in the future? Explain.

Recalling

3. What aspects of space travel did Tsiolkovsky correctly predict in his books?

Interpreting

4. Why are some imaginary space stations better known than any real satellite?
5. What piece of space equipment did Hermann Oberth predict when he said that small rockets could act as "ferries" between the earth and orbiting stations?
6. What evidence in the selection supports McAleer's statement that people became interested in space travel in the 1950's?

Applying

7. "Visionaries" often predict inventions and discoveries years before their time. Make two predictions of scientific developments that will happen before you turn thirty.

ANALYZING LITERATURE

Appreciating a Magazine Article

Magazine articles are often like miniature versions of longer nonfiction forms. They are written on a variety of topics. "Space Stations of the Mind" includes biographies, explanations of technology, a history of space travel, and a discussion of portrayals of space travel in books and movies and on television.

1. What information did McAleer include about one of the space pioneers in the article?
2. Why is this article called "Space Stations of the Mind"?
3. What qualities of a magazine article does "Space Stations of the Mind" have?

CRITICAL THINKING AND READING

Evaluating Ideas

To **evaluate** is to judge quality or value. When you evaluate ideas, you decide whether they make sense. First, you must understand the ideas. Then, support your evaluation with reasons. Tell whether the following people's ideas about space stations seem practical. Support your evaluation.

1. Edward Everett Hale
2. Konstantin Tsiolkovsky
3. Hermann Potocnik

THINKING AND WRITING

Writing an Imaginative Travel Article

In the Writing activity on the Guide for Reading page, you wrote about arriving at a space station. Use that writing to develop an article about a trip to a space station. The article will appear in a travel magazine. First, use your imagination to create the details. Then write the first draft of your article. In revising, think of your readers. Make your description so complete that they will feel as if they have been there.

LEARNING OPTIONS

1. **Community Connections.** With a group of classmates, choose one of the space pioneers described in this article. Design a monument to honor that pioneer's contribution to space travel. Write a few words for a plaque to attach to the monument. Present your idea to the class.
2. **Art.** What if you could design a space station? What would it look like? What would you include in it? How would you protect the crew from the dangers of space? With a small group of your classmates, design a space station for the future.

GUIDE FOR READING

Lee Bennett Hopkins

(1938–) taught school for six years and now spends most of his time writing and traveling around the country. He advises school systems and universities about education and literature. Hopkins has edited several outstanding poetry anthologies. One of these is *Don't You Turn Back,* a collection of poems by Langston Hughes. He has written collections of his own poetry as well as books and magazine articles about education and creative activities.

Virginia Hamilton

Interview

An **interview** is a special kind of conversation. One person, the interviewer, asks questions of another person, the subject, in order to get specific information. A magazine article based on an interview is also called an interview. Most writers try to use a conversational style in their interviews. This article by Lee Bennett Hopkins is based on an interview he had with Virginia Hamilton.

Focus

Before you read this article, choose a famous musician, actor, writer, or artist. Imagine that you have the opportunity to interview this person. What questions would you want to ask him or her? Brainstorm for a list of ten to fifteen questions to ask the person of your choice. As you read this selection, compare your questions to the ones Hopkins must have asked Virginia Hamilton.

Vocabulary

Knowing the following words will help you as you read "Virginia Hamilton."

alternate (ôl′ tər nit) *adj.*: First one and then the other; succeeding each other (p. 281)

perceive (pər sēv′) *v.*: Observe; become aware (p. 281)

clan (klan) *n.*: A group composed of several families, all claiming descent from the same ancestor (p. 282)

saga (sä′ gə) *n.*: A long story of adventure or heroic deeds (p. 282)

prodigy (präd′ ə jē) *n.*: A child of highly unusual talent or genius (p. 283)

contemplative (kən tem′ plə tiv′) *adj.*: Thoughtful (p. 284)

motivated (mōt′ ə vāt′ əd) *adj.*: Driven to move forward or to progress (p. 285)

Spelling Tip

This is a useful spelling rule: Use *i* before *e*, except after *c*. Knowing this rule will help you remember to use *e* before *i* in *perceive.*

Virginia Hamilton

Lee Bennett Hopkins

" 'Writers never tell the truth; that is, they tell more than one truth. . . .' "

Virginia Hamilton describes herself as being "chronically overweight, foul-tempered and given to alternate fits of depressions[1] and elation.[2] In sum," she continues, "I am a textbook neurotic[3] who never sleeps. I love life, freedom, lazing around and daydreaming. I read all the time—everything from Bulfinch[4] to seed catalogs."

Despite her self-analysis, she is the kind of person one loves to be around. And it's hard for me to think of her being either foul-tempered or one who might ever laze around! I know her as being bubbly and bouncy, with a never-stand-still way about her that makes one quickly perceive her sparkling, contagious enthusiasm for life.

Miss Hamilton grew up in Yellow Springs, an Ohio village that had been a station on the Underground Railroad.[5] The rural community, about sixty miles north of the Ohio River, is the home of Antioch College. The population includes descendants of abolitionists[6] and fugitive slaves.

Commenting on her childhood, she states: "I was born in a miserable corner of southern Ohio and dutifully raised there, where it is said that God, Himself, has seen the place only twice: once, when He created it; and the time He came back to apologize for what He had done. Actually, Yellow Springs, where I grew up, is quite a pretty place. My mother's Perry family came to the town before Emancipation.[7] The progenitor[8] was, of course, a runaway slave. He settled

1. depressions (dē presh′ ənz) *n.*: Feelings of sadness, gloominess, and hopelessness.

2. elation (ē lā′ shən) *n.*: Feelings of joy, pride, and high spirits.

3. textbook neurotic (no͞o rät′ ik) *n.*: A person suffering from anxiety of one sort or another, as described in medical textbooks.

4. Bulfinch (1796–1867): U.S. reteller of myths.

5. Underground Railroad: A system of safe hiding places set up by some opponents of slavery before 1861 to help slaves escape to free states or to Canada.

6. abolitionists (ab′ ə lish′ ən ists) *n.*: People in favor of doing away with slavery; people opposed to slavery.

7. Emancipation (ē man′ sə pā′ shən) *n.*: The freeing of all slaves in territory at war with the Union on January 1, 1863; slaves' freedom was granted in the Emancipation Proclamation issued by President Lincoln.

8. progenitor (prō jen′ ə tər) *n.*: Ancestor; forefather.

down on the rich land. He married, prospered; and the family grew into the large, extended Perry clan. I grew up within the warmth of loving aunts and uncles, all reluctant farmers but great storytellers. I remember the tales best of all. My own father, who was an outlander[9] from Illinois, Iowa, and points west, was the finest of the storytellers besides being an exceptional mandolinist.[10] Mother, too, could take a slice of fiction floating around the family and polish it into a saga."

Miss Hamilton was the fifth child born to Etta B. and Kenneth J. Hamilton. Her parents were "dollar-poor" in the 1930's when she was born. She describes their situation: "Franklin Roosevelt's New Deal[11] hadn't touched our household nor much of the Miami Valley where our village lay. But my parents turned acres of rich soil into a working farm with enough extra produce to sell by the bushel to the local grocer.

"By the time I was seven, I knew that life must be freedom; there was no better life than those acres and the surrounding farmlands. Being the 'baby' and bright, mind you, and odd and sensitive, I was left alone to discover whatever there was to find. No wonder then that I started to write things down at an early age. I'm a writer, I think, nearly by birth. There was no other way, really, that I could go."

As she approached college age, she was drawn to the Antioch community of books and writing, parties and dances. But at the close of these gatherings, when the students returned to their dormitories, she would return to her family's home, a mile out on the Dayton Pike.

After attending Antioch College and Ohio State University, Miss Hamilton moved to New York City where she married Arnold Adoff.

The author's first book for children, *Zeely* (Macmillan),[12] received wide critical acclaim.[13] The book tells a haunting story of eleven-year-old Elizabeth "Geeder" Perry and her brother John "Toeboy" Perry, who spend a summer on their Uncle Ross's farm. One day Geeder finds a photograph of a Watutsi queen[14] in an old magazine. The portrait reminds Geeder of Zeely, the grown daughter of Nat Tayber who rents a small part of Uncle Ross's land. Geeder decides that Zeely must also be a queen and becomes swept up in her fantasies.

The publication of *Zeely* came about via an old college friend who was working at Macmillan. The woman remembered a short story Miss Hamilton had written in college. "I had mostly forgotten it; but she reminded me about it and thought that if I tried making a book out of it, it would be a great story for children. Well, that's what I did! I took those eighteen moth-eaten pages and worked them over. It took a long time, but *Zeely* came from that. It was a happy accident—the kind of luck that hits you if you hang around New York long enough. I never really decided to write for children. It hap-

9. outlander: Someone from another area.

10. mandolinist (man′ də lin′ ist) *n.*: Someone who plays a mandolin, which is a stringed musical instrument with a long neck and a rounded body.

11. Franklin Roosevelt's New Deal: The policies of President Roosevelt's administration during the 1930's that were to advance economic recovery from the Great Depression.

12. Macmillan: A publishing company.

13. critical acclaim: Praise.

14. Watutsi (wä to͞ot′ sē) **queen:** Queen of an African tribe known for tall, handsome people.

pened about the time I was thinking about giving up being a writer since I was having trouble breaking into the adult writing field. I thought I might become an athletic instructor, or a singer—anything was better than the part-time bookkeeping, cost-accounting work I had been doing."

Her second book, *The House of Dies Drear* (Macmillan), dramatizes the history of the Underground Railroad in Ohio, viewed from the present day. It is a taut mystery, one which youngsters gulp down quickly and find hard to forget. Miss Hamilton remarked, "*The House of Dies Drear* is my favorite book, I think, because it is so full of all the things I love: excitement, mystery, black history, the strong, black family. In it I tried to pay back all those wonderful relatives who gave me so much in the past. And I tried to show the importance of the black church to my being; also the land and the good and bad of small town rural life."

Her third book, *The Time-Ago Tales of Jahdu*[15] (Macmillan), is a modern fable. The tales are told by Mama Luke, an old lady who cares for Lee Edward after school while his mother is at work. The story is set in New York's Harlem. Miss Hamilton's second Jahdu book, *Time-Ago Lost: More Tales of Jahdu* (Macmillan), was published in 1973; she commented: "Little Jahdu out on the road again. Looky there, little Brother! Here he is!"

The Planet of Junior Brown (Macmillan), her fourth book, was selected as a Newbery Honor Book[16] in 1972. As all of her works, this novel is a fine example of literary craftsmanship. The tale centers around Junior Brown, a 262-pound musical prodigy with a neurotic, overprotective mother; Buddy

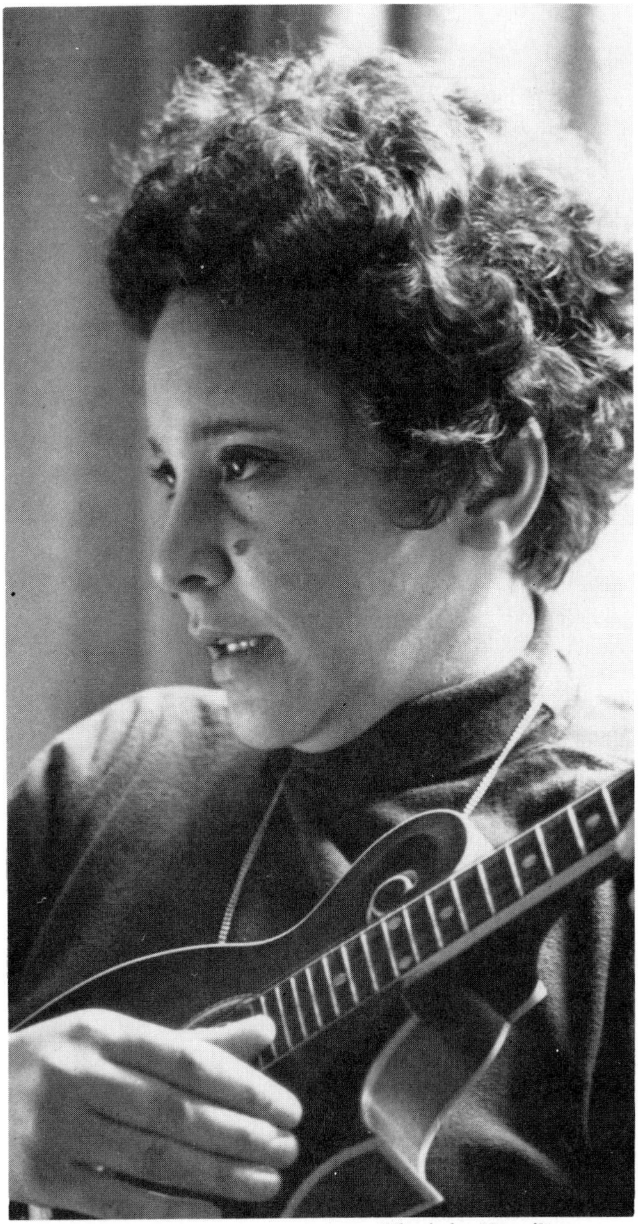

Virginia Hamilton

15. Jahdu (zhä′ du)
16. Newbery Honor Book: The John Newbery Medal is awarded each year for the book that makes the most distinguished contribution to American literature for children. The Newbery Honor Book is the runner-up.

Clark, a loner who has no family whatsoever; and Mr. Pool, once a teacher but now a janitor—the custodian of the high-school broom closet.

I asked Miss Hamilton if any of her characters are based on real people she knows or knew. She commented: "Oh, I'd say that Uncle Ross in *Zeely* is somewhat similar to my Uncle Lee who was a collector of antiques and stray cats; Geeder and Toeboy talk and act and sleep outside in much the same way my brother and I did. I don't really base any of my characters on real people. I do take the atmosphere of known people, their emotions, and give them to my characters. Zeely, of course, is completely imagined as a character. I never knew anyone like her. But then, a writer deals in possibilities. My childhood was immensely free, rural and, at times, lonely. There could have been a Zeely; it would have been fun if there had been. When I grew up, I simply rewrote the past and put Zeely into it. I think I'd have to say my characters are for the most part based on me. If you'll notice, every lead character is something of a loner, imaginative and contemplative, from Zeely up through Thomas Small in *The House of Dies Drear* to Junior Brown. My characters are the way I see the artist, the *human*, isolated, out of time, in order to reveal himself more clearly. I am tremendously interested in the human as oracle[17] and as spirit isolated. I tried to speak of that in *The Planet of Junior Brown* with the use of planets and the loneliness of mankind in the immensity of space and time. That is why Junior Brown futilely sees himself as the center of a wheel or spiral, trying desperately to find a place for his mental isolation.

"I hope children and adults will accept my characters, all of them, in the manner they were given—with love and warmth for all that is uniquely human. A child—anyone—must know me through my books. I reveal myself only reluctantly, if at all. Not that I'm trying to hide exactly, but more that I feel there is not really much to know. What I am is simply very personal and is revealed somewhat through what I write."

Like many of her characters, Miss Hamilton is a "loner; an introvert,[18] with no companions other than my immediate family. I do not like to talk, although I am called upon to do that more and more. Why is it writers are thought to be speakers as well? Writers never tell the truth; that is, they tell more than one truth, depending on what they had for breakfast or what they dreamed about the night before. I am fond of telling lies, about my age, creations, the past, and my husband!"

She then told me about her work habits: "When I get an idea, I keep it to myself until I find out whether I have a good story working. When I know that, well, then I'll read parts to my husband. A story idea simply comes to me, and I accept the wonder of that sort of thing without probing to find out where it comes from. Usually, though, I get a title in my head like *Dies Drear* or *Junior Brown* and then start thinking about it. I'm not really aware of the thinking, for it is lightning swift. I get bits and pieces of conversation, flashes of atmosphere, a location. All a jumble at first, until I begin to write it

---

17. oracle (ôr′ ə kəl) *n.*: A source of great knowledge or wisdom.

18. introvert (in′ trō vʉrt) *n.*: Someone who directs his or her attention inward toward his or her own thoughts, feelings, and experiences.

and sort it out. I rewrite very little; when I'm ready to write it out, it comes along pretty clean."

The author and her family recently returned to Yellow Springs after living in New York City for several years. The Adoffs have two children—a daughter, Leigh, "who is a high-spirited nine-year-old," and a son, Jaime, "a highly-motivated five!"

"My children take up a good deal of my time, of course, and I don't mind that one bit," Miss Hamilton said. "They are so active and creative; they want to know everything; and so I have to know everything in order to tell them. We have a good time. Life with two writers in the house is very hectic, very difficult, and often very amusing. My husband is basically a poet, although he is an anthologist,[19] too. As everyone knows, poets talk all the time—as does Arnold. He not only talks forever but he works forever as well. He has a tremendous capacity for getting things done and can juggle work on three books at once. Plus he chops down trees and generally spends a good deal of time being a gentleman farmer. Having been born in the Bronx, he took to the land like an alligator out of water. Arnold is like a whirlwind. He keeps everything all stirred up and noisy. He's never boring because he's always thinking up some outrageous new thing to do. We both work in the mornings and usually late at night. We get very little sleep. Who needs it anyway? The long last sleep is long enough."

The Adoffs live at the end of a dead-end gravel road in the middle of a two-acre field. The land was once part of the farm on which Miss Hamilton grew up. Their house has high peaks made out of redwood, one deck, and two patios. "Everything is sliding glass so that the outdoors comes right in whenever it has a mind to. My favorite possessions are mine eyes—to see the wondrous farmland surrounding us. We don't live in a neighborhood as such. My mother still lives in the old homestead just down the field and through the roses and trees." Her brother and his family still live on Grandpa Perry's farm, the original Perry settlement, near her mother's house.

"We raise a lot of flowers and lots of fuss in town," Miss Hamilton chuckled. "I'm on the local Human Relations Committee and the Committee on Equal Education. I belong to the local writers group. We are all women, and the group has been in existence for at least fifty years. There are many professional writers in town. Yellow Springs draws artists, ecologists, socialists, and other rabble-rousers like moths to a light! You can perhaps blame Antioch for that—maybe the crystalline[20] quality of the atmosphere.

"I don't feel like an adult as such. I feel maybe twelve sometimes. I feel I'd like to slow things down a bit. We work and play so hard out here that the seasons do not merely turn—they streak away."

Reader's Response

After reading this interview with Virginia Hamilton, would you want to read her books? Why or why not?

---

19. anthologist (an' thäl' ə jist) *n.*: A person who collects written works of others into one volume.

20. crystalline (kris' təl in) *adj.*: Like a crystal; clear and transparent.

RESPONDING TO THE SELECTION

Your Response

1. Whom would you want to interview and why?
2. Do you share any personality traits with Virginia Hamilton or any of her fictional characters? Explain.

Recalling

3. How did Hamilton's writing career begin?
4. Describe three of Hamilton's books.

Interpreting

5. How are Hamilton's characters related to the people she knows?
6. How are Hamilton's characters related to her own personality?
7. In what ways did Hamilton's childhood shape her career as a writer?
8. Why does Hamilton write books?

Applying

9. Hamilton says that story ideas "simply come" to her. Where could you get ideas for topics to write about?

ANALYZING LITERATURE

Understanding an Interview

An **interview** records a conversation in which the interviewer asks questions of the subject to get specific information. In this article written from an interview with Virginia Hamilton, Hopkins summarizes information and also includes quotations so that we read Virginia Hamilton's own words.

1. Find a passage in which Hopkins summarizes information from the interview or from other sources.
2. Find a quotation that is probably taken directly from Hopkins's notes or a recording of the interview.
3. What kind of information does an interview article give that might not be available elsewhere?

CRITICAL THINKING AND READING

Evaluating a Generalization

A **generalization** is a conclusion based on a number of specific examples. However, generalizations can be misleading if they try to cover too much or if they are based on too few examples. Good writers use generalizations very carefully. Most of the time, Virginia Hamilton avoids generalizations about writing and writers. Instead, she discusses the specific—herself, her writing, and her techniques. However, she makes one remarkable generalization: "Writers never tell the truth. . . ." (page 284) Explain why you think her generalization is or is not valid.

THINKING AND WRITING

Writing an Interview

Choose someone in your community to interview—perhaps a politician, teacher, or storekeeper. Write to or call your subject, requesting an interview. Next, write a list of questions to ask your subject. You may refer to the list of questions you developed in the Focus activity on page 280. Then conduct the interview, listening carefully to the answers. Be alert for new ideas your subject introduces and follow them up. Take careful notes, or record the interview. Then write an article based on your interview. Decide which topics in your notes are most important to a portrait of your subject. When you revise, refer to "Virginia Hamilton" to see how to connect ideas to make the interview read smoothly. Be sure to send a copy to your subject.

LEARNING OPTION

Speaking and Listening. Read a book by Virginia Hamilton. You might choose one mentioned in this article or one that she has published since this article was written. Prepare an oral book report and present it to your class.

Writing From Observation

How many times have you watched nature at work and wondered about its secrets? Have you observed a bird in flight and wished that you could spread your wings and take flight across the sky? Observations like these have sparked the imaginations of scientists, inventors, and artists. For instance, the Wright brothers, who invented the airplane, were inspired to recreate the power and ability of birds' wings to lift themselves into the air.

Writers also spark their imaginations by observing themselves and their environment. For example, Andrew A. Rooney observed the way he reads the newspaper and discovered that "There's nothing I do so much of that I do so badly."

Your Turn

Become an observer. You will make observations and then write about them.

Prewriting

1. Become an observer. Take ten minutes to observe something in your classroom or outside the school. Notice everything you can. Pay attention to details that appeal to different senses. List all the details you notice.

Then, working with a partner, review all your observations and select those that are important to creating a single impression or making a point. For example, if you observe the inside of your classroom, what details would give the feeling of the room?

2. Find a topic for your writing. Consider what you might write about. You can make observations about almost anything—an object, a place, a person, a habit or practice like Andrew A. Rooney's about reading the newspaper. To come up with possibilities, you might make lists. List objects around you; list people you know or see regularly; list things that interest you or "bug" you. Review your lists and select a topic you'd like to explore by observation. This will be your subject.

3. Observe your subject for a day. Make notes and a cluster diagram. One student chose his sneakers as a topic and made this cluster.

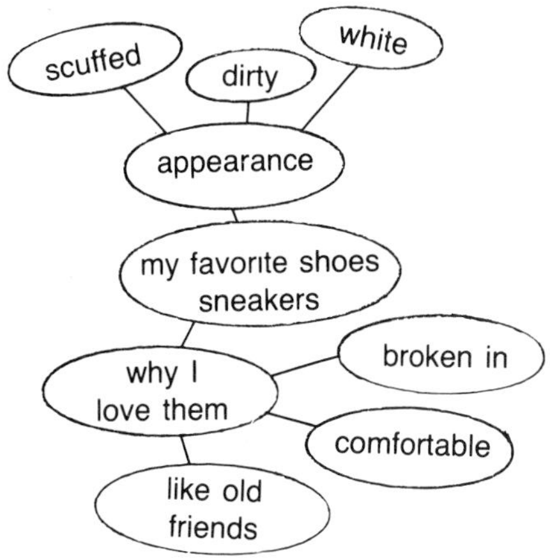

4. Make a discovery. Review your notes and your cluster diagram. Look for a pattern or a point. Can you use your observations to invent something new? Can you make a new comparison about your subject? Do your observations help you see your subject from a different point of view? Jot down some of these ideas or discoveries. Select one. Write it as a sentence. For example, the writer who observed his sneakers made this discovery: *My sneakers are more than comfortable footwear. They're friends that share my personal history.*

The discovery that you make will be the main point of your paper. This point determines what information you will keep and what information you will leave out.

Drafting

Using your notes and your discovery, write a first draft.

The following is the first draft of the student writing about his sneakers:

> I don't even have to think about putting on my sneakers. They're part of my daily routine, part of who I am. Sometimes I think they're like good friends, for these sneakers are so much a part of my life.
>
> Yet my sneakers will, even with the best of care, wear out, and I'll toss them away. They are not, after all, really good friends. Although they become more comfortable and more familiar with time, good friends never wear out or go out of style. My sneakers are my favorite shoes, but they are purchased possessions. Good friends are earned treasures.

The writer of the sample draft seems to be discovering a comparison between sneakers and friends. In future drafts he might add observations that will further develop this discovery about friends.

Revising

In addition to using the revision checklist on page 751, ask a writing partner questions such as the following:

- What do you like best about this draft?
- What might make it better?
- What other observations could I make?
- What kind of information would you like to know?

Proofreading

Consult the guidelines for proofreading on page 753. Remember to proofread especially for the kind of grammatical errors you know you're likely to make. Then write a final copy.

Reading Biographical and Personal Writing

THE YOUNG ROUTY AT CELEYRAN
Henri Toulouse-Lautrec

GUIDE FOR READING

Russell Freedman

(1929–   ) has written more than thirty books, mainly for young people. These include *Immigrant Kids, Children of the Wild West,* and *Cowboys of the Wild West,* all named notable children's books by the American Library Association. *Lincoln: A Photobiography,* a carefully researched account of the life of our sixteenth President, is a winner of the Newbery Medal for children's literature. One chapter, "A Backwoods Boy," tells of Abraham Lincoln's growing-up years.

A Backwoods Boy

Biography

A **biography** is the story of a person's life written by someone else. Biographies usually focus on the major achievements in a person's life. Often the writer, or biographer, begins by describing the subject's early life, as Freedman does in "A Backwoods Boy." Knowing about the subject's early years helps the readers understand events in later years. A biography may include illustrations, but as in all writing, the ability to paint vivid word pictures is the author's most powerful tool.

Focus

"A Backwoods Boy" tells about the experiences of Abraham Lincoln growing up on the western frontier in the 1800's. Have you heard stories about Abraham Lincoln? What have you learned about life during the 1800's? In a group of three or four, brainstorm about all the things you know about Lincoln and life during the 1800's. As you read the selection, compare the things you thought of to the things Freedman mentions.

Vocabulary

Knowing the following words will help you as you read "A Backwoods Boy."

burly (bʉr′ lē) *adj.*: Big and strong (p. 292)

makeshift (māk′ shift′) *adj.*: Used for a while as a substitute (p. 292)

precinct (prē′ siŋkt) *n.*: An election district (p. 297)

aptitude (ap′ tə to͞od′) *n.*: Natural ability (p. 297)

intrigued (in trēg′d′) *v.*: Fascinated (p. 298)

treacherous (trech′ ər əs) *adj.*: Dangerous (p. 298)

Spelling Tip

In the word *precinct,* the *s* sound and the *k* sound are both spelled with a *c.*

A Backwoods Boy

Russell Freedman

"They circled each other, then came to grips, twisting and tugging until they crashed to the ground with Lincoln on top."

"It is a great piece of folly to attempt to make anything out of my early life. It can all be condensed into a simple sentence, and that sentence you will find in Gray's Elegy[1]*— 'the short and simple annals[2] of the poor.' That's my life, and that's all you or anyone else can make out of it."* [3]

Abraham Lincoln never liked to talk much about his early life. A poor backwoods farm boy, he grew up swinging an ax on frontier homesteads in Kentucky, Indiana, and Illinois.

He was born near Hodgenville, Kentucky, on February 12, 1809, in a log cabin with one window, one door, a chimney, and a hard-packed dirt floor. His parents named him after his pioneer grandfather. The first Abraham Lincoln had been shot dead by hostile Indians in 1786, while planting a field of corn in the Kentucky wilderness.

Young Abraham was still a toddler when his family packed their belongings and moved to another log-cabin farm a few miles north, on Knob Creek. That was the first home he could remember, the place where he ran and played as a barefoot boy.

He remembered the bright waters of Knob Creek as it tumbled past the Lincoln cabin and disappeared into the Kentucky hills. Once he fell into the rushing creek and almost drowned before he was pulled out by a neighbor boy. Another time he caught a fish and gave it to a passing soldier.

Lincoln never forgot the names of his first teachers—Zachariah Riney followed by Caleb Hazel—who ran a windowless log schoolhouse two miles away. It was called a "blab school." Pupils of all ages sat on rough wooden benches and bawled out their lessons aloud. Abraham went there with his sister Sarah, who was two years older, when they could be spared from their chores at

1. **Elegy** (el′ ə jē) *n.*: A poem praising someone who has died.
2. **annals** (an′ əlz) *n.*: Historical records.
3. **"It is a great . . . out of it.":** This is a quotation from Abraham Lincoln.

home. Holding hands, they would walk through scrub trees and across creek bottoms to the schoolhouse door. They learned their numbers from one to ten, and a smattering of reading, writing, and spelling.

Their parents couldn't read or write at all. Abraham's mother, Nancy, signed her name by making a shakily drawn mark. He would remember her as a thin, sad-eyed woman who labored beside her husband in the fields. She liked to gather the children around her in the evening to recite prayers and Bible stories she had memorized.

His father, Thomas, was a burly, barrel-chested farmer and carpenter who had worked hard at homesteading since marrying Nancy Hanks in 1806. A sociable fellow, his greatest pleasure was to crack jokes and swap stories with his chums. With painful effort, Thomas Lincoln could scrawl his name. Like his wife, he had grown up without education, but that wasn't unusual in those days. He supported his family by living off his own land, and he watched for a chance to better himself.

In 1816, Thomas decided to pull up stakes again and move north to Indiana, which was about to join the Union as the nation's nineteenth state. Abraham was seven. He remembered the one-hundred-mile journey as the hardest experience of his life. The family set out on a cold morning in December, loading all their possessions on two horses. They crossed the Ohio River on a makeshift ferry, traveled through towering forests, then hacked a path through tangled underbrush until they reached their new homesite near the backwoods community of Little Pigeon Creek.

Thomas put up a temporary winter shelter—a crude, three-sided lean-to of logs and branches. At the open end, he kept a fire burning to take the edge off the cold and scare off the wild animals. At night, wrapped in bearskins and huddled by the fire, Abraham and Sarah listened to wolves howl and panthers scream.

Abraham passed his eighth birthday in the lean-to. He was big for his age, "a tall spider of a boy," and old enough to handle an ax. He helped his father clear the land. They planted corn and pumpkin seeds between the tree stumps. And they built a new log cabin, the biggest one yet, where Abraham climbed a ladder and slept in a loft beneath the roof.

Soon after the cabin was finished, some of Nancy's kinfolk arrived. Her aunt and uncle with their adopted son Dennis had decided to follow the Lincolns to Indiana. Dennis Hanks became an extra hand to Thomas and a big brother to Abraham, someone to run and wrestle with.

A year later, Nancy's aunt and uncle lay dead, victims of the dreaded "milk sickness" (now known to be caused by a poisonous plant called white snake root). An epidemic of the disease swept through the Indiana woods in the summer of 1818. Nancy had nursed her relatives until the end, and then she too came down with the disease. Abraham watched his mother toss in bed with chills, fever, and pain for seven days before she died at the age of thirty-four. "She knew she was going to die," Dennis Hanks recalled. "She called up the children to her dying side and told them to be good and kind to their father, to one another, and to the world."

Thomas built a coffin from black cherry wood, and nine-year-old Abraham whittled the pegs that held the wooden planks to-

NANCY H. LINCOLN
Lincoln Boyhood National Memorial

SARAH BUSH JOHNSTON LINCOLN
Lincoln Boyhood National Memorial

THOMAS LINCOLN
Lincoln Boyhood National Memorial

gether. They buried Nancy on a windswept hill, next to her aunt and uncle. Sarah, now eleven, took her mother's place, cooking, cleaning, and mending clothes for her father, brother, and cousin Dennis in the forlorn and lonely cabin.

Thomas Lincoln waited for a year. Then he went back to Kentucky to find himself a new wife. He returned in a four-horse wagon with a widow named Sarah Bush Johnston, her three children, and all her household goods. Abraham and his sister were fortunate, for their stepmother was a warm and loving person. She took the motherless children to her heart and raised them as her own. She also spruced up the neglected Lincoln cabin, now shared by eight people who lived, ate, and slept in a single smoky room with a loft.

Abraham was growing fast, shooting up like a sunflower, a spindly youngster with big bony hands, unruly black hair, a dark complexion, and luminous gray eyes. He became an expert with the ax, working alongside his father, who also hired him out to work for others. For twenty-five cents a day, the boy dug wells, built pigpens, split fence rails, felled trees. "My how he could chop!" exclaimed a friend. "His ax would flash and bite into a sugar tree or a sycamore, and down it would come. If you heard him felling trees in a clearing, you would say there were three men at work, the way the trees fell."

Meanwhile, he went to school "by littles," a few weeks one winter, maybe a month the next. Lincoln said later that all his schooling together "did not amount to one year." Some fragments of his schoolwork still survive, including a verse that he wrote in his homemade arithmetic book: "Abraham Lincoln/ his hand and pen/he will be good but/god knows When."

Mostly, he educated himself by borrowing books and newspapers. There are many stories about Lincoln's efforts to find enough books to satisfy him in that backwoods country. Those he liked he read again and again, losing himself in the adventures of *Robinson Crusoe* or the magical tales of *The Arabian Nights*. He was thrilled by a biography of George Washington, with its stirring account of the Revolutionary War. And he came to love the rhyme and rhythm of poetry, reciting passages from Shakespeare or the Scottish poet Robert Burns at the drop of a hat. He would carry a book out to the field with him, so he could read at the end of each plow furrow, while the horse was getting its breath. When noon came, he would sit under a tree and read while he ate. "I never saw Abe after he was twelve that he didn't have a book in his hand or in his pocket," Dennis Hanks remembered. "It didn't seem natural to see a feller read like that."

By the time he was sixteen, Abraham was six feet tall—"the gangliest awkwardest feller . . . he appeared to be all joints," said a neighbor. He may have looked awkward, but hard physical labor had given him a tough, lean body with muscular arms like steel cables. He could grab a woodsman's ax by the handle and hold it straight out at arm's length. And he was one of the best wrestlers and runners around.

He also had a reputation as a comic and storyteller. Like his father, Abraham was fond of talking and listening to talk. About this time he had found a book called *Lessons in Elocution*, which offered advice on public speaking. He practiced before his friends, standing on a tree stump as he entertained them with fiery imitations of the roving preachers and politicians who often visited Little Pigeon Creek.

Folks liked young Lincoln. They regarded him as a good-humored, easy-going boy—a bookworm maybe, but smart and willing to oblige. Yet even then, people noticed that he could be moody and withdrawn. As a friend put it, he was "witty, sad, and reflective by turns."

At the age of seventeen, Abraham left home for a few months to work as a ferryman's helper on the Ohio River. He was eighteen when his sister Sarah died early in 1828, while giving birth to her first child.

That spring, Abraham had a chance to get away from the backwoods and see something of the world. A local merchant named James Gentry hired Lincoln to accompany his son Allen on a twelve-hundred-mile flatboat voyage to New Orleans. With their cargo of country produce, the two boys floated down the Ohio River and into the Mississippi, maneuvering with long poles to avoid snags and sandbars, and to navigate in the busy river traffic.

New Orleans was the first real city they had ever seen. Their eyes must have popped as the great harbor came into view, jammed with the masts of sailing ships from distant ports all over the world. The city's cobblestone streets teemed with sailors, traders, and adventurers speaking strange languages. And there were gangs of slaves everywhere. Lincoln would never forget the sight of black men, women, and children being driven along in chains and auctioned off like cattle. In those days, New Orleans had more than two hundred slave dealers.

The boys sold their cargo and their flat-

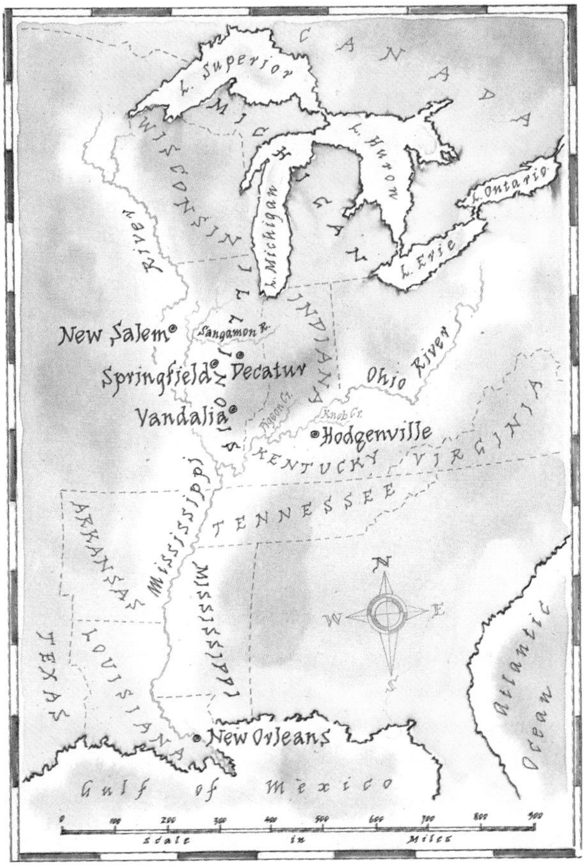

boat and returned upriver by steamboat. Abraham earned twenty-four dollars—a good bit of money at the time—for the three-month trip. He handed the money over to his father, according to law and custom.

Thomas Lincoln was thinking about moving on again. Lately he had heard glowing reports about Illinois, where instead of forests there were endless prairies with plenty of rich black soil. Early in 1830, Thomas sold his Indiana farm. The Lincolns piled everything they owned into two ox-drawn wagons and set out over muddy roads, with Abraham, just turned twenty-one, driving one of the wagons himself. They traveled west to their new homesite in central Illinois, not far from Decatur. Once again, Abraham helped his father build a cabin and start a new farm.

He stayed with his family through their first prairie winter, but he was getting restless. He had met an enterprising fellow named Denton Offutt, who wanted him to take another boatload of cargo down the river to New Orleans. Abraham agreed to make the trip with his stepbrother, John Johnston, and a cousin, John Hanks.

When he returned to Illinois three months later, he paid a quick farewell visit to his father and stepmother. Abraham was twenty-two now, of legal age, free to do what he wanted. His parents were settled and could get along without him. Denton Offutt was planning to open a general store in the flourishing village of New Salem, Illinois, and he had promised Lincoln a steady job.

Lincoln arrived in New Salem in July 1831 wearing a faded cotton shirt and blue jeans too short for his long legs—a "friendless, uneducated, penniless boy," as he later described himself. He tended the counter at Denton Offutt's store and slept in a room at the back.

The village stood in a wooded grove on a bluff above the Sangamon River. Founded just two years earlier, it had about one hundred people living in one- and two-room log houses. Cattle grazed behind split-rail fences, hogs snuffled along dusty lanes, and chickens and geese flapped about underfoot. New Salem was still a small place, but it was growing. The settlers expected it to become a frontier boom town.

With his gifts for swapping stories and making friends, Lincoln fit easily into the life of the village. He showed off his skill with an ax, competed in footraces, and got along with everyone from Mentor Graham, the schoolmaster, to Jack Armstrong, the leader of a rowdy gang called the Clary's Grove boys. Armstrong was the wrestling champion of New Salem. He quickly challenged Lincoln to a match.

On the appointed day, an excited crowd gathered down by the river, placing bets as the wrestlers stripped to the waist for combat. They circled each other, then came to grips, twisting and tugging until they crashed to the ground with Lincoln on top. As he pinned Armstrong's shoulders to the ground, the other Clary's Grove boys dived in to join the scuffle. Lincoln broke away, backed against a cliff, and defiantly offered to take them all on—one at a time. Impressed, Armstrong jumped to his feet and offered Lincoln his hand, declaring the match a draw. After that, they were fast friends.

Lincoln also found a place among the town's intellectuals. He joined the New Salem Debating Society, which met once a week in James Rutledge's tavern. The first time he debated, he seemed nervous. But as he began to speak in his high, reedy voice, he surprised everyone with the force and logic of his argument. "He was already a fine speaker," one debater recalled. "All he lacked was culture."

Lincoln was self-conscious about his meager education, and ambitious to improve himself. Mentor Graham, the schoolmaster and a fellow debater, took a liking to the young man, lent him books, and offered to coach him in the fine points of English grammar. Lincoln had plenty of time to study. There wasn't much business at Offutt's store, so he could spend long hours reading as he sat behind the counter.

When the store failed in 1832, Offutt moved on to other schemes. Lincoln had to find something else to do. At the age of twenty-three, he decided to run for the Illinois state legislature. Why not? He knew everyone in town, people liked him, and he was rapidly gaining confidence as a public speaker. His friends urged him to run, saying that a bright young man could go far in politics. So Lincoln announced his candidacy and his political platform. He was in favor of local improvements, like better roads and canals. He had made a study of the Sangamon River, and he proposed that it be dredged and cleared so steamboats could call

PECULIARSOME ABE
N. C. Wyeth
Free Library of Philadelphia

at New Salem—insuring a glorious future for the town.

Before he could start his campaign, an Indian war flared up in northern Illinois. Chief Black Hawk of the Sauk and Fox tribes had crossed the Mississippi, intending, he said, to raise corn on land that had been taken from his people thirty years earlier. The white settlers were alarmed, and the governor called for volunteers to stop the invasion. Lincoln enlisted in a militia company made up of his friends and neighbors. He was surprised and pleased when the men elected him as their captain, with Jack Armstrong as first sergeant. His troops drilled and marched, but they never did sight any hostile Indians. Years later, Lincoln would joke about his three-month stint as a military man, telling how he survived "a good many bloody battles with mosquitoes."

By the time he returned to New Salem, election day was just two weeks off. He jumped into the campaign—pitching horseshoes with voters, speaking at barbecues, chatting with farmers in the fields, joking with customers at country stores. He lost, finishing eighth in a field of thirteen. But in his own precinct, where folks knew him, he received 227 votes out of 300 cast.

Defeated as a politician, he decided to try his luck as a frontier merchant. With a fellow named William Berry as his partner, Lincoln operated a general store that sold everything from axes to beeswax. But the two men showed little aptitude for business, and their store finally "winked out," as Lincoln put it. Then Berry died, leaving Lincoln saddled with a $1,100 debt—a gigantic amount for someone who had never earned more than a few dollars a month. Lincoln called it "the National Debt," but he vowed to repay every cent. He spent the next fifteen years doing so.

To support himself, he worked at all sorts of odd jobs. He split fence rails, hired himself out as a farmhand, helped at the local gristmill.[4] With the help of friends, he was appointed postmaster of New Salem, a part-time job that paid about fifty dollars a year. Then he was offered a chance to become deputy to the local surveyor.[5] He knew nothing about surveying, so he bought a compass, a chain, and a couple of textbooks on the subject. Within six weeks, he had taught himself enough to start work—laying out roads and townsites, and marking off property boundaries.

As he traveled about the county, making surveys and delivering mail to faraway farms, people came to know him as an honest and dependable fellow. Lincoln could be counted on to witness a contract, settle a boundary dispute, or compose a letter for folks who couldn't write much themselves. For the first time, his neighbors began to call him "Abe."

In 1834, Lincoln ran for the state legislature again. This time he placed second in a field of thirteen candidates, and was one of four men elected to the Illinois House of Representatives from Sangamon County. In November, wearing a sixty-dollar tailor-made suit he had bought on credit, the first suit he had ever owned, the twenty-five-year-old legislator climbed into a stagecoach and set out for the state capital in Vandalia.

In those days, Illinois lawmakers were paid three dollars a day to cover their expenses, but only while the legislature was in

4. gristmill (grist′ mil′) *n.*: A place where grain is ground into flour.

5. surveyor (sər vā′ ər) *n.*: A person who determines the boundaries of land.

session. Lincoln still had to earn a living. One of his fellow representatives, a rising young attorney named John Todd Stuart, urged Lincoln to take up the study of law. As Stuart pointed out, it was an ideal profession for anyone with political ambitions.

And in fact, Lincoln had been toying with the idea of becoming a lawyer. For years he had hung around frontier courthouses, watching country lawyers bluster and strut as they cross-examined witnesses and delivered impassioned speeches before juries. He had sat on juries himself, appeared as a witness, drawn up legal documents for his neighbors. He had even argued a few cases before the local justice of the peace.

Yes, the law intrigued him. It would give him a chance to rise in the world, to earn a respected place in the community, to live by his wits instead of by hard physical labor.

Yet Lincoln hesitated, unsure of himself because he had so little formal education. That was no great obstacle, his friend Stuart kept telling him. In the 1830's, few American lawyers had ever seen the inside of a law school. Instead, they "read law" in the office of a practicing attorney until they knew enough to pass their exams.

Lincoln decided to study entirely on his own. He borrowed some law books from Stuart, bought others at an auction, and began to read and memorize legal codes[6] and precedents.[7] Back in New Salem, folks would see him walking down the road, reciting aloud from one of his law books, or lying under a tree as he read, his long legs stretched up the trunk. He studied for nearly three years before passing his exams and being admitted to practice on March 1, 1837.

By then, the state legislature was planning to move from Vandalia to Springfield, which had been named the new capital of Illinois. Lincoln had been elected to a second term in the legislature. And he had accepted a job as junior partner in John Todd Stuart's Springfield law office.

In April, he went back to New Salem for the last time to pack his belongings and say goodbye to his friends. The little village was declining now. Its hopes for growth and prosperity had vanished when the Sangamon River proved too treacherous for steamboat travel. Settlers were moving away, seeking brighter prospects elsewhere.

By 1840, New Salem was a ghost town. It would have been forgotten completely if Abraham Lincoln hadn't gone there to live when he was young, penniless, and ambitious.

6. legal codes: A body of laws, as for a nation or a city, arranged systematically.

7. precedents (pres′ ə dənts) *n.*: Legal cases that may serve as examples for later cases.

Reader's Response

What was the most interesting fact you learned about young Abraham Lincoln? Did anything about his early years surprise you? Explain.

Responding to the Selection

Your Response

1. What more would you like to know about young Abe Lincoln?

Recalling

2. Mention two ways eight-year-old Abraham Lincoln helped his family.

Interpreting

3. What were some early signs that Lincoln would become a great public speaker?
4. Explain what his wrestling match with Jack Armstrong proved about Lincoln.
5. How did being "a backwoods boy" affect the kind of man Lincoln became?

Applying

6. Lincoln sums up his early life as "the short and simple annals of the poor." Do you agree with these words as a description of his life? Why or why not?

Analyzing Literature

Understanding Biography

In a **biography** a writer tells the story of another person's life. In "A Backwoods Boy," Freedman paints a picture of a young man who has already begun to show some of the qualities for which he would become famous.

Read each of the following examples. Then explain what each tells about young Lincoln.

1. He fit easily into the life of the village.
2. He was elected captain of his militia company.
3. He spent fifteen years repaying a debt.

Critical Thinking and Reading

Understanding Chronological Order

The events in "A Backwoods Boy" are arranged in chronological order. **Chronological order** means that each event follows as it occurred in time. Freedman uses certain words and phrases to signal the passage of time. Some of them are "in 1816," "at the age of seventeen," or "years later."

Find five more examples of words and phrases in "A Backwoods Boy" that indicate chronological order.

Thinking and Writing

Writing a Biographical Sketch

Think of incidents in the life of someone you know that would be interesting to others. Write down a list of your thoughts about that person and the incidents. Next, write a biographical sketch using your list. First, introduce the person to your readers. Include events and examples that will help explain the character of the person. When you have finished writing a first draft, meet with two or three classmates to discuss each other's papers. Is the character of each subject revealed? Is each sketch interesting to read? Make suggestions about how each paper could be improved. Revise your paper and include as many of your classmates' suggestions for improving your sketch as you can. Then, write a final copy of your biographical sketch.

Learning Options

1. **Art.** Create an illustrated timeline that shows the events in young Abraham Lincoln's life. Begin your timeline with the year 1809—the year of Lincoln's birth. Add events as they are told in this selection. Illustrate two or three events on the timeline with drawings or pictures from old newspapers and magazines.
2. **Cross-curricular Connection.** Use the resources in your school or local library to find out about Lincoln's attempt to win a seat in the U.S. Senate in 1858. Prepare an oral report for your class in which you report on the race for the Senate and results of the election.

GUIDE FOR READING

Brenda A. Johnston

(1944–) was born in West Virginia but now lives in Cleveland, Ohio. Many of her stories have appeared in *Scholastic Magazine.* In this selection from *Between the Devil and the Sea,* Johnston tells about the early life of James Forten, a free black American of the early nineteenth century. Forten, who became the owner of the sail loft where he had worked as a boy, was one of Philadelphia's wealthiest citizens. The book has received an Honorable Mention Award from the Council of Interracial Books.

from Between the Devil and the Sea

Biographical Narrative

A **biographical narrative** is an account of someone's life told as if it were a story. A biographical narrative remains true to the major events of the subject's life, but may combine fact with fiction. In this biographical narrative, Brenda Johnston includes conversations and thoughts that fit in with the actual events in James Forten's life. However, she could not possibly know what actually was said or thought.

Focus

This selection is about fifteen-year-old James Forten, who faces frustration when he is told that he is too young to join a ship's crew. How do hearing the words "you're too young" make you feel? Write the phrase "you're too young" in the center of a sheet of paper. Then write thoughts and feelings you associate with that phrase on the page. As you read the selection, see if your feelings are similar to James's feelings.

Vocabulary

Knowing the following words will help you as you read *Between the Devil and the Sea.*

decisively (di sī′ siv lē) *adv.*: With determination (p. 301)

gait (gāt) *n.*: Manner of walking or running (p. 302)

unfalteringly (un fôl′ tər iŋ lē) *adv.*: With certainty and steadiness (p. 302)

apprehension (ap′ rə hen′ shən) *n.*: A feeling of worry (p. 302)

defied (di fīd′) *v.*: Resisted openly (p. 302)

respective (ri spek′ tiv) *adj.*: Relating separately to each of two or more (p. 304)

prospective (prə spek′ tiv) *adj.*: Expected (p. 306)

belligerent (bə lij′ ər ənt) *adj.*: Showing readiness to fight or quarrel (p. 306)

abolished (ə bäl′ isht) *v.*: Put an end to (p. 306)

loathsome (lōth′ səm) *adj.*: Disgusting (p. 308)

from Between the Devil and the Sea

Brenda A. Johnston

"James ran over to the gun crew and stood in position near the powder and balls and waited, hoping that no one would notice his trembling."

There was excitement along the harbor, and James joined the crowds watching the *Royal Lewis*, Philadelphia's own privateer,[1] bringing its captured British vessel into port. Since Philadelphia was the capital of the new nation, James witnessed many auctions[2] of captured British cargo at the wharves and marveled at the proceeds that the captain and the crew shared as a reward. The privateers were not part of the navy, but American pirate ships whose mission was to stop the British merchant ships. Their reward was patriotic glory, the wealthy cargo from the captured ships, and a small monthly allotment as well.

James wanted to join the privateer crew more than anything else in the world, but he had already learned that it was useless to plead with his mother. As he walked home from the docks, he passed the London Coffee House, where he met his friends Larry and Fred standing outside.

"Guess what?" They greeted him in excitement.

"What?" asked James coolly, careful not to betray his curiosity.

"Guess who got signed up for the *Royal Lewis*'s next trip?"

James was interested. "Not you, I know," he said, hoping with all his heart that they were not going before he could.

"Daniel Brewton," they answered him. Daniel was one of their white friends.

"I'm going to sign up, too," said James decisively.

"You're too young," said Fred.

"Daniel and I are the same age almost," said James.

"Your mother'll kill you," declared Larry. "Besides, we already tried."

James left them standing there while he approached a man sitting at a table taking

1. privateer (prī′ və tir′) *n.*: A privately owned and staffed armed ship that attacks and captures enemy ships.
2. auctions (ôk′ shəns) *n.*: Public sales where items go to the higest bidder.

down names. He stood before the man and cleared his throat.

The man looked at him inquiringly for a moment, then asked sharply, "How old are you?"

"Sixteen," said James, thinking fast. He was already nearly six feet tall and walked with a slow, self-confident gait. Black bushy eyebrows framed a lean creamed-coffee face and gave him the appearance of a scowl until one of his slow smiles broke through, lit his eyes, and showed two rows of perfect white teeth. His smiles were rare though, and most of the time his face was expressionless. He had acquired the habit of gazing unfalteringly into a person's eyes while talking, but taking care that none of his own feelings were ever reflected in his dark eyes. He now fixed his gaze on the man and waited.

The man finally shrugged his shoulders and said, "Oh, well. You're on. What's your name?"

"James Forten," he answered quickly, already wondering what he was going to tell his mother.

The man's voice broke through his thoughts. "We sail in three days, James. See you then."

He walked back to his friends and with disdain in every word said, "Well, boys, the *Royal Lewis* and I sail in three days."

They were astonished. "How?" they asked. "What did you say?"

James laughed at their dismay and patted their heads.

"I think," he said, "that you two are just a little too short." He started for home.

In spite of his apprehension about telling his mother the bad news, James was humming with joy when he reached home. His spirits were so high that even Abigail and his mother caught his mood. James put off telling his mother until he had read to her from the Bible that evening. But as he closed the book, he looked at her and started.

"Mother, can I join the crew of the *Royal Lewis*?"

She didn't answer but just returned his direct look. For a panicky moment, he wondered if someone had already told her what he had done. She acted as if she knew.

"They are taking twenty black sailors with them, Mother," he finally said.

She still would not answer. James wildly thought that either she was a mind reader or she had talked to Larry's mother.

"I'm one of the twenty," he said at last, shamefacedly.

His mother folded her arms and shook her head but did not say anything. It was the only time James had ever defied her. Now he felt sorry.

"Is it all right?" he asked, his voice pleading.

"You did what you wanted to do already, didn't you?" She sounded tired.

"Oh, I'll never get a job in the sail loft so long as the war lasts," said James. "Business keeps getting slower and slower. This way I'll get a chance to do lots of things. Travel. Defend my country." His eyes sparkled in excitement, and he suddenly laughed aloud.

"Oh, Mother," he exclaimed, "I've always wanted to ride in a ship and see the sails from the other side."

"But, James," she said, her voice almost breaking, "it's so dangerous."

"Not for our ship," said James, "the *Royal Lewis*, commanded by Captain Decatur[3]—King of the Sea."

"Promise me," his mother said, finally re-

3. Decatur (də kā′ tər)

ARCH STREET FERRY, PHILADELPHIA
William and Thomas Birch

lenting, "that you will read your Bible every night. You'll never know how much your father wanted you to be able to read."

"I promise," said James. "Only, Mother, no one can forget how to read. It's like forgetting how to walk."

Three days later James went down to the docks, taking only the clothes he wore on his back, his mother's Bible, and a bag of marbles. On the way he stopped by the sail loft to say goodbye. He was surprised that Mr. Bridges was more emotional about his leaving than his mother had been. They walked to the ship together, and Mr. Bridges stood on shore while James boarded the *Royal Lewis* and stood there waving as the ship weighed anchor and moved out to the open sea. His mother had stayed home and had waved good-bye to James from the door as if he were leaving, as always, only for the day.

Powder boy on the *Royal Lewis* was the lowest and dirtiest of jobs, and James soon realized that it consisted of more than just preparing for battle. He was often called to serve meals, act as cabin boy, and do whatever else no one in particular was assigned to do. James hid his resentment behind an expressionless face and slow smile and tried especially to make himself useful to Captain Decatur. He stood by ready to serve the captain's meals, to clear the table, or to clean the captain's quarters and was soon recognized as being reserved for the service of the captain. As a result, he escaped some of the dirtier jobs.

He was eager for his first battle, and it seemed forever until the day that the cry came from the ship's lookout that the British ship *Activist* had been spotted. The quiet *Royal Lewis* became a whirl of activity as the regular privateers, in a disciplined manner, began running to their respective posts and shouting out orders. James's head was spinning. He had forgotten all he had learned. He didn't know where to start.

"James Forten," a voice called out impatiently, sounding as if it had called him many times before. "Over here!"

James ran over to the gun crew and stood in position near the powder and balls and waited, hoping that no one would notice his trembling. The *Royal Lewis* came remarkably close to the other ship, it seemed, before the voice of the British captain broke the silence.

"This is His Majesty's frigate *Activist*," he called. "What ship is that?"

Captain Decatur's answer was to signal his men to attack. Almost immediately there was a deafening roar followed by a flash of fire from the cannon, and the deck shook under James's feet. The smell of smoke filled the air and blinded him, making him cough and sneeze. He was so frightened that he froze until a sharp nudge on his shoulder reminded him of his job. By blind instinct, he began passing the powder and cannonballs to the loader, who forced them down the muzzle with a ramrod.

Now that the battle was really on, James could see the extreme danger of his job as powder boy. When the ammunition was low, James had to run below deck to the magazine for more powder and cannonballs. He would then have to run back to his post, shielding the explosive powder from the flying sparks, which could ignite an explosion fatal to him. All around him the sparks flew, forcing him to keep moving, although he had to step over the bodies of wounded, groaning men who cried out to him for help. The battle seemed to last an eternity, and both ships appeared to be utterly destroyed.

The two ships were so close now that the crew from the *Royal Lewis* began jumping over to the deck of the *Activist* to continue the battle in man-to-man combat. James, however, stayed at his post, passing powder and balls until his arms felt like rubber. The battle finally took an upward swing when the *Activist* began burning in several places and the captain was seriously wounded. Soon the British flag was lowered in surrender, and the long battle had ended at last.

The *Activist* did not have the rich cargo that James and all the crew of the *Royal Lewis* had hoped for. As James looked around at the mangled ships and the wounded and dead men on both vessels, he wondered if it had been worth it. However, it was just the first of several battles for James, and some of the later ones brought important prisoners or goods that could be exchanged for large amounts of money. But too soon their luck changed.

One day, about three months after that first battle, as the *Royal Lewis* approached a British warship called the *Amphyon*,[4] the lookout suddenly spotted two more British vessels in the distance. Realizing the impossibility of fighting three ships at one time,

4. Amphyon (am' fē än)

the *Royal Lewis* decided to make a run for it, but the British took up the chase. Before long, they were close enough to begin firing. At the first shot, Captain Decatur immediately gave orders to strike colors. The American flag fluttered down in surrender.

It was then that James went into a complete panic. He wanted to run and scream. He knew that black sailors were never kept for prisoner exchanges but were sold into slavery in the West Indies[5] as part of the cargo. Running below to his bunk, he had just enough time to snatch up his blanket, Bible, and marbles before he was ordered on deck by one of the British officers. The crew of the *Royal Lewis* was divided into three groups and sent to the three British ships. James was with the group taken by the *Amphyon*. As the prisoners filed past the captain, James was stopped and the captain asked sharply, "What's in that bag, boy?"

"What bag?" said James in confusion, looking down. His marbles in a small cloth sack dangled from his wrist.

"How old are you?" demanded the captain.

"Fifteen," answered James quickly, forgetting his former lie.

5. West Indies: A large group of islands between North and South America.

H. M. BRIG *OBSERVER* AND AMERICAN PRIVATEER *JACK*
Culver Pictures

"I said, 'What's in that bag?' " the captain demanded again.

"Marbles," James answered, feeling very embarrassed and childish. He didn't know now what had made him bring them.

"What's your name?" asked the captain.

James figured this was the end for him. The captain probably already had a prospective buyer in mind. He stood tall and answered without faltering, "My name is James Forten."

The captain smiled and waved him on. A few hours later, while James sat with the other prisoners, a British youth with rosy cheeks, straight brown hair, and a pouting mouth approached him.

"Are you James Forten, the powder boy from the *Royal Lewis*?" he asked.

James nodded.

"I am Willie Beasley, the son of Sir John, the captain of the *Amphyon*," he said with a heavy British accent. "My father tells me that you brought a bag of marbles on board. I'm a champion. Would you like to play a game?"

James took out his marbles with great pride now and followed Willie on deck. They placed the marbles in a group on the floor between them. At first they played seriously and silently, but soon, in boyish glee, they were laughing and teasing. James was trying to decide whether or not to let Willie Beasley win, for he was sure he couldn't be beaten. His perfect aim and strong fingers had won him the neighborhood championship for years. He decided to win first and then to let Willie win. He was surprised to find out, however, that letting Willie win was no problem because he really was very good, and James had to play carefully to beat him. It was the first of many games, and in spite of themselves, the boys became fast friends, so James was in no way treated as a prisoner. At first he thought the other prisoners would be angry, but they didn't seem to notice. Sir John was glad that Willie had met someone his own age to entertain him since the trip had turned out to be a long and boring one for the boy. During one of their long days together, Willie asked James to go back to England with him. James instantly flared.

"I'll never be a traitor!" he snapped.

"What difference does it make since you're nothing but a slave in your own country anyway?" asked Willie.

"I am not a slave!" said James angrily. "I was born free."

"Well, you're just a black prisoner now," retorted Willie. "And you have only two choices. You will either be sold as a slave, or you can come to England with me as a friend." He suddenly dropped his belligerent attitude. "Oh, come on, James," he begged. "England abolished slavery. You'll get an education and live in a beautiful home. Father likes you. He thinks you have a fine mind."

James didn't answer. He was tempted, but somehow it didn't seem right. When Sir John sent for him the next day, James stood before him and refused his offer to go to England.

"You must be a fool!" exclaimed Sir John in perplexed anger.

"I am an American prisoner," said James. "I cannot be a traitor to my country."

Willie broke in. "America is not your country, James. All you are there is a slave."

"I am not a slave," answered James, quietly this time.

"Well, all you are there, then, is a servant," said Willie. "I could understand your loyalty if you were white."

This time James didn't answer.

Sir John sighed. He had spoiled Willie by trying to give him everything he wanted. Now he hated to see him disappointed. In an effort to change James's mind, he said, "You know you'll have to be sold."

James didn't know what to say. He opened his mouth to speak, but changed his mind and said nothing.

"Well?" asked Willie.

"I cannot be a traitor," James answered. Lifting his dark pain-filled eyes and looking directly at Willie, he almost whispered, "I never want to be a slave." He turned and quickly left.

The next day before the prisoner exchange, Willie Beasley approached James.

"You will be transferred to the *Jersey* with the other prisoners," he said. As soon as he started talking, his eyes filled with tears. "It is nothing but a floating death trap. No one gets off alive." He handed James a white envelope. "This is from Father to the captain of the *Jersey*. It will help you. Goodbye, James." He turned and hurried away. Looking down at the white envelope, James realized that Willie was one of the best friends he would ever have. Somehow he knew that they would never meet again.

INTERIOR OF THE PRISON SHIP *JERSEY*
The Granger Collection

When James boarded the *Jersey*, he handed the white envelope to the officer in charge, who barely glanced at it and waved him on without comment. He was sent below to the main prisoner quarters, where his nostrils were immediately assailed by the loathsome odor of human filth, and all around the dark hole he could hear the ravings and groanings of the sick and dying. James knew that he was probably the only black on board. His mind went back to Mr. Benezet, his teacher, and his school lessons on how the slaves were captured and brought to America in the pits of ships. He now knew just how they must have felt. He knew why they were so submissive and broken when they were finally sold. They said that no man sentenced to the *Jersey* survived unless he was removed in a short time, but then, James thought, most prisoners were white. He thought of his great-grandfather who had survived the slave ship and of his grandfather who had bought his freedom. From the number of African slaves in America, James realized that quite a few of them must have survived, and in a sudden surge of pride, he realized that he was of the same race. He would make it, too.

When the prisoners were brought on deck the next day, James recognized Daniel Brewton, who looked gravely ill. They were glad to see each other, and because of their past association, they quickly became friends. This relationship was hard on James because Daniel was so sickly that James ended up doing chores and hustling food for both of them. Nevertheless, James was still able to volunteer for extra jobs, and in his usual manner he picked the ones that kept him on deck and out of the stinking hole as much as possible. He loaded supplies, scrubbed the deck, and even volunteered to bring up the corpses of dead prisoners. After the first few times, this task no longer bothered him. Not only did James survive, but he also grew tough.

He never knew if it was the letter Sir John had written that prompted another prisoner to seek him out one morning while he was doing his chores. The man, who was an officer, told James he was being exchanged for a British prisoner and that he was taking a trunk with him that would hold one person. Joy flooded James's heart to think that he might finally escape, but instinct warned him not to tell Daniel. Somehow he felt like a traitor leaving him behind to die. He rudely avoided Daniel the remainder of the day. That night when Daniel sought him out in the dark pit where they usually huddled together and talked about Philadelphia, their mothers and sisters, and old times, James pretended he was sleepy.

"Leave me alone, Daniel!" he snapped.

"What's wrong?" asked Daniel.

"Nothing," James snapped again. "I'm just sick and tired of waiting to get off this boat."

"I don't think I'm ever going to get off," said Daniel. "I don't think I'm ever going to see Philadelphia or my home again." His voice cracked, and James knew that he was crying.

Long after Daniel had fallen asleep, James still lay awake, hating himself for what he knew he had to do. The next morning Daniel did not even want to go up on deck for fresh air, and James had to practically carry him up. His face was gray and his eyelids were red and swollen. His body was

THE PRISON SHIP *JERSEY*
Culver Pictures

covered with sores. His eyes seemed to be constantly pleading with James. That evening James slipped Daniel into the trunk, and the next morning he and the officer carried the trunk down to the waiting boat, which took it and the officer to freedom. As the boat disappeared toward shore, James swallowed hard and fought back the tears, knowing that it was too late to change his mind now and that a golden opportunity had slipped through his fingers.

"I can make it," he whispered to himself. "I know I can make it." He put his hand in his pocket and felt the round hardness of his bag of marbles that he had childishly clung to since leaving home. In sudden anger, he tossed them into the sea. He would never need them again. They belonged to the world of Fred and Larry, and now, Daniel. He felt like a tired old man as he turned back to the *Jersey* and wondered how he could make it through another day.

He did make it through, though. That day, and the next day, and the next—for three more months. Near the end of the war, he was freed in a general prisoner exchange. After the American ship, loaded with returning prisoners, docked in Philadelphia, James walked down the tiny streets of his boyhood home, wondering how the houses and streets could ever have looked so huge to him. A few people glanced at him curiously, some with recognition, but he barely noticed anyone. He was thinking of his mother and wondering if she knew he was on his way. He knew that even if she did know, she wouldn't be waiting at the door but would be in the kitchen cooking and would try to pretend that his walking through the door after all this time was nothing very exciting. But the smell of biscuits and gravy would soon fill the house, and her singing voice would float from the kitchen. Long before nightfall the whole neighborhood would know that Sarah Forten's boy was home.

JAMES FORTEN
Historical Society of Pennsylvania

James pushed the door open, and the aroma of cooking food filled his nostrils. She knew. When he walked into the kitchen, she didn't even look up until he whirled her around in a bear hug. In spite of herself, she could not help crying when she saw how much James looked like his father. He was now six feet two inches and thin as a rail.

"You're so skinny," she said, shaking her head.

"They don't cook like you do on the *Jersey*," replied James, laughing. "Where is Abigail?"

"Oh, she lives down the street now," said his mother. "There was no way to tell you. She's married."

"Married!" exclaimed James. To him Abigail was just a child. He couldn't imagine her married.

"Daniel Brewton was here and told us how you slipped him off the boat," his mother said. "I'm proud of you."

She piled his plate high with rice and gravy and biscuits and pork chops and okra,[6] just the way James had dreamed of her doing over and over again while he lay in the dark misery of the *Jersey*, counting off the passing days. It had taken 210 days for the dream to come true.

Reader's Response
What is your opinion of James? Would you like to have known him? Explain.

---

6. okra (ō′ krə) *n.*: A plant whose sticky green pods are used as a cooked vegetable.

RESPONDING TO THE SELECTION

Your Response

1. How do you feel about James's joining the ship's crew against his mother's wishes?
2. If you had been a friend of James's, what advice would you have given to him after he signed onto the ship's crew?

Recalling

3. What two reasons does James give for wanting to join the privateer's crew?

Interpreting

4. Compare James's feelings after the battle with the *Activist* and after the battle with the *Amphyon.*
5. James refuses to go to England with Willie and become a traitor to his country. What does this tell us about James?

Applying

6. James took "care that none of his own feelings were ever reflected in his dark eyes." Is it ever a good idea to hide your feelings? Explain.

ANALYZING LITERATURE

Understanding a Biographical Narrative

A **biographical narrative** is an account of a person's life told as if it were a story. Brenda Johnston includes several lively conversations to breathe life into James Forten. Although these conversations probably never occurred, they help us to understand James. Find an example of a conversation in the story. Then answer the following questions.

1. Who are the speakers?
2. About what are they talking?
3. What does the dialogue reveal about the people who are speaking?
4. Why do you think the author decided to use dialogue at this point in the narrative instead of description?

CRITICAL THINKING AND READING

Recognizing Fact and Fiction

A biographical narrative is a blend of **fact,** which is true, and **fiction,** which is invented. The events in a person's life are facts. For example, it is a fact that James Forten lived in Philadelphia. However, the author imagines how James Forten feels and what he thinks and says. That James was "wondering what he was going to tell his mother" is an example of fiction. We do not know what James was thinking; we can only guess based on the events at the time.

Find two examples of fact and two examples of fiction in the selection. Explain your choices.

THINKING AND WRITING

Writing a Biographical Narrative

Choose a famous person with whose life you are familiar and an important event in this person's life. What happened at that crucial time? How do you think the person felt? Write a brief biographical narrative about this event. Include dialogue. When you revise, make sure that any fictional details make sense, considering what you know actually happened. Put your biographical narrative together with those of your classmates as a classroom magazine.

LEARNING OPTIONS

1. **Speaking and Listening.** Imagine that you had an opportunity to interview James Forten when he returned to Philadelphia. Think of at least six questions to ask him. Then, with a classmate who pretends to be Forten, conduct an interview. You may wish to write an article based on your interview.
2. **Performance.** With a classmate, play the roles of James Forten's mother and a neighbor of the family. Perform two dialogues for the class. The first takes place the day after James leaves. The second occurs when he returns.

GUIDE FOR READING

Olivia (Susy) Clemens

(1872–1896) was only thirteen years old when she wrote "My Papa, Mark Twain" in her journal. Mark Twain, whose real name was Samuel Clemens, wrote the classic American novel *The Adventures of Huckleberry Finn.* Susy, the oldest of Twain's three daughters, was just twenty-four years old when she died. In his autobiography Twain says of Susy's work, "I have had no compliment, no praise, no tribute from any source that was so precious to me as this one was and still is."

My Papa, Mark Twain

Character Sketch

A **character sketch** is a short, lively, informal description in which the writer tries to show what a person is really like. The author writes about and gives examples to illustrate the subject's most important features or characteristics. For example, if the person is funny, the writer gives examples of his or her humor. If the person is brave, the writer shows his or her bravery.

Focus

As you will see in this selection, Mark Twain's daughter Susy was very proud of her father's character and sense of humor. Think about someone whose sense of humor you enjoy. Create a list of what this person says or does that you find funny. Give specific examples of jokes, actions, or looks that you find humorous. Share your list with a small group of classmates to see if they also find the person amusing. Compare your subject with Mark Twain as you read the essay.

Vocabulary

Knowing the following words will help you as you read "My Papa, Mark Twain."

profile (prō′ fīl) *n.*: A side view of the face (p. 313)
billiards (bil′ yərdz) *n.*: The game of pool (p. 313)
incessantly (in ses′ ənt lē) *adv.*: Constantly (p. 313)
marrow (mar′ ō) *n.*: The soft tissue that fills most bones (p. 315)
pauper (pô′ pər) *n.*: An extremely poor person (p. 315)

Spelling Tip

If you think of an ant as incessantly gathering food, you will remember that the word *incessantly* is spelled with *ant* in the middle.

My Papa, Mark Twain

Susy Clemens

". . . he told us the other day that he couldn't bear to hear anyone talk but himself, but that he could listen to himself talk for hours without getting tired . . ."

Mark Twain's daughter Susy wrote this short biography of her father in a journal when she was thirteen years old. As you will see, Susy's feelings about her father and his work are clear, in spite of many misspelled words.

We are a very happy family. We consist of Papa, Mamma, Jean, Clara and me. It is papa I am writing about, and I shall have no trouble in not knowing what to say about him, as he is a very striking character.

Papa's appearance has been described many times, but very incorrectly. He has beautiful gray hair, not any too thick or any too long, but just right; a Roman nose which greatly improves the beauty of his features; kind blue eyes and a small mustache. He has a wonderfully shaped head and profile. He has a very good figure—in short, he is an extrodinarily fine looking man. All his features are perfect exept that he hasn't extrodinary teeth. His complexion is very fair, and he doesn't ware a beard. He is a very good man and a very funny one. He has got a temper, but we all of us have in this family. He is the loveliest man I ever saw or ever hope to see—and oh, so absentminded.

Papa's favorite game is billiards, and when he is tired and wishes to rest himself he stays up all night and plays billiards, it seems to rest his head. He smokes a great deal almost incessantly. He has the mind of an author exactly, some of the simplest things he can't understand. Our burglar alarm is often out of order, and papa had been obliged to take the mahogany room off from the alarm altogether for a time, because the burglar alarm had been in the habit of ringing even when the mahogany-room window was closed. At length he thought that perhaps the burglar alarm might be in order, and he decided to try and see; accordingly he put it on and then went down and opened the window; consequently the alarm bell rang, it would even if the alarm had been in order. Papa went despairingly upstairs and said to mamma, "Livy the mahogany room won't go on. I have just opened the window to see."

"Why, Youth," mamma replied. "If you've opened the window, why of course the alarm will ring!"

Susy and Papa playing, Mark Twain Memorial, Hartford, Connecticut

"That's what I've opened it for, why I just went down to see if it would ring!"

Mamma tried to explain to papa that when he wanted to go and see whether the alarm would ring while the window was closed he mustn't go and open the window—but in vain, papa couldn't understand, and got very impatient with mamma for trying to make him believe an impossible thing true.

Papa has a peculiar gait we like, it seems just to suit him, but most people do not; he always walks up and down the room while thinking and between each coarse at meals.

Papa is very fond of animals particularly of cats, we had a dear little gray kitten once that he named "Lazy" (papa always wears gray to match his hair and eyes) and he would carry him around on his shoulder, it was a mighty pretty sight! the gray cat sound asleep against papa's gray coat and hair. The names that he has give our different cats are really remarkably funny, they are named Stray Kit, Abner, Motley, Fraeulein, Lazy, Buffalo Bill, Soapy Sall, Cleveland, Sour Mash, and Pestilence and Famine.

Papa uses very strong language, but I have an idea not nearly so strong as when he first married mamma. A lady acquaintance of his is rather apt to interupt what one is saying, and papa told mamma he thought he should say to the lady's husband "I am glad your wife wasn't present when the Deity said Let there be light."

Papa said the other day, "I am a mugwump[1] and a mugwump is pure from the marrow out." (Papa knows that I am writing this biography of him, and he said this for it.) He doesn't like to go to church at all, why I never understood, until just now, he told us the other day that he couldn't bear to hear anyone talk but himself, but that he could listen to himself talk for hours without getting tired, of course he said this in joke, but I've no dought it was founded on truth.

One of papa's latest books is "The Prince and the Pauper" and it is unquestionably the best book he has ever written, some people want him to keep to his old style, some gentleman wrote him, "I enjoyed Huckleberry Finn immensely and am glad to see that you have returned to your old style." That enoyed me, that enoyed me greatly, because it trobles me to have so few people know papa, I mean realy know him, they think of Mark Twain as a humorist joking at everything; "And with a mop of reddish brown hair which sorely needs the barbar brush, a roman nose, short stubby mustache, a sad care-worn face, with maney crows' feet" etc. That is the way people picture papa, I have wanted papa to write a book that would reveal something of his kind sympathetic nature, and "The Prince and the Pauper" partly does it. The book is full of lovely charming ideas, and oh the language! It is perfect. I think that one of the most touching scenes in it is where the pauper is riding on horseback with his nobles in the "recognition procession" and he sees his mother oh and then what followed! How she runs to his side, when she sees him throw up his hand palm outward, and is rudely pushed off by one of the King's officers, and then how the little pauper's conscience troubles him when he remembers the shameful words that were falling from his lips when she was turned from his side "I know you not woman" and how his grandeurs were stricken valueless and his pride consumed to

---

1. **mugwump** (mug′ wump′) *n.*: A Republican who refused to support the candidates of the party in the 1884 election.

ashes. It is a wonderfully beautiful and touching little scene, and papa has described it so wonderfully. I never saw a man with so much variety of feeling as papa has; now the "Prince and the Pauper" is full of touching places, but there is always a streak of humor in them somewhere. Papa very seldom writes a passage without some humor in it somewhere and I don't think he ever will.

Clara and I are sure that papa played the trick on Grandma about the whipping that is related in "The Adventures of Tom Sawyer": "Hand me that switch." The switch hovered in the air, the peril was desperate—"My, look behind you Aunt!" The old lady whirled around and snatched her skirts out of danger. The lad fled on the instant, scrambling up the high board fence and disappeared over it.

We know papa played "Hookey" all the time. And how readily would papa pretend to be dying so as not to have to go to school! Grandma wouldn't make papa go to school, so she let him go into a printing office to learn the trade. He did so, and gradually picked up enough education to enable him to do about as well as those who were more studious in early life.

Reader's Response

Susy Clemens writes that she wishes her father "would reveal something of his kind sympathetic nature." Do you think she successfully brings out this side of her father's character? If so, how?

Keeping a Journal

Susy Clemens wrote her biographical sketch of her father in a journal. A journal is a place for personal writing—a place to write about your experiences and your thoughts. Unless you give someone permission to read your journal, you are the only one who will see it.

If you keep a journal, you need not record what you do each day, as you might in a diary. Instead, you may write in a journal when you have something particular that you want to remember. Perhaps you might include a biographical sketch of a friend or relative, as Susy Clemens did of her father. You may jot down a recipe for cookies you ate at a friend's house; or the way you felt after winning a race, doing well on a test, or seeing a movie. Perhaps you will want to remember what someone said about a new outfit you were wearing one day or what happened when you and your best friend had an argument.

There are advantages to keeping a journal. When you must find a topic for a writing assignment, the writing in your journal can be a source of ideas. Another reason for writing in a journal is that when you write, you think. Putting thoughts and ideas down on paper demands that you organize your thoughts and really think about what you mean. Your thinking, and therefore your schoolwork, will improve as a result.

You might consider keeping a journal. Writing about your feelings and making observations will give you satisfaction and insight into your life that you might otherwise miss. In the future you will enjoy reading what you have written about events that seemed unforgettable at the time, yet would have been forgotten without a journal.

Responding to the Selection

Your Response

1. Does this essay by Susy Clemens make you wish you had known Mark Twain? Explain.

Recalling

2. List three physical features that Susy includes in her description of her father.
3. Name two things that amuse Susy about her father's relationship with the family's cats.
4. Summarize Susy's feelings about *The Prince and the Pauper.*

Interpreting

5. Why does Susy refer to the Pauper's words "I know you not woman" as "shameful"?
6. How does Susy feel about her father's not attending school? Explain.
7. This story contains many misspelled words. Why do you think the character sketch was published without correcting the errors?
8. What picture of Mark Twain emerges from Susy's description?

Applying

9. If someone were to write a character sketch about you, which of your traits would you want to have included?

Analyzing Literature

Appreciating a Character Sketch

In a **character sketch,** the writer tries to show what the subject is really like in a short, lively, informal description. In "My Papa, Mark Twain," it is clear that Susy loves her father. Yet she includes both positive and negative qualities of her famous parent.

1. List Mark Twain's good points and his faults as described by his daughter.
2. Which of Mark Twain's characteristics does Susy make most believable? How does she convince you that this characteristic is real?

Critical Thinking and Reading

Recognizing a Writer's Viewpoint

"My Papa, Mark Twain" is a character sketch written from the viewpoint of the subject's daughter. The language, style, and choice of examples are those of a thirteen year old who is related to and loves the subject.

1. In this sketch, Susy objects to some opinions others have about Twain. Find two examples where Susy's opinion of her father differs from the way she says others see him.
2. How might this sketch be different if it were told by a biographer not related to Mark Twain?

Thinking and Writing

Writing a Character Sketch

Think of someone you know who would make a good subject for a character sketch. You may choose a member of your family, a friend, or anyone else. First, jot down examples of what this person says and does. Then turn your ideas into a character sketch. Choose one or two of the person's characteristics that you can describe with examples you have jotted down. If you have chosen your examples well, your reader will understand why you feel as you do about your subject. Remember, while Susy Clemens's work was published without corrections, you must proofread and correct your sketch.

Learning Option

Speaking and Listening. Form a group with two classmates. Research to find out more about the life of Mark Twain. Then prepare a television interview with Twain and his daughter. One member of your group will take the role of Twain, another will be Susy Clemens, and the third will be the interviewer. Use your research materials to create questions and answers. When you are ready, present the interview to the class.

GUIDE FOR READING

The Platoon System

Beverly Cleary

(1916–   ) has been writing stories about children for more than thirty years. About her childhood in Oregon, she says, "I wanted to read funny stories about the sort of children I knew and I decided that someday when I grew up I would write them." Her best-loved books include *Ramona and Her Father* and *Ramona Quimby, Age 8*—both Newbery honor books. *A Girl from Yamhill* is the story of Cleary's own childhood. In this selection she describes her experiences as a seventh-grader in the 1920's.

Autobiography

An **autobiography** is a person's own account of his or her life. In an autobiography we learn not only the writer's experiences, but also special thoughts and feelings as he or she remembers them.

Focus

As a young girl, Beverly Cleary enjoyed most of her experiences in school. Yet some things about school upset her. What do you enjoy about your school? What things would you change? In a small group, create a list of the things you like about your school and a list of the things you would change. As you read this selection, note whether your likes and dislikes are similar to Cleary's.

Vocabulary

Knowing the following words will help you as you read "The Platoon System."

platoon (plə to͞on′) *n.*: A small military unit; any small group like this (p. 320)
deteriorated (di tir′ ē ə rāt′ əd) *v.*: Became worse (p. 320)
innovation (in′ ə vā′ shən) *n.*: A change; a new idea (p. 320)
consternation (kän′ stər nā′ shən) *n.*: Confusion or bewilderment; frustration (p. 321)
plagiarism (plā′ jə riz′ əm) *n.*: The taking of ideas or writing from another and passing them off as one's own (p. 321)
conformity (kən fôrm′ ə tē) *n.*: Action that follows customs, rules, popular opinion, and so on (p. 323)
intimidated (in tim′ ə dāt ′d) *v.*: Made afraid (p. 324)
perjure (pʉr′ jər) *v.*: Willfully tell a lie while expected to tell the truth (p. 324)
incandescent (in′ kən des′ ənt) *adj.*: Glowing (p. 325)
circumventing (sʉr′ kəm vent′ iŋ) *v.*: Going around (p. 325)

Spelling Tip

In some words an *s* sound is spelled *sc* when it is followed by an *e* or an *i*. Remembering this will help you spell *incandescent.*

The Platoon System

from *A Girl from Yamhill*

Beverly Cleary

"All my life, Mother had told me to use my imagination, but I had never expected to be asked, or even allowed, to use it in school."

When school started in September, girls discovered that boys, awful in the sixth grade, had become terrible in the seventh grade. They said bad words, some of which we did not understand. They tucked small mirrors under the laces of their Keds[1] and stuck their feet under girls' skirts.

Our class was supposed to be studying grammar, which included diagraming sentences from a tan book, *Grammar and Composition*, by Effie B. McFadden, with selections for seventh-grade study and memorizing. Many of us referred to this unpopular book simply as "Effie."

"After all, this is a grammar school," Miss Stone, our serious teacher, reminded us when we groaned at Effie and her grammar.

Instead of concentrating on Effie, my attention turned to a curly-haired boy named Allen who sat across the aisle from me and was more interesting than making skeletons out of sentences and labeling the bones with proper subjects, verbs, objects, and modifiers.

Allen was also more interesting than our arithmetic book, obviously the work of an educator who enjoyed torturing seventh-graders with "An ice cream can was $\frac{2}{3}$ full. After 18 dishes had been taken out, it was still $\frac{1}{16}$ full. How many dishes had been taken out?" Concealing Allen's notes from Miss Stone, who threatened to read aloud any note she intercepted, was my exercise in problem solving.

Because boys usually went in pairs for protection when one of them was interested in a girl, Allen and his friend George sometimes walked home from school with me while I wheeled my bicycle. Except for chinning themselves on any handy branch, they were almost civilized. It was George who gave me his first manual training project, a breadboard nicely rounded at one end, with a neatly bored hole for hanging it on a nail. Mother put it away for me to use "someday," and whenever she ran across it, she referred to it as "Beverly's hope chest."

---

1. **Keds:** A brand of sneakers.

In the seventh grade, changes took place, not only in boys but in the school curriculum. The platoon system was introduced. This meant we were taught some subjects—"Effie," reading, arithmetic, and United States history—in our homeroom but marched off in platoons to other rooms for music, art, nature study, library, an oddly named class called "auditorium," and double periods for domestic science or manual training. And, of course, gymnasium, where seventh graders exercised with wands or marched while Claudine played "Napoleon's Last Charge" on the piano.

Girls sewed in 7A and cooked in 7B while boys hammered, sawed, and sanded in another basement classroom. Many parents objected to the platoon system; schools should stick to basics. Mother felt the new system too strenuous. "It's just rush, rush, rush all day long," she said. At PTA[2] she complained to Miss Stone that my handwriting had deteriorated and was difficult to read. Miss Stone replied that before long most people would use typewriters.

We now had a school library with a librarian, Miss Smith, a young, brisk, well-tailored teacher who also taught reading. She taught us how to use the library and once made us line up alphabetically by our last names, as if we were books on shelves. After that, I found a place on the shelf where my book would be if I ever wrote a book, which I doubted.

Miss Smith introduced an innovation to Fernwood. Until Miss Smith entered our lives, our teachers forbade reading in the classroom, except for old copies of the *National Geographic*. No one enjoyed this except the terrible boys who knew, by ragged covers, which issues contained pictures of naked women in African tribes.

Not being able to read in school had frustrated me. During the first week, I held my reader under my desk and read it all the way through, even though teachers said repeatedly, "Do not read ahead." After that I hid books I wanted to read inside my geography, an ideal book, because of its size, for hiding other books. I was deeply grateful to Miss Smith, not only for letting us read but for letting me into the library first on the days when *St. Nicholas* magazine[3] arrived.

Miss Smith had standards. We could read, but we must read good books. Cheap series books, traded around the neighborhood, were not permitted in her classroom. Miss Smith was also strict. She once made me stay after school until I could write on the blackboard, from memory and in order, all the presidents of the United States. I do not recall what I did to deserve this judgment, but I do recall thinking it more sensible than writing "I will not talk in gymnasium" one hundred times—a penalty once meted out by Miss Helliwell, our gym teacher.

Miss Smith also gave unusual assignments. Once, without warning, she said, "I want you to pretend you live in George Washington's time and write a letter to someone describing an experience."

Write something we had not learned in a book? This was unheard of. "But that's not fair," some protested.

Miss Smith assured us that such an assignment was perfectly fair. We knew she

2. PTA: Parent-Teacher Association.

3. *St. Nicholas* magazine: A famous children's magazine.

was right. Miss Smith was always fair. Strict, but fair.

"You mean *now?*" someone asked.

"Now." Miss Smith was always firm.

"But how?" someone else asked.

"Use your imaginations," said Miss Smith, unconcerned by the consternation she had created.

I was excited. All my life, Mother had told me to use my imagination, but I had never expected to be asked, or even allowed, to use it in school. After a moment of pencil chewing, I wrote to an imaginary cousin, telling how I had sacrificed my pet chicken to help feed Washington's starving, freezing troops at Valley Forge.

The next day, Miss Smith read my letter to the class, praised me for using my imagination, and said everyone else in the class had to try again. At Fernwood any written work, even practice sentences, that did not measure up to teachers' standards was rewritten—sometimes more than once. Smugly I read a library book while my classmates struggled with letters about their sacrifices of pet lambs and calves for Washington's troops. Copycats, I thought with contempt. Mother had told me authors found their ideas in their own minds, not in the words of others. Besides, who ever heard of lambs and calves in the middle of winter? In Yamhill, they were born in springtime.

Next Miss Smith gave us homework: writing an essay about our favorite book character. This brought forth groans and sighs of resignation from most of the class. Nobody wanted to do homework, especially original homework.

That weekend, Mother happened to be visiting her parents in Banks, where Grandpa Atlee had bought back his store. (When he was seventy, after two years of retirement, he decided he was too young to be idle.) After I put together a Sunday dinner for my father, who gamely ate it and was enjoying his pipe and the Sunday paper, I sat down to write the essay. Which favorite character when I had so many? Peter Pan? Judy from *Daddy-Long-Legs*? Tom Sawyer? I finally solved this problem by writing about a girl who went to Bookland and talked to several of my favorite characters. I wrote on and on, inventing conversations that the characters might have had with a strange girl. As rain beat against the windows, a feeling of peace came over me as I wrote far beyond the required length of the essay. I had discovered the pleasure of writing, and to this day, whenever it rains, I feel the urge to write. Most of my books are written in winter.

As much as I enjoyed writing it, I thought "Journey Through Bookland" was a poor story because the girl's journey turned out to be a dream; and if there was anything I disliked, it was a good story that ended up as a dream. Authors of such stories, including Lewis Carroll,[4] were cheating, I felt, because they could not think of any other conclusion.

I was also worried because I had used characters from published books. Miss Smith had lectured us on plagiarism and said that stealing from books was every bit as wrong as stealing from a store. But how could I write about a favorite character without having him speak?

When we turned our essays in during library, I watched anxiously as Miss Smith riffled through the papers. Was I going to catch

---

4. Lewis Carroll: Author of *Alice in Wonderland*.

it? Miss Smith pulled out a paper that I recognized as mine and began to read aloud. My mouth was dry and my stomach felt twisted. When she finished, she paused. My heart pounded. Then Miss Smith said, "When Beverly grows up, she should write children's books."

I was dumbfounded. Miss Smith was praising my story-essay with words that pointed to my future, a misty time I rarely even thought about. I was not used to praise. Mother did not compliment me. Now I was not only being praised in front of the whole class but was receiving approval that

HOMEWORK
Milton Avery
Thyssen-Bornemisza Collection

was to give direction to my life. The class seemed impressed.

When I reported all this to Mother, she said, "If you are going to become a writer, you must have a steady way of earning your living." This sound advice was followed by a thoughtful pause before she continued, "I have always wanted to write myself."

My career decision was lightly made. The Rose City Branch Library—quiet, tastefully furnished, filled with books and flowers—immediately came to mind. I wanted to work in such a place, so I would become a librarian.

Miss Smith, dear brisk lady who gave unusual assignments, astonished us again by announcing one day that we were no longer to call her Miss Smith. She was now Mrs. Weaver.

"You mean you got *married?*" we asked after this news had sunk in.

With a smile, she admitted she had. A teacher getting married was unheard of to us. Some were called "Mrs.," but we thought they were widows. Our teachers never discussed their personal lives with their classes, but here was a teacher who had presumably fallen in love while she was a teacher. Astounding! Such a thing had never happened before and, in the course of my education, never happened again.

In addition to Mrs. Weaver and her surprising assignments, home economics and manual training were new to us. In sewing class, while boys were sawing away at their breadboards, girls in 7A were laboring over samplers of stitches and seams and putting them to use making cooking aprons that slipped over our heads and had bias binding properly applied to the neck and armholes, and bloomers that taught us to measure elastic without stretching it. In 7B, cooking class began by making white sauce without lumps.

Mother, who often told me how she sacrificed to give me piano lessons, gave up when we moved from Hancock Street; so once again I had school music to dread. *That* had not changed. We were still expected to sing alone.

The goals of our new art class were conformity and following directions, not creativity. The teacher passed out squared paper. She instructed us to set our pencil points on an intersection ten squares down and four squares from the left-hand edge. Her directions droned on. "Draw a line two squares over, one square down, two squares over . . ." on and on. Grimly we labored to keep up with the instructions, to pay her the attention she demanded. When she finished, those of us who had kept up had identical outlines of a rooster. We were then told which crayons to use "without scrubbing" on which squares; others, those who did not pay attention or, in the case of the terrible boys, did not want to, had something surreal.[5] Perhaps, without knowing it, they had captured the spirit of a rooster, if not the approval of the art teacher.

Auditorium was taught by Miss Viola Harrington, who stood at the rear of the auditorium while we took turns standing up straight, walking up the steps to the center of the stage, facing her, and whispering, "Can you hear me whisper?"

"Louder," said Miss Harrington. "I can't hear you."

We took deep breaths and even deeper breaths until we thought our lungs would

5. surreal (sər rē′ əl) *adj.*: Strange; distorted.

burst, until Miss Harrington could hear us at the back of the auditorium.

From that stage, speaking distinctly, we recited memorized poetry, reported on current events, and gave talks on assigned subjects. When Miss Harrington assigned me a report on "Guano," Mother said, "The idea! What a thing to talk about in public." The terrible boys whispered a different word for fertilizer supplied by birds on islands off the coast of South America. I was embarrassed to stand on the stage talking about bird droppings, no matter how rich in nitrate and phosphate. Such stuff, to me, was not valuable but something to avoid stepping in. Miss Harrington obviously had never walked across a barnyard full of chickens.

The most unusual change in curriculum was nature study, taught by Miss Lydia Crawford, an aloof[6] eccentric with long, glossy brown hair wound around her head and with the high color and glowing complexion of an outdoor woman. She always wore plain dark dresses that stopped just below her knees; she wore high brown shoes, much higher than those I had finally been allowed to abandon, which laced all the way to her knees. We were all intimidated by Miss Crawford.

Miss Crawford believed that if we were to study nature, we should have nature around us. She brought, and encouraged us to bring, exhibits to be placed on a ledge beneath the window. Plants bloomed; lichen, mosses, and minerals were displayed; chipmunks raced on wheels; and a two-headed garter snake and I stared at each other through the glass walls of its prison.

Miss Crawford told us that when she was a little girl, she was taught to recite "From the stable to the table, dirty flies!" She said women ruined their skins with face powder, which was made from talc. "See, children, this is what foolish women rub on their faces," she said, holding up a piece of the greenish mineral while her own face shone from soap and water. She told us we must always rotate our crops and never, never perjure ourselves.

The curriculum required Miss Crawford to lead us through a book with a dark blue cover entitled *Healthy Living*. We stared listlessly at drawings of correct and incorrect posture and of properly balanced meals before we began a relentless journey of a meal through the alimentary canal, beginning with food thoroughly chewed. I endured what went on in our mouths and esophagi, but I began to have doubts about the whole thing down around our stomachs, and when we reached the liver and gallbladder, the whole messy business became disgusting and, beyond those organs, too embarrassing to mention. I did not want to think of all that going on inside of *me*. Ugh.

Miss Crawford, radiating health, was apparently as bored with *Healthy Living* as her class. One day she suddenly closed the sensible text, laid it aside, and with her fingertips resting on the front desk in the center row, began to tell us a story about a man named Jean Valjean,[7] who lived in France a long time ago and who had spent nineteen years as a galley slave for stealing a loaf of bread to feed his hungry nieces and nephews. We all perked up. We knew about galley slaves from pirate movies.

Miss Crawford's cheeks grew redder, and

---

6. aloof (ə lo͞of′) *adj.*: Distant, reserved, and cool.

7. Jean Valjean (zhän väl zhän′)

her face became incandescent with excitement, as she went on and on, telling us the story in great detail. Nothing this moving had ever happened in school before. We groaned when the bell rang.

"Children," said Miss Crawford, "I shall continue the story in our next class."

Nature study became the best part of school. Chipmunks still raced, a home of a trapdoor spider was added to the nature display; but all that mattered to us was *Les Misérables*. On and on we traveled with Jean Valjean, hounded by Inspector Javert all the way. Fantine, her little daughter, Cosette, and the wicked Thénardiers all became as real as, perhaps more real than, our neighbors. We gasped when Fantine sold her beautiful hair to pay the Thénardiers for the care of Cosette. Even the most terrible boys sat still, fascinated. Unaware of social injustice in our own country, we were gripped by Victor Hugo's story of social injustice in nineteenth-century France.

Some parents—but not mine—listening to us retell at the supper table the marvelous story Miss Crawford was bringing to our imaginations, began to object. Storytelling in school was improper. We were there to learn, not to be entertained. Telephone calls and visits were made to Mr. Dorman, who was a very wise man. Of course we should be studying *Healthy Living*, and so we did. However, at least once a week Miss Crawford came to our auditorium class to continue the story.

June came, summer vacation was about to begin, and she had not finished *Les Misérables*.

"Don't worry, children," she said. "I'll be here when you return in September."

True to her word, Miss Crawford was waiting when school started, and took up where she had left off. Well into the eighth grade, the story of Jean Valjean came to an end. Miss Crawford began another novel by Victor Hugo, *Toilers of the Sea*.

By coincidence, the next year one of Mother's cousins, Verna, who had become a librarian, sent me a copy of *Les Misérables*, which she inscribed in her beautiful vertical handwriting: "A book that you may enjoy someday, if not now, Beverly." I had already lived the book and did not read it for many years. Then, as I read, Miss Crawford was before me on every page. She seemed not to have missed a single word.

I often wonder why this particular book meant so much to an eccentric Oregon teacher. Had someone in her family suffered a terrible injustice? Had her repeated warning about perjury come from some experience in her own life? Or had she perhaps spent her childhood in isolation on a farm where the works of Victor Hugo were the only books available? And why did she suddenly feel compelled to share this novel with a class of seventh-graders? Whatever her reasons, I am profoundly grateful to her—and to the wisdom of Mr. Dorman for circumventing unimaginative parents and allowing her to tell the entire book in such detail. My copy has 1,222 pages.

Reader's Response

Which of Beverly Cleary's school experiences was most like one of your own? Explain why you did or did not feel the same way about the experience that Beverly did.

Responding to the Selection

Your Response

1. Were you surprised by some of Cleary's opinions? Why or why not?

Recalling

2. Describe the platoon system.
3. Why does Beverly's mother object to the platoon system?
4. Identify two "unusual assignments" that Miss Smith gives the class.

Interpreting

5. Compare and contrast Miss Smith and the art teacher. How are they alike? How are they different?
6. Which teachers and events mentioned in the selection had the most lasting effect on Beverly Cleary? Why?
7. How do the shop and home economics classes show the different expectations people had for boys and girls?

Applying

8. Some parents object to Miss Crawford's storytelling because it is entertaining. Is it possible to be entertained while you are learning? Explain.

Analyzing Literature

Understanding Autobiography

A person's record of his or her own life is called an **autobiography**. The writers of autobiographies share their experiences and feelings in a very personal way. In "The Platoon System," you see people and events as Beverly Cleary sees them. You feel emotions as she feels them.

1. How does Cleary feel about the "terrible boys"? Find evidence from the selection to support your opinion.
2. Find a passage in which Cleary shares a strong emotion with us. Explain how she feels. Which words express her feelings?

Critical Thinking and Reading

Drawing Conclusions

A writer may suggest a feeling or an idea without actually saying it. You can draw your own conclusions from what the author does say. When Beverly says, "My mouth was dry and my stomach felt twisted," you can conclude that she was nervous. What can you conclude from each of these statements from "The Platoon System"?

1. "'If you are going to become a writer, you must have a steady way of earning your living.'"
2. "Even the most terrible boys sat still, fascinated."

Thinking and Writing

Writing an Autobiographical Sketch

Pretend you have been asked to write a humorous autobiographical sketch for a class yearbook. Think of a funny experience you have had. Begin by jotting down everything you remember about your experience. Next, turn your ideas into sentences. Then share your drafts with a writing partner. He or she may have some helpful suggestions for making your paper more amusing. Finally, rewrite your paper neatly and proofread it for spelling, grammar, and punctuation. Is it the best you can do? If so, put it together with those of your classmates in a class yearbook.

Learning Options

1. **Performance.** Choose a portion from "The Platoon System" to dramatize. Write dialogue for each of the characters in the scene and assign roles to classmates. After you have practiced, present your skit for the class.
2. **Speaking and Listening.** With a small group, role-play the meeting of the PTA during which some parents complained about the school's new program. Some of your group should support the program, while others should protest against it.

YOUR WRITING PROCESS

Writing From Personal Experience

When was the last time you told a friend about something funny that happened in class? About an exciting event in your life? About something that made you frightened or upset? Chances are that you talked about at least one personal experience recently.

Your Turn

Write about a personal experience that you consider worth sharing with readers.

Prewriting

1. Brainstorm for topic possibilities. Perhaps you can make lists of people you feel strongly about and events from your recent or distant past that you think are interesting or important. Jot down as many possibilities as you can on each list. Here are some ideas to get you started:

```
People I'll Always Remember
     -Ronnie Falcone, the
      softball coach
     -Grams, the next door
      neighbor
I'll Never Forget These Times
     -those two weeks at Y camp
     -my first piano lesson
     -last spring's softball
      season
```

Review your lists and choose a topic you want to explore. The more your topic interests you, the more it will interest your readers.

2. Focus your topic. You need to understand the significance of your topic. In a sentence, write why you've chosen it. To do that, complete this sentence: "I have chosen my topic because. . . ."

Here's an example: *I have chosen to write about Grams because she's so kind and generous.* Or, *I think I'll write about that camping trip our family took because we had such funny calamities.*

3. Gather information. Before you write, you need to fill your "writing cupboard" with information about your focused topic. Give yourself a lot of "ingredients" to choose from. One way to gather lots of information is by questioning. Ask and answer *who, what, where, when, why,* and *how* questions about your focused topic. Try to write without stopping, even if you repeat yourself or sound silly.

```
     Who is Grams? my next door
neighbor, John's mom, Mr.
Harkless's widow, my favorite old
lady, white hair, little clear
frame glasses, usually wears red
dresses with matching belts, a
little pudgy . . .
     What is Grams? my best old
```

```
person friend, like a mother or
grandmother but she doesn't tell
me what to do! someone I really
trust, good listener . . .
     Why do I think Grams is kind
and generous? those yummy chewy
peanut cookies she always makes,
letting me sit in her rocker and
read her National Geographics and
Readers Digests, lets me play her
piano. . .
```

4. Focus your topic again. Review your information. Now write another, more specific focus statement. Here is an example:

```
     Having a neighbor like Grams
is terrific. She's not only a
wonderful cookie baker, but she
also shares her home and herself
with me.
```

Remember, you want your reader to learn something about your subject. If your focus is too general or if you have no focus, your reader won't learn anything.

When you're happy with your focus statement, you're ready to begin your first draft.

Drafting

Using your notes and focus statement, draft your personal experience. Your focus statement guides your choice of what to include. For example, in "A Backwoods Boy," Russell Freedman writes about Lincoln's humble boyhood, so he does not discuss President Lincoln's stand on slavery. The student writing about Grams will not include what her house looks like.

Revising

In addition to using the revision checklist on page 751, work with a partner or a small group to revise your paper. Read your draft aloud and ask the following questions:

- What is your general impression of this draft?
- In your own words, what do you understand to be the focus of my topic?
- Keeping in mind my focus, do you hear unrelated details that I should leave out?
- Are there enough details to give you a sense of my topic? If not, what do you want to hear more about?
- Would dialogue improve this writing? Where?
- What about this draft confuses you?
- What have you learned about my subject?

Proofreading

Consult the guidelines for proofreading on page 753. Remember to proofread especially for punctuation in dialogue if you have used it.

When you have finished proofreading your paper carefully, use your best handwriting to make a clean copy of your writing.

Reading Letters

THE WINDOW
Pierre Bonnard

GUIDE FOR READING

Letter to the U.S. Government

Chief Seattle (?–1866) was chief of the Dwamish tribe of the northwest United States. When he was a boy, he saw the British explorer Vancouver sail into Puget Sound in 1792. When the Northwest became American territory, he signed the treaty of Port Elliott, which placed the Native Americans on reservations. He said, "It matters little where we pass the remnant of our days. They will not be many." The city of Seattle, Washington, is named for him.

Letter to Joan

C. S. Lewis (1898–1963) was born in Belfast, Ireland. He attended college in the United States and, for most of his life, taught at universities in England. Some of his writing took the form of science fiction fantasies about the struggle between good and evil. One of these is *Out of the Silent Planet.* He also wrote a popular series of books for young people called the *Chronicles of Narnia.* The first book in the series is *The Lion, the Witch, and the Wardrobe.* Lewis answered every one of the many letters he received from readers all around the world. Many readers, like Joan, wrote to share writing and pictures and to ask his advice.

Letter to Scottie

F. Scott Fitzgerald (1896–1940) is considered one of the greatest American fiction writers. He wrote about the Jazz Age, a period during the 1920's. Fitzgerald's first novel, *This Side of Paradise,* describes college life after World War I. His masterpiece, the novel *The Great Gatsby,* explores the dark side of success. During the 1920's, Fitzgerald, his wife Zelda, and baby daughter Frances (called "Scottie") lived in France, where other American artists were living.

Because Fitzgerald's wife was seriously ill for many years, their daughter Scottie was sent away to schools and camps. Her father, therefore, did much of his parenting by mail.

Letters

A **letter** is a written communication from one person or organization to another. Letters fall into two groups: personal and public. Public letters play an important role in business, politics, and so on. Some are written to convince someone to do something. Others state an opinion. Generally, public letters use a formal, impersonal style.

Most writers of personal letters write for an audience of one. Personal letters are usually written in a relaxed style, like a conversation. A personal letter may be written just to say hello, to pass on personal information, or just to keep in touch.

Focus

Everyone enjoys receiving letters. List five people you would like to receive letters from. What would you want them to say to you? What would you say in your return letter? As you read the following letters, try to imagine how the people who received them felt as they read them.

Vocabulary

Knowing the following words will help you read these letters.

contempt (kən tempt′) *n.*: Feeling one has toward something considered worthless (p. 335)

hideously (hid′ ē əs lē) *adv.*: Horribly (p. 336)

logic (läj′ ik) *n.*: Correct reasoning (p. 336)

implement (im′ plə mənt′) *v.*: Carry out (p. 337)

abstract (ab strakt′) *adj.*: Referring to qualities, not objects (p. 337)

concrete (kän krēt′) *adj.*: Real, in material form (p. 337)

documentation (däk′ yo͞o mən tā′ shən) *n.*: Supporting evidence (p. 338)

virtue (vʉr′ cho͞o) *n.*: The quality of goodness (p. 338)

contemporaries (kən tem′ pə rer′ ēz) *n.*: People of about the same age (p. 340)

rudimentary (ro͞o də men′ tər ē) *adj.*: Incompletely developed (p. 340)

fertile (fʉrt′ ′l) *adj.*: Rich in resources or invention (p. 340)

Spelling Tip

The word *contemporary* ends in a consonant and a *y*. Therefore, to make the word plural, change the *y* to *i* and add *es*. This is a rule you can apply to other words ending in a consonant and a *y*.

Letter to the U.S. Government

Chief Seattle

"We are part of the earth and it is part of us."

How can you buy or sell the sky, the warmth of the land? The idea is strange to us.

If we do not own the freshness of the air and the sparkle of the water, how can you buy them?

Every part of this earth is sacred to my people.

Every shining pine needle, every sandy shore, every mist in the dark woods, every clearing and humming insect is holy in the memory and experience of my people. The sap which courses through the trees carries the memories of the red man.

The white man's dead forget the country of their birth when they go to walk among the stars. Our dead never forget this beautiful earth, for it is the mother of the red man.

We are part of the earth and it is part of us. The perfumed flowers are our sisters; the deer, the horse, the great eagle, these are our brothers.

The rocky crests, the juices in the meadows, the body heat of the pony, and man—all belong to the same family.

So, when the Great Chief in Washington sends word that he wishes to buy our land, he asks much of us. The Great Chief sends word he will reserve us a place so that we can live comfortably to ourselves.

He will be our father and we will be his children. So we will consider your offer to buy our land.

But it will not be easy. For this land is sacred to us.

This shining water that moves in the streams and rivers is not just water but the blood of our ancestors.

If we sell you land, you must remember that it is sacred, and you must teach your children that it is sacred and that each ghostly reflection in the clear water of the lakes tells of events and memories in the life of my people.

The water's murmur is the voice of my father's father.

The rivers are our brothers, they quench our thirst. The rivers carry our canoes, and feed our children. If we sell you our land, you must remember, and teach your children, that the rivers are our brothers, and yours, and you must henceforth give the rivers the kindness you would give any brother.

We know that the white man does not understand our ways. One portion of land is the same to him as the next, for he is a stranger who comes in the night and takes from the land whatever he needs.

The earth is not his brother, but his enemy, and when he has conquered it, he moves on.

He leaves his father's graves behind, and he does not care. He kidnaps the earth from the children, and he does not care.

His father's grave and his children's birthright, are forgotten. He treats his mother, the earth, and his brother, the sky, as things to be bought, plundered, sold like sheep or bright beads.

His appetite will devour the earth and leave behind only a desert.

I do not know. Our ways are different from your ways.

The sight of your cities pains the eyes of the red man. But perhaps it is because the red man is a savage and does not understand.

There is no quiet place in the white man's cities. No place to hear the unfurling of leaves in spring, or the rustle of an insect's wings.

But perhaps it is because I am a savage and do not understand.

The clatter only seems to insult the ears. And what is there to life if a man cannot hear the lonely cry of the whippoorwill or the arguments of the frogs around a pond at night? I am a red man and do not understand.

The Indian prefers the soft sound of the wind darting over the face of a pond, and the smell of the wind itself, cleaned by a midday rain, or scented with the piñon pine.

The air is precious to the red man, for all things share the same breath—the beast, the tree, the man, they all share the same breath.

The white man does not seem to notice the air he breathes. Like a man dying for many days, he is numb to the stench.

But if we sell you our land, you must remember that the air is precious to us, that the air shares its spirit with all the life it supports. The wind that gave our grandfather his first breath also receives his last sigh.

And if we sell you our land, you must keep it apart and sacred, as a place where even the white man can go to taste the wind that is sweetened by the meadow's flowers.

So we will consider your offer to buy our land. If we decide to accept, I will make one condition: the white man must treat the beasts of this land as his brother.

I am a savage and I do not understand any other way.

I have seen a thousand rotting buffaloes on the prairie, left by the white man who shot them from a passing train.

I am a savage and I do not understand how the smoking iron horse can be more important than the buffalo that we kill only to stay alive.

What is man without the beasts? If all the beasts were gone, man would die from a great loneliness of spirit.

For whatever happens to the beasts, soon happens to man. All things are connected.

You must teach your children that the ground beneath their feet is the ashes of your grandfathers. So that they will respect the land, tell your children that the earth is rich with the lives of our kin.

Teach your children what we have taught our children, that the earth is our mother.

Whatever befalls the earth befalls the sons of the earth. If men spit upon the ground, they spit upon themselves.

EVER-CHANGING COLOR OF THE SEVEN YEI'S (detail)
Baje Whitethorne, Sr.

This we know: the earth does not belong to man; man belongs to the earth. This we know.

All things are connected like the blood which unites one family. All things are connected.

Whatever befalls the earth befalls the sons of the earth. Man did not weave the web of life: he is merely a strand in it. Whatever he does to the web, he does to himself.

Even the white man, whose God walks and talks with him as friend to friend, cannot be exempt from the common destiny.

We may be brothers after all.

We shall see.

One thing we know, which the white man may one day discover—our God is the same God.

You may think now that you own Him as you wish to own our land; but you cannot. He is the God of man, and His compassion is equal for the red man and the white.

This earth is precious to Him, and to harm the earth is to heap contempt on its Creator.

The whites too shall pass; perhaps sooner than all other tribes. Contaminate your bed, and you will one night suffocate in your own waste.

But in your perishing you will shine brightly, fired by the strength of the God who brought you to this land and for some special purpose gave you dominion over this land and over the red man.

That destiny is a mystery to us, for we do not understand when the buffalo are all slaughtered, the wild horses are tamed, the secret corners of the forest heavy with scent of many men, and the view of the ripe hills blotted by talking wires.[1]

Where is the thicket? Gone.

Where is the eagle? Gone.

The end of living and the beginning of survival.

Reader's Response

If you had a choice, where would you live, in the city or in the country?

1. **talking wires:** Telegraph wires.

Responding to the Selection

Your Response

1. Do you think Chief Seattle persuaded the U.S. government with his arguments? Why or why not?

Recalling

2. Why does Chief Seattle say that "every part of this earth is sacred to my people"?
3. In return for selling the land, what promises does Chief Seattle ask from the government?

Interpreting

4. **Based on this letter, contrast the attitude of white people and the attitude of Native Americans toward the environment.**
5. **Give examples to show whether or not Chief Seattle's predictions about the environment have come true.**
6. **What does Chief Seattle mean by "the end of living and the beginning of survival"?**

Applying

7. Are more or fewer people coming to agree with Chief Seattle's ideas about treating the land responsibly? Give examples to support your answer.

Analyzing Literature

Appreciating Letters

Letters are written for many reasons. Some letters, such as Chief Seattle's, are meant to move the person who receives it to do something or to believe one way or another. Because Chief Seattle's letter is a public one that is still read today, people are still being influenced by Chief Seattle's views.

1. What purposes do you think Chief Seattle had for writing this letter?
2. Who do you think Chief Seattle's true audience was?
3. How might Chief Seattle have tried to accomplish his goals today?

Letter to Joan

C. S. Lewis

" 'Good English' is whatever educated people talk; so that what is good in one place or time would not be so in another."

The Kilns,
Headington Quarry,
Oxford

[26 June 1956]

Dear Joan—

Thanks for your letter of the 3rd. You describe your Wonderful Night v.[ery] well. That is, you describe the place & the people and the night and the feeling of it all, very well—but not the *thing* itself—the setting but not the jewel. And no wonder! Wordsworth[1] often does just the same. His *Prelude* (you're bound to read it about 10 years hence. Don't try it now, or you'll only spoil it for later reading) is full of moments in which everything except the *thing* itself is described. If you become a writer you'll be trying to describe the *thing* all your life: and lucky if, out of dozens of books, one or two sentences, just for a moment, come near to getting it across.

C.S. LEWIS
THE LION, THE WITCH AND THE WARDROBE
BOOK 1 IN THE CHRONICLES OF NARNIA

1. **William Wordsworth** (1770–1850): English poet.

About *amn't I*, *aren't I*, and *am I not*, of course there are no right and wrong answers about the language in the sense in which there are right and wrong answers in Arithmetic. "Good English" is whatever educated people talk; so that what is good in one place or time w[oul]d not be so in another. *Amn't* was good 50 years ago in the North of Ireland where I was brought up, but bad in Southern England. *Aren't I* w[oul]d have been hideously bad in Ireland but very good in England. And of course I just don't know which (if either) is good in modern Florida. Don't take any notice of teachers and textbooks in such matters. Nor of logic. It is good to say "More than one passenger was hurt," although *more than one* equals at least two and therefore logically the verb ought to be plural *were* not singular *was!* What really matters is:—

1. Always try to use the language so as to make quite clear what you mean and

make sure y[ou]r. sentence couldn't mean anything else.

2. Always prefer the plain direct word to the long, vague one. Don't *implement* promises, but *keep* them.
3. Never use abstract nouns when concrete ones will do. If you mean "More people died" don't say "Mortality rose."
4. In writing, don't use adjectives which merely tell us how you want us to *feel* about the thing you are describing. I mean, instead of telling us a thing was "terrible," describe it so that we'll be terrified. Don't say it was "delightful"; make *us* say "delightful" when we've read the description. You see, all those words (horrifying, wonderful, hideous, exquisite) are only like saying to your readers "Please will you do my job for me."
5. Don't use words too big for the subject. Don't say "infinitely" when you mean "very"; otherwise you'll have no word left when you want to talk about something *really* infinite.

Thanks for the photos. You and Aslan[2] both look v.[ery] well. I hope you'll like your new home.

With love,
yours
C. S. Lewis

Reader's Response
What would your reaction be if you received this letter?

2. Aslan: The great lion in C. S. Lewis's *The Chronicles of Narnia.*

Responding to the Selection

Your Response

1. Do you agree with Lewis's advice about "good" and "bad" English?
2. What kind of person do you think Lewis was?

Recalling

3. What does Lewis like about Joan's description of her Wonderful Night?
4. What definition of "Good English" does Lewis offer Joan?
5. What three sources does Lewis consider useless in trying to decide what "Good English" is?

Interpreting

6. What reasons does Lewis probably have for giving Joan advice such as choosing plain, direct words over long, vague ones?
7. Explain how Lewis feels about differences in language like those among *amn't I, aren't I,* and *am I not.*
8. Why does Lewis object to a writer's using adjectives that "tell us how you want us to feel about the thing you are describing"?
9. Explain why Lewis would object to the following sentence. "That piece of chocolate cake was the most awesome I've ever eaten in my life."

Applying

10. Lewis advises Joan not to read Wordsworth's "Prelude" until she is older. Do you think that some works of literature or art are beyond the appreciation of young people? Explain your answer.

Learning Option

Writing. Probably at some time or another you have offered advice to someone. Using C. S. Lewis's letter as a model, write a letter to a person you wish to advise. Share your letter with a partner, and discuss your advice.

Letter to Scottie

F. Scott Fitzgerald

"All I believe in in life is the rewards for virtue . . . and the punishments *for not fulfilling your duties . . ."*

La Paix, Rodgers' Forge
Towson, Maryland
August 8, 1933

Dear Pie:[1]

I feel very strongly about you doing [your] duty. Would you give me a little more documentation about your reading in French? I am glad you are happy—but I never believe much in happiness. I never believe in misery either. Those are things you see on the stage or the screen or the printed page, they never really happen to you in life.

All I believe in in life is the rewards for virtue (according to your talents) and the *punishments* for not fulfilling your duties, which are doubly costly. If there is such a volume in the camp library, will you ask Mrs. Tyson to let you look up a sonnet of Shakespeare's in which the line occurs "*Lilies that fester smell far worse than weeds.*"

Have had no thoughts today, life seems composed of getting up a *Saturday Evening Post*[2] story. I think of you, and always pleasantly; but if you call me "Pappy" again I am going to take the White Cat out and beat his bottom *hard, six times for every time you are impertinent.* Do you react to that?

I will arrange the camp bill.

Halfwit, I will conclude.

Things to worry about:
- Worry about courage
- Worry about cleanliness
- Worry about efficiency
- Worry about horsemanship
- Worry about . . .

Things not to worry about:
- Don't worry about popular opinion
- Don't worry about dolls
- Don't worry about the past
- Don't worry about the future
- Don't worry about growing up
- Don't worry about anybody getting ahead of you
- Don't worry about triumph

1. Pie: Affectionate nickname for his daughter, Frances Scott Fitzgerald, also known as Scottie, who was away at summer camp.

2. ***Saturday Evening Post:*** A weekly magazine.

F. Scott Fitzgerald and his daughter "Scottie," 1928

Don't worry about failure unless it comes through your own fault
Don't worry about mosquitoes
Don't worry about flies
Don't worry about insects in general
Don't worry about parents
Don't worry about boys
Don't worry about disappointments
Don't worry about pleasures
Don't worry about satisfactions

Things to think about:

What am I really aiming at?

How good am I really in comparison to my contemporaries in regard to:

(a) Scholarship
(b) Do I really understand about people and am I able to get along with them?
(c) Am I trying to make my body a useful instrument or am I neglecting it?

With dearest love,

[Daddy]

P.S. My come-back to your calling me Pappy is christening you by the word Egg, which implies that you belong to a very rudimentary state of life and that I could break you up and crack you open at my will and I think it would be a word that would hang on if I ever told it to your contemporaries. "Egg Fitzgerald." How would you like that to go through life with—"Eggie Fitzgerald" or "Bad Egg Fitzgerald" or any form that might occur to fertile minds? Try it once more and I swear I will hang it on you and it will be up to you to shake it off. Why borrow trouble?

Love anyhow.

Reader's Response
What would you add to or remove from either of Fitzgerald's lists of things to worry about and not worry about?

Responding to the Selection

Your Response

1. What kind of father do you think Fitzgerald was? Explain.

Recalling

2. Identify the two things in life that Fitzgerald says he believes in.
3. Why does Fitzgerald threaten Scottie with the name "Egg Fitzgerald"?

Interpreting

4. Explain how the line "Lilies that fester smell far worse than weeds" might apply to Scottie if she does not work up to her ability level.
5. Which of the items on Fitzgerald's list of things not to worry about seem less than completely serious? Explain.
6. What tendencies in Scottie might have been worrying Fitzgerald when he wrote this letter? Give evidence for your answer.
7. How does Fitzgerald seem to feel about himself? Give evidence for your answer.

Applying

8. Do you agree with Fitzgerald that happiness and misery are things seen on the screen and printed page but never really happen to people in life? Give reasons for your opinion.

Critical Thinking and Reading

Recognizing Formal and Informal Style

Style is the way something is done. Imagine two people answering the telephone. One is eager; one is reserved. Their attitudes will show in their styles. The eager one's voice will be lively; the reserved one's voice will be calm.

In writing, there is a vast range of styles. Among them are formal and informal style. A **formal style** usually goes with a serious purpose and an **informal style** with a less serious one, though that is not always the case. A formal style usually uses "good English" as C. S. Lewis defined it—the English that educated people speak in formal situations. An informal style often uses slang and other casual ways of speaking that people use when they are in relaxed situations. Chief Seattle's letter is written in a formal style. F. Scott Fitzgerald's is written in an informal style.

1. Find an example of a formal sentence in Chief Seattle's letter. It should be a sentence that uses words or phrases a person would not be likely to use in casual conversation.
2. Find an example of an informal sentence in Fitzgerald's letter. It should be a sentence that uses words or phrases that a person would not be likely to use in a formal situation, like a speech given to the United Nations.

Thinking and Writing

Writing a Letter

Write a letter of your own. Choose the person to whom you will write. You may want to choose one of the people on the list you made earlier. Your letter may be personal or public. Before you begin writing, think about your purposes for writing. What effect do you want to have on your reader? How do you want your reader to "see" you? As you write, be aware of your purposes and think about how they affect your style. When you revise your letter, make sure that your style suits your purpose and audience. Then proofread your letter and prepare the final draft. If it is appropriate to do so, mail the letter.

MULTICULTURAL CONNECTION

Letter Writing in Different Cultures

F. Scott Fitzgerald begins his letter to Scottie by affectionately writing "Dear Pie" and closes "With dearest love." However, in many parts of the world, letters do not always start with the word *Dear* and end with words like *Love* or *Sincerely*.

Greetings and salutations. Salutations are greetings, or the way someone begins a letter. In some cultures, what you say at the beginning of a letter has religious meaning. In India, for example, people begin their letters by giving thanks to God. Then they are expected to announce that they are in excellent health and to inquire about the well-being of the person to whom the letter is addressed.

Following the rules. In many countries, letter writing is very formal. Certain terms of respect must be used to begin and end letters. In Germany, for example, it is common to begin a letter with "My Most Respected Mr. or Mrs. . . ." In France, it is polite to end a letter with a formal conclusion such as "Please accept my most respectful wishes. . . ." In China, letters are sometimes written in the classical language, which is different from the language used in modern speech. In some languages—Russian, for example—the word *you* is always capitalized when writing a letter as a sign of respect for the person being addressed. The pronoun *I*, on the other hand, is written in lowercase.

Class display. Ask relatives and friends to share with you letters or postcards from other countries. Make a display, showing different formats and conventions.

GUIDE FOR READING

How to Write a Letter

Purpose

Purpose is the author's reason for writing. A writer usually has both a general purpose and a specific purpose. The general purpose may be to explain, to inform, to describe, to narrate, to persuade, or to entertain. The specific purpose is the main point the writer wants to make about the topic. Sometimes, this main point is easy to spot; it may begin or end the writing. At other times, the main point is only hinted at here and there throughout the writing.

Garrison Keillor

(1942–) was the host of a live radio show called *A Prairie Home Companion* from 1974 to 1987. The program, which won a Peabody Award and an Edward R. Murrow Award, was filled with the gentle, folksy humor that has become Keillor's trademark. Keillor was born in Anoka, Minnesota. For many years he has contributed to *The New Yorker* and other magazines. Keillor is the author of the books *Happy to Be Here* (1982), *Lake Wobegon Days* (1985), and *We Are Still Married: Stories and Letters* (1989).

Focus

In this selection, you will read about the beauty and importance of giving and receiving letters. How do you feel about receiving and writing letters? Copy the chart below onto a sheet of paper. Fill in the chart, listing all your feelings about receiving and writing letters. As you read this essay, note whether Keillor's suggestions would help you solve problems you have writing letters.

How I Feel About Receiving Letters	People I Write To	Problems I Have Writing Letters

Vocabulary

Knowing the following words will help you as you read "How to Write a Letter."

anonymity (an′ ə nim′ ə tē) *n.*: The condition of being unknown (p. 343)

obligatory (əb lig′ ə tôr′ ē) *adj.*: Required (p. 343)

episode (ep′ ə sōd′) *n.*: A series of related events (p. 344)

sibling (sib′ liŋ) *n.*: Brother or sister (p. 344)

How to Write a Letter

Garrison Keillor

"Outrage, confusion, love—whatever is in your mind, let it find a way to the page."

We shy persons need to write a letter now and then, or else we'll dry up and blow away. It's true. And I speak as one who loves to reach for the phone, dial the number, and talk. I say, "Big Bopper here—what's shakin', babes?" The telephone is to shyness what Hawaii is to February, it's a way out of the woods, *and yet:* a letter is better.

Such a sweet gift—a piece of handmade writing, in an envelope that is not a bill, sitting in our friend's path when she trudges home from a long day spent among wahoos and savages, a day our words will help repair. They don't need to be immortal, just sincere. She can read them twice and again tomorrow: *You're someone I care about, Corinne, and think of often and every time I do you make me smile.*

We need to write, otherwise nobody will know who we are. They will have only a vague impression of us as A Nice Person, because, frankly, we don't shine at conversation, we lack the confidence to thrust our faces forward and say, "Hi, I'm Heather Hooten; let me tell you about my week." Mostly we say "Uh-huh" and "Oh, really." People smile and look over our shoulder, looking for someone else to meet.

So a shy person sits down and writes a letter. To be known by another person—to meet and talk freely on the page—to be close despite distance. To escape from anonymity and be our own sweet selves and express the music of our souls.

Same thing that moves a giant rock star to sing his heart out in front of 123,000 people moves us to take ballpoint in hand and write a few lines to our dear Aunt Eleanor. *We want to be known.* We want her to know that we have fallen in love, that we quit our job, that we're moving to New York, and we want to say a few things that might not get said in casual conversation: *Thank you for what you've meant to me, I am very happy right now.*

The first step in writing letters is to get over the guilt of *not* writing. You don't "owe" anybody a letter. Letters are a gift. The burning shame you feel when you see unanswered mail makes it harder to pick up a pen and makes for a cheerless letter when you finally do. *I feel bad about not writing, but I've been so busy,* etc. Skip this. Few letters are obligatory, and they are *Thanks for the wonderful gift* and *I am terribly sorry to hear about George's death* and *Yes, you're welcome to stay with us next month*, and not many more than that. Write those promptly if you want to keep your friends. Don't worry about the others, except love letters, of course. When your true love writes, *Dear Light of My Life, Joy of My Heart, O Lovely Pulsating Core of My Sensate*[1] *Life*, some response is called for.

Some of the best letters are tossed off in a burst of inspiration, so keep your writing stuff in one place where you can sit down for a few minutes and (*Dear Roy, I am in the middle of a book entitled* We Are Still Married *but thought I'd drop you a line. Hi to your sweetie, too*) dash off a note to a pal. Envelopes, stamps, address book, everything in a drawer so you can write fast when the pen is hot.

A blank white eight-by-eleven sheet can look as big as Montana if the pen's not so hot—try a smaller page and write boldly. Or use a note card with a piece of fine art on the front; if your letter ain't good, at least they get the Matisse.[2] Get a pen that makes a sensuous[3] line, get a comfortable typewriter, a friendly word processor—whichever feels easy to the hand.

Sit for a few minutes with the blank sheet in front of you, and meditate on the person you will write to, let your friend come to mind until you can almost see her or him in the room with you. Remember the last time you saw each other and how your friend looked and what you said and what perhaps was unsaid between you, and when your friend becomes real to you, start to write.

Write the salutation—*Dear You*—and take a deep breath and plunge in. A simple declarative sentence will do, followed by another and another and another. Tell us what you're doing and tell it like you were talking to us. Don't think about grammar, don't think about lit'ry style, don't try to write dramatically, just give us your news. Where did you go, who did you see, what did they say, what do you think?

If you don't know where to begin, start with the present moment: *I'm sitting at the kitchen table on a rainy Saturday morning. Everyone is gone and the house is quiet.* Let your simple description of the present moment lead to something else, let the letter drift gently along.

The toughest letter to crank out is one that is meant to impress, as we all know from writing job applications; if it's hard work to slip off a letter to a friend, maybe you're trying too hard to be terrific. A letter is only a report to someone who already likes you for reasons other than your brilliance. Take it easy.

Don't worry about form. It's not a term paper. When you come to the end of one episode, just start a new paragraph. You can go from a few lines about the sad state of pro football to the fight with your mother to your fond memories of Mexico to your cat's urinary-tract infection to a few thoughts on personal indebtedness and on to the kitchen sink and what's in it. The more you write, the easier it gets, and when you have a True True Friend to write to, a *compadre*,[4] a soul sibling, then it's like driving a car down a country road, you just get behind the keyboard and press on the gas.

Don't tear up the page and start over when you write a bad line—try to write your

1. sensate (sen′ sāt′) *adj.*: Appealing to the senses.
2. Matisse (mȧ tēs′): Henri (än rē′) Matisse (1869–1954), a French painter.
3. sensuous (sen′ shoo̅ əs) *adj.*: Readily grasped by the senses.

4. compadre (käm päd′ rā) *n.*: Spanish for buddy; close friend.

LAUDRENCE TYPING
Fairfield Porter
Parrish Art Museum, Southampton, New York
Gift of the Estate of Fairfield Porter

way out of it. Make mistakes and plunge on. Let the letter cook along and let yourself be bold. Outrage, confusion, love—whatever is in your mind, let it find a way to the page. Writing is a means of discovery, always, and when you come to the end and write *Yours ever* or *Hugs and kisses*, you'll know something you didn't when you wrote *Dear Pal.*

Probably your friend will put your letter away, and it'll be read again a few years from now—and it will improve with age. And forty years from now, your friend's grandkids will dig it out of the attic and read it, a sweet and precious relic of the ancient eighties that gives them a sudden clear glimpse of you and her and the world we old-timers knew. You will then have created an object of art. Your simple lines about where you went, who you saw, what they said, will speak to those children and they will feel in their hearts the humanity of our times.

You can't pick up a phone and call the future and tell them about our times. You have to pick up a piece of paper.

Reader's Response
Do you like to receive letters? Why?

Responding to the Selection

Your Response

1. How do you feel about writing letters?
2. Which advice of Keillor's was helpful to you? Explain.

Recalling

3. Why does Keillor suggest that you keep your writing materials in one place?
4. What does Keillor recommend as a first step before you begin writing to a friend?

Interpreting

5. Keillor uses many incomplete sentences and slang terms. Why does he do that?
6. Why does Keillor urge people to plunge on when they make a mistake?
7. What contrasts does Keillor make between a letter and a telephone call?

Applying

8. Of what value is writing or receiving a letter?

Analyzing Literature

Understanding the Author's Purpose

A writer's **purpose** is what the writer wants to accomplish. A writer often has more than one purpose for writing. In this essay, Keillor wants to inform, describe, persuade, and entertain.

1. What information does Keillor give to accomplish each of his general purposes?
2. Keillor also has a specific purpose, or a main point that he wants to make. What is Keillor's specific purpose in "How to Write a Letter"?

Critical Thinking and Reading

Recognizing an Author's Attitude

Most writers have an **attitude,** a particular set of feelings, toward the subjects about which they write. Some authors announce their attitudes; most do not. Attitudes influence what authors say and the way they say it. Evidence of the author's attitude appears in the selection of details and the choice of words. Garrison Keillor writes of a friend who "trudges home from a long day spent among wahoos and savages." Judging from his choice of words, he seems to regard work as annoying drudgery. What attitudes do the following passages reveal?

1. "People smile and look over our shoulder, looking for someone else to meet."
2. ". . . when you have a True True Friend to write to, . . . it's like driving a car down a country road. . . ."

Thinking and Writing

Writing a Personal Letter

Follow Keillor's advice to write a personal letter. Don't hesitate, just "take a deep breath and plunge in." You might want to begin with the sentences you wrote before reading the selection. After you have written your letter, read it and revise it. Remember that "it's not a term paper." Correct any glaring errors, but concentrate on adding anything you forgot, especially the details that will bring it to life. If you wish to mail your letter, do so.

Learning Options

1. **Art.** In order to write a letter, you must have a piece of writing paper. Create your own personal design for letter-writing stationery. Make copies of your stationery and use it to send letters to friends.
2. **Listening and Speaking.** Garrison Keillor has a story-telling style worth listening to. Find out if your local library owns tapes of Keillor's show, *A Prairie Home Companion.* Listen to Keillor's style and then practice reading "How to Write a Letter" aloud. When you are ready, read the essay aloud to your class.

YOUR WRITING PROCESS

Writing to Influence

In countless situations every day, people try to influence one another. What happens when you want to go shopping and your friend wants to play soccer? How do you decide which you will do? What happens when someone in your family wants to watch one television program and you want to watch another? Chances are you try to influence the other person. You try to change the person's mind so he or she will want to do or think as you do. You can also influence others by your writing.

Your Turn

Write a letter to someone you know well, but not someone who already shares your views about the topic. Your purpose is to influence your reader to think and feel a particular way.

Prewriting

1. Brainstorm for topic possibilities. List your favorite and least favorite in categories such as these: *book, movie, actor, singer, song, place, holiday, restaurant, pet, sport, pastime, game, hobby.*

Next exchange lists with a partner. Do you discover new ideas? Add them to your own list. Finally, star three topics you could write about.

2. Choose your topic. For each topic you consider writing about, freewrite on separate sheets of paper for five minutes each. List reasons you think and feel as you do.

Your freewriting might look like this:

```
     Having a cat--a wonderful
pet, soft, cuddly, doesn't need
to be walked in the cold, answers
when you talk to it, sits on my
lap and purrs, keeps me warm in
winter, place to rest my book
when I read in the big
chair. . . .
```

Review your freewriting, adding to it as you read. Choose the topic about which you can be most persuasive and one about which your reader does not agree with you. Be sure of the main point you want to make about your topic.

3. Consider your reader. You especially need to consider your reader when you write to influence. Therefore, picture your reader in your mind. Then ask yourself these questions and jot down your answers:

- How does my reader probably think and feel about this subject?
- How might my reader object to my views?
- How can I get my points across effectively?

Here are one student's notes:

```
--Cats, I love them. Jerry
doesn't, though. He loves dogs.
He'll probably think only dogs
```

```
are good pets, probably doesn't
care at all about cats. Since
he's my good friend, though,
he'll listen to what I have to
tell him. Might think that I
don't care about dogs, only cats,
that I'm narrow minded--better
show him I like dogs, too--show
him the good ways the two pets
are similar, then show how cats
are also special.
```

4. Make a writing plan. Use information from your freewriting to briefly outline the body of your letter.

- State your topic.
- State your thoughts and feelings about it.
- State your most persuasive reasons for feeling as you do.
- Note objections you anticipate and your responses to them.

Drafting

Use your notes and outline to compose a first draft of your letter. Use a tone to fit your reader. For example, if you are writing to a good friend, be friendly and positive, especially on points of possible disagreement. Here's an example:

```
     I know you think dogs are
terrific, the way they follow you
around and wag their tails. I
agree--dogs are terrific.
However, in their own way, cats
can be just as terrific. The pet
cat I'm talking about will greet
you at the door just like a dog.
She'll meow like crazy when
you're on the telephone, trying,
just like a dog, to get your
attention, and you'll laugh. . . .
```

Revising

In addition to using the revision checklist on page 751, work with a partner or small group to revise. Read your draft aloud and ask the following questions:

- What do you think I am trying to influence the reader to do, think, or feel?
- Do I influence you? Explain how.
- Which points are strongest? Which are weakest?
- What kind of reader does it sound like I am writing to? How can you tell?
- Is there anything you disagree with?
- What tone do you hear? Does it sound right for my topic and reader? Is the tone the same throughout the letter?

Proofreading

Consult the guidelines for proofreading on page 753. Remember to proofread especially for punctuation and capitalization in letter openings and closings.

Then use your best handwriting to make a clean copy of your letter.

Reading Essays

THE ANGLERS
Henri Rousseau

GUIDE FOR READING

Rhoda Blumberg

(1917–) has written many children's books, as well as scripts for radio and television. Her books include *The First Travel Guide to the Moon* and *More Freaky Facts.* Two of Blumberg's greatest interests are animals and research. In "The Truth About Dragons," she combines these interests to reveal why dragons have enchanted people for more than five thousand years. Writing in a clever, imaginative way, Blumberg almost convinces her readers that these creatures are real.

The Truth About Dragons

What Is an Essay?

An **essay** is a type of nonfiction. It focuses on one idea or event. This is the subject of the essay. An essay gives its writer's view of or personal experience with the subject. The author of an essay has a purpose for writing it. Sometimes the purpose may be to explain a subject or to give information about it. This is, like "The Truth About Dragons," an **explanatory essay.**

Focus

"The Truth About Dragons" is in two parts. One part is about western dragons, the ones from the western world—Europe, North America, and South America. The other part is about eastern dragons, those from the eastern world—Asia and the nearby islands. The people who live in these regions of the world have very different views about dragons. What are your views about dragons? What ideas and images come to mind when you think of these creatures? Make a cluster diagram or a word web centered on the word *dragon.* As you write down your ideas of dragons, include words and phrases that appeal to the five senses: sound, sight, smell, taste, or touch.

Then, as you read the essay, note the differences in views of western people and eastern people toward dragons.

Vocabulary

Knowing the following words will help you as you read "The Truth About Dragons."

plagues (plāgz) *n.*: Deadly diseases that spread rapidly (p. 351)

crests (krests) *n.*: Tufts on the heads of some animals or birds (p. 352)

mammoth (mam′ əth) *adj.*: Huge (p. 354)

meditate (med′ ə tāt) *v.*: Think quietly, often about mysterious or religious events (p. 356)

cater (kā′ tər) *v.*: Try hard to supply what another needs (p. 360)

boon (bo͞on) *n.*: A welcome benefit (p. 360)

The Truth About Dragons

Rhoda Blumberg

"When dragons fly through the air, their jaws and skins drip poisons that cause everything from pimples to plagues."

PART I: WESTERN DRAGONS

From ancient reports, it is clear that Western Dragons are the most terrible and terrifying of all animals. They spread disease, kill crops, and enjoy attacking and eating people. First confined to Africa and the ancient countries of Persia and Babylonia, these dangerous beasts found their way to Europe. They flew, slithered, and swam, invading Europe from Sicily to Scandinavia.

During the Middle Ages,[1] when people suffered from poverty and plagues, dragons added to their miseries. The monsters roamed the countryside, especially at night. Anything from soured milk to sudden sickness was proof that they lurked nearby.

People knew that Western Dragons could be like poison tanks. Not only their fangs, but their bodies are filled with venom. The poison of some dragons is so strong that should a man on horseback stab the monster with a spear, the venom will travel up the spear, destroying horse and rider.

When dragons fly through the air their jaws and skins drip poisons that cause everything from pimples to plagues. People often starved because a dragon's sweat and saliva had killed crops.

Fortunately, the number of dragon reports declined as centuries passed. Father Kircher, a seventeenth-century expert in earth sciences, explained that most dragons are hiding underground. In his book *The Subterranean World*, he wrote that the reptiles are rarely seen because they prefer to remain in caves and in holes beneath the earth's surface. Few dragons come out in the open. Some have lost their way. Others can't return to their lairs because an earthquake or landslide has blocked their passage home. According to Father Kircher, most of the world's dragon population remains unseen beneath our feet.

Physical Appearance

The Historie of Serpents, by Edward Topsell, published in 1608, describes three basic kinds of dragons: "There be some Dragons which have wings and no feet, some again have both feet and wings, and some neither

1. **Middle Ages:** The period of European history between ancient and modern times, A.D 476 to about A.D. 1450

feet nor wings." Those without feet and wings don't look like ordinary snakes because they have crests on their heads and yellow beards on their chins.

The most common variety of dragons has wings and two or four feet. It is a heavy reptile with bulging eyes, batlike wings, and huge jaws equipped with razor-sharp teeth. Its body is covered with rough scales, and its long pointed tail has poisonous spikes that are as sharp as daggers. Its feet have sharp curved claws for clutching victims. It has poison fangs, a forked tongue, and a stinking breath that could choke a person to death. Because its insides burn like a furnace, it spits fire, and smoke streams out of its nostrils.

The ancient Greeks were horrified by hydras, sea dragons with nine or more heads. As centuries passed, only seven-headed hydras were seen. The seventeeth-century naturalist Edward Topsell included a picture of a hydra in *The Historie of Serpents.* He wrote that a hydra, shipped from Venice to Turkey in 1530, was exhibited in public before being presented to the King of France.

Dragons with horses' heads and snakes' bodies, and with fishes' fins and crocodiles' bodies have long scared seafarers. Norwegian sailors used to throw castor oil overboard, hoping the nasty tasting stuff would keep such monsters away. They also carved their ships to look like fierce dragons, ready to devour any beast that swam close. Interestingly enough, sea dragons have been reported during the twentieth century.

Dragons are yellow, black, silver, gray, slimy green or blood-red. A few rare types are multicolored.

Dragons hiss, grunt, and roar. When injured they howl and scream.

Size

Although most Western Dragons are fifteen to twenty feet long—the size of large crocodiles—a few varieties are less than four feet long when full-grown.

Supersized dragons have always been seen more frequently than tiny terrors. One African reptile attacked the Roman army of General Regulus. According to the Roman historian Livy, "After many of the soldiers had been seized in [the dragon's] mouth, and many more crushed by the folds of its tail, its hide being too thick for javelins[2] and darts, the dragon was at last attacked by military engines and crushed by repeated blows from heavy stones."

This dragon was a midget compared with another African monster described by the geographer Iphicrates.[3] His dragon had grass growing on its back. It was so big that Iphicrates said people mistook it for a meadow.

The smallest and most fearsome of all dragons was the basilisk. This mini-monster, ranging in size from six inches to two feet, had the head of a rooster, the warts of a toad, and the body of a snake. It hid in wells and in cellars. The basilisk's death-ray eyes killed with a look. Anyone it glared at dropped dead. Once common in Europe, basilisks were killed off by clever people who used mirrors as shields. The monsters died of fright when they saw their own horrid reflections.

Habitat

Most dragons live in caves above or underground, but they also make themselves at

---

2. javelins (jav′ lins) *n.*: Light spears for throwing.
3. Iphicrates (if i′ krə tēs): A Greek general.

home in any field. The smallest varieties live almost everywhere, in holes in the ground, in trees, tombs, tunnels, wells, and cellars.

Dragons over one hundred feet long have been discovered on mountaintops. These are golden in color, with arched eyebrows and long, flowing beards. They bed down on top of gold mines or make their dens in mountain caves.

Black dragons as big as elephants have hidden in marshes. They are sluggish monsters, able to hunt only those animals and people who come near their mud-mound dwellings. Survival is a struggle, especially because the mountain dragons come down to steal their food.

Silver-colored dragons live in rivers. Other water dwellers live in the ocean. And there are fish-like reptiles that shine in the night, startling people living near large European and African lakes.

Diet

Dragons enjoy milk, maidens, cakes, birds, oxen, deer, and elephants' blood.

Milk is their favorite drink. It makes them sleepy and too drunk to harm anyone. Egyptians, Greeks, and Romans used to leave milk at the entrances to dragon caves. They

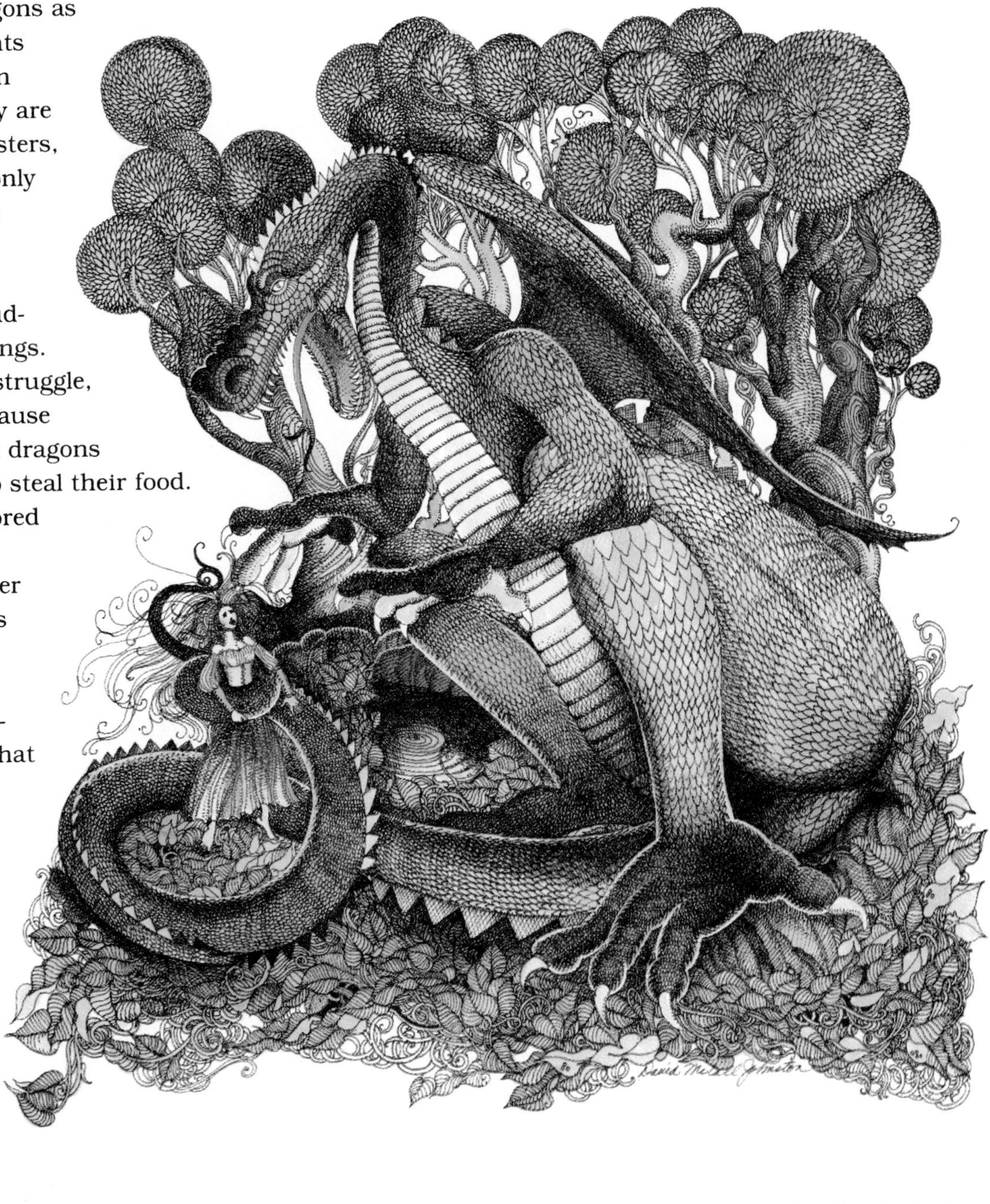

also left honey cakes to satisfy the beast's sweet tooth. European housekeepers used to leave milk outside their homes for stray, thirsty dragons. They didn't want to invite the monsters over for a visit, but they hoped that milk would make the creatures so drowsy that they wouldn't eat people. Unmarried daughters were in the gravest danger, for sweet, tender maidens are a tasty dish.

When dragons hunger for a snack, they open their jaws, lift their heads, and inhale deeply. The force of their breath creates a draft. Birds flying overhead are sucked into their mouths and down their throats.

There were reports of a mammoth maneater in Africa that would eat twice as fast as any other dragon, because it had two heads. This double-header was finally killed by lightning. What a stroke of luck!

Although their teeth are as sharp as steak knives, some full-grown dragons gulp down victims whole, without biting or chewing. After swallowing an ox or a deer they twist themselves around trees, crushing the animals they have eaten.

Old nature books claimed that dragons swallow elephants whole, and then cough up the bones. This has been questioned by experts who insist that dragons only like elephants' blood. They wait in trees until elephants pass below, then pounce upon the big gray beasts. Coiling themselves around the elephants' bodies, and biting the tips of the ears, they suck the elephants dry. The elephants become empty bags of skin and bones. The foolhardy dragons keep drinking until they blow up like balloons. When the elephants fall down dead, the dragons wrapped around them are crushed to death.

Some African dragons in search of food used to cross the Red Sea to Arabia. Four or five twisted themselves together into a floating raft. The dragons' heads were held above the water, acting as sails, as the beasts rode the waves. Once ashore, they headed for apple orchards and feasted until their bellies ached. Then they grazed for lettuce, their remedy for instant relief from indigestion.

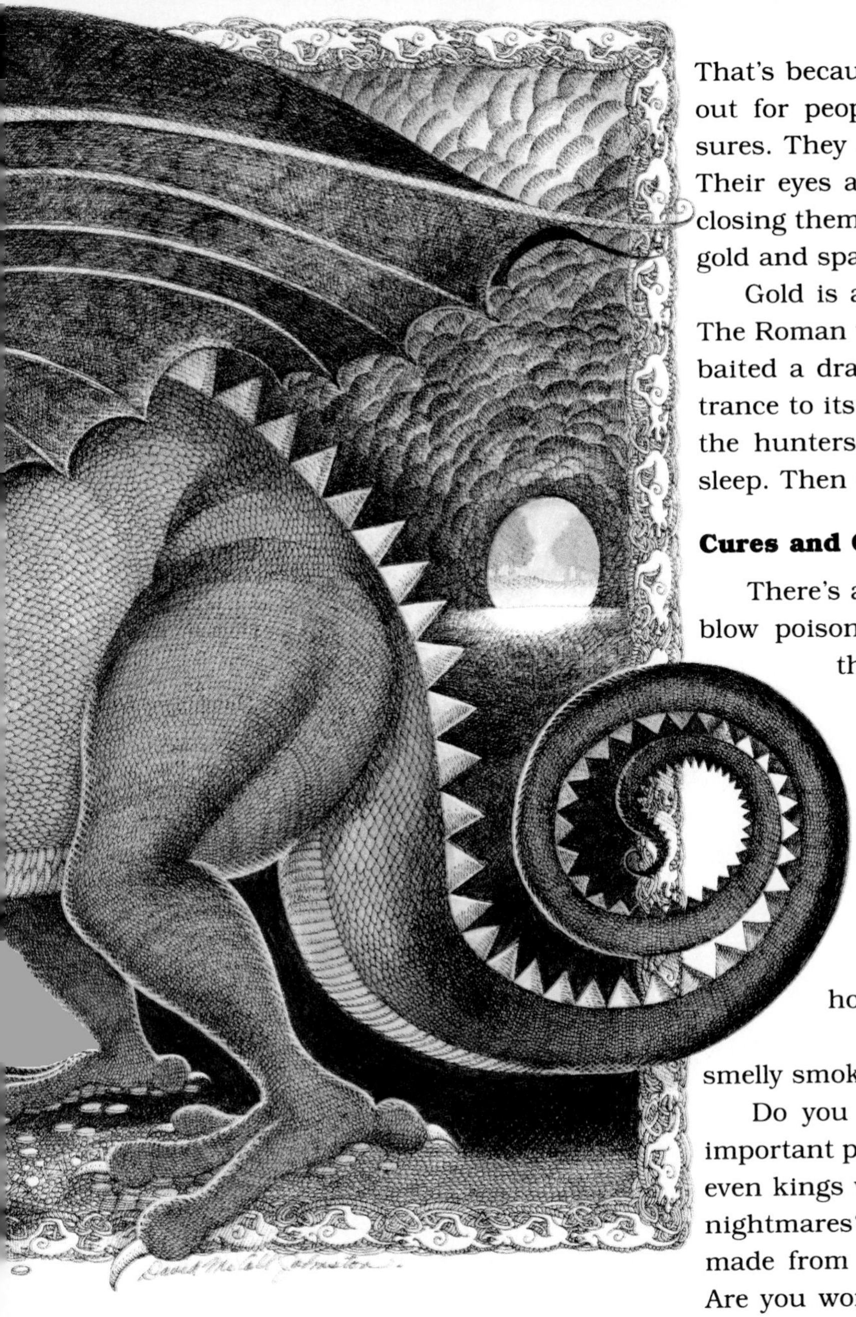

Hoarding Treasure

Western Dragons are miserable misers. Although they haven't any real use for money and jewels, they collect heaps of gold and gems. And they try to kill anyone coming near their hoard.

Miser dragons have bloodshot eyes. That's because they are always on the lookout for people who try to steal their treasures. They even sleep with their eyes open. Their eyes are red from the strain of never closing them, and from the glare of glittering gold and sparkling jewels.

Gold is a magnet that attracts dragons. The Roman writer Pliny relates that hunters baited a dragon by hanging gold at the entrance to its cave. When the beast came out, the hunters played soft music to lull it to sleep. Then they cut off its head.

Cures and Charms

There's a German saying, "A dragon can blow poison through stone walls, but not through knitted stockings." A few persons carried extra stockings to hold over their faces, in case they met a dragon. Most people used time-tested charms: salt and iron (also successful against witches and demons). They sprinkled salt around their houses, and nailed iron horseshoes over their doors. Burning bones and filth to make smelly smoke also drove dragons away.

Do you feel nervous about meeting an important person? Carry dragons' teeth, and even kings will be kind to you. Do you have nightmares? Rub yourself with an ointment made from dried dragons' eyes and honey. Are you worried about a lawsuit? Place the fat of a dragon's heart in the skin of a gazelle and tie it to your arm with deer muscle. You will win your case. This advice comes from the thirty-seven volume *Natural History* by Pliny, a first-century Roman. By mentioning that some dragons have a precious jewel inside their heads, he gave dragon hunting a boost for at least 1500 years.

PART II: EASTERN DRAGONS

Unlike the ugly, nasty, Western types, most Eastern Dragons are beautiful, friendly, and wise. They are the angels of the Orient. Instead of being hated, they are loved and worshiped. Temples and shrines have been built to honor them, for they control the rain, lakes, and seas.

Many Chinese cities have pagodas where people used to burn incense and pray to dragons. The Black Dragon Pool Chapel, near Peking, was reserved for the Empress and her court. Special worship services took place there on the first and fifteenth of every month.

Dragon shrines and altars can still be seen in many parts of the Far East. They are usually along seashores and riverbanks, because most Eastern Dragons live in water. The Isle of the Temple, in Japan's Inland Sea, has become a famous stopover for pilgrims who meditate and pray to dragons.

Everything connected with Eastern Dragons is blessed. The Year of the Dragon,

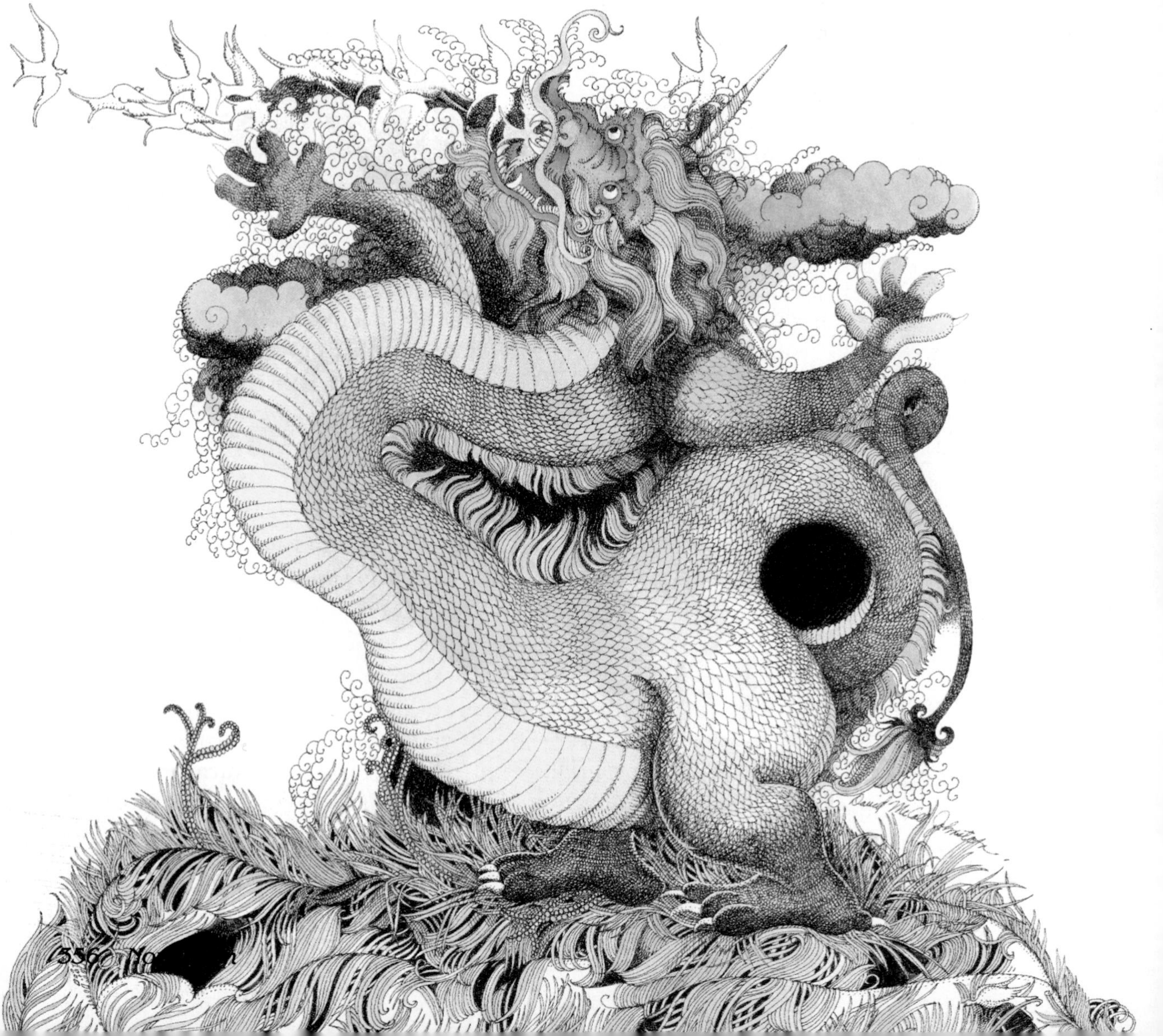

which takes place every twelve years, is lucky. Present-day Oriental astrologers claim that children born during Dragon Years enjoy health, wealth, and long life. (1964, 1976, and 1988 were Dragon Years.)

Dragons are so wise that they have been royal advisors. A thirteenth-century Cambodian king spent his nights in a golden tower, where he consulted with the real ruler of the land—a nine-headed dragon.

Eastern Dragons are vain, even though they are wise. They are insulted when a ruler doesn't follow their advice, or when people don't honor their importance. Then, by thrashing about, dragons either stop making rain and cause water shortages, or they breathe black clouds that bring storms and floods. Small dragons do minor mischief, such as making roofs leak, or causing rice to be sticky.

People set off firecrackers and carry immense paper dragons in special parades. They also race dragon-shaped boats in water—all to please and appease their dragons.

Physical Appearance

The ancient sage Wang Fu described an Eastern Dragon: "Its head is like a camel's, its ears like a cow's, its neck like a snake's, its belly like a frog's, its scales like a carp's,[4] its claws like an eagle's, and its paws like a tiger's." It has whiskers on the sides of its mouth and a bright pearl growing under its chin.

That's only one kind. Most Eastern Dragons have horns and whiskers, but their heads often resemble cows' or horses'. They never look like the horrible snake-dragons of the West. They rarely have wings, and they breathe clouds, not fire. Their voices sound like jingling coins, ringing bells, or clanging gongs.

Instead of wings, the dragon has a "poh shan," a growth on top of its head that pumps air in and out, lifting the creature high in the sky. Winds enable it to sail through the air. Some scholars claim that the pearl under its chin makes the dragon airborne, but how this works has never been explained.

There are odd-looking varieties. Horse-headed dragons have been showing up for at least 5,000 years. One specimen had wings at its side, and walked on top of the water. Another tossed its mane back and forth making noises that sounded like a flute.

Cow-heads are also common. A ten-footer, found lying on the banks of China's Yangtze River, was different from most because of its long, thick eyebrows. A Yellow River variety, seen on shore in the 1920's by a Chinese teacher, was bright blue, and as big as five cows. Both dragons crawled into the water as soon as it started to rain.

Size

Dragons are as small as silkworms and as large as mountains. Tiny ones may cluster under window ledges and on rooftops. It's possible to find them hiding in the seams of a robe.

There are almost as many Asiatic dragons as there are fish in the sea, and they come in all sizes.

Giant dragons are so big and powerful, they control the forces of nature. When they breathe, they make clouds; when they inhale water, they cause whirlpools. Underground dragons create hills by humping their backs.

---

4. carp (kärp) *n.*: A type of freshwater fish, including goldfish.

Supersized Oriental dragons are miles long. They are the biggest, grandest, most powerful animals in the whole world.

Habitat

Many dragons are year-round sea dwellers.

Land and sky dragons that don't like cold weather spend their winters at the bottom of the ocean. Their marineland vacation ends in the spring when they surface, and either float up to the sky, or go ashore. Autumn frosts have them hurrying back to their underwater homes. Whenever dragons enter and leave the sea, they disturb the air and water causing floods and hurricanes.

Every pond, lake, river, and stream has its resident dragons. Although numerous, they are rarely seen, because they're so shy that they sink when anybody watches them.

Thousands of Eastern Dragons make their homes inside mountains and under the ground. They don't like to be disturbed, and they can become so bad tempered that experts in "feng shui" are consulted before anyone digs in the soil. Feng shui is the art of placing graves, homes, and buildings in locations that won't bother dragons. Experts have a mysterious instinct for sensing just where underground dragon paths lie, even though these are out of sight. The paths must never be touched.

Diet

Bamboo, milk and cream, the flesh of swallows, and arsenic are favorite foods. Although to people it's a deadly poison, arsenic merely makes dragons fat.

In 1611 B.C., the Emperor of China appointed the Royal Dragon Feeder, whose duty was to throw food into sacred dragon ponds. Royal Dragon Feeder was an honored post for centuries.

The custom of feeding dragons was common throughout the Orient. According to the *Buddhist Records*, a dragon chapel on the banks of the Indus River had a copper vessel filled with cream for a white-eared river dragon.

As a rule, Eastern Dragons never eat people. But woe to anyone who dines on roasted swallows and rides in a boat. Dragons, detecting the scent of the digested birds, will overturn the boat and swallow the swallow-swallower.

Wise people never offer mong plants to dragons. Although mong is a delicious vegetable used in Oriental cooking, it makes dragons irritable. And when an Eastern Dragon is out of sorts, it can cause storms, floods, and earthquakes.

Enjoying Treasure

Like dragons all over the world, Eastern Dragons love jewels and precious stones. They prefer jade, coral, and pearls to gold, silver, and diamonds.

Unlike their Western cousins, Eastern Dragons are not misers. They make use of their treasure, wearing jewelry and building undersea palaces of coral and pearls. And they are so generous that they give gifts of gems to people lucky enough to meet them.

Unfortunately, although typical Eastern Dragons are gentle and giving, there are exceptions. Japanese pearl divers fear shark-dragons, which threaten to attack them as they work. Shark-dragons also patrol wrecked ships.

Nagas, the many-headed dragon snakes of India and Southeast Asia, can be killers. Although some Nagas aren't dangerous, most of them can't be trusted. They can be as nasty as Western Dragons. Nagas love to wear jewels and build palaces of gems. They are as skillful at jewel-craft as their Chinese relatives.

Cures and Charms

Dragon blood, fat, brains, saliva, teeth, and horns are miracle medicines curing everything from measles to madness. Dragon bones are the best remedies, and also easiest to find.

Until 1927 entire villages in China supported themselves by digging and selling dragon bones. Visiting scientists from the American Museum of Natural History were very upset when they saw warehouses filled with the bones, because they claimed that these were fossils of prehistoric animals. They bought and shipped huge quantities to their museum in New York City, and presented some to a museum in Peking. Thereafter, selling dragon-bone medicine was forbidden. However, an undercover dragon-bone business continues to cater to customers all over the Orient.

Here is a handy list of other useful products:

Dragon whiskers: for keeping flies and mosquitoes away; also a boon to fishermen, because they attract fish when placed in a stream. The best quality whiskers are three feet long, and deep purple.

Dragon saliva: an excellent ink for marking jade and gold; a base for the finest perfume and incense. The saliva is found floating on the ocean's surface.

Dragon meat: reserved for royal kitchens. Emperor Hwo ordered soup made from a dragon that fell on his palace grounds during a storm. He and his ministers enjoyed the broth. Emperor Chao handed his chefs a tusked dragon which he caught while fishing in the Wei River. The dragon was delicious "brain food." After eating it, Emperor Chao was able to write brilliant essays.

Dragon paths are more important than dragon products. To assure good fortune, locate your home, your business, and the family burial plot near underground dragon paths. Feng shui experts can be hired to advise you. They own round wooden compasses that point to the paths and they sometimes taste the soil before deciding upon a lucky site. People swear by them, but in some cases they swear at them.

In 1976 feng shui advisors were blamed when water pipes burst and elevators broke in a Hong Kong skyscraper. But feng shui experts must have a good record, for they have customers all over the world.

Some people are guided by the stars, others by dragon paths.

Reader's Response

Do you prefer western dragons or eastern dragons? Explain.

Responding to the Selection

Your Response

1. How do you feel about mythical monsters like dragons?

Recalling

2. Summarize the ways people used to protect themselves against western dragons.
3. Give three examples to show that eastern dragons have been treated with respect and admiration.

Interpreting

4. Why do you think the author chose this title? What is the truth about dragons?

Applying

5. Since dragons are not real, why do you think there are so many beliefs and so much information about them from all parts of the world?

Analyzing Literature

Understanding the Explanatory Essay

The purpose of an **explanatory essay** is to explain or inform. "The Truth About Dragons" is filled with specific information about these extraordinary, make-believe creatures.

1. Describe two dragons that were believed to have the features of common animals.
2. List two ways dragons were thought to affect wildlife.
3. List two ways dragons were thought to affect the weather.

Critical Thinking and Reading

Comparing and Contrasting

Comparing means finding ways in which things are alike. **Contrasting** means finding ways in which they are different. Western and eastern dragons are different in many ways, but they are similar in some ways. Compare and contrast them by making and completing a chart like the following.

	Western Dragons	Eastern Dragons
Main difference		
Size		
Sounds		
Attitude toward treasure		

Thinking and Writing

Writing an Explanatory Essay

Choose a real animal to write about. It might be one that can be kept as a pet or one that is found on a farm or in a zoo. It might be one that is on the endangered species list. First, list information about the animal: What does it look like? Where does it live? How does it get its food? What unusual things does it do? You may have to do some research to gather enough facts about the animal. Then write an explanatory essay called "The Truth About ________." Share your draft with a classmate and try to add any facts he or she thinks would improve your essay. Make a final copy.

Learning Option

Writing. Blumberg wrote about encounters that people had with make-believe dragons of long ago. How would a modern-day dragon behave? Write a brief description of a dragon that might exist today. What does this dragon look like? How does it act toward people? What does it eat? Use the cluster diagram that you developed in the Focus activity to help you write. Allow a friend to read your first draft. Use any helpful suggestions to write your final draft.

GUIDE FOR READING

Jesse Stuart

(1906–1984), Kentucky-born novelist, poet, and short-story writer, received the Thomas Jefferson Southern Award and the Academy of Arts and Sciences Award for his writing. *The Thread That Runs So True* was selected as the best book of 1949. According to *The Chicago Sunday Tribune,* Jesse Stuart's stories "all have a heart." "Old Ben" will tug at your heart as you read this recollection of a most unusual pet.

Old Ben

Narrative Essay

Some essays tell true stories. These are called **narrative essays**. The writer gives a brief and personal account of a subject that is important to him or her. This type of essay is like a selection from an autobiography. The writer, however, does not actually have to be the central character. The writer may focus on any character or characters, while including his or her own personal thoughts and feelings.

Focus

Old Ben is a snake. What are your feelings about snakes? Freewrite about the feelings you have about snakes. Include reasons for your feelings and any experiences you've had with snakes. As you read "Old Ben," see if your feelings about snakes match any of the character's feelings.

Vocabulary

Knowing the following words will help you as you read "Old Ben."

corncrib (kôrn′ krib′) *n.*: A structure used for storing corn (p. 363)

hayloft (hā′ lôft′) *n.*: An upper story in a barn or stable used for storing hay (p. 365)

partition (pär tish′ ən) *n.*: Something that separates or divides, such as an interior wall that separates one room from another (p. 366)

Spelling Tip

To spell *partition* correctly, remember this sentence: If you partition a room, you part it.

Old Ben

Jesse Stuart

"My father had always told me there was only one good snake—a dead one."

One morning in July when I was walking across a clover field to a sweet-apple tree, I almost stepped on him. There he lay coiled like heavy strands of black rope. He was a big bull blacksnake. We looked at each other a minute, and then I stuck the toe of my shoe up to his mouth. He drew his head back in a friendly way. He didn't want trouble. Had he shown the least fight, I would have soon finished him. My father had always told me there was only one good snake—a dead one.

When the big fellow didn't show any fight, I reached down and picked him up by the neck. When I lifted him he was as long as I was tall. That was six feet. I started calling him Old Ben as I held him by the neck and rubbed his back. He enjoying having his back rubbed and his head stroked. Then I lifted him into my arms. He was the first snake I'd ever been friendly with. I was afraid at first to let Old Ben wrap himself around me. I thought he might wrap himself around my neck and choke me.

The more I petted him, the more affectionate he became. He was so friendly I decided to trust him. I wrapped him around my neck a couple of times and let him loose. He crawled down one arm and went back to my neck, around and down the other arm and back again. He struck out his forked tongue to the sound of my voice as I talked to him.

"I wouldn't kill you at all," I said. "You're a friendly snake. I'm taking you home with me."

I headed home with Old Ben wrapped around my neck and shoulders. When I started over the hill by the pine grove, I met my cousin Wayne Holbrook coming up the hill. He stopped suddenly when he saw me. He started backing down the hill.

"He's a pet, Wayne," I said. "Don't be afraid of Old Ben."

It was a minute before Wayne could tell me what he wanted. He had come to borrow a plow. He kept a safe distance as we walked on together.

Before we reached the barn, Wayne got brave enough to touch Old Ben's long body.

"What are you going to do with him?" Wayne asked. "Uncle Mick won't let you keep him!"

"Put him in the corncrib," I said. "He'll have plenty of delicate food in there. The cats we keep at this barn have grown fat and lazy on the milk we feed 'em."

I opened the corncrib door and took Old Ben from around my neck because he was beginning to get warm and a little heavy.

"This will be your home," I said. "You'd better hide under the corn."

Besides my father, I knew Old Ben would have another enemy at our home. He was our hunting dog, Blackie, who would trail a snake, same as a possum or mink. He had treed blacksnakes, and my father had shot them from the trees. I knew Blackie would find Old Ben, because he followed us to the barn each morning.

The first morning after I'd put Old Ben in the corncrib, Blackie followed us. He started toward the corncrib holding his head high, sniffing. He stuck his nose up to a crack in the crib and began to bark. Then he tried to tear a plank off.

"Stop it, Blackie," Pa scolded him. "What's the matter with you? Have you taken to barking at mice?"

"Blackie is not barking at a mouse," I said. "I put a blacksnake in there yesterday!"

"A blacksnake?" Pa asked, looking unbelievingly. "A blacksnake?"

"Yes, a pet blacksnake," I said.

"Have you gone crazy?" he said. "I'll move a thousand bushels of corn to get that snake!"

"You won't mind this one," I said. "You and Mom will love him."

My father said a few unprintable words before we started back to the house. After breakfast, when Pa and Mom came to the barn, I was already there. I had opened the crib door and there was Old Ben. He'd crawled up front and was coiled on a sack. I put my hand down and he crawled up my arm to my neck and over my shoulder. When Mom and Pa reached the crib, I thought Pa was going to faint.

"He has a pet snake," Mom said.

"Won't be a bird or a young chicken left on this place," Pa said. "Every time I pick up an ear of corn in the crib, I'll be jumping."

"Pa, he won't hurt you," I said, patting the snake's head. "He's a natural pet, or somebody has tamed him. And he's not going to bother birds and young chickens when there are so many mice in this crib."

"Mick, let him keep the snake," Mom said. "I won't be afraid of it."

This was the beginning of a long friendship.

Mom went to the corncrib morning after morning and shelled corn for her geese and chickens. Often Old Ben would be lying in front on his burlap sack. Mom watched him at first from the corner of her eye. Later she didn't bother to watch him any more than she did a cat that came up for his milk.

Later it occurred to us that Old Ben might like milk, too. We started leaving milk for him. We never saw him drink it, but his pan was always empty when we returned. We know the mice didn't drink it, because he took care of them.

"One thing is certain," Mom said one morning when she went to shell corn. "We don't find any more corn chewed up by the mice and left on the floor."

July passed and August came. My father got used to Old Ben, but not until he had proved his worth. Ben had done something our nine cats couldn't. He had cleaned the corncrib of mice.

Then my father began to worry about Old Ben's going after water, and Blackie's finding his track. So he put water in the crib.

September came and went. We began wondering where our pet would go when days grew colder. One morning in early October we left milk for Old Ben, and it was there when we went back that afternoon. But Old Ben wasn't there.

"Old Ben's a good pet for the warm months," Pa said. "But in the winter months, my cats will have to do the work. Maybe Blackie got him!"

"He might have holed up for the winter in the hayloft," I told Pa after we had removed all the corn and didn't find him. "I'm worried about him. I've had a lot of pets—groundhogs, crows and hawks—but Old Ben's the best yet."

November, December, January, February, and March came and went. Of course we never expected to see Old Ben in one of those months. We doubted if we ever would see him again.

One day early in April I went to the corncrib, and Old Ben lay stretched across the floor. He looked taller than I was now. His skin was rough and his long body had a flabby appearance. I knew Old Ben needed mice and milk. I picked him up, petted him, and told him so. But the chill of early April was still with him. He got his tongue out slower to answer the kind words I was saying to him. He tried to crawl up my arm but he couldn't make it.

That spring and summer mice got scarce in the corncrib and Old Ben got daring. He went over to the barn and crawled up into the hayloft, where he had many feasts. But he made one mistake.

He crawled from the hayloft down into Fred's feed box, where it was cool. Old Fred was our horse.

There he lay coiled when the horse came in and put his nose down on top of Old Ben. Fred let out a big snort and started kicking. He kicked down a partition, and then turned his heels on his feed box and kicked it down. Lucky for Old Ben that he got out in one piece. But he got back to his crib.

Old Ben became a part of our barnyard family, a pet and darling of all. When children came to play with my brother and sisters, they always went to the crib and got Old Ben. He enjoyed the children, who were afraid of him at first but later learned to pet this kind old reptile.

Summer passed and the late days of September were very humid. Old Ben failed one morning to drink his milk. We knew it wasn't time for him to hole up for the winter.

We knew something had happened.

Pa and I moved the corn searching for him. Mom made a couple of trips to the barn lot to see if we had found him. But all we found was the rough skin he had shed last spring.

"Fred's never been very sociable with Old Ben since he got in his box that time," Pa said. "I wonder if he could have stomped Old Ben to death. Old Ben could've been crawling over the barn lot, and Fred saw his chance to get even!"

"We'll see," I said.

Pa and I left the crib and walked to the barn lot. He went one way and I went the other, each searching the ground.

Mom came through the gate and walked over where my father was looking. She started looking around, too.

"We think Fred might've got him," Pa said. "We're sure Fred's got it in for him over Old Ben getting in his feed box last summer."

"You're accusing Fred wrong," Mom said. "Here's Old Ben's track in the sand."

I ran over to where Mom had found the track. Pa went over to look, too.

"It's no use now," Pa said, softly. "Wouldn't have taken anything for that snake. I'll miss him on that burlap sack every morning when I come to feed the horses. Always looked up at me as if he understood."

The last trace Old Ben had left was in the corner of the lot near the hogpen. His track went straight to the woven wire fence and stopped.

"They've got him," Pa said. "Old Ben trusted everything and everybody. He went for a visit to the wrong place. He didn't last long among sixteen hogs. They go wild over a snake. Even a biting copperhead[1] can't stop a hog. There won't be a trace of Old Ben left."

We stood silently for a minute looking at the broad, smooth track Old Ben had left in the sand.

---

1. copperhead (käp′ ər hed′) *n.*: A poisonous snake.

Reader's Response

Have your feelings about snakes changed as a result of reading "Old Ben"? Explain.

Responding to the Selection

Your Response

1. What surprised you or interested you in this narrative essay?
2. What feelings did you experience in response to Old Ben's story?

Recalling

3. Describe Old Ben.
4. Why doesn't the narrator harm the snake when he first sees it?
5. List three examples of Old Ben's friendliness.

Interpreting

6. Compare the first reactions of Mom and Pa to Old Ben.
7. How is Old Ben helpful to the family?
8. Why is it a "mistake" for Old Ben to crawl into Fred's feed box?
9. How does the fact that Old Ben "trusted everything and everybody" lead to trouble?

Applying

10. The narrator says, "My father had always told me there was only one good snake—a dead one." Why do you think so many people have negative feelings about snakes?

Analyzing Literature

Understanding a Narrative Essay

A **narrative essay** is a brief, personal story. In this essay the focus is on Old Ben. We learn about Old Ben by what the writer says and feels about him and by the way others react to him.

1. Give specific examples from the essay to show that the narrator, his mother, and his father care about Old Ben.
2. Choose three words to describe Old Ben. Explain why you chose each word, citing examples from the story.
3. How does the narrator feel about Old Ben?

Critical Thinking and Reading

Observing and Inferring

An **inference** is a conclusion that you draw based on facts or clues. You can often form a conclusion after carefully observing what happens in a story. For each of the following situations, answer two questions: (1) What do you observe? (2) What conclusion can you make?

1. Wayne's feelings about Old Ben
2. Blackie's feelings about Old Ben
3. Old Ben's return in April

Thinking and Writing

Writing a Narrative Essay

Many popular television programs are about children and their pets. Pretend that you are submitting an idea for a new TV show. Write a brief narrative essay about the pet. It might be a pet of your own, one that belongs to a friend, or even an imaginary one. Begin by jotting down specific details to show why this pet is special. Then write your essay. Use specific verbs. Proofread your paper and write it over neatly. Finally, make up a name for this new television show and use it as the title of your essay.

Learning Options

1. **Writing.** Write an obituary for Old Ben. An obituary is a notice in the newspaper about someone's death. It usually includes a short biography of the deceased and his or her main achievements. After you have written the obituary, design a gravestone with a short poem or quotation to memorialize Old Ben.
2. **Cross-curricular Connection.** Find out more about blacksnakes at your school or local library. You may wish to call your local zoo to find out information. Find out where they live and what they eat. Present your findings to the class in an illustrated oral report.

GUIDE FOR READING

Katherine B. Shippen

(1892–1980) was a teacher who wrote her first book, *New Found World* (a Junior Literary Guild selection) when she was past fifty. "I'm very used to talking to young people and writing isn't very much different," she said. In addition to history and biography, she also wrote about medicine, aeronautics, and as in *Portals to the Past,* archaeology. In this selection from that work, you will learn about the many attempts to uncover the truth behind one of the world's great mysteries.

The Strange Geometry of Stonehenge

Descriptive Essay

A **descriptive essay** is a relatively short piece of nonfiction in which the author describes a particular subject. Whether describing people, scenery, or things, the writer uses colorful language and specific details to make the essay come alive. In this essay Shippen describes a collection of enormous stones arranged in the middle of an English countryside.

Focus

This essay describes Stonehenge—one of the greatest mysteries of all time. How do people uncover mysteries? One of the things they do is ask questions. Think of a topic that you would like to know more about. List questions you would like answered on this topic. As you read this selection, note the type of questions the researchers might have asked as they worked to unlock the mystery of Stonehenge.

Vocabulary

Knowing the following words will help you as you read "The Strange Geometry of Stonehenge."

geometry (jē äm′ ə trē) *n.*: The branch of mathematics that deals with shapes (p. 369)

immemorial (im′ me môr′ ē əl) *adj.*: Ancient; extending back before memory (p. 369)

recumbent (ri kum′ bənt) *adj.*: Lying down; leaning (p. 370)

colossal (kə läs′ əl) *adj.*: Huge; gigantic (p. 370)

obliterated (ə blit′ ər āt′ əd) *adj.*: Blotted out (p. 370)

encroaching (en krōch′ iŋ) *adj.*: Extending in a gradual way beyond limits (p. 370)

inscrutable (in skro͞ot′ ə b'l) *adj.*: Mysterious (p. 370)

antiquarian (an′ ti kwer′ ē ən) *n.*: A person who studies ancient works of art (p. 371)

Spelling Tip

To spell *encroaching,* remember this rule, "When two vowels go walking, the first one does the talking." In other words, the *o* is the one you sound, so it comes before the *a*.

The Strange Geometry of Stonehenge

Katherine B. Shippen

"Rough, colossal, inscrutable, the strange geometric pattern kept its secrets through the passing centuries."

In 1918 Sir Cecil Chubb of Salisbury[1] made a unique gift to the English government. The gift was Stonehenge, a group of rough-hewn stones that stand on the chalk downs[2] of Salisbury Plain. When he presented them to England, Sir Cecil did not know exactly what he was giving. He did not know how these stones came to be in the middle of the plain, or who had dragged them there, or why they were arranged as they were. The only thing he knew was that they had stood there since time immemorial.

The huge cluster of upright stones which he had given his country stands in the center of a level circular space 300 feet wide, surrounded by a ditch and an earthwork. A grassy road which is now called "the Avenue" enters this space from the northeast and a single rough boulder called the "Hele Stone" stands in the center of this road.

Within the outer circle the stones are carefully arranged in four series. First there is a circle of enormous "sarsen" stones, some of them 13 feet tall and weighing more than 40 tons. (The word "sarsen," which comes from "Saracen," meant anything heathenish to the people of the Middle Ages. None but

1. Salisbury (sôlz′ ber ē): City in south central England.
2. chalk downs: Areas of open, grassy plains situated over limestone (chalky) deposits.

the devil himself could have moved them, it was said.) Originally the sarsens in this great circle were joined by a line of lintels[3] fastened with crude stone tenons and mortises.[4]

With the passing of time, winds and storms have blown down the lintels. Some of them still lie on the ground. The stones of the circle inside the first are somewhat smaller and of a different kind. They are "bluestones."

Inside the bluestone circle there are sarsen stones again, and here they are arranged in a big horseshoe. The stones of the horseshoe have been put up in pairs, each pair topped by a stone lintel. Each group forms a trilithon.[5]

The trilithons are graduated in size; the tallest one, which stands opposite the opening of the horseshoe, is more than 22 feet high, with a lintel 16 feet long and 4 feet thick. Only two trilithons are standing today; originally there were probably eleven.

Finally, inside the horseshoe there are more bluestones, but only a few of them. Enough remain, however, to show that they were once arranged in an oval pattern.

At the heart of it all is a great recumbent stone which generations of men have called the "Altar Stone." But whether or not it was an altar, or for what god it was made, no one can say.

What did it mean, this gigantic exercise in geometry, these circles within circles, this colossal horseshoe? Who came here in the days when the patterns of these rocks were understood? What did they do here? Once a wide road led across the down to this place, a highway broad enough for glittering processions—but processions of whom? Were they soldiers? Or priests? Unused as the ages passed, the highway nearly disappeared, obliterated by the encroaching grass. Only very recently were the vague outlines of the road found again by the penetrating eye of a camera carried in an airplane.

Rough, colossal, inscrutable, the strange geometric pattern kept its secrets through the passing centuries. Legends about it have abounded. Some said the wizard Merlin[6] got the devil to whisk these stones from Ireland in a single night. Others said that Queen Boadicea[7] was buried here. A brave and beautiful British woman, she died leading her people in a revolt against the Roman legions. But there was nothing to prove that this was her monument.

Again it was said that this was a monument for Hengist and Horsa,[8] who had come from Jutland to help fight off the Picts and Scots[9] and had stayed to conquer the country for themselves. But nothing remains to show that Hengist and Horsa were buried there, either.

King James I[10] in the seventeenth century apparently wanted to have done with legends. He sent his architect Inigo Jones to

---

3. lintels (lint′ əls) *n.*: Horizontal crosspieces over a door or some other opening.

4. tenons (ten′ əns) **and mortises** (môr′ tis ez): Joints made by fitting extending parts (tenons) into adjoining holes (mortises).

5. trilithon (tri lith′ än) *n.*: Group of three stones, consisting of two uprights with the third as a lintel across the top.

6. Merlin (mur′ lin): In the legends of King Arthur, a magician and advisor to King Arthur.

7. Queen Boadicea (bō′ ad ə sē′ ə): Queen of a tribe in ancient Britain who died in A.D. 62.

8. Hengist (hen′ gist) **and Horsa:** Brothers who were chiefs of a tribe that had come from Jutland (now Denmark). They died in A.D. 488 and 455, respectively.

9. Picts and Scots: People of ancient Great Britain who were driven into Scotland by the Britons and the Romans.

10. James I: King of England from 1603–1625.

examine Stonehenge. Inigo Jones announced that without any doubt it was a Roman temple.

But the theory of Roman origin for the structure did not content the patriotic English. Charles II[11] asked John Aubrey, a noted antiquarian, to investigate further. Aubrey lived not far from Stonehenge in Avebury, where there was another large circle of standing stones. It was generally believed that those stones marked the meeting place of the Druids,[12] the mysterious bards[13] and priests who had been such a powerful influence in England at the time of the Roman occupation. Stonehenge was built by the Druids too, Aubrey announced.

The more he investigated, the more Aubrey was sure the Druids had built Stonehenge. The Roman writers with whose work he was familiar had described the Druid ceremonies; it was said the Druids were accus-

11. Charles II: King of England, Scotland, and Ireland from 1660–1685.

12. Druids (dro͞o′ idz): Members of an order of priests in ancient Britain, who appear in legends as prophets and sorcerers.

13. bards (bärds) *n.*: Poets and singers.

tomed to performing human sacrifices. Did they slaughter their victims here on the Altar Stone? Examining the earth inside the great circle enclosed by the ditch and earthwork, Aubrey found a series of depressions in the ground. Undoubtedly these had been deeper holes which time had filled with silt[14] and earth. Had the Druids once burned the bodies of their victims in these holes? The "Aubrey Holes" fired the imagination of all who came to Stonehenge now, and seemed to make it more certain that Stonehenge had been built by the Druids.

William Stukely, Secretary of the Society of Antiquaries in 1718, was as sure as anyone else that the Druids had built Stonehenge. He was a doctor of medicine but he was also a minister of the Christian Church, and he was greatly interested in trying to reconcile the Druids' beliefs with the Christians'. Perhaps the Druids had not been so savage, after all, he said; the only accounts of them were those written by the Romans who wanted to eradicate them. Stukely considered the Druids poets and moral teachers, and he rehearsed all the traditions that made the oak tree and the mistletoe sacred to them. There was no doubt in his mind that they had constructed Stonehenge, as he went methodically making the first survey of the place.

Now no one thought of any other origin for Stonehenge, and when in the eighteenth century people became interested in the esoteric wisdom of the East, it was maintained that the Druids were astrologers and that Stonehenge was a stellar[15] observatory. But there was no more to prove this than that it had been Boadicea's tomb.

The years passed and Stonehenge continued to hold a fascination for antiquarians, who tried again and again to understand it. In the nineteenth century a "Mr. Cunnington" made a great effort but had no success. Sure that he would not be the last one to seek an explanation for the great stones, he hid a bottle of good port wine under the Altar Stone for the refreshment of those who came after. It was not found again till 1920. And all this time people were more and more sure that Stonehenge had been built by the Druids.

Archeological methods took a great step forward in the twentieth century, and various sciences were now joined together in investigation. Astronomy was one of these.

For some time it had been observed that if you stood behind the Altar Stone at dawn on Midsummer Day and looked straight through the great horseshoe and along the Avenue you would see the sun come up behind the Hele Stone. Scholars believed this orientation proved that the great design must have been made by sun worshipers. Sir Norman Lockyer, the British Royal Astronomer, was much interested in this. It was known that with the slightly irregular movement of the earth the exact point at which the sun rises on a given date each year varies slightly, and by precise calculations it is possible to determine exactly how much. If Stonehenge was oriented to the rising sun on Midsummer Day, it would be possible to find out by astronomical calculations in what year it was built.

In 1901 Sir Norman made these astronomical calculations. Stonehenge was built at a date "lying between 1900 and 1500

14. silt (silt) *n.*: Particles of sand, rock, and so forth, that accumulate on the bottom of rivers or other bodies of water.

15. stellar (stel' ər): *adj.*: Of the stars.

B.C.," he announced. But that was a thousand years before anyone ever mentioned Druids in England. If Sir Norman's conclusions were right, the whole fabric of the belief in the Druid construction of Stonehenge was destroyed. And those who looked up at the mammoth stones were more than ever at a loss to understand them.

Astronomy was not the only tool that was used to banish the idea that the Druids had built Stonehenge. While Sir Norman was working out the year in which the sun first rose over the Altar Stone, an archeologist named Gowland began to excavate. He dug carefully at six different points so that he could compare the things he found at one place with those he found at another. As he dug he noted the exact depth of every man-made object that he found. In all six places there were coins in the first ten-inch layer—a penny of George III, a half-penny of George I, a pewter farthing of James II[16]—and below these were coins of Roman date.

Now Gowland dug deeper. Two or three feet down he found tools of flint, then axes and hammerstones of sandstone, and finally massive pounding hammers, or mauls—the tools that had pounded the great menhirs[17] of Stonehenge into shape. But these were

16. a penny . . . James II: Coins of Great Britain dating from about 1685–1820. King George III was king from 1760–1820, George I from 1714–1727, and James II from 1685–1688.

17. menhirs (men′ hirs) *n.*: Huge, rough, upright stones.

not all. At last, near one of the trilithons, he found a chip of sarsen stone with a small green stain of oxidized copper. This artifact indicated that the builders had lived in the Bronze Age.[18]

Astronomy and archeology had now confirmed each other. Stonehenge had not been built by the Druids, but a thousand years before their time. In 1950 this date was established in a third way, for charcoal dug from one of the Aubrey Holes confirmed it. Carbon-14 dating[19] placed the construction at 1847 B.C., with a possible variation of 225 years.

So the cool, precise work of the scientists put an end to legends and superstitions. There could be no more talk of Druids at Stonehenge now. Nevertheless, the ancient structure was as mysterious as it had ever been. Whence had the great stones come? Why were they of two different kinds?

Geology was another science that helped find an answer to these questions. Geological study now proved that the sarsen stones of gray sandstone must have been brought from the Marlborough Downs 24 miles away. But the bluestones were another matter. The nearest place that bluestone was to be found was in the Prescelly mountains in South Wales, 150 miles from Stonehenge. Why these stones were chosen, and how they were transported over the hills and valleys, and across the rivers, no one has been able to say.

Stuart Piggott, an eminent British archeologist, is working at Stonehenge now. He started to excavate in 1950, carefully leaving more than half the area untouched, for he held that the diggers of the future would

---

18. Bronze Age: Period of time from about 3500 to about 1000 B.C.

19. Carbon-14 dating: Method of dating archeological finds by measuring the amount of radioactive carbon-14 remaining in them.

undoubtedly develop techniques superior to his own and he did not want to spoil their work.

After working some time Piggott announced that the earthworks and big stone circles and the horseshoe were not all put up at the same time. Successive groups came and went, he held, building and destroying and building up again over a period of about four hundred years. He thought the ditch and earthwork, the circle of Aubrey Holes, the Avenue, and the Hele Stone were all part of the original construction built about 1847 B.C. Another group of people made the two rings of bluestones, and later the huge sarsen circle and the trilithon horseshoe were put up. These were the last to be built, and they were made about 1500 B.C.

In all three phases the line between the center of the Altar Stone and the center of the Hele Stone was preserved, proving that all the builders had been sun worshipers and that this was not a monument or a meeting place, but a temple to the sun.

Up to 1953 no more could be found out about Stonehenge and its builders, even with the most modern scientific research. And then, by accident, a new discovery was made. It was late on a June afternoon, and the sun's rays were striking the surface of one of the sarsens obliquely. They cast small shadows wherever there were scratches or indentations on the stone's surface. One of the excavators noticed what seemed to be a pattern scratched on the stone. He looked more closely and observed that two images had been cut there. One was that of an ax. Its form was familiar enough, for many axes of this type had been uncovered in digging around the sarsens. But the other image was startling. For there, neatly etched, was a dagger—a dagger with a round handle and a long pointed blade. The English had never used daggers of this kind. This was the sort of weapon carried by the Mycenaean Greeks who influenced the culture of the Eastern Mediterranean at the time of the Trojan war.[20] This finding seemed to indicate that the builders of Stonehenge had gone to the Eastern Mediterranean to employ an architect. Here, carved on the stone, was his symbol.

With the finding of the dagger other facts that had been casually observed became significant. There was, for instance, the shape of the sarsens; they bulged slightly, just as the pillars of the Greek temples did. And there was the technique of shaping the stone blocks. They had been banged with the heavy stone mauls which had been found in the ground near them. The granite obelisks[21] of Egypt had been fashioned in exactly the same way.

Was it an architect from the Eastern Mediterranean who was commissioned to design Stonehenge? Did the fame of the Mycenaean Greek builders extend all the way to Britain thirty-five hundred years ago? Was their reputation so great the Britons wanted a "foreigner" to design their precious temple to the sun? The sun itself, striking the stone with the slanting rays of the late afternoon, had posed new questions.

Reader's Response

Which explanation for the existence of Stonehenge do you find most interesting? Why?

---

20. Trojan War: In Greek legend, the war waged against Troy by the Greeks; it took place from 1260–1250 B.C.

21. obelisks (äb′ ə lisks) *n.*: Tall, slender, four-sided stone pillars tapering toward their tops, which are shaped like pyramids.

Responding to the Selection

Your Response

1. What more would you like to know about Stonehenge after reading this article?

Recalling

2. What are the "sarsen stones"?
3. Describe the "bluestones."

Interpreting

4. Why is Stonehenge referred to as a "gigantic exercise in geometry"?
5. How did Sir Norman's new evidence add to the mystery of Stonehenge?
6. Contrast the two images that were discovered by accident in 1953.
7. Reread the last paragraph. What does it suggest about Stonehenge?

Applying

8. It has been said that the more we learn, the more we realize how little we really know. How does this apply to Stonehenge? Has this ever been true in your life? Explain.

Analyzing Literature

Understanding a Descriptive Essay

A **descriptive essay** draws a picture in words. It includes lively, colorful language and specific details to describe its subject. After reading Katherine Shippen's description of the "rough-hewn stones," you should have a clear picture of Stonehenge.

1. The author says, "A grassy road . . . enters this space from the northeast and a single rough boulder . . . stands in the center of this road." Find two more examples of specific detail in the essay.
2. Katherine Shippen says that "the penetrating eye of a camera" revealed the hidden road. Why is this wording better than saying that "the photographs" revealed the hidden road?

Critical Thinking and Reading

Drawing Conclusions From Evidence

A **conclusion** is an idea that follows logically from another idea or group of ideas. There have been many conclusions about Stonehenge stated over the years. To be believable, a conclusion must be supported by evidence. Evidence is factual information. What evidence is there to support each of the following conclusions? How believable is each conclusion?

1. Queen Boadicea is buried in Stonehenge.
2. Stonehenge was built by the Druids.
3. Stonehenge was built between 1900 and 1500 B.C., during the Bronze Age.
4. Builders of Stonehenge had gone to the Eastern Mediterranean to find an architect.

Thinking and Writing

Writing a Descriptive Essay

Pretend that you have been digging in the ground of a vacant lot. Suddenly your shovel hits something hard and you begin digging faster. You have uncovered something amazing! Describe what you have found. Use specific details to give a clear picture. Offer a possible explanation for what you have found. Test your word picture by asking a classmate to read your essay and then draw a picture of your discovery. Did your reader "get the picture"? If not, bring the fuzzy parts into focus by adding more specific details.

Learning Option

Art. Based on the detailed description that Shippen gives in her essay, make a map of Stonehenge. Use Shippen's explanations of what the different types of stone structures look like and even the direction that Stonehenge faces. Make a legend that includes symbols for the different types of stones. Be sure to include a direction indicator on your map.

Writing to Inform

"How can I find your cousin's house?" "How do you make these wonderful cookies?" "What do you know about Argentina?" The answers to all these questions would provide information or an explanation. If the answers were written down, they would all be examples of informative writing.

Readers sometimes fear that informative writing is dull writing. That's not so if it's effective writing. Does Jesse Stuart's "Old Ben" bore you? How could it! Not only do you learn important and interesting information about blacksnakes, but you also read the moving tale of the family's pet. Do you yawn through "The Truth About Dragons"? More likely you chuckle at Rhoda Blumberg's detailed descriptions and laugh at how people create "dragons" to take the blame for unexplained events. After all, effective writing captures its readers' interest—regardless of its purpose.

Your Turn

Write a composition that informs. Your purpose is to interest readers and inform them about your topic. If you entertain them, too, that's fine.

Prewriting

1. Brainstorm for topic possibilities. Pick something you know more about than most of your readers. Don't bore readers with what they already know. List at least three possibilities for each of the following categories:

Any imaginary or real creatures about which you know a lot. For example, do you know about elves that play tricks on your family? Does a bathroom elf steal caps from toothpaste tubes and a kitchen elf put used cups in the sink?

Any true story that has a beginning, middle, and end. Then your structure is built in. If you choose a story you've already enjoyed sharing with friends, you'll already have "composed" early drafts. Examples include stories around a family pet, a holiday, trip, or memorable event. Also, this is a foolproof way to find a topic nobody else knows about, since it's your own experience.

Any other topic. Think about when your friends have said, "Wow, you know a lot about that" or "I wish I knew as much about that as you do."

2. Choose a topic. Look at your list of possibilities. Put a star by the two or three topics you know best. Put a star by the two or three topics about which your classmates would most enjoy reading. Put a star by another two or three best topics. Then look at your starred topics. Pick one for your writing topic.

3. Gather and organize information. Use a graphic organizer. Use a time line such as the one that follows if your topic has a beginning, middle, and end, or if it's a how-to-do-something topic. Draw the time line on a single sheet of paper turned horizontally. Along the line, insert all information that might be important. Later you will pick which information to use.

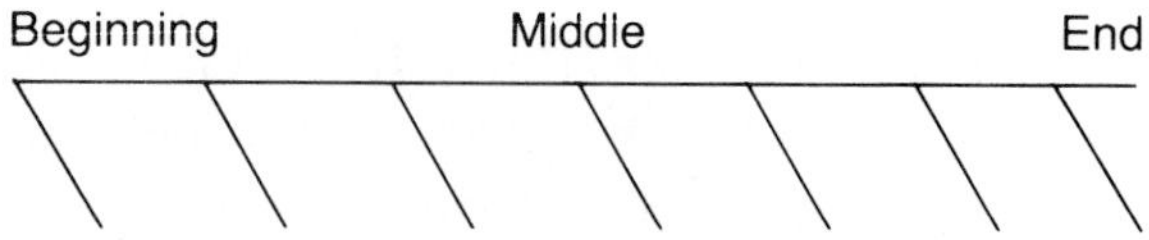

Use a cluster diagram if you have decided to write about a person, place, or thing.

Drafting

Use information from your time line or cluster diagram to compose a first draft. Choose only important and interesting details. Constantly ask yourself, "Is this really important?" "Is this really interesting?" If not, don't use it. If it's already in, cross it out. If you think of other details to add, add them. Be flexible. Here's one student's early draft:

> Would you like to know about the different kind of elves there are? Some people think elves are imaginary, but I insist they're not. Elves are actually living among us as you read this! They seem to live in little families in different rooms in our house. Just yesterday I walked into the bathroom, and there on the floor was a dirty hand towel. I knew a bathroom elf had struck again. What a pain! Sometimes, my brother or I actually get blamed for what the bathroom elf does. That elf also. . . .

Revising

Use the revision checklist on page 751. In addition, read your draft aloud to a writing partner and ask questions such as the following ones:

- What's your first reaction to this?
- What's the most interesting part of this composition? Why is it most interesting?
- What's the least interesting part? Explain. Do you think I should leave it out or should I fix it up? How might I fix it?
- What have you learned about my subject?
- Do you have enough information to feel informed? If not, what do you need to hear more about?
- Do you need to have anything clarified?

You might wish to trade papers with your partner and respond in writing.

Proofreading

Consult the guidelines on page 753 for proofreading. Remember to see that you start new paragraphs often enough. Then make a final copy. If illustrations will make your paper more effective, go ahead and illustrate it.

Reading Essays in the Content Areas

THE ARTIST'S DAUGHTER
Frederick Carl Frieseke
Brooklyn Museum

GUIDE FOR READING

Hattie Clark

(1930–) grew up in the small Ohio town of Cuyahoga Falls. Clark wrote feature stories for a newspaper and taught in Native American schools in the Southwest. Later, she wrote for the *Christian Science Monitor* newspaper at both the Boston and Chicago bureaus. "Raising my sons, Keith and Wyn, has been my major accomplishment," Clark says. Raising her sons also gave Clark an interest in writing for children. Some of her work, including this selection, has appeared in the children's magazine *Highlights*.

Paul Klee

Setting a Purpose for Reading

A **purpose** is a reason for doing something. Setting a purpose before you begin reading will help you in many ways. It will focus your attention while you read. It will help you remember what you have read. It will help you be sure you understand what you read. One way to set a purpose is to ask questions. You can start with a reporter's classic questions: Who? What? When? Where? Why? and How?

Look at the essay you are about to read. You will see that it is about an artist, Paul Klee. Be sure to look at his puppet and painting (pages 381 and 382). Glancing at them before you begin will give you a general sense of his art. Form the questions in your mind. You might wonder who Paul Klee was, what he did, when and where he lived, how he lived and worked, and why his work is appreciated.

Focus

The illustrations that accompany this essay show that Paul Klee was an imaginative artist. To help you form questions about Klee and his work, make a cluster diagram about the puppet and the painting. Write the word *puppet* or *painting* in the center of a sheet of paper. Then, jot down all the words and phrases that come to mind as you look at these illustrations. As you read the essay, add more phrases to your cluster diagram.

Vocabulary

Knowing the following words will help you as you read "Paul Klee."

complex (käm pleks′) *adj.*: Not simple; complicated (p. 382)

meander (mē an′ dər) *v.*: Wander aimlessly; ramble (p. 382)

Spelling Tip

In the word *complex,* the *ks* sound is spelled with an *x.*

Paul Klee[1]

Hattie Clark

". . . his imagination always turned cartwheels and played with clouds."

Take a long look at the paintings and the puppets on these pages.

Ah, they were done by a little kid, you say.

Your guess couldn't be more wrong. These works are the creative products of Paul Klee. This artist, who spent much of his life in Switzerland, lived from 1879 to 1940.

Klee was a master at line drawing and painting. Sometimes his lines were slender as a spider's web, sometimes as thick as a little finger. He made his lines slide, skitter, and squiggle across the canvas. But he never let them go too far. He never stopped them too soon. Nor did he let his lines stray. Klee made both his lines and his colors the servants of his ideas.

Many artists paint what they see around them, but Klee painted what he saw *within* his imagination. And his imagination was a castle filled with treasures . . . with clowns and gardens . . . with birds and beasts and make-believe creatures . . . with moons and funny machines, and even ghosts. These fantastic forms fill his paintings. And his paintings are sprinkled with humor, because humor was at the core of Klee's being.

At the same time he was deeply serious. He put into his painting his intense feelings about human life and what was going on in the world.

Puppet by Paul Klee

1. **Paul Klee** (klā)

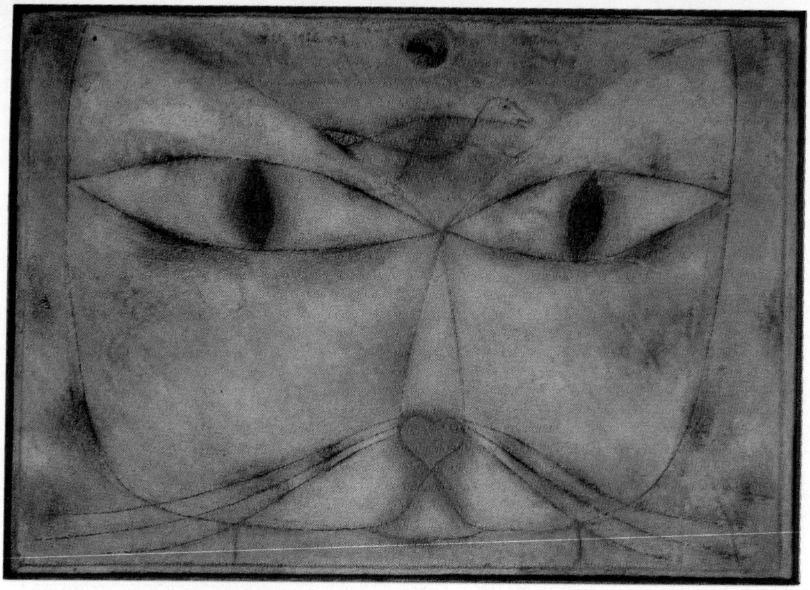

CAT AND BIRD
Paul Klee
Sidney and Harriet Janis Collection
Museum of Modern Art, New York

Three-year-olds put their ideas and feelings into their artwork, too. But not in the same way as Klee. A young child usually works quite quickly. But Klee worked slowly. His paintings were built idea by idea, line by line. Sometimes he sat for hours without painting a stroke. And often he worked on several paintings at once. When he was finally finished, complex ideas had been carefully worked into his canvasses.

In Klee's studio there was a table littered with what some would call clutter. But to him, they were objects of beauty, objects that triggered his imagination: a bird's egg, a pine cone, an odd-shaped root, coral, wire, wood, scraps of cloth.

Many such "finds" went into decorating the puppets that Klee made for his son, Felix. The first eight were given to Felix on his ninth birthday. In all, Klee created about fifty puppets from papier mâché[2] and plaster.

Among the puppets were a grandmother, a farmer, a policeman, a clown, a monk, and a ghost who was supposed to have escaped from an electrical outlet. Felix and his father spent many wonderful hours with these strange and wonderful "people."

Whether Klee made puppets or paintings, his imagination always turned cartwheels and played with clouds. Why not start your imagination working? Take a line for a walk as Klee did. Put your pencil on a paper. Draw a line. Make your line skip. Now run. Lead your line into an imaginary valley, over a mountain, and through a stream. Your line meets another line. Now you have two lines to work with. Together they meander through a forest. They hurry past a monster. Don't quit now. Keep going . . . going . . . going.

Reader's Response
What do you think of Klee's art?

---

2. papier-mâché (pā′ pər mə shā′) *n.*: A material made of paper pulp mixed with glue that is easily molded when moist and that dries strong and hard.

Responding to the Selection

Your Response

1. If you were an artist, what would you choose as subjects? Why?
2. What questions would you have asked Paul Klee if you could have met him?

Recalling

3. Where did Klee find his inspiration and subjects?
4. Describe Klee's working methods.

Interpreting

5. Explain how, according to Clark, Klee's artwork differs from a child's.
6. Do you agree or disagree with Clark's statement that humor figures prominently in Klee's painting? Why?
7. What evidence supports Clark's statement that Klee "put into his painting his intense feelings about human life"?

Applying

8. Try following the suggestion at the end of the essay. Then interpret your drawing, explaining what thoughts influenced it.

Reading in the Content Areas

Setting a Purpose for Reading

One way to set a purpose for your reading is to ask the questions a reporter would ask: Who? What? When? Where? Why? and How? After using this method with this essay about Paul Klee, you should have the answers to the following questions.

1. Who was Paul Klee?
2. What type of painting did he do?
3. When did Klee live?
4. Where did Paul Klee live and work?
5. Why is Klee's work highly regarded?
6. How did Klee work?

Critical Thinking and Reading

Comparing and Contrasting Pieces of Art

Comparing works of art means looking at their similarities. **Contrasting** them is examining their differences. Comparing works by the same artist will give you insight into the artist's underlying ideas, feelings, attitudes, and style. Contrasting them will help you appreciate each work as a unique expression. Study the puppet and the painting by Paul Klee. Then compare and contrast them according to the following instructions.

1. Compare the subjects of the puppet and the painting. How is the puppet similar to the subject of the painting?
2. Contrast the subjects of the puppet and the painting. How are they different?

Thinking and Writing

Writing About Art

Working in a group with your classmates, discuss your reactions to Klee's puppet and painting. Begin by discussing your comparisons and contrasts between the two works. Then discuss the works, using the following aspects: materials, style, and methods. Use what you learn from the discussion to write a brief statement of your opinion of Klee's work. Get together again with your group to hear the writers read their work.

Learning Option

Art. In the final paragraph of the essay, Hattie Clark suggests how you can start your imagination working. Try the techniques that she presents to create an illustration. When you have finished, write a brief explanation of how the techniques worked for you. Ask your teacher to post your illustration and explanation on the bulletin board or wall.

GUIDE FOR READING

Carrol Alice Stout

(1904–) was born in Loveland, Colorado, and attended Colorado State Teachers College. She started teaching in a rural Colorado school. After fifteen years she moved to California, continued teaching, and became principal of a school there. After her retirement Stout started writing a family history, as well as articles like "The Giants of Easter Island." "Writing makes my retirement more interesting," she says.

The Giants of Easter Island

Taking Notes

Taking notes will help you remember the most important information from your reading—if your notes are good. Before you start to take notes, look over the selection to get a general idea of it. Then read the piece carefully. When you take notes, you select important points and key details and write them down. You omit everything else. Often, these points will be signaled by words and phrases, such as *in conclusion, most important,* and *the causes of.* Do not use complete sentences. Leave out articles (the words *a, an, the*), and use abbreviations. Review your notes after writing them so that you will remember them.

Focus

Suppose that you have been sailing across the Pacific Ocean. One day, you come upon an isolated island. All along the shoreline, you see enormous stone heads like the ones pictured on page 387. Brainstorm with a small group of classmates about the origin, meaning, and purpose of these heads. As you read this selection, see how your guesses match what scientists know.

Vocabulary

Knowing the following words will help you as you read "The Giants of Easter Island."

primitive (prim′ i tiv) *adj.*: Having simplicity suggesting the earliest times (p. 385)

archeologist (är′ kē äl′ ə jist) *n.*: A scientist who studies evidence of the life and culture of ancient peoples (p. 385)

elevated (el′ ə vāt′ id) *adj.*: Lifted up (p. 388)

anthropology (an′ thrō päl′ ə jē) *n.*: The scientific study of the physical and cultural development of human beings (p. 388)

Spelling Tip

Notice that the *k* sound in archeology is spelled *ch.*

The Giants of Easter Island

Carrol Alice Stout

"For more than two hundred years, scientists have wondered how the huge statues—some weighing as much as twenty-five tons—had been carved with primitive tools and moved across the island."

When the stone carvers had "released" the giant *moai*[1] from the rock atop the dead volcano, the workmen laid down their stone picks and returned to their village, about four miles across the small Pacific Ocean island. Then the twelve-foot-high moai, or statue, "came to life," walked across the island, and climbed onto a stone platform that had been built for it near the village.

That was the story the people on Easter Island told the Norwegian archeologist Thor Heyerdahl when, in the 1950's, he led an expedition to investigate the mysterious stone statues found there. For more than two hundred years, scientists have wondered how the huge statues—some weighing as much as twenty-five tons—had been carved with primitive tools and moved across the island.

The story didn't make sense, though. Statues don't "come to life." Besides, these long-nosed, long-eared, blank-eyed statues with long-fingered hands clasped under their stomachs had no legs!

When the Dutch admiral Jacob Roggeveen[2] "discovered" the island on Easter Sunday in 1722, he saw many of these statues

1. ***moai*** (mō' ī) *n.*: Giant stone statues.

2. **Jacob Roggeveen** (räg' ə vēn')

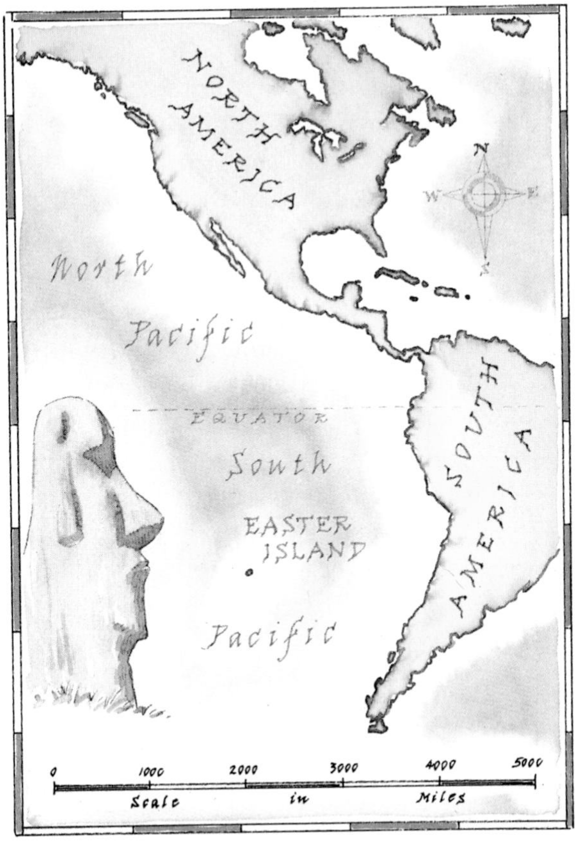

standing on platforms of stone. Fifty-two years later, when the English explorer Captain James Cook visited Easter Island, most of the statues lay face down at the base of their platforms. Cook also noticed that the people of the island did not seem as lively and healthy as Roggeveen had reported them to be.

When Heyerdahl's expedition got there, no statues were standing. For months the scientists and helpers in his expedition examined the statues and looked for clues to the past. They found that people had lived on the island much earlier than most scientists had believed. Wood from a statue platform was dated by the carbon-14 method.[3] The test showed that the platform had been built sometime between nine hundred and thirteen hundred years ago.

Almost three hundred years ago, according to legends and to clues that have been found, a war took place on the island. One of the two groups of people who lived on the island was wiped out except for one man. This group was known as the "long ears" because of their custom of lengthening their ear lobes by making holes in them and putting in weights.

Heyerdahl made friends with the island's mayor, Pedro Atán. Atán said that he was descended from the only long ear to survive the war, a man named Ororoine. Heyerdahl asked Atán if he knew how the statues were carved.

"Yes," he said. "I will carve you a statue. My relatives and I. Only a real long ear can carve a statue."

Many people in the camp didn't think that the mayor could keep his promise, but Heyerdahl believed him. Late the following night, Heyerdahl sat in his tent with two companions talking about their work. Suddenly they heard a faint humming sound. It was a strange kind of singing. It grew louder. Through the tent opening they could see men, each with a feathery crown, huddled in a circle in the middle of the camp. Each was hitting the ground with something he held—a war club, a paddle, or a stone pick.

Soon two people wearing bird masks could be seen dancing to the low-pitched song of the men and the shrill voice of an old woman. After the ceremony, when Heyerdahl told the mayor how much he had enjoyed it, the mayor said that the ceremony had not been performed to entertain the expedition members. The song was for the blessing of God, *Atua*.[4]

Next day Atán and five of his relatives took a few expedition members to the quarry atop the crater of the dead volcano, called Rano Raraku. There, hundreds of partly finished statues had remained for centuries since an unknown day when the stonecutters had laid down their stone picks and never returned.

The long ears began collecting some of the hundreds of stone picks scattered over the quarry. The picks looked like flat front teeth of some giant animal. The mayor's men went right to work. They spread out their picks along the base of the rocky wall. Each man set a gourd of water near him. The mayor, still wearing his fern leaf crown, measured the rock facing using his outstretched arms and outspread fingers as a ruler. With a pick he marked the stone.

3. carbon-14 method: Measuring the amount of radioactive carbon-14 remaining in fossils or archeological specimens in order to date them.

4. *atua* (ə to͞o′ ə)

The mayor gave a signal, and the men lined up in front of the wall and suddenly began singing. They began hitting the wall in rhythm with the song. It was the first time in centuries that the sound of stonecutting had been heard at Raraku. One tall old man become so excited that he danced as he sang and hit the rock. Slowly, the marks grew deeper under the men's picks.

Without breaking the rhythm, a worker would grab his gourd and splash water on the rock to soften it and to keep rock splinters from flying into his eyes.

After they had worked three days, you could see the outlines of the statue. Whenever one of the men threw aside a dull pick, the mayor grabbed it and stuck it against another pick on the ground to sharpen it again.

At the end of the third day the stonecutters stopped. They were wood carvers, and not trained to carve stone for long periods of time. Atán said that it probably would have taken twelve months, with two teams working all day, to finish a statue. An archeologist with the expedition agreed. But Atán had shown how a huge statue could be carved from hard stone using only tools the islanders had used centuries ago.

Heyerdahl asked the mayor if he also knew how the statues were lifted to the platforms. "Of course," said Atán.

Heyerdahl decided to call the man's bluff. He offered to pay Atán $100 on the day that the largest statue lying on its face in the sand at Anakena Bay stood again on its platform. Right away, the mayor accepted the challenge.

To raise a statue, Atán needed twelve men, three poles, and a huge pile of pebbles and boulders. To begin, three men put the ends of their poles under the statue and pushed down on the other ends, using the poles as levers to lift the statue. The figure did not stir. They kept prying. Finally, a tiny space could be seen between the ground and the statue. The mayor, lying on his stomach beside the statue, quickly shoved tiny pebbles under it. Steadily the process went on. Lift, push stones under the statue, rest, and lift again. Now everyone except the lifters was gathering rocks. Larger and larger ones were needed as the huge figure gradually rose.

When men could no longer reach the ends of the poles, they pulled on ropes fastened to them. Men had to climb up the stone pile to place new stones under the statue. One false move and the statue and the stones would topple.

The old woman brought special egg-shaped stones. She and the mayor placed them in a circle, thinking their magic would help.

The mayor passed ropes around the stone head and fastened them to stakes driven into the ground, to hold the statue on the platform.

After eighteen days of work, the statue was finally eased into an upright position. The pile of stones was taken apart.

The mayor had done what he said he would do. A statue had been lifted to a platform by men using the same kind of tools Easter Islanders of long ago might have used.

Since the mayor had shown that he knew so much about statues, Heyerdahl asked whether he knew how they were moved from Rano Raraku crater, where they were carved, to different places around the island.

The mayor said, "They walked."

Heyerdahl kept asking and the mayor admitted that possibly a *miro manga erua*—a kind of sledge[5] made out of a forked tree trunk—had been used. He knew they were used to move heavy stones into position on top of the platforms. He knew how to make one, but he did not have enough relatives to move a statue, and other Easter Islanders were not interested in helping.

At the camp two large oxen were killed and barbecued. Everyone on the island was invited. After the people had enjoyed the food and fun of a good picnic, it was not difficult to get nearly two hundred of them to help move the statue.

They put the sledge in place under a twelve-foot statue that had been left long ago on a road. Carefully they lashed the statue to the sledge with strong ropes, and pulled the giant over the ground.

In this way, scientists got an idea of *how* the giant statues may have been carved, carried across the island, and raised to their platforms. *Why* they were made is another question. Present-day islanders believe that the statues represented ancestors of the people who made them, and that those people thought the statues had "supernatural" powers.

The statues are not the only remains found on the island. There are many elevated tombs, hundreds of stone towers that must have marked land boundaries, caves lined with stones fitted together, rocks with pictures carved into their sides, and the remains of stone houses and farmyards. There are also wooden tablets carved with a writing like no other writing known today.

These accomplishments seem astonishing to Dr. William Mulloy, a professor of anthropology at the University of Wyoming, at Laramie. Dr. Mulloy has been studying the remains on Easter Island for thirteen years, and is now directing efforts to restore many of the giant statues to their platforms.

He believes that the small island could never have had more than three or four thousand people living on it. And he doubts that many visitors could have reached the remote island bringing new ideas with them. Yet the island people must have developed a fairly complicated way of living to produce the things they did before war almost wiped them out.

5. sledge (slej) *n.*: A type of sled.

By studying the remains left by these people, scientists may learn more about how they lived, worked, played, and worshiped. But unless someone finds the "key" to the writing on the tablets and learns to read their messages, the mystery of Easter Island may remain at least partly unsolved.

Reader's Response
Why do you think the Easter Islanders built the huge statues? What do you think caused their destruction?

Responding to the Selection

Your Response

1. What more would you like to learn about the great stone heads of Easter Island?

Recalling

2. Describe the Easter Island statues.
3. How did scientists in Heyerdahl's expedition decide how long people had lived on Easter Island?

Interpreting

4. What probably happened between Roggeveen's and Cook's visits?
5. What might account for the story that the statues "walked" across the island?

Applying

6. Why is it important for people today to find out what happened to ancient civilizations?

Reading in the Content Areas

Taking Notes

Taking notes will help you remember the important ideas in your reading. The following notes cover the first four paragraphs of "The Giants of Easter Island."

Story told by Easter Islanders—stone statues walked from volcano to platforms

Roggeveen "discovery" of the island in 1722—statues standing; people lively and healthy

Cook visit 52 years later—statues toppled; islanders not healthy

Now follow these instructions:

1. Review the rest of the essay and take notes on it.
2. Compare your notes with the essay. Be sure you have recorded only important ideas.

Critical Thinking and Reading

Drawing Conclusions from Evidence

When people are presented with a fact or group of facts—evidence—it is natural for them to draw a conclusion. For example, in "The Giants of Easter Island," Heyerdahl's expedition concludes from evidence—the mayor's demonstration—that the statues could have been carved using only crude stone tools.

1. What conclusion do you draw from the fact that the mayor accepted money for showing how to raise a statue?
2. What mistaken conclusion did Heyerdahl reach about the ceremony and singing? What evidence did he use to reach this mistaken conclusion?

Thinking and Writing

Writing an Anthropological Report

Suppose that you have come from another culture to report on the customs of ours. Try to look at our culture with the eye of an outsider. Write a report that you could deliver as a lecture when you return home. In writing your talk, remember that your audience knows nothing about what you have seen. Work with a partner to revise your report. Take particular care to see that your explanations are complete.

GUIDE FOR READING

Bill Cosby

(1937–) starred in and produced the *Cosby Show* on television. Cosby has also starred in other television series and several movies and has made more than twenty musical and comedy records. He is the author of *The Wit and Wisdom of Fat Albert, Bill Cosby's Personal Guide to Power Tennis,* and *Fatherhood.* His recordings and television work have won him eight Grammy awards and four Emmy awards. In this selection Cosby, who has a doctorate in education, gives advice about how to read faster.

How to Read Faster

Outlining

Outlining means organizing content to show the main ideas and supporting details. A formal outline might look like this:

I. First main idea
  A. First major detail
    1. First minor detail
    2. Second minor detail
  B. Second major detail
II. Second main idea {The outline continues in this way.}

By dividing an essay into its main ideas and supporting details, you will understand and remember the connections between ideas.

Focus

Choose a partner. Select an author biography from any Guide for Reading page in this book and have your partner do the same. As you each read your biography, select and list ten key words or phrases in order on a sheet of paper. Exchange lists and quiz each other to see if you remember details from the biography. As you read "How to Read Faster," find the technique that reminds you of this activity.

Vocabulary

Knowing the following words will help you as you read "How to Read Faster."

correspondence (kôr′ ə spän′ dəns) *n.*: Letters (p. 391)
techniques (tek nēks′) *n.*: Systematic methods or ways of doing something (p. 391)
efficiently (e fish′ ənt lē) *adv.*: In a way producing the best result with the least effort (p. 391)
comprehension (käm′ prē hen′ shen) *n.*: Understanding; knowledge (p. 392)
successive (sək ses′ iv) *adj.*: Following one after another in order (p. 392)

Spelling Tip

Notice that neither of the two *k* sounds in the word *techniques* is spelled with a *k*. One is spelled *ch* and the other is spelled *qu.*

How to Read Faster

Bill Cosby

"With enough practice, you'll be able to handle more *reading at school or work—and at home—*in less time.*"*

When I was a kid in Philadelphia, I must have read every comic book ever published. (There were fewer of them then than there are now.)

I zipped through all of them in a couple of days, then reread the good ones until the next issues arrived.

Yes indeed, when I was a kid, the reading game was a snap.

But as I got older, my eyeballs must have slowed down or something! I mean, comic books started to pile up faster than my brother Russell and I could read them!

It wasn't until much later, when I was getting my doctorate,[1] I realized it wasn't my eyeballs that were to blame. Thank goodness. They're still moving as well as ever.

The problem is, there's too much to read these days, and too little time to read every word of it.

Now, mind you, I still read comic books. In addition to contracts,[2] novels, and newspapers. Screenplays, tax returns and correspondence. Even textbooks about how people read. And which techniques help people read more in less time.

I'll let you in on a little secret. There are hundreds of techniques you could learn to help you read faster. But I know of three that are especially good.

And if I can learn them, so can you—and you can put them to use *immediately.*

They are common-sense, practical ways to get the meaning from printed words, quickly and efficiently. So you'll have time to enjoy your comic books, have a good laugh with Mark Twain or a good cry with *War and Peace*. Ready?

Okay. The first two ways can help you get through tons of reading material—fast—*without reading every word.*

They'll give you the *overall meaning* of what you're reading. And let you cut out an awful lot of *unnecessary* reading.

1. Preview—If It's Long and Hard

Previewing is especially useful for getting a general idea of heavy reading like long magazine or newspaper articles, business reports, and nonfiction books.

1. **doctorate** (däk′ tər it) *n.*: The highest level of degree given by a university.
2. **contracts** (kän′ trakts′) *n.*: Legal agreements between people.

It can give you as much as half the comprehension in as little as one tenth the time. For example, you should be able to preview eight or ten 100-page reports in an hour. After previewing, you'll be able to decide which reports (or which *parts* of which reports) are worth a closer look.

Here's how to preview: Read the entire first two paragraphs of whatever you've chosen. Next read only the *first sentence* of each successive paragraph. Then read the entire last two paragraphs.

Previewing doesn't give you all the details. But it does keep you from spending time on things you don't really want—or need—to read.

Notice that previewing gives you a quick, overall view of *long, unfamiliar* material. For short, light reading, there's a better technique.

2. Skim—If It's Short and Simple

Skimming is a good way to get a general idea of light reading—like popular magazines or the sports and entertainment sections of the paper.

You should be able to skim a weekly popular magazine or the second section of your daily paper in less than *half* the time it takes you to read it now.

Skimming is also a great way to review material you've read before.

Here's how to skim: Think of your eyes as magnets. Force them to move fast. Sweep them across each and every line of type. Pick up *only a few key words in each line.*

Everybody skims differently.

You and I may not pick up exactly the same words when we skim the same piece, but we'll both get a pretty similar idea of what it's all about.

To show you how it works, I circled the words I picked out when I skimmed the following story. Try it. It shouldn't take you more than ten seconds.

> My brother Russell thinks monsters live in our bedroom closet at night. But I told him he is crazy.
>
> "Go and check then," he said.
>
> I didn't want to. Russell said I was chicken.
>
> "Am not," I said.
>
> "Are so," he said.
>
> So I told him the monsters were going to eat him at midnight. He started to cry. My Dad came in and told the monsters to beat it. Then he told us to go to sleep.
>
> "If I hear any more about monsters," he said, "I'll spank you."
>
> We went to sleep fast. And you know something? They never did come back.

Skimming can give you a very good *idea* of this story in about half the words—and in *less* than half the time it'd take to read every word.

So far, you've seen that previewing and skimming can give you a *general idea* about content—fast. But neither technique can promise more than 50 percent comprehension, because you aren't reading all the words. (Nobody gets something for nothing in the reading game.)

To *read faster and understand most*—if not all—of what you read, you need to know a third technique.

THE CRITIC
The Inland Printer (Japanese)
Free Library, Philadelphia

3. Cluster—To Increase Speed *and* Comprehension

Most of us learned to read by looking at each word in a sentence—*one at a time.*

Like this:

My—brother—Russell—thinks—monsters . . .

You probably still read this way sometimes, especially when the words are difficult. Or when the words have an extra-special meaning—as in a poem, a Shakespearean play, or a contract. And that's OK.

But word-by-word reading is a rotten way to read faster. It actually *cuts down* on your speed.

Clustering trains you to look at *groups* of words instead of one at a time—to increase your speed enormously. For most of us, clustering is a *totally different way of seeing what we read.*

Here's how to cluster: Train your eyes to see *all* the words in clusters of up to three or four words at a glance.

Here's how I'd cluster the story we just skimmed.

(My brother Russell)(thinks monsters) (live in)(our bedroom closet)(at night.) (But I told him)(he is crazy.)

("Go and)(check then,")(he said.)

(I didn't want to,)(Russell said)(I was chicken.)

("Am not,")(I said.)

("Am so,")(he said.)

(So I told him)(the monsters)(were going to)(eat him)(at midnight.)(He started to cry.)(My Dad came in)(and told the monsters)(to beat it.)(Then he told us)(to go to sleep.)

("If I hear)(any more about)(monsters," he said,)("I'll spank you.")

(We went)(to sleep fast.)(And you know something?)(They never did come back.)

Learning to read clusters is not something your eyes do naturally. It takes constant practice.

Here's how to go about it: Pick something light to read. Read it as fast as you can. Concentrate on seeing three to four words at once rather than one word at a time. Then reread the piece at your normal speed to see what you missed the first time.

Try a second piece. First cluster, then reread to see what you missed in this one.

When you can read in clusters without missing much the first time, your speed has increased. Practice fifteen minutes every day and you might pick up the technique in a week or so. (But don't be disappointed if it takes longer. Clustering *everything* takes time and practice.)

So now you have three ways to help you read faster. Preview to cut down on unnecessary heavy reading. Skim to get a quick, general idea of light reading. And cluster to increase your speed *and* comprehension.

With enough practice, you'll be able to handle *more* reading at school or work—and at home—*in less time.* You should even have enough time to read your favorite comic books—and *War and Peace*!

Reader's Response

Which of these methods for increasing your reading speed would work best for you?

Responding to the Selection

Your Response

1. Will you practice these methods? Why or why not?

Recalling

2. Which of the techniques helps you get a general idea of a long, "heavy" piece of writing?
3. Which of the techniques helps you increase your reading speed?
4. Which of the techniques helps you quickly get the general idea of lighter reading?

Interpreting

5. Why does Cosby begin an essay about reading faster with a story about his childhood?
6. Describe how Cosby's choice of words, sentence structure, and choice of examples affect the selection.
7. To whom does Cosby seem to be addressing his advice? Is his presentation effective? Explain.

Applying

8. What are the benefits of being able to read fast?

Reading in the Content Areas

Outlining

Outlining means organizing the content of a piece of writing to show the main ideas and supporting details. The following is an outline of the first part of the "Preview" section of "How to Read Faster."

I. Usefulness of previewing
  A. Appropriate types of reading
    1. Long articles
    2. Business reports
    3. Nonfiction books

Complete the outline of the "Preview" section of the essay.

Critical Thinking and Reading

Applying Reading Techniques

Review "How to Read Faster" to be sure that you understand the uses of each of the three techniques Cosby discusses. Then list five specific pieces of writing that you intend to read over the next few days. Answer the following questions about the items in your list.

1. For which pieces of writing would it be appropriate to use previewing?
2. For which pieces of writing would it be appropriate to use skimming?
3. For which pieces of writing would it be appropriate to use clustering?

Thinking and Writing

Explaining How

Everyone is an expert at something. It might be sailing a boat or getting along with younger brothers or sisters. Choose something that you do well, and then write an article telling someone else how to do it. Take a lighthearted approach, as Bill Cosby does. Try to think of shortcuts or "trade secrets" that you can pass on, like the three techniques Cosby gives. In revising your article, be sure that you have chosen words, sentence structures, and examples that give your piece a lively, upbeat tone.

Learning Options

1. **Art.** Suppose that you want to describe the process of preparing a favorite food, such as a Dagwood sandwich or a frozen yogurt sundae. Make a flowchart showing all the steps in the process. Remember to show the steps in order, and indicate any steps that occur at the same time.
2. **Writing.** Suppose that you are a newspaper editor. A reporter has sent you a news story, but it was accidentally put into the office paper shredder. All you can find in the shredder are these words and phrases: *Today, High Dam, Rivertown, washed away, on the roofs of their homes, rescuers in canoes and motorboats, Ellen Jones, hero, Red Cross, shelters.* Write the news story from the "skimmed" facts. When you have finished, compare your story with those written by your classmates.

GUIDE FOR READING

Jean Craighead George

(1919–) was born in Washington, D.C. She has been a newspaper reporter, magazine illustrator, teacher, and editor. She is the author of more than thirty books, including *My Side of the Mountain, Julie of the Wolves, Spring Comes to the Ocean,* and *Journey Inward,* her autobiography. Nearly all her works are about nature. She even calls her works of fiction "documentary novels" because the investigations into nature within them are carefully researched and scientifically accurate.

The Hatchling Turtles

Summarizing

Summarizing is restating something briefly in different words. Summaries can be useful when you do research and can help you remember what you read and help you study for tests.

Before you begin to write a summary, read the text thoroughly and make sure you understand it. Next decide what to include and what to leave out to be sure that the summary is short but accurate. To help you decide, make a list of the most important ideas, events, and facts in the text. Include these in your summary. Then list any supporting ideas needed to make the ideas understandable.

Focus

Before you begin reading, think about nature and natural events for a moment. What has impressed, puzzled, or amused you? With a small group of classmates, make a list of strange facts about nature. As you read, decide whether you will add the turtles to your list.

Vocabulary

Knowing the following words will help you as you read "The Hatchling Turtles."

hatchling (hach′ liŋ) *adj.*: Recently brought forth from an egg (p. 397)

rites (rīts) *n.*: Formal ceremonies or acts carried out according to fixed rules (p. 397)

ancestral (an ses′ trəl) *adj.*: Inherited from ancestors (p. 397)

laboriously (lə bôr′ ē əs lē) *adv.*: In a manner requiring much hard work (p. 397)

instinctively (in stiŋk′ tiv lē) *adv.*: Using inborn knowledge and ability (p. 398)

feat (fēt) *n.*: An act showing unusual daring or skill (p. 398)

phosphorescent (fäs′ fə res′ ənt) *adj.*: Giving off light (p. 399)

Spelling Tip

Notice that twice in *phosphorescent* an *f* sound is spelled *ph.*

The Hatchling Turtles

Jean Craighead George

". . . they were to perform a feat so mysterious that men still study and wonder how they accomplish it."

The rites of spring in the ocean are strange to man but none is so wondrous as the journey of the little turtles to the sea.

In February green turtles go to their ancestral beaches through dark seas and over miles of unmarked water. The backs of these great creatures heave above the surface as, swiftly and silently, they find unerringly the sand where they were hatched.

Near the sponges' rock a green turtle paddled her streamlined flippers against the ocean as she swam toward Bimini Island, in the Bahamas.[1] It was time to lay her eggs. Three years had passed since she had last sought this sparkling island. All these years she had lived in mysterious depths by day, and come to the surface at night to hang with her head out of the water and sleep. Now, in the rhythm of the green turtle, she was returning to the little coral island in the sea.

She lumbered ashore unsteadily, because the land felt strange and too firm under her feet. Dragging and pulling herself, she crawled to the top of the beach. She looked about, then went on, thumping laboriously over grass and sticks. She came to a log, heaved over it and flopped into the sand.

1. **Bahamas** (bə hä′ məz): A group of more than 700 islands in the Atlantic Ocean southeast of Florida. Bimini (bim′ ə nē) is a major island in the northwest section of the Bahamas.

Slowly her back flippers dug a deep well in the sand. All day she worked. When night fell, she pushed the sand back again, covering a dozen or so newly laid eggs.

And now the land took over the green turtle's work. The days of sunshine, warming the sand, changed the fertilized eggs from one cell to many, until one morning each small turtle fought for freedom within its shell.

They hatched two feet down in the sand, all of them on the same day. As they broke out, their shells collapsed, leaving a small room of air for them to breathe. It wasn't much of a room, just big enough for them to wiggle in and move toward the sky. As they wiggled they pulled the sand down from the ceiling and crawled up on it. In this manner the buried room began to rise, slowly, inch by inch.

Within a week the whole nest chamber of little turtles was almost to the surface, as the young beasts instinctively clawed at the sand above their heads. All week they had struggled against the heavy grains a few minutes at a time. Then they would rest. In this astonishing manner they moved toward the sun.

One evening the sand behind a log on Bimini Island began to quake and tremble. A small foot, webbed, and covered with scales, broke into the air. A pointed head with beautiful markings and peering eyes pushed out of the sand. A hatchling green turtle had clambered into the world.

He was followed within minutes by about a dozen others. They rested. Some looked about, for now they were to perform a feat so mysterious that men still study and wonder how they accomplish it.

The turtles came out of the ground at twilight, the tide was low, and the waves were breaking far out. The hatchling turtles looked at the sky and the sand. They could not see the water but, alone, untaught, they must find it. And find it quickly, for they are food for almost all the birds and animals that comb[2] the beaches.

The first turtle to move started the wrong way. He walked a few inches, then suddenly swung all the way around and went back. Something had told him his direction was incorrect. A log lay in the direction he must go. He struggled forward and as he did, all the other hatchling turtles moved with him, looking, feeling. They crawled over the log and tumbled onto the sand below. They got up, and plodded up a hill and hurtled through grass on their way to the sea. No man knows what lights or stars or guide-posts called them, but in clusters, in single file, in spurts and rests, they crossed the sand, going in the correct direction.

It would not have mattered what the weather—storm or sun, light or shadow—some deep instinct told these little reptiles where to put their feet.

Beyond the grass they moved faster, reaching instinctively to the flat planes of the sea and sky. Some lifted their heads and looked, others just plodded on and on. They went down the long beach. They struck the tidal flat![3]

The feel of the flat, so different from high dry sand, threw them all into a frenzy of excitement. As if they knew what was coming next, they dropped to their bellies and tried to swim. This got them nowhere. Quickly they got to their feet again, and ran, fell, swam, down the tidal slope. The sea was ahead!

Other things inspired them to hurry—things they had never seen before: the phosphorescent animals that lit the edges of the sea, the wind, the heave of the breakers far beyond. The hatchling turtles saw and felt and sensed—and ran faster.

The first turtle suddenly felt the foamy wetness of a reaching wave. He tried to throw his feet back and up, flapping them in the manner of a flying bird. The wave slipped away. He ran on. A stronger wave slid over him—and he exploded into his swimming stroke. The wave slipped out. The turtle fell on his belly. He was stranded, but he did not try to walk again. It was as if the touch of the sea had erased the memory of walking. Flippers back and up, he waited. Another wave rolled in. He swam a few inches only to be dropped on the sand again as the wave swirled out. And again he waited for the sea.

At last he was picked up by a large wave. He was in deep water—and swimming. He needed no practice. He knew exactly what to do—go under the water. Presently he emerged, breathed, and looked around as if to take his bearings. Then out to sea, on and on, until he reached the breakers.

He plunged on toward a piling wave. He had never seen one before or experienced its swirling force, and it seemed that he would be caught up in it and thrown back on the beach. He swam up to it. His body sensed the rhythm of its cresting, for he back-watered until the dynamics were just right. Then he dove. His head went down. Boiling currents carried him to the bottom, where

2. comb (cōm) *v.*: Search thoroughly.
3. tidal flat: The level sand that is covered with water at high tide, but not at low tide.

he found gentle eddies to wait in until the wave passed and broke on the shore. Behind the first turtle came the others, plunging into the wave at just the right time. Then they were gone! Their paddling would keep up for a week, a week that would take them to some unknown part of the sea.

The spring of the turtle was done. The hatchlings were on their way to the deep ocean, far from the sands of Bimini. It would be many years before they would return, and then it would be only the females who would come to the island again.

Reader's Response
What do the hatchling turtles make you wonder about turtles and about life?

Sea Turtles' Survival—Problems and Progress

All six species of sea turtles found in the waters around the United States are endangered or threatened. Development along beaches, erosion, and ocean pollution are causing the number of sea turtles to decrease. Turtles lose nesting sites when development or erosion occurs. They die when they eat plastic bags, mistaking them for jellyfish. Tar, fishing lines, and other debris have also been found in the stomachs of dead turtles.

Concern for the survival of the sea turtles has resulted in efforts to preserve them. For many years the state of Florida had a program called Head Start to help more sea-turtle eggs hatch and more hatchlings survive. Eggs were gathered from their nests on Florida beaches and taken to hatcheries where they were safe from predators, such as raccoons, opossums, and armadillos. When the eggs hatched, some hatchlings were tagged for identification and kept at the hatcheries for up to a year. This gave them time to grow so that they would be more likely to survive. Now state officials are waiting to see how many of the tagged turtles return to nest on Florida beaches.

Meanwhile, in areas such as the Hobe Sound National Wildlife Refuge on the Atlantic coast of Florida, workers remove predators and protect beaches from erosion. Thus they provide a safe place for sea turtles to lay their eggs.

Responding to the Selection

Your Response

1. This essay may seem like a science subject. Do you think it is an appropriate essay for an English class to read? Explain.

Recalling

2. Describe the turtles' struggle to dig their way to the surface of the sand.
3. How do the turtles react as soon as they feel the wetness of a wave?

Interpreting

4. Why do the hatchlings wait until twilight to clamber out into the world?
5. Predict what the females from this group of hatchlings will do when they return.

Applying

6. George calls the journey of the little turtles "wondrous." What other feats of nature inspire wonder or amazement?

Reading in the Content Areas

Summarizing

Summarizing is restating something briefly. When you write a summary, use a clear, direct style. Keep the ideas in your summary in the same order in which they appear in the original. You may also feel free to use key words and phrases from the original in your summary.

Summarize "The Hatchling Turtles" in a paragraph of approximately 250 words.

Critical Thinking and Reading

Inferring from Observation

Observing is the act of noting and recording facts and events. For example, when Jean George describes the first turtle walking the wrong way, stopping, and turning toward the water, she is making an observation.

Inferring means drawing a conclusion—often from observations. For example, after observing that the first turtle turned around, George makes the inference that "Something had told him his direction was incorrect."

Look around the room where you are. Make an observation about something in the room. Then make an inference based on your observation. Write down your observation and your inference. Discuss them with your classmates.

Thinking and Writing

Describing a Natural Occurrence

The wonders of nature are not limited to the Bahamas; they are all around us, from changes in the weather to the way ants build tunnels.

Choose a natural occurrence you would like to write about. It could be as simple an occurrence as a sunset. Observe the event closely and do some research, if necessary, to find out more about it. Use your notes as a source of ideas for the first draft of a paper describing this occurrence. Before you revise your paper, have a classmate read it. Does your classmate think your descriptions and main ideas are clear? Revise your paper after listening to your classmate's suggestions for improving it. Prepare a final draft and share it with your classmates.

Learning Options

1. **Cross-curricular Connection.** In a small group, choose a wild animal that you find interesting. Research the life cycle of that animal in your school or public library. Then, prepare an illustrated report about that animal to present to the class.
2. **Speaking and Listening.** Imagine that you could interview a hatchling turtle about its experience. With a partner, write several questions you would ask the turtle. Then, do an interview with one of you pretending to be a turtle, and the other an interviewer.

How Can You Read Your Textbooks?

Think back to the time when you were a very young child. How did you learn? One good way was probably by asking questions. You asked many, many questions! Sometimes these questions were answered immediately by someone who knew the answer. That was great; you were able to move on to use your new knowledge. Then there were times you had a question in your mind and you needed to find the answer for yourself. That was when you had to search for the answer. Your search might have raised even more questions. The answer to "How can you read your textbooks?" is, for example, another question.

How do you ask questions?

The thinking, questioning, and searching you do when you read a textbook is much like any other type of learning. In order to begin a search for answers, you must have a question! And sometimes the question changes as your search becomes more specific. Suppose you are going to read in your social studies textbook about ancient Egypt. One of your questions might be, "How did the Egyptians live?" As you read and find answers, other questions may arise that cause you to change your original question. Perhaps now you ask, "What were the religious beliefs of the ancient Egyptians?" You may also become interested in a part of the topic for which you have no question. A new question might be, "Why was mummification so important to the ancient Egyptians?" As you form questions and gather facts and ideas, keep a record of what you are doing by using lists, groups, and labels in many forms. It is much like taking notes.

Your list might look like this.

```
Ancient Egypt
mummies
pharaohs were kings
tombs
pyramids
Nile River
King Tut
artifacts are protected
hieroglyphics
```

You might decide to group all of the words associated with death (mummies, tombs, pyramids, Nile River, King Tut, artifacts) together with the question, "How did the ancient Egyptians view death?" or "What did the ancient Egyptians do to prepare for death?" At this point you might be tempted to throw away the word *hieroglyphics*, but don't do that yet! This may be just the idea that interests you the most when you do more reading. Save good words and put them into other lists as you read. The word hieroglyphics may prompt other lists and cause you to ask questions about the topic. Here is what one sixth grader thought:

```
What are hieroglyphics and why
were they used?
writings on tomb walls
papyrus
scribes
pictures with meanings
Is a hieroglyphic a sound or
   meaning?
How long were they used?
Were the same symbols used by
   everyone?
```

Notice that the student knew some information, but then began to ask questions about the question because she wanted to learn more about the topic of hieroglyphics.

What do you already know or need to know?

Before you try to form questions, think about what you already know. You already know some facts and ideas about the topics you study in school textbooks. You can use this knowledge to help develop new ideas.

As you look into the library that is your mind, it is also important to understand that in order to answer a question effectively, you may have to ask, "What do I need to know?" This is the most important step in finding important information. How the question is asked is like a road sign for your information gathering. It directs you to the sources that may contain your answer. A good questioning strategy can help you study everything from literature to social studies to science material.

Let's examine your social studies textbook. History and geography books can be full of exciting stories. Sometimes, however, they are not written in the readable and thrilling way of a literature book. That makes your job as a learner more difficult, but not impossible. With these books, you can use the active reading strategies of forming questions, making predictions, clarifying, summarizing, and responding to what you read. These are the same strategies you use to read any nonfiction selection.

Remember to begin with what you already know and then ask questions as you read. Good questions will lead you to the right answers.

YOUR WRITING PROCESS

Writing to Explore a Content Area

An important local, national, or international event occurs. Perhaps a water main breaks. Your newspaper carries stories, the radio brings you updates, and television shows you what is going on. You become curious about what a water main is and how it operates. You wonder why a water main breaks or how it's repaired—or where the water comes from, or where used water goes. You might seek more information about your interest. Perhaps the newspaper has related science articles. Writing to explore a content area offers the chance to shape your knowledge for yourself and to share it with others.

Your Turn

Explore a content area in writing. Your purpose is to learn something you do not know about one of your school subjects. Perhaps you can write to fulfill an assignment.

Prewriting

1. Consider possible topics. Unless you are going to write to fulfill a specific assignment from a teacher, research topic ideas. You need at least a day to look for topic possibilities. Use recent issues of the newspaper. Watch television news programs and listen to the radio news. Ask yourself, "What do I want to find out more about?"

Keep a journal of possible topics—in question form—to share with classmates. Use the following content areas as possibilities, and write a second question for each:

geography—Why was the growing season so short this year?
education—What do you have to do to become a lawyer?
outer space—What is a black hole?
politics—Why did the town council vote against lighting the town softball field for night play?
environmental studies—Should our community have a bottle bill?
science—How does water travel from the reservoir to home faucets?
mathematics—What is Newton's theory of gravity?
history—Who first lived around here, and what was it like?
the arts—Why does it cost so much to make a movie?
physical education—How is a basketball made?

2. Choose a topic. Look at your list of possibilities. With a partner, discuss which two or three topics you'd like to know more about and why. Choose one to write about.

3. Find out about your topic. Formulate as many specific questions about your topic as you can. For example, if you're going to find out how basketballs are made, you might write the following questions: Where are basketballs made? What machinery is needed to make them? What are they made of? How are they filled with air? Why are some basketballs more expensive than others?

Use the library. Check encyclopedias and nonfiction books. Talk to appropriate experts like the mayor, or a representative of the mayor's office, on the telephone or in person. If the event is timely, use newspapers, magazines, and the radio.

Take notes on paper divided into two columns. Use the left column for notes. Use the right column to indicate sources and personal comments. Take lots of notes. Until you focus your topic, you can't be sure which notes will be helpful.

4. Focus your topic. For example, if you're writing about basketball, focus on one idea, such as how the ball is made, the history of the game, or what makes a player excel.

5. Make an informal outline. Your outline will keep you on track. An informal outline can have phrases or sentences, and it can be fully developed or brief, depending on what is most helpful to you as a writer.

6. Write an introductory paragraph. It should make your topic and the focus of your paper clear. The introductory paragraph may also give any background information your readers will need to understand your paper.

Drafting

Compose your first draft. Use information from your notes and outline. As you write, you might need to get more information. (That doesn't mean you didn't do enough research, just that you're discovering holes in your knowledge.) Also remember to do more than summarize information. As you tell about your subject, your attitude toward it should come through. If you find facts impressive, let your enthusiasm show. Why have a draft that sounds as though a robot wrote it!

Revising

Use the revision checklist on page 751. In addition, share your draft with a writing partner and ask questions such as the following:

- In your own words, what's this paper about?
- Are there holes in my information? What should I find out more about?
- Are there any terms I've used that I need to define or explain more?
- Do you hear my voice in this, or does it sound like I just summarized information from outside sources?

Proofreading

Consult the guidelines for proofreading on page 753. Remember to use quotation marks and bibliographic information if you have quoted directly. Then make a final copy.

READING AND RESPONDING

Nonfiction

Nonfiction deals with real people, places, things, and events. The nonfiction writer usually keeps several things in mind while writing: an idea to present (the topic), the purpose for presenting the idea, and an audience. To appreciate nonfiction fully, you respond to the elements of nonfiction and the writer's techniques.

RESPONDING TO PURPOSE Purpose refers to the reason for writing. A writer usually has both a general purpose and a specific purpose. The general purpose may be to explain or inform, to descibe, to persuade, or to entertain. The specific purpose may be to explain the effect of an incident on the writer's life. It may be to make you marvel at a natural event. Your response to the writer's purpose will affect your understanding of the work.

RESPONDING TO IDEAS AND SUPPORT The main ideas are the most important points the writer wants to make. Main ideas can be facts or opinions. Support is the information the writer uses to develop or illustrate the main ideas. Support includes facts to back up opinions, reasons to explain events, examples to illustrate ideas, and descriptive details to help you form a mental picture of the topic. As you read, you respond to these ideas.

RESPONDING TO ORGANIZATION Writers organize their ideas to accomplish their purpose. The information may be arranged in chronological order, spatial order, order of importance, or any other order that will best convey the message of the piece.

RESPONDING TO TECHNIQUES Writers may use a variety of techniques to accomplish their purpose. They may use description or comparison and contrast. They may use emotional language to arouse your feelings. They may include stories or quotations, or they may use unexpected grammatical or sentence structure to create an effect. Notice the author's techniques as you read.

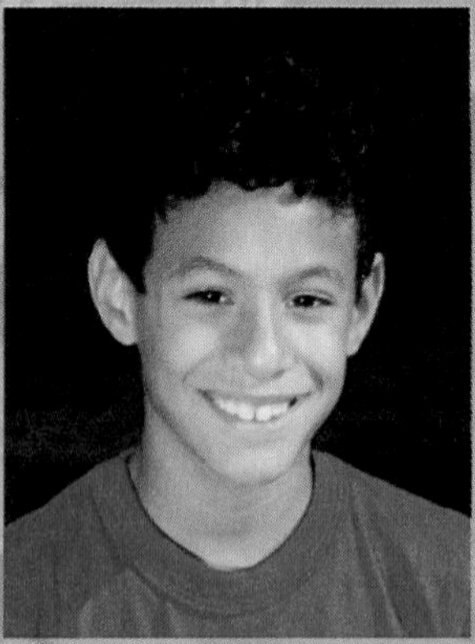

On pages 407–412, you will see how Justin Williams from the Thomas Jefferson Middle School in Teaneck, New Jersey read and responded to "The Horse Snake." The notes in the side column include Justin's thoughts and responses while he read this story. What are your thoughts as you read "The Horse Snake"?

MODEL

The Horse Snake

Huynh Quang Nhuong

"Because of their bone-breaking squeeze and fatal bite they are one of the most dangerous creatures of the uplands."

Despite all his courage there was one creature in the jungle that Tank[1] always tried to avoid—the snake. And there was one kind of snake that was more dangerous than other snakes—the horse snake. In some areas people called it the bamboo snake because it was as long as a full-grown bamboo tree. In other regions, the people called it the thunder or lightning snake, because it attacked so fast and with such power that its victim had neither time to escape nor strength to fight it. In our area, we called it the horse snake because it could move as fast as a thoroughbred.[2]

One night a frightened friend of our family's banged on our door and asked us to let him in. When crossing the rice field in front of our house on his way home from a wedding, he had heard the unmistakable hiss of a horse snake. We became very worried; not only for us and our friend, but also for the cattle and other animals we raised.

It was too far into the night to rouse all our neighbors and go to search for the snake. But my father told my cousin to blow three times on his buffalo horn, the signal that a dangerous wild beast was loose in the hamlet.[3] A few seconds later we heard three long quivering sounds of a horn at the far end of the hamlet answering our warning. We presumed that the whole hamlet was now on guard.

Ideas and Support: *Tank sounds brave because he's not scared of all these jungle animals.*

Purpose: *Why does the author want to tell us about these snakes?*

Support: *If I were him, I would also be scared after hearing the horse snake's hiss.*

Technique: *The writer is telling a story from real life. He knows all the facts of village life.*

Support: *I think the horn is a great way of communicating. It's a great signal.*

---

1. **Tank:** The author's pet water buffalo.
2. **thoroughbred** (thur′ ō bred′): A pure-bred horse known for its speed.
3. **hamlet** (ham′ lit): A very small, enclosed village.

Ideas: *I wonder how old the cousin is. He must have been older than the narrator because he had the responsibility of helping the father protect the family.*

Technique: *It must be a giant horse snake if it can kill a horse in that way. The author keeps showing how dangerous the snake is.*

I stayed up that night, listening to all the sounds outside, while my father and my cousin sharpened their hunting knives. Shortly after midnight we were startled by the frightened neighing of a horse in the rice field. Then the night was still, except for a few sad calls of nocturnal[4] birds and the occasional roaring of tigers in the jungle.

The next day early in the morning all the able-bodied men of the hamlet gathered in front of our house and divided into groups of four to go and look for the snake. My father and my cousin grabbed their lunch and joined a searching party.

They found the old horse that had neighed the night before in the rice field. The snake had squeezed it to death. Its chest was smashed, and all its ribs broken. But the snake had disappeared.

Everybody agreed that it was the work of one of the giant horse snakes which had terrorized our area as far back as anyone could remember. The horse snake usually eats small game, such as turkeys, monkeys, chickens, and ducks, but for unknown reasons sometimes it will attack people and cattle. A fully grown horse snake can reach the size of a king python.[5] But, unlike pythons, horse snakes have an extremely

---

4. nocturnal (näk tʉr′ nəl) *adj.*: Active during the night.
5. python (pī′ thän′): A large, nonpoisonous snake that crushes its prey to death.

poisonous bite. Because of their bone-breaking squeeze and fatal bite they are one of the most dangerous creatures of the uplands.

The men searched all day, but at nightfall they gave up and went home. My father and my cousin looked very tired when they returned. My grandmother told them to go right to bed after their dinner and that she would wake them up if she or my mother heard any unusual sounds.

Organization: *This story is in chronological order. It wouldn't make sense in any other order.*

The men went to bed and the women prepared to stay up all night. My mother sewed torn clothing and my grandmother read a novel she had just borrowed from a friend. And for the second night in a row, they allowed my little sister and me to stay awake and listen with them for as long as we could. But hours later, seeing the worry on our faces, my grandmother put aside her novel and told us a story:

Technique: *Why does the writer have the grandmother tell a story?*

> Once upon a time a happy family lived in a small village on the shore of the South China Sea. They respected the laws of the land and loved their neighbors very much. The father and his oldest son were woodcutters. The father was quite old, but he still could carry home a heavy load of wood.
>
> One day on his way home from the jungle he was happier than usual. He and his son had discovered a wild chicken nest containing twelve eggs. Now he would have something special to give to his grandchildren when they pulled his shirtsleeves and danced around him to greet him when he came home.

Ideas: *I wonder if the 12 eggs are snake eggs and not chicken eggs.*

> The father looked at the broad shoulders of his son and his steady gait under a very heavy load of wood. He smiled. His son was a good son, and he had no doubt that when he became even older still his son would take good care of him and his wife.
>
> As he was thinking this he saw his son suddenly throw the load of wood at a charging horse snake that had come out of nowhere. The heavy load of wood crashed into the snake's head and stunned it. That gave them enough time to draw their sharp woodcutting knives. But instead of attacking the horse snake

Technique: *The story is making me more scared now because they are alone and there could be more horse snakes in the area.*

from the front, the elder shouted to his son to run behind the big bush of elephant grass nearby while he, who was a little too old to run fast, jumped into the front end of the bush. Each time the snake passed by him the old man managed to hit it with his knife. He struck the snake many times. Finally it became weak and slowed down; so he came out of his hiding place and attacked the snake's tail, while his son attacked the snake's head. The snake fought back furiously, but finally it succumbed to the well-coordinated attack of father and son.

Ideas and Support: *The horse snake is a fighter. That's why it took so long to die.*

When the snake was dead, they grabbed its tail and proudly dragged it to the edge of their village. Everyone rushed out to see their prize. They all argued over who would have the honor of carrying the snake to their house for them.

The old woodcutter and his son had to tell the story of how they had killed the snake at least ten times, but the people never tired of hearing it, again and again. They all agreed that the old woodcutter and his son were not only brave but clever as well. Then and there the villagers decided that when their chief, also a brave and clever man, died, the old woodcutter was the only one who deserved the honor of replacing him.

Technique: *I wouldn't be scared after hearing the grandmother's story. The children might have thought that the family could defeat the snake with knives they kept in the house.*

When my grandmother finished the story, my little sister and I became a bit more cheerful. People could defeat this dangerous snake after all. The silent darkness outside became less threatening. Nevertheless, we were still too scared to sleep in our room, so my mother made a makeshift bed[6] in the sitting room, close to her and our grandmother.

Ideas and Support: *I think some people should still stay on guard. It looks like the horse snake is still around.*

When we woke up the next morning, life in the hamlet had almost returned to normal. The snake had not struck again that night, and the farmers, in groups of three or four, slowly filtered back to their fields. Then, late in the afternoon, hysterical cries for help were heard in the direction of the western

---

6. makeshift bed: A temporary bed.

part of the hamlet. My cousin and my father grabbed their knives and rushed off to help.

It was Minh,[7] a farmer, who was crying for help. Minh, like most farmers in the area, stored the fish he had caught in the rice field at the end of the rainy season in a small pond. That day Minh's wife had wanted a good fish for dinner. When Minh approached his fish pond he heard what sounded like someone trying to steal his fish by using a bucket to empty water from the pond. Minh was very angry and rushed over to catch the thief, but when he reached the pond, what he saw so petrified him that he fell over backward, speechless. When he regained control he crawled away as fast as he could and yelled loudly for help.

The thief he saw was not a person but a huge horse snake, perhaps the same one that had squeezed the old horse to death two nights before. The snake had hooked its head to the branch of one tree and its tail to another and was splashing the water out of the pond by swinging its body back and forth, like a hammock. Thus, when the shallow pond became dry, it planned to swallow all the fish.

Technique: *Comparing the snake's swinging to a hammock is a simile.*

All the villagers rushed to the scene to help Minh, and our village chief quickly organized an attack. He ordered all the men to surround the pond. Then two strong young men approached the snake, one at its tail and the other at its head. As they crept closer and closer, the snake assumed a striking position, its head about one meter above the pond, and its tail swaying from side to side. It was ready to strike in either direction. As the two young men moved in closer, the snake watched them. Each man tried to draw the attention of the

Ideas: *The snake must be very smart because of the way he tried to get the fish.*

---

7. Minh (min)

Technique: *Here is another simile.*

Purpose: *One theme in this story seems to be to show how a village can work together.*

Purpose: *I think many things you do in life involve team work. This story is a good example of team work. It shows how you can achieve your goal by working together. This also reminds me of how my parents always tell me to work with others and to be a team player.*

snake, while a third man crept stealthily to its side. Suddenly he struck the snake with his long knife. The surprised snake shot out of the pond like an arrow and knocked the young man unconscious as it rushed by. It broke through the circle of men and went into an open rice field. But it received two more wounds on its way out.

The village chief ordered all the women and children to form a long line between the open rice field and the jungle and to yell as loudly as they could, hoping to scare the snake so that it would not flee into the jungle. It would be far easier for the men to fight the wounded snake in an open field than to follow it there.

But now there was a new difficulty. The snake started heading toward the river. Normally a horse snake could beat any man in a race, but since this one was badly wounded, our chief was able to cut off its escape by sending half his men running to the river. Blocked off from the river and jungle, the snake decided to stay and fight.

The hunting party surrounded the snake again, and this time four of the best men attacked the snake from four different directions. The snake fought bravely, but it perished. During the struggle one of the men received a dislocated shoulder, two had bruised ribs, and three were momentarily blinded by dirt thrown by the snake. Luckily all of them succeeded in avoiding the fatal bite of the snake.

We rejoiced that the danger was over. But we knew it would only be a matter of time until we would once again have to face our most dangerous natural enemy—the horse snake.

Huynh Quang Nhuong was born in Vietnam. During the Vietnam War, Huynh was a student at Saigon University. After graduating with a degree in chemistry, he was drafted into the South Vietnamese army. A gunshot wound he received on the battlefield left Huynh permanently paralyzed. In 1969, he came to the United States for additional medical treatment. Huynh remained in America. He earned additional degrees at Long Island University and at the University of Missouri. He now lives in Columbia, Missouri.

Reader's Response
At what point did you feel the most suspense? Explain.

RESPONDING TO THE SELECTION

Your Response

1. How did you feel about snakes before you read this selection? Have your feelings changed? Explain.

Recalling

2. Identify two other names people called the horse snake. Why did they use each name?
3. What signal did the villagers use to alert people of a dangerous animal?
4. What happened to the four men who surrounded the snake and killed it?

Interpreting

5. Why did the men not run out into the field when they heard the frightened neighing of the horse?
6. Explain why the children were allowed to stay up late at night.
7. Identify two messages of the grandmother's story.
8. Why were the villagers concerned about the snake heading toward the river?

Applying

9. The villagers killed the snake by working together. What problems in your community could be solved if people cooperated? Explain.

ANALYZING LITERATURE

Reviewing the Essay

An **essay** is a type of nonfiction that focuses on one idea or event. In an essay, a writer expresses his or her views and experiences. An essay writer's general purpose is to inform, to describe, to persuade, or to entertain.

1. What experience does Huynh's essay describe?
2. How did the author feel about the experience at that time? How do you know?
3. What is Huynh's purpose for writing this essay?

CRITICAL THINKING AND READING

Making Inferences About Culture

An **inference** is a logical conclusion reasoned from evidence. Writers do not always tell you directly about the setting or culture they are writing about. Often you must infer this information from clues in the essay. These clues can be names, events, customs, celebrations, objects that are described—in short, anything that gives you a hint about the culture.

1. Where do the events of this essay take place? How do you know?
2. What kind of culture did the author come from?

THINKING AND WRITING

Writing About a Conflict

Write an narrative essay about a dangerous animal. You may tell a true incident, or you may imagine one. Tell the events in the order in which they occurred. Include background, setting, and any other relevant information.

LEARNING OPTIONS

1. **Speaking and Listening.** Form a group with four other students. Four of the group members will pretend to be one of the people that killed the snake. The fifth group member will interview each of these village heroes to find out how they stalked the snake and how it felt. Perform the interview for the class.
2. **Cross-curricular Connection.** Find out more about large, dangerous snakes. Consult an encyclopedia for information about the size, appearance, habitat, and feeding habits. What kind of snake do you think the horse snake is? Present your findings to the class in an oral report.

BRIDGING FORMS

THE HOUSE OF DIES DREAR
by Virginia Hamilton

"Thomas had the queerest notion that he was not alone. In front of him, between him and the steps of the veranda, something waited.

'Papa?' he said. He heard something.

The sound went, 'Ahhh, ahhh, ahhh.' It was not moaning, nor crying. It wasn't laughter, but something forlorn and lost and old.

Thomas backed away. 'No,' he said. 'Oh please!' "

If you want to find out what happens to Thomas, read *The House of Dies Drear,* a novel that weaves a modern mystery story with the period of history when runaway slaves were helped to freedom along the Underground Railroad. Novels like *The House of Dies Drear* bridge the gap between fiction and nonfiction by using historical facts and, sometimes, historical characters in a fictional story.

You were introduced to Virginia Hamilton, the author of *The House of Dies Drear,* in the selection by Lee Bennett Hopkins on page 281. In the article, Hamilton reveals her interest in connecting fact with fiction. She strives to bridge the gap between readers of today and courageous black families from the past. Hamilton also explains some of the numerous connections between *The House of Dies Drear* and her own family history and her community, which contains many houses that once harbored fugitive slaves. Hamilton also states that *The House of Dies Drear* is her favorite book.

Secret Passages, Hidden Doors

The House of Dies Drear is a mystery set in a small town in present-day Ohio. Thomas Small and his family move from North Carolina into the dark, rambling house of Dies Drear. Dies Drear was an abolitionist; that means he was active in the movement to abolish slavery. He built his house more than one hundred years earlier as a station for the Underground Railroad. In order to

FUGITIVE SLAVES ESCAPING FROM EASTERN SHORE OF MARYLAND
The Granger Collection

hide slaves, it contained secret passages, hidden doors, and false walls. The history of the house is full of mystery and sorrow. Dies Drear and two slaves had been murdered in the house and the ghosts of all three were believed to haunt it still.

Thomas, being a naturally inquistive thirteen-year-old, immediately sets out to explore every passage in the house and dispel the mystery. Despite some scares, Thomas and his father find most of the hidden buttons, sliding doors, and secret passages. However, mysterious events continue to frighten and annoy the family, who feel that someone is trying to scare them away. Could this be Pluto, the strange and mysterious caretaker? Or perhaps the unfriendly Darrow family? The answers to these questions can be found in the novel.

"My Stories Are . . . Pieces of Me"

Virginia Esther Hamilton is noted for her works of fiction for young adults and preteens. She has also collected and rewritten stories that were orginally told by slaves. You can find one of these, "He Lion, Bruh Bear, and Bruh Rabbit," on page 605.

Hamilton's style of writing, which she calls the writer's personality, includes a careful choice of words. She has said, "My stories are little pieces of me." She uses herself, as well as her parents, aunts, uncles, and cousins as the basis for many of her characters. Throughout her work, Hamilton communicates a sensitivity to and a love for her black heritage.

The Mystery Continues

Virginia Hamilton once commented that people and objects in her books tend to turn into emblems, objects that represent a broader group or idea. As you read *The House of Dies Drear*, think about prominent characters or objects. Could they represent groups of people or broad ideas? Also, think about the history you learn as you read. Would you like to discover more about the Underground Railroad, fugitive slaves, or the abolition movement? If so, explore on your own material related to the historical events in *The House of Dies Drear*.

The story of Dies Drear is continued in a subsequent book, *The Mystery of Drear House: The Conclusion of the Dies Drear Chronicle*. If you enjoy *The House of Dies Drear*, you might read this one, too.

FOCUS ON READING
Recognizing Main Ideas

Everything you read contains a message for you. Writers use certain methods to help you understand their messages. They organize what they have to say in paragraphs. A paragraph usually contains one main idea and information that supports, or explains, that idea.

Just as the writers must organize the writing to make their meaning clear to the readers, so the readers must think about the selection in order to understand it.

First, you will notice that the selection has a topic, a subject about which the author is writing. Next, you will discover that the author has information or opinions about the topic to share with the reader. These are the main ideas expressed in the writing.

Stated Main Ideas

Sometimes, main ideas are stated directly in one sentence in a paragraph. The following paragraph from "The Drive-In Movies" contains a main idea stated directly in the first sentence. Each of the other sentences in the paragraph gives details to support the main idea.

> One Saturday I decided to be extra good. When she came out of the bedroom tying her robe, she yawned a hat-sized yawn and blinked red eyes at the weak brew of coffee I had fixed for her. I made her toast with strawberry jam spread to all the corners and set the three boxes of cereal in front of her. If she didn't care to eat cereal, she could always look at the back of the boxes as she drank her coffee.

A directly stated main idea is called the topic sentence of a paragraph. A topic sentence may be the first sentence in the paragraph, or it may appear at the end or in the middle.

Activity 1

Find the main idea in each of the following paragraphs. Each main idea is stated directly.

1. Miss Smith also gave unusual assignments. Once, without warning, she said, "I want you to pretend you live in George Washington's time and write a letter to someone describing an experience."

2. The toughest letter to crank out is one that is meant to impress, as we all know from writing job applications; if it's hard work to slip off a letter to a friend, maybe you're trying too hard to be terrific. A letter is only a report to someone who already likes you for reasons other than your brilliance. Take it easy.
3. By the time he was sixteen, Abraham was six feet tall—"the gangliest awkwardest feller . . . he appeared to be all joints," said a neighbor. He may have looked awkward, but hard physical labor had given him a tough, lean body with muscular arms like steel cables. He could grab a woodsman's ax by the handle and hold it straight out at arm's length. And he was one of the best wrestlers and runners around.

Implied Main Ideas

Sometimes, writers do not state main ideas directly. Instead, you the reader will have to figure out the main idea from the details presented. Each paragraph need not contain an implied main idea. In fact, there may be only one or two in a whole selection. What is the implied main idea of the following paragraph?

> My father said a few unprintable words before we started back to the house. After breakfast, when Pa and Mom came to the barn, I was already there. I had opened the crib door and there was Old Ben. He'd crawled up front and was coiled on a sack. I put my hand down and he crawled up my arm to my neck and over my shoulder. When Mom and Pa reached the crib, I thought Pa was going to faint.

By the way Pa acts, you can see that the implied main idea is that he does not like snakes.

Activity 2

Determine the implied main idea in the following paragraph.

> When the Dutch admiral Jacob Roggeveen "discovered" the island on Easter Sunday in 1722, he saw many of these statues standing on platforms of stone. Fifty-two years later, when the English explorer Captain James Cook visited Easter Island, most of the statues lay face down at the base of their platforms. Cook also noticed that the people of the island did not seem as lively and healthy as Roggeveen had reported them to be.

YOUR WRITING PROCESS

Preparing a Class News Publication

Do you want to read an interesting, entertaining, and informative class news publication? Who doesn't! Here's an opportunity to produce one.

Your Turn

Prepare a class news publication. Your purpose is to cooperate with your classmates to produce a publication that contains interesting, informative, and entertaining articles. Your audience will be your classmates.

Prewriting

1. Brainstorm for article ideas. Work as a whole class or in small groups to brainstorm for ideas. Have a recorder note all ideas on the chalkboard for class consideration. Since this is a starting point, accept all ideas. The strangest idea might spark one that will be everyone's favorite. Ideas for articles might include the following:

interview with a foreign-born classmate
statistical profile of the class
interview with a teacher
students' favorite recipes
information about school sports
movie reviews
book reviews
student survey about a controversial issue
an advice column
class fashion notes
a how-to column

2. Evaluate article ideas. Evaluate each suggested idea. Keep in mind that just as few people read a newspaper from cover to cover, not everyone will be interested in reading every article. For example, you might have enjoyed Neil McAleer's "Space Stations of the Mind," but a classmate with little knowledge of space exploration might find it hard going. That doesn't mean it shouldn't be in this unit, or that a specialized article doesn't belong in your publication. If it's a well-written article on a subject that appeals to many readers, seriously consider it.

To evaluate each idea, ask questions such as the following, putting a checkmark by ideas that seem especially interesting or attractive:

- Will there be enough readers interested in this?
- Will this present new information or a new slant on a topic? If not, is there a slant we can suggest?
- Can this be done in the time frame we have?

In deciding which articles to include, also consider whether there's enough variety of subject matter and purpose. Readers like to be informed, entertained, and persuaded.

3. Consider additional tasks. Thinking up articles is just the beginning. Next, as a whole class, brainstorm for other tasks people must do. Have a recorder write ideas on the chalkboard. Examples might include the following:

Set and enforce deadlines.
Accept work as it's finished each step of the way and get it to the right people for the next step.
Revise.
Proofread.
Type.
Duplicate and distribute.
Arrange articles and art on the pages.
Check facts.
Be in charge of the whole project.
Do research for writers.
Write articles.
Act as recorder at meetings.
Do artwork.

Finally, recruit volunteers to carry out the tasks. Consider insuring against illness and emergencies—assign more articles than you actually need. Be sure a recorder keeps track of projects and people from the start.

Guidelines for Writing Articles

First, gather the information you will need for the article you have chosen to write. Perhaps you will need to interview a classmate or someone in the community for information. If so, prepare the questions you want to ask in advance, and take careful notes during the interview.

Next, organize the information you have gathered in an effective way. You may want to write the article in chronological order. Perhaps writing from the least important to the most important information will be more effective.

Finally, write a first draft of the article. Keep in mind that you are trying to be both informative and entertaining.

Revising

As each article comes in, editors should review it at a meeting with its author. Ways of improving the article should be discussed and agreed upon. The author should use the editors' suggestions to revise the article. When considering each article, editors should use the revision checklist on page 749 and should consider the following points:

- Does this really tell readers what they don't already know?
- Why will this piece appeal to readers?
- Are there terms that need to be defined?
- Is the opening catchy?
- Is important information missing?
- Would quotations make this a better piece?
- Would more description make this more effective?

Proofreading

Proofreaders should consult the guidelines on page 751 for proofreading. They must be sure there are no typographical, grammatical, or spelling errors in the copy. Errors take away from the finished product.

Publishing

Publishing day! Either duplicate the publication on school equipment or arrange to have it duplicated. Then, distribute the class news publication.

BOOKSHELF

If you are looking for a good book to read, try one of these. Some of these are nonfiction, some are fiction by writers in this unit, and some are fiction that reads like nonficton.

SADAKO AND THE THOUSAND PAPER CRANES, Eleanor Coerr, A Dell Yearling Book, 1977. Sadako was two years old when an atomic bomb was dropped on Hiroshima during World War II. Ten years later Sadako discovers that she has developed leukemia from the radiation. Despite her pain, Sadako's courage made her a heroine in Japan.

THE LION, THE WITCH, AND THE WARDROBE, C. S. Lewis, Collier Books, Macmillan Publishing Company, 1970 (first published in 1950). Enter the magical world of Narnia with Peter, Susan, Edmund, and Lucy as they join Aslan the lion in fighting the wicked White Witch.

WRAPPED FOR ETERNITY: The Story of the Egyptian Mummy, Mildred Pace, McGraw-Hill Book Company, 1974. Explore the way ancient Egyptians prepared dead rulers for eternity. Pace tells what was found when scientists carefully unwrapped mummies to see how they had been preserved.

A GATHERING OF DAYS, Joan W. Blos, Aladdin Books, Macmillan Publishing Company, 1979. This fictional journal of a young New England girl shows how a girl from New Hampshire spent her time from 1830 to 1832.

AMOS FORTUNE, FREE MAN, Elizabeth Yates, Puffin Books, 1989 (first published in 1950). This is a biography of an African prince sold into slavery in America. Yates not only portrays Amos Fortune's life vividly but also the time and place in which he lived.

THE TALKING EARTH, Jean Craighead George, Harper & Row, 1983. The fascinating and mysterious Florida Everglades are the setting for this novel. A young girl enters them alone to search for her Native American heritage and learns to listen to the earth. This is an opportunity to visit a fascinating area that few people get to explore in real life.

UNIT ACTIVITIES

Writing

1. Think of people who have played an important role in American history. Choose one and, in a library, conduct research into his or her childhood years. Take notes and keep a careful record of the books where you find your information. Write a draft telling about the person's childhood years and the characteristics that enabled him or her to play such an important role in history.

Writing

2. Write a letter to someone you know, giving him or her advice. Decide on the person who will receive the letter and the advice you want to give. Freewrite a list of points you wish to make. Then write the letter, following the proper form for a personal letter. You may wish to mail the letter when you have finished it.

Cooperative Learning

3. Working with a group of your classmates, choose an animal that appears on the endangered species list. Divide responsibility among group members for research. Find reasons why the animal is endangered, ways people are trying to protect the animals that remain, ways people are trying to encourage an increase in the numbers of the animals, and problems that exist for the animals' future. Prepare a report on the group's findings. Each member of the group should be responsible for writing, revising, or proofreading part of the report.

Speaking and Listening

4. Prepare a speech and demonstration showing your classmates how to do something. Your topic might be how to build a birdhouse, how to make an apple pie, or how to polish your shoes. Start by choosing your topic and listing any props you will need in class for your demonstration. Practice describing the process at home before presenting it to your classmates.

Speaking and Listening

5. Interview an older member of your family, a neighbor, or a friend about how growing up was different in his or her youth. Before interviewing, prepare a list of questions to ask. Either take notes or tape record the interview. Share your findings with your classmates during a class discussion.

THE LEGEND OF THE WHITE DEER
Tamas Galambos
Private Collection

POETRY

The language of poetry is not the language of everyday speech. It is written in a special kind of language. Poetic language is compact; each word is selected with the utmost care. The words often suggest more than they say directly. Elements like rhythm and rhyme make the language of poetry more musical than everyday language. Poetry also looks different in writing, using verses and stanzas much as everyday language uses sentences and paragraphs. Finally, poetry can be about any subject you can imagine. In this unit you will find poems about animals, nature, school subjects, feelings and ideas, even about everyday activities like soccer and skateboarding. Enjoy them!

HOW TO READ A POEM

Poetry is a special form of writing. It is different from other forms of writing in its appearance, its use of words, and its musical qualities. Poets use language imaginatively to create images, tell stories, explore feelings and experiences, and suggest meanings. They choose and combine words carefully to enable you to see your world in a new and fresh way. Poets also use rhythm and rhyme to create musical effects in a poem.

The language and sounds of poetry work together to create the poetic experience of a poem. To fully appreciate and enjoy poetry, like other forms of literature, use the following active reading strategies.

QUESTION Ask what the poem is saying. Why does the writer include certain words and details? Look for answers to your questions as you read.

USE YOUR SENSES What images is the poet creating? How are these images developed? Let your imagination see the pictures in your mind, and let your senses take in the poet's language.

LISTEN Much poetry is musical. Read the poem aloud so that you can hear the sound of it and feel its rhythm. Often the words and rhythm suggest a mood or feeling. Let the sound of the poem pull you into it. How does the sound affect you?

CONNECT Bring your own experience and knowledge to the poem. What images and sounds are familiar? Which are new to you? Try putting the poem in your own words. When you can express a poem in your own words, you will better understand its meaning.

RESPOND How does the poem make you feel as you read? Go beyond the poet's meaning and add your own. What does the poem say to *you*?

Try to use these strategies as you read the poems in this unit. They will help you increase your enjoyment and understanding of poetry.

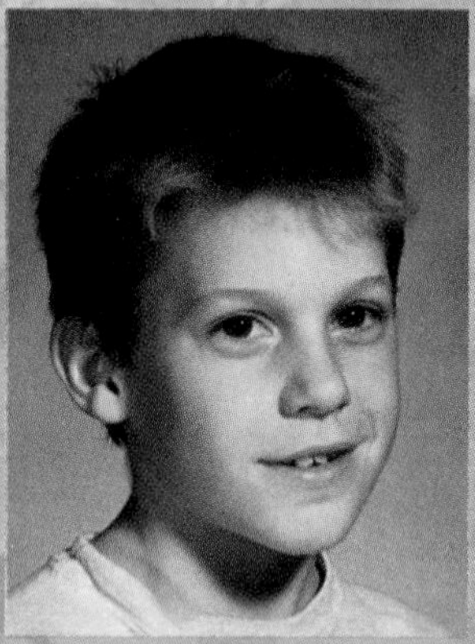

Charles Smith from the Dedham Middle School in Dedham, Massachusetts, actively read "Abuelito Who" on pages 425 and 426. The notes in the side column include Charles's thoughts and comments. How are your thoughts and responses similar to and different from Charles's?

MODEL

Abuelito[1] Who

Sandra Cisneros

Paraphrase: *The title means Grandfather Who.*

Abuelito who throws coins like rain
and asks who loves him
who is dough and feathers
who is a watch and glass of water
whose hair is made of fur
is too sad to come downstairs today
who tells me in Spanish you are my diamond
who tells me in English you are my sky
whose little eyes are string
can't come out to play
sleeps in his little room all night and day
who used to laugh like the letter k
is sick
is a doorknob tied to a sour stick
is tired shut the door
doesn't live here anymore
is hiding underneath the bed
who talks to me inside my head

Senses: *The grandfather has soft hair.*

Connect: *The grandfather loves his grandchild.*

Question: *Does this mean he is blind?*

Connect: *He must be very old—maybe 90 years old. He also must be sick.*

Question: *What does this mean—that he has a cane?*

Question: *Does this mean he is dying?*

1. **Abuelito** (ä bwĕ lē′ tō): In Spanish, an affectionate term for a grandfather.

Connect: *Spoons remind me of medicine.*

Respond: *I felt sadness and love in the poem. The grandfather really loves his grandchild. The narrator remembers how he got old and sick.*

Respond: *The image of how the grandfather got old and sick is most real to me. The line that says he doesn't live here anymore made me think that maybe he died.*

is blankets and spoons and big brown shoes
who snores up and down up and down up and down again
is the rain on the roof that falls like coins
asking who loves him
who loves him who?

Reader's Response
Which image of the grandfather is most vivid to you?

Sandra Cisneros (1954–) was raised in Chicago. Because her parents were from Mexico, Cisneros grew up speaking both English and Spanish. Her writing draws on her Mexican heritage and her life experiences, especially her childhood. Cisneros has also taught creative writing to students in elementary school, high school, and college. She has published two collections of poems, *Bad Boys* and *My Wicked, Wicked Ways*, as well as a novel, *The House on Mango Street.*

EZRA DAVENPORT, 1929 (detail)
Clarence Holbrook Carter
Courtesy of the Artist

Responding to the Selection

Your Response

1. Does Abuelito remind you of anyone you know? Explain.
2. How would someone like Abuelito make you feel? Explain.

Recalling

3. What does Abuelito ask?
4. Why can't Abuelito come out to play?

Interpreting

5. Why does Abuelito speak to the narrator in Spanish and English?
6. What are the narrator's feelings toward Abuelito? Support your answer.
7. Compare the images the poet uses to describe Abuelito in lines 3–5 with the images she uses in lines 10–16. How has Abuelito changed? Explain.

Applying

8. In what ways does this poem honor all grandparents?

Analyzing Literature

Appreciating Images

Images are pictures poets create with words that appeal to our five senses. Cisneros uses images related to sight, sound, and touch in her poem. For example, Abuelito is "dough and feathers," he laughs "like the letter k," and his "hair is made of fur." These images are vivid because you can see, hear, and touch these things in your imagination.

1. Find another example of an image that appeals to the sense of sight. What specific words create this image?
2. Abuelito "snores up and down up and down up and down." To what sense does this image appeal?

Critical Thinking and Reading

Making Inferences About Images

An **inference** is a reasonable conclusion you draw from stated information. In this poem you make inferences about the title character based on the images that the author uses. For example, the author says that Abuelito is "a doorknob tied to a sour stick." This image makes you think of someone thin and sickly.

1. Is the Abuelito described in the first five lines of the poem healthy or sick? Support your answer.
2. What images tell you that Abuelito loves the narrator of the poem?

Thinking and Writing

Using Images to Describe People

Vivid images can describe a person more accurately than facts and figures. For example, saying that someone is a "whirlwind" tells you more about his or her manner and style than a list of accomplishments could. Choose a famous person and write a series of images to describe the person, but do not mention the person's name.

When you have finished writing your description, share your images with your classmates to see if they can recognize the person you have described.

Learning Options

1. **Art.** Create a collage about grandfathers. You may have your collage represent grandfathers in general or a specific one, like your own. You may use pictures cut from magazines, photographs, or any other items on your collage.
2. **Writing.** Write the message to go into a birthday card to "Abuelito," to your own grandfather, or to any special older person you know. The message should communicate the special feelings you have for this person. You may create the whole card as well.

The Elements of Poetry

LAURENCE AT THE PIANO
Fairfield Porter
Hirschl & Adler

GUIDE FOR READING

The Geese

Richard Peck (1934–) was born in Decatur, Illinois. Peck is best known for his young-adult novels such as *Ghosts I Have Been, Dreamland Lake,* and *Secrets of the Shopping Mall.* Since he gave up teaching in 1972 with the publication of his first novel, *Don't Look and It Won't Hurt,* Peck has published more than fifteen novels dealing with concerns of teenagers. Difficult relationships, the meaning of friendship, and the joys and sorrows of love are just a few of the themes in his books. Now Peck spends much of his time visiting schools and talking with young people. "The Geese" describes not a young person but a father's actions and feelings.

Dust of Snow

Robert Frost (1875–1963) is considered a New England poet even though he was born thousands of miles away in San Francisco. When Frost moved to New England, he found the land that would be his home for most of his life. Beginning with his first book of poetry, *A Boy's Will* (1913), Frost painted moving portraits of nature and rural life. In "Dust of Snow," you will get a small sample of the work of a poet who won the Pulitzer Prize four times, more than any other poet.

Adventures of Isabel

Ogden Nash (1902–1971) is considered by many to be the best writer of light, humorous verse in America. Nash held many different jobs, from teaching school to working on Wall Street, before he turned to writing verse. Like many new writers, Nash was not sure of his talent. He threw out his first attempt at a poem, then retrieved it and sent it to a magazine, which published it. Among his long list of books are *Parents Keep Out: Elderly Poems for Youngerly Readers* and *Custard and Company: Poems by Ogden Nash.* You will see his playful touch in "Adventures of Isabel."

Stanza and Verse

A **stanza** is a group of lines of poetry, usually similar in length and pattern and separated by spaces. Much like a paragraph in prose, each stanza usually develops one idea.

A **verse** is a single line of poetry. It may be a complete sentence, but most of the time it is only part of a sentence. The word *verse* also refers to poetry in general.

X. J. Kennedy divided his poem "Lighting a Fire" into two stanzas with three verses each:

One quick scratch
Of a kitchen match
And giant flames unzip!

How do they store
So huge a roar
In such a tiny tip?

In each stanza the three lines (verses) are part of a single sentence. Note how each of the two stanzas contains its own main idea.

Focus

Poets can have very different views of animals and the natural world. Where one poet may see animals as noble and powerful, another may view them as comical or with human characteristics. Make a chart like the one below, and write your views of geese, the crow, and the bear. As you read the poems that follow, compare your views with those of the three poets in this section.

Geese	Crow	Bear

Vocabulary

Knowing the following words will help you read these poems.

lure (lo͞or) *n.*: Anything that attracts or tempts (p. 433)

rued (ro͞od) *v.*: Regretted (p. 434)

ravenous (rav′ ə nəs) *adj.*: Greedily hungry (p. 435)

cavernous (kav′ ər nəs) *adj.*: Deep and empty (p. 435)

scurry (skʉr′ ē) *v.*: To run hastily (p. 435)

rancor (raŋ′ kər) *n.*: Bitter hate or ill will (p. 435)

hideous (hid′ ē əs) *adj.*: Very ugly (p. 435)

concocter (kən käkt′ ər) *n.*: Inventor (p. 436)

GEESE IN FLIGHT
Roy Mason
The Genesee Country Museum
Mumford, New York

The Geese

Richard Peck

My father was the first to hear
The passage of the geese each fall,
Passing above the house so near
He'd hear within his heart their call.

And then at breakfast time he'd say:
"The geese were heading south last night,"
For he had lain awake till day,
Feeling his earthbound soul take flight.

Knowing that winter's wind comes soon
After the rushing of those wings,
Seeing them pass before the moon,
Recalling the lure of faroff things.

Reader's Response

What special feelings or thoughts do you associate with fall?

Responding to the Selection

Interpreting

1. Which images in each stanza suggest the coming of winter?
2. What feelings does hearing the passage of the geese stir up in the father?
3. Of what might the father be thinking when he recalled "the lure of faroff things"?

Applying

4. Have you ever felt "the lure of faroff things"? Have you been filled with a desire to wander? Explain your answer.

Analyzing Literature

Understanding Stanza

A **stanza** is a group of lines that present one main idea in a poem. You can tell by the break after lines 4 and 8 that there are three stanzas in "The Geese."

1. State the main idea of each stanza.
2. How do the main ideas of the separate stanzas develop the theme of the poem?

BEFORE THE WIND
Sheila Gardner
Collection of Mrs. Glenn C. Janss

Dust of Snow

Robert Frost

The way a crow
Shook down on me
The dust of snow
From a hemlock tree

Has given my heart
A change of mood
And saved some part
Of a day I had rued.

Responding to the Selection

Your Response

1. Has a small incident like the one in the poem ever made a difference in the way you felt? Explain your answer.

Recalling

2. Describe what happens in the first stanza.
3. How does the person react in the second stanza to what happened in the first stanza?

Interpreting

4. What contrasts in color can you see in the first stanza?
5. Why do you think the person reacts as he does in the second stanza?

Applying

6. What are some of the things that help to cheer you up when you are sad?

Learning Options

1. **Speaking and Listening.** The punctuation in a poem and the space between the stanzas often help you read a poem more meaningfully. Choose a partner and read "Dust of Snow" aloud to each other. Let the meaning and punctuation guide your reading. Notice that the poem consists of one sentence. The first stanza contains the subject of the sentence, and the second stanza contains the predicate. The stanza break does not have any punctuation that would signal a pause.
2. **Writing.** "Dust of Snow" is written from the viewpoint of a human being. Write another version of the poem—from the crow's point of view. Pretend that you are the crow, and you have just been startled by the appearance of a person passing your tree. Reveal your feelings about the situation and mention your reason for shaking the snow down onto the person.

Adventures of Isabel

Ogden Nash

Isabel met an enormous bear,
Isabel, Isabel, didn't care;
The bear was hungry, the bear was ravenous,
The bear's big mouth was cruel and cavernous.
The bear said, Isabel, glad to meet you,
How do, Isabel, now I'll eat you!
Isabel, Isabel, didn't worry,
Isabel didn't scream or scurry.
She washed her hands and she straightened her hair up,
Then Isabel quietly ate the bear up.

Once in a night as black as pitch
Isabel met a wicked old witch.
The witch's face was cross and wrinkled,
The witch's gums with teeth were sprinkled.
Ho ho, Isabel! the old witch crowed,
I'll turn you into an ugly toad!
Isabel, Isabel, didn't worry,
Isabel didn't scream or scurry,
She showed no rage and she showed no rancor,
But she turned the witch into milk and drank her.

Isabel met a hideous giant,
Isabel continued self-reliant.
The giant was hairy, the giant was horrid,
He had one eye in the middle of his forehead.
Good morning Isabel, the giant said,
I'll grind your bones to make my bread.
Isabel, Isabel, didn't worry,
Isabel didn't scream or scurry.
She nibbled the zwieback[1] that she always fed off,
And when it was gone, she cut the giant's head off.

---

1. zwieback (swē′ bak) *n.*: A kind of bread or biscuit that is sliced and toasted after being baked.

Isabel met a troublesome doctor,
He punched and he poked till he really shocked her.
The doctor's talk was of coughs and chills
And the doctor's satchel bulged with pills.
The doctor said unto Isabel,
Swallow this, it will make you well.
Isabel, Isabel, didn't worry,
Isabel didn't scream or scurry.
She took those pills from the pill concocter,
And Isabel calmly cured the doctor.

Reader's Response

Which adversary in the poem would you least like to face? Why?

RESPONDING TO THE SELECTION

Your Response

1. Would you enjoy knowing someone like Isabel? Why or why not?
2. Have you ever wanted to be like Isabel? Explain your answer.

Recalling

3. Identify who or what Isabel meets in each stanza.
4. What does each person or thing threaten to do to Isabel?
5. Describe how Isabel takes care of each person or thing.

Interpreting

6. Explain how you know Isabel does not panic when she meets someone or something who wants to harm her.
7. Why do you think the poet does not describe Isabel but does describe the other characters?
8. At what line in each stanza do you begin to think that she will triumph over the opponent?

Applying

9. As we read this poem, we side with Isabel, who seems to be an underdog—the weaker person or team in a struggle or contest. Why do we often tend to root for the underdog?

CRITICAL THINKING AND READING

Recognizing the Effects of Connotation

Connotation is the emotional response that a word produces in a reader. Denotation is the dictionary meaning of a word. For example, the denotation of "enormous" is "very large." However, "enormous" means much more to us when we hear it. We picture tremendous size that can take our breath away. This emotional response is the connotation of the word.

1. For each of the following words from the poem, describe the connotation—the emotional response each word brings to mind.
   a. horrid b. nibbled c. bulged
2. For each word in question 1, substitute a word that has nearly the same meaning. For example, substitute the word *devoured* for the word *nibbled.* Explain how the connotation of each new word changes the feeling of the line.

THINKING AND WRITING

Writing Another Stanza

Write an additional stanza describing another of Isabel's adventures. Start by brainstorming for ideas about who her opponent should be, how the opponent would threaten her, and how she could overcome the opponent. As you write your first draft, use the same pattern that each stanza in the poem follows: (1) Isabel meets opponent; (2) Opponent is described; (3) Opponent speaks; (4) "Isabel, Isabel, didn't worry . . ."; (5) Isabel takes action and triumphs. As you revise, change or add words so that your lines resemble those in "Adventures of Isabel." Proofread your stanza and prepare a final draft. Perhaps you could draw a picture of the adventure to accompany your final draft.

Share your stanza with your classmates.

LEARNING OPTIONS

1. **Art.** Make a copy of "Adventures of Isabel." Mount the poem on two sheets of paper. Next to each stanza, draw a picture that illustrates what is happening in the stanza. When you have finished illustrating the poem, display your work in the classroom.
2. **Writing.** Pretend that you are Isabel. Write a diary entry for each adventure in the poem. Explain how you felt about each of your adversaries and tell whether or not you were really scared when you met them. Share your diary entries with the class.

GUIDE FOR READING

The Shark

John Ciardi (1916–1986) was an American writer who published his first book of children's poetry, *The Reason for the Pelican,* in 1959. Three years later he won the Junior Book Award from the Boys' Club of America for another book, *The Man Who Sang the Sillies.* In addition to his children's books, John Ciardi wrote books, primarily poetry and translations, for adults. Much of his children's verse, including "The Shark," is marked by humor based in part on nonsense.

Door Number Four

Charlotte Pomerantz (1930–   ) was born in Brooklyn, New York. Her books for children have been very well received. In fact, she won the Jane Addams' Children's Book Award in 1975 for *The Princess and the Admiral.* In 1984 she won a Christopher Award for *Posy.* Charlotte Pomerantz's fascination with language, not just English, can be seen in two of her books: *The Tomarindo Puppy* and *If I Had a Paka,* which is the source of "Door Number Four." This poem inventively combines the English language with the Indonesian language.

Books Fall Open

David McCord (1897–   ) was born in New York City but has spent much of his life in Boston, Massachusetts. In his long literary career, he has written books of poems, essays, and nonfiction, as well as many remarkable books of children's poems. Although he published his first adult book in 1926, his first book of children's poems was not published until 1952. David McCord believes that poetry is rhythm, "just as the planet Earth is rhythm." "Books Fall Open" is an example of his sense of rhythm and his sense of wordplay.

Rhyme and Rhythm

Rhyme is the repetition of sounds at the ends of words. For example, *bleak* and *streak* rhyme. The most common type of rhyme in poetry is end rhyme, where the words at the ends of the lines rhyme. Words can also rhyme within a line. In many poems the rhyming lines in each stanza follow the same pattern. For example, if a poem has stanzas of four lines each, the rhyme pattern could be that alternate lines rhyme. Of course, not all poems contain rhyme.

Rhythm is the sound pattern created by stressed and unstressed syllables. Stressed syllables receive more emphasis than unstressed syllables. The stressed syllables are underlined in the following familiar song:

Twinkle, twinkle, little star.
How I wonder what you are.

This pattern of stressed and unstressed syllables gives the poem a rhythm, a beat. The rhythm helps give poetry its musical quality.

Focus

"Books fall open,/you fall in." These are the opening lines of one of the poems you are about to read. Suppose you are about to fall into one of these poems about sharks, finding friendship, or reading books. Which poem would you choose? In a small group, discuss your choice. Then write a brief paragraph telling why you would like to be inside that poem. As you read each poem, think about whether your expectations about the poem were accurate. Would you choose a different poem? Why or why not?

Vocabulary

Knowing the following words will help you read these poems.

drab (drab) *adj.*: Dull; dreary (p. 440)

delver (delv′ ər) *n.*: Investigator (p. 443)

wherewithal (hwer′ with ôl′) *n.*: Necessary means to do something (p. 443)

venture (ven′ chər) *v.*: Do or go at some risk (p. 443)

hanker (haŋ′ kər) *v.*: Crave; long (p. 443)

Spelling Tip

You will have few problems with the spelling of *wherewithal* if you break the word into its parts: *where + with + al.*

The Shark

John Ciardi

My dear, let me tell you about the shark.
Though his eyes are bright, his thought is dark.
He's quiet—that speaks well of him.
So does the fact that he can swim.
But though he swims without a sound,
Wherever he swims he looks around
With those two bright eyes and that one dark thought.
He has only one but he thinks it a lot.
And the thought he thinks but can never complete
Is his long dark thought of something to eat.
Most anything does. And I have to add
That when he eats his manners are bad.
He's a gulper, a ripper, a snatcher, a grabber.
Yes, his manners are drab. But his thought is drabber.
That one dark thought he can never complete
Of something—anything—somehow to eat.

Be careful where you swim, my sweet.

Reader's Response
What is your attitude about sharks? Does it mirror the poet's attitude? Why or why not?

Responding to the Selection

Your Response

1. Has this poem changed your feelings toward sharks? Explain.

Recalling

2. What qualities "speak well" of the shark?

Interpreting

3. Why is the shark's "one dark thought" never satisfied?
4. What point does the repetition of the phrase "one dark thought" make about the shark?
5. What is the effect of the poem's final line?
6. Imagine you are a storyteller reading this poem aloud to a group of students. What tone of voice would you use? Why? What words would you emphasize? Why?

Applying

7. This poem makes fun of something that terrifies us. Why do you think human beings

POSTER FROM THE MOVIE *JAWS*

ridicule things that are really frightening? Have you ever done this? If so, explain.

ANALYZING LITERATURE

Understanding Rhyme

Rhyme is the repetition of sounds at the ends of words. The rhymes in this poem are **end rhymes.** The lines are arranged in couplets—pairs of rhymed lines. The rhymes give the poem a playful quality, despite its subject and warning. It also makes the poem more pleasurable to read aloud.

1. Each of the couplets expresses a complete thought. How does the rhyme pattern make it easier to understand these thoughts?
2. What is the effect of the change in the rhyme pattern of the final line?

Door Number Four

Charlotte Pomerantz

Above my uncle's grocery store
is a pintu,
is a door.
On the pintu
is a number,
nomer empat,
number four.
In the door
there is a key.
Turn it,
enter quietly.
Hush hush, diam-diam,
quietly.
There, in lamplight,
you will see
a friend,
teman,
a friend
who's me.

RESPONDING TO THE SELECTION

Your Response

1. Would you like the speaker in the poem to be your friend? Why or why not?

Recalling

2. What do these Indonesian words mean?
   a. pintu d. diam
   b. nomer e. empat
   c. teman

Interpreting

3. Why does the poet say to "enter quietly"?
4. Do you think this poem takes place in a city or in the country? Why?

Applying

5. Why are friends more willing to do things for each other than for strangers?

ANALYZING LITERATURE

Recognizing Rhythm

Rhythm is created by using stressed and unstressed syllables to create a sound pattern. In the first line of "Door Number Four," for example, you will find the following stressed and unstressed syllables (stressed syllables are underlined):

Above my uncle's grocery store

1. Write down lines 4–8 and underline the stressed syllables.
2. Read "Door Number Four" aloud to a partner. Try to find a comfortable, natural rhythm. Read it again. You might tap out the rhythm as you read. When you are listening to your partner, listen to the rhythm created by the stressed and the unstressed syllables.

Books Fall Open

David McCord

Books fall open,
you fall in,
delighted where
you've never been;
hear voices not once
heard before,
reach world on world
through door on door;
find unexpected
keys to things
locked up beyond
imaginings.
What *might* you be,
perhaps *become*,
because one book
is somewhere? Some
wise delver into
wisdom, wit,
and wherewithal
has written it.

True books will venture,
dare you out,
whisper secrets,
maybe shout
across the gloom
to you in need,
who hanker for
a book to read.

ESBJORN, from A FAMILY
Carl Larsson

Responding to the Selection

Your Response

1. Does this poem describe how you feel about books? Explain.

Recalling

2. From the first stanza, describe three discoveries you might find when you read.
3. How do "True books" affect you?

Interpreting

4. What does the poet mean when he says that you "fall in" to a book?
5. Briefly summarize the poet's attitude toward reading.

Applying

6. The first two lines of the poem make it sound as if finding worthwhile things to read is accidental. Do you think that is true? Explain.
7. How has reading affected you? Name some books, stories, or articles that have influenced you and explain how.

Playing With Words

We all have fun playing with words. Poets play with the sounds and meanings of words all of the time. Part of poetry is, after all, word play.

Your Turn

You can join in the word play of poetry by writing a humorous, two-line synonym poem. The first line of a synonym poem mentions a subject and gives three or four synonyms or related words. The second line completes a thought about the subject. The lines should have about the same rhythm, and the last words in each line should rhyme.

Prewriting

1. Write your subject on the top of a sheet of paper. Your subject may be an idea or a thing, but it should be a word that has a lot of synonyms. Underneath, list all the synonyms and related words you can think of. For example, Sylvester chose *BIG* as a subject, and wrote the following synonyms and related words: *large, huge, great, giant, immense, colossal, blimp.*

2. Complete the thought. Look over your list of synonyms. What associations do the words call up? List these, and choose one to complete the thought in the second line of the poem. Sylvester's list reminded him of how his belly felt after he ate pizza.

Drafting

From your synonym list, choose the best three or four words for the first line of your poem. The last word in the line should be only one or two syllables, so you can more easily find a word to rhyme with it. Sylvester chose *huge, great, colossal.*

Your second line should complete a thought about the subject, rhyme with the first line, and have about the same rhythm as the first line. With these guidelines, Sylvester wrote the following synonym poem:

Pizza

Big, huge, colossal, great
My belly shows how much I ate.

Revising

Ask yourself or ask a partner the following questions:

- Are the words in the first line vivid and expressive?
- Does the second line complete a thought or make a clever statement related to the first line?
- Do the final words in each line rhyme?
- Do the two lines have the same rhythm?

Use the answers to revise your poem. Play with the words to make it even better.

The Language of Poetry

DREAM SAFARI
Marcy Cook, student
Highlands Ranch, Colorado
From the 1991–1992 Crayola Dream-Makers Collection, property of Binney & Smith, Inc.
Reprinted with permission.

GUIDE FOR READING

Simile: Willow and Ginkgo

Eve Merriam (1916–1992) was born in Philadelphia. Because her family was always interested in books and reading, Merriam began her lifelong fascination with poetry at an early age. She said, "I remember being enthralled by the sound of words, by their musicality . . . And, of course, there is a special magic about rhyme, the chime that rings with time." Her interest in poetry led to a life-long writing career for both children and adults that included numerous collections of poetry as well as fiction, nonfiction, and drama. Her first book of poetry for adults, *Family Circle,* was awarded the Yale Series of Younger Poets Prize in 1946. In 1962 Merriam's first book of poetry for children, *There is No Rhyme for Silver,* was published. Merriam felt that poetry for young people should be fun yet memorable. She also felt that "poetry is closer to painting than any other form of literature." Notice how Merriam uses words to create pictures in "Simile: Willow and Ginkgo."

Sun

Valerie Worth (1933–   ) began a series of poems whose subjects are "small" things with her first poetry book for children, appropriately titled *Small Poems.* She has also published a collection of magic spells and incantations, *The Crone's Book of Words.* Worth was born in Philadelphia and was graduated from Swarthmore College. Her hobbies, gardening and astronomy, reflect an interest in things that change slowly. Indeed, she has written that the "stuff of poetry" is "that which changes slowly. . . ." "Sun" is about one of the things in our world that never changes, the sun's warmth.

Simile

Poets use language imaginatively to help you see or feel things in a new way. One technique that poets use is the **simile.** A simile is a comparison in which a similar quality is pointed out in two basically unlike things. Similes make comparisons using the words *like* or *as*. We frequently use similes in our everyday speech. For example, perhaps you have heard someone say, "She ran like the wind," in which the speed of a girl is compared to the speed of the wind; or, "His head is as hard as a rock," in which a boy's head is compared to the hardness of a rock.

By showing a similarity between two basically unlike things, the writer creates an unusual and memorable picture. In the following stanza from the poem "On Our Way," poet Eve Merriam uses three similes to suggest ways of moving:

What kind of walk shall we take today?
Leap like a frog? Creep like a snail?
Scamper like a squirrel with a furry tail?

By comparing the movements of basically unlike things—people and frogs, people and snails, people and squirrels—Merriam creates a vivid comparison that is easy to remember and to understand.

Focus

In the poems "Simile: Willow and Gingko" and "Sun" you will find similes that help you visualize the authors' descriptions of trees and the sun. Similes are not used just in poetic language. People often use similes to describe everyday events. Create a "simile diary" by writing similes that tell about your day. For example, when you woke up you might have "stretched like a cat." Write at least four similes in your diary. As you read the poems, look for the similes these poets used.

Vocabulary

Knowing the following words will help you read these poems.

sleek (slēk) *adj.*: Smooth and shiny (p. 449)

streaming (strēm′ iŋ) *v.*: Floating; flying (p. 449)

thrives (thrīvz) *v.*: Grows successfully and strong (p. 450)

Spelling Tip

Both *sleek* and *streaming* have the long *e* sound; however, *sleek* is spelled with two *e*'s while *streaming* is spelled with *ea.*

Simile: Willow and Ginkgo[1]

Eve Merriam

The willow is like an etching,[2]
Fine-lined against the sky.
The ginkgo is like a crude sketch,
Hardly worthy to be signed.

The willow's music is like a soprano,[3]
Delicate and thin.
The ginkgo's tune is like a chorus
With everyone joining in.

The willow is sleek as a velvet-nosed calf;
The ginkgo is leathery as an old bull.
The willow's branches are like silken thread;
The ginkgo's like stubby rough wool.

The willow is like a nymph[4] with streaming hair;
Wherever it grows, there is green and gold and fair.
The willow dips to the water,
Protected and precious, like the king's favorite daughter.

---

1. ginkgo (giŋ′ kō) *n.*: An Asiatic tree with fan-shaped leaves.
2. etching (ech′ iŋ) *n.*: A print of a drawing or design made on metal, glass, or wood.
3. soprano (sə pran′ ō) *n.*: The highest singing voice of women, girls, or young boys.
4. nymph (nimf) *n.*: A goddess of nature, thought of as a beautiful maiden.

The ginkgo forces its way through gray concrete;
Like a city child, it grows up in the street.
Thrust against the metal sky,
Somehow it survives and even thrives.

My eyes feast upon the willow,
But my heart goes to the ginkgo.

Reader's Response
Are you more like the willow or the ginkgo? Explain.

Responding to the Selection

Your Response

1. Is there a tree in your neighborhood or park that you like? Explain why you like this tree.
2. Did you enjoy reading this poem? Why or why not?

Recalling

3. List all the things to which the willow is compared.
4. List all the things to which the ginkgo is compared.

Interpreting

5. What traits does the willow have? What traits does the ginkgo have? Compare the willow's and the ginkgo's traits.
6. Why do the poet's eyes go out to the willow? Why does the poet's heart go out to the ginkgo?

Applying

7. Does a person need the qualities of both the willow and the ginkgo? Explain.
8. If you were going to compare each tree to an animal, which animals would you choose? Why?

Analyzing Literature

Understanding Simile

When a writer uses a **simile,** he or she points out a similar quality in two things that seem to be unlike. These comparisons use the words *like* or *as.*

1. List three similes from the poem. What qualities are compared in each?
2. What qualities do the similes of the willow have in common? What do these qualities indicate about the willow?
3. What qualities do the similes of the ginkgo have in common? What do these qualities indicate about the ginkgo?
4. Explain how "like an etching" is a better simile than "like a drawing." Why does "like the king's favorite daughter" work better than "like a daughter"?

Learning Option

Speaking and Listening. Work with a partner or a group to read this poem aloud in two parts. First decide who will read the lines about the willow and who will read the lines about the ginkgo. Remember that the willow is ". . . like a soprano,/Delicate and thin," while "The ginkgo's tune is like a chorus." Be sure to follow the punctuation and stanza breaks rather than the line breaks. Present your reading to your classmates.

AT LEAST FOR NOW
Leslie Baker

Sun

Valerie Worth

The sun
Is a leaping fire
Too hot
To go near,

But it will still
Lie down
In warm yellow squares
On the floor

Like a flat
Quilt, where
The cat can curl
And purr.

Responding to the Selection

Your Response

1. Which of Worth's descriptions of the sun do you like better? Explain.

Recalling

2. What is the sun in the first stanza? What is the sun compared to in the final stanza?

Interpreting

3. How does the description of the sun change from the first stanza to the second stanza?
4. Why do you think the poet uses the word *quilt* rather than, say, *blanket*?
5. What do the actions of the cat suggest?

Applying

6. To what other things can you compare the different strengths of the sun's heat?

Thinking and Writing

Writing a Poem of Contrast

The first stanza of "Sun" gives a strong image of the sun as "Too hot/To go near." The rest of the poem, however, changes that image, showing the sun as a "flat/Quilt, where/The cat can curl." Try to write a poem that begins with one image but that ends with an opposite one.

Work with a partner to brainstorm for ideas for your poem. Try to think of things that can be contrasted from the start of the poem to the end. For example, a day starts with brightness but ends with darkness, or a cat hunts mice and birds yet likes to have you rub its ears and belly. As you write your first draft, try to use similes to create vivid and memorable images. Read your first draft aloud to your partner, and use any of your partner's helpful suggestions in your revision.

GUIDE FOR READING

Ankylosaurus

Jack Prelutsky (1940–) was born in Brooklyn, New York, but has lived in Albuquerque, New Mexico, for a number of years. Before he turned to writing full time, Prelutsky was a cab driver, a furniture mover, and a potter. Then, at the urging of a friend, Prelutsky submitted a collection of nonsense verses to a publisher. This resulted in his first book of children's verses, *A Gopher in the Garden and Other Animal Poems* (1967). He has since published many books of his own verse as well as books of verse he translated from German. Prelutsky has many talents and interests in addition to writing. One of these talents is singing, and he has appeared in summer opera companies and the musical play *Fiddler on the Roof.* His other hobbies include book collecting, making wooden toys, and inventing word and board games. "Ankylosaurus" reveals another of Jack Prelutsky's interests, dinosaurs.

How to Write a Poem About the Sky

Leslie Marmon Silko (1948–) was raised on the Laguna Pueblo reservation in New Mexico. Her poetry reflects the Pueblo Indians' respect for nature and story telling. "How to Write a Poem About the Sky" is about a landscape very different from the deserts of New Mexico where Silko grew up. This poem describes the tundra—a cold, barren geographic region in western Alaska.

Metaphor

Like a simile, a **metaphor** suggests a similarity between two generally unlike things. A metaphor, however, does not use the words *like* or *as.* Instead, a metaphor describes something as though it were something else. For example, if you take a test that has easy questions to answer, you might say that the test was "a piece of cake." You don't mean this literally, of course—the test isn't really a piece of cake. But by showing the similarity between a test and a piece of cake, which is delicious and therefore easy to eat, the metaphor shows how easy the test was to take.

Focus

The two poems you are about to read are about dinosaurs and the sky. What images come to mind when you think about dinosaurs or the sky? In a group of three of four, make a word web for either dinosaur or sky. Use the models below to help you get started. When you are finished, use your word web to write two or three metaphors about your word. For example, if your word is sky, you might write, "the sky is a door to the universe." As you read the poems, compare your metaphors with the metaphors the poets have made.

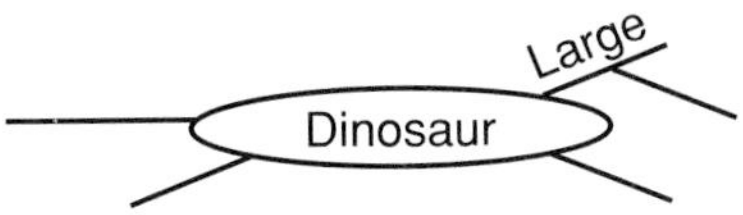

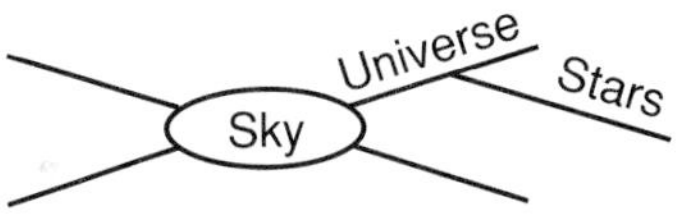

Vocabulary

Knowing the following words will help you read "Ankylosaurus" and "How to Write a Poem About the Sky."

inedible (in ed′ ə b'l) *adj.*: Not fit to be eaten (p. 454)

minuscule (min′ ə skyo͞ol′) *adj.*: Tiny (p. 454)

cudgel (kuj′ əl) *n.*: A short, thick stick or club (p. 454)

gristle (gris′ 'l) *n.*: Cartilage; tough, elastic tissue that is part of the skeleton (p. 454)

membranes (mem′ brāns) *n.*: Thin, flexible layers, especially of animal or plant tissue (p. 456)

Spelling Tip

Notice that *minuscule* contains the word *minus.* Remember this to help you spell it.

Ankylosaurus[1]

Jack Prelutsky

Clankity Clankity Clankity Clank!
Ankylosaurus was built like a tank,
its hide was a fortress as sturdy as steel,
it tended to be an inedible meal.

It was armored in front, it was armored behind,
there wasn't a thing on its minuscule mind,
it waddled about on its four stubby legs,
nibbling on plants with a mouthful of pegs.

Ankylosaurus was best left alone,
its tail was a cudgel of gristle and bone,
Clankity Clankity Clankity Clank!
Ankylosaurus was built like a tank.

1. **Ankylosaurus** (aŋ′ kə lō sôr′ əs) *n.*: A heavily armored, short-legged dinosaur.

Responding to the Selection

Your Response

1. Do you find this description of the ankylosaurus humorous?

Recalling

2. Give two reasons why the ankylosaurus was an inedible meal.

Interpreting

3. What sort of personality did the ankylosaurus have?
4. Why was the ankylosaurus best left alone?

Applying

5. Dinosaurs are very popular among young people. Can you suggest a reason for this popularity?

Analyzing Literature

Understanding Metaphor

A **metaphor** suggests a similarity between two things that seem dissimilar. Through such comparisons, a poet emphasizes certain qualities in the things being compared.

1. The ankylosaurus was "built like a tank." Find two metaphors in the poem that develop this comparison. How do these metaphors help you visualize this extinct beast?
2. For this poem, why are the similarities between the ankylosaurus and a tank more important than the differences?
3. How do lines 1 and 11 add to the overall comparison developed in the poem?

ONE WRITER'S PROCESS

Jack Prelutsky and "Ankylosaurus"

An Accidental Poet Jack Prelutsky began writing poems "quite by accident." His first poems were written to accompany his drawings of imaginary creatures. Prelutsky says that "these first poems were 'nonsense' poems because the creatures were strange and silly." A friend encouraged Prelutsky to show his drawings and poems to an editor. Prelutsky recalls that the editor "hated my drawings, but loved my verses, and encouraged me to write poems about real animals." He then went on to write his first book, *A Gopher in the Garden.*

Fascination with Dinosaurs Prelutsky reports that he has always been fascinated by dinosaurs. "When I was a kid," he says, "I frequently visited The Museum of Natural History, where I was delighted and awed by skeletons and fragments of tyrannosaurus, brontosaurus, and many others."

DRAFTING

A Humorous Poem Prelutsky knew that "Ankylosaurus" was going to be humorous, like the rest of his poems in *Tyrannosaurus Was a Beast.* "I almost never write a poem in one sitting, and 'Ankylosaurus' was no exception," he reports. He believes that "Ankylosaurus" was "composed over a period of days."

REVISING

A Dozen Revisions Prelutsky is fortunate in that rhyming, a chief device of his poems, comes easily to him. Still, he finds it necessary to revise his work. Although he remembers writing "Ankylosaurus" with little difficulty, he adds that he "probably rewrote it at least a dozen times" before he was satisfied.

PUBLISHING

Putting Words to Music "I've often performed 'Ankylosaurus' as a song," Prelutsky says, "setting it to the music of 'Sweet Betsy from Pike.' When I sing it for children, I add a 'clankity-clankity-clankity-clank' chorus and have them join in."

Advice to Young Writers Prelutsky offers this advice to young writers:

"Keep your eyes and ears open, and try to be aware of what's going on around you. *Notice things.*

"Always carry a notebook, and as soon as you see, hear, or remember something that seems special, *write it down.*

"*Read! Read! Read!* The more you read, the more you'll learn about writing.

"*Write, write, write!* The more you practice, the better you'll get."

THINKING ABOUT THE PROCESS

1. Prelutsky says he often performs "Ankylosaurus" as a song. How would singing the poem change your feelings about it?
2. **Cooperative Activity** Together with several classmates, study a picture or figurine of an animal. What writing ideas does it give you? Share your ideas with the class.

How to Write a Poem About the Sky

Leslie Marmon Silko

for the students of the Bethel Middle School, Bethel, Alaska—Feb. 1975

You see the sky now
colder than the frozen river
so dense and white
little birds
walk across it.

You see the sky now
but the earth
is lost in it
and there are no horizons.
It is all
a single breath.

You see the sky
but the earth is called
by the same name
                    the moment
                    the wind shifts
sun splits it open
and bluish membranes
push through slits of skin.

You see the sky

VOICES OF THE CLOUDS
Jessie Lee Geiszler
Courtesy of the Artist

RESPONDING TO THE SELECTION

Your Response

1. Describe the mood of this poem.
2. What does the sky make you think of?

Interpreting

3. Why is there no horizon in the landscape?
4. Why is the phrase "the moment/the wind shifts" placed where it is on the page?

Applying

5. How does knowing that this poem describes an Alaskan landscape clarify its metaphors?

CRITICAL THINKING AND READING

Analyzing the Details of a Metaphor

Metaphors must make sense if they are to be memorable. Are the things being compared really similar in the way the poet suggests? Does the metaphor help you look at the subject with new understanding?

1. To what does the poet compare the sky in lines 16–19?
2. Does the poem suggest a new way of looking at the sky? Explain your answer.

THINKING AND WRITING

Writing Metaphors

Write metaphors that describe people you know. First list four or five people. Next to each name write a character trait that you wish to describe. Then choose an animal or an object that shares that same trait. Finally, write a metaphor that suggests the similarity between each person and the animal or object you have chosen.

GUIDE FOR READING

April Rain Song

Langston Hughes (1902–1967) was born in Joplin, Missouri, and was raised in Illinois and Ohio. After attending classes at Columbia University for a year, Hughes left school and traveled to Europe and Africa working on merchant ships. He returned to the United States and settled in Harlem, a section of New York City. While living in Harlem, Hughes was exposed to jazz and blues, music which came to influence his poetry. Among Hughes's best-known collections of poetry are *The Weary Blues* (1926), *The Dream Keeper* (1932), and *Montage of a Dream Deferred* (1951). He also wrote fiction, plays, movie screenplays, and autobiographical sketches. Although much of Hughes's poetry addresses the difficulties of life for urban blacks, "April Rain Song" shows a gentle side of living in the city.

Winter Poem

Nikki Giovanni (1943–   ) spent a happy childhood in Knoxville, Tennessee, where she was born. Although her poetry often voices her concern for the black community, she considers herself an individualist, who writes about love and life and a person's fight for survival. Her poems and articles have appeared in many newspapers and magazines. Giovanni's work earned her a National Book Award nomination as well as inclusion in the Ohio Women's Hall of Fame. She says that "children are an exciting audience to both read to and write for . . . I hope my poetry reaches both the heart and the mind of a child who is a child and the adult who still nurtures the child within." You will notice her vivid imagination, sensitivity, and eye for detail when you read "Winter Poem."

Personification

Poets may give human qualities to objects or ideas. This technique is called **personification,** a long word that contains a shorter word, person. Personification can add life to writing by making us see common things in a new way. For example, you might have heard someone describe the frigid winter air as "biting cold" or an eroding shoreline as being "eaten away by the water." Of course, cold air cannot really bite, and water cannot really eat, but giving these nonhuman elements human qualities makes the descriptions more striking. Writers use personification to emphasize qualities in ways we have not thought of. Yet when you read these examples of personification, you are struck by their appropriateness and vividness.

Focus

The two poems in this group use personification. In the first poem, rain is personified; in the second, snow. Think about the human qualities rain and snow might have. Then think of other elements of nature. Copy the chart below onto a sheet of paper. With a group of three or four classmates, list at least five elements of nature. Describe one or two things that this element does. Then write a personification of the element. Try to think of personifications that are unique or unusual. As you read "April Rain Song" and "Winter Poem," ask yourself how personification helps you to see or feel a poet's description.

Element of Nature	What It Does	Personification
Wind	*Shakes trees.*	*Wind is a bully.*

Vocabulary

Knowing the following words will help you read "April Rain Song" and "Winter Poem."

gutter (gut′ ər) *n.*: A narrow channel along the side of a road or street, to carry off water (p. 461)

engulfed (in gulft′) *v.*: Overwhelmed (p. 463)

RAINY NIGHT
Charles Burchfield
San Diego Museum of Art

April Rain Song

Langston Hughes

Let the rain kiss you.
Let the rain beat upon your head with silver
  liquid drops.
Let the rain sing you a lullaby.

The rain makes still pools on the sidewalk.
The rain makes running pools in the gutter.
The rain plays a little sleep-song on our roof
  at night—

And I love the rain.

Reader's Response
How does the rain make you feel?

Responding to the Selection

Your Response

1. Do you have different feelings about the rain at different times? Explain.
2. Has Hughes's poem changed your opinion of the rain?

Recalling

3. What three things are we asked to let the rain do to us?

Interpreting

4. To what feelings or emotions does the first stanza appeal?
5. Contrast what the rain does in the first stanza to what it does in the second stanza.
6. Why is the last line of the poem a logical ending? Why does it stand alone?

Applying

7. In what way does the sound of rain sometimes have the same effect as a lullaby or song?
8. Think of a time when you experienced rain as Hughes describes it. Then think of other kinds of rain. Describe some of the different kinds of rain that you've experienced.

Analyzing Literature

Understanding Personification

Personification is a way of speaking in which human qualities are given to a nonhuman subject.

1. What three human abilities is the rain given in the first stanza?
2. How do these human qualities help you to imagine the description of the rain?
3. Replace the three uses of personification with words that do not use personification. For example, you might change line 1 to read "Let the rain fall on you." How do these changes affect the poem?

Critical Thinking and Reading

Paraphrasing a Poem

Paraphrasing means putting a poem or a story into your own words. Paraphrasing a poem may help you to understand it better. Paraphrasing is never a substitute for the poem, but it helps you understand what the poet is saying.

Here is a paraphrase of the first stanza of "April Rain Song": The rain is as gentle as a kiss, drops of liquid, and a lullaby.

1. Paraphrase the second stanza of the poem.
2. Compare your paraphrase with the poem. Can you explain why the poem is more moving than your paraphrase?

Learning Options

1. **Art.** Look at the picture on page 460. What is the mood of the painting? Is the mood of the painting the same as the mood of the poem? Divide a sheet of paper into two columns. Head the first column "poem" and the other "painting." In each column, write how you think the poem or the painting portrays the rain. Then write a brief paragraph explaining whether or not the artist and the poet agree.
2. **Cross-curricular Connection.** Use your local or school library to find a piece of music to accompany "April Rain Song." You may wish to ask a music teacher for help. Be sure to choose a piece that reflects the mood of the poem. Then, read the poem aloud and play your chosen piece of music for the class.

MULTICULTURAL CONNECTION

The Importance of Rain

A Vietnamese story. There is a story in Vietnam about a king who once ruled in the sky and wanted to punish a young couple for a minor offense. He ordered the young man and woman to stay on opposite sides of the river, away from each other, and meet only once a year. Even today when they meet, they are so happy that they cannot stop crying for joy. This is why, according to Vietnamese legend, it always rains on that day—the seventh day of the seventh lunar month of each year.

Exploring and Sharing

You are probably familiar with such sayings as "It's raining cats and dogs" or "Keep something for a rainy day." Find other sayings and proverbs about rain and share them with the class. Ask classmates from other countries to tell you about their special customs related to rain.

Winter Poem

Nikki Giovanni

once a snowflake fell
on my brow and i loved
it so much and i kissed
it and it was happy and called its cousins
and brothers and a web
of snow engulfed me then
i reached to love them all
and i squeezed them and they became
a spring rain and i stood perfectly
still and was a flower

Responding to the Selection

Your Response

1. How does the sight of snow affect you?

Recalling

2. How are the snow and the person changed at the end of the poem?

Interpreting

3. Were you surprised by the ending of the poem? Why?
4. Do you think the ending of the poem is appropriate for the rest of the poem? Why?
5. What might the poet be saying in the poem about the power of love?

Applying

6. Have you ever had an experience with snow or rain that changed the way you thought about that type of weather? Explain.

Thinking and Writing

Writing a Dream Poem

Nikki Giovanni's "Winter Poem" describes an imaginary transformation, that is, a complete change, of a person into a flower. Can you imagine what it might be like to transform into something different? Try to imagine such an experience. It can be a wonderful transformation or a scary one, a humorous episode or a serious experience. Write a poem modeled after "Winter Poem" describing your transformation. Describe your change in simple, clear language and build toward a surprise at the end. Before writing a final copy, proofread to remove any words that do not contribute directly to the main idea. Also eliminate punctuation and capital letters. If you are uncomfortable writing a poem, you may write a narrative describing your transformation.

GUIDE FOR READING

Fireflies

Paul Fleischman (1952–), born in Monterey, California, is the son of children's author Sid Fleischman. You may have read some of his father's books, such as *Humbug Mountain* or *By the Great Horn Spoon.* As Paul relates, "My father, as it happens, writes children's books—books he read aloud to us chapter by chapter as he wrote them. So, writing for children always seemed an honorable and possible profession." "Fireflies" is a poem from one of his books of poems for two voices, *Joyful Noise,* which is a Newbery Medal winner. These poems for two voices reflect Fleischman's keen interest in music, as the poems are to be read at the same time, as in a musical duet.

The Fairies' Lullaby

William Shakespeare (1564–1616) is the most highly regarded poet and playwright in the English language. He was born in the English town of Stratford-on-Avon and went to London when he was a young man. There he began writing and acting in plays. Shakespeare wrote thirty-seven plays, along with several long, narrative poems and over one hundred and fifty shorter poems called sonnets. Among his most famous plays are *Romeo and Juliet, Macbeth,* and *Hamlet.* "The Fairies' Lullaby" appears in *A Midsummer Night's Dream,* a delightful comedy written around 1600. This lullaby is sung by a group of fairies to Titania, the queen of the fairies, to lull her to sleep in the forest.

hist whist

E. E. Cummings (1894–1962) was born in Cambridge, Massachusetts. After graduating from Harvard University in 1915, he served as an ambulance driver in World War I. When the war was over, Cummings returned to the United States to work as a painter and a poet. Probably the first thing that will strike you about Cummings's poems is his original use of language and the unusual look of the poem on the page. Cummings wrote this way so that the appearance of the poem on the page contributes to the meaning of the words. Despite their appearance, Cummings's poems, like "hist whist," are delightful language experiences.

Sound Devices: Alliteration and Onomatopoeia

In poetry, sound is an essential element. All poets work with the sounds of words when writing poems. Sound can mean rhyme but it also means much more than that. Two other types of sound devices are alliteration and onomatopoeia. These devices add to the "music" and to the meaning of the poem.

Alliteration is the repetition of the consonant sound at the beginning of words. For example, "Peter Piper picked a peck of pickled peppers" repeats the consonant *p* at the beginnings of words.

Onomatopoeia is the use of words that imitate sounds. Words like *buzz, hiss,* and *screech* are examples of onomatopoeia.

Focus

The three poems you are about to read use the sounds of words to communicate images. With two or three classmates, create a special chant or poem to call an animal or insect to you. Use alliteration, onomatopoeia, and rhyme as much as possible.

As you read the poems that follow, notice how each writer uses sound in his poem.

Vocabulary

Knowing the following words will help you as you read these poems.

parchment (pärch′ mənt) *n.*: The skin of an animal prepared as a surface on which to write (p. 466)

flitting (flit′ iŋ) *v.*: Flying lightly and rapidly (p. 466)

glimmering (glim′ ər iŋ) *v.*: Giving a faint, flickering light (p. 466)

calligraphers (kə lig′ rə fʉrz) *n.*: People who use artistic handwriting (p. 466)

graffiti (grə fēt′ ē) *n.*: A drawing on a public surface (p. 466)

offense (ə fens′) *n.*: Crime; hurtful act (p. 468)

tingling (tiŋ′ gliŋ) *adj.*: Stinging, as from excitement (p. 471)

tweeds (twēdz) *n.*: Clothes made of a rough, multicolored-fabric (p. 471)

scuttling (skut′ ′l iŋ) *adj.*: Quickly moving (p. 471)

rustle (rus′ ′l) *v.*: Make soft sounds (p. 471)

Spelling Tip

Notice that when you add *-ing* to verbs ending in *e,* like *tingle* and *scuttle,* the *e* is dropped.

Fireflies

Paul Fleischman

Light	Light
	is the ink we use
Night	Night
is our parchment	
	We're
	fireflies
fireflies	flickering
flitting	
	flashing
fireflies	
glimmering	fireflies
	gleaming
glowing	
Insect calligraphers	Insect calligraphers
practicing penmanship	
	copying sentences
Six-legged scribblers	Six-legged scribblers
of vanishing messages,	
	fleeting graffiti
Fine artists in flight	Fine artists in flight
adding dabs of light	
	bright brush strokes
Signing the June nights	Signing the June nights
as if they were paintings	as if they were paintings
	We're
flickering	fireflies
fireflies	flickering
fireflies.	fireflies.

Reader's Response
What memories or feelings does this poem call up in you?

RESPONDING TO THE SELECTION

Your Response

1. What images come to mind when you watch fireflies?

Recalling

2. To what does the poet compare light and night in lines 1–4?
3. Explain two comparisons in lines 14–19.

Interpreting

4. In what way are fireflies artists?
5. What are the "vanishing messages,/fleeting graffiti"?
6. Visualize a firefly's appearance at night. Why do you think the poet places some words—*fireflies, flashing, flickering,* for example—by themselves?

Applying

7. There is a magical quality about watching fireflies' lights on a warm summer evening. Can you think of any other scenes from nature that evoke this kind of magic? Explain.

ANALYZING LITERATURE

Understanding Alliteration

Alliteration is the repetition of the initial consonant sounds in words. For example, the lines "fireflies/flickering/flitting/flashing" repeat the initial consonant *f.* The sound "f" suggests the sound of short, quick movements or of movement through the air. The alliteration adds to the meaning and the "music" of the poem.

Find two other examples of alliteration in "Fireflies."

LEARNING OPTION

Speaking and Listening. "Fireflies" is a poem that was written to be read by two people. Read "Fireflies" with a partner. One of you reads the part on the left and the other reads the part on the right. When words appear on the same line, both of you read your lines together. Otherwise, you each read the words on your side. To start, you read "Light" together. Then the person who reads the right side reads, "is the ink we use," and so forth. Watch your partner's part, as well as your own, so you know when not to read. Practice reading this poem for two voices and then present it to the class.

The Fairies' Lullaby
from A Midsummer Night's Dream
William Shakespeare

Fairies. You spotted snakes with double tongue,
Thorny hedgehogs, be not seen.
Newts and blindworms,[1] do no wrong,
Come not near our fairy Queen.
Chorus. Philomel,[2] with melody
Sing in our sweet lullaby;
Lulla, lulla, lullaby, lulla, lulla, lullaby.
Never harm,
Nor spell, nor charm,
Come our lovely lady nigh.[3]
So, good night, with lullaby.

Fairies. Weaving spiders, come not here.
Hence,[4] you long-legged spinners, hence!
Beetles black, approach not near.
Worm nor snail, do no offense.
Chorus. Philomel, with melody
Sing in our sweet lullaby;
Lulla, lulla, lullaby, lulla, lulla, lullaby.
Never harm,
Nor spell, nor charm,
Come our lovely lady nigh.
So, good night, with lullaby.

---

1. newts and blindworms (no͞ots) *n.*: Newts are salamanders, animals that look like lizards but are related to frogs. Blindworms are legless lizards. In myths, salamanders were said to live in fire.
2. philomel (fil′ ō mel′) *n.*: A nightingale.
3. nigh (nī) *adv.*: Near.
4. hence (hens) *adv.*: Go away from this place.

Who Is William Shakespeare?

"Friends, Romans, countrymen, lend me your ears!" "To be, or not to be: that is the question," "All's well that ends well." Have you ever heard any of these quotations? They are all from the plays of William Shakespeare, considered by many to be the greatest writer who ever lived. Perhaps the most important reason for Shakespeare's reputation is his understanding of human nature.

The feelings and emotions portrayed by the characters in Shakespeare's plays are as real as they are timeless. Jealousy, ambition, love, and laughter are as true to audiences today as they were to audiences 350 years

Responding to the Selection

Your Response

1. What title would you give this lullaby? Explain.

Interpreting

2. What tone of voice would the Fairies use? What tone of voice would the Chorus use?
3. Why might creatures like newts, blindworms, and weaving spiders be considered creepy and scary in Shakespeare's time?

Applying

4. How is this lullaby different from ones you are familiar with? How is it similar?

Analyzing Literature

Appreciating Refrain

A **refrain** is a regularly repeated line or group of lines after each stanza in a poem or song. The refrain contributes to the music and emphasizes ideas in a poem or a song.

1. What part of "Fairies' Lullaby" makes up the refrain?
2. What ideas or feelings are emphasized by the refrain?
3. How are the feelings or ideas expressed in the refrain different from those in the other lines?
4. How might songs or poems be different without a refrain?

Thinking and Writing

Modernizing a Poem

The lines spoken by the Fairies in each stanza refer to things like "spotted snakes" and "thorny hedgehogs." These might not frighten a modern reader. Rewrite the poem, making its content more modern. First paraphrase the poem, rewriting it in your own words. Then begin rewriting the Fairies' lines, deciding what frightening or unpleasant things you would want to protect the queen from. You might include things like unknown space creatures, toxic waste, or grizzly bears. You could also change the Chorus's lines. As you work on your poem, try to imitate the rhythm and rhyme that Shakespeare used.

ago. Shakespeare's characters are also distinctly individual and, therefore, unforgettable.

Shakespeare presents characters and situations in an amazing variety. He even includes supernatural creatures such as the fairies who sing "A Fairies' Lullaby." Nearly every level of society, from kings to gatekeepers, is reflected in his dramas. Nearly every social or political situation, from teenage love to murderous kings, is played out in the course of his plays. These situations represent problems we all face in life. Yet Shakespeare succeeds in presenting these problems in an individual and highly entertaining way.

For example, although *Romeo and Juliet* is set in Italy hundreds of years ago, this tale about a "pair of star-cross'd lovers" has many of the emotions and problems common today: the wonderful and terrible feelings associated with first love, the pain and confusion of young people whose wishes are different from those of their parents, the regret for actions or statements made in anger. As a result, the play is one of the best-known love stories of all time. It has been modernized in the popular play and movie *West Side Story*.

Shakespeare's understanding of human nature enabled him to create characters who are individual yet universal. As the great English writer Samuel Johnson said of Shakespeare, "His drama is the mirror of life."

hist whist

E. E. Cummings

hist   whist
little ghostthings
tip-toe
twinkle-toe

WITCH AND GOBLINS
Arthur Rackham
New York Public Library

little twitchy
witches and tingling
goblins
hob-a-nob   hob-a-nob

little hoppy happy
toad in tweeds
tweeds
little itchy mousies

with scuttling
eyes   rustle and run   and
hidehidehide
whisk

whisk   look out for the old woman
with the wart on her nose
what she'll do to yer
nobody knows

for she knows the devil   ooch
the devil   ouch
the devil
ach   the great

green
dancing
devil
devil

devil
devil

wheeEEE

Reader's Response

Do you think this is a frightening poem or a funny one? Explain.

Responding to the Selection

Your Response

1. Do you think the art on page 470 is a good illustration for this poem? Why or why not?

Recalling

2. With whom do the goblins "hob-a-nob"?
3. What advice does the poet give "little itchy mousies"?

Interpreting

4. Imagine what a toad looks like. Why is the toad described as "in tweeds/tweeds"?
5. What do you think is the setting—the time and place of the poem?
6. What does the final line contribute to the meaning or the mood of the poem?

Applying

7. Why do we like being entertained by things that we find terrifying?

Analyzing Literature

Recognizing Onomatopoeia

Onomatopoeia is the use of a word that imitates a sound. For example, "rustle" suggests the sound made by the "itchy mousies" in dried leaves. Onomatopoeia adds vividness to the poem by using sounds that create an effect.

1. Find three other examples of onomatopoeia in "hist whist."
2. Why is onomatopoeia so useful in poetry?

Learning Option

Writing. Rewrite a newspaper article in E. E. Cummings's poetic style. You might create something like this from an article about a tornado:

whir   whirling winding wind
wonderfully weird
i worry i may be
maybe
whisked away

GUIDE FOR READING

Arithmetic

Carl Sandburg (1878–1967), born in Galesburg, Illinois, is as well known for his six-volume biography of Abraham Lincoln and his books on the Civil War as he is for his poetry. In fact Sandburg won the Pulitzer Prize for both poetry and history. Before he could support himself as a writer, Sandburg worked as a milk delivery boy, a house painter, and a newspaper reporter. He also volunteered for the army in 1898 to fight in the Spanish-American War. All this experience enabled him to capture the spirit of working people in the industrial age, the subject of many of his poems. "Arithmetic," however, shows another side of Sandburg: his whimsical sense of humor.

The Sidewalk Racer

Lillian Morrison (1917–) spent nearly forty years working in the New York Public Library. Born in Jersey City, New Jersey, Morrison has written a number of poetry books, including *The Sidewalk Racer and Other Poems of Sports and Motion,* and *The Break Dance Kids.* Morrison has said, "I love rhythms, the body movement implicit in poetry, explicit in sports . . . I am drawn to athletes, dancers, drummers, jazz musicians, who transcend misery and frustration and symbolize for us something joyous, ordered, and possible in life." Her love of the rhythms of music and sports is apparent in the rhythm and movement of "The Sidewalk Racer."

Images

An **image** is a picture the poet creates with words. To create images, poets use words or phrases that appeal to one or more of our five senses—sight, sound, smell, taste, and touch. For example, in this excerpt from the poem "The Harbor," Carl Sandburg uses words that appeal to our senses of sight, sound, and touch.

On a blue burst of lake,
Long lake waves breaking under the sun
On a spray-flung curve of shore;
And a fluttering storm of gulls,
Masses of great gray wings
And flying white bellies
Veering and wheeling free in the open.

The scene in this poem is a lake shore on a sunny day with birds flying above. By using images like "blue burst of lake," or "Veering and wheeling" that appeal to sight, "spray-flung" that appeals to touch, and "fluttering" that appeals to sound, Sandburg creates a description that is vivid and sharp.

Sometimes writers arrange the poem's words in a shape, often one that looks like the subject. A poem that has words arranged to form a visual image is called a concrete poem.

Focus

The authors of the following poems use language to bring vivid images to mind about arithmetic and skateboarding. Make a cluster diagram that describes a school subject or a sport. Write your subject in the center of a sheet of paper and circle it. Then around your subject add ideas related to it and circle them. Connect your circles with lines to show how your ideas branch out from the main topic. Include specific words—concrete details—that create sharp images. Then as you read the poems, notice the images the poets have created.

Vocabulary

You probably know the dictionary meanings of most of the words in these poems. However, as you read, take time to think about the meanings suggested and the images created by these words.

Arithmetic

Carl Sandburg

Arithmetic is where numbers fly like pigeons in and out of
your head.
Arithmetic tells you how many you lose or win if you know
how many you had before you lost or won.
Arithmetic is seven eleven all good children go to heaven—or
five six bundle of sticks.[1]
Arithmetic is numbers you squeeze from your head to your
hand to your pencil to your paper till you get the answer.
Arithmetic is where the answer is right and everything is nice
and you can look out of the window and see the blue sky—
or the answer is wrong and you have to start all over and
try again and see how it comes out this time.
If you take a number and double it and double it again and
then double it a few more times, the number gets bigger
and bigger and goes higher and higher and only arithmetic can tell you what the number is when you decide to
quit doubling.
Arithmetic is where you have to multiply—and you carry the
multiplication table in your head and hope you won't lose it.
If you have two animal crackers, one good and one bad, and
you eat one and a striped zebra with streaks all over him
eats the other, how many animal crackers will you have if
somebody offers you five six seven and you say No no no
and you say Nay nay nay and you say Nix nix nix?
If you ask your mother for one fried egg for breakfast and she
gives you two fried eggs and you eat both of them, who is
better in arithmetic, you or your mother?

---

1. **seven eleven . . . bundle of sticks:** This line is a reference to children's counting rhymes.

Reader's Response

How do you feel about arithmetic? Why?

Responding to the Selection

Your Response

1. What images come to mind when you think about arithmetic?

Recalling

2. According to the poem, how do numbers get from your head to the paper?

Interpreting

3. In line 10, what does Sandburg mean when he says, "You can look out the window and see blue sky"?
4. Summarize Sandburg's attitude toward arithmetic.
5. Which of the sentences are nonsensical? Explain your choices.
6. Why does the poet mix realistic images about arithmetic with nonsensical images?

Applying

7. We do not typically think of arithmetic in connection with a poem. What are some other unusual uses for arithmetic and numbers?

Analyzing Literature

Understanding Images

Images are word pictures that allow you to "see" in your imagination what the poet is writing about.

Divide a sheet of paper into five sections, labeling each section with one of the five senses: sight, sound, taste, touch, and smell. Read "Arithmetic" again, looking for words and phrases that appeal to your senses. Then list these words or phrases in the appropriate section of your paper. For example, under "Sight," you might include the opening line of the poem. You will find more images for some senses than for others.

1. Identify one image for each of the following senses: sight, touch, hearing.
2. How do the images add to the poem?
3. Create two images about arithmetic, one appealing to the sense of taste and one to the sense of smell.

Critical Thinking and Reading

Recognizing Generalizations

A **generalization** is a broad statement intended to be true of a group of situations, objects, or people. For example, "Young people enjoy rock music" is a generalization. Careful writers avoid making generalizations because they can be misleading or false unless they are supported with facts. Poets, however, sometimes make generalizations without supporting them to create images. For example, Carl Sandburg makes this generalization: "Arithmetic is where numbers fly in and out of your head."

1. Find three other generalizations in the poem.
2. Write three of your own generalizations about math, showing how you feel about the subject.

Thinking and Writing

Writing a List Poem

"Arithmetic" is a list poem. It explains and describes its subject by listing some of its qualities and giving examples in concrete terms.

Write your own list poem. To begin, brainstorm a subject. Something related to school—teachers, science, school lunch—might be a good idea. Next, jot down examples or qualities of your subject. Now work on these examples and qualities, creating images with words that appeal to the senses. When you have listed six or seven examples, go over them to see if the images are clear. Place them in the order you think best conveys your subject. When you revise, eliminate any unnecessary words—words that do not contribute directly to your poem. Proofread your poem and make a final copy.

Responding to the Selection

Your Response

1. How did reading this poem make you feel?
2. Have you ever ridden a skateboard? Describe what it was like.

Recalling

3. As the speaker skims the "asphalt sea," what else does he or she do? (lines 3–4)
4. Identify the three things the speaker feels he or she is.

Interpreting

5. Which of the poet's comparisons in lines 6–12 do you think most accurately describes a "sidewalk racer"? Explain your answer.
6. How can the speaker be both "the sailor/ and the sail" or "the driver and the wheel"?
7. When you read this poem aloud, you can imagine the feeling of speed or movement. What words or phrases cause this feeling?

Applying

8. Lillian Morrison has said that "there are emotions connected with sports . . . one wants to catch." What are some of the emotions she catches in "The Sidewalk Racer"? What are some emotions you connect with sports?

The Sidewalk Racer
or
On the Skateboard
Lillian Morrison

Skimming
an asphalt sea
I swerve, I curve, I
sway; I speed to whirring
sound an inch above the
ground; I'm the sailor
and the sail, I'm the
driver and the wheel
I'm the one and only
single engine
human auto
mobile.

Analyzing Literature

Understanding Concrete Poetry

A **concrete poem** is a poem whose words are arranged into a shape, usually a shape that looks like the subject of the poem. This creates a visual image to go along with the word images in the poem. Concrete poems are often lighthearted and playful, with the shape of the poem contributing to this lighthearted tone.

1. How does the shape of "The Sidewalk Racer" add to its impact on the reader?
2. Would the poem be more or less interesting if it were shaped in regular lines of the same length as in a traditional poem? Why?
3. Look at the photograph on page 476. How is this image similar to and different from the images in the concrete poem?

Thinking and Writing

Writing a Concrete Poem

Before you begin writing a concrete poem, brainstorm subjects whose shapes suggest something about them. A telephone receiver, a car, or a roller coaster are possibilities. When you are ready to begin writing, concentrate on the rhythm of your phrases and lines. Try to have your rhythm match the effect you are trying to create with your poem. As you revise, do your best to have the words, phrases, rhythm, and shape all contribute to the effect.

GUIDE FOR READING

Two Riddles

Ian Serraillier (1912–) was born in London, England, and spent much of his life there as a teacher. He has a strong interest in old English ballads and legends, writing poems about and adaptations of *Beowulf, Sir Gawain and the Green Knight,* and *The Adventures of Robin Hood.* Many of his poems have been broadcast on the radio in the United States, as well as in England, New Zealand, and Australia. His most famous work, *The Silver Sword,* was made into a series for children on British radio.

Mary Austin (1868–1934) lived most of her life in the Southwest and in California. She spent years living with Native Americans in the desert and studying their way of life. Several of Austin's works reflect her concern for the rights of the American Indian. Austin wrote numerous novels, short stories, poems, articles, and plays. In contrast to her riddle, Mary Austin is perhaps best remembered for her collections of regional sketches of the Southwest.

Riddles

Riddles are like puzzles. A good riddle will have clues that challenge you and make you think but will not give away the answer. The words in riddles often have more than one meaning. Be prepared to read a riddle a few times before you understand a clue or find the appropriate meaning to a word.

Focus

The following riddles use personification; they give human qualities to nonhuman things. Think of a riddle you know. Write your riddle down and trade it with a partner. See if you can guess each other's riddle. Then, think about what made the riddles hard or easy to solve. Did the riddle use personification, simile, or metaphor? Read the riddles on page 479 carefully and see if you can guess the answers.

Vocabulary

Knowing the following words will help you read these riddles.

devours (di vo͞orz′) *v.*: Swallows greedily; destroys (p. 479)

stoutest (stout′ est) *adj.*: Strongest (p. 479)

Two Riddles

In the dripping gloom I see
A creature with broad antlers,
Motionless. It turns its head;
One gleaming eye devours the dark.
I hear it cough and clear its throat;
Then, with a hungry roar, it charges into
the night
And is swallowed whole.

Ian Serraillier

(A motorcycle)

I come more softly than a bird,
And lovely as a flower;
I sometimes last from year to year
And sometimes but an hour.

I stop the swiftest railroad train
Or break the stoutest tree.
And yet I am afraid of fire
And children play with me.

Mary Austin

(Snow)

Responding to the Selection

Your Response

1. Which of these riddles did you find more difficult? Explain.

Recalling

2. Identify three beastlike qualities of the motorcycle.

Interpreting

3. Do you think the comparison of a motorcycle to a creature is a good one? Why or why not?
4. How are contrasts used in the second riddle?
5. If you guessed either riddle, what clues helped you the most? Why?

Applying

6. Share some of the riddles you know. How are they similar to or different from these riddles?

Thinking and Writing

Writing a Riddle

Try to write your own riddle. You should not try to trick the reader; rather, do what Ian Serraillier does. He uses a metaphor, that is, he describes a motorcycle in terms of an animal. He describes the handlebars as "broad antlers" and the headlight as "One gleaming eye."

Think of a subject for your riddle. Something concrete like a marble or a comb would probably work best. Next, jot down metaphors that describe your subject. Finally, put it all together in a poem. Revise your riddle. Do your metaphors clearly suggest your answer? Proofread your revised poem and prepare a final copy. Challenge your classmates and your teacher by reading your riddle aloud.

Playing With Images

Good poetry is vivid, alive, and full of images that let you use your senses to understand and to feel what the poet is saying. You can create your own images and play with them to form an original poem.

Your Turn

An enjoyable way to play with images is to write an "opposite poem." An "opposite poem" is made up of four to six lines. The first line usually names your subject in a manner similar to the following: "What is the opposite of ______ ?" The remaining lines define your subject by giving images that are the opposite of the subject.

Prewriting

1. Decide on a subject. A subject can be an idea, stated as an adjective, or a thing, stated as a noun. Adjectives like *large, good,* or *kind* make good subjects because they suggest many ideas for opposites. If you choose a noun, make sure it has opposites.

2. Make a chart. On the top of a sheet of paper write "What is the opposite of ______?" Write your subject in the blank. Divide the paper into five sections and label each section with one of the five senses. For each section, think of at least one image that is the opposite of your subject. One student's chart looked like this:

Topic: What is the opposite of large?

Sight	Sound	Smell	Touch	Taste
a pin hole a flea a grain of sand	a mosquito's buzz a pin dropping	the odor of dust wood smoke from a distance leaves in the fall	a fuzzy caterpillar a feather a slight summer breeze	a snowflake on my tongue bubbles in soda

Drafting

Begin by writing the first line. Then use specific, concrete words for your opposite images. Try to keep the rhythm of each line about the same. If you wish, use rhyme. Here is an example of one student's first draft:

```
What is the opposite of large?
A single snowflake on my lips,
A caterpillar tickling my finger
tips.
The drop of a pin on the floor,
A grain of sand from the shore.
```

Revising

Share your poem with a partner. Keep the following questions in mind when discussing revisions:

- Do the images clearly suggest the opposite of the subject?
- Do the images appeal to more than one of the senses?
- Can any words be replaced with more concrete or specific words?

Types of Poetry

FOREST SCENE
Marck Frueh
Sal Barracca & Associates

GUIDE FOR READING

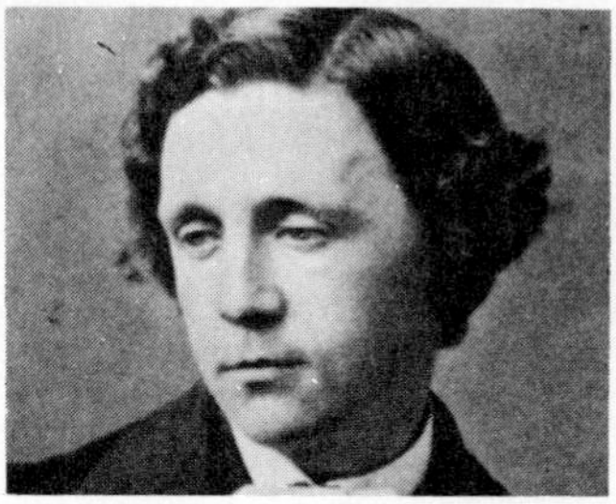

Lewis Carroll

(1832–1898) is the pen name of Charles Lutwidge Dodgson, a professor of mathematics. Under the name of Lewis Carroll he wrote books and long nonsense poems to amuse the children of some friends. "The Walrus and the Carpenter" is from one of his two famous books, *Alice's Adventures in Wonderland* and *Through the Looking Glass.* These works are known for their clever wordplay and fantasy. Both wordplay and fantasy are prominent elements of "The Walrus and the Carpenter."

The Walrus and the Carpenter

Narrative Poetry

Narrative poetry is poetry that tells a story. A narrative poem presents events in much the same way that a short story does, using plot, characters, and dialogue. Notice that dialogue plays an important part in this poem. "The Walrus and the Carpenter" tells its story in chronological order, that is, the order in which things happen in time.

Focus

"The Walrus and the Carpenter" is an amusing nonsense story in rhyme. What words come to mind when you think of walruses and carpenters? In a small group, make two word webs—one for the word *walrus* and another for the word *carpenter.* Use the models below to help you get started. As you read this poem, see if any of the words or thoughts in your word webs are mentioned.

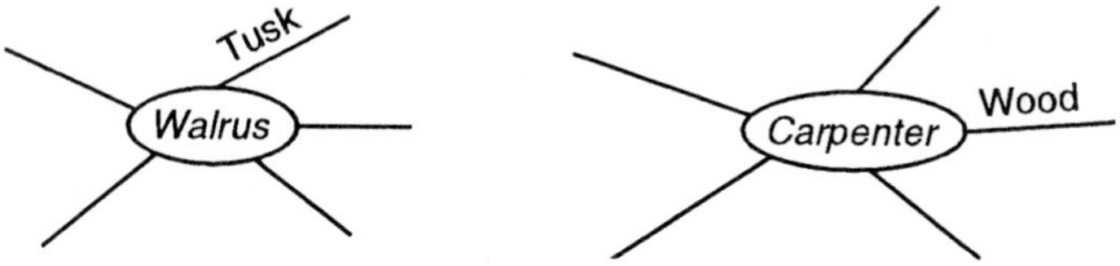

Vocabulary

Knowing the following words will help you read "The Walrus and the Carpenter."

billows (bil′ ōz) *n.*: Large, swelling masses, like waves (p. 483)

sulkily (sulk′ ə lē) *adv.*: Gloomily; poutingly (p. 483)

beseech (bi sēch′) *v.*: To beg for (p. 484)

frothy (frôth′ ē) *adj.*: Foamy (p. 484)

dismal (diz′ m'l) *adj.*: Depressing; miserable (p. 486)

Spelling Tip

Notice that the adverb *sulkily* is formed by changing the *y* in sulky to *i* before adding *-ly.*

The Walrus and the Carpenter

Lewis Carroll

The sun was shining on the sea,
  Shining with all his might:
He did his very best to make
  The billows smooth and bright—
And this was odd, because it was
  The middle of the night.

The moon was shining sulkily,
  Because she thought the sun
Had got no business to be there
  After the day was done—
"It's very rude of him," she said,
  "To come and spoil the fun!"

The sea was wet as wet could be,
  The sands were dry as dry.
You could not see a cloud, because
  No cloud was in the sky:
No birds were flying overhead—
  There were no birds to fly.

The Walrus and the Carpenter
  Were walking close at hand:
They wept like anything to see
  Such quantities of sand:
"If this were only cleared away,"
  They said, "it would be grand!"

From ALICE THROUGH THE LOOKING GLASS
John Tenniel

"If seven maids with seven mops
   Swept it for half a year,
Do you suppose," the Walrus said,
   "That they could get it clear?"
"I doubt it," said the Carpenter,
   And shed a bitter tear.

"O Oysters, come and walk with us!"
   The Walrus did beseech.
"A pleasant walk, a pleasant talk,
   Along the briny beach:
We cannot do with more than four,
   To give a hand to each."

The eldest Oyster looked at him,
   But never a word he said:
The eldest Oyster winked his eye,
   And shook his heavy head—
Meaning to say he did not choose
   To leave the oyster-bed.

But four young Oysters hurried up,
   All eager for this treat:
Their coats were brushed, their faces washed,
   Their shoes were clean and neat—
And this was odd, because, you know,
   They hadn't any feet.

Four other Oysters followed them,
   And yet another four;
And thick and fast they came at last,
   And more, and more, and more—
All hopping through the frothy waves,
   And scrambling to the shore.

The Walrus and the Capenter
   Walked on a mile or so,
And then they rested on a rock
   Conveniently low:
And all the little Oysters stood
   And waited in a row.

"The time has come," the Walrus said,
"To talk of many things:
Of shoes—and ships—and sealing wax—
Of cabbages—and kings—
And why the sea is boiling hot—
And whether pigs have wings."

"But wait a bit," the Oysters cried,
"Before we have our chat;
For some of us are out of breath,
And all of us are fat!"
"No hurry!" said the Carpenter.
They thanked him much for that.

"A loaf of bread," the Walrus said,
"Is what we chiefly need:
Pepper and vinegar besides
Are very good indeed—
Now, if you're ready, Oysters dear,
We can begin to feed."

From ALICE THROUGH THE LOOKING GLASS
John Tenniel

From ALICE THROUGH THE LOOKING GLASS
John Tenniel

"But not on us!" the Oysters cried,
  Turning a little blue.
"After such kindness, that would be
  A dismal thing to do!"
"The night is fine," the Walrus said.
  "Do you admire the view?

"It was so kind of you to come!
  And you are very nice!"
The Carpenter said nothing but
  "Cut us another slice.
I wish you were not quite so deaf—
  I've had to ask you twice!"

"It seems a shame," the Walrus said,
  "To play them such a trick.
After we've brought them out so far,
  And made them trot so quick!"
The Carpenter said nothing but
  "The butter's spread too thick!"

"I weep for you," the Walrus said:
  "I deeply sympathize."
With sobs and tears he sorted out
  Those of the largest size,
Holding his pocket-handkerchief
  Before his streaming eyes.

"O Oysters," said the Carpenter,
  "You've had a pleasant run!
Shall we be trotting home again?"
  But answer came there none—
And this was scarcely odd, because
  They'd eaten every one.

Reader's Response
How do you feel about the trick the Walrus and the Carpenter play on the Oysters?

RESPONDING TO THE SELECTION

Your Response

1. If you had been an oyster, would you have followed the Walrus and the Carpenter? Explain.

Recalling

2. Why is it odd that the sun is shining? (lines 5–6)
3. What do the Walrus and the Carpenter do with the Oysters?

Interpreting

4. Why does the eldest Oyster refuse to follow the Walrus and the Carpenter?
5. The Walrus and the Carpenter rest on a rock that is "conveniently low." For what is the rock "conveniently low"?
6. At what point do you begin to think the Walrus and the Carpenter might mean to harm the Oysters?
7. Why don't the Oysters run away once they learn what the Walrus and the Carpenter plan to do with them?
8. What is funny about the dialogue between the Walrus and the Carpenter?

Applying

9. Do you think this poem is funny or sad? Can it be both? Explain your answer.

ANALYZING LITERATURE

Understanding Narrative Poetry

Narrative poetry tells a story using plot, character, and setting. The two main characters in this narrative poem are, of course, the Walrus and the Carpenter.

1. Describe the characters of the Walrus, the Carpenter, and the Oysters.
2. Why is the setting of the story important?
3. List six events in the plot.
4. Why do the regular rhythm and the end rhymes add to the fun of reading the poem?

CRITICAL THINKING AND READING

Appreciating Nonsense

Nonsense poetry is exactly what it sounds like, poetry that does not make any sense. To enjoy nonsense poetry, you should not try to figure it out. Its humor comes from the contrast between realistic situations and the nonsensical situations or statements in the poem. For example, in the first stanza "the sun was shining," although it was "the middle of the night."

1. List four other things in the poem that do not make any sense.
2. Do each of the four things strike you as funny? Why or why not?

THINKING AND WRITING

Writing Another Ending

Over the years, some readers have expressed disappointment with the ending of "The Walrus and the Carpenter." In fact, in the musical play, *Alice,* the Walrus and the Carpenter are visited in their sleep by the ghosts of two oysters who are seeking revenge. Write a brief description of a different ending. Make sure each of the characters is represented. Try to maintain the humor, rhyme, and story line of the original poem. Share your ending with the class.

LEARNING OPTION

Speaking and Listening. "The Walrus and the Carpenter" is a wonderful poem to read aloud in a group. Form a small group and designate three people to read each of the major parts: the Narrator, the Walrus, and the Carpenter. The rest of the group can take the part of the Oysters. Practice reading the poem, trying to capture the characters' personalities by speaking as you imagine the characters would speak. When you're ready, read the poem aloud to the class.

GUIDE FOR READING

Arnold Adoff

(1935–) was born and raised in New York City. He also worked there as a teacher for twelve years. Since moving to Ohio, Adoff has produced a number of poetry books and picture books. He has also edited numerous collections of short stories and poems, mostly written by and about Black Americans. Since 1960 Adoff has been married to noted writer Virginia Hamilton. Their two children helped inspire Adoff to write a book of sports poems that includes "Alone In The Nets," a poem about soccer.

Alone In The Nets

Speaker

A character telling a poem is called the **speaker.** It is the voice of the speaker you hear in a poem, not that of the poet. In "Alone In The Nets," the speaker tells a story of an experience during a soccer game. The speaker refers to himself or herself as "I." Remember, the speaker is not the poet but an imaginary person.

Focus

"Alone In The Nets" is about a soccer game. What sports do you enjoy playing? What sports do you enjoy watching? How do you feel when you are playing or watching your favorite sport? Make a cluster diagram about the feelings you have while playing or watching your favorite sport. Use the sample cluster diagram below to get started. Write the name of the sport in the center of a sheet of paper. Draw a circle around the word and begin jotting down the feelings and experiences you associate with it. Then draw circles around each idea and connect them with lines to show their relationship with the central idea. As you read "Alone In The Nets," compare your diagram with the ideas in the poem.

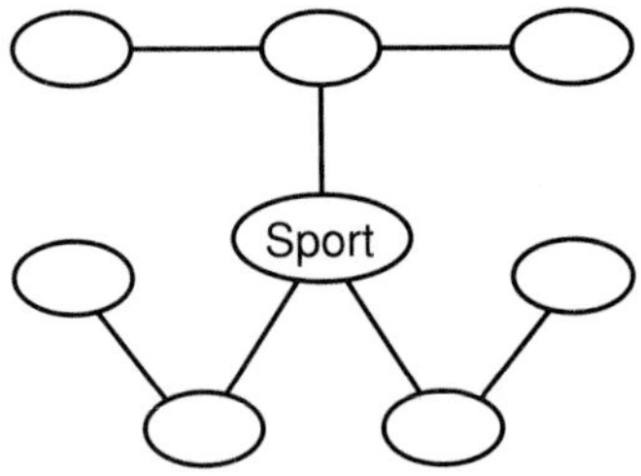

Vocabulary

Knowing the following words will help you read "Alone In The Nets."

opposition (äp′ ə zish′ ən) *n.*: Here, the other team (p. 489)
cleats (klētz) *n.*: Pieces of wood, plastic, or metal fastened to the underside of a shoe to prevent slipping (p. 489)
evaporate (i vap′ ə rāt′) *v.*: To disappear like vapor (p. 492)

Alone In The Nets

Arnold Adoff

Alone In The Nets.

I

am

alone of course,
in the nets, on this cold and raining afternoon,
and our best defending fullback
is lying on the wet ground out of position.
Half the opposition is pounding
down the field,
and their lead forward is gliding
so fast, she can just barely keep
the ball in front of her sliding
foot.

Her cleats are expensive,
and her hair b o u n c e s
neatly
like the after
girls in the shampoo commercials.
There is a big grin
on her face.

Now: In This Frozen Moment On This Moving World Through Space

is the right time to ask why am I here just standing
in my frozen place?
Why did I get up on time this morning?
Why did I get up at all?
Why did I listen to the coach and agree to play
this strange position in a r e a l game
in a strange town on this wet and moving world?

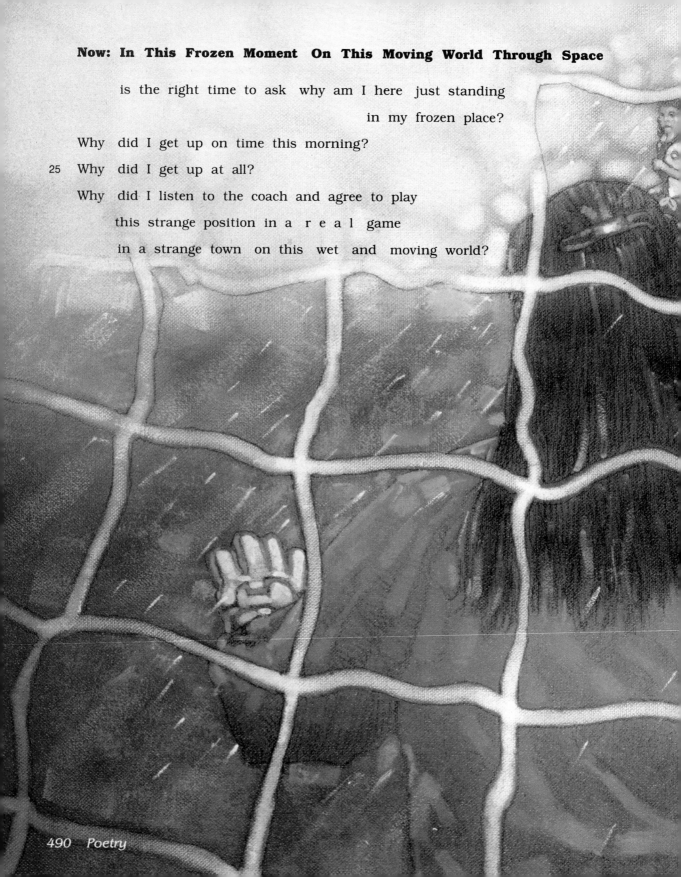

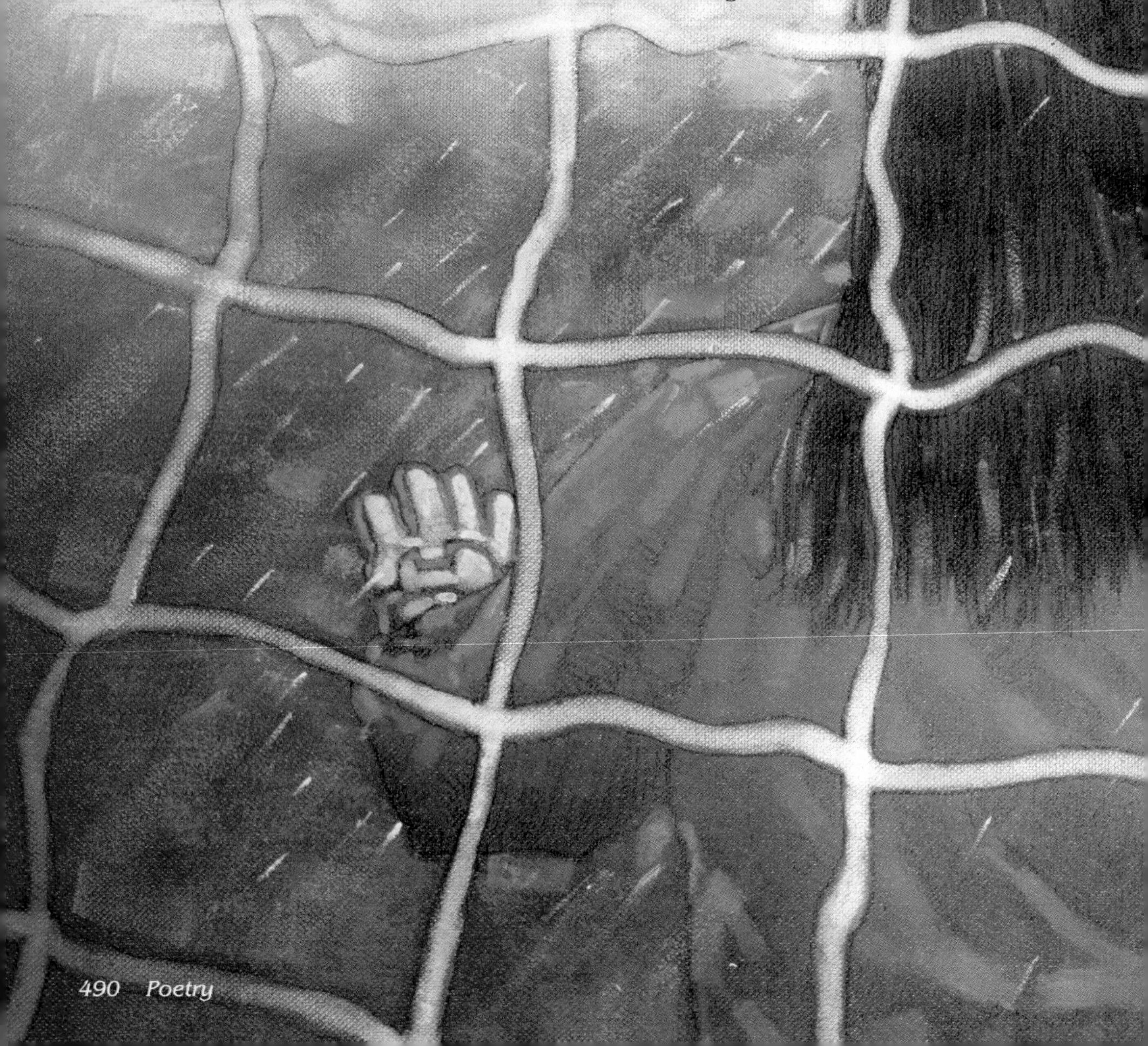

Why is it raining?
Why is it raining so h a r d?
Where
are all of our defenders?
Why do all of our players
do all of the falling
down?

Why am I here?

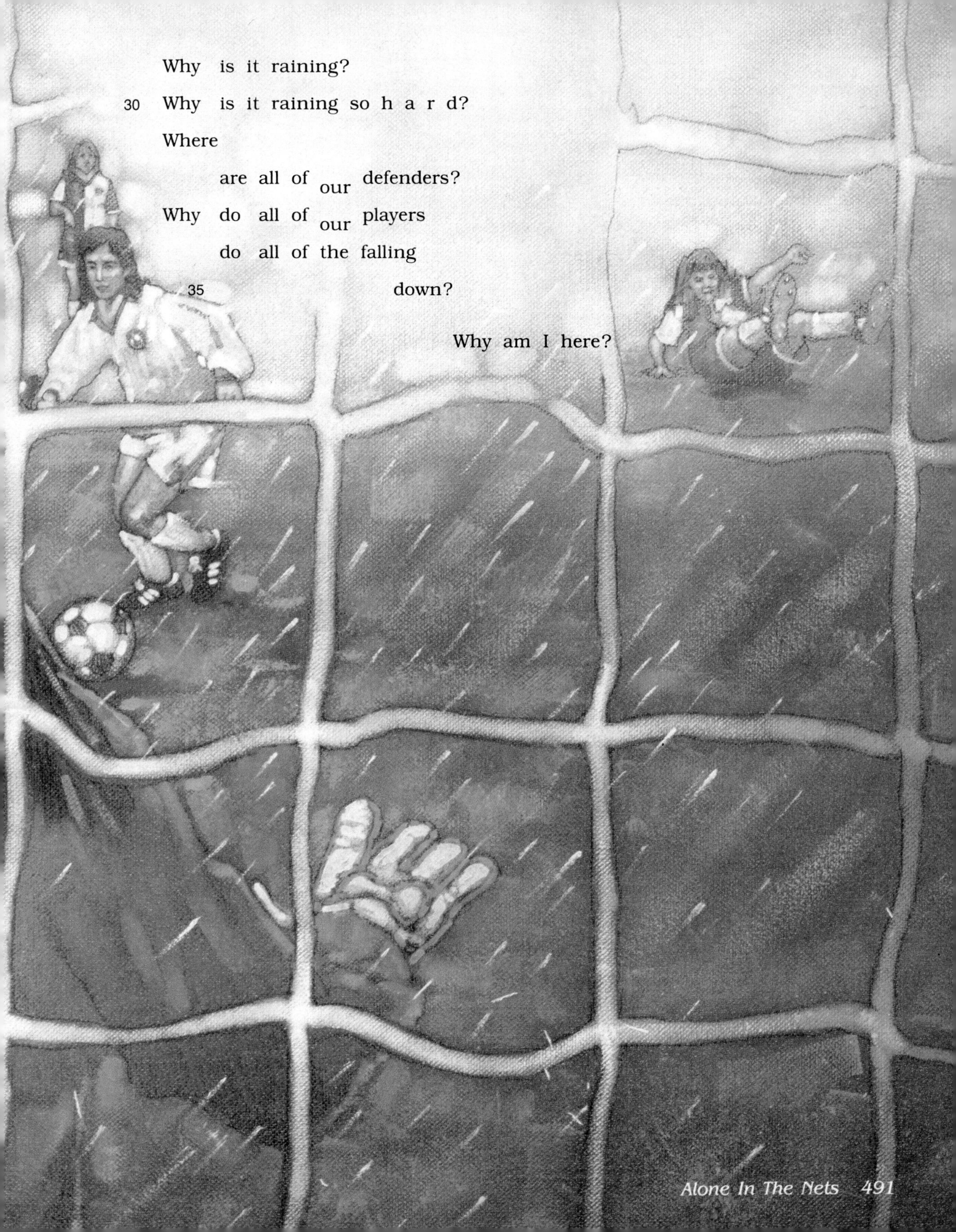

But Frozen Moments Can Unfreeze And I Can Stretch

and reach for the ball flying to the corner of
our
goal.

I can reach and jump
and dive into the s p a c e

between my out
stretched
hands
and the outside poles

of the nets.

My fears evaporate like my sweat in this chilling
breeze,

and I can move with this moving world

and pace my steps

like that old
movie

high
noon sheriff in his just

right

time.

That grinning forward gets her shot away too soon,

and I am there, on my own time, in the air,

to meet the ball,

and fall on it

for the save.

I wave my happy ending wave and get up.

The game goes on.

Reader's Response
Were you able to share the speaker's thoughts and feelings? Why or why not?

Responding to the Selection

Your Response

1. Have you ever felt alone the way the speaker in this poem does? Explain.

Recalling

2. What did the coach talk the speaker into doing? (lines 26–27)

Interpreting

3. Summarize the speaker's feelings about being alone in the nets. (lines 21–36)
4. How does the repetition of "why" in lines 21–36 affect the poem?
5. What does the speaker mean by a "frozen moment"? What does she mean when she says, "But Frozen Moments Can Unfreeze"?
6. What do you think the poet was trying to show by arranging the words in lines 1–4, 15, and 19 in unusual ways?
7. How does the speaker's attitude change from the beginning of the poem to the end?

Applying

8. Although this poem is about soccer, that's not the only time you can feel "alone in the nets." Describe some other situations where people lack confidence and feel alone.

Analyzing Literature

Understanding Speaker

It is important to remember that the **speaker** in the poem is not the poet, because the speaker's thoughts and feelings might be different from those of the poet. It is possible that Arnold Adoff has never played soccer or been alone in the nets. The speaker in this poem does let us know something about herself. By referring to herself as "I," we feel the speaker is talking or thinking out loud, much as we all do.

Read "Alone In The Nets" aloud. Then read it again, but substitute "she" for "I." (Change the verb when necessary, like "am" to "is" in line 3.)

1. How is the poem different without a speaker?
2. Do you like the poem better with or without the speaker? Explain your answer.

Critical Thinking and Reading

Making Inferences About the Speaker

An **inference** is a reasonable conclusion you draw from given information. For example, if your friend is yawning a lot and has dark circles under his eyes, you could make the inference that he is tired. You have come to a reasonable conclusion based on observed information.

Likewise, we can make inferences about the speaker in "Alone In The Nets" based on the information given. You could infer, for example, that the speaker is a girl because the opposition is a girls' team.

1. What information lets you infer that the speaker is playing soccer?
2. What inference can you make about how the speaker feels about "their lead forward"? (lines 14–20)
3. Make three other inferences about the speaker's feelings about playing goalie.

Thinking and Writing

Writing a Monologue

Imagine yourself as a player or a spectator at a sporting event. Then imagine your thoughts during the game. You may be feeling excited, tense, bored, nervous, or even angry. Write one or two paragraphs of your thoughts as they go through your head. An account of your thoughts as they occur is called a monologue. Like the speaker in "Alone In The Nets," your thoughts may jump around as the action changes. When you have finished, read your monologue to a small group of classmates.

GUIDE FOR READING

Light and Water

Juan Ramón Jiménez (1881–1958) is considered one of Spain's finest modern poets. He is noted for his complete devotion to poetry and for his encouragement of the many younger poets who were constantly with him. Born in Moguer, Spain, Jiménez's interest in writing began at an early age. He sent poems to newspapers and had his first poem published at age seventeen. In 1939 the turmoil of the Spanish Civil War forced Jiménez to leave the country. He traveled in Latin America and the United States before settling in Puerto Rico. It was there that he received the Nobel Prize in Literature two years before his death.

How soft a Caterpillar steps—

Emily Dickinson (1830–1886) lived all her life in Amherst, Massachusetts. Always a shy and private person, Dickinson kept more and more to herself as she grew older. During her final years, she dressed only in white and did not leave her house. Eventually, she rarely even left her room. Because of her shyness, only a handful of her nearly 2000 poems were published during her lifetime. Indeed, her own family was not even aware that she had written so many poems. Yet she is now considered one of the finest American poets. "How soft a Caterpillar steps—" is a good example of how closely Emily Dickinson studied the things of nature.

Beauty

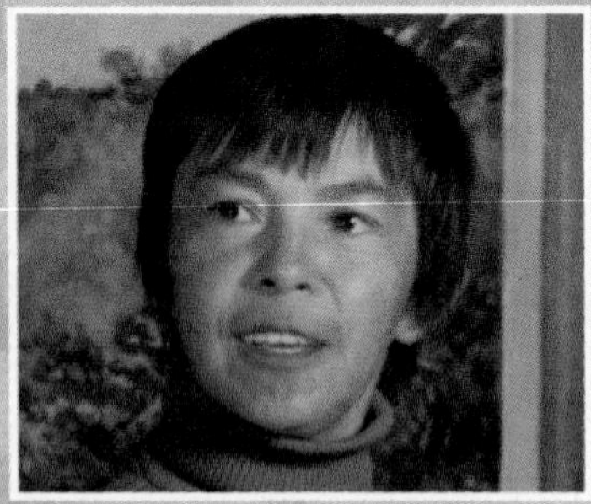

E-Yeh-Shure (1928–) was born and raised in a pueblo, a Native American village in New Mexico. Her Indian name means "Blue Corn." E-Yeh-Shure is also known as Louise Abeita Chewiwi, her non-Indian name. She has taught on different Indian reservations for over twenty years. When she was ten years old, E-Yeh-Shure wrote *I Am a Pueblo Indian Girl,* a book about her people and their way of life. "Beauty" is from this book and reflects her strong connection with nature.

Lyric Poetry

A **lyric poem** is one that expresses the poet's observations and feelings. Lyric poems tend to be musical in nature. In fact, lyric poems got their name from the lyre, a harp-like musical instrument whose music was used to accompany such poems in ancient Greece.

A lyric poet can speak about a variety of subjects, but each poem generally focuses on a single strong emotion or observation. For example, Jiménez writes about the reflections of light on water, Dickinson writes about a caterpillar, and E-Yeh-Shure writes about what she sees as truly beautiful.

Focus

Each of the poems in this section reflects the poets' ideas of beauty. What do you find beautiful? For some people, nature is a source of beauty. For others, beauty is found in people's kindness. Some may feel that a perfect pass in a football game is a thing of beauty. On a separate sheet of paper, copy the word web below. Complete the web by adding the things and feelings you find most beautiful in your world. Then as you read the poems, compare your ideas of beauty with those of the poets.

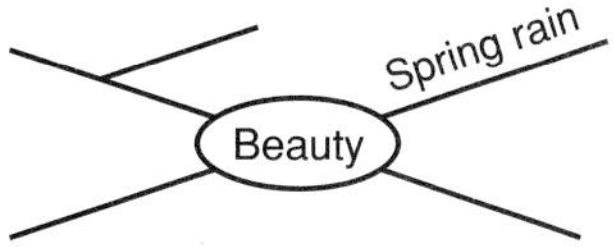

Vocabulary

Knowing the following words will help you read these poems.

vapors (vā′ pərz) *n.*: Visible moisture floating in air (p. 496)

vanish (van′ ish) *v.*: Disappear (p. 496)

velvet (vel′ vit) *adj.*: Smooth or soft like velvet fabric (p. 498)

arrest (ə rest′) *v.*: To catch and keep one's attention (p. 498)

terrestrial (tə res′ trē əl) *adj.*: Having a worldly or commonplace quality (p. 498)

intent (in tent′) *adj.*: Firmly directed (p. 498)

in earnest (ʉr′ nist) *adv.*: Seriously and sincerely (p. 499)

Spelling Tip

It might help you to remember the spelling of the adjective *terrestrial* by splitting the word into two parts: *terres* and *trial.*

Light and Water

Juan Ramón Jiménez

translated by H. R. Hays

The light above—golden, orange, green—
Among the misty clouds.

Oh trees without leaves,
Rooted in water,
Branching in the light!

Below, the water—green, orange, golden—
Among the misty vapors.

Among the misty vapors, among the misty clouds,
Light and water—what magics!—vanish.

Luz y Agua

La luz arriba—oro, naranja, verde—,
entre las nubes vagas.

¡Ay, árboles sin hojas;
raíces en el agua,
ramajes en la luz!—

Abajo, el agua—verde, naranja, oro—,
entre la vaga bruma.

Entre la bruma vaga, entre las vagas nubes,
luz y agua—; ¡qué májicas—se van.

REFLECTIONS OF SUN ON THE WATER
André Derain
Musée de l'Annonciade, St. Tropez

RESPONDING TO THE SELECTION

Your Response

1. Does the poem remind you of a place you have seen? Explain.

Recalling

2. What happens to the light and water?

Interpreting

3. Why do you think that both the light above and the water below are the same colors?
4. Describe the image this poem brings to mind.

Applying

5. Have you ever viewed a scene from nature that seemed mysterious or magical to you?

ANALYZING LITERATURE

Understanding Lyric Poetry

A **lyric poem** expresses the poet's emotions, thoughts, and observations in language that is vivid and musical. For example, the line "Branching in the light!" creates an image of a tree's branches bathed in sunlight.

1. Words that describe colors are examples of vivid language. What color words does Jiménez use in the poem? How do they help you to see what he is describing?
2. What words does Jiménez repeat in the poem? How are these words important in creating the image?
3. How would you describe the poet's feelings about his subject? Explain your answer.

How soft a Caterpillar steps—

Emily Dickinson

How soft a Caterpillar steps—
I find one on my Hand
From such a velvet world it comes
Such plushes at command
Its soundless travels just arrest
My slow—terrestrial eye
Intent upon its own career
What use has it for me—

Responding to the Selection

Your Response

1. Have you ever looked closely at something in nature and been surprised by what you found? Explain your experience.
2. Does the poem make you feel differently about caterpillars? Explain.

Recalling

3. Where is the caterpillar?
4. What word describes the caterpillar's world?

Interpreting

5. Find a word that appeals to the sense of touch and a word that appeals to the sense of sound. What images do these words create?
6. How do you think the speaker feels about the caterpillar? Explain your answer.

Applying

7. Explain why looking closely at something for the first time often causes you to see it in a different light.

Learning Option

Writing. This poem reveals the poet's sudden awareness of the caterpillar—but how does the caterpillar feel about the poet? Write a brief poem from the caterpillar's point of view. Think about the caterpillar as it suddenly finds itself on a person's hand instead of a branch.

Beauty

E-Yeh-Shure

Beauty is seen
In the sunlight,
The trees, the birds,
Corn growing and people working
Or dancing for their harvest.

Beauty is heard
In the night,
Wind sighing, rain falling,
Or a singer chanting
Anything in earnest.

Beauty is in yourself.
Good deeds, happy thoughts
That repeat themselves
In your dreams,
In your work,
And even in your rest.

Reader's Response

How would you complete the sentence "Beauty is . . ."?

Responding to the Selection

Your Response

1. Do you see beauty in the same things the poet does? Explain.

Recalling

2. How can "Beauty" be in yourself?

Interpreting

3. How do the first lines in each stanza relate to the remaining lines in the stanza?

Applying

4. Why is it important to see beauty within yourself as well as in things outside of yourself?

Critical Thinking and Reading

Recognizing Sensory Words

Poets use **sensory words,** which appeal to your senses of sight, hearing, touch, taste, or smell. These words give you a striking impression of the physical world.

1. The first line of "Beauty" alerts us to look for words that appeal to our sense of sight. Find three words or phrases in the stanza that appeal to your sense of sight.
2. To what sense does the first line in the second stanza tell you to be alert?
3. Find three words or phrases in the second stanza that appeal to this sense.

Thinking and Writing

Writing a Lyric Poem

Look at the word web you made in the Focus activity in the Guide for Reading and add anything else you feel about beauty. Try to make the details specific and vivid, using words that appeal to the senses. Use your web to write a lyric poem. Arrange the words in a logical order, perhaps according to senses. Write your first draft. Then revise it, cutting out any unnecessary words. Read your revised poem to a partner, and apply any of your partner's constructive comments when you write your final draft.

GUIDE FOR READING

Two Limericks

These two limericks, like many of the form, were created anonymously. That simply means that the author could not or did not wish to be named. The limericks may have been written down by their authors or they may have been passed down by word of mouth. Though named after the county Limerick in Ireland, the origin of limericks is unknown. Edward Lear popularized limericks in print with his famous collection of limericks, *Book of Nonsense,* printed in 1846. Since that time many famous and not-so-famous poets have written limericks.

Limericks

A **limerick** is a type of light, humorous verse. Often nonsensical in nature, it is a five-line poem in which lines 1, 2, and 5 rhyme, as do lines 3 and 4. The rhythm of a limerick is equally important. The lines that rhyme also have the same rhythm, as well as the same number of syllables. So lines 1, 2, and 5 sound alike, as do lines 3 and 4. The purpose of most limericks is to make you laugh, and the rhyme and rhythm add much to a limerick's humor.

Focus

Limericks are usually written about silly or nonsensical subjects. Read the two lines below and copy them into your notebook. Fill in the blanks with two words that rhyme, and you have started your own limerick. In a group of two or three, brainstorm for a list of places and hobbies that rhyme. You may wish to change other words in the two lines to suit your choice of places or hobbies. After you read the limericks on the facing page, complete the one you have started.

I once knew a woman from ___________
Her hobbies were sailing and ___________

Vocabulary

Knowing the following words will help you read these poems.

flue (flo͞o) *n.*: A tube for the passage of smoke, as in a chimney (p. 501)

flaw (flô) *n.*: Break; crack (p. 501)

Two Limericks

Anonymous

A flea and a fly in a flue
Were caught, so what could they do?
Said the fly, "Let us flee."
"Let us fly," said the flea.
So they flew through a flaw in the flue.

There was a young fellow named Hall,
Who fell in the spring in the fall;
'Twould have been a sad thing
If he'd died in the spring,
But he didn't—he died in the fall.

Responding to the Selection

Your Response

1. Do you find these limericks amusing? Why or why not?

Interpreting

2. The first limerick uses words that sound similar, beginning with the letters *fl*. How do these words contribute to the fun of the poem?
3. The first limerick also contains words that sound alike but are spelled differently. Explain how these words add to the humor.
4. In the second limerick, why did the poet choose the name Hall for the young fellow?

Applying

5. Think of some other examples of limericks, tongue twisters, or other nonsensical poems or songs. Why do we enjoy such things?

Analyzing Literature

Understanding Limericks

Limericks are short, humorous poems with a specific form: They are five lines long, with the first, second, and fifth lines rhyming, and the third and fourth lines rhyming. Limericks usually contain ridiculous characters and situations.

1. What is the source of the humor of the first limerick?
2. What is unexpected about the final line in the second limerick?
3. Put one of the limericks into your own words. Do you like your version of the limerick? How do the rhythm and rhyme add to the humor?

GUIDE FOR READING

Two Haiku

Haiku

Haiku is a form of poetry that developed in Japan. Haiku has seventeen syllables in three lines, five in the first line, seven in the second line, and five in the third line. The haiku poet usually tries to capture a simple scene from nature and to suggest a strong feeling about it. A good haiku enables you to see an entire scene and experience a strong feeling or emotion.

Focus

A famous person once sent a telegram to an author explaining what he thought of the author's latest work. The telegram simply said: "!" Haiku is rather like that brief telegram. Haiku lets the reader understand the writer's emotional response in a few words. Usually, the writer uses words that appeal to the senses. Think of something in nature that you find beautiful. In a chart like the one below, list words to describe the effect of that natural object or event on each of your senses. Note the way the poets appeal to your senses in the haiku that follow.

Topic: ______________________

Sight	Sound	Smell	Touch	Taste

Vocabulary

In haiku simple words are used to create vivid images. As you read each haiku, think about both the literal meaning of the word and the implied meaning of the word.

Matsuo-Bashō

(1644–1694) was born near Kyoto, Japan. He is acknowledged to be one of the masters of the haiku. His poem illustrates the qualities of a good haiku, particularly the striking picture of nature that he presents.

Muso-Soseki

(1275–1351) was one of the most important religious leaders of his time in Japan. Although only one book of his poetry was published, many people consider his haiku to be among his best work.

Two Haiku

An old silent pond . . .
A frog jumps into the pond,
splash! Silence again.

Bashō

Over the wintry
forest, winds howl in a rage
with no leaves to blow.

Soseki

FROG
Meika Gafu
Courtesy of the Trustees of the British Museum

Responding to the Selection

Your Response

1. Which of these haiku do you prefer? Why?

Recalling

2. Where does each haiku take place?
3. Find a specific sound-word in each poem.

Interpreting

4. Contrast the scenes in each haiku.
5. Describe the feelings in each haiku. How are they different?

Applying

6. Why do you think that brief descriptions or brief statements are sometimes more effective than long ones?

Analyzing Literature

Understanding Haiku

Haiku is a Japanese verse form with seventeen syllables in three lines. The skill in writing haiku is in capturing a moment in nature and its associated feelings within this small structure.

1. Describe the scenes in both haiku.
2. What feelings do you associate with the first haiku? With the second haiku?
3. What words contribute to these feelings?

Learning Option

Writing. Choose some aspect of nature as the subject of your own haiku. Use the chart you prepared in the Focus activity in the Guide for Reading to write your haiku. Be sure to follow the form of the haiku described on page 502. When you have finished writing your haiku, you may wish to illustrate the poem for your readers.

Playing With Forms

You have no difficulty telling which selections in this book are poems and which are not. After all, poetry *looks* different because poetry follows forms that are different from other types of literature.

Your Turn

Write a poem that has a specific form. Look at the poems in this book for ideas.

Prewriting

1. Choose a form to imitate. You might select a haiku, a limerick, a concrete poem, or you might try a different form such as a diamante poem. For this form, you place two nouns with opposite meanings at opposite ends of the diamond. Fill in the lines with the kinds of words suggested to describe a progression between the nouns:

_____ (noun #1)
_____ _____ (adjectives)
_____ _____ _____ ("ing" words)
_____ _____ *_____ _____ (nouns)
_____ _____ _____ ("ing" words)
_____ _____ (adjectives)
_____ (noun #2)

*Place the *key word* here. The *key word* switches the thought of the poem toward the second noun.

Whatever form you plan to use, make the shape of it on your paper.

2. Choose a subject for your poem that matches the form. For example, limericks are humorous, and concrete poems have a shape that suggests the meaning.

3. Brainstorm for the words and ideas to use in your poem.

Drafting

Put your ideas into the appropriate form. While it is important to keep form in mind, don't forget that you are trying to write a good poem. Focus on meaning as well as form. Brenda wrote the following diamante:

```
              Winter
           Cold   Gray
   Chilling   Snowing   Darkening
     Ice    Snow   *March   Rain
Brightening   Melting   Growing
           Warm   Sunny
              Summer
```

Revising

Keep these questions in mind as you revise:

- Have I correctly followed the form of poetry I chose?
- Are my images specific? Do they appeal to the senses?
- If I used rhyme, does the rhyme seem natural or does it distract from the poem?

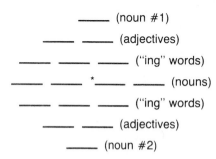

Themes in Poetry

AFTER THE SHOWER
John Atkinson Grimshaw
Christopher Wood Gallery

GUIDE FOR READING

One

James Berry (1925–   ) was born in Jamaica, an island in the Caribbean Sea. When he was 23 years old, he immigrated to Great Britain. Berry was working in the British school system when he noticed there was an absence of books for and about children of African and Caribbean heritages. He decided to fill that gap and began writing stories and poems about the Caribbean. In addition, he wrote about the experiences of minority children in Great Britain. Berry published several short story and poetry collections in the 1980's. The poem "One" is from *When I Dance: Poems,* a poetry anthology published in 1988. *When I Dance* won the *Signal* Poetry Award in 1989. Berry also teaches and is fond of telling his students, "I am not going to teach poetry; I'm not teaching anything, because you are already poets."

Sea Songs

Myra Cohn Livingston (1926–   ) was born in Omaha, Nebraska. *Whispers and Other Poems,* her first book of poetry, was published when she was in her first year of college. Following graduation from college, Livingston wrote book reviews and did public relations work in Hollywood. Since that time she has published many highly praised books for children. Much of her poetry for young people is drawn from her own happy childhood, and from her experiences with her young children. She says ". . . I still see with the eyes of a child. Each of us must live life anew and discover the simple things of childhood." Livingston believes that all things in nature are part of a natural cycle of life and decay. "Sea Songs" describes the natural cycle of life around the sea.

Theme

In literature, **theme** is the underlying meaning of a work, the idea it presents about people or about life. In poetry, as in short stories, the theme is sometimes stated directly, but more often it is suggested by the content of the poem. The theme reflects the poet's concerns or feelings about the subject. In the poem "One," James Berry shares his thoughts about individuality. "Sea Songs" has a theme that deals with the world of nature.

Focus

Two different themes are explored in the following poems. The titles of the poems, "One" and "Sea Songs," suggest what the theme of each poem might be. What comes to mind when you think of the word "one"? What does the phrase "sea songs" mean to you? Form a group of three or four classmates. Choose the title of one poem, and create a cluster diagram of your thoughts and feelings about that title. Write the title in the center of a sheet of paper and circle it. Around the title, jot down all the words and phrases that come to mind. Circle each word or phrase and connect related ideas with lines. As you read these poems, compare your ideas with the poets' ideas.

Vocabulary

Knowing the following words will help you read these poems.

mimic (mim′ ik) *v.*: to imitate or copy (p. 508)

tentacles (ten′ tə k'lz) *n.*: Flexible, slender growths about the head or mouth, used like arms to grasp and hold (p. 510)

lashed (lasht) *adj.*: Whipped; struck (p. 511)

galleons (gal′ ē ənz) *n.*: Large Spanish warships from the fifteenth and sixteenth centuries (p. 511)

heaving (hēv′ iŋ) *adj.*: Rising and falling rhythmically (p. 511)

buffeted (buf′ it 'd) *v.*: Thrust or tossed about (p. 511)

furrows (fur′ ōz) *n.*: Narrow grooves (p. 513)

splaying (splā′ iŋ) *v.*: Spreading out (p. 513)

kaleidoscopes (kə lī′ də skōps) *n.*: Constantly changing sets of color (p. 513)

Spelling Tip

Remember to insert an e in *galleon* or you will have *gallon* instead.

One

James Berry

Only one of me
and nobody can get a second one
from a photocopy machine.

Nobody has the fingerprints I have.
Nobody can cry my tears, or laugh my laugh
or have my expectancy when I wait.

But anybody can mimic my dance with my dog.
Anybody can howl how I sing out of tune.
And mirrors can show me multiplied
many times, say, dressed up in red
or dressed up in gray.

Nobody can get into my clothes for me
or feel my fall for me, or do my running.
Nobody hears my music for me, either.

I am just this one.
Nobody else makes the words
I shape with sound, when I talk.

But anybody can act how I stutter in a rage.
Anybody can copy echoes I make.
And mirrors can show me multiplied
many times, say, dressed up in green
or dressed up in blue.

LITTLE WILLIE
Raymond Lark
Courtesy of Edward Smith & Company

Responding to the Selection

Your Response

1. What would you like to tell the poet about your individuality?

Recalling

2. How is the speaker in this poem a unique person?
3. In what ways can the speaker be copied?

Interpreting

4. What moods do you think the speaker is in when he dresses in red, gray, green, or blue?
5. What feelings do you think the poet has about individuality? Explain.

Applying

6. Do you think more people try to be individuals or to fit in with the crowd? Explain.

Analyzing Literature

Understanding Theme

The **theme** of a poem is the central idea, or underlying meaning. It is often a comment about life or about human nature. Usually you can state a theme in one sentence. The theme is not the same as the subject but is often a general comment related to the subject. In this poem the subject is implied, or suggested, by the title, "One."

1. What point is the poet making about individuality?
2. What information from the poem supports the point?
3. State the theme of the poem in one sentence.

THE WAVE
Marsden Hartley
Worcester Art Museum

Sea Songs

Myra Cohn Livingston

Crashing on dark shores, drowning, pounding
breaker swallows breaker. Tide follows
tide. Lost in her midnight witchery
moon watches, cresting tall waves, pushing
through mist and blackness the cold waters.

Moon, you have worked long.
Now rest . . .

Mermaids curl in coral beds. Kraken[1]
wind long tentacles, weave tales of lost
sailors sleeping in beams of sunken
ships; tales of bright treasure buried in
silt and the glittering of doubloons.[2]

Moon, you have gone mad.
Be still . . .

---

1. kraken (krä′ kən) *n.*: A legendary sea monster said to resemble a giant squid.
2. doubloons (du blo͞ons′) *n.*: Old Spanish gold coins.

Caravels,[3] lashed by tails of mermen
carry old dreams. Galleons, shouldered on
scaly arms, bound over the breakers.
Clouds gather in white mist. All is still.
Pale stars disappear in darkling sky.

Moon, you speak in
strange riddles . . .

Wind rises. Drizzle turns to raindrop.
Sea and sky split with thunder, gale howls.
Heaving ships, plunged into black waters,
vomit saltspray back to hissing seas,
sailing over, up and ever on.

Moon, you cry out with
nightmare . . .

This, Columbus saw beneath ocean
stretching from dark shores to wide, bright sands,
tossed and buffeted by strong iron
chains rusted with blood-red; yet never
waking from dream, he sailed in madness.

Moon, your tale is told
Now sleep . . .

Drowned in foam, faded in the gray mist,
phantoms disappear. A sandpiper
prints the clean morning sand. Pelicans
plunge dive the whitecaps. Across distant
sea swells, sun gurgles, rising in light.

Moon, your shadow
still watches . . .

Fishermen unwind tangled nets, cast
trawls[4] into marbled waters, snaring

---

3. caravels (kar′ ə velz′) *n.*: Small sailing ships used in the sixteenth century.

4. trawls (trôlz) *n.*: Fishing nets.

THE CALM AFTER THE STORM
Edward Moran
Private Collection

schools of fish in their tarred, wet purses,
chumming and charming with live wriggling
anchovy and herring, a day's catch.

Sun, you watch behind
thin clouds.

Tilted umbrellas nod in soft sand.
Patchworks of bright towels sprawl beach picnics.
Surfboards ride the foaming surf. Painted
pails pour water into moated castles,
buried in the lost digs of summer.

Sun, you climb higher
and higher.

Ketches and sloops color the blue days.
Spinnakers of red rig for racing.
Dinghies and catamarans[5] bobbing,
jumbles of masts and booms in dizzy
patterns, billow with walloping sails.

---

5. Ketches and sloops . . . and catamarans: Ketches, sloops, dinghies, and catamarans are types of sailboats. Spinnakers are large, triangular forward sails used on some boats for racing.

Sun, you smile on
your play.

Wind blows the water into furrows.
Waves leap toward the shore, the crests foaming
white, the whitecaps spraying, splaying,
dashing against pitted rocks, dying
slowly in the thirsty, sponging sands.

Sun, you sink as
you watch.

Under the sand, below the water
sun in spring feeds the floating plankton,
forking light on the drifting seaweeds,
multiplying herring, menhaden,[6]
churning over the salts of the sea.

Sun, you bring life,
you bring food.

Cries of porpoise and dolphin echo
through dark submarine canyons and shelves.
Shrimp crackle, small croakers and drums hiss.
Huge rubber men pry from barnacles
giant scallops and swim with gray sharks.

Here, sun, you can
still see.

Deeper than this, dwell darkness and cold.
Sun cannot probe these underground dungeons
locked by sea devils and dragonfish,
flashing with light, turning on eerie
torches, kaleidoscopes of color.

No sun, no moon
sees here.

GOOD SAILING
Montague Dawson

6. menhaden (men hād′ 'n) *n.*: A sea fish related to the herring.

Who cries of what lies beyond, beneath
bottom realms? Volcanoes rising from
ocean floor, golden with shells, gray wash
showered from earth, red clay, and wind dust?
Who speaks of mysterious red tides?

Moon, you return
once more . . .

Ghosts raise galley ships on crimson tides.
Sun flees. Foghorn cries to lighthouse.
Wind blows wild storms and over dark waves
mermaids sing bewitching sea songs to
sailors steering wildly toward the moon.

Moon, speak once more
the dreams . . .

MULTICULTURAL CONNECTION

Ideas About the Sea

For people who live by the sea and depend on it for their livelihood, the sea has always been mysterious. Its surface can turn into rolling mountains of water, and dangerous creatures lurk in its depths. So great is the power of the sea that every early culture believed the sea was ruled by gods. The Chinese believed that storms were produced by dragons that lived in palaces under the sea. To the Greeks, a god named Poseidon, the king of the ocean, called up storms.

The mysterious tides. Ancient peoples did not know that tides are caused by the attraction of the moon. They thought that there was a connection between the tides and life and death. Along the Atlantic coast of Europe, especially in France and Spain, peasants believed that children were born only when the tide was coming in and that people who died of old age would do so only as the tide went out. The Haidas, a Native American group on the west coast of Canada, believed that dead friends sailed in on the tide to greet those who were about to die and then carried them off on the ebb tide.

A myth from Nova Scotia. The most spectacular tides occur in Nova Scotia, Canada. Because the Bay of Fundy is ninety-four miles long and relatively narrow, it acts almost like a funnel. The incoming tide rises rapidly and may go as high as seventy feet. Indian groups who lived in Nova Scotia said this was the god Glooscap's attempt to keep beavers from building a dam across the bay.

Exploring and Sharing

Do you know someone who has lived by the sea? Interview this person to find out about his or her attitudes toward the sea. Organize your notes and share them with the class.

Reader's Response

If you could go to the sea and experience some of the things in this poem, what would you choose to experience? Why?

Responding to the Selection

Your Response

1. Has reading this poem changed the way you feel about the sea? Explain.

Recalling

2. Summarize the cycle of night and day at the sea described in the poem.

Interpreting

3. What moods and feelings are conveyed in the stanzas that are followed by the "Moon" refrain? In the stanzas that are followed by the "Sun" refrain?
4. The poem describes the progression from night to day to night. Think about the descriptions of ships, people, and sea creatures. What ships, people, and sea creatures are associated with the night? With the day?

Applying

5. The seas of the world have been a source of wonder, mystery, and excitement throughout time. For what reasons are people fascinated with our oceans and seas?

Analyzing Literature

Finding Meaning

You find meaning in a poem by responding to it in your own personal way. Your own experiences and memories influence your interpretation of theme. Therefore, the meaning you find in a poem—or any piece of literature—is personal. For example, "Sea Songs" might remind a sailor of his sea experiences, making him feel happy. Another person, who has never seen the sea, might feel wonder and awe at the mysterious life and activity of the sea.

To find meaning in a poem, read it carefully, think about the theme, and think about how you feel about the theme.

1. Summarize what "Sea Songs" means to you.
2. What are some of your experiences and memories that helped shape this meaning?

Critical Thinking and Reading

Supporting an Interpretation

Your **interpretation** of a poem is your explanation of the poet's theme. When you make an interpretation, you should be able to support it with evidence from the poem. For example, one interpretation of "Sea Songs" might be "The variety of life in the sea is wonderful." The poem is filled with descriptions of sea creatures, ships, birds, and even sea monsters. It describes the mysteries and joys of the sea.

1. Find evidence from the poem to support this interpretation.
2. What might be another interpretation of "Sea Songs"? Provide evidence to support it.

Thinking and Writing

Writing a Letter

Write a letter to a friend describing a scene in nature that moves you. It could be a description of the sea; it could be a mountain range. It could also be about a tree or a patch of flowers in a city park. Freewrite about your subject, focusing on its appearance and the feelings you associate with it. You might want to observe your subject while you are writing. Circle the words and phrases that best describe the subject and your feelings about it. Organize these into a rough outline and use them as you write the first draft. As you revise, be sure you have details that enable your friend to see your subject clearly and understand how you feel about it. Remember, be specific.

GUIDE FOR READING

If I Were in Charge of the World

Judith Viorst was born in Newark, New Jersey, but has lived in Washington, D.C. for much of her life. At age seven she began writing "terrible poems about dead dogs mostly." Her first book of poems, *The Village Square,* was published in 1965. Judith Viorst says most of her children's books are for or about her own children. "If I Were in Charge of the World" expresses wishes that we can all understand.

Change

Charlotte Zolotow (1915–) was born in Norfolk, Virginia. She became convinced that she wanted to be a writer when her fourth grade teacher praised one of her short stories. Since she wrote her first book for children in 1944, Zolotow has written more than sixty-five other books. "Change" reflects her interest in how "the sounds of the words communicate the meanings of the words."

Daydreamers

Born in North Carolina, **Eloise Greenfield** (1929–) has written biography and fiction as well as poetry. In fact, she wrote an award-winning biography of Rosa Parks, the woman who helped start the Civil Rights movement in the 1960's by refusing to give up her bus seat to a white man. She has also won the Jane Addams Children's Book Award and the 1978 Coretta Scott King Award. *Under the Sunday Tree* is her most recent book of poems. She now lives in Washington, D.C., where she teaches creative writing.

Whatif

Chicago born **Shel Silverstein** (1932–) grew up wanting to become a dancer or a baseball player. Instead he became a cartoonist and a writer. He is best known for his excellent books of poetry, *Where the Sidewalk Ends* and *A Light in the Attic.* Although he does not like to be interviewed, Silverstein has vowed to "keep on communicating." His poem "Whatif" communicates some feelings that all of us experience at one time or another.

Theme

The **theme** of a poem is its general idea about or insight into life or human nature. Many themes in poetry have to do with the "inside world"; that is, the inner thoughts and feelings of people. For example, the following poem, "Days," by Karle Wilson Baker, describes the speaker's inner world.

Some days my thoughts are just cocoons—all cold, and dull and blind,
They hang from dripping branches in the grey woods of my mind;
And other days they drift and shine—such free and flying things!
I find the gold-dust in my hair, left by their brushing wings.

The description of different kinds of thoughts also suggests the feelings that accompany them. You can feel the boredom and sadness that accompany "cocoon" thoughts and the wonder and joy that accompany thoughts that "drift and shine." You could say that the theme of this poem is: Some thoughts are almost magical in their effect on people. Part of the enjoyment of reading poems about the "inner" world is realizing that others have thoughts and feelings similar to your own.

Focus

The poems in this group are about the "inner world" of thoughts and feelings. Imagine you were inviting adults on a tour of the mind of a person your age. What would you want to show them? What kinds of things do you think are typical of most young people? With a group of classmates, list three or four stops you would make on "A Tour of the Young Person's Mind." As you read the poems in this group, think about the thoughts and feelings the authors are writing about.

Vocabulary

Knowing the following vocabulary words will help you read these poems.

crimson (krim′ z'n) *n.*: Deep red (p. 520)

promenade (präm′ ə näd) *v.*: Parade; march (p. 521)

pranced (pranst) *v.*: Moved gaily and with confidence (p. 524)

If I Were in Charge of the World

Judith Viorst

If I were in charge of the world
I'd cancel oatmeal,
Monday mornings,
Allergy shots, and also
Sara Steinberg.

If I were in charge of the world
There'd be brighter night lights,
Healthier hamsters, and
Basketball baskets forty-eight inches
lower.

If I were in charge of the world
You wouldn't have lonely.
You wouldn't have clean.
You wouldn't have bedtimes.
Or "Don't punch your sister."
You wouldn't even have sisters.

If I were in charge of the world
A chocolate sundae with whipped cream
and nuts would be a vegetable.
All 007 movies[1] would be G.
And a person who sometimes forgot to
brush,
And sometimes forgot to flush,
Would still be allowed to be
In charge of the world.

1. 007 movies: Popular spy-adventure movies featuring James Bond, agent 007.

Reader's Response
What would you change if you were in charge of the world?

Responding to the Selection

Your Response

1. Do you think it is good to think about what you want to change in the world? Why or why not?

Interpreting

2. How does the speaker feel about the things that he or she would get rid of?
3. How does the speaker feel about the things he or she would simply change?
4. Describe the speaker in this poem.

Applying

5. Do you think that the speaker would really do everything in the poem if he or she were able to? Explain your answer.
6. Almost everyone has daydreams about being in charge of the world. Discuss some of the problems that would come with being in charge of the world.

Critical Thinking and Reading

Comparing and Contrasting Ideas

Comparing means looking at the similarities between two or more things. **Contrasting** means looking at the differences between two or more things.

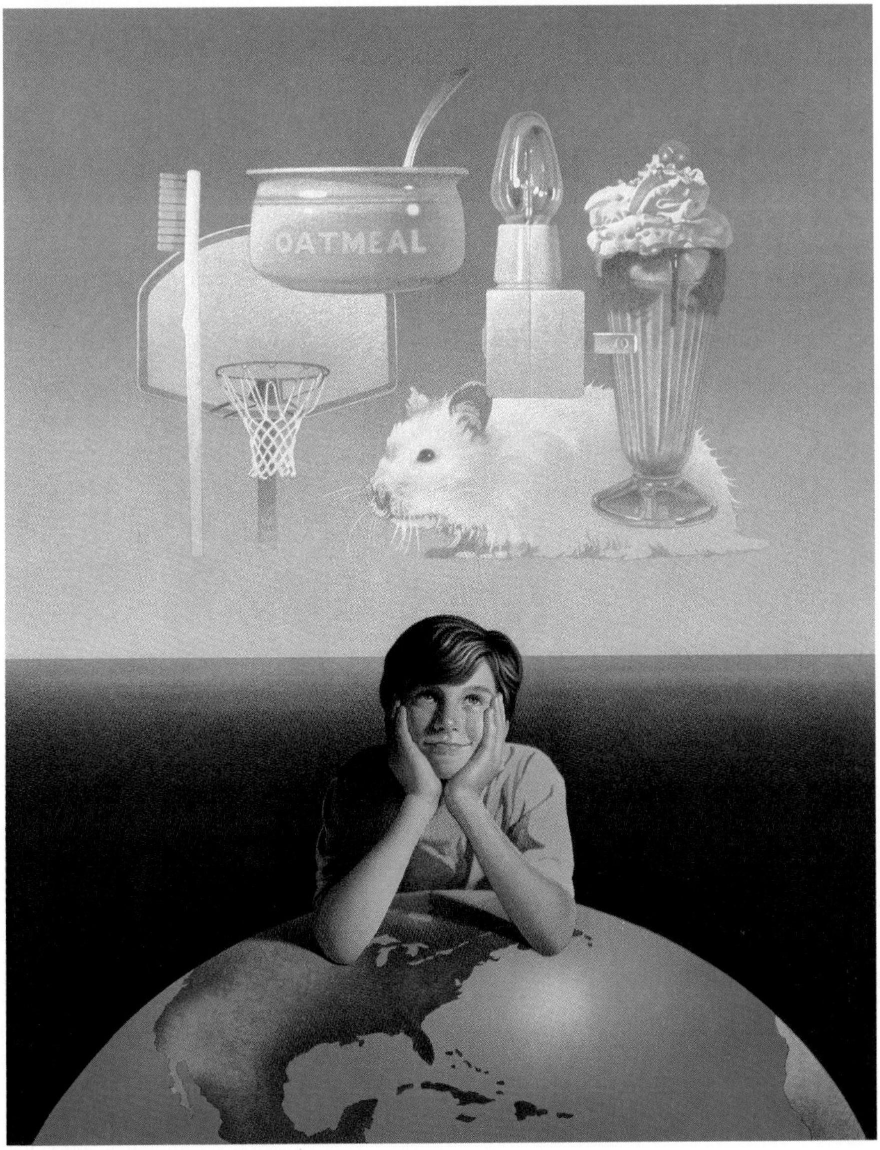

"If I Were in Charge of the World" is a poem about changes the speaker would like to make if he or she were in charge of the world. Imagine that you are in charge of the world and compare and contrast the speaker's wishes with your own.

1. Of the changes described by the speaker, which would you also make?
2. Which of the changes described by the speaker would you not make?
3. What other changes would you make if you were in charge of the world?

Change

Charlotte Zolotow

The summer
still hangs
heavy and sweet
with sunlight
as it did last year.

The autumn
still comes
showering gold and crimson
as it did last year.

The winter
still stings
clean and cold and white
as it did last year.

The spring
still comes
like a whisper in the dark night.

It is only I
who have changed.

Reader's Response

How have you changed since this time last year?

RESPONDING TO THE SELECTION

Your Response

1. In what ways would you like to change in the coming year?

Recalling

2. How is the summer the same? The autumn? The winter? The spring?

Interpreting

3. How does the speaker of the poem feel about change? Explain.
4. How are the first four stanzas similar?
5. The length and structure of the final stanza are different from the other stanzas. How does this difference reinforce the idea of change?

Applying

6. Why is it important that all things continue to grow and change?

ANALYZING LITERATURE

Recognizing Feelings

Feelings are an important part of many poems that reflect on our "inner" world. For example, you might say that the speaker in "Change" has happy, content feelings about summer because she says it "hangs/heavy and sweet/with sunlight."

1. What personal feelings or memories do these descriptions of the seasons bring out in you?
2. What feeling does the speaker suggest about change? How does this feeling contrast with the other feelings in the poem? What theme is conveyed through this contrast?
3. What does this poem make you think about change?

Daydreamers

Eloise Greenfield

Daydreamers . . .

holding their bodies still
for a time
letting the world turn around them

while their dreams hopscotch,
doubledutch, dance,

thoughts rollerskate,
crisscross,
bump into hopes and wishes.

Dreamers
thinking up new ways,
looking toward new days,

planning new tries,
asking new whys.
Before long,
hands will start to move again,
eyes turn outward,
bodies shift for action,
but for this moment they are still,

they are
the daydreamers,
letting the world dizzy itself
without them.

Scenes passing through their minds
make no sound
glide from hiding places
promenade and return
silently

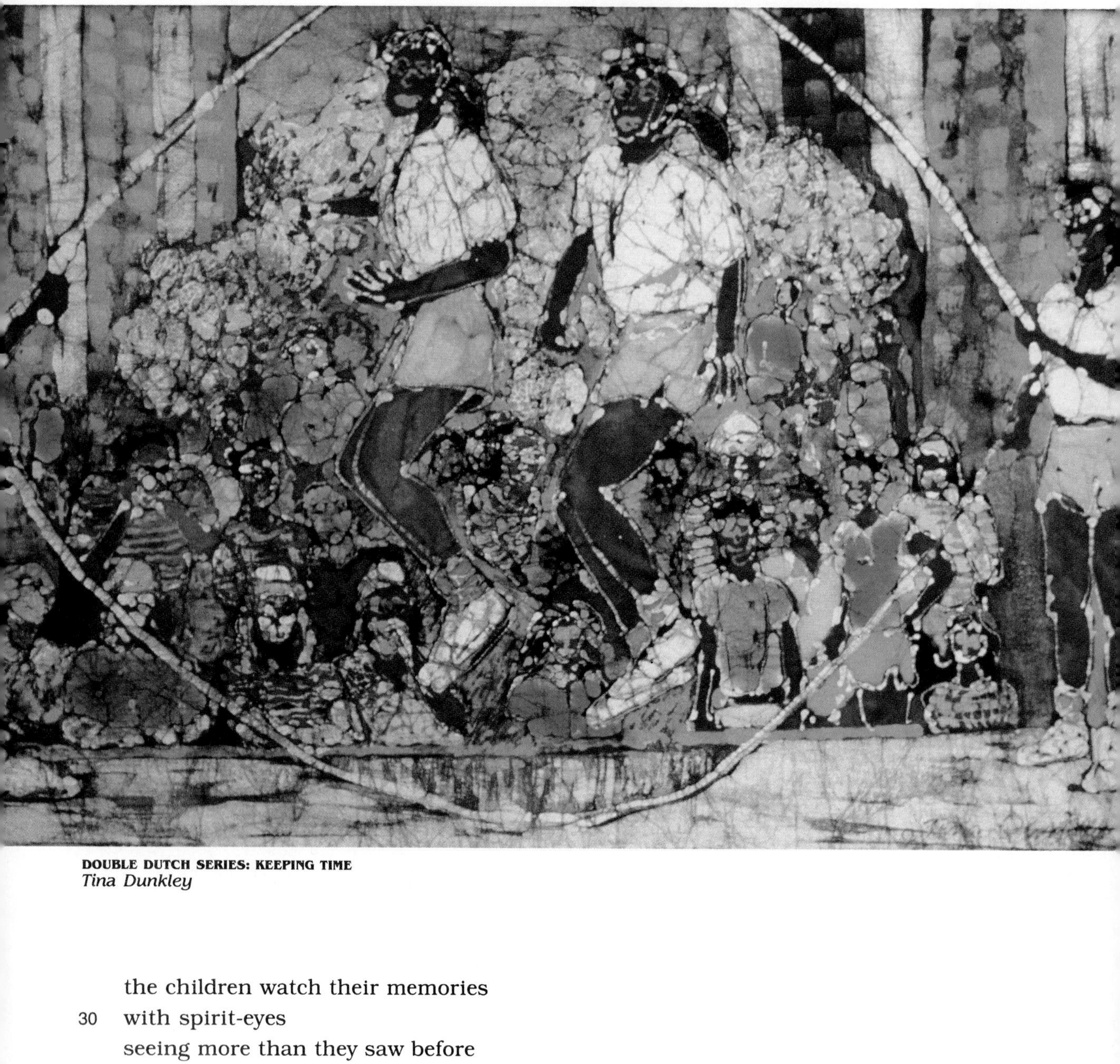

DOUBLE DUTCH SERIES: KEEPING TIME
Tina Dunkley

the children watch their memories
with spirit-eyes
seeing more than they saw before

feeling more
or maybe less
than they felt the time before
reaching with spirit-hands
to touch the dreams
drawn from their yesterdays

They will not be the same
after this growing time,
this dreaming.
In their stillness they have moved
forward

toward womanhood
toward manhood.
This dreaming has made them
new.

Reader's Response
Do you agree with the speaker about the way daydreamers change? Why or why not?

Responding to the Selection

Your Response

1. Do you think daydreaming is a waste of time? Explain.

Recalling

2. Name three things dreamers do.
3. How do daydreamers change?

Interpreting

4. What words create a feeling of movement in lines 1–9?
5. What do you think "spirit-eyes" and "spirit-hands" might be?
6. Explain the meaning of the final sentence.

Applying

7. Why is it important for people to hold on to their hopes and dreams?

Learning Options

1. **Art.** Everyone has daydreams. Think of one or two of your daydreams or those described in the poem. Using magazine pictures, scraps of cloth, or other items, create a collage to illustrate these daydreams.
2. **Performance.** In a group of three or four, dramatize the stanzas of this poem. To prepare, read the poem and highlight lines that suggest action. Decide how your group can best dramatize that action using the resources available in the classroom. Then practice reading the poem, coordinating the action with the words. When you are ready, perform the poem for your class.

Whatif

Shel Silverstein

Last night, while I lay thinking here,
Some Whatifs crawled inside my ear
And pranced and partied all night long
And sang their same old Whatif song:
Whatif I'm dumb in school?
Whatif they've closed the swimming pool?
Whatif I get beat up?
Whatif there's poison in my cup?
Whatif I start to cry?
Whatif I get sick and die?
Whatif I flunk that test?
Whatif green hair grows on my chest?
Whatif nobody likes me?
Whatif a bolt of lightning strikes me?
Whatif I don't grow taller?
Whatif my head starts getting smaller?
Whatif the fish won't bite?
Whatif the wind tears up my kite?
Whatif they start a war?
Whatif my parents get divorced?
Whatif the bus is late?
Whatif my teeth don't grow in straight?
Whatif I tear my pants?
Whatif I never learn to dance?
Everything seems swell, and then
The nighttime Whatifs strike again!

Reader's Response
Have you ever experienced the Whatifs?

Responding to the Selection

Your Response

1. What do you think is the most serious Whatif in this poem? Explain your answer.

Interpreting

2. Why do the Whatifs come at night?
3. Why do you think so many of the Whatifs concern school and appearance?
4. How does repetition add to the playful effect of the poem?

Applying

5. Why do you think that everyone experiences the Whatifs every now and then?

Thinking and Writing

Adding to "Whatif"

Write your own whatifs to fit in the middle of Shel Silverstein's poem. Think about some of your own whatifs and jot them down. As in the poem, your whatifs can be feelings you have actually experienced or they can be silly or nonsensical. Next, try to arrange your whatifs in pairs of rhymed lines. You can make up as many rhymed pairs as you desire. Finally, insert your whatifs into the poem and read them aloud. Do the lines rhyme? Do they fit in with the rest of the poem? Make any final changes for your final draft.

Learning Option

Art. Illustrate two or three Whatifs from this poem. You may create your own drawings or use pictures from old magazines and newspapers. Write the appropriate lines from the poem somewhere on your illustrations.

YOUR WRITING PROCESS

Reflective Writing

Have you ever found yourself thinking seriously and carefully about how you feel about someone or something? This kind of thinking is called reflection. Poems such as "Whatif" and "April Rain Song" are reflective. The speakers have reflected on their feelings and expressed them in a poem. We respond to poems like these because they deal with feelings or emotions we all share.

Your Turn

Write your own reflective poem about something that you have strong feelings for.

Prewriting

1. Choose a subject. It doesn't necessarily have to be your innermost thoughts, which are not always easy to reveal. You can write about other things that you think about, such as why things happen as they do, or your anger when you see people littering.

2. Freewrite about your subject, letting out your thoughts and feelings about it. For example, Linda reflected on her grandmother and did the following freewriting:

```
     My grandma always knows the
answers to questions I ask her,
and I ask her a lot. She likes to
make things to give as presents,
like the woolly orange sweater
she gave me for my birthday. She
always smiles. Everything she
does shows she cares about others.
```

Drafting

Look over your freewriting and choose those words and phrases that best sum up your feelings. Pull out these words and arrange them in a way that seems logical. Here is the first draft of Linda's poem.

```
My grandma
Always
   knows the answer
   has a smile
   gives to others
   listens
What would I do without her?
```

Revising

This is the best part of writing a poem, when you get to tinker with the words. Read what you have written. You'll probably need to add words to connect thoughts from one line to the next and replace general words or phrases with specific ones. Above all, don't be afraid to play with the words, phrases, and images. Experiment! When you are happy with what your poem says and how it says it, write your final copy.

Reading and Responding

Poetry

Robert Frost has written, "A poem . . . begins in delight and ends in wisdom." Perhaps you experienced these feelings as you read and responded to the poems in this unit.

There is no precise definition for poetry, but it has special qualities that set it apart from other forms of literature. The language is imaginative, musical, and compact. The form may be unusual. Images and sound devices give you special insights into a poem.

Your active reading strategies enable you to respond fully to poetry.

On pages 527 and 528, you can see an example of reading and responding by Markus Putnam from The Northeast Center for Creative Arts in Grand Rapids, Michigan. The notes in the side column include Marcus's thoughts and comments as he responded to "The Naming of Cats." Your responses may be different as you read.

RESPONDING TO LANGUAGE Poets use language to create new ways of seeing things. In doing so, they often use figurative language, language that is not intended to be understood literally. These figures of speech enable you to see or think about something in a new and imaginative way. What does the language make you think about? How does it make you feel?

RESPONDING TO APPEARANCE Poetry can take a variety of forms. What does it look like on the page? Is its appearance related to the type of poetry it is, such as narrative or lyric? How does its appearance affect your expectations and understanding?

RESPONDING TO IMAGERY Poets appeal to your senses by developing images. Use your imagination and your senses to take in the images. What senses do you use to respond to the images?

RESPONDING TO SOUND The music of poetry is created by sound devices. Read poems aloud and let the rhythm and the rhyme flow naturally. Listen to alliteration, onomatopoeia, and other musical devices. What is the effect of these sound devices? How do they contribute to the meaning of the poem?

RESPONDING TO THEME Many poems convey an important idea or insight about life. What do you think is the message of the poem? What special meaning does the poem have for you? How can you connect it to your life?

MODEL

The Naming of Cats

T. S. Eliot

Theme: *Will the poem be about cats' names?*

The Naming of Cats is a difficult matter,
It isn't just one of your holiday games;
You may think at first I'm as mad as a hatter
When I tell you, a cat must have THREE DIFFERENT NAMES.
First of all, there's the name that the family use daily,
Such as Peter, Augustus, Alonzo or James,
Such as Victor or Jonathan, George or Bill Bailey—
All of them sensible everyday names.
There are fancier names if you think they sound sweeter,
Some for the gentlemen, some for the dames:
Such as Plato, Admetus, Electra, Demeter—
But all of them sensible everyday names.

Appearance: *This poem looks hard to read because the lines are long and there are no breaks, but it's not so hard.*

Sound: *I like the way all these names sound when they're read in a row.*

Theme: *Naming cats sounds more complicated than I thought.*

CHUCK AND LOUISE
Mary Lake-Thompson

Imagery: *This is how a cat looks when it's feeling proud—a stiff tail and wide whiskers.*

Language: *The poet thinks cats have a secret one-of-a-kind name.*

Language: *There are a lot of long words, but they have nice sounds.*

Theme: *The ending says that names are special. Maybe the theme of this poem is that what you call someone or something is important. It shows how much you respect a person or thing.*

Response: *When I name something, I think of what it looks like or reminds me of. Some people I know are named for people in their family. My friend is named Henry after his grandfather.*

But I tell you, a cat needs a name that's particular,
  A name that's peculiar, and more dignified,
Else how can he keep up his tail perpendicular,
  Or spread out his whiskers, or cherish his pride?
Of names of this kind, I can give you a quorum,[1]
  Such as Munkustrap, Quaxo, or Coricopat,
Such as Bombalurina, or else Jellylorum—
  Names that never belong to more than one cat.
But above and beyond there's still one name left over,
  And that is the name that you never will guess;
The name that no human research can discover—
  But THE CAT HIMSELF KNOWS, and will never confess.
When you notice a cat in profound meditation,
  The reason, I tell you, is always the same:
His mind is engaged in a rapt contemplation
  Of the thought, of the thought, of the thought of his name:
    His ineffable effable
    Effanineffable[2]
Deep and inscrutable singular Name.

Reader's Response

Have you ever chosen the name for anything—a pet, a doll, or a team, for instance? How do you go about choosing a name?

1. quorum (kwôr′ əm) *n.*: The presence at a meeting of a minimum number of members necessary for an organization or group to carry on with business.

2. ineffable (in ef′ ə b′l) *adj.*: **. . . Effanineffable:** *Ineffable* means "inexpressible." *Effable* has the opposite meaning. In line 30 Eliot playfully combines both words and makes a new word whose meaning makes sense only in this poem.

T. S. Eliot (1888–1965) was born in St. Louis, Missouri; however, he moved to England in 1914 and thirteen years later became a citizen of that country. He worked for a publishing house in London as he developed his reputation as a poet, critic, and dramatist. In 1948 Eliot was awarded the Nobel Prize for Literature. Eliot's poetry and drama are often very serious and difficult; yet he also wrote *Old Possum's Book of Practical Cats*, a favorite book of verse. This book, which includes "The Naming of Cats," was the basis of the celebrated Broadway musical, *Cats*.

Responding to the Selection

Your Response

1. What name would you choose for a cat?

Recalling

2. How many names must a cat have?
3. Of what types are the names?
4. Which is the name that the cat is thinking about when it is in "rapt contemplation"?

Interpreting

5. Explain why a cat needs "a name that's peculiar, and more dignified."
6. How might the different names for a single cat correspond to different moods?

Applying

7. Do you have a nickname? Do you prefer to use the name your parents gave you? In what ways is your name important to you?

Analyzing Literature

Appreciating Repetition

Repetition is the use of words or phrases over and over in the same poem. While we may not like people who repeat themselves when speaking, repetition in poetry can enhance the meaning and the musical quality. Eliot repeats the words *name(s)* or *naming* in this poem. He also lists specific names, a kind of repetition.

1. How many times are the words *name, names,* or *naming* used in the poem?
2. What effect does this repetition have on the poem?

Thinking and Writing

Writing About a Name Change

Write a paragraph in which you tell how you would change your first name and explain why. In your prewriting, consider the following questions: What would you change your first name to? Why would you change your name? What is it about your name that you do not like? Begin your paragraph by revealing the name you have chosen and use the reasons from your prewriting to explain. As you revise, be sure your reasons are in a logical order. If you would not like to change your first name, write a paragraph explaining why your name suits you.

BRIDGING FORMS

GHOSTS I HAVE BEEN
by Richard Peck

"Many's the ignorant person who claims that spirits and haunts have forsaken the modern age in this new twentieth century. But what they do not know would fill a book. And this is the book." So begins the novel *Ghosts I Have Been* by Richard Peck.

Some of the writers in this unit do not limit themselves to writing poetry. In fact, some writers are better known for other forms of literature. For example, William Shakespeare is best known for his plays, and Lewis Carroll is best known for the novels *Alice in Wonderland* and *Through the Looking Glass*.

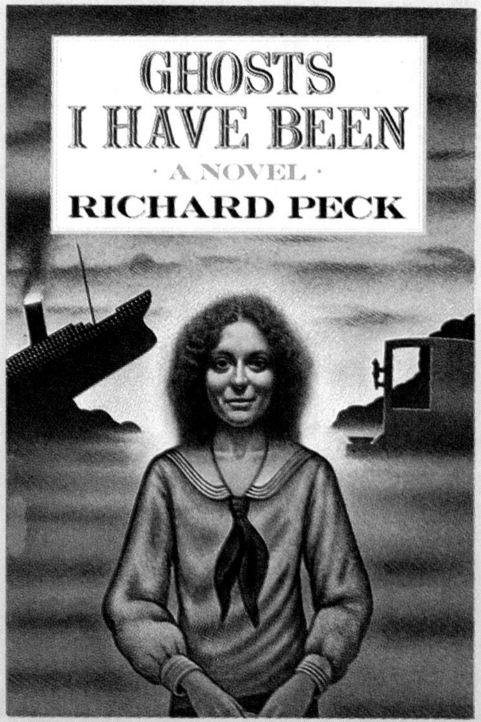

A contemporary writer who bridges forms of literature is Richard Peck. His poem "The Geese" is in this unit. Although the poem focuses on the thoughts of a father, Peck is better known for his novels focusing on young people. One of these novels is *Ghosts I Have Been*.

The Adventures of Blossom Culp

Ghosts I Have Been tells of a young girl's adventures with ghosts. The main character in the novel is a charmingly clever young lady named Blossom Culp, who lives in Bluff City, mid-America. Blossom is a fourteen-year-old who feels she is different from the other children in town. Like her mother, Blossom has Gypsy blood, and it has made her psychic—she can see the unseen and experience the past and future. This "gift" combined with Blossom's independent, feisty disposition lead her through some exciting and humorous adventures.

Her adventures include experiences with ghosts and with seeing things in the past and in the future. Some of these experiences are not very pleasant—for example, she relives the sinking of the Titanic, and she has a glimpse of the terrible war, World War I, that is to come in Europe. Blossom comes to realize that knowing the future is not without its problems and sorrows. But her strength of character and especially her sense of humor help her to come to terms with her amazing gift.

A Novelist for Young Readers

Richard Peck is an accomplished writer for young adults, having published more than fifteen novels dealing with the concerns of teenagers. One of the reasons for his success is that Peck writes for his audience, not to it. He uses language and dialogue that is realistic and appealing to young readers. Peck is also praised for the emotional depth of his characters and themes. At times, you feel he must be a teenager himself. He once commented, "Growing up is not just one problem at a time. It is a great many, often quiet problems . . . books are mainly about human relationships, friendships, family life, and trying to grow up the best way you know how." Peck's writings reflect this insight.

Read On!

When you read *Ghosts I Have Been*, you will notice how different it is from "The Geese." You will get a broader picture of the author—his style, his outlook, and his ideas. You will discover themes very different from ideas in "The Geese." If you enjoy *Ghosts I Have Been*, you might want to read another by Peck. Search out other works and read on!

FOCUS ON READING

Making Inferences

The skill of making inferences is very useful in reading poetry. Because a poem is usually made up of very few words, many of its ideas and meanings are suggested rather than stated directly. To help you to understand a poem you make inferences. An **inference** is a reasonable conclusion based on evidence. The evidence can be concrete images, sensory words, other details in the poem, or it can be your own background knowledge and experience. Both types of evidence must be carefully weighed to determine if they support the inference that is being made. Making inferences can help you to gain more meaning from a poem and help you to understand the poem's central message, or theme.

Inferences

Think about "Alone in the Nets," for example. What inferences can you make to help you understand the poem? First, you can infer that the speaker is a girl, and that she is playing goalie in a soccer game. These facts are never stated directly, but you probably inferred them without even trying. How did you infer these facts? You probably noted the title "Alone in the Nets" and you looked at the illustration to infer that the speaker is a goalie. Perhaps you inferred that the speaker is a girl because she refers to other players as "she" and your own experience is that girls usually compete separately from boys in soccer. Another inference you could make is that she is not happy about playing goalie because she has never before played the position. You can make this inference from words and phrases such as "alone of course" and all of the lines beginning "Why."

However, the speaker's mood seems to change from sad to happy, from miserable to confident, about halfway through the poem when the speaker makes a save. Again, you could make this inference based on words and phrases such as "But Frozen Moments Can Unfreeze," "My fears evaporate," and "I wave my happy ending wave."

Activity

Read the following poem, "Simple-Song," by Marge Piercy, and answer the questions that follow it.

When we are going toward someone we say
you are just like me
your thoughts are my brothers
word matches word
how easy to be together.

When we are leaving someone we say
how strange you are
we cannot communicate
we can never agree
how hard, hard and weary to be together.

We are not different nor alike
but each strange in his leather body
sealed in skin and reaching out clumsy hands
and loving is an act
that cannot outlive
the open hand
the open eye
the door in the chest standing open.

1. What does the speaker mean by "going toward someone"? Give evidence to support your answer.
2. What does the speaker mean by "leaving someone"? Give evidence to support your answer.
3. What can you infer about the meaning of the final five lines? Give evidence to support your answer.

Compiling a Poetry Anthology

An anthology is a collection of literature selections in one book. The textbook you are reading is an anthology containing short stories, plays, nonfiction, poems, tales from the oral tradition, and a novel. Some anthologies contain only one type of literature, such as poetry.

Poetry anthologies are organized in any number of ways. They might include poets from a specific part of the country, or poets born after or before a certain date. Some are more general, grouping poems according to themes and topics. Some of the books suggested on page 536 are anthologies.

Your Turn

Why not create a class poetry anthology made up of the poems you have written for class? You can contribute two poems, a favorite that you have already written, and one that you write especially for the anthology.

Choosing an Editorial Staff

Before you begin to choose poems, you should select an editorial staff. You should choose one, two, or three student editors depending on the size of your class. Together with your teacher, editors will be responsible for making sure that everyone contributes to the project. They will also make final decisions about how the poems will be arranged in the anthology.

You should also choose a production manager, who will be responsible for supervising the printing of the anthology.

Choosing a Poem

Even if you aren't a member of the editorial staff, your part in the anthology is extremely important. After all, there wouldn't be an anthology without the poets. As a contributor to the collection, begin by carefully looking over all the poems you have written, even those you have not handed in to your teacher. Choose your favorite poem for your first contribution to the anthology.

Revising an Old Poem or Writing a New One

For your second contribution, you may wish to revise a draft of a poem that you wrote but were unsatisfied with, or you may write another, entirely new poem.

1. Revising an old poem. If you choose to revise a poem you've already written, work with a small group of other students who are doing the same. Share your poems and ask for suggestions for revision. You might work from the following checklist:

- Have you included vivid words that appeal to the senses?
- Does the poem have a regular rhythm?

- Does the poem make sense? Are the ideas clear?
- Are any similes and metaphors original, yet understandable to the reader?

2. Writing a new poem. If you choose to write a new poem, consider both what you want to write about and a form appropriate for your topic. For example, if you choose to write about an experience you had last summer, you might want to write a narrative poem.

Follow appropriate prewriting, writing, and revising strategies for the subject and the type, or form, of your poem. For a narrative poem, for example, you could begin by writing down the sequence of events, choosing the best of these to include in a story form of your poem. Then by eliminating unnecessary words and arranging your story into lines and stanzas, you could mold your story into a rough draft of a poem. You could then share the draft with a partner, revise it, and prepare a final draft.

Choosing a Format

When your poems are ready, submit them to the editorial staff. The editorial staff will review the poems and come up with ideas on how to arrange them in the collection. Perhaps poems could be arranged by similar form—limericks, opposites, narratives; perhaps by author, theme, or topic. Editors will discuss their ideas with the class and all of you will decide on your format.

In addition to choosing a format, the class must make these decisions.

1. Will artwork be included? If so, what kind? Who should contribute the art?
2. What should be the title of your anthology? A name is very important. It can be poetic, yet it must also reflect the content of the anthology.
3. What should the cover of your anthology look like?
4. Who will compose the table of contents for the anthology?
5. Who will compose an introduction to the anthology?

After the class makes these decisions and carries them out, all the material can be submitted to the editorial staff to organize and prepare for publication.

Publishing Your Class Anthology

Decide on the number of copies to produce. You might want to give complimentary copies to people such as the principal and a copy or two to the librarian for use in the library. Do you want one copy for the classroom, or a copy for each student?

The production manager should find out the best method available to reproduce your anthology. Possible methods include school computers and printers, school photocopying machines or mimeograph machines. Whatever method is used, the production manager will probably need assistance in copying and assembling the anthologies.

You might like to read more poetry on your own. Try some of these books. In each book you'll find a rich variety of emotion and experience.

ALL THE COLORS OF THE RACE by Arnold Adoff. Lothrop, Lee and Shepard Books, 1982. These poems reveal the inner thoughts and feelings of a young person's special point of view. Full of love, hope, and optimism, *All The Colors of the Race* is a celebration of the spirit.

BRONZEVILLE BOYS AND GIRLS by Gwendolyn Brooks. Harper and Row, 1956. Although set in Chicago, this collection speaks for and about young people everywhere. Gwendolyn Brooks shows the varied feelings and experiences of the young with sensitivity and warmth.

DON'T YOU TURN BACK by Langston Hughes. Alfred A. Knopf, 1967. Selected by Lee Bennett Hopkins, this collection of relatively short poems was chosen specifically for young people. The poems speak with honesty and humor of emotions common to us all—love, hate, hope, despair.

A LIGHT IN THE ATTIC by Shel Silverstein. Harper, 1981. If you enjoyed "Whatif," try this collection of imaginative poems. Read about Geraldine shaking a cow, the Dragon of Grindly Grun, Thumb Face, the Homework Machine, the hippo who wanted to fly, and many others.

THE PLACE MY WORDS ARE LOOKING FOR compiled by Paul B. Janeczko. Bradbury Press, 1990. This collection provides more than most poetry anthologies. In it, poets like Eve Merriam, Myra Cohn Livingston, and Jack Prelutsky share their thoughts and inspirations, as well as their poems.

THESE SMALL STONES selected by Norma Farber and Myra Cohn Livingston. Harper & Row, 1987. This collection of delightful poems is about small things from the real and imagined world. Valerie Worth, Shel Silverstein, and many other poets are represented in this collection.

UNIT ACTIVITIES

Writing

1. Write a letter to the speaker of one of your favorite poems. In your letter, explain why you enjoyed it. Give advice to or ask questions of the speaker that are appropriate to what you found out from the poem.

Speaking and Listening

2. Prepare an oral presentation of your favorite poem. As you practice, use your hands, your face, and your voice to express what the poem means to you. When you are ready, recite the poem to your class.

Speaking and Listening

3. Work with a partner to create an interview situation with a character or speaker from a poem. First, choose a character or speaker you both find interesting. Then brainstorm for questions and answers to questions about things such as the subject's adventures, attitudes, or feelings. Decide who will play the part of the interviewer and who will play the part of the speaker. Practice your interview. When you are ready, present the interview to the class.

Cooperative Learning

4. Working in groups of three, write a poem that tells of different episodes, or adventures, of some character. As a group, decide on the character, the tone (humorous, exciting), and a structure (number of lines, rhythm) for your poem. Then, each student should write one or two stanzas. Work together to combine individual stanzas into a single poem. Make sure the poem follows a uniform structure.

Creative Response

5. Choose a favorite image or scene from a poem in the unit. Create a picture of this scene or image. Your picture can be a painting, a photograph, a drawing, or some other form. If you choose a poem with a series of images, perhaps you could create a collage of these images.

Creative Response

6. Create a "Found Poem." Thumb through magazines and newspapers. Cut out words and phrases that appeal to you. Then select related words and phrases and arrange them in a poem. Tape your poem to a sheet of paper and share it with the class.

TA MATETE
Paul Gauguin

THE ORAL TRADITION

Long before there were books, there were stories—stories to explain what people didn't understand, stories to teach lessons. Each society, country, and family had its tales. These stories were told again and again and passed orally from one generation to the next. The passing on of stories in this way is known as the oral tradition.

The oral tradition consists of many kinds of stories—folk tales, fables, myths, and legends. The characters may be animals, ordinary or extraordinary people, heroes, gods and goddesses. In these tales animals may talk, monsters appear, unusual events take place, yet through all these strange occurrences, the tales reveal something about human nature.

Most of these tales have no known authors, but in recent times, people have listened to them and written them down. Stories from the oral tradition are available from all cultures. This unit introduces you to a sampling from all over the world.

Map of Tales from the Oral Tradition

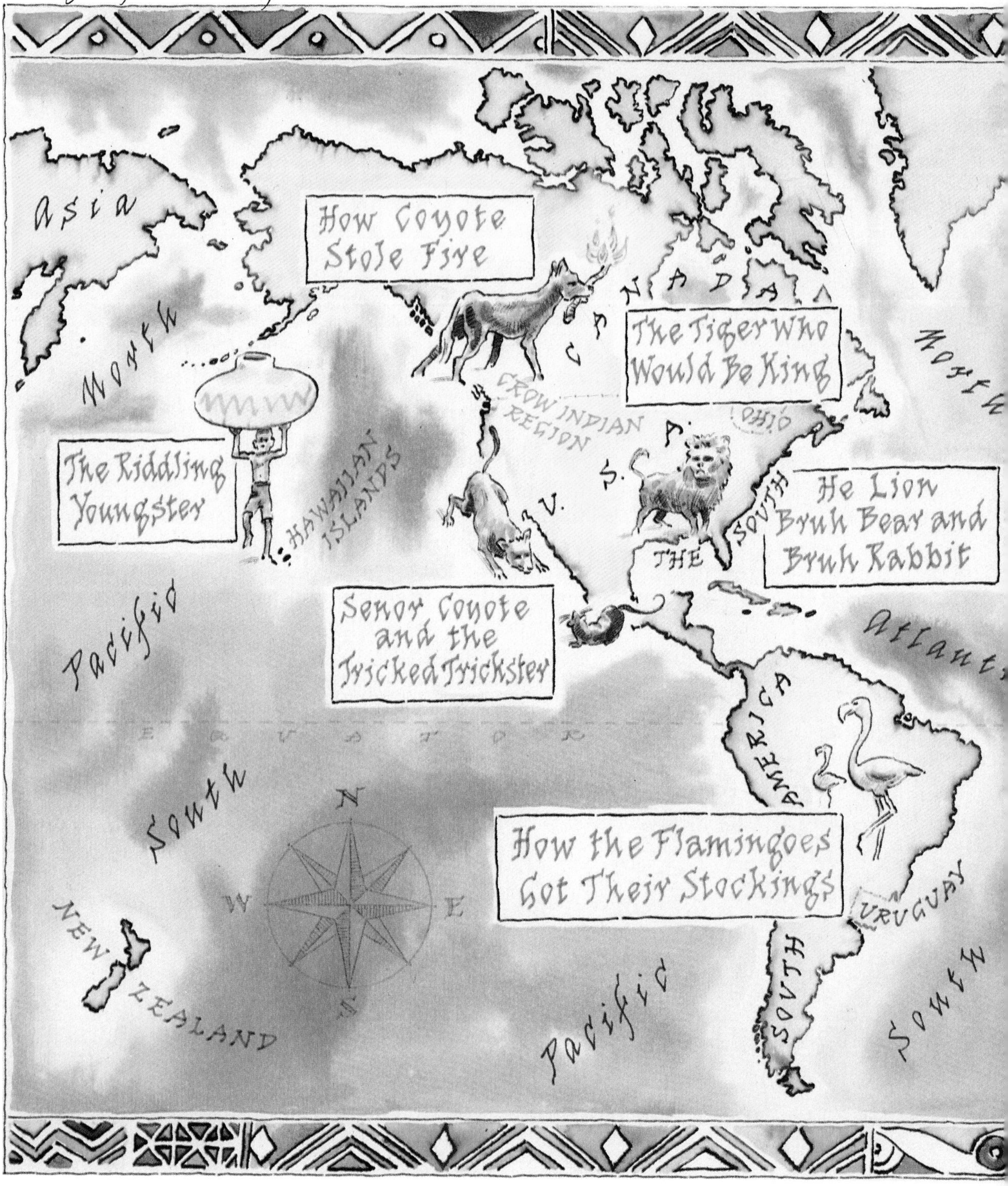

Iduna and the Magic Apples
NORWAY
SWEDEN
The Gorgon's Head
Orpheus
Arachne
GREECE
The Living Kuan-yin
老婆の知恵
The Wise Old Woman
CHINA
JAPAN
The Cow-tail Switch
Osebo's Drum
The Fly
VIETNAM
GHANA
LIBERIA
Atlantic
Indian Ocean
AUSTRALIA
Mufaro's Beautiful Daughters
0 1000 2000 3000 4000 5000 6000 7000 8000
Scale in Miles

HOW TO READ FOLK LITERATURE

Folk tales, myths, and legends are among the oldest forms of literature. They were made up and handed down orally from generation to generation. These tales, myths, and legends reflect the traditions, beliefs, and values of common people—the folk—all over the world. Folk literature can be entertaining, but it also introduces you to cultures across the world. Although these tales originated long ago, they convey thoughts and feelings common to people today.

When you read folk literature, you will often find elements of fantasy and exaggeration—animals speak, and supernatural events occur. Yet you always know what to expect. The stories move in a predictable pattern toward an end in which the good characters are rewarded and the bad punished. Folk literature is clear and simple.

Use your active reading strategies to help you read the folk literature in this section.

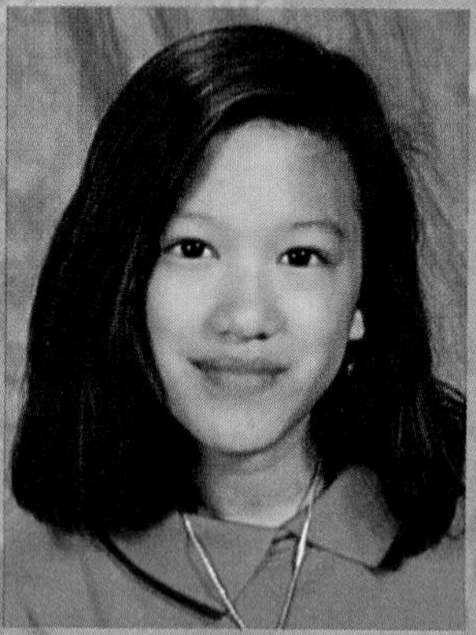

Adine Le of Joseph Kerr Middle School in Elk Grove, California, actively read and responded to "The Fly." The comments in the margins on pages 543–547 include Adine's thoughts and comments. You may share some of Adine's thoughts, or you may have your own entirely different ones.

QUESTION Ask questions about the characters. What is the goal of each? Why does each character behave as he or she does? What does the story suggest about the culture portrayed? As you read, look for the answers to your questions.

VISUALIZE Use the details of the story to build pictures in your mind. What does the setting look like? How do the characters act? Adjust your visualization as you learn more about the story.

PREDICT You will notice patterns and common elements in folk literature. Characters frequently behave in predictable ways. Once you have read the opening of the tale, predict what you think will happen.

CONNECT Make connections between your life and any familiar elements in the story. What similar issues do people of today face? What message is in the story?

RESPOND How do you feel and what do you think about the characters and their actions? What have you learned about the beliefs, values, or attitudes of the people who originated the tale? What does the tale say to you?

The Fly
from Vietnam
Mai Vo-Dinh

" '. . . my father has gone to cut living trees and plant dead ones and my mother is at the market place selling the wind and buying the moon.' "

Everyone in the village knew the usurer,[1] a rich and smart man. Having accumulated a fortune over the years, he settled down to a life of leisure in his big house surrounded by an immense garden and guarded by a pack of ferocious dogs. But still unsatified with what he had acquired, the man went on making money by lending it to people all over the county at exorbitant rates. The usurer reigned supreme in the area, for numerous were those who were in debt to him.

Question: *I wonder what the people needed the money for?*

One day, the rich man set out for the house of one of his peasants. Despite repeated reminders, the poor laborer just could not manage to pay off his long-standing debt. Working himself to a shadow, the peasant barely succeeded in making ends meet. The moneylender was therefore determined that if he could not get his money back this time, he would proceed to confiscate some of his debtor's most valuable belongings. But the rich man found no one at the peasant's house but a small boy of eight or nine playing alone in the dirt yard.

Respond: *This man is ruthless. He doesn't care about people's feelings.*

Connect: *I've had debts, but people were more understanding than this.*

"Child, are your parents home?" the rich man asked.

"No, sir," the boy replied, then went on playing with his sticks and stones, paying no attention whatever to the man.

"Then, where are they?" the rich man asked, somewhat irritated, but the little boy went on playing and did not answer.

1. **usurer** (yo͞o′ zho͞o rər) *n.*: A person who lends money at high interest rates.

Visualize: *Are they really doing these strange things?*

When the rich man repeated his query, the boy looked up and answered, with deliberate slowness, "Well, sir, my father has gone to cut living trees and plant dead ones and my mother is at the market place selling the wind and buying the moon."

"What? What in heaven are you talking about?" the rich man commanded. "Quick, tell me where they are, or you will see what this stick can do to you!" The bamboo walking stick in the big man's hand looked indeed menacing.

Predict: *The moneylender is lying. He won't erase the debt.*

After repeated questioning, however, the boy only gave the same reply. Exasperated, the rich man told him, "All right, little devil, listen to me! I came here today to take the money your parents owe me. But if you tell me where they really are and what they are doing, I will forget all about the debt. Is that clear to you?"

"Oh, sir, why are you joking with a poor little boy? Do you expect me to believe what you are saying?" For the first time the boy looked interested.

"Well, there is heaven and there is earth to witness my promise," the rich man said, pointing up to the sky and down to the ground.

But the boy only laughed. "Sir, heaven and earth cannot talk and therefore cannot testify. I want some living thing to be our witness."

Catching sight of a fly alighting on a bamboo pole nearby, and laughing inside because he was fooling the boy, the rich man proposed, "There is a fly. He can be our witness. Now, hurry and tell me what you mean when you say that your father is out cutting living trees and planting dead ones, while your mother is at the market selling the wind and buying the moon."

Question: *Why does the boy keep saying such silly things?*

Looking at the fly on the pole, the boy said, "A fly is a good enough witness for me. Well, here it is, sir. My father has simply gone to cut down bamboos and make a fence with them for a man near the river. And my mother . . . oh, sir, you'll keep your promise, won't you? You will free my parents of all their debts? You really mean it?"

"Yes, yes, I do solemnly swear in front of this fly here." The rich man urged the boy to go on.

Respond: *This boy is very clever.*

"Well, my mother, she has gone to the market to sell fans so she can buy oil for our lamps. Isn't that what you would call selling the wind to buy the moon?"

Shaking his head, the rich man had to admit inwardly that the boy was a clever one. However, he thought, the little genius still had much to learn, believing as he did that a fly could be a witness for anybody. Bidding the boy good-by, the man told him that he would soon return to make good his promise.

A few days had passed when the moneylender returned. This time he found the poor peasant couple at home, for it was late in the evening. A nasty scene ensued, the rich man claiming his money and the poor peasant apologizing and begging for another delay. Their argument awakened the little boy who ran to his father and told him, "Father, father, you don't have to pay your debt. This gentlemen here has promised me that he would forget all about the money you owe him."

Connect: *I knew the moneylender was lying. Guys like him don't care who they hurt.*

"Nonsense," the rich man shook his walking stick at both father and son. "Nonsense, are you going to stand there and listen to a child's inventions? I never spoke a word to this boy. Now, tell me, are you going to pay or are you not?"

Question: *Why doesn't the rich man just give them more time? He has enough money.*

The whole affair ended by being brought before the mandarin[2] who governed the county. Not knowing what to believe, all the poor peasant and his wife could do was to bring their son with them when they went to court. The little boy's insistence about the rich man's promise was their only encouragement.

The mandarin began by asking the boy to relate exactly what had happened between himself and the moneylender. Happily, the boy hastened to tell about the explanations he gave the rich man in exchange for the debt.

Respond: *I think the boy should have gotten a better witness than a fly.*

"Well," the mandarin said to the boy, "if this man here has indeed made such a promise, we have only your word for it. How do we know that you have not invented the whole story yourself? In a case such as this, you need a witness to confirm it, and you have none." The boy remained calm and declared that naturally there was a witness to their conversation.

---

2. mandarin (man′ də rin) *n.*: A high official who has the power to make decisions of law.

"Who is that, child?" the mandarin asked.

"A fly, Your Honor."

"A fly? What do you mean, a fly? Watch out, young man, fantasies are not to be tolerated in this place!" The mandarin's benevolent face suddenly became stern.

"Yes, Your Honor, a fly. A fly which was alighting on this gentleman's nose!" The boy leapt from his seat.

"Insolent little devil, that's a pack of lies!" The rich man roared indignantly, his face like a ripe tomato. The fly was *not* on my nose; *he was on the housepole . . .*" But he stopped dead. It was, however, too late.

Respond: *The boy is smarter than I thought.*

The majestic mandarin himself could not help bursting out laughing. Then the audience burst out laughing. The boy's parents too, although timidly, laughed. And the boy, and the rich man himself, also laughed. With one hand on his stomach, the mandarin waved the other hand toward the rich man:

"Now, now, that's all settled. You have indeed made your promises, dear sir, to the child. *Housepole or no housepole, your conversation did happen after all!* The court says you must keep your promise."

And still chuckling, he dismissed all parties.

Respond: *I didn't think the boy was very clever to use a fly as a witness. Although I knew that somehow the userer would be made to keep his promise, I didn't guess how the boy would use the fly to win his case.*

Reader's Response

When you began this tale, did you think the boy was clever when he agreed to have a fly as a witness? Why or why not?

Mai Vo-Dinh grew up in Vietnam, was educated in France and now lives in the United States. By the age of ten, like many other Vietnamese children, he knew many of his country's folk tales. As an adult, he remembers them vividly and retells many of them in his collection, *The Toad is the Emperor's Uncle: Animal Folk Tales From Viet-Nam*, from which this story was taken. Vo-Dinh is also a book illustrator and an artist whose oil paintings and woodcuts have been exhibited in the United States and abroad.

Responding to the Selection

Your Response

1. Do you think the boy was clever or just lucky? Explain.

Recalling

2. Why does the rich man go to the poor boy's house?
3. How does the boy succeed in freeing his parents from debt?

Interpreting

4. Why do you think the boy at first avoids giving the rich man a direct answer?
5. If the boy tells him what he means by his answer, the rich man swears to forget the family's debt. What does he hope to gain by this?
6. A witness is one who testifies to the truth. Is the fly a good witness? Why or why not?

Applying

7. Why do people enjoy stories about the poor outsmarting the wealthy?

Analyzing Literature

Appreciating the Oral Tradition

The **oral tradition** refers to the folk tales and other stories that are handed down by word of mouth from one generation to the next. These tales express the history, values, and beliefs of a culture. Eventually these tales were written so that we can read them today.

1. Oral tales survive because they are appealing in some way. Why might "The Fly" have survived for so many centuries?
2. What is this folk tale telling us about the values of the Vietnamese?

Critical Thinking and Reading

Understanding Metaphors

A **metaphor** is a way of speaking that shows a likeness between apparently unlike things. Using metaphors often involves speaking of one thing in terms of another. In "The Fly," the boy answers the rich man's questions in metaphors. He describes his parents' activities in terms other than what they are really doing.

1. What metaphors does the boy use to describe his father's activity? What is his father really doing?
2. What metaphor describes his mother's activity? What is she really doing?
3. Using metaphors in your response, answer the following questions:
   a. What did you do yesterday after school?
   b. What do you want to be doing ten years from now?

Thinking and Writing

Summarizing a Folk Tale

Summarizing a story means retelling it in a shortened form, noting only the most important events in the correct order. Summarize "The Fly," using your own words.

First reread the story. Then decide what the key developments are. Write down each of these events as briefly as possible, without quoting directly what was said. Be sure you explain why the boy managed to outsmart the rich man. As you revise your summary, remember that it must be understandable to someone who has not read the tale.

Learning Options

1. **Speaking and Listening.** Practice reading "The Fly" aloud. Develop different voices for each character and use hand and face gestures to express the events in the story. After you have finished rehearsing, read the story for your class.
2. **Performance.** Work with a classmate to create an interview with the fly. First think of how the fly would have viewed the story. Next make a list of questions the interviewer will ask and answers the fly will give. Then practice your interview. Finally, perform the interview for the class.

How Things Began

CORN KACHINA
Clifford Brycelea
21st Century Art Investment

GUIDE FOR READING

Douglas Hill and Gail Robinson,

a Canadian couple, lived among Native Americans for many years and heard their tales firsthand. One character who appears in many tales they heard is Coyote. Hill and Robinson collected these tales in *Coyote the Trickster.* "How Coyote Stole Fire" is well known among the Crow Indians. It shows Coyote's typical behavior.

How Coyote Stole Fire

Origin Tale

An **origin tale** is a story from the oral tradition that seeks to explain the beginnings of certain natural events. Different cultures have passed on varying tales about how the seasons began, how the world began, why the sun travels across the sky, and why animals act as they do. "How Coyote Stole Fire" is a Crow Indian version of how humans came to have fire.

Focus

This origin tale tells how Coyote obtained fire for human beings. The tale also reveals certain aspects of the relationship between nature and humans. Why do you think people considered obtaining fire an important event? In a small group, brainstorm for a list of reasons why humans need fire. Then discuss whether you think fire is as important today as it was thousands of years ago. As you read "How Coyote Stole Fire," notice the importance of fire to the Crow Indians.

Vocabulary

Knowing the following words will help you as you read "How Coyote Stole Fire."

sacred (sā′ krid) *adj.*: Religious; respected (p. 551)
mourning (môr′ niŋ) *n.*: Sorrowing for the dead (p. 551)
expense (ik spens′) *n.*: Cost or sacrifice (p. 551)
glinted (glint′ əd) *v.*: Gleamed or flashed (p. 551)
skulking (skulk′ iŋ) *v.*: Sneaking around or hiding in (p. 552)
rivulets (riv′ yo͞o litz) *n.*: Little streams (p. 552)
scorched (skôrch'd) *v.*: Burned slightly (p. 554)
pursued (pər so͞od′) *v.*: Chased (p. 554)

Spelling Tip

Remember that *mourning* has a "u" after the "o" unlike its homophone *morning.*

How Coyote Stole Fire

from the Crow Indians

Gail Robinson and Douglas Hill

". . . Coyote lunged from the bushes, snatched up a glowing portion of fire, and sprang away down the mountainside."

Long ago, when man was newly come into the world, there were days when he was the happiest creature of all. Those were the days when spring brushed across the willow tails, or when his children ripened with the blueberries in the sun of summer, or when the goldenrod bloomed in the autumn haze.

But always the mists of autumn evenings grew more chill, and the sun's strokes grew shorter. Then man saw winter moving near, and he became fearful and unhappy. He was afraid for his children, and for the grandfathers and grandmothers who carried in their heads the sacred tales of the tribe. Many of these, young and old, would die in the long, ice-bitter months of winter.

Coyote, like the rest of the People, had no need for fire. So he seldom concerned himself with it, until one spring day when he was passing a human village. There the women were singing a song of mourning for the babies and the old ones who had died in the winter. Their voices moaned like the west wind through a buffalo skull, prickling the hairs on Coyote's neck.

"Feel how the sun is now warm on our backs," one of the men was saying. "Feel how it warms the earth and makes these stones hot to the touch. If only we could have had a small piece of the sun in our teepees during the winter."

Coyote, overhearing this, felt sorry for the men and women. He also felt that there was something he could do to help them. He knew of a faraway mountaintop where the three Fire Beings lived. These Beings kept fire to themselves, guarding it carefully for fear that man might somehow acquire it and become as strong as they. Coyote saw that he could do a good turn for man at the expense of these selfish Fire Beings.

So Coyote went to the mountain of the Fire Beings and crept to its top, to watch the way that the Beings guarded their fire. As he came near, the Beings leaped to their feet and gazed searchingly round their camp. Their eyes glinted like bloodstones, and their hands were clawed like the talons of the great black vulture.

"What's that? What's that I hear?" hissed one of the Beings.

"A thief, skulking in the bushes!" screeched another.

The third looked more closely, and saw Coyote. But he had gone to the mountaintop on all-fours, so the Being thought she saw only an ordinary coyote slinking among the trees.

"It is no one, it is nothing!" she cried, and the other two looked where she pointed and also saw only a gray coyote. They sat down again by their fire and paid Coyote no more attention.

So he watched all day and night as the Fire Beings guarded their fire. He saw how they fed it pine cones and dry branches from the sycamore trees. He saw how they stamped furiously on runaway rivulets of flame that sometimes nibbled outwards on edges of dry grass. He saw also how, at night, the Beings took turns to sit by the fire. Two would sleep while one was on guard; and at certain times the Being by the fire would get up and go into their teepee, and another would come out to sit by the fire.

Coyote saw that the Beings were always jealously watchful of their fire except during one part of the day. That was in the earliest morning, when the first winds of dawn arose on the mountains. Then the Being by the fire would hurry, shivering, into the teepee calling, "Sister, sister, go out and watch the fire." But the next Being would always be slow to go out for her turn, her head spinning with sleep and the thin dreams of dawn.

Coyote, seeing all this, went down the mountain and spoke to some of his friends among the People. He told them of hairless man, fearing the cold and death of winter. And he told them of the Fire Beings, and the warmth and brightness of the flame. They all

COYOTE
Rufino Tamayo
Art Institute of Chicago

agreed that man should have fire, and they all promised to help Coyote's undertaking.

Then Coyote sped again to the mountaintop. Again the Fire Beings leaped up when he came close, and one cried out, "What's that? A thief, a thief!"

But again the others looked closely, and saw only a gray coyote hunting among the bushes. So they sat down again and paid him no more attention.

Coyote waited through the day, and watched as night fell and two of the Beings went off to the teepee to sleep. He watched as they changed over at certain times all the night long, until at last the dawn winds rose.

Then the Being on guard called, "Sister, sister, get up and watch the fire."

And the Being whose turn it was climbed slow and sleepy from her bed, saying, "Yes, yes, I am coming. Do not shout so."

But before she could come out of the teepee, Coyote lunged from the bushes, snatched up a glowing portion of fire, and sprang away down the mountainside.

Screaming, the Fire Beings flew after him. Swift as Coyote ran, they caught up with him, and one of them reached out a clutching hand. Her fingers touched only the tip of the tail, but the touch was enough to turn the hairs white, and coyote tail-tips are white still. Coyote shouted, and flung the fire away from him. But the others of the People had gathered at the mountain's foot, in case they were needed. Squirrel saw the fire falling, and caught it, putting it on her back and fleeing away through the tree tops. The fire scorched her back so painfully that her tail curled up and back, as squirrels' tails still do today.

The Fire Beings then pursued Squirrel, who threw the fire to Chipmunk. Chattering with fear, Chipmunk stood still as if rooted until the Beings were almost upon her. Then, as she turned to run, one Being clawed at her, tearing down the length of her back and leaving three stripes that are to be seen on chipmunks' backs even today. Chipmunk threw the fire to Frog, and the Beings turned towards him. One of the Beings grasped his tail, but Frog gave a mighty leap and tore himself free, leaving his tail behind in the Being's hand—which is why frogs have had no tails ever since.

As the Beings came after him again, Frog flung the fire on to Wood. And Wood swallowed it.

The Fire Beings gathered round, but they did not know how to get the fire out of Wood. They promised it gifts, sang to it and shouted at it. They twisted it and struck it and tore it with their knives. But Wood did not give up the fire. In the end, defeated, the Beings went back to their mountaintop and left the People alone.

But Coyote knew how to get fire out of Wood. And he went to the village of men and showed them how. He showed them the trick of rubbing two dry sticks together, and the trick of spinning a sharpened stick in a hole made in another piece of wood. So man was from then on warm and safe through the killing cold of winter.

Reader's Response

The Fire Beings possessed something that no other beings had. Do you think it was right for Coyote to steal something that was not his? Why or why not?

Responding to the Selection

Your Response

1. People can legally own land and water, but do you think anyone could own fire? Why or why not?

Recalling

2. Why do the women of the village moan "like the west wind through a buffalo skull"?
3. How do the Fire Beings keep their fire going?
4. How does Coyote steal fire from the Fire Beings?

Interpreting

5. Why does Coyote decide to help the humans?
6. According to the Crow Indians, Coyote is one of the People, a race of powerful, supernatural beings who usually appear as animals. What human and animal characteristics do the People demonstrate? What powers and abilities do they show?
7. Why can't the Fire Beings get the fire back from Wood?

Applying

8. Aside from warmth, what other benefits has fire given to humans?

Analyzing Literature

Appreciating an Origin Tale

An **origin tale** provides an imaginative explanation of the way certain things began. The Crow Indians, who passed down this folk tale, saw the origin of many natural events in the actions or teachings of the animal-gods, or the People.

1. Summarize the origin of fire as presented by the Crow Indians.
2. Why have people of different cultures made up tales to explain natural events?

Critical Thinking and Reading

Recognizing Cause and Effect

A **cause** is what brings about a result, or **effect.** In this tale for instance, Coyote teaches humans to rub two dry sticks together to make a spark that will create fire. This action (cause) produces a fire (effect). According to this tale, what is the cause for each of the following effects?

1. The tips of coyotes' tails are white.
2. Squirrel tails always curl up.
3. Chipmunks have three white stripes on their backs.
4. Frogs have no tails.

Thinking and Writing

Writing an Origin Tale

Write your own origin tale modeled after "How Coyote Stole Fire." Choose a natural event and think of an animal-god who could be responsible for bringing this event about. What action might the animal-god take to cause this event? How do the humans then learn that this event was caused by a particular animal-god? Use vivid action verbs whenever you can. As you revise, think about whether you have made clear the cause and effect.

Learning Options

1. **Listening and Speaking.** Work with a partner to develop a list of questions that an interviewer might ask a Fire Being after the incident in the tale. Then play the roles of the interviewer and the Fire Being. Rehearse your interview and present it to the class.
2. **Art.** Based on the story, what do you think the Fire Beings looked like? Draw a Fire Being. Use your imagination to add details not provided by the authors.

GUIDE FOR READING

Harold Courlander

(1908–), who was born in Indianapolis and raised in the Midwest, has been a specialist in folk tales and folklore since the 1930's. He has compiled many books of folk tales from the Caribbean, Africa, the United States, and Asia. A number of his collections came from research he did while working for the United Nations and while doing field studies for various foundations and research institutes. His collection of African tales, as in "Osebo's Drum," features animals as well as humans in a variety of situations.

Osebo's Drum

Animal Tales

Animal tales are among the oldest types of folk story. The characters are animals who behave according to their animal characteristics, but who also have human characteristics. Many of these tales are "why" stories—stories that give explanations for why things are as they are. Often they follow a predictable pattern in which the smaller, weaker animal becomes the hero of the story.

Focus

In this tale, Nyame the Sky God challenges the animals of the earth to take a drum from a ferocious leopard named Osebo. Among the animals who try to perform this task are the elephant, the lion, the antelope, the crocodile, and the turtle. Which of the animals do you think will be successful? In a group of five, make a chart with the name of each animal. Choose one animal each and take turns listing the reasons why your animal will be the one to get the drum from Osebo. As you read the story, see if your predictions were accurate.

Vocabulary

Knowing the following words will help you as you read "Osebo's Drum."

admired (əd mīr' d') *v.*: Highly regarded (p. 557)

ambitions (am bish' ənz) *n.*: Strong desires (p. 557)

ceremony (ser' ə mō' nē) *n.*: A formal ritual or occasion (p. 557)

pitifully (pit' i fəl lē) *adv.*: Sorrowfully, regretfully (p. 558)

embers (em' bərz) *n.*: Smoldering or burning remains of a fire (p. 559)

abuse (ə byo͞oz') *v.*: To mistreat or to misuse (p. 559)

Spelling Tip

Remember that there are two *e*'s in *ceremony.*

Osebo's Drum
from Ghana
Harold Courlander

" 'Nyame, the Sky God, has built himself a great new drum . . . It is so large that he can enter into it and be completely hidden.' "

Osebo,[1] the leopard, once had a great drum which was admired by all animals and gods. Although everyone admired it, no one ever hoped to own it, for Osebo was then the most powerful of animals on earth, and he was feared. Only Nyame,[2] the Sky God, had ambitions to get the drum from the leopard.

It happened one time that Nyame's mother died, and he began the preparations for a spectacular funeral. He wondered what he could do to make the ceremony worthy of his family. People said to him: "For this ceremony we need the great drum of Osebo."

And Nyame said: "Yes, I need the drum of Osebo."

But Nyame didn't know how he could get the drum. At last he called the earth animals before him, all but the leopard himself. Nyame's stool was brought out, and he sat upon it, while his servants held over his head the many-colored parasol[3] which is called the rainbow. He said to the animals:

"For the funeral ceremonies I need the great drum of the leopard. Who will get it for me?"

Esono,[4] the elephant, said: "I will get it." He went to where the leopard lived and tried to take the drum, but the leopard drove him away. The elephant came back to the house of the Sky God, saying: "I could not get it."

Then Gyata,[5] the lion, said: "I will get the drum." He went to the place of the leopard and tried to take the drum, but the leopard drove him off. And Gyata, the lion, returned to the house of the Sky God, saying: "I could not get it."

Adowa,[6] the antelope, went, but he couldn't get it. Odenkyem,[7] the crocodile, went, but he couldn't get it. Owea,[8] the tree bear, went, but he couldn't get it. Many animals went, but the leopard drove them all away.

Then Akykyigie,[9] the turtle, came for-

1. **Osebo** (ō sē′ bō)
2. **Nyame** (nī′ a mē)
3. **parasol** (par′ ə sôl′) *n.*: A light umbrella held as a sunshade.
4. **Esono** (ē sō′ nō)
5. **Gyata** (gī ät′ ä)
6. **Adowa** (a dō′ wä)
7. **Odenkyem** (ō′ den kē′ əm)
8. **Owea** (ō wē′ ä)
9. **Akykyigie** (a′ kē kē′ ə gē)

TURTLE AND ROCKS from MOJAVE
Wendell Minor

ward. In those days the turtle had a soft back like other animals. He said to the Sky God: "I will get the drum."

When people heard this, they broke into a laugh, not even bothering to cover their mouths. "If the strong creatures could not get Osebo's drum," they said, "how will you, who are so pitifully small and weak?"

The turtle said: "No one else has been able to bring it. How can I look more foolish than the rest of you?"

And he went down from the Sky God's house, slowly, slowly, until he came to the place of the leopard. When Osebo saw him coming, he cried out: "Are you too a messenger from Nyame?"

The turtle replied: "No, I come out of curiosity. I want to see if it is true."

The leopard said: "What are you looking for?"

"Nyame, the Sky God, has built himself a great new drum," the turtle said. "It is so large that he can enter into it and be completely hidden. People say his drum is greater than yours."

Osebo answered: "There is no drum greater than mine."

Akykyigie, the turtle, looked at Osebo's drum, saying: "I see it, I see it, but it is not so large as Nyame's. Surely it isn't large enough to crawl into."

Osebo said angrily: "Why is it not large enough?" And to show the turtle, Osebo crawled into the drum.

The turtle said: "It is large indeed, but your hind quarters are showing."

The leopard squeezed further into the drum.

The turtle said: "Oh, but your tail is showing."

The leopard pulled himself further into the drum. Only the tip of his tail was out.

"Ah," the turtle said, "a little more and you will win!"

The leopard wriggled and pulled in the end of his tail.

Then the turtle plugged the opening of the drum with an iron cooking pot. And while the leopard cried out fiercely, the turtle tied the drum to himself and began dragging it slowly, slowly, to the house of Nyame, the Sky God. He dragged for a while; then he stopped to beat the drum as a signal that he was coming.

When the animals heard the great drum of Osebo, they trembled in fear, for they thought surely it was Osebo himself who was playing. But when they saw the turtle coming, slowly, slowly, dragging the great drum behind him, they were amazed.

The turtle came before the Sky God and said: "Here is the drum. I have brought it. And inside the drum is Osebo himself. What shall I do with him?"

Inside the drum Osebo heard, and he feared for his life. He said: "Let me out, and I will go away in peace."

The turtle said: "Shall I kill him?"

The animals all said: "Yes, kill him!"

But Osebo called out: "Do not kill me; allow me to go away. The drum is for the Sky God, and I won't complain."

So the turtle removed the iron pot which covered the opening in the drum. Osebo came out frightened. He came hurriedly. And he came out backwards, tail first. Because he couldn't see where he was going, he fell into the Sky God's fire, and his hide was burned in many little places by the hot embers. He leaped from the fire and hurried away. But the marks of the fire, where he was burned, still remain, and that is why all leopards have dark spots.

The Sky God said to the turtle: "You have brought the great drum of Osebo to make music for the funeral of my mother. What can I give you in return?"

The turtle looked at all the other animals. He saw that they were jealous of his great deed. And he feared that they would try to abuse him for doing what they could not do. So he said to Nyame: "Of all things that could be, I want a hard cover the most."

So the Sky God gave the turtle a hard shell to wear on his back. And never is the turtle seen without it.

Reader's Response

How did you feel when you knew that the turtle was going to bring Osebo's drum to the Sky God? Why?

Responding to the Selection

Your Response

1. If you had been the turtle, what would you have asked the Sky God for? Explain.

Recalling

2. Why does the Sky God want Osebo's drum?
3. Why do the other animals laugh at the turtle?
4. Why does the turtle want a hard shell?

Interpreting

5. Why do the other animals fail to get Osebo's drum? What characteristics do they display?
6. What is the leopard's weakness? How does his weakness lead to his defeat?
7. The turtle is very clever, but he also has other qualities. What are they, and when does he show them?

Applying

8. Why is cleverness more important than size or strength?

Analyzing Literature

Appreciating Animal Tales

The main characters in many folk tales are animals who talk and behave like humans. Some animal tales explain the appearances and habits of the animals and follow a predictable pattern in which a small, weak character accomplishes what larger, stronger characters cannot.

1. What led you to believe that the turtle would get Osebo's drum for the Sky God?
2. What animal appearances or habits does this tale explain?

GUIDE FOR READING

Horacio Quiroga

(1878–1937), who was born in Salto, Uruguay, was a writer best known for his short stories about the Argentinian jungle. Although born in Uruguay, Quiroga lived most of his life as a pioneer farmer in the tropical forest of northern Argentina. He incorporated the tropical setting, which he knew so well, into his writing. His tales often have animals that illustrate human behavior, as do the animals in this tale.

How the Flamingoes Got Their Stockings

Origin Tale

Origin tales explain how or why things happen in nature. Although most origin tales are hundreds or thousands of years old, this one is more recent. Quiroga creates his own origin tale, in which he explains certain animal characters to make a point about human behavior. This tale pokes fun at excessive pride or vanity.

Focus

Vanity is a trait common to all people. Almost everyone knows someone who has too much vanity. What are the signs of vanity? Copy into your notebook the diagram below. Around the word "vanity," add more examples of things people do that show they are vain. As you read, note whether the things on your diagram were mentioned in the story.

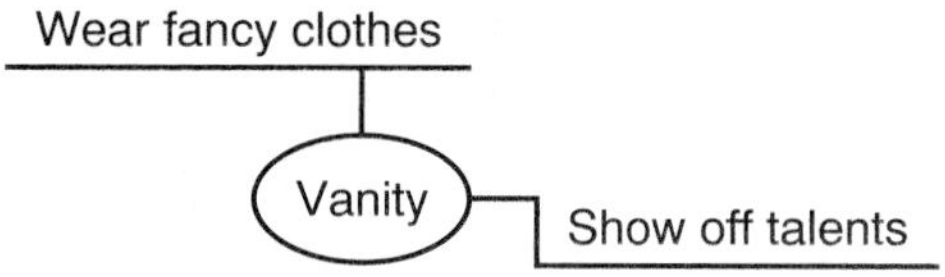

Vocabulary

Knowing the following words will help you as you read "How the Flamingoes Got Their Stockings."

determined (di tʉr′ mənd) *adj.*: Having one's mind made up (p. 561)

gauze (gôz) *n.*: A very thin, transparent, loosely woven material (p. 561)

envious (en′ vē əs) *adj.*: Feeling jealousy toward someone who possesses something that one desires for oneself (p. 562)

pirouetting (pir′ o͞o wet′ iŋ) *v.*: Spinning around on one foot (p. 562)

writhed (rīth'd) *v.*: Squirmed or twisted (p. 562)

accommodate (ə käm′ ə dāt) *v.*: To help; to do a favor for (p. 563)

Spelling Tip

Remember that *accommodate,* a commonly misspelled word, has two *c*'s and two *m*'s.

How the Flamingoes Got Their Stockings

from Uruguay

Horacio Quiroga

" 'We must go and get some stockings for our legs . . . like the coral snakes themselves—then they will fall in love with us!' "

Once the snakes decided that they would give a costume ball; and to make the affair a truly brilliant one they sent invitations to the frogs, the toads, the alligators and the fish.

The fish replied that since they had no legs they would not be able to do much dancing; whereupon, as a special courtesy to them, the ball was held on the shore of the Paraná.[1] The fish swam up to the very beach and sat looking on with their heads out of water. When anything pleased them they splashed with their tails.

To make as good an appearance as possible, the alligators put necklaces of bananas around their throats; and they came to the ball smoking big Paraguay cigars. The toads stuck fish scales all over their bodies; and when they walked, they moved their forelegs out and in as though they were swimming. They strutted up and down the beach with very glum, determined faces; and the fish kept calling to them, making fun of their scales. The frogs were satisfied to leave their smooth green skins just as they were; but they bathed themselves in perfume and walked on their hind legs. Besides, each one carried a lightning bug, which waved to and fro like a lantern, at the end of a string in the frog's hand.

But the best costumes of all were worn by the snakes. All of them, without exception, had dancing gowns of the color of their skins. There were red snakes, and brown snakes, and pink snakes, and yellow snakes—each with a garment of tulle[2] to match. The *yarara*,[3] who is a kind of rattler, came in a single-piece robe of gray tulle with brick-colored stripes—for that is the way the *yarara* dresses even when he is not going to a ball. The coral snakes were prettier still. They draped themselves in a gauze of reds, whites and blacks; and when they danced, they wound themselves round and round like corkscrews, rising on the tips of their tails, coiling and uncoiling, balancing this way and that. They were the most graceful

1. **Paraná** (pä′ *rä* nä′): A river in South America.

2. **tulle** (to͞ol) *n.*: A thin, fine netting of material.

3. ***yarara*** (yä rä *rä*′)

JUNGLE SCENE
Robert Giusti

and beautiful of all the snakes, and the guests applauded them wildly.

The flamingoes were the only ones who seemed not to be having a good time. Stupid birds that they were, they had not thought of any costumes at all. They came with the plain white legs they had at that time and the thick, twisted bills they have even now. Naturally they were envious of all the gowns they saw, but most of all, of the fancy dress of the coral snakes. Every time one of these went by them, curtsying, pirouetting, balancing, the flamingoes writhed with jealousy. For no one, meanwhile, was asking them to dance.

"I know what we must do," said one of the flamingoes at last. "We must go and get some stockings for our legs—pink, black and white like the coral snakes themselves—then they will all fall in love with us!"

The whole flock of them took wing immediately and flew across the river to a village nearby. They went to the store and knocked:

"Tan! Tan! Tan!"

"Who is it?" called the storekeeper.

"We're the flamingoes. We have come to get some stockings—pink, black, and white."

"Are you crazy?" the storekeeper answered. "I keep stockings for people, not for silly birds. Besides, stockings of such colors! You won't find any in town, either!"

The flamingoes went on to another store:

"Tan! Tan! Tan! We are looking for stockings—pink, black and white. Have you any?"

"Pink, black and white stockings! Don't you know decent people don't wear such things? You must be crazy! Who are you, anyway?"

"We are the flamingoes," the flamingoes replied.

"In that case you are silly flamingoes! Better go somewhere else!"

They went to still a third store:

"Tan! Tan! Pink, black and white stockings! Got any?"

"Pink, black and white nonsense!" called the storekeeper. "Only birds with big noses like yours could ask for such a thing. Don't make tracks on my floor!"

And the man swept them into the street with a broom.

So the flamingoes went from store to store, and everywhere people called them silly, stupid birds.

However, an owl, a mischievous *tatu*,[4] who had just been down to the river to get some water, and had heard all about the ball and the flamingoes, met them on his way back and thought he would have some fun with them.

"Good evening, good evening, flamingoes," he said, making a deep bow, though, of course, it was just to ridicule the foolish birds. "I know what you are looking for. I doubt if you can get any such stockings in town. You might find them in Buenos Aires;[5] but you would have to order them by mail. My sister-in-law, the barn owl, has stockings like that, however. Why don't you go around and see her? She can give you her own and borrow others from her family."

"Thanks! Thanks, ever so much!" said the flamingoes; and they flew off to the cellar of a barn where the barn owl lived.

"Tan! Tan! Good evening, Mrs. Owl," they said. "A relation of yours, Mr. Tatu, advised us to call on you. Tonight, as you know, the snakes are giving a costume ball, and we have no costumes. If you could lend us your pink, black and white stockings, the coral snakes would be sure to fall in love with us!"

"Pleased to accommodate you," said the barn owl. "Will you wait just a moment?"

She flew away and was gone some time. When she came back she had the stockings with her. But they were not real stockings. They were nothing but skins from coral snakes which the owl had caught and eaten during the previous days.

"Perhaps these will do," she remarked. "But if you wear them at the ball, I advise you to do strictly as I say: dance all night long, and don't stop a moment. For if you do, you will get into trouble, I assure you!"

The flamingoes listened to what she said; but, stupidly, did not try to guess what she could have meant by such counsel. They saw no danger in the pretty stockings. Delightedly they doubled up their claws like fists, stuck them through the snakeskins, which were like so many long rubber tubes, and flew back as quickly as they could to the ball.

When the guests at the dance saw the flamingoes in such handsome stockings, they were as jealous as could be. You see, the coral snakes were the lions[6] of the evening, and after the flamingoes came back, they would dance with no one but the flamingoes.

---

4. *tatu* (tä too̅′): Bird.

5. Buenos Aires (bwā′ nəs er′ ēz): The capital of Argentina, which is a country in South America.

6. the coral snakes . . . lions: The most popular guests or the main attraction.

Remembering the instructions of the barn owl, the flamingoes kept their feet going all the time, and the snakes could not see very clearly just what those wonderful stockings were.

After a time, however, they grew suspicious. When a flamingo came dancing by, the snakes would get down off the ends of their tails to examine its feet more closely. The coral snakes, more than anybody else, began to get uneasy. They could not take their eyes off those stockings, and they got as near as they could, trying to touch the legs of the flamingoes with with the tips of their tongues—for snakes use their tongues to feel with, much as people use their hands. But the flamingoes kept dancing and dancing all the while, though by this time they were getting so tired they were about ready to give up.

The coral snakes understood that sooner or later the flamingoes would have to stop.

CARIBBEAN SCENE WITH FLAMINGO
Wilson McLean

So they borrowed the lightning bugs from the frogs, to be ready when the flamingoes fell from sheer exhaustion.

And in fact, it was not long before one of the birds, all tired out, tripped over the cigar in an alligator's mouth, and fell down on her side. The coral snakes all ran toward her with their lanterns, and held the lightning bugs up so close that they could see the feet of the flamingo as clearly as could be.

"Aha! Aha! Stockings, eh? Stockings, eh?" The coral snakes began to hiss so loudly that people could hear them on the other side of the Paraná.

The cry was taken up by all the snakes: "They are not wearing stockings! We know what they have done! The flamingoes have been killing brothers of ours, and they are wearing their skins as stockings! Those pretty legs each stand for the murder of a coral snake!"

At this uproar, the flamingoes took fright and tried to fly away. But they were so tired from all the dancing that not one of them could move a wing. The coral snakes darted upon them, and began to bite at their legs, tearing off the false stockings bit by bit, and, in their rage, sinking their fangs deep into the feet and legs of the flamingoes.

The flamingoes, terrified and mad with pain, hopped this way and that, trying to shake their enemies off. But the snakes did not let go till every last shred of stocking had been torn away. Then they crawled off, to rearrange their gauze costumes that had been much rumpled in the fray. They did not try to kill the flamingoes then and there; for most coral snakes are poisonous; and they were sure the birds they had bitten would die sooner or later anyway.

But the flamingoes did not die. They hopped down to the river and waded out into the water to relieve their pain. Their feet and legs, which had been white before, had now turned red from the poison in the bites. They stood there for days and days, trying to cool the burning ache, and hoping to wash out the red.

But they did not succeed. And they have not succeeded yet. The flamingoes still pass most of their time standing on their red legs out in the water. Occasionally they go ashore and walk up and down for a few moments to see if they are getting well. But the pain comes again at once, and they hurry back into the water. Even there they sometimes feel an ache in one of their feet; and they lift it out to warm it in their feathers. They stand that way on one leg for hours, I suppose because the other one is so stiff and lame.

That is why the flamingoes have red legs instead of white. And the fishes know it too. They keep coming up to the top of the water and crying "Red legs! Red legs! Red legs!" to make fun of the flamingoes for having tried to borrow costumes for a ball. On that account, the flamingoes are always at war with the fishes. As they wade up and down, and a fish comes up too close in order to shout "Red legs" at them, they dip their long bills down and catch it if they can.

Reader's Response

What advice would you have given the flamingoes if you were a kinder barn owl? Explain.

RESPONDING TO THE SELECTION

Your Response

1. Do you feel sorry for the flamingoes in this story? Why or why not?

Recalling

2. Give three reasons why the flamingoes are called stupid, silly birds.
3. Whom do the flamingoes see to get their stockings? Whose advice do they follow?
4. How do the coral snakes figure out that the flamingoes are wearing snakeskins?

Interpreting

5. What human behavior do the fish, alligators, toads, and frogs demonstrate?
6. What kind of people do the flamingoes represent?
7. What comment is the writer making about silly vanity?

Applying

8. Give examples from everyday life in which excessive vanity causes trouble.

ANALYZING LITERATURE

Understanding the Origin Tale

Origin tales explain the cause or origin of certain natural occurrences. In "How the Flamingoes Got Their Stockings," the author gives an imaginative explanation for why flamingoes have red feet and legs but, on a deeper level, he criticizes a common human failing—vanity.

1. Name three of the flamingoes' behaviors and give the origins of each.
2. What human behavior is Quiroga criticizing in this tale? Why does he use animal characters to criticize human behavior?

CRITICAL THINKING AND READING

Examining Consequences of Actions

Some actions of characters in stories have specific consequences. When the flamingoes, for example, put on snakeskin stockings, their action has unfortunate consequences. It angers the coral snakes, who attack them. Sometimes unfortunate consequences can be avoided if people think carefully about the possible outcomes of their actions.

1. How might the flamingoes have avoided angering the coral snakes?
2. What hint should they have paid more attention to?
3. Why is it important to consider the possible consequences of one's actions?

THINKING AND WRITING

Writing a Letter of Advice

"How the Flamingoes Got Their Stockings" illustrates the consequences of excessive vanity. Perhaps the flamingoes would have acted differently if they had received better advice. Imagine you are giving the flamingoes advice about the party. Write a letter to the flamingoes explaining how to act in order to get along with the coral snakes. Be sure to think through your advice and anticipate what the consequences of your advice might be. Give your paper to a peer to read. Ask him or her if your advice is good and sound. Revise your first draft and write a final copy.

LEARNING OPTIONS

1. **Writing.** Some of the problems the flamingoes had at the ball might have been solved if everyone had behaved properly. Write a book of etiquette to describe the proper dress and behavior at a Snake's Ball. Include the appropriate way to address the various animals present and what to do when it is time to leave.
2. **Art.** Retell this story in comic book form. With a group of classmates, decide which scenes of the story would be best to illustrate. Decide which members will draw and which will create dialogue and narrative. Show your finished product to the class.

Retelling a Story

Think about when you've told family or friends about something that happened to you. You told the story as you saw and experienced it. Now imagine that instead of you, one of the other people—or someone who observed the event—tells the story. That person, too, will tell the story as he or she saw and experienced it. In other words, that person will retell the story from his or her point of view. How might each version of the story be similar? How might they differ?

Stories you have read can also be retold from a different point of view—perhaps from that of another character or an imagined onlooker. For example, imagine how the wolf in "Little Red Riding Hood" might tell his side of the story. Perhaps he would try to convince people that the grandmother is really the villain. From his version you would get a very different picture of the event.

Your Turn

Retell a story from another character's point of view. You may choose a story from this unit or choose any folk or fairy tale most classmates know. Your purpose is to entertain your readers by telling a familiar story in a fresh way. Your audience is your classmates.

Prewriting

1. Select a tale and a character. From whose point of view will you write the story? You might enjoy retelling "Osebo's Drum," for example, from the point of view of the turtle, the leopard, or the Sky God.

2. Make a list of traits. Part of the fun of retelling the story is creating a voice for your character. With your character in mind, jot down a list of descriptive notes to help you get "into the skin" of that character.

3. Make a time line. To keep the events of the story in order, make a time line showing the events of the story you must include. This will be your general outline to refer to as you write. Put in just the main details to keep you on track, and add other details as you go.

4. Freewrite. Write for five or ten minutes, telling the story, or just freewrite to get used to your character's voice and point of view. Refer to your time line if you want, but remember that you can just experiment right now.

Here's what one student wrote as the leopard in "Osebo's Drum":

```
What a dummy I am! I can't
believe I let a tacky turtle
trick me. After all, I used to be
such a big deal. Let me tell you
about it. You see I made this
fabulous drum. I made it because
everyone thought I was so great,
and I wanted to have just one
```

```
thing that would make everyone
think I was, well, even
greater. . . .
```

Notice that the leopard uses *I* when he speaks. Your character, too, will use *I*.

Drafting

Write the first draft of your story. You might want to continue your freewriting, or you might begin again. Following is an example of a rough draft the same student wrote:

```
As soon as word got out about my
fantastic deal of a drum,
everyone was actually after it.
You know the elephant? Well he
turned up on my very
doorstep--then the lion, and
then every other animal in town.
Fortunately, they all failed to
steal my drum.
```

Revising

Use the revision checklist on page 751. In addition, read your draft to a small group or partner. Then ask questions such as the following:

- Who is telling this story? How do you know?
- Is the story fun to listen to? What do you suggest I do to make it more fun? Should I make the character's voice more obvious?
- Does the voice of the character telling the story stay the same throughout? If not, where do you hear the character's voice begin to change?
- Do you want more details about anything in the story?

Using the suggestions your partner or group made, revise your draft.

Proofreading

Consult the guidelines for proofreading on page 753. Although you may not be using standard English, be sure that your punctuation and spelling are accurate. Then make a final copy, incorporating the revisions you made in the preceding stage.

Publishing

Tell your tale to your classmates. Invite listeners to share with you what they liked about your version. Then make a classroom collection of your tales.

Riddles and Questions

THE INDIGO SNAKE
Romare Bearden
Freedom Place Collection

GUIDE FOR READING

Carol Kendall

(1917–), who was born in Ohio, is an award-winning writer; she won the Newbery Honor Book award for *The Gammage Cup.* Its sequel, *The Whisper of Glocken,* is also a Newbery Honor Book.

Yao-wen Li

(1924–) was born and raised in Canton, China. In 1947 she moved to America. "The Living Kuan-yin" is one of many traditional Chinese tales Yao-wen Li collected on a return visit to China in 1973.

The Living Kuan-yin

Folk Tale

A **folk tale** is a story told by common people—the folk—that has been handed down by word of mouth and eventually written down. Folk tales may entertain, explain a wonder of nature, or express the values or beliefs of a culture. "The Living Kuan-yin" is based on one of the most-loved Chinese goddesses—Kuan-yin.

Focus

In this story, Po-wan, the main character, visits the Living Kuan-yin, a goddess who can tell the past and the future. The Living Kuan-yin will answer only three questions. What three questions would you ask a goddess? Write three questions that you would ask the Living Kuan-yin. As you read "The Living Kuan-yin," compare your list of questions with the questions that Po-wan asks.

Vocabulary

Knowing the following words will help you as you read "The Living Kuan-yin."

destitute (des′ tə to͞ot′) *adj.*: Extremely poor (p. 571)
dwindled (dwin′ d'ld) *v.*: Shrunk; became less (p. 571)
ponder (pän′ dər) *v.*: Think deeply about; consider carefully (p. 571)
extravagantly (ik strav′ ə gənt lē) *adv.*: Excessively; beyond reasonable limits (p. 571)
reluctance (ri luk′ təns) *n.*: Unwillingness; hesitation (p. 573)
inadvertently (in′ əd vʉr′ tənt lē) *adv.*: Unintentionally, not purposefully (p. 573)
prevail (pri vāl′) *v.*: Take advantage of (p. 573)
amiable (ā′ mē ə b'l) *adj.*: Friendly (p. 573)

Spelling Tip

Remember that *extravagant* ends with *ant* and *inadvertent* ends with *ent.*

The Living Kuan-yin
from China
Carol Kendall and Yao-wen Li

"The Living Kuan-yin allowed but three questions, and he had . . . accumulated four questions."

Even though the family name of Chin means *gold*, it does not signify that everyone of that name is rich. Long ago, in the province of Chekiang,[1] however, there was a certain wealthy Chin family of whom it was popularly said that its fortune was as great as its name. It seemed quite fitting, then, when a son was born to the family, that he should be called Po-wan, "Million," for he was certain to be worth a million pieces of gold when he came of age.

With such a happy circumstance of names, Po-wan himself never doubted that he would have a never-ending supply of money chinking through his fingers, and he spent it accordingly—not on himself, but on any unfortunate who came to his attention. He had a deep sense of compassion for anyone in distress of body or spirit: a poor man had only to hold out his hand, and Po-wan poured gold into it; if a destitute widow and her brood of starvelings[2] but lifted sorrowful eyes to his, he provided them with food and lodging and friendship for the rest of their days.

In such wise did he live that even a million gold pieces were not enough to support him. His resources so dwindled that finally he scarcely had enough food for himself; his clothes flapped threadbare on his wasted frame; and the cold seeped into his bone marrow for lack of a fire. Still he gave away the little money that came to him.

One day, as he scraped out half of his bowl of rice for a beggar even hungrier than he, he began to ponder on his destitute state.

"Why am I so poor?" he wondered. "I have never spent extravagantly. I have never, from the day of my birth, done an evil deed. Why then am I, whose very name is A Million Pieces of Gold, no longer able to find even a copper to give this unfortunate creature, and have only a bowl of rice to share with him?"

He thought long about his situation and at last determined to go without delay to the South Sea. Therein, it was told, dwelt the all-merciful goddess, the Living Kuan-yin,[3] who

1. Chekiang (jä jē′ äng): An eastern province of China on the coast of the East China Sea.

2. starvelings (stärv′ liŋz) *n.*: Children who are thin and weak from lack of food.

3. Kuan-yin (kwän yin): The Buddhist goddess of goodness and mercy.

could tell the past and future. He would put his question to her and she would tell him the answer.

Soon he had left his home country behind and traveled for many weeks in unfamiliar lands. One day he found his way barred by a wide and furiously flowing river. As he stood first on one foot and then on the other, wondering how he could possibly get across, he heard a commanding voice calling from the top of an overhanging cliff.

"Chin Po-wan!" the voice said, "if you are going to the South Sea, please ask the Living Kuan-yin a question for me!"

"Yes, yes, of course," Po-wan agreed at once, for he had never in his life refused a request made of him. In any case, the Living Kuan-yin permitted each person who approached her three questions, and he had but one of his own to ask.

Craning his head towards the voice coming from above, he suddenly began to tremble, for the speaker was a gigantic snake with a body as large as a temple column. Po-wan was glad he had agreed so readily to the request.

"Ask her then," said the snake, "why I am not yet a dragon even though I have practiced self-denial[4] for more than one thousand years?"

"That I will do, and gl-gladly," stammered Po-wan, hoping that the snake would continue to practice self-denial just a bit longer. "But, your . . . your Snakery . . . or your Serpentry, perhaps I should say . . . that is . . . you see, don't you . . . first I must cross this raging river, and I know not how."

"That is no problem at all," said the

MOUNTAINOUS LANDSCAPE WITH SAILBOAT
Chi-Fong Lei
Courtesy of the Artist

4. self-denial (self di nī′ əl) *n.*: The act of giving up one's own desires or pleasures, often for the benefit of others.

snake. "I shall carry you across, of course."

"Of course," Po-wan echoed weakly. Overcoming his fear and his reluctance to touch the slippery-slithery scales, Chin Po-wan climbed on to the snake's back and rode across quite safely. Politely, and just a bit hurriedly, he thanked the self-denying serpent and bade him good-bye. Then he continued on his way to the South Sea.

By noon he was very hungry. Fortunately a nearby inn offered meals at a price he could afford. While waiting for his bowl of rice, he chatted with the innkeeper and told him of the Snake of the Cliff, which the innkeeper knew well and respected, for the serpent always denied bandits the crossing of the river. Inadvertently, during the exchange of stories, Po-wan revealed the purpose of his journey.

"Why then" cried the innkeeper, "let me prevail upon your generosity to ask a word for me." He laid an appealing hand on Po-wan's ragged sleeve. "I have a beautiful daughter," he said, "wonderfully amiable and pleasing of disposition. But although she is in her twentieth year, she has never in all her life uttered a single word. I should be very much obliged if you would ask the Living Kuan-yin why she is unable to speak."

Po-wan, much moved by the innkeeper's plea for his mute daughter, of course promised to do so. For after all, the Living Kuan-yin allowed each person three questions, and he had but one of his own to ask.

Nightfall found him far from any inn, but there were houses in the neighborhood, and he asked for lodging at the largest. The owner, a man obviously of great wealth, was pleased to offer him a bed in a fine chamber, but first begged him to partake of a hot meal and good drink. Po-wan ate well, slept soundly, and, much refreshed, was about to depart the following morning, when his good host, having learned that Po-wan was journeying to the South Sea, asked if he would be kind enough to put a question for him to the Living Kuan-yin.

"For twenty years," he said, "from the time this house was built, my garden has been cultivated with the utmost care, yet in all those years, not one tree, not one small plant, has bloomed or borne fruit, and because of this, no bird comes to sing nor bee to gather nectar. I don't like to put you to a bother, Chin Po-wan, but as you are going to the South Sea anyway, perhaps you would not mind seeking out the Living Kuan-yin and asking her why the plants in my garden don't bloom?"

"I shall be delighted to put the question to her," said Po-wan. For after all, the Living Kuan-yin allowed each person three questions, and he had but . . .

Traveling onward, Po-wan examined the quandary[5] in which he found himself. The Living Kuan-yin allowed but three questions, and he had somehow, without quite knowing how, accumulated four questions. One of them would have to go unasked, but which? If he left out his own question, his whole journey would have been in vain. If, on the other hand, he left out the question of the snake, or the innkeeper, or the kind host, he would break his promise and betray their faith in him.

"A promise should never be made if it cannot be kept," he told himself. "I made the promises and therefore I must keep them. Besides, the journey will not be in vain, for at least some of these problems will be solved by the Living Kuan-yin. Furthermore, assisting others must certainly be counted as a

5. quandary (kwän′ drē) *n.*: A confusing situation.

good deed, and the more good deeds abroad in the land, the better for everyone, including me."

At last he came into the presence of the Living Kuan-yin.

First, he asked the serpent's question: "Why is the Snake of the Cliff not yet a dragon, although he has practiced self-denial for more than one thousand years?"

And the Kuan-yin answered: "On his head are seven bright pearls. If he removes six of them, he can become a dragon."

Next, Po-wan asked the innkeeper's question: "Why is the innkeeper's daughter unable to speak, although she is in the twentieth year of her life?"

And the Living Kuan-yin answered: "It is her fate to remain mute until she sees the man destined to be her husband."

Last, Po-wan asked the kind host's question: "Why are there never blossoms in the rich man's garden, although it has been carefully cultivated for twenty years?"

And the Living Kuan-yin answered: "Buried in the garden are seven big jars filled with silver and gold. The flowers will bloom if the owner will rid himself of half the treasure."

Then Chin Po-wan thanked the Living Kuan-yin and bade her good-bye.

On his return journey, he stopped first at the rich man's house to give him the Living Kuan-yin's answer. In gratitude the rich man gave him half the buried treasure.

Next Po-wan went to the inn. As he approached, the innkeeper's daughter saw him from the window and called out, "Chin Po-wan! Back already! What did the Living Kuan-yin say?"

Upon hearing his daughter speak at long last, the joyful innkeeper gave her in marriage to Chin Po-wan.

TWO BUDDHIST SAINTS (detail)
Unknown artist
Lizzadro Museum of Lapidary Art
Elmhurst, Illinois

Lastly, Po-wan went to the cliffs by the furiously flowing river to tell the snake what the Living Kuan-yin had said. The grateful snake immediately gave him six of the bright pearls and promptly turned into a magnificent dragon, the remaining pearl in his forehead lighting the headland like a great beacon.

And so it was that Chin Po-wan, that generous and good man, was once more worth a million pieces of gold.

Reader's Response

Whose question—the snake's, the innkeeper's, the rich man's, or his own—did you think Po-wan would omit? Why?

Responding to the Selection

Your Response

1. What qualities of Po-wan's character do you admire? Explain.

Recalling

2. Why does Po-wan lose all his gold?
3. Before he sets out on his journey, what three things does Po-wan know about Kuan-yin?
4. What are the three requests made of Po-wan?
5. What answers does Kuan-yin give to Po-wan?

Interpreting

6. Name three ways in which Po-wan and Kuan-yin are similar.
7. Why does the goddess Kuan-yin grant the wishes of the snake, the innkeeper, and the rich man? What good qualities do they have?

Applying

8. Po-wan cites the proverb, or saying, "A promise should never be made if it cannot be kept." What does this proverb imply about the values of the people who told this tale?

Analyzing Literature

Understanding Folk Tales

Folk tales are stories made up long ago and handed down by word of mouth. Many of these tales reveal the values or beliefs of a culture. Folk tales may include details that are strange or extraordinary. For example, this tale combines the religious beliefs of many Chinese with extraordinary events.

1. What strange or extraordinary events happen to Po-wan?
2. What do these events indicate about the beliefs of this culture?

Critical Thinking and Reading

Recognizing a Culture's Values

Values are the ideas, qualities, and behaviors that a culture holds important. Folk tales can tell much about the values and beliefs of the ordinary people of a certain country. For example, as the goddess of mercy, Kuan-yin represents one of the essential beliefs of Buddhism—one of the main religions in China.

1. Describe the kind of person Po-wan is.
2. What behavior and qualities of Po-wan are rewarded? What values does this story encourage? Explain your answer.
3. Why do you think this folk tale has lasted for so many years?

Thinking and Writing

Writing a Letter

This tale illustrates a characteristic many Chinese value—generosity. Think of what values Americans hold dear. Write a letter to someone in which you describe an incident that illustrates this value. Give your paper to a partner to read. Ask him or her if your incident illustrates the value. Make any necessary revisions. Write a final draft.

Learning Options

1. **Writing.** Suppose that you are a reporter on Po-wan's hometown newspaper. Po-wan has just returned to town. Write a news story telling about what happened to this local hero.
2. **Performance.** With a small group of classmates, choose one scene in this story. Assign the roles in the scene to members of your group. When you have practiced the dialogue and the action, perform the scene for your class.

GUIDE FOR READING

Yoshiko Uchida

(1921–1992), a Japanese-American writer, was born and raised in California. Her interest in writing began early. When she was just ten, she wrote stories in books she made of brown wrapping paper. She went on to write twenty-eight books, mostly for young people. Much of her writing reflects the experience of many Japanese living in the United States, particularly during the 1930's and 1940's. In addition, to give other Japanese Americans a sense of their heritage, Uchida collected and retold many Japanese tales like "The Wise Old Woman."

The Wise Old Woman

Theme

A **theme** is the central idea of a story, or the general idea about life that a story reveals. Folk tales often contain themes, which express ideas about life or living that are important either to a particular culture or to all people. In "The Wise Old Woman," the theme expresses an important idea about old people.

Focus

Many cultures place great value on the wisdom of old people. The expression "live and learn" means that the longer people live, the more they learn. Can you imagine a world where there were no older people? In a group, think of several older people you know. What have you learned from them? Try to think of examples that demonstrate the wisdom of these people. Then write down the advantages and disadvantages of a world without older people. As you read "The Wise Old Woman," think of the value of older people in our society.

Vocabulary

Knowing the following words will help you as you read "The Wise Old Woman."

arrogant (ar′ ə gənt) *adj.*: Proud, overbearing (p. 577)
haughtily (hôt′ ə lē) *adv.*: Proudly, arrogantly (p. 577)
decree (di krē′) *v.*: Issue an official order or decision (p. 577)
banished (ban′ isht) *v.*: Sent away to get rid of (p. 577)
deceive (di sēv′) *v.*: Mislead; to make a person believe something that is not true (p. 577)
conquer (kän′ kər) *v.*: Take control over (p. 578)
bewilderment (bi wil′ dər mənt) *n.*: Confusion; puzzlement (p. 580)
commended (kə mend′ əd) *v.*: Praised (p. 580)
summoned (sum′ ən'd) *v.*: Called forth (p. 580)

Spelling Tip

When you spell *deceive,* remember this rule: Use *i* before *e* except after *c*.

The Wise Old Woman
from Japan
Yoshiko Uchida

". . . he kept his mother safely hidden and no one in the village knew that she was there."

Many long years ago, there lived an arrogant and cruel young lord who ruled over a small village in the western hills of Japan.

"I have no use for old people in my village," he said haughtily. "They are neither useful nor able to work for a living. I therefore decree that anyone over seventy-one must be banished from the village and left in the mountains to die."

"What a dreadful decree! What a cruel and unreasonable lord we have," the people of the village murmured. But the lord fearfully punished anyone who disobeyed him, and so villagers who turned seventy-one were tearfully carried into the mountains, never to return.

Gradually there were fewer and fewer old people in the village and soon they disappeared altogether. Then the young lord was pleased.

"What a fine village of young, healthy and hard-working people I have," he bragged. "Soon it will be the finest village in all of Japan."

Now there lived in this village a kind young farmer and his aged mother. They were poor, but the farmer was good to his mother, and the two of them lived happily together. However, as the years went by, the mother grew older, and before long she reached the terrible age of seventy-one.

"If only I could somehow deceive the cruel lord," the farmer thought. But there were records in the village books and everyone knew that his mother had turned seventy-one.

Each day the son put off telling his mother that he must take her into the mountains to die, but the people of the village began to talk. The farmer knew that if he did not take his mother away soon, the lord would send his soldiers and throw them both into a dark dungeon to die a terrible death.

"Mother—" he would begin, as he tried to tell her what he must do, but he could not go on.

Then one day the mother herself spoke of the lord's dread decree. "Well, my son," she said, "the time has come for you to take me to the mountains. We must hurry before the lord sends his soldiers for you." And she did not seem worried at all that she must go to the mountains to die.

"Forgive me, dear mother, for what I must do," the farmer said sadly, and the next morning he lifted his mother to his shoulders and set off on the steep path toward the mountains. Up and up he climbed, until the trees clustered close and the path was gone. There was no longer even the sound of birds, and they heard only the soft wail of the wind in the trees. The son walked slowly, for he could not bear to think of leaving his old mother in the mountains. On and on he climbed, not wanting to stop and leave her behind. Soon, he heard his mother breaking off small twigs from the trees that they passed.

"Mother, what are you doing?" he asked.

"Do not worry, my son," she answered gently. "I am just marking the way so you will not get lost returning to the village."

The son stopped. "Even now you are thinking of me?" he asked, wonderingly.

The mother nodded. "Of course, my son," she replied. "You will always be in my thoughts. How could it be otherwise?"

At that, the young farmer could bear it no longer. "Mother, I cannot leave you in the mountains to die all alone," he said. "We are going home and no matter what the lord does to punish me, I will never desert you again."

So they waited until the sun had set and a lone star crept into the silent sky. Then in the dark shadows of night, the farmer carried his mother down the hill and they returned quietly to their little house. The farmer dug a deep hole in the floor of his kitchen and made a small room where he could hide his mother. From that day, she spent all her time in the secret room and the farmer carried meals to her there. The rest of the time, he was careful to work in the fields and act as though he lived alone. In this way, for almost two years, he kept his mother safely hidden and no one in the village knew that she was there.

Then one day there was a terrible commotion among the villagers for Lord Higa of the town beyond the hills threatened to conquer their village and make it his own.

"Only one thing can spare you," Lord Higa announced. "Bring me a box containing one thousand ropes of ash and I will spare your village."

The cruel young lord quickly gathered together all the wise men of his village. "You are men of wisdom," he said. "Surely you can tell me how to meet Lord Higa's demands so our village can be spared."

But the wise men shook their heads. "It is impossible to make even one rope of ash, sire," they answered. "How can we ever make one thousand?"

"Fools!" the lord cried angrily. "What good is your wisdom if you cannot help me now?"

And he posted a notice in the village square offering a great reward of gold to any villager who could help him save their village.

But all the people in the village whispered, "Surely, it is an impossible thing, for ash crumbles at the touch of the finger. How could anyone ever make a rope of ash?" They shook their heads and sighed, "Alas, alas, we must be conquered by yet another cruel lord."

The young farmer, too, supposed that this must be, and he wondered what would happen to his mother if a new lord even more terrible than their own came to rule over them.

When his mother saw the troubled look

on his face, she asked, "Why are you so worried, my son?"

So the farmer told her of the impossible demand made by Lord Higa if the village was to be spared, but his mother did not seem troubled at all. Instead she laughed softly and said, "Why, that is not such an impossible task. All one has to do is soak ordinary rope in salt water and dry it well. When it is burned, it will hold its shape and there is your rope of ash! Tell the villagers to hurry and find one thousand pieces of rope."

The farmer shook his head in amazement. "Mother, you are wonderfully wise," he said, and he rushed to tell the young lord what he must do.

"You are wiser than all the wise men of the village," the lord said when he heard the farmer's solution, and he rewarded him with many pieces of gold. The thousand ropes of ash were quickly made and the village was spared.

In a few days, however, there was another great commotion in the village as Lord Higa sent another threat. This time he sent a log with a small hole that curved and bent seven times through its length, and he demanded that a single piece of silk thread be threaded through the hole. "If you cannot perform this task," the lord threatened, "I shall come to conquer your village."

The young lord hurried once more to his wise men, but they all shook their heads in

THE ROAD TO SHU
Matsumura Goshun
Margaret Watson Parker Art Collection
University of Michigan Museum of Art

bewilderment. "A needle cannot bend its way through such curves," they moaned. "Again we are faced with an impossible demand."

"And again you are stupid fools!" the lord said, stamping his foot impatiently. He then posted a second notice in the village square asking the villagers for their help.

Once more the young farmer hurried with the problem to his mother in her secret room.

"Why, that is not so difficult," his mother said with a quick smile. "Put some sugar at one end of the hole. Then, tie an ant to a piece of silk thread and put it in at the other end. He will weave his way in and out of the curves to get to the sugar and he will take the silk thread with him."

"Mother, you are remarkable!" the son cried, and he hurried off to the lord with the solution to the second problem.

Once more the lord commended the young farmer and rewarded him with many pieces of gold. "You are a brilliant man and you have saved our village again," he said gratefully.

But the lord's troubles were not over even then, for a few days later Lord Higa sent still another demand. "This time you will undoubtedly fail and then I shall conquer your village," he threatened. "Bring me a drum that sounds without being beaten."

"But that is not possible," sighed the people of the village. "How can anyone make a drum sound without beating it?"

This time the wise men held their heads in their hands and moaned, "It is hopeless. It is hopeless. This time Lord Higa will conquer us all."

The young farmer hurried home breathlessly. "Mother, Mother, we must solve another terrible problem or Lord Higa will conquer our village!" And he quickly told his mother about the impossible drum.

His mother, however, smiled and answered, "Why, this is the easiest of them all. Make a drum with sides of paper and put a bumblebee inside. As it tries to escape, it will buzz and beat itself against the paper and you will have a drum that sounds without being beaten."

The young farmer was amazed at his mother's wisdom. "You are far wiser than any of the wise men of the village," he said, and he hurried to tell the young lord how to meet Lord Higa's third demand.

When the lord heard the answer, he was greatly impressed. "Surely a young man like you cannot be wiser than all my wise men," he said. "Tell me honestly, who has helped you solve all these difficult problems?"

The young farmer could not lie. "My lord," he began slowly, "for the past two years I have broken the law of the land. I have kept my aged mother hidden beneath the floor of my house, and it is she who solved each of your problems and saved the village from Lord Higa."

He trembled as he spoke, for he feared the lord's displeasure and rage. Surely now the soldiers would be summoned to throw him into the dark dungeon. But when he glanced fearfully at the lord, he saw that the young ruler was not angry at all. Instead, he was silent and thoughtful, for at last he realized how much wisdom and knowledge old people possess.

"I have been very wrong," he said finally. "And I must ask the forgiveness of your mother and of all my people. Never again will I demand that the old people of our village be sent to the mountains to die. Rather, they will be treated with the respect and honor

TAKETORI MONOGATARI, THE BAMBOO CUTTER OR THE TALE OF THE SHINING PRINCESS
Metropolitan Museum of Art

they deserve and share with us the wisdom of their years."

And so it was. From that day, the villagers were no longer forced to abandon their parents in the mountains, and the village became once more a happy, cheerful place in which to live. The terrible Lord Higa stopped sending his impossible demands and no longer threatened to conquer them, for he too was impressed. "Even in such a small village there is much wisdom," he declared, "and its people should be allowed to live in peace."

And that is exactly what the farmer and his mother and all the people of the village did for all the years thereafter.

Reader's Response

Who do you think is the hero of this tale, the old woman or her son? Explain your answer.

MULTICULTURAL CONNECTION

Growing Up and Leaving Home

Leaving home is a rite of passage that most young Americans go through as they grow to maturity. Whether they go off to college, get a job, or marry, young people in the United States reach an age when they are ready to leave their parents' home and strike out on their own.

In Asian and Hispanic cultures. In some other cultures, however, this may never happen. Even after reaching adulthood, young people still live in the house where they grew up. In many Asian and Hispanic cultures, women are expected to stay in their parents' house until they marry. Then they go to live with their new husband and his family. If a woman does not marry, she may continue to live in her family home for the rest of her life.

Children who stay at home are often surrounded by a large extended family that may include not only parents but grandparents, aunts, uncles, and cousins. Such large families keep customs and traditions alive and ensure the care and support of young children and old people.

There are many advantages for children who stay at home. They can experience the satisfaction of helping to support their parents' household after years of being supported themselves. They can appreciate and draw on the wisdom and experience of their grandparents. Their own children can learn skills and hear stories from the older adults, and child care is never a problem.

In the former Soviet Union. In countries like the former Soviet Union, housing is scarce and young people have little choice but to stay at home. "Home" in cities like Moscow is often a cramped apartment which may even be shared by another family. This situation can breed conflict between family members, or foster warmth and togetherness.

In the United States. Leaving home is not so prevalent in the United States as it once was. In recent years, economic problems have caused many young men and women to stay at home. Even people in their thirties who have left home are coming back to live with Mom and Dad to save on expenses and enjoy family life.

Discussing the Pros and Cons

Discuss with classmates the advantages and disadvantages of living at home as an adult.

Responding to the Selection

Your Response

1. Do you think that the young lord deserved to be saved by the wise old woman? Why or why not?

Recalling

2. Explain the crisis that threatens the village after the old people are banished.

Interpreting

3. What details in the story illustrate the deep love the farmer and his mother have toward one another?
4. Why do you think the wise men could not find ways to meet Lord Higa's demands but the old woman could?
5. When the farmer presents a way to fulfill the first demand, why isn't Lord Higa satisfied?

Applying

6. Describe some ways that you see older people contributing their wisdom to our society.

Analyzing Literature

Understanding Theme

In a folk tale, the **theme** often expresses values upheld by the culture from which the story comes. The theme is generally a lesson about life or living. In "The Wise Old Woman," the theme is expressed by the lord, who learns that an old woman has saved the village.

1. Express the theme of this tale in your own words.
2. Is the theme of this folk tale universal—important to all cultures? Explain.

Critical Thinking and Reading

Identifying Clues to Outcome

Throughout this folk tale, there are clues that the old woman's wisdom will somehow influence the young lord to reverse his decision to banish all old people. The title itself is a clue, since it implies that the woman is the central character and will somehow show her wisdom.

1. At what point in the folk tale did you figure out what the outcome would be? What details led you to your prediction?
2. Find a clue that illustrates the old woman's wisdom even before she presents solutions to Lord Higa's demands.
3. Why is the old woman's success in fulfilling the lord's demands a clue to the outcome?

Thinking and Writing

Writing from a Different View

This folk tale is told in such a way that you share the farmer's feelings and reactions, not those of the young lord or the old woman. Think about how you could write this story from another character's view of the events. Rewrite the events as though the lord or the old woman is telling them, describing only what that character could know about. As you revise, check to make sure you have included all the important developments from the original tale.

Learning Options

1. **Writing.** Pretend that you are the young lord. Write a letter to the wise old woman apologizing for your treatment of the old people in the village and thanking her for what she did.
2. **Multicultural Activity.** Research to find out how older people are honored in one or two other cultures. You might gather information by interviewing people of different cultures in your community. Then create a poster illustrating how people around the world honor their elders.

GUIDE FOR READING

Vivian L. Thompson,

a writer of stories for young people and a longtime resident of Hawaii, has spent many years searching out Hawaiian tales and legends. *Hawaiian Legends of Tricksters and Riddlers,* from which this story was taken, is the first published collection of such tales from Hawaii. Thompson has published many books for young readers, including *Hawaiian Myths of Earth, Sea, and Sky, Faraway Friends, Camp-in-the-Yard, Sand Day,* and *Glad Day.*

The Riddling Youngster

Conflict

Conflict is the struggle between opposing sides or forces. Just as it is in short stories, conflict is the basis for action in a folk tale. In "The Riddling Youngster," conflict develops between a brave young riddler and a proud chief. On a deeper level, the conflict is between good and evil.

Focus

What is the best riddle you know? Get into a small group and share a riddle. After each person in your group has told a riddle, spend a few minutes analyzing the riddles. Which was the funniest? The most clever? Why? What makes a riddle clever or funny?

In "The Riddling Youngster," you will read about a clever young boy who challenged a chief to a riddling contest. Notice the skill and cleverness it takes to create and solve riddles.

Vocabulary

Knowing the following words will help you as you read "The Riddling Youngster."

refuge (ref′ yo͞oj) *n.*: Shelter; safe retreat (p. 587)
avenge (ə venj′) *v.*: Take revenge on behalf of, as for a wrong (p. 588)
defiance (di fī′ əns) *n.*: Bold behavior intended to challenge (p. 588)
impudence (im′ pyo͞o dəns) *n.*: Disrespectful behavior; rudeness (p. 588)
malice (mal′ is) *n.*: Desire to do harm to others (p. 589)
mocking (mäk′ iŋ) *adj.*: Imitating (p. 593)
sacrifice (sak′ rə fīs′) *v.*: Give up on; surrender (p. 593)

Spelling Tip

Remember that *defiance* ends with *ance* and *impudence* ends with *ence.*

The Riddling Youngster
from Hawaii
Vivian L. Thompson

"A shudder ran through Kai. He had lost. His bones would now join those of his father . . ."

It was riddling time for Halepaki[1] and his son, Kai-palaoa.[2] Each morning they spent long hours together in the giving and answering of riddles, in the creating of chants, in the matching of wits.

Halepaki had scarcely seated himself when his son began. "I have a fine riddle for you this morning, my father! Listen!

The back is thin,
The front is thin,
The bones outside,
The skin inside,
It flies but cannot walk."

Halepaki buried his face in his hands. "A strange animal, this one, with bones on the outside and skin on the inside," he murmured.

"You can't guess it! I've caught you at last!" Kai cried.

His father raised his head. "I wonder . . ." he began slowly, "could it be . . . a kite?"

Kai's face fell. "How did you guess it?"

Halepaki's eyes twinkled. "This riddle—it is one you learned from your mother, eh?"

Kai nodded. "How could you know that?"

"Because it is one she learned from me."

Father and son broke into laughter. Kai said, "Here is another. This one you have not heard. I made it up myself:

Green as grass,
White as snow,
Red as fire,
Black as lava,
It tastes good to the tongue."

Halepaki repeated the words softly to himself, was silent for a moment, then asked, "Could it be the watermelon?"

"Ae,[3] watermelon!" Kai shouted. "Your favorite fruit!"

"So it is." Halepaki chuckled. "Now let me ask you one, my sharp-witted son.

Useful to man,
Though full of holes;
The more holes you add,
The more it can carry."

---

1. **Halepaki** (hä′ lē pä′ kē)
2. **Kai-palaoa** (kī′ pä lä′ ō ä)
3. **Ae** (ī′ ā): Yes.

MAHANA MAO, 1898
Paul Gauguin
Art Museum of Ateneum, Helsinki

Kai frowned. "Useful yet full of holes! A sieve? But a sieve carries nothing!"

"True. But you swim in the right direction, Clever One."

Kai whispered the last line again. "The more holes you add, the more it can carry . . . I have it! A fishnet!"

"Aia la![4] You will be a better riddler than your father, before long!" Halepaki cried.

"Not so," Kai protested. "You are the finest riddler in the islands!"

"Ah, no," Halepaki answered. "Kalani,[5] High Chief of Kauai,[6] is counted champion. But someday when I have learned enough, I shall challenge the great Kalani."

"And then you will be champion riddler of the islands," Kai said confidently.

"And you, the riddling youngster," said Halepaki.

The day soon came when Halepaki set out to challenge the champion. Kai and his mother stood on the beach watching his father's canoe make its way past Mokuola,[7] the tiny islet in the bay, then head out into deep water toward the island of Kauai in the western sea.

The new moon grew to roundness and moved on to smallness, once . . . twice . . . three times . . . and four, and no word came from Halepaki.

Kai and his mother stared out to sea, straining for a glimpse of Halepaki's canoe beyond the waving coco palms of Mokuola. Island of Refuge, it was called, and there, one in trouble could flee from any island, for refuge. But for Kai and his mother there was no refuge from anxiety.

"Some evil has surely befallen your father or he would have sent word before this," Kai's mother said sorrowfully.

"I will go in search of him," said Kai. "But before I set foot on the island of the riddling champion I must learn all that I can of my father's art. Will you teach me what you know of riddling, my mother?"

Kai learned all that his mother could teach him, of the things above and the things below, of life in the uplands and life in the lowlands, of distant places on his island and their special characteristics. Then she said, "Now you must go to your aunt in Kohala.[8] She married my brother who was a fine riddler, and she has lived on the island of Kauai and can teach you much that I do not know."

So Kai journeyed to Kohala and learned from his aunt all that she could teach him, of things that happen by day and things that happen by night, of good and of evil, of life and of death, of distant places on the island of Kauai and their special characteristics. When she had taught him all she knew, he was classed as an expert although he was still a youngster.

Then Kai carefully chose the largest calabash[9] he could find, and packed it with a variety of articles that might be helpful to him in his mission. He bade farewell to his aunt and mother, stepped into his canoe, and went in search of his father.

When he reached the island of Kauai, a fleet of fishing canoes was unloading its catch. Standing on the beach, watching, was a handsome youth about his own age. Kai

---

4. Aia la (ī′ ä lä): There! I told you so!

5. Kalani (kä lä′ nē)

6. Kauai (kou′ ī): An island of Hawaii, northwest of the island of Oahu.

7. Mokuola (mō′ ko͞o ō′ lä)

8. Kohala (kō hä′ lä): A district of the island of Hawaii.

9. calabash (kal′ ə bash) *n.*: The dried, hollow shell of a gourd such as squash, melon, or pumpkin, used as a bowl, as a cup, or as a large carrier.

approached him and said, "I am Kai-palaoa of Hawaii.[10] Can you give me news of Halepaki the riddler who came to challenge your High Chief four moons ago?"

The youth gave him a strange look and pointed. "The flag of the High Chief still flies; his kapu stick[11] still stands," he said. "Halepaki challenged and lost. His bones lie bleaching in the High Chief's House-of-Bones, his teeth in his Fence-of-Teeth."

Kai's heart grew heavy at the news.

"What was this man Halepaki to you?" the youth asked.

"He was my father." Kai thought he saw a look of compassion cross the stranger's face but it was gone in a flash and the youth said nothing more. Kai drew a deep breath. He knew now that he must challenge the High Chief of Kauai; avenge his father . . . or join him.

He turned and went to the head fisherman. "I am a stranger who has come on a long journey," he said. "Can you spare me a few fish?"

"Take what you need," said the man.

Kai studied the catch carefully, then chose two fish. The first was black with a reddish-yellow top fin that gave it the name "waving flag." The second was one whose name meant "brave challenge."

"You take but two," the fisherman commented. "You have a small hunger."

"Not so," Kai replied. "My hunger is great, but for revenge, not food. Tell me, who is that youth?"

"He is Kelii[12]—Young Chief, younger brother of Kalani the High Chief."

Kai turned for another look but Kelii had disappeared. Kai strode to the chief's flagstaff, tore down the chief's flag and hung in its place his fish called "waving flag." He snatched the white kapa ball[13] from the chief's kapu stick and replaced it with his fish, "brave challenge."

Soon a messenger appeared in answer to this defiance. He called down, "The High Chief orders you to come up, young braggart!"

Kai replied, "The stranger orders you to come down, middle-aged braggart!"

Amused at his impudence, the chief's messenger came down and escorted Kai, with his riddler's calabash, to the High Chief. At the door of the riddling house he was challenged by Keeper of the Bones.

"Who are you and what do you seek?"

"I am Kai-palaoa, son of Halepaki the riddler, of Hawaii. I come to challenge your chief to a contest of wits."

"Ho! Listen to the riddling youngster!" jeered Keeper of the Bones. "If it is a contest you want, a contest you shall have. But you are too young to enter the riddling house. You shall remain outside. Outside you shall compete, outside eat and sleep, and outside die."

"If I am too young to enter the riddling house, your chief is too old to leave it. He shall remain inside. Inside he shall compete, inside eat and sleep, and inside die."

At this, the angry voice of the High Chief was heard from inside. "Enough! Am I to spend the time of the contest shut up in here while this youngster is free to come and go? The young braggart has outwitted you! Bid him enter."

Scowling, Keeper of the Bones moved aside and Kai entered. He saw the High

---

10. Hawaii (hə wä' ē)

11. kapu (kä' pōō): Forbidden.

12. Kelii (ka lē' ē)

13. kapa (kä' pä) **ball**: A ball made out of cloth made from bark.

MATAMOE
Paul Gauguin
The Pushkin Museum of Fine Arts, Moscow

Chief seated on a platform covered with fine woven matting. Behind him stood six warriors. On his left stood Keeper of the Teeth.

Keeper of the Bones, instead of taking his place on the chief's right, proceeded to tear up the matting from one half of the floor. Then he spilled out the contents of a water gourd, turning the earthen floor to mud. Taking his place on the matting-covered platform he said with a look of malice, "We regret that we have no fine mat like the chief's to offer the stranger."

Kai calmly opened his calabash, took out handfuls of grass and threw them down upon the muddly floor. He covered the grass, first with a coarse kapa,[14] then with a finely-made, sweetly-scented kapa, and answered, "I regret that I have no fine kapa like mine, to offer the chief."

The High Chief's face grew dark. "You would challenge me to a contest of wits, knowing that your father's skill was not

14. kapa (kä′ pä) *n.*: Cloth made from bark.

enough to save him?" he demanded.

"I would," Kai replied.

"For what stakes?"

"My bones against your bones."

The High Chief looked startled. Keeper of the Bones said with an evil grin, "O Chief, your House-of-Bones and Fence-of-Teeth lack but one set each. This one's bones are young and soft, his teeth short and white, but they will do."

Kai grinned. "The chief's bones are old and brittle, his teeth long and yellow, but they will do."

The High Chief gave an angry bellow. "Begin the contest!"

Keeper of Teeth said to Kai, "As challenger, you have the choice of referee. My services are available."

"Mahalo,"[15] said Kai curtly. "I have another choice."

The chief and his two attendants studied him uneasily. "Who is your choice?" Keeper of Teeth demanded.

"Kelii," Kai answered.

The three looked amused. Kai felt a chill of dread. Had he mistaken the look of sympathy in Kelii's face? Even so, Kai felt him to be a better choice than Keeper of Teeth.

Kelii was summoned. He looked straight at Kai as he entered but his face remained expressionless. The three showed no doubt of Kelii's support as he took his place upon the platform.

Keeper of Bones said smoothly, "Before such an important event, it is fitting that we drink of ceremonial awa[16] and eat of baked pig."

He turned to Keeper of Teeth. "Check the imu.[17] See if our pig is ready while I prepare the awa root."

Keeper of Teeth went out. Soon Kai smelled the appetizing aroma of roasting pork. Calmly he reached into his calabash and chose what he needed: pebbles, kindling, fire sticks, and a small wooden pig wound about with string. He dug a small hole in the earthen floor, built a small imu, lighted a small fire. Then, taking up his small wooden pig, he pulled the string. It unwound with a squealing sound.

"Such a noisy one, this pig!" Kai exclaimed. He went through the motions of killing and cleaning it. In the hollow center he tucked a portion of baked pork he had brought with him. Then he placed his miniature pig in his miniature imu, covered it with pebbles, grass, and damp kapa mats, and sat back on his heels with a sigh of satisfaction.

"Now while my pig bakes, I shall prepare my awa," he said. From the calabash came pieces of awa root already pounded, and his stone pounder. He gave the roots a few token strokes, placed them in a piece of palm fiber and adding water, strained the liquid into his drinking bowl.

While Keeper of Bones was still pounding awa root for the High Chief's ceremonial drink, Kai was already making his offering to his gods and drinking his. While Keeper of Teeth was still watching the chief's imu, Kai was taking his miniature pig from his miniature imu, removing the portion of baked pork, and eating with good appetite.

But when the royal meal was ready, the High Chief took little pleasure in it, for Kai,

---

15. Mahalo (mä hä′ lō): Thank you.

16. awa (ä′ vä): A ceremonial drink made from the root of a shrub.

17. imu (ē′ mo͞o): Earth oven; an oven that is made by digging a pit in the earth, placing hot stones in it, and covering the opening with leaves, bark, and so on.

who should have been watching, hungry and envious, was instead finishing his own tasty meal.

"Clear this away!" the chief ordered. "Let the contest begin!"

Kelii came forward and announced in a cold voice, "A contest of wits between Kalani, High Chief of the island of Kauai, and Kaipalaoa, riddling youngster from the island of Hawaii. Five rounds to be played. If tied score, another contest tomorrow. The stakes, their bones. Winner to go free, loser to be baked in the imu. First, let each compose a chant telling of the wonders to be found only on his own island. The High Chief goes first."

The High Chief thought for a moment, then began his chant:

"How beautiful is the island of Kauai!
Island of the barking sand,
Island of the spouting horn,
Island of the great canyon
And the mountain of rippling waters."

Kai nodded his appreciation and responded:

"How beautiful is Hawaii!

TAHITIAN LANDSCAPE
Paul Gauguin
The Minneapolis Institute of Arts

Island of the black sand,
Island of the white mountain,
Island of five volcanoes
And the home of eternal fire."

Kelii announced a tie. "First round . . . pai a pai.[18] Now let us have a round of match and top."

The High Chief looked smug and began at once: "I speak of an animal of great wisdom. The yellow-backed crab is small and must go crawling. But he carries his bones on the outside to protect the meat inside. His legs are ten."

Kai retorted, "I speak of an animal of great wisdom. The red rock lobster is small and must go crawling. But he carries his bones on the outside to protect the meat inside. His legs are fourteen."

"Second round . . . pai a pai," Kelii droned. "Now let us hear of foods that grow below ground."

To himself, the High Chief counted some off on his fingers, then began:

"Below the ground,
Below the ground,
These do grow below the ground:
The root of the potato,
The root of the sweet potato,
The root of the yam,
And the arrowroot."

Kai responded promptly:

"Below the ground,
Below the ground,
These do grow below the ground:
The root of sweet fern,
The root of wetland taro,[19]
The root of dryland taro,
And the awa root
Which makes man forget all others."

"Third round . . . pai a pai," said Kelii. "Now of foods that grow above ground."

High Chief was full of assurance. He began at once:

"Above the ground,
Above the ground,
These do grow above the ground:
Fruit of the banana,
Fruit of the mountain apple,
Fruit of the sugar cane,
And the breadfruit."

Kai's answer came swiftly:

"Above the ground,
Above the ground,
These do grow above the ground:
Fruit of the palm—the coconut,
Fruit of the bird—the egg,
Fruit of the night—the moon,
Fruit of the day—the sun,
Which nourishes all other fruits."

There was no doubt about that round. Kai's last line had certainly matched and topped the High Chief's. "Fourth round . . . still a tie. One round to go," Kelii declared. "Let us hear now of canoe travels."

High Chief thought for a moment, then a sly grin spread across his face. Arrogantly he began his chant;

"My canoe sails to the islands:
To Niihau,[20] *to Kauai,*
To Oahu[21] *and Molokai,*[22]

18. pai a pai (pä′ ē ä pä′ ē): Tied score.
19. taro (tä′ rō) *n.*: A large plant cultivated for its edible roots.
20. Niihau (nē′ hou): An island of Hawaii.
21. Oahu (ō ä′ hōō): An island of Hawaii.
22. Molokai (mō′ lō kī′ ē): An island of Hawaii.

To Lanai[23] and Kahoolawe,[24]
To Maui[25] and Hawaii,
And then turns home—
For there are no more islands."

This time, Kai seemed to have no ready answer. He sat, head in hands, lost in thought. High Chief nodded triumphantly. Keeper of Bones rubbed his hands, as if already preparing Kai's bones for the chief's monstrous house. Keeper of Teeth licked his lips expectantly. Kelii's face remained expressionless.

High Chief began a mocking chant:

"The answer is yet to come.
It is for you to answer;
It is for us to listen.
We wait, but hear nothing."

Slowly Kai raised his head and began repeating the words of the chief's earlier chant. The riddling house grew still as death.

"My canoe sails to the islands:
To Niihau, to Kauai,
To Oahu and Molokai,
To Lanai and Kahoolawe,
To Maui and Hawaii,
And then turns home—
To Mokuola, Island of Refuge
For all the islands!"

Kai had surely topped the High Chief's chant, but his life now depended on Kelii's decision. Would Young Chief give a fair verdict, even though it meant death for his older brother? The riddling house seemed filled with flashing lightning as High Chief, Keeper of Bones, and Keeper of Teeth sent unspoken messages flying through the air to Kelii.

Young Chief's face was a carved mask. Suddenly, he pointed . . . to High Chief and his men!

A shudder ran through Kai. He had lost. His bones would now join those of his father; and his mother, waiting beyond the Island of Refuge, would never see husband or son again.

The Kai heard Young Chief's words. "Mea i poho[26] . . . the loser!"

Kai saw Kelii's hand rise and fall . . . not once, but three times. He saw the warriors move in swiftly and carry out High Chief . . . Keeper of Bones . . . Keeper of Teeth, to the waiting imu.

Kai approached the platform and knelt before Young Chief. "I owe my life to you," he said.

Kelii's face lost its frozen look. He shook his head. "Your father's life I could not save," he said. "Yours I could not sacrifice. Now that I am High Chief, there will be no more riddling for such stakes on the island of Kauai. When you have taken your father's bones home for burial, the House-of-Bones and Fence-of-Teeth will be destroyed."

Then Kai-palaoa the riddling youngster who had become riddling champion, having accomplished what he had set out to do, gathered up the bones of his father for their last sad journey home.

23. Lanai (lä nī′ ē): An island of Hawaii.
24. Kahoolawe (kä′ hō ō lä′ vē): An island of Hawaii.
25. Maui (mou′ ē): An island of Hawaii.

26. Mea i poho (mē′ ä ē pō hō′): The loser.

Reader's Response
Would you have taken on the challenge Kai took up? Why or why not?

RESPONDING TO THE SELECTION

Your Response

1. Do you think that Kelii will be a better chief than his brother? Why or why not?
2. Do you think that Kai was right to take vengeance on the chief?

Recalling

3. Why does Kai leave his island? Why does he go first to his aunt's island?
4. How does Kai issue his challenge to the chief?
5. Why does Kai pick Kelii as referee?
6. Explain how Kai gains an advantage over the chief even before the contest begins.

Interpreting

7. Describe the relationship between Kai and his father. Why does the father spend so much time teaching riddles to his son?
8. Name two ways in which Kai represents the forces of good.
9. Name two ways in which the chief and his attendants represent evil.

Applying

10. Riddles played an important role in ancient Hawaii. Are riddles important in our culture? What role do riddles play in other cultures?

ANALYZING LITERATURE

Understanding Conflict

Conflict is the struggle between opposing forces. It is a crucial element of a story because it causes the action and helps create suspense. In this tale, there are several conflicts: youth against age, commoner against ruler, good against evil.

1. Which do you think is the major conflict? Describe it in your own words.
2. How is this conflict resolved?
3. How does the conflict add suspense in the story?

CRITICAL THINKING AND READING

Analyzing Riddling

A **riddle** is a problem or puzzle that requires some thought or cleverness to answer or to understand. In this folk tale, riddling is more than just giving and answering puzzling statements. It involves imitating words and actions, matching and topping another's cleverness, making plays on words, and composing chants.

1. Give an example of the use of cleverness in imitating words and actions.
2. Why is riddling so important to this story?

THINKING AND WRITING

Writing a Letter to Persuade

Imagine that you want to persuade a television producer to make a film of "The Riddling Youngster." Write a letter to this producer. First make a list for yourself of the most important, exciting moments of the story. Then draft your letter to the television producer, explaining why this story would make a good film and using some of the events and details from your list. Also explain the conflict of the story and the ways in which it becomes suspenseful and exciting. As you revise, make sure you have convinced the producer that other young people will be eager to see the film.

LEARNING OPTIONS

1. **Writing.** Work with your classmates to make a book of riddles. Choose both silly riddles and classic rhyming riddles. You can look in the library for examples of riddles or read pages 595–596 for advice.
2. **Cross-curricular Connection.** One of the most famous riddles in history is the riddle of the Sphinx. Do some research about this famous riddle. Copy the riddle—and the solution—on a piece of drawing paper. Illustrate the riddle with your own drawing of the Sphinx.

Writing a Riddle

Can you think of a riddle you enjoy telling? What makes a riddle fun to solve? Like many people you probably enjoy telling and solving riddles with your friends. From the folk tales in this section, you know that people from all over the world have enjoyed making and solving riddles for centuries.

Riddles are fun to make up, and you can create a riddle of your own once you know how. All you have to do is describe something without naming what it is.

Your Turn

Create original riddles for a class riddle collection. Your purpose is to challenge your listeners. Your audience is your classmates.

Prewriting

Do you remember this riddle in "The Riddling Youngster"?

"Green as grass,
White as snow,
Red as fire,
Black as lava,
It tastes good to the tongue."

When you discovered the riddle was describing a watermelon, did you think to yourself, "Of course, how obvious!"?

You, too, can create a riddle. Follow these steps to come up with an original riddle that will test your classmates' wits.

1. Find a subject for your riddle. On a sheet of paper, list as many possible topics for a riddle as you can. Select one. For example, you might list, among others, watermelon, orange, candle, and butter. Select one possibility.

2. Identify the characteristics. On the left half of a sheet of paper, list as many characteristics as you can, so you have several from which to choose. If you choose an orange, for example, your list of characteristics might look like this:

round
cool to the touch
bumpy and tough
orange color

3. Describe each characteristic. On the right side of the paper list words and phrases that describe each characteristic of your object or action. For example, for the orange you might begin your list as follows:

round	shape of a ball
cool to the touch	warmer than an ice cube
bumpy and tough	feels like leather
orange color	like a pale sunset

Is your riddle taking shape? It should be.

If not, choose another subject from your objects or action list, and try prewriting again.

Drafting

Look over your notes. Select several characteristics from the right column, and try them in different combinations. Do they describe something without naming it?

Here is one student's riddle using the prewriting started earlier:

```
What looks like a ball, feels
like leather, is warmer than an
ice cube, and is the color of a
pale sunset?
```

As a challenge, you might like to set up your riddle in rhyming lines.

Revising

Work with writing partners to test your riddle. Read it aloud. Then ask your listeners, "What am I describing?"

If everyone guesses your riddle right away, it might be too easy, so you may want to take away some of your hints or change them.

If nobody solves your riddle, add hints one at a time from your prewriting list. If you run out of hints and still nobody has solved your riddle, tell the answer. Then ask, "Now that you know the answer, was it obvious?" If not, share your prewriting with your partners. Ask them for suggestions about new hints. It might be that your riddle just won't work. Then choose another subject and begin again.

Proofreading

Consult the guidelines for proofreading on page 753. Because a riddle is short, a riddle writer needs to proofread especially carefully. Mistakes easily distract readers and might lead them away from solving your riddle.

Publishing

Write your riddle on one side of an index card in your neatest printing. On the other side, print the answer in parentheses. If you have more than one riddle, make a separate card for each one.

Consider inviting another class to a riddle festival. If they enjoy riddles, you can also teach them how to create them.

Tricksters, Heroes, and Other Characters

THE TURTLE
Alain Thomas

GUIDE FOR READING

I. G. Edmonds

(1917–), a collector of folk tales, was born and raised in Texas. As a soldier in the South Pacific during World War II, Edmonds became interested in folklore when he heard a native chief's story of how his island was created. Edmonds then collected and recorded folk tales from every country he visited during his twenty-three-year service with the Air Force. Among the tales he collected were many about a trickster character, which he published in *Trickster Tales.*

Señor Coyote and the Tricked Trickster

The Trickster

The trickster is one of the best-loved characters in folk tales. The **trickster** relies on wit and intelligence, rather than strength, to outsmart bigger or more powerful opponents. The trickster character is most often an animal. Although the rabbit may seem like an obvious trickster, other animals such as the turtle and the spider have also been cast in the trickster role. In this story, the coyote believes himself to be a great trickster but his skills are put to the test by another quick-witted creature—the mouse.

Focus

In this story, Coyote, Mouse, and Rattlesnake find themselves in predicaments in which they need help. Think of times when you have needed help. How did you go about asking for help? Did the person who helped you expect anything in return? Write down one or two instances in which you asked for help and tell whether you had to do anything in return for the help. As you read this story, think about why it is important for people to help each other.

Vocabulary

Knowing the following words will help you as you read "Señor Coyote and the Tricked Trickster."

spirited (spir′ it id) *adj.*: Lively (p. 599)

gnaw (nô) *v.*: To bite and wear away bit by bit with the teeth (p. 599)

ungrateful (un grāt′ fəl) *adj.*: Not thankful (p. 599)

reproachfully (ri prōch′ fəl lē) *adv.*: With blame (p. 599)

indignantly (in dig′ nənt lē) *adv.*: Angrily (p. 601)

welfare (wel′ fer′) *n.*: Well-being (p. 602)

protested (prə test′ id) *v.*: Objected to strongly (p. 602)

Spelling Tip

Remember that *gnaw,* like *gnat, gnarl,* and *gnome,* begins with a silent *g.*

Señor Coyote and the Tricked Trickster

from Mexico

I. G. Edmonds

"He worked all day and dreamed all night of how he could trick his way out of his troubles."

One day long ago in Mexico's land of sand and giant cactus *Señor*[1] Coyote and *Señor* Mouse had a quarrel.

None now alive can remember why, but recalling what spirited *caballeros*[2] these two were, I suspect that it was some small thing that meant little.

Be that as it may, these two took their quarrels seriously and for a long time would not speak to each other.

Then one day Mouse found Señor Coyote caught in a trap. He howled and twisted and fought, but he could not get out. He had just about given up when he saw Señor Mouse grinning at him.

"Mouse! *Mi viejo amigo*[3]—my old friend!" he cried. "Please gnaw this leather strap in two and get me out of this trap."

"But we are no longer friends," Mouse said. "We have quarreled, remember?"

"Nonsense!" Señor Coyote cried. "Why I love you better than I do Rattlesnake, Owl, or anybody in the desert. You must gnaw me loose. And please hurry for if the *peon*[4] catches me I will wind up a fur rug on his wife's kitchen floor."

Mouse remembered how mean Señor Coyote had been to him. He was always playing tricks on Mouse and his friends. They were very funny to Señor Coyote for he was a great trickster, but often they hurt little Mouse.

"I'd like to gnaw you free," he said, "but I am old and my teeth tire easily."

"Really, Señor Mouse, you are ungrateful," said Señor Coyote reproachfully. "Remember all the nice things I have done for you."

"What were they?"

"Why——" Coyote began and stopped. He was unable to think of a single thing. There was a good reason for this. He had done nothing for Mouse but trick him.

But Señor Coyote is a sly fellow. He said quickly, "Oh, why remind you of them. You remember them all."

1. ***Señor*** (sen yôr′): Spanish title used like "mister."
2. ***caballeros*** (kä bä yer′ ōs): Spanish for "gentlemen."
3. ***Mi viejo amigo*** (mē vē ā′ hō ä mē′ gō)
4. ***peon*** (pe′ än): Spanish for "worker"—an unskilled laborer.

"I fear my memory of yesterday is too dim," Mouse said, "but I could remember very well what you could do for me tomorrow."

"Tomorrow?" Coyote asked.

"Yes, tomorrow. If I gnaw away the leather rope holding you in the trap, what will you do for me tomorrow, and the day after tomorrow and the day after the day after tomorrow and the day——"

"Stop!" Señor Coyote cried. "How long is this going on?"

"A life is worth a life. If I save your life, you should work for me for a lifetime. That is the only fair thing to do."

"But everyone would laugh at a big, brave, smart fellow like me working as a slave for a mere mouse!" Señor Coyote cried.

"Is that worse than feeling sad for you because your hide is a rug in the peon's kitchen?"

Señor Coyote groaned and cried and argued, but finally agreed when he saw that Mouse would not help him otherwise.

"Very well," he said tearfully, "I agree to work for you until either of us dies or until I have a chance to get even by saving your life."

Mouse said with a sly grin, "That is very fine, but I remember what a great trickster

COYOTE AND MOON from MOJAVE
Wendell Minor

you are. So you must also promise that as soon as I free you that you will not jump on me, threaten to kill me, and then save my life by letting me go!"

"Why, how can you suggest such a thing!" Coyote cried indignantly. And then to himself he added, "This mouse is getting *too* smart!"

"Very well, promise," Mouse said.

"But I am not made for work," Señor Coyote said tearfully. "I live by being sly."

"Then be sly and get out of the trap yourself," Mouse retorted.

"Very well," Señor Coyote said sadly. "I will work for you until I can pay back the debt of my life."

And so Mouse gnawed the leather strap in two and Coyote was saved. Then for many days thereafter Señor Coyote worked for Mouse. Mouse was very proud to have the famous Señor Coyote for a servant. Señor Coyote was greatly embarrassed since he did not like being a servant and disliked working even more.

There was nothing he could do since he had given his promise. He worked all day and dreamed all night of how he could trick his way out of his troubles. He could think of nothing.

Then one day Baby Mouse came running to him. "My father has been caught by Señor Snake!" he cried. "Please come and save him."

"Hooray!" cried Coyote. "If I save him, I will be released from my promise to work to for him."

He went out to the desert rocks and found Señor Rattlesnake with his coils around Señor Mouse.

"Please let him go and I will catch you two more mice," Coyote said.

"My wise old mother used to tell me that a bird in the hand is worth two in the bush," Snake replied. "By the same reasoning, one mouse in Snake's stomach is worth two in Coyote's mind."

"Well, I tried, Mouse," Coyote said. "I'm sorry you must be eaten."

"But you must save me, then you will be free from your promise to me," Mouse said.

"If you're eaten, I'll be free anyway," Coyote said.

"Then everyone will say that Coyote was not smart enough to trick Snake," Mouse said quickly. "And I think they will be right. It makes me very sad for I always thought Señor Coyote the greatest trickster in the world."

This made Coyote's face turn red. He was very proud that everyone thought him so clever. Now he just *had* to save Mouse.

So he said to Snake, "How did you catch Mouse anyway?"

"A rock rolled on top of him and he was trapped," Mouse said. "He asked me to help him roll it off. When I did he jumped on me before I could run away."

"That is not true," Snake said. "How could a little mouse have the strength to roll away a big rock. There is the rock. Now you tell me if you think Mouse could roll it."

It was a very big rock and Coyote admitted that Mouse could not possibly have budged it.

"But it is like the story *Mamacita*[5] tells her children at bedtime," Mouse said quickly. "Once there was a poor burro who had a load of hay just as large as he could carry. His master added just one more straw and the poor burro fell in the dirt. Snake did

---

5. *Mamacita* (mä mə sē′ tä): Spanish for "mommy."

MOUSE from MOJAVE (detail)
Wendell Minor

not have quite enough strength to push the rock off himself. I came along and was like that last straw on the burro's back and together we rolled the rock away."

"Maybe that is true," Snake said, "but by Mouse's own words, he did only a very little of the work. So I owe him only a very little thanks. That is not enough to keep me from eating him."

"Hmmm," said Coyote. "Now you understand, Snake, that I do not care what happens myself. If Mouse is eaten, I will be free of my bargain anyway. I am only thinking of your own welfare, Snake."

"Thank you," said Señor Rattlesnake, "but I do enough thinking about my welfare for both of us. I don't need your thoughts."

"Nevertheless," Coyote insisted, "everyone is going to say that you ate Mouse after he was kind enough to help you."

"I don't care," Snake said. "Nobody says anything good of me anyway."

"Well," said Coyote, "I'll tell you what we should do. We should put everything back as it was. Then I will see for myself if Mouse was as much help as he said he was or as little as you claim. Then I can tell everyone that you were right, Snake."

"Very well," said Señor Snake. "I was lying like this and the rock was on me—"

"Like this?" Coyote said, quickly rolling the rock across Snake's body.

"Ouch!" said Snake. "That is right."

"Can you get out?" Coyote asked.

"No," said Snake.

"Then turn Mouse loose and let him push," said Coyote.

This Snake did, but before Mouse could push, Coyote said, "But on second thought if Mouse pushes, you would then grab him again and we'd be back arguing. Since you are both as you were before the argument started, let us leave it at that and all be friends again!"

Then Coyote turned to Mouse. "So, my friend, I have now saved your life. We are now even and my debt to you is paid."

"But mine is such a *little* life," Mouse protested. "And yours is so much *larger*. I don't think they balance. You should still pay me part."

"This is ridiculous!" Coyote cried. "I—"

"Wait!" Snake put in hopefully. "Let me settle the quarrel. Now you roll the rock away. I'll take Mouse in my coils just the way we were when Coyote came up. We'll be then in a position to decide if—"

"Thank you," said Mouse. "It isn't necessary to trouble everyone again. Señor Coyote, we are even."

Reader's Response
Which character did you identify with most? Why?

Responding to the Selection

Your Response

1. Which character do you think is the most clever? Explain.

Recalling

2. Why is Mouse reluctant to help the trapped Coyote?
3. Why does Coyote work as Mouse's servant, despite his embarrassment?

Interpreting

4. Why is Coyote surprised that Mouse can outwit him?
5. Which of Coyote's characteristics does Mouse appeal to in persuading Coyote to save him from Snake?
6. What common failing do Coyote and Snake share? Why does this failing make them easily tricked?

Applying

7. Trickster tales appear in folk literature all over the world. Why do you think the trickster is a popular character?

Analyzing Literature

Understanding the Trickster

The **trickster** in folk tales is a character who relies on cleverness to outsmart bigger, more powerful opponents. In many tales the trickster is a small animal. In this story, all of the animals are tricksters.

1. Describe the way Coyote tricks Snake.
2. What lesson is in this tale about Coyote, a trickster himself, who gets tricked by Mouse?

Critical Thinking and Reading

Evaluating the Qualities of a Trickster

Trickster characters share typical qualities. They are, above all, clever. They know how to take advantage of the weaknesses of their opponents, can anticipate how an opponent might react, and know how to bargain. Tricksters are also persistent, trying a different approach when a first effort fails, such as when Coyote asks Mouse to remember the times he had been nice.

1. What characteristics of a trickster does each character use in tricking another?
2. Which character—Mouse, Coyote, or Snake—do you think is the best trickster? Why?

Thinking and Writing

Writing a Dialogue

Imagine that you are Snake. Horse wants to hire a trickster to trick Dog in some way. Horse asks whether you would recommend Coyote or Mouse as the best trickster. Coyote is a famous trickster but his pride gets in the way sometimes. Mouse outwitted Coyote and yet got caught by you. Create a conversation with Horse in which you explain the qualities of both Mouse and Coyote and give your opinion about which one ought to be hired.

Learning Options

1. **Multicultural Activity.** Make a list of the Spanish words and phrases in this story. Arrange the words in alphabetical order. Then, create a mini Spanish-English dictionary by writing the English definition next to each Spanish word.
2. **Speaking and Listening.** Suppose that someone comes by and rescues Señor Rattlesnake. What do you think Snake would have to say about what happened? Write a dialogue between Snake and his rescuer. Remember that Snake's version of the story may be very different from that of Coyote or Mouse.

GUIDE FOR READING

Virginia Hamilton

(1936–) was born, raised, and still lives on her family's land in southwestern Ohio. She is an acclaimed writer of books for children and young adults. More recently she has collected and written two books of folk tales. *In the Beginning* is a collection of creation stories, and *The People Could Fly* is a collection of tales told by enslaved Africans. "He Lion, Bruh Bear, and Bruh Rabbit" is one of these. Although they originated with enslaved Africans, these tales, "like all folk tales, belong to all of us," she says.

He Lion, Bruh Bear, and Bruh Rabbit

Personification

Personification is the giving of human characteristics to nonhuman subjects. Folk tales often use personification with animal characters, who are given human abilities and personalities. In this folk tale, he Lion, Bruh Bear, and Bruh Rabbit have the characteristics of speech and reason.

Focus

Animals are personified differently in different cultures. Many Americans, for example, see the spider as a sinister creature, trapping innocent victims in its web, but many Africans consider the spider to be wise and clever. Each culture looks at nature from a point of view that comes from its history and its customs. The lion and the rabbit are key characters in the story you are about to read. On a separate sheet of paper, copy the two diagrams that follow. On the lines around each diagram, write the qualities that you associate with each animal.

As you read "He Lion, Bruh Bear, and Bruh Rabbit," compare the characteristics on your diagrams with those of the lion and the rabbit in the story.

Vocabulary

Knowing the following words will help you read "He Lion, Bruh Bear, and Bruh Rabbit."

cordial (kôr′ jəl) *adj.*: Warm and friendly (p. 606)

scrawny (skrô′ nē) *adj.*: Very thin; skinny and bony (p. 607)

He Lion, Bruh Bear, and Bruh Rabbit

African American

Virginia Hamilton

" 'ME AND MYSELF. ME AND MYSELF. Nobody tell me what not to do,' he said. 'I'm the King of the forest' . . ."

Say that he Lion would get up each and every mornin. Stretch and walk around. He'd roar, "ME AND MYSELF. ME AND MYSELF," like that. Scare all the little animals so they were afraid to come outside in the sunshine. Afraid to go huntin or fishin or whatever the little animals wanted to do.

"What we gone do about it?" they asked one another. Squirrel leapin from branch to branch, just scared. Possum[1] playin dead, couldn't hardly move him.

He Lion just went on, stickin out his chest and roarin, "ME AND MYSELF. ME AND MYSELF."

The little animals held a sit-down talk, and one by one and two by two and all by all, they decide to go see Bruh[2] Bear and Bruh Rabbit. For they know that Bruh Bear been around. And Bruh Rabbit say he has, too.

So they went to Bruh Bear and Bruh Rabbit. Said, "We have some trouble. Old he Lion, him scarin everybody, roarin every mornin and all day, 'ME AND MYSELF. ME AND MYSELF,' like that."

"Why he Lion want to do that?" Bruh Bear said.

"Is that all he Lion have to say?" Bruh Rabbit asked.

"We don't know why, but that's all he Lion can tell us and we didn't ask him to tell us that," said the little animals. "And him scarin the children with it. And we wish him to stop it."

"Well, I'll go see him, talk to him. I've known he Lion a long kind of time," Bruh Bear said.

"I'll go with you," said Bruh Rabbit. "I've known he Lion most long as you."

That bear and that rabbit went off through the forest. They kept hearin somethin. Mumble, mumble. Couldn't make it out. They got farther in the forest. They heard it plain now. "ME AND MYSELF. ME AND MYSELF."

"Well, well, well," said Bruh Bear. He wasn't scared. He'd been around the whole forest, seen a lot.

1. **Possum** (päs′ ə m): Colloquial for "opossum," a small, tree-dwelling mammal that pretends to be dead when it is trapped.
2. **Bruh** (bru): Black American dialect for "brother."

"My, my, my," said Bruh Rabbit. He'd seen enough to know not to be afraid of an old he lion. Now old he lions could be dangerous, but you had to know how to handle them.

The bear and the rabbit climbed up and up the cliff where he Lion had his lair. They found him. Kept their distance. He watchin them and they watchin him. Everybody actin cordial.

"Hear tell you are scarin everybody, all the little animals, with your roarin all the time," Bruh Rabbit said.

"I roars when I pleases," he Lion said.

"Well, might could you leave off the noise first thing in the mornin, so the little animals can get what they want to eat and drink?" asked Bruh Bear.

"Listen," said he Lion, and then he roared: "ME AND MYSELF. ME AND MYSELF. No-

LION WITH LANDSCAPE
A. J. Taylor
Shelburne Museum, Shelburne, Vermont

body tell me what not to do," he said. "I'm the king of the forest, *me and myself.*"

"Better had let me tell you somethin," Bruh Rabbit said, "for I've seen Man, and I know him the real king of the forest."

He Lion was quiet awhile. He looked straight through that scrawny lil Rabbit like he was nothin atall. He looked at Bruh bear and figured he'd talk to him.

"You, Bear, you been around," he Lion said.

"That's true," said old Bruh Bear. "I been about everywhere. I've been around the whole forest."

"Then you must know somethin," he Lion said.

"I know lots," said Bruh Bear, slow and quiet-like.

"Tell me what you know about Man," he Lion said. "He think him the king of the forest?"

"Well, now, I'll tell you," said Bruh Bear, "I been around, but I haven't ever come across Man that I know of. Couldn't tell you nothin about him."

So he Lion had to turn back to Bruh Rabbit. He didn't want to but he had to. "So what?" he said to that lil scrawny hare.

"Well, you got to come down from there if you want to see Man," Bruh Rabbit said. "Come down from there and I'll show you him."

He Lion thought a minute, an hour, and a whole day. Then, the next day, he came on down.

He roared just once, "ME AND MYSELF. ME AND MYSELF. Now," he said, "come show me Man."

So they set out. He Lion, Bruh Bear, and Bruh Rabbit. They go along and they go along, rangin the forest. Pretty soon, they come to a clearin. And playin in it is a little fellow about nine years old.

"Is that there Man?" asked he Lion.

"Why no, that one is called Will Be, but it sure is not Man," said Bruh Rabbit.

So they went along and they went along. Pretty soon, they come upon a shade tree. And sleepin under it is an old, olden fellow, about ninety years olden.

"There must lie Man," spoke he Lion. "I knew him wasn't gone be much."

"That's not Man," said Bruh Rabbit. "That fellow is Was Once. You'll know it when you see Man."

So they went on along. He Lion is gettin tired of strollin. So he roars, "ME AND MYSELF. ME AND MYSELF." Upsets Bear so that Bear doubles over and runs and climbs a tree.

"Come down from there," Bruh Rabbit tellin him. So after a while Bear comes down. He keepin his distance from he Lion, anyhow. And they set out some more. Goin along quiet and slow.

In a little while they come to a road. And comin on way down the road, Bruh Rabbit sees Man comin. Man about twenty-one years old. Big and strong, with a big gun over his shoulder.

"There!" Bruh Rabbit says. "See there, he Lion? There's Man. You better go meet him."

"I will," says he Lion. And he sticks out his chest and he roars, "ME AND MYSELF. ME AND MYSELF." All the way to Man he's roarin proud, "ME AND MYSELF, ME AND MYSELF!"

"Come on, Bruh Bear, let's go!" Bruh Rabbit says.

"What for?" Bruh Bear wants to know.

"You better come on!" And Bruh Rabbit takes ahold of Bruh Bear and half drags him to a thicket. And there he makin the Bear hide with him.

For here comes Man. He sees old he Lion real good now. He drops to one knee and he takes aim with his big gun.

Old he Lion is roarin his head off: "ME AND MYSELF! ME AND MYSELF!"

The big gun goes off: PA-LOOOM!

He Lion falls back hard on his tail.

The gun goes off again. PA-LOOOM!

He Lion is flyin through the air. He lands in the thicket.

"Well, did you see Man?" asked Bruh Bear.

"I seen him," said he Lion. "Man spoken to me unkind, and got a great long stick him keepin on his shoulder. Then Man taken that stick down and him speakin real mean. Thunderin at me and lightnin comin from that stick, awful bad. Made me sick. I had to turn around. And Man pointin that stick again and thunderin at me some more. So I come in here, cause it seem like him throwed some stickers at me each time it thunder, too."

"So you've met Man, and you know zactly what that kind of him is," says Bruh Rabbit.

"I surely do know that," he Lion said back.

Awhile after he Lion met Man, things were some better in the forest. Bruh Bear knew what Man looked like so he could keep out of his way. That rabbit always did know to keep out of Man's way. The little animals could go out in the mornin because he Lion was more peaceable. He didn't walk around roarin at the top of his voice all the time. And when he Lion did lift that voice of his, it was like, "Me and Myself and Man. Me and Myself and Man." Like that.

Wasn't too loud atall.

Reader's Response

Do you agree with Bruh Rabbit's decision to let he Lion meet Man face-to-face rather than watch from the bushes? Explain.

MULTICULTURAL CONNECTION

Bruh Rabbit

The character Bruh or Brer Rabbit originally came from the rich folklore of Africa. There Rabbit represented what Africans valued—the notion that intelligence can defeat brute force.

When Africans were enslaved and brought to America, they brought with them their unique oral tradition. Here, Rabbit as trickster took on a larger and more meaningful role. Slaves held Rabbit in high esteem because of his cunning and deception—skills that slaves often found necessary for survival.

In 1880, stories about Brer Rabbit were written and published in Joel Chandler Harris's *Uncle Remus, His Songs and Sayings.* In this collection, Uncle Remus, an elderly slave, tells the adventures of Brer Rabbit to a boy who lives on a southern plantation.

Many stories about Rabbit's adventures are still being told, and through the years, Rabbit has remained a popular character.

Exploring on Your Own

1. Other animals have played a similar role in different cultures. What animals do you know that have played as large a role in a culture's folklore as Rabbit has in African American folk tales?
2. Explore the tradition of the Spanish *cuentos* in the Southwest. What roles do animals play in these folk tales?

Responding to the Selection

Your Response

1. Does the rabbit in the story have the qualities that you associate with rabbits? Explain.
2. Do you feel that he Lion deserved what he got? Why or why not?

Recalling

3. Why does he Lion want to see Man?
4. What happens when he Lion confronts Man?

Interpreting

5. Why is Bruh Rabbit not afraid to seek out he Lion?
6. Why does he Lion roar, "Me and Myself"?
7. Why is he Lion so surprised by Man's actions?
8. How does he Lion change after he meets Man?

Applying

9. Why do some people feel the need to roar like lions?

Analyzing Literature

Appreciating Personification

Personification is a way of speaking that gives human traits to a nonhuman subject. In this folk tale, for example, the animals are given the human abilities to speak and reason.

1. The bear, the lion, and the rabbit have specific human characteristics. What kind of person does each animal represent?
2. In this folk tale, what human traits are admired or valued, and which ones are not?

Critical Thinking and Reading

Interpreting a Tale

Animal tales were the most well known among enslaved Africans. By using animals to represent different kinds of people, enslaved storytellers could secretly describe what their world was like. Personification was an essential technique for them because they could tell tales about their slave owner without directly referring to him. These tales often presented a message.

1. Why was Bruh Rabbit such an important figure to the enslaved Africans and their storytellers?
2. What message does this folk tale present for enslaved Africans?

Thinking and Writing

Writing a Tale

Bruh Rabbit learned from experience to avoid Man. Think of an incident in which you learned a lesson the hard way—through experience. Write a tale, using animal characters, in which you portray the lesson you learned. As you revise, be sure that the lesson is clearly expressed. Write a final draft.

Learning Options

1. **Language.** Dialect is the special variation of language spoken by people of a particular region or group. In the tale you have just read, the author uses the dialect of the enslaved Africans who told the stories. For example, Bruh Bear says "Couldn't tell you nothin about him." In standard English he would say, "I couldn't tell you anything about him." Rewrite the first page of the story in standard English.
2. **Speaking and Listening.** Dialect can best be appreciated when it is read aloud. Practice reading he Lion's description of his encounter with Man. When you are ready, read the passage aloud to the class.
3. **Performance.** Choose a scene from this tale and, with two or three classmates, act it out. You may write a script first, or you can memorize the lines of dialogue from your book. Let your portrayals emphasize the individual qualities of each character.
4. **Art.** Draw or paint a scene from this tale. Share your work with the class.

GUIDE FOR READING

Harold Courlander

(1908–   ) first published this folk tale in 1947 when few African stories from the oral tradition had been written down. Since then, this folklore specialist, novelist, and journalist has collected and published folk tales from around the world, including Africa, the Caribbean, and the Far East.

George Herzog

(1901–   ) is the joint author of *The Cow-Tail Switch and Other West African Stories,* from which "The Cow-Tail Switch" was taken.

The Cow-Tail Switch

Common Elements in Folk Tales

Although "The Cow-Tail Switch" comes from Liberia, on the west coast of Africa, it contains elements found in folk tales around the world. One common element is that often the hero is the youngest son or daughter in a family. This child performs some important task that others are unable to do. Other common elements include a search and a reward.

Focus

One of the ideas expressed in this folk tale is that "a man is not truly dead until he is forgotten." Write this statement on a sheet of paper. In a group of three or four students, write all the ideas that this phrase brings to mind. Decide whether you agree with the statement. As you read "The Cow-Tail Switch," consider whether Ogaloussa was ever truly dead.

Vocabulary

Knowing the following words will help you as you read "The Cow-Tail Switch."

seeped (sēp't) *v.*: Gradually passed through openings (p. 611)

hover (huv′ ər) *v.*: Hang over, linger (p. 611)

mortars (môr′ tərz) *n.*: Hard bowls in which grain is pounded (p. 611)

detained (di tān′ ′d) *v.*: Kept; held back (p. 611)

sinews (sin′ yo͞oz) *n.*: Tendons that give power and strength to muscles (p. 612)

clamor (klam′ ər) *n.*: Outcry; shouting (p. 614)

Spelling Tip

Although their endings sound alike when spoken, remember that the endings of *hover, mortar,* and *clamor* are spelled *er, ar,* and *or,* respectively.

The Cow-Tail Switch

from Liberia

Harold Courlander and George Herzog

"'They brought me back from the land of the dead. . . . I will give this cow-tail switch . . . to the one who did the most to bring me home.'"

Near the edge of the Liberian[1] rain forest,[2] on a hill overlooking the Cavally[3] River, was the village of Kundi.[4] Its rice and cassava[5] fields spread in all directions. Cattle grazed in the grassland near the river. Smoke from the fires in the round clay houses seeped through the palmleaf roofs, and from a distance these faint columns of smoke seemed to hover over the village. Men and boys fished in the river with nets, and women pounded grain in wooden mortars before the houses.

In this village, with his wife and many children, lived a hunter by the name of Ogaloussa.[6]

One morning Ogaloussa took his weapons down from the wall of his house and went into the forest to hunt. His wife and his children went to tend their fields, and drove their cattle out to graze. The day passed, and they ate their evening meal of manioc[7] and fish. Darkness came, but Ogaloussa didn't return.

Another day went by, and still Ogaloussa didn't come back. They talked about it and wondered what could have detained him. A week passed, then a month. Sometimes Ogaloussa's sons mentioned that he hadn't come home. The family cared for the crops, and the sons hunted for game, but after a while they no longer talked about Ogaloussa's disappearance.

Then, one day, another son was born to Ogaloussa's wife. His name was Puli.[8] Puli grew older. He began to sit up and crawl. The time came when Puli began to talk, and the first thing he said was, "Where is my father?"

---

1. Liberian (lī bir′ ē ən) *adj.*: In Liberia, a country on the west coast of Africa.

2. rain forest: A dense forest in a tropical region that has an abundant rainfall throughout the year.

3. Cavally (kä vä′ lē)

4. Kundi (kun′ dē)

5. cassava (kə sä′ və): A tropical plant with edible starchy roots; also called manioc.

6. Ogaloussa (ō′ gä lo͞o′ sä)

7. manioc (man′ ē äk′): The edible starchy roots of the cassava plant.

8. Puli (po͞o′ lē)

African art: staff with seated male figure atop
Dogon or Bozo Mali metalwork, bronze
Metropolitan Museum of Art

The other sons looked across the rice-fields.

"Yes," one of them said. "Where is Father?"

"He should have returned long ago," another one said.

"Something must have happened. We ought to look for him," a third son said.

"He went into the forest, but where will we find him?" another one asked.

"I saw him go," one of them said. "He went that way, across the river. Let us follow the trail and search for him."

So the sons took their weapons and started out to look for Ogaloussa. When they were deep among the great trees and vines of the forest they lost the trail. They searched in the forest until one of them found the trail again. They followed it until they lost the way once more, and then another son found the trail. It was dark in the forest, and many times they became lost. Each time another son found the way. At last they came to a clearing among the trees, and there on the ground scattered about lay Ogaloussa's bones and his rusted weapons. They knew then that Ogaloussa had been killed in the hunt.

One of the sons stepped forward and said, "I know how to put a dead person's bones together." He gathered all of Ogaloussa's bones and put them together, each in its right place.

Another son said, "I have knowlege too. I know how to cover the skeleton with sinews and flesh." He went to work, and he covered Ogaloussa's bones with sinews and flesh.

A third son said, "I have the power to put blood into a body." He went forward and put blood into Ogaloussa's veins, and then he stepped aside.

Another of the sons said, "I can put breath into a body." He did his work, and when he was through they saw Ogaloussa's chest rise and fall.

"I can give the power of movement to a body," another of them said. He put the power of movement into his father's body, and Ogaloussa sat up and opened his eyes.

"I can give him the power of speech," another son said. He gave the body the power of speech, and then he stepped back.

Ogaloussa looked around him. He stood up.

"Where are my weapons?" he asked.

They picked up his rusted weapons from the grass where they lay and gave them to him. They then returned the way they had come, through the forest and the ricefields, until they had arrived once more in the village.

Ogaloussa went into his house. His wife prepared a bath for him and he bathed. She prepared food for him and he ate. Four days he remained in the house, and on the fifth day he came out and shaved his head, because this was what people did when they came back from the land of the dead.

Afterwards he killed a cow for a great feast. He took the cow's tail and braided it. He decorated it with beads and cowry shells[9] and bits of shiny metal. It was a beautiful thing. Ogaloussa carried it with him to important affairs. When there was a dance or an important ceremony he always had it with him. The people of the village thought it was the most beautiful cow-tail switch they had ever seen.

Soon there was a celebration in the

9. cowry (kou′ rē) **shells:** Brightly colored, glossy sea shells.

village because Ogaloussa had returned from the dead. The people dressed in their best clothes, the musicians brought out their instruments, and a big dance began. The drummers beat their drums and the women sang. The people drank much palm wine. Everyone was happy.

Ogaloussa carried his cow-tail switch, and everyone admired it. Some of the men grew bold and came forward to Ogaloussa and asked for the cow-tail switch, but Ogaloussa kept it in his hand. Now and then there was a clamor and much confusion as many people asked for it at once. The women and children begged for it too, but Ogaloussa refused them all.

Finally he stood up to talk. The dancing stopped and people came close to hear what Ogaloussa had to say.

"A long time ago I went into the forest," Ogaloussa said. "While I was hunting I was killed by a leopard. Then my sons came for me. They brought me back from the land of the dead to my village. I will give this cow-tail switch to one of my sons. All of them have done something to bring me back from the dead, but I have only one cow tail to give. I shall give it to the one who did the most to bring me home."

So an argument started.

"He will give it to me!" one of the sons said. "It was I who did the most, for I found the trail in the forest when it was lost!"

"No, he will give it to me!" another son said. "It was I who put his bones together!"

"It was I who covered his bones with sinews and flesh!" another said. "He will give it to me!"

"It was I who gave him the power of movement!" another son said. "I deserve it most!"

Another son said it was he who should have the switch, because he had put blood in Ogaloussa's veins. Another claimed it because he had put breath in the body. Each of the sons argued his right to possess the wonderful cow-tail switch.

Before long not only the sons but the other people of the village were talking. Some of them argued that the son who had put blood in Ogaloussa's veins should get the switch, others that the one who had given Ogaloussa's breath should get it. Some of them believed that all of the sons had done equal things, and they they should share it. They argued back and forth this way until Ogaloussa asked them to be quiet.

"To this son I will give the cow-tail switch, for I owe most to him," Ogaloussa said.

He came forward and bent low and handed it to Puli, the little boy who had been born while Ogaloussa was in the forest.

The people of the village remembered then that the child's first words had been, "Where is my father?" They knew that Ogaloussa was right.

For it was a saying among them that a man is not really dead until he is forgotten.

Reader's Response

What surprised you most about this folk tale?

Responding to the Selection

Your Response

1. Do you think Puli deserved the switch? Explain.

Recalling

2. Describe the way each son reacts to Ogaloussa's disappearance.
3. Why does everyone want the cow-tail switch?

Interpreting

4. What typical human traits do you see displayed in the argument between the sons?
5. How does Puli's question do the most to bring his father back to life?
6. What does the last sentence of the story mean in the context of this tale?

Applying

7. Puli is rewarded for starting the process that brought his father back to life. Do you think people deserve rewards for performing services to others?

Analyzing Literature

Recognizing Common Elements in Folk Tales

Folk tales from around the world have some elements in common. One is that the hero is often the youngest son or daughter.

1. Why is the youngest son or daughter frequently a hero in folk tales?
2. Name other folk tales or fairy tales in which the youngest son or daughter is the hero.
3. What other elements in this folk tale have you noticed in other tales?

Critical Thinking and Reading

Finding Realistic and Unrealistic Details

Realistic details in a story are details that are true to life—things that can actually happen. **Unrealistic details** are strange events that seem impossible in real life. In "The Cow-Tail Switch," most details, such as the description of the Jabo village, are realistic but a few important ones are not.

1. Give three examples of realistic details.
2. What important details seem unrealistic?
3. Why do you think the writer includes unrealistic details?

Thinking and Writing

Extending a Folk Tale

Write a continuation of this folk tale. Imagine that Puli is now your age. Ogaloussa, who kept the cow-tail switch wrapped up while Puli was very young, gives it to Puli so he can take it to a ceremony for the first time. Some other boys are jealous. Describe what happens. How does Puli, a thoughtful and caring boy, respond? Try to include details in your story that suggest it is set in an African village. Carefully proofread your story. Write a final draft.

Learning Options

1. **Performance.** Form a group with several classmates. Together, choose a scene from "The Cow-Tail Switch" that you would like to dramatize. One group member should be the narrator and the others should read the words of the characters. Try to imitate the way you think the characters would speak. After you have practiced, present the scene for your classmates.
2. **Speaking and Listening.** With a partner, make a list of questions you would have liked to ask Ogaloussa after he was brought back to life. Then choose the roles you wish to play and do an interview with Ogaloussa. Use the interview to write an article for the village newspaper.

GUIDE FOR READING

James Thurber

(1894–1961), who was born in Columbus, Ohio, was a noted humorist and illustrator. As a young boy, Thurber was in an archery accident which left him blind in one eye. Despite his disability, Thurber pursued a career as a journalist. While a staff writer for *The New Yorker* magazine, Thurber published many of his contemporary fables. Like all fables, "The Tiger Who Would Be King," is on one level an entertaining tale, but on another level teaches a lesson about life.

The Tiger Who Would Be King

Fables

Fables are brief tales, in prose or verse, that teach a lesson. Usually the lesson, or moral, of a fable is stated at the end. Fables frequently show the failings or weaknesses of people in an entertaining manner. Some fables have human characters, while others, such as Thurber's "The Tiger Who Would Be King," feature animals who act like people.

Focus

Do you remember the last time you got into an argument with someone because you both wanted the same thing? How did the argument make you feel? Were you satisfied because you got what you wanted or disappointed because you did not? Did you feel bad about having an argument? In the center of a piece of paper, write the word "argument." Then around the word write all the words and phrases that come to mind when you think about your last argument. As you read "The Tiger Who Would Be King," decide whether arguing is the best way to solve a problem.

Vocabulary

Knowing the following words will help you as you read "The Tiger Who Would Be King."

prowled (prould) *v.*: Quietly and secretly crawled (p. 617)
inquired (in kwīrd′) *v.*: Asked (p. 617)
repulse (ri puls′) *v.*: To drive back; to repel an attack (p. 618)
fevered (fē′ vərd) *adj.*: In a state of heightened intensity (p. 618)
gibbous (gib′ əs) *adj.*: Half or partially illuminated (p. 618)
monarch (män′ ərk) *n.*: Supreme ruler (p. 618)
surveyed (sər vā′ d) *v.*: Saw; looked at (p. 618)

The Tiger Who Would Be King

James Thurber

It was a terrible fight. . . . All the animals of the jungle joined in, some taking the side of the tiger and others the side of the lion.

One morning the tiger woke up in the jungle and told his mate that he was king of beasts.

"Leo, the lion, is king of beasts," she said.

"We need a change," said the tiger. "The creatures are crying for a change."

The tigress listened but she could hear no crying, except that of her cubs.

"I'll be king of beasts by the time the moon rises," said the tiger. "It will be a yellow moon with black stripes, in my honor."

"Oh, sure," said the tigress as she went to look after her young, one of whom, a male, very like his father, had got an imaginary thorn in his paw.

The tiger prowled through the jungle till he came to the lion's den. "Come out," he roared, "and greet the king of beasts! The king is dead, long live the king!"

Inside the den, the lioness woke her mate. "The king is here to see you," she said.

"What king?" he inquired, sleepily.

"The king of beasts," she said.

TIGER
Morris Hirshfield
Abby Aldrich Rockefeller Fund
Museum of Modern Art, New York

"I am the king of beasts," roared Leo, and he charged out of the den to defend his crown against the pretender.

It was a terrible fight, and it lasted until the setting of the sun. All the animals of the jungle joined in, some taking the side of the tiger and others the side of the lion. Every creature from the aardvark[1] to the zebra took part in the struggle to overthrow the lion or to repulse the tiger, and some did not know which they were fighting for, and some fought for both, and some fought whoever was nearest, and some fought for the sake of fighting.

"What are we fighting for?" someone asked the aardvark.

"The old order,"[2] said the aardvark.

"What are we dying for?" someone asked the zebra.

"The new order,"[3] said the zebra.

When the moon rose, fevered and gibbous,[4] it shone upon a jungle in which nothing stirred except a macaw[5] and a cockatoo,[6] screaming in horror. All the beasts were dead except the tiger, and his days were numbered and his time was ticking away. He was monarch of all he surveyed, but it didn't seem to mean anything.

MORAL: *You can't very well be king of beasts if there aren't any.*

---

1. **aardvark** (ärd′ värk′) *n.*: A burrowing African mammal with a long snout for feeding on ants and termites.
2. **old order:** The existing government with the lion as the ruler.
3. **new order:** The new government of which the tiger wants to be the ruler.
4. **gibbous** (gib′ əs) *adj.*: More than half but less than completely illuminated.
5. **macaw** (mə kô′) *n.*: A large parrot of Central or South America with bright colors and a harsh voice.
6. **cockatoo** (käk′ ə to͞o′) *n.*: A crested parrot of Australia and the East Indies, with white plumage tinged with yellow or pink.

Responding to the Selection

Your Response

1. If you could have negotiated with the lion and the tiger, what would you have suggested they do?

Recalling

2. Why does the Tiger suddenly decide he wants to be king? What support does he have to claim the kingship?

Interpreting

3. The Tiger's son, who is said to be like his father, is ailing from an imaginary thorn in his paw. What does this detail imply about both father and son?
4. Some animals fought for the Tiger, some for the Lion, and others "fought for the sake of fighting." What does this suggest about the jungle animals? About people?

Applying

5. Why might a fable with animal characters teach a lesson better than a tale with human characters?

Analyzing Literature

Understanding a Fable

A **fable** is a short tale, in prose or verse, that teaches a lesson called a moral. In this fable Thurber uses animals who act like humans. By examining the animals' behavior, we can learn a valuable lesson about life.

1. State the moral of this fable in your own words.
2. Explain why you agree or disagree with it.

YOUR WRITING PROCESS

Inventing an Animal Tale

Are you familiar with cartoons? If you are, then you probably have a favorite cartoon character, such as Roadrunner or Bugs Bunny. Each episode of the cartoon shows the characters' behavior that gets them in and out of difficult situations. After seeing a few shows, you can usually predict how the characters will get themselves into and out of trouble.

Similarly in folk literature you read about characters getting into and out of trouble. Coyote, for example, appears in two different tales in this unit. Although the stories are from different countries, his character is basically the same. Sly, clever Coyote is not evil, but he does try to get away with whatever he can. He uses his wits to get out of trouble or to accomplish something. His actions may benefit someone else—like the mouse in "Señor Coyote and the Tricked Trickster"—but his actions almost always benefit himself as well.

These characters are all animals, but they do have characteristics shared by humans. This is one reason why audiences enjoy these characters. As they get into and out of situations, we can put ourselves into their places and perhaps learn something from their mistakes or behaviors.

You, too, can create a character and put him or her into tough situations.

Your Turn

Invent a character and make up a folk tale about it. Your goal is to write a tale about an animal who gets into a tough situation. Your audience is everyone who enjoys folk tales.

Prewriting

1. Choose any animal. On a sheet of paper, list the animal's main characteristics. If a certain quality is generally associated with it, list that quality. If you say wolf, for example, most people think "crafty." Then list the other human characteristics you want your animal to have.

2. Shape an episode. Use the following prompts as the structure of your episode. You can use whole sentences, or you can jot down notes for the story.

- Describe your character walking down a road or path somewhere. Describe as much of the setting as you want.
- Your character sees another character coming from the opposite direction. This character is an enemy. Describe this character.
- The other character threatens your character.
- Suddenly some awful disaster occurs to both of them in the same place.
- Your character gets them out of the dilemma.
- Both continue along the road together.

Here is a part of one student's notes using this formula:

```
     --pig walking along the
road--light rain falling; he
enjoys slopping barefoot through
the mud
     --pig looks up, coming from
the other direction is a wolf!
Trouble! Wolves eat pigs!
     --pig thinks fast, decides
to be nice to the wolf--maybe
the wolf won't bother him
     "Hi, wolf," says the pig.
"What's up?"
     "Your life is up, you silly
pig!" answers the wolf.
     "No, wolf, please! Don't
gobble me up!" screams the pig.
     --suddenly rain increases,
lightning strikes. A tree falls,
pins down the pair
     "Well, pig. What do we do
now? I can't very well gobble you
up, but I have a feeling neither
of us is going to get out of
here!"
     "Well, wolf. I can show you
how to get out of here if you
promise not to hurt me."
```

Drafting

Write a draft of your story. Put all your notes into complete sentences. Add details that will help develop your tale.

Revising

Use the revision checklist on page 751. In addition, read your draft to a writing partner and ask questions such as the following:

- Who are the characters?
- What are the characteristics of each?
- Would you like to hear more details about either of the characters?
- Would you like to know more details about the animals' difficult situation?

Using your partner's responses, write another draft of your story.

Proofreading

Consult the guidelines for proofreading on page 753. Remember to proofread especially for punctuation in dialogue. Make a final copy of your folk tale.

Publishing

Have a group read-around. Select those tales your group likes best. Prepare a dramatic reading or a Readers Theater of these tales, and record them on tape. Add sound effects if you like. Lend your tape to another class to enjoy.

Classic Myths

THE CHARIOT OF APOLLO
Odilon Redon

GUIDE FOR READING

Olivia E. Coolidge

(1908–) grew up and was educated in London, England. She spent several years as a teacher of English, Latin, and Greek in both the United States and in Europe. She has written many stories, myths, and biographical sketches for young people. Some of her works include *Lives of Famous Romans* and *The Presidency of Abraham Lincoln.* The story "Arachne" is included in her book, *Greek Myths.*

Arachne

Myth

A **myth** is an ancient story created to explain natural events. Gods, goddesses, and heroes are among the characters in myths. In addition to explaining events in nature, some myths also present a lesson on how to live, or serve as a warning to follow society's rules. This myth explains the origin of the spider and teaches about the consequences of boasting.

Focus

Sometimes pride is considered a virtue, a good quality; sometimes it is a vice, a weakness. For example, it is fine to be proud of your family or your school, but it is not so admirable to be proud of your good looks. With a small group of classmates, make a list of the things one should be proud of and the things one should be modest about. As you read about what happened to Arachne, think of what advice you would have given her about pride.

Vocabulary

Knowing the following words will help you as you read "Arachne."

obscure (əb skyoor′) *adj.*: Unknown; hidden (p. 623)
indignantly (in dig′ nənt lē) *adv.*: Done with anger about something that seems unfair (p. 623)
immortal (i môr′ t'l) *adj.*: Living forever (p. 625)
mortal (môr′ t'l) *adj.*: Referring to humans, who must eventually die (p. 625)
obstinacy (äb′ stə nə sē) *n.*: Stubbornness (p. 625)
skeins (skānz) *n.*: Coils of thread or yarn (p. 625)
resorted (ri zôrt′ id) *v.*: Turned to for help (p. 626)

Spelling Tip

Remember this rule: Place *i* before *e* except after *c* or when sounded like *a* as in *neighbor* or *weigh. Skein* is sounded like *a*, so you spell it with *e* before *i.*

Arachne

from ancient Greece

Olivia E. Coolidge

" 'If Athene herself were to come down and compete with me, she could do no better than I.' "

Arachne[1] was a maiden who became famous throughout Greece, though she was neither wellborn nor beautiful and came from no great city. She lived in an obscure little village, and her father was a humble dyer of wool. In this he was very skillful, producing many varied shades, while above all he was famous for the clear, bright scarlet which is made from shellfish, and which was the most glorious of all the colors used in ancient Greece. Even more skillful than her father was Arachne. It was her task to spin the fleecy wool into a fine, soft thread and to weave it into cloth on the high, standing loom within the cottage. Arachne was small and pale from much working. Her eyes were light and her hair was a dusty brown, yet she was quick and graceful, and her fingers, roughened as they were, went so fast that it was hard to follow their flickering movements. So soft and even was her thread, so fine her cloth, so gorgeous her embroidery, that soon her products were known all over Greece. No one had ever seen the like of them before.

At last Arachne's fame became so great that people used to come from far and wide to watch her working. Even the graceful nymphs[2] would steal in from stream or forest and peep shyly through the dark doorway, watching in wonder the white arms of Arachne as she stood at the loom and threw the shuttle from hand to hand between the hanging threads, or drew out the long wool, fine as a hair, from the distaff[3] as she sat spinning. "Surely Athene[4] herself must have taught her," people would murmur to one another. "Who else could know the secret of such marvelous skill?"

Arachne was used to being wondered at, and she was immensely proud of the skill that had brought so many to look on her. Praise was all she lived for, and it displeased her greatly that people should think anyone, even a goddess, could teach her anything. Therefore when she heard them murmur, she would stop her work and turn round indignantly to say, "With my own ten fingers I gained this skill, and by hard practice from

---

1. **Arachne** (ä räk′ nē)

2. **nymphs** (nimfz) *n.*: Minor nature goddesses, thought of as beautiful maidens living in rivers, trees, and so on.

3. **distaff** (dis′ taf) *n.*: A stick on which flax or wool is wound for use in spinning.

4. **Athene** (ə thē′ nə): The Greek goddess of wisdom, skills, and warfare.

early morning till night. I never had time to stand looking as you people do while another maiden worked. Nor if I had, would I give Athene credit because the girl was more skillful than I. As for Athene's weaving, how could there be finer cloth or more beautiful embroidery than mine? If Athene herself were to come down and compete with me, she could do no better than I."

One day when Arachne turned round with such words, an old woman answered her, a gray old woman, bent and very poor,

ARACHNE from GREEK GODS AND HEROES
Arvis Stewart

who stood leaning on a staff and peering at Arachne amid the crowd of onlookers. "Reckless girl," she said, "how dare you claim to be equal to the immortal gods themselves? I am an old woman and have seen much. Take my advice and ask pardon of Athene for your words. Rest content with your fame of being the best spinner and weaver that mortal eyes have ever beheld."

"Stupid old woman," said Arachne indignantly, "who gave you a right to speak in this way to me? It is easy to see that you were never good for anything in your day, or you would not come here in poverty and rags to gaze at my skill. If Athene resents my words, let her answer them herself. I have challenged her to a contest, but she, of course, will not come. It is easy for the gods to avoid matching their skill with that of men."

At these words the old woman threw down her staff and stood erect. The wondering onlookers saw her grow tall and fair and stand clad in long robes of dazzling white. They were terribly afraid as they realized that they stood in the presence of Athene. Arachne herself flushed red for a moment, for she had never really believed that the goddess would hear her. Before the group that was gathered there she would not give in; so pressing her pale lips together in obstinacy and pride, she led the goddess to one of the great looms and set herself before the other. Without a word both began to thread the long woolen strands that hang from the rollers, and between which the shuttle[5] moves back and forth. Many skeins lay heaped beside them to use, bleached white, and gold, and scarlet, and other shades, varied as the rainbow. Arachne had never thought of giving credit for her success to her father's skill in dyeing, though in actual truth the colors were as remarkable as the cloth itself.

Soon there was no sound in the room but the breathing of the onlookers, the whirring of the shuttles, and the creaking of the wooden frames as each pressed the thread up into place or tightened the pegs by which the whole was held straight. The excited crowd in the doorway began to see that the skill of both in truth was very nearly equal, but that, however the cloth might turn out, the goddess was the quicker of the two. A pattern of many pictures was growing on her loom. There was a border of twined branches of the olive, Athene's favorite tree, while in the middle, figures began to appear. As they looked at the glowing colors, the spectators realized that Athene was weaving into her pattern a last warning to Arachne. The central figure was the goddess herself competing with Poseidon[6] for possession of the city of Athens; but in the four corners were mortals who had tried to strive with gods and pictures of the awful fate that had overtaken them. The goddess ended a little before Arachne and stood back from her marvelous work to see what the maiden was doing.

Never before had Arachne been matched against anyone whose skill was equal, or even nearly equal to her own. As she stole glances from time to time at Athene and saw the goddess working swiftly, calmly, and always a little faster than herself, she became angry instead of frightened, and an evil thought came into her head. Thus as Athene stepped back a pace to watch Arachne fin-

---

5. shuttle (shut′ 'l) *n.*: In weaving, a device to carry the woof thread back and forth between warp threads.
6. Poseidon (pō sī′ d'n): Greek god of the seas and oceans.

ishing her work, she saw that the maiden had taken for her design a pattern of scenes which showed evil or unworthy actions of the gods, how they had deceived fair maidens, resorted to trickery, and appeared on earth from time to time in the form of poor and humble people. When the goddess saw this insult glowing in bright colors on Arachne's loom, she did not wait while the cloth was judged, but stepped forward, her gray eyes blazing with anger, and tore Arachne's work across. Then she struck Arachne across the face. Arachne stood there a moment, struggling with anger, fear, and pride. "I will not live under this insult," she cried, and seizing a rope from the wall, she made a noose and would have hanged herself.

The goddess touched the rope and touched the maiden. "Live on, wicked girl," she said. "Live on and spin, both you and your descendants. When men look at you they may remember that it is not wise to strive with Athene." At that the body of Arachne shriveled up, and her legs grew tiny, spindly, and distorted. There before the eyes of the spectators hung a little dusty brown spider on a slender thread.

All spiders descend from Arachne, and as the Greeks watched them spinning their thread wonderfully fine, they remembered the contest with Athene and thought that it was not right for even the best of men to claim equality with the gods.

Reader's Response

If you were Arachne, would you have challenged the goddess Athene? Why or why not?

MULTICULTURAL CONNECTION

Goddesses of Wisdom

The Greek goddess Athene. In the story of Arachne, the goddess Athene is an expert spinner and weaver. Although she was the patron of arts and crafts, Athene was better known as the goddess of war and as the goddess of wisdom. You know that Athene was a warrior goddess because she is often shown wearing a helmet and armor. She protected the Greeks in battle by showing them how to outwit their enemies. Because Athene was often accompanied by an owl, Greek soldiers were always happy to see an owl during battle. They believed it was a sign that the goddess was present to protect them. The owl's reputation for wisdom is due to its being associated with the goddess.

Goddesses of wisdom in other cultures. The Romans had a set of gods and goddesses who closely resembled those of the Greeks. Wisdom was ruled by Minerva. She was, like Athene, a warrior.

In Celtic Britain, there was a witch-goddess named Ceridwen. She brewed a potion that would give universal knowledge.

The ancient Armenians had Anahit, who represented fertility and wisdom. The Armenians called her "mother of all knowledge."

In India, the Hindu religion has Sarasvati, a goddess of wisdom, speech, and art and favored deity of those who wish to learn.

Exploring and Sharing

While many ancient religions had goddesses of wisdom, others had gods of wisdom. Find out who Thoth (or Thot), Mimir, and Omoigane were, and which groups worshiped them. Share your findings with your classmates.

Responding to the Selection

Your Response

1. Do you feel Arachne deserved the punishment she received? Why or why not?

Recalling

2. Describe Arachne's skills.
3. Who is the "gray old woman" who appears in the crowd? What advice does she offer Arachne?
4. Describe the cloths woven by Arachne and Athene. What is depicted on each cloth?
5. How does Athene give Arachne a last warning?

Interpreting

6. Explain why Arachne refuses to accept the advice from the old woman.
7. Summarize the "sentence" Athene imposes on Arachne at the end of the myth. What lesson might the Greeks have learned from this myth?

Applying

8. Pride can be both helpful and harmful. Give examples of situations that show both possibilities.

Analyzing Literature

Understanding Myth

Myths have many purposes. They explain acts of nature, they entertain, and they may also teach a lesson about the way to live.

1. What in nature does this myth explain?
2. What lesson about ways to live does this myth illustrate?
3. How is this myth entertaining?

Critical Thinking and Reading

Comparing and Contrasting Characters

The characters portrayed in this myth display similarities as well as differences in personality and behavior. When you examine characters' similarities, you are **comparing** them. When you examine their differences, you are **contrasting** them. Sometimes you can come to a better understanding of yourself or others by comparing and contrasting personalities and behaviors.

1. In what two ways are Arachne and Athene alike?
2. How do the two women seem to contrast?
3. Which woman do you think was the stronger personality, Arachne or Athene? Explain.

Thinking and Writing

Writing About Spiders

Write a paper in which you take a stand on whether the nature of spiders is beautiful or ugly. Begin by making a cluster of your notions of spiders. Include all of your impressions of spiders. Write a draft of your paper, making sure to give reasons for your opinions. Exchange your paper with a writing partner. Share ideas on how to improve each other's writing. Write a final draft.

Learning Options

1. **Speaking and Listening.** Choose a partner and imagine that the two of you are journalists covering the contest between Athene and Arachne. Create a "play-by-play" radio-style commentary for the event. You may wish to listen to a radio broadcast of a sporting event to get some ideas. Practice your dialogue before reading it for the class.
2. **Cross-curricular Connection.** Arachne wove images of the misdeeds of the gods and goddesses of Greece. What was in the weaving that made Athene so angry? Locate a book about Greek mythology in your library. Find one or two incidents that Arachne might have portrayed in her weaving. Share your information with the class.

GUIDE FOR READING

Alice Low

(1926–   ) has written seventeen children's books and is currently the editor of Children's Choice book club. Low grew up around children's books; her mother was also a children's book author. Low spent her youth making books and puppets, giving plays, and singing. Since then, she has written scripts for numerous filmstrips, a musical play for children, and articles for young adult magazines.

Orpheus

Myth

Myths are stories about gods, goddesses, and heroes passed from one generation to another. Many Greek myths were taken over by the Romans. Greek and Roman myths have had a great deal of influence on our culture. For centuries writers, artists, and musicians have used the myths or mythological characters as the basis of their own work. "Orpheus" has influenced writers, musicians, and filmmakers around the world.

Focus

To the ancient Greeks, the underworld was the place of the dead. When a person died, he or she was ferried across the river Styx by Charon, the ferryman. Once in the underworld, a person could not return to the world of the living except under very special circumstances. The underworld was also a place of punishment and reward. The Greeks were highly imaginative when it came to creating appropriate punishments for the wicked and rewards for the good. Form a group of four students. Brainstorm about what you think Hades, the underworld of the Greek myths, was like. As you read "Orpheus," compare your group's ideas to the underworld in the myth.

Vocabulary

Knowing the following words will help you as you read "Orpheus."

inspiration (in′ spə rā′ shən) *n.*: Something that brings on creative ability; motivation (p. 629)

lyre (līr) *n.*: A small stringed instrument, similar to a harp (p. 629)

entranced (in transt′) *v.*: Charmed; put into a trance (p. 629)

condemned (kən dem'd′) *v.*: Doomed (p. 630)

summoned (sum′ ən'd) *v.*: Sent for; called forth (p. 630)

Spelling Tip

Notice that in the word *condemned* the consonant *n* is silent.

Orpheus

from ancient Greece

Alice Low

"When stern Hades heard Orpheus's song, he began to weep."

There were nine goddesses called Muses. Born of Zeus[1] and a Titan[2] named Mnemosyne,[3] each muse presided over a different art or science.

Calliope,[4] one of these sisters, was the inspiration of poets and musicians. She was the mother of Orpheus[5] (a mortal because his father was one) and gave to her son a remarkable talent for music.

Orpheus played his lyre so sweetly that he charmed all things on earth. Men and women forgot their cares when they gathered around him to listen. Wild beasts lay down as if they were tame, entranced by his soothing notes. Even rocks and trees followed him, and the rivers changed their direction to hear him play.

Orpheus loved a young woman named Eurydice,[6] and when they were married, they looked forward to many years of happiness together. But soon after, Eurydice stepped on a poisonous snake and died.

Orpheus roamed the earth, singing sad melodies to try to overcome his grief. But it was no use. He longed for Eurydice so deeply that he decided to follow her to the underworld. He said to himself, "No mortal has ever been there before, but I must try to bring back my beloved Eurydice. I will charm Persephone[7] and Hades[8] with my music and win Eurydice's release."

He climbed into a cave and through a dark passage that led to the underworld. When he reached the river Styx,[9] he plucked his lyre, and Charon,[10] the ferryman, was so charmed that he rowed him across. Then he struck his lyre again, and Cerberus,[11] the fierce three-headed dog who guarded the gates, heard the sweet music and lay still to let him pass.

---

1. Zeus (zo͞os): Ruler of heaven and earth, of all gods and all humans.

2. Titan (tīt′ ′n): A giant god; one of a race of giant gods who warred with the gods of Olympus.

3. Mnemosyne (nē mäs′ i nē)

4. Calliope (kə lī′ ə pē)

5. Orpheus (ôr′ fē us)

6. Eurydice (yo͞o rid′ i sē)

7. Persephone (pər sef′ ə nē): Queen of Hades; the daughter of Zeus and Demeter.

8. Hades (hā′ dēz): Name for the underworld. Also, the name for the god of the underworld; husband of Persephone.

9. Styx (stiks): The river which flows around Hades nine times. It is the river across which Charon ferries the dead.

10. Charon (ker′ ən): A god of the underworld. For a fee placed in the mouth of the dead at the time of burial, Charon would ferry the souls over the river Styx to Hades. Few passed Charon without proper burial, except Orpheus, who charmed him with his lyre.

11. Cerberus (sʉr′ bər əs)

Orpheus continued to play his lyre tenderly as he made his way through the gloomy underworld. The ghosts cried when they heard his sad music. Sisyphus,[12] who had been condemned to roll a rock uphill forever, stopped his fruitless work to listen. Tantalus,[13] who had been sentenced to stand in a pool of receding water, stopped trying to quench his thirst. And even the wheel to which Ixion[14] was tied as punishment stopped turning for one moment.

At last Orpheus came to the palace of Hades and Persephone, king and queen of the underworld. Before they could order him to leave, he began his gentle song, pleading for Eurydice.

When stern Hades heard Orpheus's song, he began to weep. Cold Persephone was so moved that, for the first time in all her months in the underworld, her heart melted.

"Oh, please, my husband," she said to Hades, "let Eurydice be reunited with Orpheus."

And Hades replied, "I, too, feel the sadness of Orpheus. I cannot refuse him."

They summoned Eurydice, and the two lovers clasped each other and turned to leave.

"Wait!" said Hades to Orpheus. "Eurydice is yours to take back to earth on one condition."

"What is that?" asked Orpheus.

"She must follow you, and you must not look back at her until you are on earth again."

"I understand," said Orpheus. "And I am forever grateful."

Orpheus and Eurydice left the underworld and made their way through the dark passage that led to the upper world. At last they reached the cave through which Orpheus had descended.

"I can see daylight ahead," called Orpheus to Eurydice. "We are almost there." But Eurydice had not heard him, and so she did not answer.

---

12. Sisyphus (sis′ ə fəs): Condemned for the crimes of stealing, killing, and insulting Hades, the god of the underworld.

13. Tantalus (tan′ tə ləs): Condemned for stealing a favorite golden dog of Zeus; giving mortals ambrosia and nectar—the food and drink of the gods; and killing his own son and serving him to the gods for food.

14. Ixion (iks′ ī än): Claimed to be the first murderer; he murdered his father-in-law.

ORPHEUS from GREEK GODS AND HEROES
Arvis Stewart

Orpheus turned to make sure that she was still following him. He caught one last glimpse of her with her arms stretched out to him. And then she disappeared, swallowed up by darkness.

"Farewell," he heard her cry as she was carried back to the underworld.

Orpheus tried to follow her, but this time the gods would not allow it. And so he wandered the earth alone. He sang his sad songs to the rocks and the trees and longed for the time when he, too, would die and be reunited with his beloved Eurydice in the underworld.

Reader's Response
If you were Orpheus, would you have looked back to see if Eurydice was following? Why or why not?

RESPONDING TO THE SELECTION

Your Response

1. What message do you think this myth was intended to convey?

Recalling

2. What effect does Orpheus's music have on people and gods? Give three examples.
3. Why does Orpheus decide to rescue his wife from the underworld?
4. Why does Orpheus look back to see if Eurydice is following him?

Interpreting

5. Sisyphus, Tantalus, and Ixion are three people condemned to punishment in the underworld. What do their punishments suggest about the gods' attitude toward mortals?
6. What reasons might the gods have for allowing Orpheus and Eurydice to be reunited?
7. Explain why the gods put a condition on permitting Orpheus and his bride to return to earth.

Applying

8. This myth has been a source of inspiration for writers, artists, and musicians through the ages. Why do you think this myth has been so popular?

ANALYZING LITERATURE

Understanding Myth

Myths are ancient stories about gods and heroes. Some myths tell of the relationship between the gods and humans.

1. To whom does Orpheus owe his talent? Why was he able to win the sympathy of the gods?
2. In what situations were the gods willing to help humans? What limitations were put on their help?

THINKING AND WRITING

Writing Lyrics

Orpheus was a great musician. Imagine that as he planned his return to the underworld, he hired you as a lyricist to help him write the perfect persuasive song—the one that would convince the gods to give him a second chance to take Eurydice back to earth. Draft the lyrics to his song. You may put your lyrics to either a familiar or an original melody. Begin by listing words associated with the myth and with your purpose of persuading Hades and Persephone. Then write your song, using some of the words from your list. Allow another person to read and comment on your lyrics. Make any changes you think would strengthen the message in your song. Then write a final draft.

GUIDE FOR READING

Anne Terry White

(1896–   ), who was born in Russia, has worked as a teacher, a social worker, and a translator of Russian literature. White has spent many years writing literature for children and young adults. Her collection of Greek myths, such as "The Gorgon's Head," are among her best-loved children's tales.

The Gorgon's Head

The Hero

One of the most familiar figures in oral tradition is the **hero**, a character of great courage and nobility. The hero goes on quests, rescues people in trouble, wins battles with enemies, and overcomes other seemingly impossible obstacles. The hero's ability to cope with perils and monsters sets him apart from other humans. Often in the Greek myths, the gods were known to favor as well as challenge the heroes. One well-known hero whom the gods favor is Perseus.

Focus

Many myths are based on the idea that people cannot avoid their fate or destiny. Do you believe that this is true? In a small group, make a list of reasons why you believe—or do not believe—in fate. As you read "The Gorgon's Head," consider the role of fate in this myth.

Vocabulary

Knowing the following words will help you as you read "The Gorgon's Head."

evade (i vād′) *v.*: Avoid; escape (p. 633)

perilous (per′ əl əs) *adj.*: Dangerous (p. 634)

venomous (ven′ əm əs) *adj.*: Poisonous (p. 636)

abashed (ə basht′) *v.*: Ashamed (p. 636)

appease (ə pēz′) *v.*: Satisfy; gratify; please (p. 636)

valorous (val′ ər əs) *adj.*: Brave (p. 636)

dowry (dou′ rē) *n.*: Property that a woman brings to her husband at marriage (p. 637)

Spelling Tip

Perilous, venomous, and *valorous* end with *-ous,* a suffix that means "full of" or "having much." These adjectives are formed by adding *ous* to the root words, *peril, venom,* and *valor.*

The Gorgon's Head

from ancient Greece

Anne Terry White

". . . none may look upon the Gorgons and live[.] The sight of them . . . turns men to stone."

Acrisius,[1] King of Argos,[2] came home from Delphi[3] with a heavy heart, for he had received a dreadful oracle.[4]

"No sons shall be born to you," the priestess had told him. "But you shall have a grandson, and by his hand you shall die."

Now the king had an only daughter, who was yet a maiden. So in his distress he thought: "I will evade my fate. I will shut Danae[5] up away from the sight of men in a house of bronze all sunk underground." And he carried out his cruel plan.

But Acrisius forgot to take the gods into account. Part of the roof of the house was open to the sky. And one day, as lovely Danae sat sadly looking up at the passing clouds, Zeus[6] beheld the maiden. Changing himself into a shower of gold, he stormed into her chamber.

When afterwards a son was born to Danae, she hid him from her father's sight. Nevertheless, the king discovered the baby and was more than ever filled with fear. He dared not kill the little Perseus[7] directly lest the gods avenge the murder. Instead, he had a great chest built, placed Danae and her boy in it, and set them adrift upon the sea.

All day and all night the chest tossed upon the waves. Danae lulled her child with song, and he slept. But when dawn came, a great wave picked up the chest and carried it close to the tiny island of Seraphos.[8]

It happened that a fisherman, Dictys[9] by name, saw the chest bobbing on the waves close to the shore. He dragged the box to land and opened it. When he beheld the pitiful mother with the helpless little child, his heart was moved. He took them both to his wife, for Dictys was childless, and there in the kindly fisherfolk's humble home Perseus grew up.

Now Danae had been a beautiful maiden.

1. Acrisius (ə kris′ ē əs)
2. Argos (är′ gōs): A city in Greece.
3. Delphi (del′ fī): The site of the most famous oracle of Apollo. The ancient Greeks believed that Delphi was the middle of the earth.
4. oracle (ôr′ ə k′l) *n.*: A prophecy or message. Also, a person of great knowledge or wisdom.
5. Danae (dan′ ā ē): Daughter of Acrisius.
6. Zeus (zo͞os)
7. Perseus (pʉr′ sē us)
8. Seraphos (sə ri′ fōs): An island in the Aegean Sea.
9. Dictys (dik′ tis)

And when Perseus was grown into a fine tall youth, she was still beautiful. So it was not strange that King Polydectes,[10] who was Dictys' brother, fell in love with her and made her his wife. But the King hated the youth—just because Danae doted on him—and sought some way to be rid of him.

At last Polydectes said to his stepson, "The time has come, Perseus, for you to win glory for yourself in some bold adventure."

Young Perseus thought so, too. But what should the adventure be?

"I think," the wily Polydectes said, "it would be a good idea for you to cut off the Medusa's[11] head. That would bring you the greatest fame."

All unsuspecting, Perseus set off to find the Medusa, not knowing in the least how perilous an adventure he had undertaken. For the Medusa was one of the three Gorgons, terrible winged monsters who lived alone on an island. They had teeth like the tusks of a boar, hands of brass, and snakes instead of hair. Perseus did not know where to look for the Gorgons. Nor did he know which of them was Medusa. And this was important, for Medusa was the only one of the three that could be slain.

From place to place the prince went in his quest, getting more and more discouraged. Then one day he beheld a young man of great beauty, wearing winged sandals and a winged cap, and carrying in his hand a wand around which two golden serpents twined. Perseus knew at once that this was Hermes[12] and was overjoyed when the god said:

"Perseus, I approve the high adventure you have in mind. But you must be properly equipped for it. Without the winged sandals, the magic wallet, and the helmet of invisibility which the Nymphs[13] of the North possess, you can never succeed. Now, I cannot tell you where the Nymphs live, but I will take you to the Gray Women.[14] You can find out from them."

"And will they indeed tell me?" Perseus asked.

"Not willingly," Hermes replied. "But you can make them do it. They have but one eye among the three. Snatch it from them as they pass it from one to another and none can see. And do not give it back till they tell you what you want to know."

With that, Hermes gave Perseus a magnificent curved sword.

"You will need it," he said, "for the Medusa's scales are hard as metal."

Perseus had just taken the sword when there was a sudden brightness in the sky, and he beheld the goddess Athene[15] descending toward them.

"Of what use will be your sword, my brother," she said to Hermes, "when none may look on the Gorgons and live? The sight of them, as you well know, turns men to stone. Take my bright shield, Perseus. Look into it instead of at the monster as you approach to do battle, and you will see the Medusa reflected as in a mirror."

So saying, the goddess disappeared, and the brightness with her.

On and on with his god-companion Perseus journeyed, farther than man had ever been. At last they came to the end of the

10. Polydectes (päl ē dək′ tēz)

11. Medusa's (mə do͞o′ säz)

12. Hermes (hʉr′ mēz): The messenger of the gods.

13. Nymphs (nimfz): Minor nature goddesses, thought of as beautiful maidens living in rivers, trees, and so on.

14. Gray Women: Also called Graeae (grē′ ē′). Three old sisters who act as guards for the Gorgons and have only one eye and one tooth to share among them.

15. Athene (ə thē′ nä): Goddess of wisdom, skills, and warfare.

earth. There the weird Gray Women sat, passing their eye from one to another just as Hermes had said. Danae's son knew what to do. He left the god and crept quietly towards them, waited till one had taken the eye from her forehead, and snatched it away as she passed it to her sister.

The Gray Women raised a fearful clamor when they realized that a stranger had their eye. They howled and they threatened. But without the eye they were helpless, and in the end they grudgingly told Perseus the way to the Nymphs of the North.

So again Perseus went on, this time to find the happy beings who possessed the three priceless things he needed. And when the Nymphs heard the reason he wanted them, they were willing to give him the winged shoes, the helmet that would make him invisible, and the magic wallet that would become the right size for whatever he wished to carry.

Fully equipped now, Perseus lightly sped through the air over land and over sea to the fearful island of the Gorgons. As he approached, he could see, scattered in the fields and along the roads, statues of men and beasts whom the sight of the Gorgons had turned to stone. And, at last, from high above, he beheld the monsters themselves reflected in his shield. Their scale-covered bodies glistened in the sun, their great wings were folded, the snakes that were their hair lay hideously coiled and intertwined. The Gorgons were asleep.

But which of the three was Medusa? Perseus could see no

difference among them.

Suddenly he heard Athene's voice:

"Descend, Perseus, and strike! The Gorgon nearest the shore is Medusa."

Perseus swept down, and still gazing into the shield, boldly swung his blade. With one stroke he cut off the grisly head. Then, springing into the air, he thrust his prize, all writhing and hissing, into the magic wallet.

Up leaped the Gorgon sisters, for they heard the rattle of Medusa's scales as the severed body thrashed about. They turned their snaky heads and when they saw Perseus, they roared with fury. Flapping their great wings, they set off in pursuit. But they could not outstrip the winged sandals.

Over lands and peoples the hero flew, on and on. He had lost his way now, for Hermes had left him. Below, the Lybian[16] desert stretched endlessly. Perseus did not know what those sands were, nor did he guess that the ruby drops falling from Medusa's head were turning into venomous snakes that would inhabit the desert forever. But now he saw a sight that made his heart beat fast with excitement and wonder.

Fastened by chains to a cliff by the sea was a beautiful maiden. Had it not been that a slight breeze stirred her hair and that tears flowed from her eyes, he would have thought her a statue. Perseus almost forgot to keep his winged sandals moving, so struck was he by her rare beauty.

"Lovely maiden, you should not wear such chains as these," he stammered out, "but rather those which bind the hearts of lovers. I pray you, tell me your name and why you are bound like this."

At first the girl made no reply, so abashed was she before the youth. But when he urged her again and again to speak, she told him all her story.

"I am Andromeda,"[17] she said, "daughter of Cepheus,[18] King of the Ethiopians.[19] The beautiful Cassiopeia[20] is my mother. It is her beauty that has chained me here. For the gods are jealous, and in nothing may we mortals surpass them. Woe, woe the day my mother vaunted[21] herself fairer than the daughters of Nereus![22] The sea god has sent a serpent to prey upon our people, and my death alone can appease his anger. So says the oracle."

She had scarcely finished speaking when the loud roaring of the waves announced that the monster was on his way. Andromeda shrieked. At her cry, her frantic father and mother came running. They clung to their daughter and lamented.[23]

"Enough of tears!" Perseus said to them sternly. "I am Perseus, son of Zeus and Danae. Now I will make this contract with you—that Andromeda shall be mine if I save her from the serpent."

"Indeed, indeed, valorous youth, she

16. **Lybian** (lib′ ē ən): In Lybia, a country in northern Africa, west of Egypt.

17. **Andromeda** (an dräm′ ə dä)

18. **Cepheus** (sē′ fē us)

19. **Ethiopians** (ē′ thē ō′ pē ənz): Peoples of Ethiopia, a country in northeastern Africa.

20. **Cassiopeia** (kas ē ō pē′ ä)

21. **vaunted** (vänt′ əd) *v.*: Boasted or bragged.

22. **Nereus** (nē′ rē us): A god of great kindliness; also called the Old Man of the Sea and Nereus the Truthful. The father of the Nereids, the nymphs of the sea.

23. **lamented** (lə men′ tid) *v.*: Mourned for, as if for someone dead.

shall be yours! Only save her from the monster, and you shall have our kingdom as well as our daughter."

The monster was coming on, his breast parting the waves like a swift ship. Suddenly Perseus sprang into the air and shot high up in the clouds. Seeing the youth's shadow upon the sea, the monster attacked it in fury. Then Perseus swooped like an eagle from the sky and buried his sword up to the hilt in the beast's right shoulder. The creature reared upright, then plunged beneath the water, and turned around and around like some fierce wild boar in the midst of baying hounds.

Nimbly avoiding the snapping jaws, Perseus dealt blow after blow wherever he had the chance to strike. Red blood poured from the monster's mouth. The air was so filled with spray that the hero's winged sandals grew heavy. He dared not trust himself to them longer. Spying a rock over which the waves were breaking, he braced himself against it with his left hand, and four times he drove his sword into the monster's side.

As the creature sank to its death, Perseus heard shouts of joy from the shore. And when he looked, Andromeda already stood free beside her parents.

"I will take this fair maiden without dowry," Perseus said.

And that very day the wedding was celebrated. Torches were tossed in the air, incense was thrown on the flames. Garlands were hung from the palace roof. And everywhere the sound of lyres and pipes and singing was heard.

Now while the marriage feast was at its height, the door of the banquet hall was suddenly flung open, and in burst a mob of shouting, riotous men. Foremost stood Andromeda's uncle, Phineas,[24] javelin in hand.

"Behold, I am here!" he cried. "I have come to avenge the theft of my promised bride."

"What are you doing, brother?" the fa-

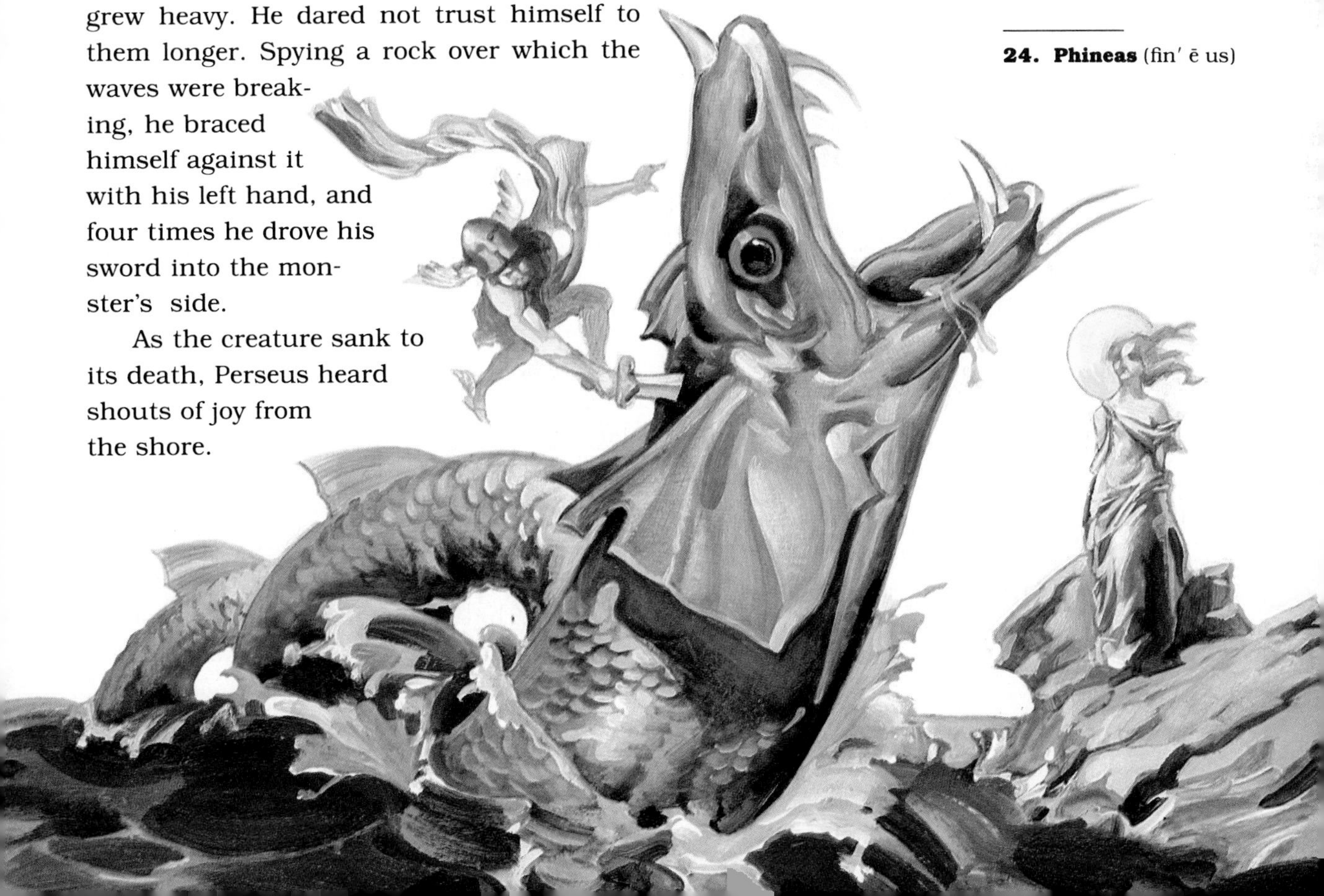

24. Phineas (fin′ ē us)

ther cried. "Do you, who stood by and watched while Andromeda was put in chains and did nothing to help her, dare to be indignant because another has snatched the prize? Let the man who rescued her have the reward he was promised! He has not been chosen in preference to you, but in preference to certain death."

Phineas said not a word. He looked from the king to Perseus, undecided at which to aim his weapon, then hurled it at the hero. The spear struck in Perseus' couch.

Perseus leaped up from the cushions, wrenched out the spear, and hurled it back at his foe. Had Phineas not taken refuge behind the altar, he would have perished. As it was, one of his followers received the weapon full in his forehead.

Then the rioters went wild. Weapons were hurled, and the feast turned into a battle. Thick as hail, javelins sped by Perseus' ears. He set his shoulders against a great stone column and struck down one man after another. But at last he realized that valor could not withstand the numbers against him.

"If I have any friends here, let them hide their faces!" he shouted.

With this he drew Medusa's head out of the wallet. One of the attackers was just preparing to cast his javelin, but before he could cast, he was turned to stone. Another, who was about to thrust his sword through Perseus, stood frozen with it in his hand. A third was turned to stone even as he uttered a taunt. Two hundred men became stony statues before Phineas yielded, crying:

"Put away your horrible weapon. Hide it! Grant me only my life and may the rest be yours!"

"What I can give you, most cowardly Phineas, I will!" Perseus replied. "You shall be a lasting monument here in the palace of my father-in-law."

The unhappy Phineas tried to turn away his eyes, but even as he did so, his flesh turned to stone.

When at the year's end, Perseus sailed home with Andromeda, Polydectes' hatred had in no way lessened. The King was furious that his stepson had returned, and refused to believe that he had actually slain the Medusa. With scornful taunts he upbraided the young man for having come home empty-handed.

It was more than Perseus could bear.

"I shall prove to you that what I say is true!" he cried. "Hide your eyes, all you who are my friends!" And he showed the Gorgon's head to cruel Polydectes.

That was the last time Perseus ever used the horrible head. He gave it most willingly to Athene, who kept it ever after.

Now that Polydectes was dead, Danae yearned to go home again and be reconciled to her father. So Perseus made the fisherman Dictys king of the island and sailed with his mother and Andromeda to Greece.

But it happened that when they came to Argos, King Acrisius was away from home. Games were being held in Larissa,[25] and Perseus, hearing of them, decided to go there and take part. And there at the games it was that the oracle which Acrisius had received at Delphi was strangely fulfilled. For when it came Perseus' turn to throw the discus, he threw it so that it swerved to one side. It landed among the spectators and killed an old man. That old man was King Acrisius, who had gone to such cruel lengths to avoid the fate which the gods had ordained.

---

25. Larissa (lä ris′ ä): The acropolis—the fortified upper part of an ancient Greek city—at Argos.

Reader's Response

Do you think Perseus could have succeeded in killing Medusa without the gods' help? Why or why not?

RESPONDING TO THE SELECTION

Your Response

1. Did the ending of this story surprise you? Why or why not?

Recalling

2. What is the "dreadful oracle" that is delivered to King Acrisius?
3. What adventure does Polydectes suggest that Perseus undertake?
4. List three perilous encounters Perseus experiences during his adventure.
5. Explain how the oracle given to King Acrisius is fulfilled.

Interpreting

6. What is Polydectes's true motive in sending Perseus to kill Medusa?
7. Medusa is beheaded by Perseus, yet her head continues to have power. Explain how the evil gorgon's head is beneficial to Perseus.

Applying

8. Heroes are universal. What purpose and value do heroes have in society?

ANALYZING LITERATURE

Appreciating the Hero

The **hero** in a myth is a character whose actions are noble and inspiring. A hero often goes on a quest, a journey undertaken to accomplish some noble or heroic task. The way that a hero handles the difficulties on a quest sets him apart from ordinary mortals.

1. What heroic characteristics does Perseus have?
2. What help does he get on his quest?
3. How does Perseus's quest enable him to prove himself a hero?

CRITICAL THINKING AND READING

Inferring a Culture's Values

Heroes like Perseus serve as models for what is respected and good in a culture. By examining the kind of person the hero is, as well as who or what the hero conquers, readers can infer a culture's values.

1. What qualities in a person do you think the ancient Greeks hold in high esteem?
2. What do King Acrisius, the gorgons, and the sea serpent represent? What can you infer about the values of the ancient Greeks from these characters whom Perseus defeats?

THINKING AND WRITING

Writing a Scene for a Movie

Movie scriptwriters occasionally use Greek myths as the basis of their stories by keeping the story's plot and characters but changing the setting. Imagine that you are proposing a script based on "The Gorgon's Head" and you must provide the producer with one scene for the movie. Brainstorm with classmates on possible new settings and time periods for "The Gorgon's Head." Then choose the scene on which you will base your movie. Write the script for this scene, including dialogue and screen directions.

LEARNING OPTION

Speaking and Listening. How do you think the Gorgons viewed their encounter with Perseus? With two classmates, write questions you would like to ask the Gorgons. Then choose the roles you wish to play and perform the interview for your class.

GUIDE FOR READING

Marianna Mayer

(1945–   ) is a writer and illustrator of children's books. She has retold many fairytale classics, including *Beauty and the Beast,* the *Adventures of Pinocchio,* and *Aladdin and the Enchanted Lamp.* Her book *The Unicorn and the Lake* was a "Children's Choice" and winner of two children's book awards. "Iduna and the Magic Apples" combines elements of fairytales and the myths of the Norse.

Iduna and the Magic Apples

Characters in Myth

The **characters** in "Iduna and the Magic Apples" are Norse gods. Many Norse myths, like this one, focus on the conflict between the gods and the evil giants. You can understand these characters by observing what each one says and does, what the storyteller says about each one, and what the characters say about one another.

Focus

This myth is a classic tale of good versus evil. Iduna's garden and her magic apples represent the goodness in the world. The giant Thiassi represents evil. In today's world, the forces of good often have to work against the forces of evil. With a small group make two lists. On one list, write down all the things that are good in the world. On the other list, write down the things that are evil. Then, try to think of ways to work against the evil things in the world. As you read this selection, notice how some characters are tempted by evil and how others resist it.

Vocabulary

Knowing the following words will help you as you read "Iduna and the Magic Apples."

menacing (men′ is iŋ) *adj.*: Threatening; sinister (p. 643)
compelling (kəm pel′ liŋ) *adj.*: Irresistible; forceful (p. 643)
thwart (thwôrt) *v.*: Prevent from happening (p. 643)
calamity (kə lam′ ə tē) *n.*: Disaster (p. 643)
inevitable (in ev′ ə tə b′l) *adj.*: Certain to happen (p. 643)
ominous (äm′ ə nəs) *adj.*: Threatening; frightful (p. 643)
impassively (im pas′ iv lē) *adv.*: Calmly (p. 646)
vigil (vij′ əl) *n.*: Watch (p. 647)

Spelling Tip

If a word ends with a consonant-vowel-consonant pattern, like *compel,* you usually double the final consonant before adding *ing.*

Iduna and the Magic Apples

from ancient Norse lands

Marianna Mayer

" '*What if Odin is right and Iduna's apples* are *the reason that we are all strong and youthful?*' "

In an ancient time, when the Norse[1] gods dwelt in the land called Asgard,[2] the wind blew through the halls of their splendid palaces and listened to their tales. The wind was young as a summer breeze, blowing from wild, wooded gardens to lush green valleys where only the gods walked. Although such times are past, the wind remembers the stories of the gods. If you listen carefully, you may hear it whisper the tale of Iduna[3] and the magic apples . . . how her treasure of golden apples kept the great god Odin,[4] his brother Loki,[5] and all the other gods from growing old . . . but the wicked giant Thiassi[6] envied the gods and sought to bring ruin upon them . . . once upon a time . . .

Of all the gardens in Asgard, none was more beautiful than Iduna's. The great lord Odin and the other gods named it Everlasting, for from the moment Iduna entered it, nothing withered, nothing died. Flowers blue and lavender, crimson and yellow, palest pink and fairest white, grew in glorious abundance, rivaling each other in radiance. Trees bore throughout the year—brilliant blossoms and sweet fruit together upon the same bough. The grass was fair and tender green, as in the first few days of spring, and in Iduna's garden it was *always* spring.

The wind's gentle breezes blew through the grove and whispered softly to the fresh young flowers. *Dance as I blow. Toss your pretty heads this way and that. You'll never tire. You'll never fade. Iduna looks after you.* Hearing the wind's song, the birds took up the chant and sang it as they flew throughout the garden.

In this splendid garden, Iduna was a fitting mistress. Her sweet temper and natural beauty drew the wild swans to rest their heads upon her lap. The birds always sang their best songs for her. Indeed, all the wild beasts loved her. Even the fish in the lake grew tame at the sight of her strolling by the water and came swimming to the surface to gaze at her with love.

1. **Norse** (nôrs) *adj.*: Scandinavian.
2. **Asgard** (as′ gärd)
3. **Iduna** (i do͞o′ nə)
4. **Odin** (ō′ din): King of the gods and goddesses; god of war, wisdom, and art.
5. **Loki** (lō′ kē): God of fire; a trickster and sky traveler.
6. **Thiassi** (thī as′ ē)

"Of all the gardens in Asgard, none was more beautiful than Iduna's."
Illustration from IDUNA AND THE MAGIC APPLES
Laszlo Gal

In all the time she had lived in the garden, Iduna had never left it. It was her sanctuary.[7] So long as she remained within its walls, no harm could come to her or those she loved. But should she leave . . . what then? Many things would change.

This little paradise was a happy place. Odin and the other gods often visited, marveling at Iduna's kindness and delighting in her humor and her wit. Yet there was another reason that they came: Iduna pos-

---

7. sanctuary (saŋk′ cho͞o wer′ ē) *n.*: A safe place of refuge or protection.

sessed a special treasure—a golden chest of magic apples that kept all those who ate them ever young. Truly it was the precious fruit that kept the gods immortal. Odin knew the value of these apples. He never ventured on a journey without a few to take along.

This very day he had come with his half brother Loki to see Iduna. They were setting off on foot to tour the ordinary world disguised as peasants, wishing to observe it unrecognized. Iduna made them a gift of all the magic apples she had. But no sooner had she emptied the chest than it refilled itself.

It was late afternoon when Iduna said farewell to her friends and walked down to the riverbank. There she sat, watching the sky reflected on the slowly moving water. Dreamily she looked on as the mirrored faces of the clouds changed from rose to crimson in the setting sun.

All at once, a startling shadow fell across the water. It was huge and dark with widespread wings. Iduna looked up and gasped in horror. A monstrous figure—a bird with a menacing human face—glowered at her. She tried to look away, she tried to run, but the creature's piercing gaze was too compelling. She could not move.

Then abruptly the monster drew itself up and, curling its sharp talons, flew higher and higher into the sky. The power of Iduna's garden had protected her. The monster wished to capture her, but he would have to find another way. Soon the evil figure was a mere speck receding into the blood red clouds.

As it disappeared, a few stray black feathers floated down and changed into black insects with pointed wings and poisonous stingers. Suddenly they encircled Iduna and attacked. She fought them off, but one crept into the folds of her gown and stung her to the heart. The swarm knew that one had succeeded and, satisfied, withdrew and flew away. The poison left behind was working to sap Iduna's strength. From that moment on, things began to go wrong.

Unaware of any danger to Iduna, Odin and Loki had departed on their journey. The travelers were a strange pair. Though half brothers, they could not have been more different. Odin was a mightly ruler careful to temper his great power with reason and compassion. Loki was a selfish mischief maker, capable of changing his shape as easily as his loyalties. He managed to stir up trouble whenever Odin was away. This time, hoping to thwart calamity, Odin had invited Loki to join him. Unfortunately, even a wise plan cannot prevent what is inevitable.

That evening, having traveled far, the two companions found a spot in the wilderness to rest for the night. Hungry, they set about building a fire to roast some meat for their supper. When the fire seemed quite hot, Odin covered the meat with the burning embers to hasten its cooking.

Presently, an ominous black bird, the very one that had plagued Iduna, soundlessly alighted in a tall tree above them. There, hidden in the shadows, the evil creature watched and waited, a vicious sneer twisting its human lips.

At last, Loki exclaimed, "I'm starving! It's been hours since that meat went in the fire. Surely it's cooked by now."

Odin answered, "It *has* been long enough. See if it's ready to eat."

But when they looked, the meat was raw. Disgusted, Loki sat back again to wait. More time passed, and again they checked the roast, but it was as before: The meat was too raw to eat.

Odin raised his eyes to Loki and frowned, saying, "However long we wait, this meat will not cook. No doubt there is some dark magic at work tonight."

His words brought a harsh laugh from the shadows. "Unless you share your meat with me," said the huge black bird, "I can assure you, you'll not eat tonight."

Odin knew at once that this was no real bird. He suspected that it was Thiassi, for the wicked giant often disguised himself as a bird of prey. But Odin could not be absolutely certain and, wishing to avoid trouble, agreed to the bird's demand. At once, the roast was ready to eat, whereupon Odin motioned to the bird to take its share. The creature flew down, took the very best portion, and left almost nothing for Odin and Loki.

Outraged, Loki seized a stick and struck the intruder. Instantly the bird took flight, carrying the stick in its talons with the startled Loki, his hands held fast, clinging to the other end. No matter how hard he tried, he could not let go.

"[Odin] suspected that [the bird] was Thiassi, for the wicked giant often disguised himself as a bird of prey."

Illustration from IDUNA AND THE MAGIC APPLES
Laszlo Gal

The bird *was* Thiassi, and by his evil magic he held Loki bound. Thiassi flew low, dragging his helpless victim across the ground and through the trees. Bruised and bleeding, Loki pleaded for mercy. But Thiassi was the enemy of all the gods of Asgard. He had failed to capture Iduna, and thus he was delighted to carry off Loki, for he had a plan.

"I will set you free on one condition," said the giant as he flew dangerously close to a row of jagged cliffs.

"*Anything!* Anything you wish!" shouted Loki, his voice filled with terror at the sight of this new danger.

The giant laughed and said, "You are a coward, Loki, but you'll have your freedom, if you promise to deliver Iduna and her treasure of magic apples to me."

Loki agreed at once, without a thought to the consequences for Iduna or the gods, and visited the Everlasting Garden at the first opportunity.

He found Iduna alone, sitting in her apple orchard deep in thought. She did not see Loki until he sat down beside her.

"Iduna, guess where I have been," said Loki as he eyed her closely. "If you like, I'll tell you. But first, let me have one of your marvelous apples."

Iduna reached into the golden chest and handed him a shining apple.

But Loki tossed it from one hand to the other, without taking a bite. Giving her a sidelong glance, he frowned and said, "It's just as I suspected. Poor innocent girl, your apples are nothing compared to some I've seen recently."

Iduna was startled, but she tried to smile. "Surely you're mistaken," said Iduna.

"Odin, who has traveled the world over, insists there are no apples to compare to these."

Loki laughed slyly, and the sound made the maiden uneasy. "Well, Odin is mistaken. He'll soon change his mind, I assure you."

His harsh words hurt her, and she stood up quickly. As she did, a sharp pain, like the point of a stinger, jabbed at her heart. She pressed her hand to the spot. "It would be better not to talk of this," she said, and started to walk away.

Loki knew the power of his words and hastened after her. "All right, don't listen to me. But you'll be sorry when your garden is forgotten and everyone is going to this new one for its apples. Alas, my dear, then it will be too late."

Iduna sighed. The poisoned stinger had done its work. She felt too weak to shake off these taunting words. As her strength ebbed away, Iduna's mind grew dark and confused.

Quickly, like a viper[8] moving in for the kill, Loki continued. "Perhaps I should take you to this orchard—it's close by—so you can see for yourself if what I say is true. You mustn't take *my word* for it! Together we could gather all of the apples. Then I'll help you plant their seeds here in your own orchard. It'll be our secret. I swear I'll not tell anyone." With that, Loki came close to Iduna and took her hand in his, saying, "Oh, but you must come now, Iduna. We will go at once, before it's *too late*."

Iduna looked into Loki's eyes and asked, "Is it truly a short distance? I shouldn't leave my garden, but if you promise we'll return quickly . . . perhaps there is no harm."

"*Quickly!*" Loki exclaimed with a laugh. "We'll be back in no time at all. Don't tell me you can't leave this garden even for a few moments. I'm doing you a favor. Surely you won't refuse me?"

Resigned at last, Iduna reached for the chest and said, "All right, but we must hurry."

Still holding firmly to Iduna's hand, Loki began to run down the path toward the gate, heedless of whether she stumbled or struggled to catch her breath. She had no time to think as he pulled her along behind him. He didn't stop until they had reached the gate that shut the garden off from the rest of the world.

Iduna hesitated and tried to step back, but Loki tugged at her roughly, forcing her through the gate and out of the garden. In that final second she heard all the life in the garden cry out to her. *Iduna, don't abandon us! Oh, Iduna, please. Come back. Come back!*

But it was too late. The gate banged shut behind her. She stood with Loki on the other side of all she loved.

The sun was low on the horizon. An overgrown path ahead was deep in shadow. A chilly night wind blew through Iduna's hair, stung her cheeks, and made her shiver.

"We must be quick," Iduna whispered, "so I may come back soon."

Loki did not answer.

She looked at him, and his face was turned away from her, toward the dark sky above them. She followed his gaze and quaked with terror at what she saw. There looming over her was the wicked Thiassi, his wings spread wide. As he dropped lower and lower, his huge shadow fell over her like a cloak. Before she could find breath to cry out, the creature's black talons clasped her and she was lifted higher and higher into the sky.

---

8. viper (vī′ pər) *n.*: A snake.

Loki watched impassively till they vanished, then shrugged and said, "It's nothing to me if Thiassi wishes to make Iduna his captive. I will never be suspected."

Yet something disturbed him. Walking on, eyes fixed upon the ground, Loki tried to dismiss Iduna from his thoughts. He could not. Finally, he paused and asked himself, "What if Odin is right and Iduna's apples *are* the reason that we are all strong and youthful? Might *I* suffer and grow old without Iduna's magic apples? *Impossible!*" Yet he shuddered.

Loki heard a sound and looked up to see his daughter, Hela,[9] mistress of the dead, drifting past him. She stopped a moment and glanced at Loki. The sight of her never failed to strike fear in her father. One side of her face was quite beautiful but deathly pale; the other, the white bones of death itself.

It was not long before the gods knew that Iduna had vanished, for almost at once the Everlasting Garden began to die. The flowers dropped their petals and withered, the leaves faded, and a harsh north wind howled through the grove and tore them from their branches. Dense gray clouds hung overhead, hiding all traces of the sun. The strong wind brought rain that soon changed to snow, smothering everything under a thick white mantle.

No matter where Loki turned, there were worried looks and anxious questions. "Where can Iduna have gone?" "How can it be that she has left her garden without a word to any of us?" *"Is there not one of us who knows more than he is saying?"*

Little by little, day by day, Iduna's absence took its toll on all of them. Lines of worry deepened into wrinkles. Their hair lost its luster and soon turned white. Sapped of their vigor, the once-immortal gods grew old.

It was then that Loki's daughter, Hela, appeared in Odin's palace, Valhalla.[10] Odin commanded her to leave, but Hela laughed and answered, "I'll claim all of you soon enough. Without Iduna's apples to keep you young, none of you are safe from death. Your time grows short. I will leave, but only to make a place for you in my land of the *dead!*"

When she had gone, Bragi,[11] Odin's son, spoke out. "We have ourselves to blame, if we cannot find Iduna. Many months have passed, and yet not one of us has gone to search for her. Tell me, are we all too feeble to risk our lives for her? Well, I am not."

Odin spoke up quickly. "Bragi is right. He and I will go at once to the three sisters of fortune. They'll tell us where to seek Iduna."

The sisters of fortune could tell the past, the present, and the future, but they answered in riddles that only the wise Odin could decipher. From them he and Bragi learned that it was Loki who had helped Thiassi steal Iduna. The sisters declared that only Loki could rescue her and undo the evil he had caused, and to reach the giant's ice palace he must fly there, using falcon wings.

Loki refused. The thought of facing the giant again was too terrible for such a coward. But the gods threatened him with death unless he agreed. Reluctantly, he let them fasten the mantle of falcon feathers upon his shoulders. At once, he was transformed into a bird and flew up into the sky toward Thiassi's castle.

As Loki drew closer and closer to his destination, the sky turned steel gray and the frosty air grew even colder. Finally, he saw

---

9. **Hela** (he′ lä): Goddess of the underworld.

10. **Valhalla** (väl häl′ ə)

11. **Bragi** (brä′ gē): God of poetry.

the icy mountains that encircled Thiassi's domain; indeed, it was a land made totally of ice, dull and without luster, for the sun would not shine. Loki had never seen such a place. The entire castle was carved from the side of a huge ice mountain. Here the giant had imprisoned Iduna.

Fearing that the gods might one day discover her, Thiassi had shut Iduna in a chamber without light or fresh air, where she passed each day isolated and alone, seeing no one but Thiassi.

Once a day he visited to ask the same question. "When will you grant me what I ask, Iduna? I'll have the magic apples and *you* as my bride, mark my words! Sooner or later you must agree," roared the giant.

Iduna trembled but bravely resisted him and firmly said *no*, regardless of his threats. To give the magic apples to Thiassi, Iduna knew, would be disastrous, for in his hands their powers for good would turn to evil. He would have taken the apples by force, but they shrank to tiny seeds and slipped through his fingers whenever he reached into the golden chest. There in the corners they hid until Iduna placed her hand in the chest. Then the apples grew full and ripe again.

One morning, the giant went off across the ocean. Relieved to be free of him for a little while, Iduna went to the tiny crevice where, if she pressed her ear, she could hear the moaning of the sea far below. Oh, she thought, if only I could return to my own sweet garden.

Just then, she heard her name called. There outside the tiny opening was Loki, his falcon wings spread wide to steady himself against the gusty wind.

"Quickly," he shouted. "Get the golden chest."

"I have it," she answered, and Loki spoke a few words of magic. Instantly she was changed into a small gray bird, and the precious golden chest became a tiny locket hidden beneath her feathers.

Out of the narrow window like an arrow came Iduna. The wind tore at her fragile wings, but she pressed on against the current.

"Follow me or we will both be lost forever," Loki shouted back at her. "This way lies the land of Asgard."

The thought of home and her beloved friends gave Iduna fresh strength, and her heart swelled with courage. "Thiassi shall not triumph!" she whispered, and with these determined words the little bird picked up speed.

But they had not gone far when they heard screams of rage behind them. It was the giant, who had returned to discover that Iduna had escaped. Turning himself back into a giant bird, he flew in pursuit.

For three long days and nights he chased them. Though they had had a head start, his speed exceeded theirs and he was narrowing the distance. Soon he would snatch up the tiny bird in his sharp talons.

Ever since Loki's departure, the gods had kept a vigil on Valhalla's high tower, watching for a sign. On the fourth night, the sharp-eyed Odin spotted a falcon and another, much smaller bird pursued by a massive black-winged creature.

Calculating the speed at which they each traveled, sadly he told the others, "They will not escape. Thiassi will seize Iduna before she can reach us."

Odin ordered fires set. By the time the flames were raging, the travelers were very close. Now all could see that the giant would seize Iduna before she could reach safety.

Illustration from IDUNA AND THE MAGIC APPLES
Laszlo Gal

"The flames hungrily caught [Thiassi's] sweeping wings, and he tumbled to his doom in the blaze."

Suddenly, the falcon rose to escape the wall of flames. The small gray bird lifted herself to follow. But the giant black bird was too heavy to rise. The flames hungrily caught his sweeping wings, and he tumbled to his doom in the blaze.

With Iduna's last effort she passed over the clouds of smoke and came to rest at Odin's feet. He lifted her up with the touch of his hand, and Iduna was restored to her true form.

A glorious celebration soon followed. Songs were written that day of Iduna's triumph over Thiassi. In the halls of Valhalla the minstrels sang with such feeling that the walls rang with their music. A great feast was spread across the polished banquet table. Iduna opened the golden chest and gave each of the gods a magic apple. As they ate, new vigor flowed into their veins and they were made strong and young once more.

At the close of the feasting, Iduna returned to the Everlasting Garden. The instant she reentered, the sun shone bright and warm again, and what had seemed dead in her absence was reborn. Springtime in all its beauty unfolded once more. The fair young trees grew tall and green and the flowers lifted their radiant heads at the sight of her. The wind's fragrant breezes blew softly through the grove in a song of praise for her, and the birds took up the melody, singing joyously of their beloved Iduna's return.

Reader's Response

What do you think of Loki's actions? Would you trust him? Explain your answers.

Responding to the Selection

Your Response

1. Do you think Loki deserved to be punished? Why or why not?

Recalling

2. Why is Iduna's garden so important?
3. How does Loki trick Iduna into leaving her garden? Why does he want her to leave?
4. Describe what happens when Iduna leaves the Everlasting Garden.
5. How does Loki save Iduna from Thiassi?

Interpreting

6. Why does Loki first assist Thiassi in capturing Iduna and then rescue her?
7. What do you think would have happened if Iduna had turned the golden apples over to Thiassi?
8. Like many other myths, Norse myths illustrate the values of their culture. What values does this tale show?

Applying

9. If you had access to magic apples that would keep you young forever, would you eat them? What benefits and problems could come from living forever?

Analyzing Literature

Understanding Characters in Myth

Myths, like novels and short stories, contain **characters** with a variety of personalities and traits.

1. What do you learn about Iduna when she refuses to turn over her apples to Thiassi?
2. What do Loki's actions tell about him? Is he indeed a mischief-maker? Explain.

Critical Thinking and Reading

Understanding Chronological Order

The events in this story are in **chronological order**, the order in which they occur.

1. List the major events of this myth in chronological order.
2. Would this myth be as effective if the order of the events were changed and you knew from the beginning the outcome of the story? Why or why not?

Thinking and Writing

Writing a Character Description

Choose one character from "Iduna and the Magic Apples" to write about in a descriptive paragraph. You can describe your character's physical appearance, behavior, personality, and so on. Write a topic sentence that gives an overall description of the character you choose. In your paragraph you should mention at least three incidents from the story that support the description of your character. At the end of your paragraph, write a sentence that summarizes the personality of the character. Revise and write a final draft.

Learning Option

Speaking and Learning. A readers theater is a dramatic reading of a piece of literature. It is like a play but lines are read aloud from a script and few props are used. Prepare a readers theater presentation for a section from "Iduna and the Magic Apples." One section might be the scene in which Loki tricks Iduna into leaving her garden. Write the script for the scene you choose. In your script, include directions for the actors' facial expressions, voice variations, and gestures. Act out the scene for the class.

YOUR WRITING PROCESS

Writing a Hero Tale

What is your idea of a hero? The heroes in the Classic Myths section all portray a similar type of person. In the hero tales in this section, the hero (1) wants to achieve a goal, (2) meets challenges or tests which he must pass to meet his goal, (3) is up against high stakes, and (4) either wins or loses, depending on the hero's original intentions. What makes these stories so exciting, however, is the conflict between the hero and someone or something else.

Your Turn

Model your hero after one of the myths in this section or another hero from stories you have read. Your purpose is to write a tale about a hero who wants to achieve a goal. Your audience is your classmates.

Prewriting

1. Examine the patterns of a hero tale. To pattern your hero tale after another story, first examine that story to determine the pattern it follows. Following is one student's brief analysis of the patterns of the myths in this section:

Arachne

Arachne wants to be known as the best, most skillful weaver in the world (goal). She insists she is better even than the goddess Athene. She competes in a spinning and weaving contest with the goddess herself (test). If she wins, she will be declared the best. If she loses, anything might happen, for Athene is, after all, a powerful goddess (stakes). Arachne loses and her punishment is given (conclusion).

The Gorgon's Head

Perseus wants to prove himself to his stepfather, King Polydectes (goal). The King challenges him to cut off the head of the Medusa (test). Finding the Medusa and killing her proves extraordinarily difficult and dangerous (challenge). With the help of the gods, he succeeds (conclusion).

2. Create a hero. Your hero may be male or female, from any time period, or from any place. Then read or reread the myth upon which you will model your own tale and examine it, noting its pattern.

3. Determine the basic facts for your tale. Develop the details about your character and events.

Following is an example of a chart one student developed for Orpheus:

<u>The hero</u>: Orpheus

<u>The hero's goal</u>: Orpheus wants his beloved dead wife back with him on earth.

<u>The test</u>: Through his skill, he gains his way to the underworld, where he convinces the gods to grant his desire. He must lead his wife out of the underworld without looking back at her. He must have faith in the gods.

<u>The stakes</u>: If Orpheus looks back to see if his wife is following him, she returns to the underworld.

<u>How the hero performs</u>: Orpheus loses faith and looks back.

<u>The conclusion</u>: He loses his wife forever.

Drafting

Use your prewriting notes to write your first draft. Be as creative and imaginative as you wish. Just be sure to keep to the basic elements of a hero seeking a goal and being tested in order to achieve it.

Revising

Use the revision checklist on page 751. In addition, read your draft to a small group and ask questions such as the following to confirm that your story is clearly told:

- Do I adequately describe my hero? What additional information would you like to know about him or her?
- Is the hero's test clearly defined?
- Are the hero's stakes clearly defined?
- What additional details and conflict should I include?
- Does my tale have a clear and believable conclusion?
- What is the most exciting part of my tale?

Using the suggestions your partner makes, rewrite your draft.

Proofreading

Consult the guidelines for proofreading on page 753. Then make a final copy of your tale to share with your classmates.

Publishing

Read your tale to your classmates. Invite them to share with you what they liked about it.

READING AND RESPONDING

The Oral Tradition

The oral tradition is rich and varied. Folk literature of this tradition introduces you to cultures across the world. While these tales entertain you, they also give you insight into what people from different places and different times hold important.

As an active reader of folk literature, you question, predict, clarify, and summarize while reading. You pay attention to the characters and the action. You also consider the following elements, which are especially important to the oral tradition: the source of the tale, its purpose, and the way it develops. Finally, you respond personally to the tale as you do to all literature. In this way you put together your knowledge of the elements of folk literature.

Dorothulia Davis of the Redford School in Detroit, Michigan, actively read and responded to "Mufaro's Beautiful Daughters." The notes in the side columns on pages 653–660 include Dorothulia's responses. How are your responses similar to and different from Dorothulia's?

RESPONDING TO SOURCE Where does the story come from? Consider the source of the tale and its original tellers. What do you learn about the people who composed the tale? What does it reveal about the culture? What ideas does it have in common with stories from other places?

RESPONDING TO PURPOSE Tales from the oral tradition entertained listeners, but they often had another purpose as well. Some tales answered questions about nature. Some illustrated what the people believed and valued. Others showed how people should behave, and they set up heroes as models. Think about the purpose of the tale you are reading.

RESPONDING TO CHARACTERS The characters in folk literature are varied—animals, wise and clever people, heroes, gods and goddesses. Sometimes animal characters are used to convey ideas about human behavior. Often the human characters are out of the ordinary—they have powers or abilities that most people do not have.

RESPONDING TO DEVELOPMENT The original tellers used their imaginations in their stories. The stories in folk literature often develop through fantasy, magic, or other unrealistic details. Yet the outcome is predictable. Soon after you are introduced to the characters and situation, you know who will do well and who will be disappointed or defeated.

MODEL

Mufaro's Beautiful Daughters

John Steptoe

" '*Only a king can choose between two such worthy daughters.*' "

A long time ago, in a certain place in Africa, a small village lay across a river and half a day's journey from a city where a great king lived. A man named Mufaro[1] lived in this village with his two daughters, who were called Manyara and Nyasha.[2] Everyone agreed that Manyara and Nyasha were very beautiful.

Source: *How far back was a long time ago?*

Manyara was almost always in a bad temper. She teased her sister whenever their father's back was turned, and she had been heard to say, "Someday, Nyasha, I will be a queen, and you will be a servant in my household."

Character: *I think Nyasha will get the better half and Manyara will be the servant in her household.*

"If that should come to pass," Nyasha responded, "I will be pleased to serve you. But why do you say such things? You are clever and strong and beautiful. Why are you so unhappy?"

"Because everyone talks about how kind *you* are, and they praise everything you do," Manyara replied. "I'm certain that Father loves you best. But when I am a queen, everyone will know that your silly kindness is only weakness."

Character: *I think Manyara is jealous of Nyasha.*

Nyasha was sad that Manyara felt this way, but she ignored her sister's words and went about her chores. Nyasha kept a small plot of land, on which she grew millet,[3] sunflowers, yams,[4] and vegetables. She always sang as she worked,

Development: *Nyasha feels sadness for her sister after their spat.*

1. **Mufaro** (mo͞o fär′ ō)
2. **Manyara** (man yär′ ə) **. . . Nyasha** (nī äsh′ ə)
3. **millet** (mil′ it) *n.*: A cereal grass used for food.
4. **yams** (yamz) *n.*: Sweet potatoes.

and some said it was her singing that made her crops more bountiful[5] than anyone else's.

Development: *Nyasha is so kind that a snake allows her to pet it.*

One day, Nyasha noticed a small garden snake resting beneath a yam vine. "Good day, little Nyoka,"[6] she called to him. "You are welcome here. You will keep away any creatures who might spoil my vegetables." She bent forward, gave the little snake a loving pat on the head, and then returned to her work.

Development: *They have a beautiful friendship.*

From that day on, Nyoka was always at Nyasha's side when she tended her garden. It was said that she sang all the more sweetly when he was there.

Purpose: *Mufaro is naive to what's going on with his daughters.*

Mufaro knew nothing of how Manyara treated Nyasha. Nyasha was too considerate of her father's feelings to complain, and Manyara was always careful to behave herself when Mufaro was around.

Development: *Does the queen also have to be intelligent?*

Early one morning, a messenger from the city arrived. The Great King wanted a wife. "The Most Worthy and Beautiful Daughters in the Land are invited to appear before the King, and he will choose one to become Queen!" the messenger proclaimed.

Purpose: *Why is Mufaro so sure that one of his daughters will get picked?*

Mufaro called Manyara and Nyasha to him. "It would be a great honor to have one of you chosen," he said. "Prepare yourselves to journey to the city. I will call together all our friends to make a wedding party. We will leave tomorrow as the sun rises."

Purpose: *Manyara is trying to coax her father into not letting Nyasha go. That way Manyara has first chance at being queen.*

"But, my father," Manyara said sweetly, "it would be painful for either of us to leave you, even to be wife to the king. I know Nyasha would grieve to death if she were parted from you. I am strong. Send me to the city, and let poor Nyasha be happy here with you."

Development: *Why doesn't Mufaro know what's going on?*

Mufaro beamed with pride. "The king has asked for the most worthy and the most beautiful. No, Manyara, I cannot send you alone. Only a king can choose between two such worthy daughters. Both of you must go!"

That night, when everyone was asleep, Manyara stole quietly out of the village. She had never been in the forest at

---

5. bountiful (boun′ tə fəl) *adj.*: Plentiful.
6. Nyoka (nī ō′ kə)

Character: *Manyara is very stupid. She doesn't know what she is getting into.*

Development: *Where did the little boy come from?*

Character: *Manyara is evil.*

Development: *Who is this old woman? Where did she come from?*

Purpose: *The old woman is very wise.*

Character: *Manyara shows no respect for the elderly.*

Purpose: *Manyara doesn't use her head, and she disobeyed what was told to her.*

Purpose: *Where did the man with his head tucked under his arm come from? What does this mean?*

night before, and she was frightened, but her greed to be the first to appear before the king drove her on. In her hurry, she almost stumbled over a small boy who suddenly appeared, standing in the path.

"Please," said the boy. "I am hungry. Will you give me something to eat?"

"I have brought only enough for myself," Manyara replied.

"But, please!" said the boy. "I am so *very* hungry."

"Out of my way, boy! Tomorrow I will become your queen. How dare you stand in my path?"

After traveling for what seemed to be a great distance, Manyara came to a small clearing. There, silhouetted[7] against the moonlight, was an old woman seated on a large stone.

The old woman spoke. "I will give you some advice, Manyara. Soon after you pass the place where two paths cross, you will see a grove of trees. They will laugh at you. You must not laugh in return. Later, you will meet a man with his head under his arm. You must be polite to him."

"How do you know my name? How dare you advise your future queen? Stand aside, you ugly old woman!" Manyara scolded, and then rushed on her way without looking back.

Just as the old woman had foretold, Manyara came to a grove of trees, and they did indeed seem to be laughing at her.

"I must be calm," Manyara thought. "I will *not* be frightened." She looked up at the trees and laughed out loud. "I laugh at you, trees!" she shouted, and she hurried on.

It was not yet dawn when Manyara heard the sound of rushing water. "The river must be up ahead," she thought. "The great city is just on the other side."

But there, on the rise, she saw a man with his head tucked under his arm. Manyara ran past him without speaking. "A queen acknowledges[8] only those who please her," she said to herself. "I will be queen. I will be queen," she chanted, as she hurried on toward the city.

Nyasha woke at the first light of dawn. As she put on her finest garments, she thought how her life might be changed

---

7. silhouetted (sil′ o͞o et′ əd) *adj.*: Seen as a dark shape against a light background.

8. acknowledges (ak näl′ ij əz) *v.*: Recognizes and greets.

forever beyond this day. "I'd much prefer to live here," she admitted to herself. "I'd hate to leave this village and never see my father or sing to little Nyoka again."

Purpose: *Nyasha is simple and good in contrast with her sister.*

Her thoughts were interrupted by loud shouts and a commotion from the wedding party assembled outside. Manyara was missing! Everyone bustled about, searching and calling for her. When they found her footprints on the path that led to the city, they decided to go on as planned.

As the wedding party moved through the forest, brightly plumed birds darted about in the cool green shadows beneath the trees. Though anxious about her sister, Nyasha was soon filled with excitement about all there was to see.

They were deep in the forest when she saw the small boy standing by the side of the path.

"You must be hungry," she said, and handed him a yam she had brought for her lunch. The boy smiled and disappeared as quietly as he had come.

Character: *Without thinking about it, Nyasha knew the boy was hungry, and she gave him food because of her kindness.*

Later, as they were approaching the place where the two paths crossed, the old woman appeared and silently pointed the way to the city. Nyasha thanked her and gave her a small pouch filled with sunflower seeds.

Purpose: *Does Nyasha know what is going to happen to her?*

The sun was high in the sky when the party came to the grove of towering trees. Their uppermost branches seemed to bow down to Nyasha as she passed beneath them.

Purpose: *The trees bowing down to her suggest a good end to this story for her.*

At last, someone announced that they were near their destination.

Nyasha ran ahead and topped the rise before the others could catch up with her. She stood transfixed[9] at her first sight of the city. "Oh, my father," she called. "A great spirit must stand guard here! Just look at what lies before us. I never in all my life dreamed there could be anything so beautiful!"

Arm in arm, Nyasha and her father descended the hill, crossed the river, and approached the city gate. Just as they entered through the great doors, the air was rent by piercing cries, and Manyara ran wildly out of a chamber at the center of the enclosure. When she saw Nyasha, she fell upon her, sobbing.

---

9. transfixed (trans fikst') *adj.*: Motionless in wonder.

Development: *What has happened?*

"Do not go to the king, my sister. Oh, please, Father, do not let her go!" she cried hysterically.[10] "There's a great monster there, a snake with five heads! He said that he knew all my faults and that I displeased him. He would have swallowed me alive if I had not run. Oh, my sister, please do not go inside that place."

---

10. hysterically (hi ster′ ik lē) *adv.*: With wild, uncontrolled emotion.

It frightened Nyasha to see her sister so upset. But, leaving her father to comfort Manyara, she bravely made her way to the chamber and opened the door.

Purpose: *Nyasha always does what is right.*

On the seat of the great chief's stool lay the little garden snake. Nyasha laughed with relief and joy.

"My little friend!" she exclaimed. "It's such a pleasure to see you, but why are you here?"

"I am the king," Nyoka replied.

And there, before Nyasha's eyes, the garden snake changed shape.

"I am the king. I am also the hungry boy with whom you shared a yam in the forest and the old woman to whom you made a gift of sunflower seeds. But you know me best as Nyoka. Because I have been all of these, I know you to be the Most Worthy and Most Beautiful Daughter in the Land. It would make me very happy if you would be my wife."

And so it was that, a long time ago, Nyasha agreed to be married. The king's mother and sisters took Nyasha to their house, and the wedding preparations began. The best weavers in the land laid out their finest cloth for her wedding garments. Villagers from all around were invited to the celebration, and a great feast was held. Nyasha prepared the bread for the wedding feast from millet that had been brought from her village.

Purpose: *Manyara got what she deserved.*

Mufaro proclaimed to all who would hear him that he was the happiest father in all the land, for he was blessed with two beautiful and worthy daughters—Nyasha, the queen; and Manyara, a servant in the queen's household.

Response: *Nyasha's almost too good to be true, but I still like her. Manyara is sneaky and mean. She deserved to end up a servant.*

Reader's Response
What is your opinion of each daughter? Why?

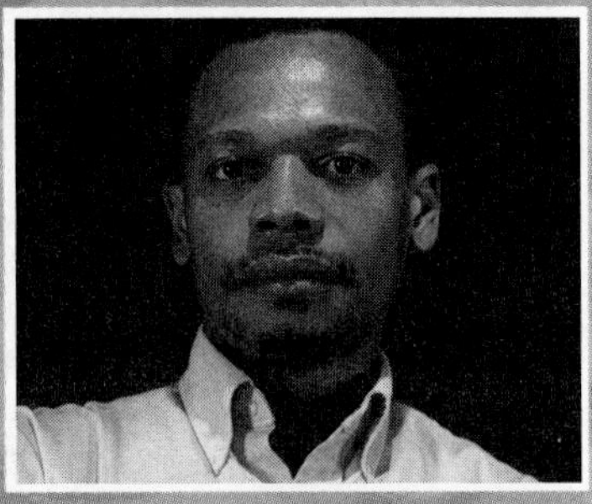

John Steptoe (1950–1989) grew up in the Bedford-Stuyvesant section of Brooklyn, New York. He began drawing pictures and telling stories when he was a small boy. He published his first book, *Stevie,* at the age of nineteen. Steptoe received the *Boston Globe* Horn Book Award for "Mufaro's Beautiful Daughters." Upon accepting the award, he said, "I wanted to create a book that included some of the things that were left out of my own education about the people who were my ancestors."

Responding to the Selection

Your Response

1. How would you react if you had a sister like Manyara?
2. If you were Nyasha, would you want Manyara to be a servant in your household? Why or why not?

Recalling

3. What reason did Manyara give for feeling unhappy?
4. Who was the garden snake?
5. What frightened Manyara?

Interpreting

6. Why did Manyara behave herself when Mufaro was around?
7. Was Manyara's concern for her sister sincere when she said that Nyasha would grieve to death if she were parted from her father? How do you know?
8. Why did Manyara want to be the first to appear before the king?

Applying

9. How could you apply the lesson taught by this folk tale to your own life?

Analyzing Literature

Understanding Folk Tales

Folk tales have certain elements in common. For example, most folk tales have a purpose. The purpose of "Mufaro's Beautiful Daughters" is to teach a lesson about proper behavior. Characters in folk tales often have unusual or magical powers. The plot of the tales may involve magic or fantasy. Finally, no matter how fantastic the tale is, the ending is predictable. Good always triumphs over evil.

1. What lesson do you think this tale intended to teach?
2. Describe the special powers of one character in "Mufaro's Beautiful Daughters."
3. At what point in the story were you able to predict what the ending would be?

Critical Thinking and Reading

Understanding Characters Through Dialogue

Dialogue is the conversation between characters in a story. Dialogue may reveal the characters' personality or traits of characters. By paying close attention to the dialogue, you can tell whether a character is being honest or dishonest, sincere or insincere. Does the character always do what he or she says, or does the character say one thing and do another?

1. What does Manyara say early in the story that reveals her jealousy toward Nyasha?
2. Identify dialogue that shows that Mufaro does not know Manyara's true character.
3. Reread the story to find dialogue in which Manyara reveals two of her faults.

Thinking and Writing

Writing a Folk Tale

Write your own folk tale. Use your personal experience as a source for the plot. You may base your tale on something that happened in your experience.

Include the elements of a folk tale. Your purpose will be to teach a lesson to the reader. Your characters should have special powers. Fantasy or magic may play a role in the development of the story, and your ending should be predictable early in the story.

Learning Option

Performance. Work with a partner or small group to write a skit for a scene to take place after this story ends. It may be the wedding scene or another scene at some point in the future in Nyasha's household. Practice your skit and perform it for your class.

BRIDGING FORMS

The Trojan War
by Bernard Evslin

We are all familiar with comic strip and cartoon heroes. Superman, who is among the most well-known contemporary heroes, fights against evil in his never-ending battle for truth and justice. Despite his super-human strength, however, Superman does have one weakness—kryptonite, a mineral that renders him powerless whenever he is near it.

Superman, like other heroes, is modeled after classic Greek heroes. Achilles and Ulysses, two main characters in Bernard Evslin's, *The Trojan War*, are such models.

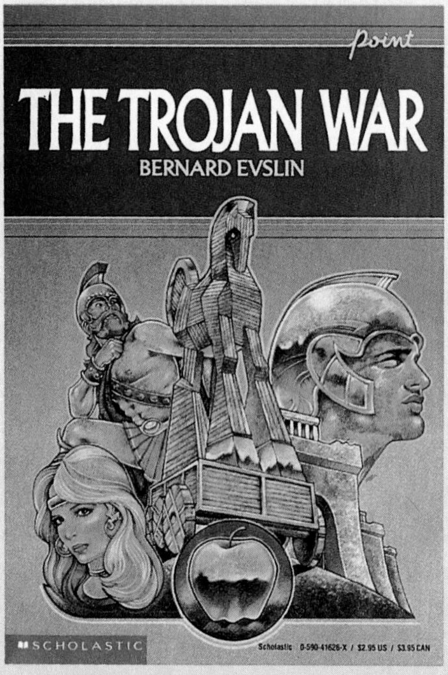

The Oral Tradition

The Trojan War is based on historical fact. No one knows for sure what really happened during the war between the Greeks and the Trojans. This legend, which began in the oral tradition thousands of years ago, was later written down by Homer, a Greek poet. In a great epic poem, *The Iliad*, Homer recounts his vision and interpretation of the events that took place thousands of years before. In *The Trojan War*, Evslin retells Homer's epic poem. In doing so he bridges time and forms.

Achilles' Heel

Scholars debate the actual cause of the destruction of Troy. About all historians know for certain is that there was a war between the Greeks and the Trojans. The details surrounding this event have been widely interpreted and written about in such works of literature as *The Iliad* and *The Trojan War*.

According to tradition, the Trojan war began after Paris abducted the Greek queen Helen. Helen's husband King Menelaus and his army set out for Troy to bring her home.

THE PROCESSION OF THE TROJAN HORSE INTO TROY
G. D. Tiepolo
The Granger Collection

The fighting continued for ten years, with both sides threatening periodic victory, amid much meddling from the gods. Achilles, the greatest of the Greek warriors, became angry at the commander's treatment of him and refused to fight, thereby weakening Greece's army. Finally, he returned to the field, but was struck down when Paris thrust an arrow into his only vulnerable spot—the tendon behind his right heel.

Ulysses, a clever Greek hero, growing impatient with the long battle, suggested a final plan to win the war. To discover his plans and which side wins the war, you must read *The Trojan War*.

Evslin's Work

Bernard Evslin is a full-time professional writer, who has written and produced plays for Broadway, including *Geranium Hat*. Evslin has received the National Education Association Award in 1961 for best television documentary on an educational theme for *Face of the Land*. He primarily retells the myths of ancient Rome and Greece. His other work includes *Merchants of Venus, The Greek Gods, The Adventures of Ulysses*, and a series called *Monsters of Mythology*.

Understanding the Oracle

Riddles, tricks, and oracles play important roles in mythology, as you learned while reading the selections in the Oral Tradition unit. As you read *The Trojan War*, look for the clues that help Ulysses solve the riddle:

"Could is should . . .
Should is would,
would is wood, of course.
What began with an apple
Must end with a horse."

What are the key words that helped Ulysses understand the riddle? What kind of thinking enabled Ulysses to solve the mystery?

If you are interested in reading more myths, consult your teacher or librarian. Many more adventures of the gods and heroes have been written. You will find several featured in the Bookshelf on page 668.

FOCUS ON READING
Distinguishing Fact from Nonfact

Most material that you read contains statements of fact and statements that are not facts. By determining which statements are facts and which are not, you will gain a greater understanding of what the author is saying and can decide whether you agree with it. In other words, you will be able to evaluate the material and become a more active, critical reader.

Facts

A fact is something that happened or is really true. If a statement is fact, you can check its truth in an encyclopedia, almanac, or other reference book. In addition, you can prove something through observation. For example, you can prove whether it's raining outside by looking outside. Look at the following sentences:

Riddles were a form of debate in ancient Hawaii.

Spiders weave webs.

A warrior named Arthur lived in Britain many centuries ago.

Both sentences contain facts that can be checked by looking them up.

Nonfact

Nonfactual information cannot be proved. Nonfactual information might include opinions, predictions, attitudes, evaluations, or other statements. It might also include details or statements that are imaginary or fantastic. Notice the differences between the following sentences:

A usurer is someone who lends money with interest.

No one likes the usurer.

The first sentence tells what a usurer is. You can look up the definition in the dictionary. It is factual. The second sentence states an opinion. You cannot prove this statement. You might find someone who does like the usurer.

Signals

Sometimes distinguishing between fact and nonfact can be difficult. Sentences may contain both, and some sentences that seem to be factual may prove to be opinions instead. Looking for signals can help you distinguish fact from nonfact.

For instance, when writers state their opinions they often use words that signal their intentions. For example, they might use such phrases as "I (we) think," and "I (we) feel."

Other clues to watch for are words that describe something in a positive or negative way. Positive judgments are indicated by words such as "the finest," "wonderful," or "convenient"; whereas negative judgments are suggested by words such as "awful," "dreadful," or "unhealthy."

If such signals are not present, look carefully at the statement and ask yourself these questions: Can I prove this statement? If so, where might I find proof? Most likely if you cannot check the truth of a statement, it is not fact.

Guidelines

- If the statement can be proven to be true, it is a fact.
- If the statement expresses a belief, opinion, prediction, or judgment, it is nonfact.
- If the statement contains words such as "think," "great," "horrible," or "never," it is usually nonfact.

Activity 1

Read each of the following statements. Identify each as either fact (F) or nonfact (N).

1. Turtles once lived without their protective shells.
2. Many Chinese believe in the legend of Kuan-yin.
3. I think all animal gods were good.
4. Orpheus was the best musician in Greece.
5. Mandarins are high Chinese officials.

Activity 2

Being a critical reader and being able to distinguish fact from nonfact can help you in your everyday life. Every day you are faced with distinguishing fact from nonfact, sometimes without even being aware of it. Keep a log for one week. As you are watching television commercials, reading newspapers or magazines, or listening to speeches, jot down the details that are factual and those that are not. An entry for a toothpaste commercial, for example, might look like this:

Fact	Nonfact
cleans teeth	tastes great
helps prevent tooth decay	you will love it
helps reduce plaque	makes teeth whiter and brighter

YOUR WRITING PROCESS

Preparing a Collection of Folk Tales

Reading folk literature that others have collected can be fun. But putting together your own collection adds a whole new dimension to the activity. Who knows—you may even collect and publish some tales that have never been published before.

Are there stories that float around your community—stories "everyone" tells, and perhaps many insist are true? Maybe, for example, you have heard tales your parents or grandparents heard as children, or tales about the disappearing hitchhiker—a man picked up near the cemetery, who suddenly disappears. Researchers call the latter type of tale urban folk tales, or tales from the city, that are now being recorded and published.

Similarly, you can record urban or traditional tales you've heard.

Your Turn

Prepare a collection of folk tales. Your goal is to record a traditional or urban tale that someone else has told you. Your audience is your classmates and everyone who enjoys folk tales.

Prewriting

1. Brainstorm for ideas. Work as a whole class or in small groups to brainstorm for ways to gather tales. Have a recorder note all ideas on the chalkboard for class consideration.

Ideas might include the following:

- Interview the elderly in nursing homes.
- Invite guests to come to class and tell folk tales.
- Interview people from other countries.
- Interview family members.
- Interview friends.
- Interview local writers.

2. Evaluate your ideas. Evaluate each suggested idea by asking the following questions. Put a check mark by those ideas you like the best.

- Did I choose the best way to gather information for my story?
- What if this way leads to a dead end? Where do I go next?
- Can our research be done in the time frame we have?

In deciding how to shape your collection, remember your readers. If you consider sharing your collection with the school community, or perhaps with your families, what would they enjoy most?

3. Consider additional tasks. As a whole class, decide tasks. Have a recorder write ideas on the chalkboard. Examples might include the following:

- Set and enforce deadlines.
- Interview people.
- Collect information for biographies of people who are interviewed.
- Write thank-you notes for interviews.
- Write stories and biographies of tellers.
- Write introductions.
- Type or print tales.
- Do artwork.
- Arrange articles and art on the pages.
- Duplicate and distribute stories.

Add other tasks as you think of them. Then assign each task to a student or group of students. Be sure a recorder keeps track of all assigned projects and deadlines from the start.

4. Conducting the interviews. If you decide to interview members of the community, you might write a letter requesting the interview first. Explain your purpose and how long you think you will need. Be sure to write thank-you notes afterward. Take careful and accurate notes or tape record or video tape the interview. Also ask the interviewee for information about his or her life to include in a brief biography.

Drafting

Introduce each folk tale with information about its time and place. Then using your notes, write the story you heard. Be sure to punctuate the dialogue correctly. Also be sure to use vivid verbs and adjectives.

Revising

Revise your own work. Then submit it to your editor. In revising, editors and writers should consult the checklist on page 751 and consider the following questions:

- Is this tale complete? What information or details are missing?
- Does this tale capture my interest? If not, why not? What would make it more exciting?
- Is the story punctuated correctly?
- Does the writer use vivid verbs and adjectives?

Proofreading

Proofreaders should consult the guidelines for proofreading on page 753. They must be sure there are no typographical, grammatical, or spelling errors in the copy.

Publishing

Introduce the collection with a statement of purpose for your publication. Bind your tales in a class collection and display it in the classroom. You might consider inviting other classes to come to a storytelling session in which you can read your folk tales aloud.

BOOKSHELF

THE PEOPLE COULD FLY, AMERICAN BLACK FOLKTALES by Virginia Hamilton. Alfred A. Knopf, 1985. In this collection, Newbery Medal winner Virginia Hamilton will delight you with more tales of Bruh Rabbit's adventures. In addition to animal tales, Hamilton includes tales of fantasy, the supernatural, and freedom—the freedom of the human spirit.

THE TOAD IS THE EMPEROR'S UNCLE, ANIMAL FOLKTALES FROM VIETNAM by Mai Vo-Dinh. Doubleday and Company, Inc., 1970. During his childhood, Mai Vo-Dinh heard the stories included in this collection of Vietnamese folk tales. Vo-Dinh will introduce you to the beliefs of the people and the nature of his country as you travel through the imaginary world of animals and tricksters and the Vietnam of the past.

HEROES AND MONSTERS OF GREEK MYTH by Bernard Evslin, Dorothy Evslin, and Ned Hoopes. Scholastic, Inc., 1967. The legends of ancient Greece are brought to life in this collection of tales. Read about Perseus, Daedalus, Theseus, and Atalanta—some of Greece's greatest mythological heroes—as they defy the gods and battle hideous monsters.

BROTHER TO THE WIND by Mildred Pitts Walter. Lothrop, Lee & Shepard Books, 1985. Mildred Pitts Walter tells the story of Emeke—an African American boy who wishes he could fly. This tale, which is illustrated by Diane and Leo Dillon, will delight your senses and captivate your imagination.

MEXICAN FOLKTALES FROM THE BORDERLAND by Riley Aiken. Southern Methodist University Press, 1980. In this collection of forty-nine stories, Riley Aiken retells many of the folk tales from Mexico and its bordering states and Spain. In these stories you will be sent to the imaginative and often humorous worlds of a variety of characters.

THE GIRL WHO LOVED WILD HORSES by Paul Goble. Bradbury Press, 1978. This book tells the story of a Native American girl's love of horses and her life among them.

UNIT ACTIVITIES

Writing

1. Many of the stories in this unit are set in exotic and often fantastic places. Select your favorite story or setting from the tales in this unit. Design and write a travel brochure for the place in which it is set. Describe the setting and what type of adventures and sites a traveler might expect to encounter. Also include pictures and travel information. Display your brochures on a bulletin board in your classroom.

Speaking and Listening

2. Have a "Character Day" in which you come to class dressed as one of the characters in the Oral Tradition unit. Dress in costume. You must remain "in character" throughout the day and speak and act only as that character would.

Speaking and Listening

3. Before tales were written down, storytellers captured the attention and imagination of their audiences. The art of storytelling involved memorizing the story and acting the parts of each character. Select one tale from this unit. Be able to recite the tale without reading it. Then practice delivering the lines of the characters and the part of the narrator. When appropriate, add gestures that imitate the actions of the characters. Perform your story for classmates.

Creative Response

4. Design a T-shirt or sweat shirt with a picture illustrating your favorite folk tale or myth from this unit. For example, you might create a picture that illustrates or represents the theme of a tale, or, perhaps, a tale's setting or a character.

Cooperative Learning

5. Work with three to five classmates. Research the customs of one of the cultures represented in the Oral Tradition unit. Organize a day for the class in which you celebrate a holiday or festival particular to that culture. Decorate the room appropriately, serve that culture's special foods, and plan activities that were typical of the holiday or festival.

Cooperative Learning

6. In small groups, design and create a board game related to one of the tales in the Oral Tradition unit. For example, you might create a game based on "The Riddling Youngster" in which players must solve riddles before advancing their game pieces.

SUN, MANANA, MONHEGAN
Rockwell Kent
Bowdoin College Museum of Art

THE NOVEL

Many readers often wish that novels they really enjoyed never ended; they don't want to leave the characters and the worlds behind. Why are readers drawn into these worlds? Along with other elements of good literature, perhaps the length of a novel draws us into it. A novel is like a short story but is much longer. Therefore, in a novel there can be more characters, and you get to know the main characters much better. The plot is often more complicated; much more happens. Also, there is sometimes more than one setting in a novel, and the time can stretch over weeks, years, or even decades. Because of its length, you become more involved in the characters' lives. By the end of the novel, you feel as if you know the characters and the settings personally.

How to Read a Novel

Tuck Everlasting

When you read a novel, you enter another world. You meet new people, visit strange places, learn about different ideas, and experience a variety of emotions and events. Like a short story, a novel is a work of fiction with characters, plot, setting, and theme. However, a novel usually cannot be read in one sitting because of its length. Because you spend more time with the characters and the plot, you are usually drawn more deeply into a novel than into a short story.

BACKGROUND The setting of *Tuck Everlasting* is a small, rural town and its surrounding area. The time is late summer in 1880. Against this backdrop of rural America, you will meet a young girl, Winnie Foster, and an extraordinary family, the Tucks. The ideas and issues that Winnie considers from her experiences with the Tucks still have meaning today. You will find yourself asking the same questions that she asks as you read along.

READING STRATEGIES The length of a novel has advantages and disadvantages in comparison with a short story. You can get to know the characters better in a novel because they are more fully developed over a longer period of time. The theme can also be developed more fully. Apply your active reading strategies to a novel just as you would to a short story. Question what's happening and why the author includes information. After you complete a chapter or section of the novel, summarize it to help you to remember what you have read and to see how the information fits together with the rest of the novel. Make predictions. This strategy is especially helpful when reading *Tuck Everlasting.* The beginning of the novel in particular raises many questions and provides many hints about what is to come. Think carefully about these questions and hints, and predict what might happen as a result. Allow yourself to respond. How do you feel about the characters and the ideas?

THEMES You will encounter these themes in *Tuck Everlasting.*

- The challenge of handling events that are out of the ordinary
- The importance of humans' place in the cycle of life
- The importance of independence as a step toward maturity
- The difficulty sometimes encountered in doing what one believes to be right
- The consequences of greed
- Turning points on the road to maturity

Tuck Everlasting

SCENE AT HOUGHTON
Winslow Homer
Hirshhorn Museum and Sculpture Garden
Washington, D.C.

GUIDE FOR READING

Tuck Everlasting, Prologue–Chapter 6

Natalie Babbitt

(1932–) began her career in the field of children's books as an illustrator, and she continues to illustrate many of her own books. Babbitt writes for young people because she feels they respond to experiences and ideas in books in a way that older readers cannot. She says, "I believe that children are far more perceptive and wise than American books give them credit for." The main character in *Tuck Everlasting* proves to be both perceptive and extremely wise when she meets a family with an amazing secret.

Foreshadowing

Foreshadowing is the use of hints suggesting events to come. The hints may be comments made by the narrator, experiences or feelings of the characters, or even events in the plot. For example, in the Prologue to *Tuck Everlasting,* the narrator says, "One day . . . three things happened and at first there appeared to be no connection between them." This statement suggests that there *is* a connection, and you want to read on to find out what it is.

Focus

The novel you are about to read discusses the issue of trust. Whom do you trust? Why? Make a word web like the one below. Write down all the words and ideas that you associate with the word *trust.* As you read *Tuck Everlasting,* note which characters display the characteristics that appear on your word web.

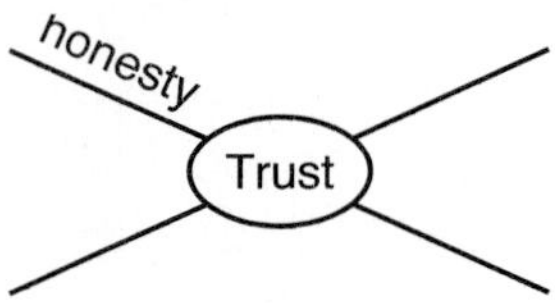

Vocabulary

Knowing the following words will help you as you read the beginning of *Tuck Everlasting.*

tangent (tan′ jənt) *n.*: A sudden change of course (p. 675)

forlorn (fər lôrn′) *adj.*: Pitiful (p. 676)

rueful (ro͞o′ fəl) *adj.*: Regretful or sorrowful (p. 678)

grimace (grim′ əs) *v.*: To twist the face in fun or in a look of pain or disgust (p. 679)

exasperated (ig zas′ pə rāt′ ’d) *adj.*: Irritated; annoyed (p. 680)

self-deprecation (self dep′ rə kā′ shən) *n.*: Expressing lack of importance of oneself (p. 681)

galling (gôl′ iŋ) *adj.*: Causing extreme irritation (p. 683)

implored (im plôrd′) *v.*: Begged (p. 688)

Tuck Everlasting

Natalie Babbitt

"Mae Tuck . . . had looked exactly the same for eighty-seven years."

Prologue

The first week of August hangs at the very top of summer, the top of the live-long year, like the highest seat of a Ferris wheel when it pauses in its turning. The weeks that come before are only a climb from balmy spring, and those that follow a drop to the chill of autumn, but the first week of August is motionless, and hot. It is curiously silent, too, with blank white dawns and glaring noons, and sunsets smeared with too much color. Often at night there is lightning, but it quivers all alone. There is no thunder, no relieving rain. These are strange and breathless days, the dog days, when people are led to do things they are sure to be sorry for after.

One day at that time, not so very long ago, three things happened and at first there appeared to be no connection between them.

At dawn, Mae Tuck set out on her horse for the wood at the edge of the village of Treegap. She was going there, as she did once every ten years, to meet her two sons, Miles and Jesse.

At noontime, Winnie Foster, whose family owned the Treegap wood, lost her patience at last and decided to think about running away.

And at sunset a stranger appeared at the Fosters' gate. He was looking for someone, but he didn't say who.

No connection, you would agree. But things can come together in strange ways. The wood was at the center, the hub of the wheel. All wheels must have a hub. A Ferris wheel has one, as the sun is the hub of the wheeling calendar. Fixed points they are, and best left undisturbed, for without them, nothing holds together. But sometimes people find this out too late.

Chapter 1

The road that led to Treegap had been trod out long before by a herd of cows who were, to say the least, relaxed. It wandered along in curves and easy angles, swayed off and up in a pleasant tangent to the top of a small hill, ambled down again between fringes of bee-hung clover, and then cut sidewise across a meadow. Here its edges blurred. It widened and seemed to pause, suggesting tranquil bovine picnics: slow chewing and thoughtful contemplation of the infinite. And then it went on again and came at last to the wood. But on reaching the shadows of the first trees, it veered sharply, swung out in a wide arc as if, for

VICTOR'S PRIDE (detail)
JoAnn Wold
Courtesy of Artique, Ltd.

the first time, it had reason to think where it was going, and passed around.

On the other side of the wood, the sense of easiness dissolved. The road no longer belonged to the cows. It became, instead, and rather abruptly, the property of people. And all at once the sun was uncomfortably hot, the dust oppressive, and the meager grass along its edges somewhat ragged and forlorn. On the left stood the first house, a square and solid cottage with a touch-me-not appearance, surrounded by grass cut painfully to the quick and enclosed by a capable iron fence some four feet high which clearly said, "Move on—we don't want *you* here." So the road went humbly by and made its way, past cottages more and more frequent but less and less forbidding, into the village. But the village doesn't matter, except for the jailhouse and the gallows. The first house only is important; the first house, the road, and the wood.

There was something strange about the wood. If the look of the first house suggested that you'd better pass it by, so did the look of the wood, but for quite a different reason. The house was so proud of itself that you wanted to make a lot of noise as you passed, and maybe even throw a rock or two. But the wood had a sleeping, otherworld appearance that made you want to speak in whispers. This, at least, is what the cows must have thought: "Let it keep its peace; *we* won't disturb it."

Whether the people felt that way about the wood or not is difficult to say. There were some, perhaps, who did. But for the most part the people followed the road around the wood because that was the way it led. There was no road *through* the wood. And anyway, for the people, there was another reason to leave the wood to itself: it belonged to the Fosters, the owners of the touch-me-not cottage, and was therefore private property in spite of the fact that it lay outside the fence and was perfectly accessible.

The ownership of land is an odd thing when you come to think of it. How deep, after all, can it go? If a person owns a piece of land, does he own it all the way down, in ever narrowing dimensions, till it meets all other pieces at the center of the earth? Or does ownership consist only of a thin crust under which the friendly worms have never heard of trespassing?

In any case, the wood, being on top—except, of course, for its roots—was owned bud and bough by the Fosters in the touch-me-not cottage, and if they never went there, if they never wandered in among the trees, well, that was their affair. Winnie, the only child of the house, never went there, though she sometimes stood inside the fence, carelessly banging a stick against the iron bars, and looked at it. But she had never been curious about it. Nothing ever seems interesting when it belongs to you—only when it doesn't.

And what is interesting, anyway, about a slim few acres of trees? There will be a dimness shot through with bars of sunlight, a great many squirrels and birds, a deep, damp mattress of leaves on the ground, and all the other things just as familiar if not so pleasant—things like spiders, thorns, and grubs.

In the end, however, it was the cows who were responsible for the wood's isolation, and the cows, through some wisdom they were not wise enough to know that they possessed, were very wise indeed. If they had made their road through the wood instead of around it, then the people would have followed the road. The people would have noticed the giant ash tree at the center of the wood, and then, in time, they'd have noticed the little spring bubbling up among its roots in spite of the pebbles piled there to conceal it. And that would have been a disaster so immense that this weary old earth, owned or not to its fiery core, would have trembled on its axis like a beetle on a pin.

Chapter 2

And so, at dawn, that day in the first week of August, Mae Tuck woke up and lay for a while beaming at the cobwebs on the ceiling. At last she said aloud, "The boys'll be home tomorrow!"

Mae's husband, on his back beside her, did not stir. He was still asleep, and the melancholy creases that folded his daytime face were smoothed and slack. He snored gently, and for a moment the corners of his mouth turned upward in a smile. Tuck almost never smiled except in sleep.

Mae sat up in bed and looked at him tolerantly. "The boys'll be home tomorrow," she said again, a little more loudly.

Tuck twitched and the smile vanished. He opened his eyes. "Why'd you have to wake me up?" he sighed. "I was having that dream again, the good one where we're all in heaven and never heard of Treegap."

Mae sat there frowning, a great potato of a woman with a round, sensible face and calm brown eyes. "It's no use having that dream," she said. "Nothing's going to change."

"You tell me that every day," said Tuck, turning away from her onto his side. "Anyways, I can't help what I dream."

"Maybe not," said Mae. "But, all the same, you should've got used to things by now."

Tuck groaned. "I'm going back to sleep," he said.

"Not me," said Mae. "I'm going to take the horse and go down to the wood to meet them."

"Meet who?"

"The boys, Tuck! Our sons. I'm going to ride down to meet them."

"Better not do that," said Tuck.

"I know," said Mae, "but I just can't wait to see them. Anyways, it's ten years since I went to Treegap. No one'll remember me. I'll ride in at sunset, just to the wood. I won't go into the village. But, even if someone did see me, they won't remember. They never did before, now, did they?"

"Suit yourself, then," said Tuck into his pillow. "I'm going back to sleep."

Mae Tuck climbed out of bed and began to dress: three petticoats, a rusty brown skirt with one enormous pocket, an old cotton jacket, and a knitted shawl which she pinned across her bosom with a tarnished metal brooch. The sounds of her dressing were so familiar to Tuck that he could say, without opening his eyes, "You don't need that shawl in the middle of the summer."

Mae ignored this observation. Instead, she said, "Will you be all right? We won't get back till late tomorrow."

Tuck rolled over and made a rueful face at her. "What in the world could possibly happen to me?"

"That's so," said Mae. "I keep forgetting."

"*I* don't," said Tuck. "Have a nice time." And in a moment he was asleep again.

Mae sat on the edge of the bed and pulled on a pair of short leather boots so thin and soft with age it was a wonder they held together. Then she stood and took from the washstand beside the bed a little square-shaped object, a music box painted with roses and lilies of the valley. It was the one pretty thing she owned and she never went anywhere without it. Her fingers strayed to the winding key on its bottom, but glancing at the sleeping Tuck, she shook her head, gave the little box a pat, and dropped it into her pocket. Then, last of all, she pulled down over her ears a blue straw hat with a drooping, exhausted brim.

But, before she put on the hat, she brushed her gray-brown hair and wound it into a bun at the back of her neck. She did this quickly and skillfully without a single glance in the mirror. Mae Tuck didn't need a mirror, though she had one propped up on the washstand. She knew very well what she would see in it; her reflection had long since ceased to interest her. For Mae Tuck, and her husband, and Miles and Jesse, too, had all looked exactly the same for eighty-seven years.

Chapter 3

At noon of that same day in the first week of August, Winnie Foster sat on the bristly grass just inside the fence and said to the large toad who was squatting a few yards away across the road, "I will, though. You'll see. Maybe even first thing tomorrow, while everyone's still asleep."

It was hard to know whether the toad was listening or not. Certainly, Winnie had given it good reason to ignore her. She had come out to the fence, very cross, very near the boiling point on a day that was itself near to boiling, and had noticed the toad at once. It was the only living thing in sight except for a stationary cloud of hysterical gnats suspended in the heat above the road. Winnie had found some pebbles at the base of the fence and, for lack of any other way to show how she felt, had flung one at the toad. It missed altogether, as she'd fully intended it should, but she made a game of it anyway, tossing pebbles at such an angle that they passed through the gnat cloud on their way to the toad. The gnats were too frantic to notice these intrusions, however, and since every pebble missed its final mark, the toad continued to squat and grimace without so much as a twitch. Possibly it felt resentful. Or perhaps it was only asleep. In either case, it gave her not a glance when at last she ran out of pebbles and sat down to tell it her troubles.

"Look here, toad," she said, thrusting her arms through the bars of the fence and plucking at the weeds on the other side. "I don't think I can stand it much longer."

At this moment a window at the front of the cottage was flung open and a thin voice—her grandmother's—piped, "Winifred! Don't sit on that dirty grass. You'll stain your boots and stockings."

And another, firmer voice—her mother's—added, "Come in now, Winnie. Right away. You'll get heat stroke out there on a day like this. And your lunch is ready."

"See?" said Winnie to the toad. "That's just what I mean. It's like that every minute. If I had a sister or a brother, there'd be someone else for them to watch. But, as it is, there's only me. I'm tired of being looked at all the time. I want to be by myself for a change." She leaned her forehead against the bars and after a short silence went on in a thoughtful tone. "I'm not exactly sure what I'd do, you know, but something interesting—something that's all mine. Something that would make some kind of difference in the world. It'd be nice to have a new name, to start with, one that's not all worn out from being called so much. And I might even decide to have a pet. Maybe a big old toad, like you, that I could keep in a nice cage with lots of grass, and . . ."

At this the toad stirred and blinked. It gave a heave of muscles and plopped its heavy mudball of a body a few inches farther away from her.

"I suppose you're right," said Winnie. "Then you'd be just the way I am, now. Why should you have to be cooped up in a cage, too? It'd be better if I could be like you, out in the open and making up my own mind. Do you know they've hardly ever let me out of this yard all by myself? I'll never be able to do anything important if I stay in here like this. I expect I'd better run away." She paused and peered anxiously at the toad to see how it would receive this staggering idea, but it showed no signs of interest. "You think I wouldn't dare, don't you?" she said accusingly. "I will, though. You'll see. Maybe even first thing in the morning, while everyone's still asleep."

"Winnie!" came the firm voice from the window.

"All *right!* I'm coming!" she cried, exas-

MANDY'S SUNHAT
Robert Duncan

perated, and then added quickly, "I mean, I'll be right there, Mama." She stood up, brushing at her legs where bits of itchy grass clung to her stockings.

The toad, as if it saw that their interview was over, stirred again, bunched up, and bounced itself clumsily off toward the wood. Winnie watched it go. "Hop away, toad," she called after it. "You'll see. Just wait till morning."

Chapter 4

At sunset of that same long day, a stranger came strolling up the road from the village and paused at the Fosters' gate. Winnie was once again in the yard, this time intent on catching fireflies, and at first she didn't notice him. But, after a few moments of watching her, he called out, "Good evening!"

He was remarkably tall and narrow, this stranger standing there. His long chin faded off into a thin, apologetic beard, but his suit was a jaunty yellow that seemed to glow a little in the fading light. A black hat dangled from one hand, and as Winnie came toward him, he passed the other through his dry, gray hair, settling it smoothly. "Well, now," he said in a light voice. "Out for fireflies, are you?"

"Yes," said Winnie.

"A lovely thing to do on a summer evening," said the man richly. "A lovely entertainment. I used to do it myself when I was your age. But of course that was a long, long time ago." He laughed, gesturing in self-deprecation with long, thin fingers. His tall body moved continuously; a foot tapped, a shoulder twitched. And it moved in angles, rather jerkily. But at the same time he had a kind of grace, like a well-handled marionette.[1] Indeed, he seemed almost to hang suspended there in the twilight. But Winnie, though she was half charmed, was suddenly reminded of the stiff black ribbons they had hung on the door of the cottage for her grandfather's funeral. She frowned and looked at the man more closely. But his smile seemed perfectly all right, quite agreeable and friendly.

"Is this your house?" asked the man, folding his arms now and leaning against the gate.

"Yes," said Winnie. "Do you want to see my father?"

"Perhaps. In a bit," said the man. "But I'd like to talk to you first. Have you and your family lived here long?"

"Oh, yes," said Winnie. "We've lived here forever."

"Forever," the man echoed thoughtfully.

It was not a question, but Winnie decided to explain anyway. "Well, not forever, of course, but as long as there've been any people here. My grandmother was born here. She says this was all trees once, just one big forest everywhere around, but it's mostly all cut down now. Except for the wood."

"I see, said the man, pulling at his beard. "So of course you know everyone, and everything that goes on."

"Well, not especially," said Winnie. "At least, *I* don't. Why?"

The man lifted his eyebrows. "Oh," he said, "I'm looking for someone. A family."

"I don't know anybody much," said Winnie, with a shrug. "But my father might. You could ask him."

---

1. marionette (mar′ ē ə net′) *n.*: A puppet moved by strings from above.

"I believe I shall," said the man. "I do believe I shall."

At this moment the cottage door opened, and in the lamp glow that spilled across the grass, Winnie's grandmother appeared. "Winifred? Who are you talking to out there?"

"It's a man, Granny," she called back. "He says he's looking for someone."

"What's that?" said the old woman. She picked up her skirts and came down the path to the gate. "What did you say he wants?"

The man on the other side of the fence bowed slightly. "Good evening, madam," he said. "How delightful to see you looking so fit."

"And why shouldn't I be fit?" she retorted, peering at him through the fading light. His yellow suit seemed to surprise her, and she squinted suspiciously. "We haven't met, that I can recall. Who are you? Who are you looking for?"

The man answered neither of these questions. Instead, he said, "This young lady tells me you've lived here for a long time, so I thought you would probably know everyone who comes and goes."

The old woman shook her head. "I *don't* know everyone," she said, "nor do I want to. And I don't stand outside in the dark discussing such a thing with strangers. Neither does Winifred. So . . ."

And then she paused. For, through the twilight sounds of crickets and sighing trees, a faint, surprising wisp of music came floating to them, and all three turned toward it, toward the wood. It was a tinkling little melody, and in a few moments it stopped.

"My stars!" said Winnie's grandmother, her eyes round. "I do believe it's come again, after all these years!" She pressed her wrinkled hands together, forgetting the man in the yellow suit. "Did you hear that, Winifred? That's it! That's the elf music I told you about. Why, it's been ages since I heard it last. And this is the first time you've *ever* heard it, isn't it? Wait till we tell your father!" And she seized Winnie's hand and turned to go back into the cottage.

"Wait!" said the man at the gate. He had stiffened, and his voice was eager. "You've heard that music before, you say?"

But, before he could get an answer, it began again and they all stopped to listen. This time it tinkled its way faintly through the little melody three times before it faded.

"It sounds like a music box," said Winnie when it was over.

"Nonsense. It's elves!" crowed her grandmother excitedly. And then she said to the man at the gate, "You'll have to excuse us now." She shook the gate latch under his nose, to make sure it was locked, and then, taking Winnie by the hand once more, she marched up the path into the cottage, shutting the door firmly behind her.

But the man in the yellow suit stood tapping his foot in the road for a long time all alone, looking at the wood. The last stains of sunset had melted away, and the twilight died, too, as he stood there, though its remnants clung reluctantly to everything that was pale in color—pebbles, the dusty road, the figure of the man himself—turning them blue and blurry.

Then the moon rose. The man came to himself and sighed. His expression was one of intense satisfaction. He put on his hat, and in the moonlight his long fingers were graceful and very white. Then he turned and disappeared down the shadowy road, and as he went he whistled, very softly, the tinkling little melody from the wood.

Chapter 5

Winnie woke early next morning. The sun was only just opening its own eye on the eastern horizon and the cottage was full of silence. But she realized that sometime during the night she had made up her mind: she would not run away today. "Where would I go, anyway?" she asked herself. "There's nowhere else I really want to be." But in another part of her head, the dark part where her oldest fears were housed, she knew there was another sort of reason for staying at home: she was afraid to go away alone.

It was one thing to talk about being by yourself, doing important things, but quite another when the opportunity arose. The characters in the stories she read always seemed to go off without a thought or care, but in real life—well, the world was a dangerous place. People were always telling her so. And she would not be able to manage without protection. They were always telling her that, too. No one ever said precisely what it was that she would not be able to manage. But she did not need to ask. Her own imagination supplied the horrors.

Still, it was galling, this having to admit she was afraid. And when she remembered the toad, she felt even more disheartened. What if the toad should be out by the fence again today? What if he should laugh at her secretly and think she was a coward?

Well, anyway, she could at least slip out, right now, she decided, and go into the wood. To see if she could discover what had really made the music the night before. That would be something, anyway. She did not allow herself to consider the idea that making a difference in the world might require a bolder venture. She merely told herself consolingly, "Of course, while I'm in the wood, if I decide never to come back, well then, that will be that." She was able to believe in this because she needed to; and, believing, was her own true, promising friend once more.

It was another heavy morning, already hot and breathless, but in the wood the air was cooler and smelled agreeably damp. Winnie had been no more than two slow minutes walking timidly under the interlacing branches when she wondered why she had never come here before. "Why, it's nice!" she thought with great surprise.

For the wood was full of light, entirely different from the light she was used to. It was green and amber and alive, quivering in splotches on the padded ground, fanning into sturdy stripes between the tree trunks. There were little flowers she did not recognize, white and palest blue; and endless, tangled vines; and here and there a fallen log, half rotted but soft with patches of sweet green-velvet moss.

And there were creatures everywhere. The air fairly hummed with their daybreak activity: beetles and birds and squirrels and ants, and countless other things unseen, all gentle and self-absorbed and not in the least alarming. There was even, she saw with satisfaction, the toad. It was squatting on a low stump and she might not have noticed it, for it looked more like a mushroom than a living creature sitting there. As she came abreast of it, however, it blinked, and the movement gave it away.

"See?" she exclaimed. "I told you I'd be here first thing in the morning."

The toad blinked again and nodded. Or

perhaps it was only swallowing a fly. But then it nudged itself off the edge of the stump and vanished in the underbrush.

"It must have been watching for me," said Winnie to herself, and was very glad she had come.

She wandered for a long time, looking at everything, listening to everything, proud to forget the tight, pruned world outside, humming a little now, trying to remember the pattern of the melody she had heard the night before. And then, up ahead, in a place where the light seemed brighter and the ground somewhat more open, something moved.

Winnie stopped abruptly and crouched down. "If it's really elves," she thought, "I can have a look at them." And, though her instinct was to turn and run, she was pleased to discover that her curiosity was stronger. She began to creep forward. She would go just close enough, she told herself. Just close enough to see. And *then* she would turn and run. But when she came near, up behind a sheltering tree trunk, and peered around it, her mouth dropped open and all thought of running melted away.

There was a clearing directly in front of her, at the center of which an enormous tree thrust up, its thick roots rumpling the

IN THE WOODS
William Trost Richards
Bowdoin College Museum of Art

ground ten feet around in every direction. Sitting relaxed with his back against the trunk was a boy, almost a man. And he seemed so glorious to Winnie that she lost her heart at once.

He was thin and sunburned, this wonderful boy, with a thick mop of curly brown hair, and he wore his battered trousers and loose, grubby shirt with as much self-assurance as if they were silk and satin. A pair of green suspenders, more decorative than useful, gave the finishing touch, for he was shoeless and there was a twig tucked between the toes of one foot. He waved the twig idly as he sat there, his face turned up to gaze at the branches far above him. The golden morning light seemed to glow all around him, while brighter patches fell, now on his lean, brown hands, now on his hair and face, as the leaves stirred over his head.

Then he rubbed an ear carelessly, yawned, and stretched. Shifting his position, he turned his attention to a little pile of pebbles next to him. As Winnie watched, scarcely breathing, he moved the pile carefully to one side, pebble by pebble. Beneath the pile, the ground was shiny wet. The boy lifted a final stone and Winnie saw a low spurt of water, arching up and returning, like a fountain, into the ground. He bent and put his lips to the spurt, drinking noiselessly, and then he sat up again and drew his shirt sleeve across his mouth. As he did this, he turned his face in her direction—and their eyes met.

For a long moment they looked at each other in silence, the boy with his arm still raised to his mouth. Neither of them moved. At last his arm fell to his side. "You may as well come out," he said, with a frown.

Winnie stood up, embarrassed and, because of that, resentful. "I didn't mean to watch you," she protested as she stepped into the clearing. "I didn't know anyone would be here."

The boy eyed her as she came forward. "What're *you* doing here?" he asked her sternly.

"It's my wood," said Winnie, surprised by the question. "I can come here whenever I want to. At least, I was never here before, but I *could* have come, any time."

"Oh," said the boy, relaxing a little. "You're one of the Fosters, then."

"I'm Winnie," she said. "Who are you?"

"I'm Jesse Tuck," he answered. "How do." And he put out a hand.

Winnie took his hand, staring at him. He was even more beautiful up close. "Do you live nearby?" she managed at last, letting go of his hand reluctantly. "I never saw you before. Do you come here a lot? No one's supposed to. It's our wood." Then she added quickly, "It's all right, though, if *you* come here. I mean, it's all right with *me*."

The boy grinned. "No, I don't live nearby, and no, I don't come here often. Just passing through. And thanks, I'm glad it's all right with you."

"That's good," said Winnie irrelevantly. She stepped back and sat down primly a short distance from him. "How old are you, anyway?" she asked, squinting at him.

There was a pause. At last he said, "Why do you want to know?"

"I just wondered," said Winnie.

"All right. I'm one hundred and four years old," he told her solemnly.

"No, I mean really," she persisted.

"Well then," he said, "if you must know, I'm seventeen."

"Seventeen?"

"That's right."

"Oh," said Winnie hopelessly. "Seventeen. That's old."

"You have no idea," he agreed with a nod.

Winnie had the feeling he was laughing at her, but decided it was a nice kind of laughing. "Are you married?" she asked next.

This time he laughed out loud. "No, I'm not married. Are you?"

Now it was Winnie's turn to laugh. "Of course not," she said. "I'm only ten. But I'll be eleven pretty soon."

"And *then* you'll get married," he suggested.

Winnie laughed again, her head on one side, admiring him. And then she pointed to the spurt of water. "Is that good to drink?" she asked. "I'm thirsty."

Jesse Tuck's face was instantly serious. "Oh, that. No—no, it's not," he said quickly. "You mustn't drink from it. Comes right up out of the ground. Probably pretty dirty." And be began to pile the pebbles over it again.

"But *you* drank some," Winnie reminded him.

"Oh. Did you see that?" He looked at her anxiously. "Well, me, I'll drink anything. I mean, I'm used to it. It wouldn't be good for *you*, though."

"Why not?" said Winnie. She stood up. "It's mine, anyway, if it's in the wood. I want some. I'm about dry as dust." And she went to where he sat, and knelt down beside the pile of pebbles.

"Believe me, Winnie Foster," said Jesse, "it would be terrible for you if you drank any of this water. Just terrible. I can't let you."

"Well, I still don't see why not," said Winnie plaintively. "I'm getting thirstier every minute. If it didn't hurt you, it won't hurt me. If my papa was here, he'd let me have some."

"You're not going to tell him about it, are you?" said Jesse. His face had gone very pale under its sunburn. He stood up and put a bare foot firmly on the pile of pebbles. "I knew this would happen sooner or later. *Now* what am I going to do?"

As he said this, there was a crashing sound among the trees and a voice called, "Jesse?"

"Thank goodness!" said Jesse, blowing out his cheeks in relief. "Here comes Ma and Miles. They'll know what to do."

And sure enough, a big, comfortable-looking woman appeared, leading a fat old horse, and at her side was a young man almost as beautiful as Jesse. It was Mae Tuck with her other son, Jesse's older brother. And at once, when she saw the two of them, Jesse with his foot on the pile of pebbles and Winnie on her knees beside him, she seemed to understand. Her hand flew to her bosom, grasping at the old brooch that fastened her shawl, and her face went bleak. "Well, boys," she said, "here it is. The worst is happening at last."

Chapter 6

Afterward, when she thought about it, it seemed to Winnie that the next few minutes were only a blur. First she was kneeling on the ground, insisting on a drink from the spring, and the next thing she knew, she was seized and swung through the air, open-mouthed, and found herself straddling the bouncing back of the fat old horse, with Miles and Jesse trotting along on either side, while Mae ran puffing ahead, dragging on the bridle.

Winnie had often been haunted by visions of what it would be like to be kidnapped. But none of her visions had been like this, with her kidnappers just as alarmed as she was herself. She had always pictured a troupe of burly men with long black moustaches who would tumble her into a blanket and bear her off like a sack of potatoes while she pleaded for mercy. But, instead, it was *they*, Mae Tuck and Miles and Jesse, who were pleading.

"Please, child . . . dear, dear child . . . don't you be scared." This was Mae, trying to run and call back over her shoulder at the same time. "We . . . wouldn't harm you . . . for the world."

"If you'd . . . yelled or anything"—this was Jesse—"someone might've heard you and . . . that's too risky."

And Miles said, "We'll explain it . . . soon as we're far enough away."

Winnie herself was speechless. She clung to the saddle and gave herself up to the astonishing fact that, though her heart was pounding and her backbone felt like a pipe full of cold running water, her head was fiercely calm. Disconnected thoughts presented themselves one by one, as if they had been waiting their turn in line. "So this is what it's like to ride a horse—I was going to run away today anyway—what will they say when I'm not there for breakfast—I wish the toad could see me now—that woman is worried about me—Miles is taller than Jesse—I'd better duck if I don't want this next branch to knock me off."

They had come to the edge of the wood now, with no sign of slowing their rapid jog. The road, where it angled across the meadow, was just ahead, dazzling white in the open sunlight. And there, standing on the road, was the man from the night before, the man in the yellow suit, his black hat on his head.

Discovering him, seeing his surprise, and presented at once with choices, Winnie's mind perversely went blank. Instead of crying out for help, she merely goggled at him as they fled past the spot where he stood. Mae Tuck was the only one who spoke, and the most she could offer was: "Teaching our little girl . . . how to ride!" Only then did it come to Winnie that she ought to shout, wave her arms, do *something*. But the man had fallen away behind by that time, and she was afraid to let go of the saddle, afraid to turn around, lest she fall off the horse. In another moment it was too late. They had sped up the hill and down its other side, and the opportunity was lost.

After another few minutes, the road led them to a place where, off to the left, a shallow stream looped near, with willows and sheltering, scrubby bushes. "Stop!" cried Mae. "We'll stop here!" Miles and Jesse grabbed at the horse's harness and he pulled up abruptly, nearly toppling Winnie off over his neck. "Lift the poor child down," Mae gasped, her chest heaving. "We'll go catch our breath by the water and try to put things straight before we go on."

But the explanation, once they had stumbled to the banks of the stream, came hard. Mae seemed embarrassed, and Miles and Jesse fidgeted, glancing at their mother uneasily. No one knew how to begin. For her part, Winnie, now that the running was over, began to comprehend what was happening, and with the comprehension her throat closed and her mouth went dry as paper. This was no vision. This was real. Strangers were taking her away; they might do anything; she might never see her mother again. And then, thinking of her mother, she saw herself as small, weak, and helpless, and she began to cry, suddenly, crushed as much by outrage as by shock.

Mae Tuck's round face wrinkled in dismay. "Dear Lord, don't cry! Please don't cry, child!" she implored. "We're not bad people, truly we're not. We *had* to bring you away—you'll see why in a minute—and we'll take you back just as soon as we can. Tomorrow. I promise."

When Mae said, "Tomorrow," Winnie's sobs turned to wails. Tomorrow! It was like being told she would be kept away forever. She wanted to go home now, at once, rush back to the safety of the fence and her mother's voice from the window. Mae reached out to her, but she twisted away, her hands over her face, and gave herself up to weeping.

"This is awful!" said Jesse. "Can't you do something, Ma? The poor little tad."

"We ought to've had some better plan than *this*," said Miles.

"That's the truth," said Mae helplessly. "The dear Lord knows there's been time enough to think of one, and it had to happen sooner or later. We been plain bone lucky it hasn't before now. But I never expected it'd be a *child!*" She reached distractedly into the pocket of her skirt and took out the music box and, without thinking, twisted the winding key with trembling fingers.

When the tinkling little melody began, Winnie's sobbing slowed. She stood by the stream, her hands still over her face, and listened. Yes, it was the same music she had heard the night before. Somehow it calmed her. It was like a ribbon tying her to familiar things. She thought, "When I get home, I'll tell Granny it wasn't elf music after all." She wiped her face as well as she could with her wet hands and turned to Mae. "That's the music I heard last night," she managed between recovering snuffles. "When I was out in my yard. My granny said it was elves."

"Dear me, no," said Mae, peering at her hopefully. "It's only my music box. I didn't suppose anyone could hear it." She held it out to Winnie. "Do you want to take a look at it?"

"It's pretty," said Winnie, taking the little box and turning it over in her hands. The winding key was still revolving, but more and more slowly. The melody faltered. Another few widely spaced notes plinked, and then it stopped.

"Wind it up if you want to," said Mae. "Clockwise."

Winnie turned the key. It clicked faintly. And then, after several more turns, the music began to play again, brisk from its fresh winding, and merry. No one who owned a thing like this could be too disagreeable. Winnie examined the painted roses and lilies of the valley, and smiled in spite of herself. "It's pretty," she repeated, handing it back to Mae.

The music box had relaxed them all. Miles dragged a handkerchief from a back pocket and mopped at his face, and Mae sank down heavily on a rock, pulling off the blue straw hat and fanning herself with it.

"Look here, Winnie Foster," said Jesse. "We're friends, we really are. But you got to help us. Come sit down, and we'll try to tell you why."

Reader's Response

What would you be thinking and doing if you were Winnie? Would you be scared? Would you be planning your escape? Explain your answer.

Responding to the Selection

Your Response

1. Before the kidnapping, Winnie says she wants to do something that would make a difference in the world. Have you ever felt that way? Explain.

Recalling

2. What does the stranger want to know?
3. Why do the Tucks react as they do to Winnie's being in the wood?

Interpreting

4. The music from the wood affects Winnie, her grandmother, and the stranger differently. What is its effect on each?
5. What about the man in the yellow suit makes him seem odd?
6. Both the Tucks and Winnie behave differently from what you would expect in a kidnapping situation. Explain the differences.

Applying

7. We often hear about adults who do great things and help others. Do you know anyone who has made a difference in the world? Explain.

Analyzing Literature

Understanding Foreshadowing

Foreshadowing is the use of hints and clues about what is yet to happen. Foreshadowing raises your curiosity, making you want to read on to find out what happens. For example, the narrator states that if the spring in the wood were discovered, "that would have been a disaster so immense that this weary old earth . . . would have trembled on its axis like a beetle on a pin." (p. 677)

1. What does this statement make you wonder about?
2. What actions and statements of the Tucks make you curious?
3. Identify three other statements that seem to foreshadow events to come. Explain why.

Critical Thinking and Reading

Making Predictions

Predictions are statements about what you think will happen in the future. When you read, you make predictions based on foreshadowing, on what you know has happened in other stories, or on your own experience. Predict what the Tucks will tell Winnie. Base your prediction on the following statements:

1. "For Mae Tuck, and her husband, and Miles and Jesse too, had all looked exactly the same for eighty-seven years."
2. Jesse says to Winnie, "It would be terrible for you if you drank any of this water. Just terrible."
3. Mae Tuck says to her sons, "Here it is. The worst is happening at last."

Thinking and Writing

Writing a Diary Entry

What qualities about yourself do you value and hope are of benefit to others? Write a diary entry reflecting on your character strengths. Begin by listing the qualities you value in yourself—not abilities but qualities such as generosity or thoughtfulness. Use your list as the basis for your entry. As you write your first draft, describe the qualities and indicate how they have made you a better person. As you revise, add examples and details that show how others benefit from your qualities.

Learning Options

1. **Art.** The author describes the clearing in the wood in some detail. Draw a picture of the clearing as you visualize it from the author's description.
2. **Writing.** Suppose that you were a police officer in charge of making a wanted poster for the kidnappers of Winnie Foster. Create a poster using the author's description of the Tucks. Do not forget to describe Winnie Foster as well.

GUIDE FOR READING

Tuck Everlasting, Chapters 7–13

Characters

Characters in a novel, like all characters in fiction, reveal what they are like through their thoughts, words, and actions. Because a novel is longer than a story, characters have more opportunities to act in different situations. Therefore, you get to know them better.

Winnie, the main character in *Tuck Everlasting,* changes and grows throughout the novel. The other important characters, Mae, Angus Tuck, Miles, and Jesse, do not change. You will find out why they do not change when you read this section of the novel.

Focus

In these chapters, Angus Tuck describes "the wheel of life." The wheel begins with a person's birth and ends with his or her death. Draw a wheel with at least five spokes. On the spokes, fill in major events that the average person experiences from birth to death.

As you read these chapters, compare the wheel you have drawn with the Tucks' description of the wheel of life.

Vocabulary

Knowing the following words will help you as you read Chapters 7–13 of *Tuck Everlasting.*

peculiar (pi kyo͞ol′ yər) *adj.*: Odd (p. 691)

parson (pär′ s'n) *n.*: Clergyman (p. 693)

shimmered (shim′ ərd) *v.*: Shone with an unsteady light (p. 695)

vanity (van′ ə tē) *n.*: Too much concern for one's appearance (p. 695)

hoarding (hôr′ diŋ) *v.*: Storing away (p. 695)

scoured (skourd) *v.*: Cleaned by hard rubbing with something rough (p. 697)

indomitable (in däm′ it ə b'l) *adj.*: Not easily discouraged or defeated (p. 697)

mirage (mi räzh) *n.*: Something that seems real but is not (p. 698)

elation (i lā′ shən) *n.*: High spirits (p. 700)

Spelling Tip

You might find it easier to spell *indomitable* if you split it into parts: *in + domit + able.*

" 'It's a big, dangerous secret. We got to have your help to keep it.' "

Chapter 7

It was the strangest story Winnie had ever heard. She soon suspected they had never told it before, except to each other—that she was their first real audience; for they gathered around her like children at their mother's knee, each trying to claim her attention, and sometimes they all talked at once, and interrupted each other, in their eagerness.

Eighty-seven years before, the Tucks had come from a long way to the east, looking for a place to settle. In those days the wood was not a wood, it was a forest, just as her grandmother had said: a forest that went on and on and on. They had thought they would start a farm, as soon as they came to the end of the trees. But the trees never seemed to end. When they came to the part that was now the wood, and turned from the trail to find a camping place, they happened on the spring. "It was real nice," said Jesse with a sigh. "It looked just the way it does now. A clearing, lots of sunshine, that big tree with all those knobby roots. We stopped and everyone took a drink, even the horse."

"No," said Mae, "the cat didn't drink. That's important."

"Yes," said Miles, "don't leave that out. We all had a drink, except the cat."

"Well, anyway," Jesse went on, "the water tasted—sort of strange. But we camped there overnight. And Pa carved a T on the tree trunk, to mark where we'd been. And then we went on."

They had come out of the forest at last, many miles to the west, had found a thinly populated valley, had started their farm. "We put up a house for Ma and Pa," said Miles, "and a little shack for Jesse and me. We figured *we'd* be starting families of our own pretty soon and would want our own houses."

"That was the first time we figured there was something peculiar," said Mae. "Jesse fell out of a tree . . ."

"I was way up in the middle," Jesse interrupted, "trying to saw off some of the branches before we cut her down. I lost my balance and I fell . . ."

"He landed plum on his head," said Mae with a shudder. "We thought for sure he'd broke his neck. But come to find out, it didn't hurt him a bit!"

"Not long after," Miles went on, "some hunters come by one day at sunset. The horse was out grazing by some trees and they shot him. Mistook him for a deer, they said. Can you fancy that? But the thing is, they didn't kill him. The bullet went right on through him, and didn't hardly even leave a mark."

"Then Pa got snake bite . . ."

"And Jesse ate the poison toadstools . . ."

"And I cut myself," said Mae. "Remember? Slicing bread."

But it was the passage of time that worried them most. They had worked the farm, settled down, made friends. But after ten years, then twenty, they had to face the fact that there was something terribly wrong. None of them was getting any older.

"I was more'n forty by then," said Miles sadly. "I was married. I had two children. But, from the look of me, I was still twenty-two. My wife, she finally made up her mind I'd sold my soul to the Devil. She left me. She went away and she took the children with her."

"I'm glad *I* never got married," Jesse put in.

"It was the same with our friends," said Mae. "They come to pull back from us. There was talk about witchcraft. Black magic. Well, you can't hardly blame them, but finally we had to leave the farm. We didn't know where to go. We started back the way we come, just wandering. We was like gypsies. When we got this far, it'd changed, of course. A lot of the trees was gone. There was people, and Treegap—it was a new village. The road was here, but in those days it was mostly just a cow path. We went on into what was left of the wood to make a camp, and when we got to the clearing and the tree and the spring, we remembered it from before."

"*It* hadn't changed, no more'n we had," said Miles. "And that was how we found out. Pa'd carved a T on the tree, remember, twenty years before, but the T was just where it'd been when he done it. That tree hadn't grown one whit in all that time. It was exactly the same. And the T he'd carved was as fresh as if it'd just been put there."

Then they had remembered drinking the water. They—and the horse. But not the cat. The cat had lived a long and happy life on the farm, but had died some ten years before. So they decided at last that the source of their changelessness was the spring.

"When we come to that conclusion," Mae went on, "Tuck said—that's my husband, Angus Tuck—he said he had to be sure, once and for all. He took his shotgun and he pointed it at hisself the best way he could, and before we could stop him, he pulled the trigger." There was a long pause. Mae's fingers laced together in her lap, twisted with the tension of remembering. At last she said, "The shot knocked him down. Went into his heart. It *had* to, the way he aimed. And right on through him. It scarcely even left a mark. Just like—*you* know—like you shot a bullet through water. And he was just the same as if he'd never done it."

"After that we went sort of crazy," said Jesse, grinning at the memory. "Heck, we was going to live forever. Can you picture what it felt like to find that out?"

"But then we sat down and talked it over . . ." said Miles.

"We're still talking it over," Jesse added.

"And we figured it'd be very bad if everyone knowed about the spring," said Mae. "We begun to see what it would mean." She peered at Winnie. "Do you understand, child? That water—it stops you right where you are. If you'd had a drink of it today, you'd stay a little girl forever. You'd never grow up, not ever."

"We don't know how it works, or even why," said Miles.

"Pa thinks it's something left over from—well, from some other plan for the way the world should be," said Jesse. "Some plan that didn't work out too good. And so everything was changed. Except that the spring was passed over, somehow or other. Maybe he's right. *I* don't know. But you see, Winnie Foster, when I told you before I'm a hundred and four years old, I was telling the truth. But I'm really only seventeen. And, so far as I know, I'll stay seventeen till the end of the world.

Chapter 8

Winnie did not believe in fairy tales. She had never longed for a magic wand, did not expect to marry a prince, and was scornful—most of the time—of her grandmother's elves. So now she sat, mouth open, wide-eyed, not knowing what to make of this extraordinary story. It couldn't—not a bit of it—be true. And yet:

"It feels so fine to tell somebody!" Jesse exploded. "Just think, Winnie Foster, you're the only person in the world, besides us, who knows about it!"

"Hold on now," said Miles cautiously. "Maybe not. There might be a whole lot of others, for all we know, wandering around just like us."

"Maybe. But *we* don't know them," Jesse pointed out. "We've never had anyone but us to talk about it to. Winnie—isn't it peculiar? And kind of wonderful? Just think of all the things we've seen in the world! All the things we're going to see!"

"That kind of talk'll make her want to rush back and drink a gallon of the stuff," warned Miles. "There's a whole lot more to it than Jesse Tuck's good times, you know."

"Oh, stuff," said Jesse with a shrug. "We might as well enjoy it, long as we can't change it. You don't have to be such a parson all the time."

"I'm not being a parson," said Miles. "I just think you ought to take it more serious."

"Now, boys," said Mae. She was kneeling by the stream, splashing her face and hands with cool water. "Whew! Such weather!" she exclaimed, sitting back on her heels. She unfastened the brooch, took off her shawl, and toweled her dripping face. "Well, child," she said to Winnie, standing up, "now you share our secret. It's a big, dangerous secret. We got to have your help to keep it. I expect you're full of questions, but we can't stay here no longer." She tied the shawl around her waist then, and sighed. "It pains me to think how your ma and pa will worry, but there's just no way around it. We got to take you home with us. That's the plan. Tuck—he'll want to talk it out, make sure you see why you can't tell no one. But we'll bring you back tomorrow. All right?" And all three of them looked at her hopefully.

"All right," said Winnie. For, she decided, there wasn't any choice. She would have to go. They would probably make her go, anyway, no matter what she said. But she felt there was nothing to be afraid of, not really. For they seemed gentle. Gentle and—in a strange way—childlike. They made her feel old. And the way they spoke to her, the way they looked at her, made her feel special. Important. It was a warm, spreading feeling, entirely new. She liked it, and in spite of their story, she liked them, too—especially Jesse.

But it was Miles who took her hand and said, "It's really fine to have you along, even if it's only for a day or two.

Then Jesse gave a great whoop and leapt into the stream, splashing mightily. "What'd you bring for breakfast, Ma?" he cried. "We can eat on the way, can't we? I'm starving!"

So, with the sun riding high now in the sky, they started off again, noisy in the August stillness, eating bread and cheese. Jesse sang funny old songs in a loud voice and swung like a monkey from the branches of trees, showing off shamelessly for Winnie, calling to her, "Hey, Winnie Foster, watch me!" and "Look what I can do!"

PATH IN THE WOODS IN SUMMER
Camille Pissarro
Musée d'Orsay, Paris, France

And Winnie, laughing at him, lost the last of her alarm. They were friends, *her* friends. She was running away after all, but she was not alone. Closing the gate on her oldest fears as she had closed the gate of her own fenced yard, she discovered the wings she'd always wished she had. And all at once she was elated. Where were the terrors she'd been told she should expect? She could not recognize them anywhere. The sweet earth opened out its wide four corners to her like the petals of a flower ready to be picked, and it shimmered with light and possibility till she was dizzy with it. Her mother's voice, the feel of home, receded for the moment, and her thoughts turned forward. Why, she, too, might live forever in this remarkable world she was only just discovering! The story of the spring—it might be true! So that, when she was not rolling along on the back of the fat old horse—by choice, this time—she ran shouting down the road, her arms flung out, making more noise than anybody.

It was good. So good, in fact, that through it all, not one of them noticed that the man they had passed on the road, the man in the yellow suit, had crept up to the bushes by the stream and heard it all, the whole fantastic story. Nor did they notice that he was following now, beside the road far behind, his mouth, above the thin, gray beard, turned ever so slightly toward a smile.

Chapter 9

The August sun rolled up, hung at mid-heaven for a blinding hour, and at last wheeled westward before the journey was done. But Winnie was exhausted long before that. Miles carried her some of the way. The tops of her cheeks were bright pink with sunburn, her nose a vivid, comic red, but she had been rescued from a more serious broiling by Mae, who had finally insisted that she wear the blue straw hat. It came down far over her ears and gave her a clownish appearance, but the shade from its brim was so welcome that Winnie put vanity aside and dozed gratefully in Miles's strong arms, her own arms wound around his neck.

The pastures, fields, and scrubby groves they crossed were vigorous with bees, and crickets leapt before them as if each step released a spring and flung them up like pebbles. But everything else was motionless, dry as biscuit, on the brink of burning, hoarding final reservoirs of sap, trying to hold out till the rain returned, and Queen Anne's lace[1] lay dusty on the surface of the meadows like foam on a painted sea.

It was amazing, then, to climb a long hill, to see ahead another hill, and beyond that the deep green of a scattered pine forest, and as you climbed, to feel the air ease and soften. Winnie revived, sniffing, and was able to ride the horse again, perched behind Mae. And to her oft-repeated question, "Are we almost there?" the welcome answer came at last: "Only a few more minutes now."

A wide stand of dark pines rose up, loomed nearer, and suddenly Jesse was crying, "We're home! This is it, Winnie Foster!" And he and Miles raced on and disappeared among the trees. The horse followed, turning onto a rutted path lumpy with roots, and it was as if they had slipped in under a giant colander. The late sun's brilliance could penetrate only in scattered glimmers, and everything was silent and untouched, the ground muffled with moss and sliding needles, the graceful arms of the pines stretched out pro-

1. **Queen Anne's lace:** A common weed with clusters of white flowers.

MAKING PEA TRELLISES
Camille Pissarro
Musée Faure, Aix-les-Bains, France

tectively in every direction. And it was cool, blessedly cool and green. The horse picked his way carefully, and then ahead the path dropped down a steep embankment; and beyond that, Winnie, peering around Mae's bulk, saw a flash of color and a dazzling sparkle. Down the embankment they swayed and there it was, a plain, homely little house, barn-red, and below it the last of the sun flashing on the wrinkled surface of a tiny lake.

"Oh, *look!*" cried Winnie. "Water!"

At the same time, they heard two enormous splashes, two voices roaring with pleasure.

"It don't take 'em more'n a minute to pile

into that pond," said Mae, beaming. "Well, you can't blame 'em in heat like this. You can go in, too, if you want."

Then they were at the door of the little house and Tuck was standing there. "Where's the child?" he demanded, for Winnie was hidden behind his wife. "The boys say you brung along a real, honest-to-goodness, natural child!"

"So I did," said Mae, sliding down off the horse, "and here she is."

Winnie's shyness returned at once when she saw the big man with his sad face and baggy trousers, but as he gazed at her, the warm, pleasing feeling spread through her again. For Tuck's head tilted to one side, his eyes went soft, and the gentlest smile in the world displaced the melancholy creases of his cheeks. He reached up to lift her from the horse's back and he said, "There's just no words to tell you how happy I am to see you. It's the finest thing that's happened in . . ." He interrupted himself, setting Winnie on the ground, and turned to Mae. "Does she know?"

"Course she knows," said Mae. "That's why I brung her back. Winnie, here's my husband, Angus Tuck. Tuck, meet Winnie Foster."

"How do, Winnie Foster," said Tuck, shaking Winnie's hand rather solemnly. "Well, then!" He straightened and peered down at her, and Winnie, looking back into his face, saw an expression there that made her feel like an unexpected present, wrapped in pretty paper and tied with ribbons, in spite of Mae's blue hat, which still enveloped her head. "Well, then," Tuck repeated, "seeing you know, I'll go on and say this is the finest thing that's happened in—oh—at least eighty years."

Chapter 10

Winnie had grown up with order. She was used to it. Under the pitiless double assaults of her mother and grandmother, the cottage where she lived was always squeaking clean, mopped and swept and scoured into limp submission. There was no room for carelessness, no putting things off until later. The Foster women had made a fortress out of duty. Within it, they were indomitable. And Winnie was in training.

So she was unprepared for the homely little house beside the pond, unprepared for the gentle eddies of dust, the silver cobwebs, the mouse who lived—and welcome to him! —in a table drawer. There were only three rooms. The kitchen came first, with an open cabinet where dishes were stacked in perilous towers without the least regard for their varying dimensions. There was an enormous black stove, and a metal sink, and every surface, every wall, was piled and strewn and hung with everything imaginable, from onions to lanterns to wooden spoons to washtubs. And in a corner stood Tuck's forgotten shotgun.

The parlor came next, where the furniture, loose and sloping with age, was set about helter-skelter. An ancient green-plush sofa lolled alone in the center, like yet another mossy fallen log, facing a soot-streaked fireplace still deep in last winter's ashes. The table with the drawer that housed the mouse was pushed off, also alone, into a far corner, and three armchairs and an elderly rocker stood about aimlessly, like strangers at a party, ignoring each other.

Beyond this was the bedroom, where a vast and tipsy brass bed took up most of the space, but there was room beside it for the washstand with the lonely mirror, and opposite its foot a cavernous oak wardrobe from which leaked the faint smell of camphor.[2]

Up a steep flight of narrow stairs was a dusty loft—"That's where the boys sleep when they're home," Mae explained—and that was all. And yet it was not quite all. For there was everywhere evidence of their activities, Mae's and Tuck's. Her sewing: patches and scraps of bright cloth; half-completed quilts and braided rugs; a bag of cotton batting with wisps of its contents, like snow, drifting into cracks and corners; the arms of the sofa webbed with strands of thread and dangerous with needles. His wood carving: curly shavings furring the floor, and little heaps of splinters and chips; every surface dim with the sawdust of countless sandings; limbs of unassembled dolls and wooden soldiers; a ship model propped on the mouse's table, waiting for its glue to dry; and a stack of wooden bowls, their sides smoothed to velvet, the topmost bowl filled with a jumble of big wooden spoons and forks, like dry, bleached bones. "We make things to sell," said Mae, surveying the mess approvingly.

And still this was not all. For, on the old beamed ceiling of the parlor, streaks of light swam and danced and wavered like a bright mirage, reflected through the windows from the sunlit surface of the pond. There were bowls of daisies everywhere, gay white and yellow. And over everything was the clean, sweet smell of the water and its weeds, the chatter of a swooping kingfisher, the carol and trill of a dozen other kinds of bird, and occasionally the thrilling bass note of an unastonished bullfrog at ease somewhere along the muddy banks.

Into it all came Winnie, eyes wide, and very much amazed. It was a whole new idea to her that people could live in such disarray, but at the same time she was charmed. It was . . . comfortable. Climbing behind Mae up the stairs to see the loft, she thought to herself: "Maybe it's because they think they have forever to clean it up." And this was followed by another thought, far more revolutionary: "Maybe they just don't care!"

"The boys don't be home very much," said Mae as they came up into the half light of the loft. "But when they are, they bed up here. There's plenty of room." The loft was cluttered, too, with all kinds of odds and ends, but there were two mattresses rolled out on the floor, and fresh sheets and blankets were folded almost neatly on each, waiting to be spread.

"Where do they go when they're away?" asked Winnie. "What do they do?"

"Oh," said Mae, "they go different places, do different things. They work at what jobs they can get, try to bring home some of their money. Miles can do carpentering, and he's a pretty fair blacksmith, too. Jesse now, *he* don't ever seem too settled in himself. Course, he's young." She stopped and smiled. "That sounds funny, don't it? Still, it's true, just the same. So Jesse, he does what strikes him at the moment, working in the fields, or in saloons, things like that, whatever he comes across. But they can't stay on in any one place for long, you know. None of us can. People get to wondering." She sighed. "We been in this house about as long as we dare, going on twenty years. It's a right nice place. Tuck's got so's he's real attached to it. Then, too, it's off by itself, plenty of fish in the pond, not too far from the towns around. When we need things, we

---

2. camphor (kam′ fər) *n.*: A strong-smelling crystal-like substance used as a moth repellent.

THE REAPER
Winslow Homer

go sometimes to one, sometimes the next, so people don't come to notice us much. And we sell where we can. But I guess we'll be moving on, one of these days. It's just about time."

It sounded rather sad to Winnie, never to belong anywhere. "That's too bad," she said, glancing shyly at Mae. "Always moving around and never having any friends or anything."

But Mae shrugged off this observation. "Tuck and me, we got each other," she said, "and that's a lot. The boys, now, they go their separate ways. They're some different, don't always get on too good. But they come home whenever the spirit moves, and every ten years, first week of August, they meet at the spring and come home *together* so's we can be a family again for a little while. That's why we was there this morning. One way or another, it all works out." She folded her arms and nodded, more to herself than to Winnie. "Life's got to be lived, no matter how long or short," she said calmly. "You got to take what comes. We just go along, like everybody else, one day at a time. Funny—we don't feel no different. Leastways, I don't. Sometimes I forget about what's happened to us, forget it altogether. And then sometimes it comes over me and I wonder why it happened to *us*. We're plain as salt, us Tucks. We don't deserve no blessings—if it is a blessing. And, likewise, I don't see how we deserve to be cursed, if it's a curse. Still—there's no use trying to figure why things fall the way they do. Things just are, and fussing don't bring changes. Tuck, now, he's got a few other ideas, but I expect he'll tell you. There! The boys are in from the pond."

Winnie heard a burst of voices downstairs, and in a moment Miles and Jesse were climbing to the loft.

"Here, child," said Mae hastily. "Hide your eyes. Boys? Are you decent? What'd you put on to swim in? I got Winnie up here, do you hear me?"

"For goodness' sake, Ma," said Jesse, emerging from the stairwell. "You think we're going to march around in our altogether with Winnie Foster in the house?"

And Miles, behind him, said, "We just jumped in with our clothes on. Too hot and tired to shed 'em."

It was true. They stood there side by side with their wet clothes plastered to their skins, little pools of water collecting at their feet.

"Well!" said Mae, relieved. "All right. Find something dry to put on. Your pa's got supper nearly ready." And she hustled Winnie down the narrow stairs.

Chapter 11

It was a good supper, flapjacks, bacon, bread, and applesauce, but they ate sitting about in the parlor instead of around a table. Winnie had never had a meal that way before and she watched them carefully at first, to see what rules there might be that she did not know about. But there seemed to be no rules. Jesse sat on the floor and used the seat of a chair for a table, but the others held their plates in their laps. There were no napkins. It was all right, then, to lick the maple syrup from your fingers. Winnie was never allowed to do such a thing at home, but she had always thought it would be the easiest way. And suddenly the meal seemed luxurious.

After a few minutes, however, it was clear to Winnie that there was at least one rule: As long as there was food to eat, there was no conversation. All four Tucks kept their eyes and their attention on the business at hand. And in the silence, given time to think, Winnie felt her elation, and her thoughtless pleasure, wobble and collapse.

It had been different when they were out-of-doors, where the world belonged to everyone and no one. Here, everything was theirs alone, everything was done their way. Eating, she realized now, was a very personal thing, not something to do with strangers. *Chewing* was a personal thing. Yet here she was, chewing with strangers in a strange place. She shivered a little, and frowned, looking round at them. That story they had told her—why, they were crazy, she thought harshly, and they were criminals. They had kidnapped her, right out of the middle of her very own wood, and now she would be expected to sleep—*all night*—in this dirty, peculiar house. She had never slept in any bed but her own in her life. All these thoughts flowed at once from the dark part of her mind. She put down her fork and said, unsteadily, "I want to go home."

The Tucks stopped eating, and looked at her, surprised. Mae said soothingly, "Why, of course you do, child. That's only natural. I'll take you home. I promised I would, soon's we've explained a bit as to why you got to promise you'll never tell about the spring. That's the only reason we brung you here. We got to make you see why."

Then Miles said, cheerfully and with sudden sympathy, "There's a pretty good old rowboat. I'll take you out for a row after supper."

"No, *I* will," said Jesse. "Let *me*. I found her first, didn't I, Winnie Foster? Listen, I'll show you where the frogs are, and . . ."

"Hush," Tuck interrupted. "Everyone hush. *I'll* take Winnie rowing on the pond. There's a good deal to be said and I think we better hurry up and say it. I got a feeling there ain't a whole lot of time."

Jesse laughed at this, and ran a hand roughly through his curls. "That's funny, Pa. Seems to me like time's the only thing we got a lot of."

But Mae frowned. "You worried, Tuck? What's got you? No one saw us on the way up. Well, now, wait a bit—yes, they did, come to think of it. There was a man on the road, just outside Treegap. But he didn't say nothing."

"He knows me, though," said Winnie. She had forgotten, too, about the man in the yellow suit, and now, thinking of him, she felt a surge of relief. "He'll tell my father he saw me."

"He knows you?" said Mae, her frown deepening. "But you didn't call out to him, child. Why not?"

"I was too scared to do *anything*," said Winnie honestly.

Tuck shook his head. "I never thought we'd come to the place where we'd be scaring children," he said. "I guess there's no way to make it up to you, Winnie, but I'm sure most awful sorry it had to happen like that. Who was this man you saw?"

"I don't know his name," said Winnie. "But he's a pretty nice man, I guess." In fact, he seemed supremely nice to her now, a kind of savior. And then she added, "He came to our house last night, but he didn't go inside."

"Well, that don't sound too serious, Pa," said Miles. "Just some stranger passing by."

"Just the same, we got to get you home again, Winnie," said Tuck, standing up decisively. "We got to get you home just as fast as we can. I got a feeling this whole thing is going to come apart like wet bread. But first we got to talk, and the pond's the best place. The pond's got answers. Come along, child. Let's go out on the water."

Chapter 12

The sky was a ragged blaze of red and pink and orange, and its double trembled on the surface of the pond like color spilled from a paintbox. The sun was dropping fast now, a soft red sliding egg yolk, and already to the east there was a darkening to purple. Winnie, newly brave with her thoughts of being rescued, climbed boldly into the rowboat. The hard heels of her buttoned boots made a hollow banging sound against its wet boards, loud in the warm and breathless quiet. Across the pond a bullfrog spoke a deep note of warning. Tuck climbed in, too, pushing off, and, settling the oars into their locks, dipped them into the silty bottom in one strong pull. The rowboat slipped from the bank then, silently, and glided out, tall water grasses whispering away from its sides, releasing it.

Here and there the still surface of the water dimpled, and bright rings spread noiselessly and vanished. "Feeding time," said Tuck softly. And Winnie, looking down, saw hosts of tiny insects skittering and skating on the surface. "Best time of all for fishing," he said, "when they come up to feed."

He dragged on the oars. The rowboat slowed and began to drift gently toward the farthest end of the pond. It was so quiet that Winnie almost jumped when the bullfrog spoke again. And then, from the tall pines and birches that ringed the pond, a wood thrush caroled. The silver notes were pure and clear and lovely.

"Know what that is, all around us, Winnie?" said Tuck, his voice low. "Life. Moving, growing, changing, never the same two minutes together. This water, you look out at it every morning, and it *looks* the same, but it ain't. All night long it's been moving, coming in through the stream back there to the west, slipping out through the stream down east here, always quiet, always new, moving on. You can't hardly see the current, can you? And sometimes the wind makes it look like it's going the other way. But it's always there, the water's always moving on, and someday, after a long while, it comes to the ocean."

They drifted in silence for a time. The bullfrog spoke again, and from behind them, far back in some reedy, secret place, another bullfrog answered. In the fading light, the trees along the banks were slowly losing their dimensions, flattening into silhouettes clipped from black paper and pasted to the paling sky. The voice of a different frog, hoarser and not so deep, croaked from the nearest bank.

"Know what happens then?" said Tuck. "To the water? The sun sucks some of it up right out of the ocean and carries it back in clouds, and then it rains, and the rain falls into the stream, and the stream keeps moving on, taking it all back again. It's a wheel, Winnie. Everything's a wheel, turning and turning, never stopping. The frogs is part of it, and the bugs, and the fish, and the wood thrush, too. And people. But never the same ones. Always coming in new, always growing and changing, and always moving on. That's the way it's supposed to be. That's the way it *is*."

The rowboat had drifted at last to the end of the pond, but now its bow bumped into the rotting branches of a fallen tree that thrust thick fingers into the water. And though the current pulled at it, dragging its stern sidewise, the boat was wedged and could not follow. The water slipped past it, out between clumps of reeds and brambles, and gurgled down a narrow bed, over stones and pebbles, foaming a little, moving swiftly now after its slow trip between the pond's wide banks. And, farther down, Winnie could see that it hurried into a curve, around a leaning willow, and disappeared.

"It goes on," Tuck repeated, "to the ocean. But this rowboat now, it's stuck. If we didn't move it out ourself, it would stay here forever, trying to get loose, but stuck. That's what us Tucks are, Winnie. Stuck so's we

SUMMER NIGHT
Eilif Peterssen
Nasjonalgalleriet, Oslo, Norway

can't move on. We ain't part of the wheel no more. Dropped off, Winnie. Left behind. And everywhere around us, things is moving and growing and changing. You, for instance. A child now, but someday a woman. And after that, moving on to make room for the new children."

Winnie blinked, and all at once her mind was drowned with understanding of what he was saying. For she—yes, even she—would go out of the world willy-nilly someday. Just go out, like the flame of a candle, and no use protesting. It was a certainty. She would try very hard not to think of it, but sometimes, as now, it would be forced upon her. She raged against it, helpless and insulted, and blurted at last, "I don't want to die."

"No," said Tuck calmly. "Not now. Your time's not now. But dying's part of the wheel, right there next to being born. You can't pick out the pieces you like and leave the rest. Being part of the whole thing, that's the blessing. But it's passing us by, us Tucks. Living's heavy work, but off to one side, the way *we* are, it's useless, too. It don't make sense. If I knowed how to climb back on the wheel, I'd do it in a minute. You can't have living without dying. So you can't call it living, what we got. We just *are*, we just *be*, like rocks beside the road."

Tuck's voice was rough now, and Winnie, amazed, sat rigid. No one had ever talked to her of things like this before. "I want to grow again," he said fiercely, "and change. And if that means I got to move on at the end of it, then I want that, too. Listen, Winnie, it's something you don't find out how you feel until afterwards. If people knowed about the spring down there in Treegap, they'd all come running like pigs to slops. They'd trample each other, trying to get some of that water. That'd be bad enough, but afterwards—can you imagine? All the little ones little forever, all the old ones old forever. Can you picture what that means? *Forever?* The wheel would keep on going round, the water rolling by to the ocean, but the people would've turned into nothing but rocks by the side of the road. 'Cause they wouldn't know till after, and then it'd be too late." He peered at her, and Winnie saw that his face was pinched with the effort of explaining. "Do you see, now, child? Do you understand? Oh, Lord, I just got to make you understand!"

There was a long, long moment of silence. Winnie, struggling with the anguish of all these things, could only sit hunched and numb, the sound of the water rolling in her ears. It was black and silky now; it lapped at the sides of the rowboat and hurried on around them into the stream.

And then, down the length of the pond, a voice rang out. It was Miles, and every word, across the water, came clearly to their ears. "Pa! Pa, come back! Something's happened, Pa. The horse is gone. Can you hear me? Someone's stole the horse."

Chapter 13

Sometime later, the man in the yellow suit slipped down from the saddle and tied the Tucks' old horse to a bar of the Fosters' fence. He tried the gate. It was unlocked. He pushed through and strode up the path to the door of the cottage. Though it was very late now, almost midnight, the windows glowed golden: the family had not gone to bed. The man in the yellow suit took off his hat and smoothed his hair with long white fingers. Then he knocked at the door. It was opened at once by Winnie's grandmother, and before she could speak, the man said quickly, "Ah! Good evening! May I come in? I have happy news for you. I know where they've taken the little girl."

Reader's Response

What do you think of the Tucks' story? Do you believe it? Why or why not?

Responding to the Selection

Your Response

1. Would you want to be immortal like the Tucks? Why or why not?

Recalling

2. How did the Tucks become immortal?

Interpreting

3. Why is Winnie astounded by the Tucks' home? How is it different from her own?
4. Explain why the Tucks cannot stay together as a family or stay in one place for long.
5. Why does Tuck choose the pond as the place for his talk with Winnie?
6. Explain what Tuck means when he says that life is like a wheel.
7. What do you think the man in the yellow suit plans to do?

Applying

8. Angus Tuck predicts that if people knew about the spring they would "trample each other, trying to get some of that water." Why does immortality appeal to people?

Analyzing Literature

Understanding Character

The **characters** in a novel reveal themselves through what they say and do and the way they interact with each other. For example, you know that Winnie has courage because when she is kidnapped you are told that "though her heart was pounding . . . her head was fiercely calm."

1. What does Angus's decision to test his immortality by shooting himself reveal about him and the way he feels about immortality?
2. Jesse says of immortality, "We might as well enjoy it, long as we can't change it." What does this statement reveal about him?
3. What does Mae's statement that "Life's got to be lived, no matter how long or short" indicate about her?

Critical Thinking and Reading

Comparing and Contrasting Characters

When you **compare** characters, you find similarities between them. When you **contrast** them, you point out differences between them. Comparing and contrasting characters can help you to understand them better.

1. How do Jesse's and Miles's attitudes toward life differ?
2. Would it be possible for Mae Tuck and Granny Foster to be friends under other circumstances? Defend your answer by comparing and contrasting them.

Thinking and Writing

Responding to a Quotation

On page 692, Jesse says, ". . . we was going to live forever. Can you picture what it felt like to find that out?" Imagine you are one of the Tucks and write a description of your thoughts and feelings when you realized you were going to live forever. Begin by freewriting about your thoughts and feelings at that moment. Then circle the words and phrases that best describe your reaction. Use these as the basis of your first draft. Revise, adding details to make your description accurate. Prepare a final draft.

Learning Options

1. **Speaking and Listening.** Dialogue refers to the words that characters say to each other. These words appear in quotation marks. Use the description of the characters in *Tuck Everlasting* to imagine how they would speak. Then, with four other students, read the dialogue between the Tucks and Winnie that begins as Tuck tells his family that he will take Winnie rowing on the pond (page 701).
2. **Writing.** Write a diary entry as Winnie Foster describing what happened to her on the day she met the Tuck family.

GUIDE FOR READING

Tuck Everlasting, Chapters 14–19

Motivation

Motivation refers to the reason—an impulse, an emotion, or a desire—that causes a person to act a certain way, to make certain decisions. Like real people, characters in fiction act according to their motives. Winnie's motive for venturing into the wood, for example, was her desire to "be by myself for a change." The action in a work of literature develops as characters with different motives interact.

Focus

You have probably been making predictions about what will happen in *Tuck Everlasting.* Do you trust the man in the yellow suit? Why or why not? Form a small group and discuss this stranger. What is he up to? Is he a danger to Winnie and the Tucks? Predict what the man in the yellow suit will do. As you read Chapters 14–19, compare your predictions with what actually happens.

Vocabulary

Knowing the following words will help you as you read Chapters 14–19 of *Tuck Everlasting.*

earnestly (ʉr′ nist lē) *adv.*: Seriously (p. 709)

illiterates (i lit′ ər its) *n.*: Those who do not know how to read or write (p. 709)

ordeal (ôr dēl′) *n.*: A severely difficult experience (p. 710)

wheezed (hwēz′d) *v.*: Breathed hard with a whistling sound (p. 710)

roust (roust) *v.*: Stir or drive out; bring out of sleep (p. 710)

in cahoots (kə ho͞ots′) *n.*: In partnership, usually in doing something dishonest (p. 710)

companionable (kəm pan′ yən ə b′l) *adj.*: Friendly (p. 710)

accommodations (ə käm′ ə dā′shənz) *n.*: Lodgings (p. 711)

petulance (pech′ oo ləns) *n.*: Unreasonable irritability (p. 719)

extraordinary (ik strôr′ d′n er′ ē) *adj.*: Very unusual (p. 720)

Spelling Tip

Notice that *extraordinary* is a compound word made up of *extra-* + *ordinary.* You might find it easier to spell if you divide it into these two words.

Chapter 14

There had been nothing for the Tucks to do but go to bed. It was too dark now to go out looking for the horse thief, and anyway, they had no idea when he had done his thieving or which way he had gone.

"That beats all, though, don't it, Pa," said Jesse, "coming up to a person's house and stealing their horse right out from under their nose!"

"I got to give you that," said Tuck. "But the question is, was it just some ordinary thief, or was it someone that had some special reason? I don't like it. I got a bad feeling about the whole thing."

"Hush now, Tuck," said Mae. She was spreading a quilt on the old sofa, making it into a bed for Winnie. "You're too much of a worrier. There's nothing we can do about it now, so there's no sense fussing. You got no reason to think there's anything peculiar about it, anyway. Come on, we'll get a good night's sleep and figure it out in the morning when we're fresh. Boys, up you go, and don't get talking—you'll keep us awake. Winnie, child, you bed down, too. You'll sleep first-rate on the sofa here."

But Winnie did not sleep at all, not for a long, long time. The cushions of the sofa were remarkably lumpy and smelled like old newspapers; and the chair pad Mae had given her for a pillow was thin and hard, and rough under her cheek. But far worse than this was the fact that she was still in her clothes, for she had firmly refused the offer of Mae's spare nightgown, with its seeming miles of faded cotton flannel. Only her own nightgown would do, and the regular bedtime routine; without them, she was painfully lonely for home. Her joy on the road that morning had completely disappeared; the wide world shrank and her oldest fears rolled freely in her consciousness. It was unbelievable that she should be in this place; it was an outrage. But she was helpless to do anything about it, helpless to control it, and exhausted by the conversation in the rowboat.

Was it true? Could they really never die, these Tucks? It had evidently not occurred to them that she might not believe it. They were only concerned that she keep the secret. Well, she did not believe it. It was nonsense. Wasn't it? Well, wasn't it?

Winnie's head whirled. Remembering the man in the yellow suit was the only thing that kept her from weeping. "He's told them by now," she thought, rehearsing it. "They've been looking for me for hours. But they don't know where to look! No. The man saw which way we were headed. Papa will find me. They're out looking for me right now."

She went over it again and again, lying wrapped in the quilt, while outside the moon rose, turning the pond to silver. There was a hint of mist, now that the air was cooler, and the frogs talked comfortably. Crickets soon joined in with their shrill, rhythmic song. In the table drawer, the mouse rustled softly, enjoying the supper of flapjack crumbs Mae had put there for him. And at last these things were clearer in Winnie's ears than the voice of her thoughts. She began to relax listening to the sound-filled silence. Then, just as she was drifting into sleep, she heard soft footsteps and Mae was beside her. "You resting easy, child?" she whispered.

"I'm all right, thank you," said Winnie.

"I'm sorry about everything," said Mae. "I just didn't know no other way but to bring you back with us. I know it ain't very happy for you here, but . . . well . . . anyway, you have a good talk with Tuck?"

"I guess so," said Winnie.

"That's good. Well. I'm going back to bed. Get a good sleep."

"All right," said Winnie.

But still Mae lingered. "We been alone so long," she said at last, "I guess we don't know how to do with visitors. But still and all, it's a good feeling, you being here with us. I wish you was . . . ours." She put out an awkward hand then and touched Winnie's hair. "Well," she said, "good night,"

"Good night," said Winnie.

Tuck came, too, a little later, to peer down at her anxiously. He was wearing a long white nightshirt and his hair was rumpled. "Oh!" he said. "You still awake? Everything all right?"

"Yes," said Winnie.

"I didn't mean to go disturbing you," he said. "But I been laying in there thinking I ought to be setting out here with you till you went to sleep."

"You don't have to do that," said Winnie, surprised and touched. "I'm all right."

He looked uncertain. "Well . . . but if you want something, will you holler? I'm just in the next room—I'd be out here like a shot." And then he added, gruffly, "It's been quite a time since we had a natural, growing child in the house . . ." His voice trailed off. "Well. Try to get some sleep. That sofa there, I guess it ain't the kind of thing you're used to."

"It's fine," said Winnie.

"The bed's no better, or I'd switch with you," he said. He didn't seem to know how to finish the conversation. But then he bent and kissed her quickly on the cheek, and was gone.

Winnie lay with her eyes wide. She felt cared for and—confused. And all at once she wondered what would happen to the Tucks when her father came. What would he do to them? She would never be able to explain how they had been with her, how they made her feel. She remembered guiltily that at supper she had decided they were criminals. Well, but they *were*. And yet . . .

And then a final visitor made her confusion complete. There was a creaking on the loft stairs and Jesse was looking down at her, very beautiful and eager in the faint blue moonlight. "Hey, Winnie Foster," he whispered. "You asleep?"

This time she sat up, pulling the quilt around her in sudden embarrassment, and answered, "No, not yet."

"Well then, listen." He knelt beside her, his curls tumbled and his eyes wide. "I been thinking it over. Pa's right about you having to keep the secret. It's not hard to see why. But the thing is, you knowing about the water already, and living right next to it so's you could go there any time, well, listen how'd it be if you was to wait till you're seventeen, same age as me—heck, that's only six years off—and then you could go and drink some, and then you could go away with me! We could get married, even. That'd be pretty good, wouldn't it! We could have a grand old time, go all around the world, see everything. Listen, Ma and Pa and Miles, they don't know how to enjoy it, what we got.

Why, heck, Winnie, life's to enjoy yourself, isn't it? What else is it good for? That's what *I* say. And you and me, we could have a good time that never, never stopped. Wouldn't that be something?"

Once more Winnie adored him, kneeling there beside her in the moonlight. He wasn't crazy. How could he be? He was just—amazing. But she was struck dumb. All she could do was stare at him.

"You think on it, Winnie Foster," Jesse whispered earnestly. "Think on it some and see if it don't sound good. Anyway, I'll see you in the morning. All right?"

"All right," she managed to whisper in return. He slipped away then, back up the creaking steps, but Winnie sat upright, wide awake, her cheeks burning. She could not deal with this remarkable suggestion, she could not "think on it." For she didn't know what to believe about anything. She lay down again, finally, and stared into the moonlight for another half an hour before she fell asleep.

Chapter 15

In Treegap, the same moonlight silvered the roof of the touch-me-not cottage, but inside, the lamps were burning. "That's right," said the man in the yellow suit. "I know where she is." He sat back in his chair in the Fosters' spotless parlor, crossing his long, thin legs, and the suspended foot began a rhythmic jiggling. He hung his hat on his knee and smiled, his eyes nearly closed. "I followed them, you see. She's with them now. As soon as I saw they'd arrived at their destination, I turned around and came directly back. I thought you'd be staying up. You've been looking for her all day, of course. It must be quite a worry."

He lifted a hand then, ignoring their exclamations, and began to smooth the thin hairs of his beard. "You know," he said thoughtfully, "I've come a long way, looking for a wood exactly like the one you've got next door here. It would mean a great deal to me to own it. And how pleasant to have neighbors like yourselves! Now, understand, I wouldn't cut down many of the trees. I'm no barbarian, you can see that. No, just a few. You wouldn't find it different at all, really." He gestured with his long, white fingers and smiled, his face crinkling pleasantly. "We'd be good friends, I think. Why, the little girl and I, we're friends already. It would be a great relief to see her safely home again, wouldn't it?" He clicked his tongue and frowned. "Dreadful thing, kidnapping. Isn't it fortunate that I was a witness! Why, without me, you might never have heard a word. They're rough country people, the ones that took her. There's just no telling what illiterates like that might do. Yes," he sighed, lifting his eyebrows and smiling again, "it looks as if I'm the only person in the whole world who knows where to find her."

And then the man in the yellow suit sat forward. His long face took on a hard expression. "Now, I don't have to spell things out for people like yourselves. Some types one comes across can't seem to cut their way through any problem, and that does make things difficult. But you, I don't have to explain the situation to *you*. I've got what you want, and you've got what I want. Of course, you might find that child without me, but . . . you might not find her in time. So: I want the wood and you want the child. It's a trade. A simple, clear-cut trade."

He looked around at the three shocked faces, and as if he were seeing nothing there but calm agreement, he smiled delightedly and rubbed his hands together. "Done and done," he said. "I knew right away, I said to myself, 'Now here is a group of intelligent, reasonable people!' I'm seldom wrong as a judge of character. Very seldom disappointed. So! All that remains is to write it up on paper, giving me the wood, and to sign it. It's best, don't you agree, to keep things legal and tidy. The rest is easy. Nothing to it. You go for your local constable, and he and I ride out and bring back the child *and* the criminals. No—oh, no, Mr. Foster—I understand your concern, but you mustn't come along. We'll do this business my way. There now! Your terrible ordeal is as good as over, isn't it? I'm so thankful I was here to help you out!"

Chapter 16

The constable was fat, and he was sleepy. He wheezed when he spoke. And he spoke quite a bit as they started off, he and the man in the yellow suit. "First they roust me out of bed in the middle of the night after I been out since sun-up looking for that child, and now I s'pose you're going to try to run me all the way," he said sourly. "I got to tell you this horse of mine is none too strong. I don't have to hurry her as a rule, so most of the time it don't matter. Seems to me we could've waited till dawn, anyway."

The man in the yellow suit was as courteous as always. "The Fosters have been waiting since yesterday morning," he pointed out. "Naturally, they're very upset. The sooner we get there, the sooner that child will be with them again."

"How come *you're* so deep in it?" asked the constable suspiciously. "Maybe you're in cahoots with the kidnappers, how do I know? You should of reported it right off, when you saw her get snatched."

The man in the yellow suit sighed. "But of course I had to find out where they were taking her," he explained patiently. "I came right back after that. And the Fosters are friends of mine. They've—uh—sold me their wood."

The constable's eyes went round. "I'll be!" he said. "What do you know about that! I didn't suppose they'd ever do a thing like that, friend or no friend. They're the first family around here, you know. Proud as peacocks, all of 'em. Family-proud, and land-proud, too. But they sold off, did they? Well, well." And he whistled in amazement.

They thumped along in silence for a while, out around the wood and across the star-lit meadow. Then the constable yawned deeply and said, "You ready to tell me how long this is going to take? How far we got to go?"

"Twenty miles north," said the man in the yellow suit.

The constable groaned. "Twenty miles!" He shifted the shotgun that rested across his saddle, and groaned again. "Clear up in the foothills? That's a fair way, all right."

There was no reply to this. The constable ran his fingers down the glistening barrel of the shotgun. Then he shrugged, and slumped a little in the saddle. "Might as well relax," he wheezed, suddenly companionable. "We'll be riding three, four hours."

Still there was no reply.

"Yessir," said the constable, trying again. "It's something new for these parts, kidnapping. Never had a case like this before that I know of, and I been in charge going on fifteen years."

He waited.

"You don't say so," his companion said at last.

"Yep, that's a fact," said the constable,

GREEN AND GOLD
Ogden M. Pleissner
Shelburne Museum, Shelburne, Vermont

with evident relief. Maybe now there would be some conversation! "Yep, fifteen years. Seen a lot of trouble in fifteen years, but nothing quite like this. 'Course, there's a first time for everything, as they say. We got a brand-new jailhouse, did you notice? Listen, it's a dandy! Give those folks nice clean accommodations." He chuckled. " 'Course, they won't be there long. Circuit judge'll be coming through next week. He'll send 'em over the Charleyville, most likely, to the county jail. That's what they do for your serious crimes. 'Course, we got a gallows[1] of our own, if we ever need it. Keeps down trouble, *I* think, just having it there. Ain't ever used it yet. That's because they take care of the serious stuff over to Charleyville, like I say."

The constable paused to light a cigar, and went on cheerfully: "What you got planned for that piece of Foster land? Going to clear her? Put up a house, or a store, maybe?"

"No," said the man in the yellow suit.

The constable waited for more, but there was no more. His sour mood returned. He frowned and shook the ashes from his cigar. "Say," he said. "You're kind of a close-lipped feller, ain't you?"

The man in the yellow suit narrowed his eyes. His mouth, above the thin gray beard, twitched with annoyance. "Look here," he said tightly. "Would you mind if I rode on ahead? I'm worried about that child. I'll tell you how to get there, and I'll go on ahead and keep watch."

"Well," said the constable grudgingly, "all right, if you're in such a ding-danged hurry. But don't do nothing till I get there. Those folks are likely dangerous. I'll try to keep up, but this horse of mine, she's none too strong. Don't see as how I could get her to a gallop, even if I tried."

"That's right," said the man in the yellow suit. "So I'll go on ahead, and wait outside the house till you get there."

He explained the route carefully, then dug his heels into the flanks of the fat old horse, cantering off into the darkness where just a hint of dawn glowed on the edges of the hills far ahead.

The constable chewed on the end of his cigar. "Humph," he said to his horse. "Did you get a gander at that suit of clothes? Oh, well, it takes all kinds, as they say." And he followed slowly after, yawning, the gap between him and the man ahead lengthening with every mile.

1. gallows (gal′ ōz) *n.*: A frame with a crossbeam used to hang criminals.

Chapter 17

For the second morning in a row, Winnie Foster woke early. Outside, in the ring of trees around the pond, the birds were celebrating, giving the new day a brass band's worth of greeting. Winnie freed herself from the twisted quilt and went to a window. Mist lay on the surface of the water, and the light was still pale. It looked unreal, and she felt, herself, unreal, waking where she had, with her hair wild and her dress all crumpled. She rubbed her eyes. Through the dewy weeds below the window, a toad hopped suddenly into view and Winnie peered at it eagerly. But no—of course it wasn't the same toad. And remembering that other toad—*her* toad, she thought now, almost fondly—it seemed to her that she had been away from home for weeks. Then she heard a step on the loft stairs and thought, "Jesse!" At once her cheeks flamed.

But it was Miles. He came into the parlor, and when he saw that she was up, he smiled and whispered, "Good! You're awake. Come on—you can help me catch some fish for breakfast."

This time, Winnie was careful not to make a noise when she climbed into the rowboat. She made her way to her seat in the stern, and Miles handed her two old cane poles—"Watch out for the hooks!" he warned—and a jar of bait: pork fat cut into little pieces. A big brown night moth fluttered out from under the oar blades propped beside her on the seat, and wobbled off toward nowhere through the fragrant air. And from the bank, something plopped into the water. A frog! Winnie caught just a glimpse of it as it scissored away from shore. The water was so clear that she could see tiny brown fish near the bottom, flicking this way and that.

Miles pushed the rowboat off and sprang in, and soon they were gliding up toward the near end of the pond, where the water came in from the stream. The locks grated as the oars dipped and swung, but Miles was skillful. He rowed without a single splash. The dripping from the blades, as they lifted, sent rows of overlapping circles spreading silently behind them. It was very peaceful. "They'll take me home today," thought Winnie. She was somehow certain of this, and began to feel quite cheerful. She had been kidnapped, but nothing bad had happened, and now it was almost over. Now, remembering the visits of the night before, she smiled—and found that she loved them, this most peculiar family. They were her friends,

THE BOATMAN
Winslow Homer
The Brooklyn Museum

after all. And hers alone.

"How'd you sleep?" Miles asked her.

"All right," she said.

"That's good. I'm glad. Ever been fishing before?"

"No," she told him.

"You'll like it. It's fun." And he smiled at her.

The mist was lifting now, as the sun poked up above the trees, and the water sparkled. Miles guided the rowboat near a spot where lily pads lay like upturned palms on the surface. "We'll let her drift some here," he said. "There'll be trout down in those weeds and stems. Here—give me the poles and I'll bait the hooks for us."

Winnie sat watching him as he worked. His face was like Jesse's, and yet not like. It was thinner, without Jesse's rounded cheeks, and paler, and his hair was almost straight, clipped neatly below the ears. His hands were different, too, the fingers thicker, the skin scrubbed-looking, but black at the knuckles and under the nails. Winnie remembered then that he worked sometimes as a blacksmith, and indeed his shoulders, under his threadbare shirt, were broad and muscled. He looked solid, like an oar, whereas Jesse—well, she decided, Jesse was like water: thin, and quick.

Miles seemed to sense that she was watching him. He looked up from the bait jar and his eyes, returning her gaze, were soft. "Remember I told you I had two children?" he asked. "Well, one of 'em was a girl. I took her fishing, too." His face clouded then, and he shook his head. "Her name was Anna. Lord, how sweet she was, that child! It's queer to think she'd be close to eighty now, if she's even still alive. And my son—he'd be eighty-two."

Winnie looked at his young, strong face, and after a moment she said, "Why didn't you take them to the spring and give them some of the special water?"

"Well, of course, we didn't realize about the spring while we was still on the farm," said Miles. "Afterwards, I thought about going to find them. I wanted to, heaven knows. But, Winnie, how'd it have been if I had? My wife was nearly forty by then. And the children—well, what was the use? They'd have been near growed theirselves. They'd have had a pa close to the same age *they* was. No, it'd all have been so mixed up and peculiar, it just wouldn't have worked. Then Pa, he was dead-set against it, anyway. The fewer people know about the spring, he says, the fewer there are to tell about it. Here—here's your pole. Just ease the hook down in the water. You'll know when you get a bite."

Winnie clutched her pole, sitting sidewise in the stern, and watched the baited hook sink slowly down. A dragonfly, a brilliant blue jewel, darted up and paused over the lily pads, then swung up and away. From the nearest bank, a bullfrog spoke.

"There certainly are a lot of frogs around here," Winnie observed.

"That's so," said Miles. "They'll keep coming, too, long as the turtles stay away. Snappers, now, they'll eat a frog soon as look at him."

Winnie thought about this peril to the frogs, and sighed. "It'd be nice," she said, "if nothing ever had to die."

"Well, now, I don't know," said Miles. "If you think on it, you come to see there'd be so many creatures, including people, we'd all be squeezed in right up next to each other before long."

Winnie squinted at her fishing line and

tried to picture a teeming world. "Mmm," she said, "yes, I guess you're right."

Suddenly the cane pole jerked in her hands and bent into an arch, its tip dragged down nearly to the water's surface. Winnie held on tight to the handle, her eyes wide.

"Hey!" cried Miles. "Look there! You got a bite. Fresh trout for breakfast, Winnie."

But just as suddenly the pole whipped straight again and the line went slack. "Shucks," said Miles. "It got away."

"I'm kind of glad," Winnie admitted, easing her rigid grip on the butt of the pole. "*You* fish, Miles. I'm not so sure I want to."

And so they drifted for a little longer. The sky was blue and hard now, the last of the mist dissolved, and the sun, stepping higher above the trees, was hot on Winnie's back. The first week of August was reasserting itself after a good night's sleep. It would be another searing day.

A mosquito appeared and sat down on Winnie's knee. She slapped at it absently, thinking about what Miles had said. If all mosquitoes lived forever—and if they kept on having babies!—it would be terrible. The Tucks were right. It was best if no one knew about the spring, including the mosquitoes. She would keep the secret. She looked at Miles, and then she asked him, "What will you do, if you've got so much time?"

"Someday," said Miles, "I'll find a way to do something important."

Winnie nodded. That was what *she* wanted.

"The way I see it," Miles went on, "it's no good hiding yourself away, like Pa and lots of other people. And it's no good just thinking of your own pleasure, either. People got to do something useful if they're going to take up space in the world."

"But what will you *do?*" Winnie persisted.

"I don't know yet," said Miles. "I ain't had no schooling or nothing, and that makes it harder." Then he set his jaw and added, "I'll find a way, though. I'll locate something."

Winnie nodded. She reached out and ran her fingers across a lily pad that lay on the water beside the boat. It was warm and very dry, like a blotter, but near its center was a single drop of water, round and perfect. She touched the drop and brought her fingertip back wet; but the drop of water, though it rolled a little, remained as round and perfect as before.

And then Miles caught a fish. There it flopped, in the bottom of the boat, its jaw working, its gills fanning rapidly. Winnie drew up her knees and stared at it. It was beautiful, and horrible too, with gleaming, rainbow-colored scales, and an eye like a marble beginning to dim even as she watched it. The hook was caught in its upper lip, and suddenly Winnie wanted to weep. "Put it back, Miles," she said, her voice dry and harsh. "Put it back right away." Miles started to protest, and then, looking at her face, he picked up the trout and gently worked the barbed hook free. "All right, Winnie," he said. He dropped the fish over the edge of the boat. If flipped its tail and disappeared under the lily pads.

"Will it be all right?" asked Winnie, feeling foolish and happy both at once.

"It'll be all right," Miles assured her. And then he said, "People got to be meat-eaters sometimes, though. It's the natural way. And that means killing things."

"I know," said Winnie weakly. "But still."

"Yes," said Miles. "I know."

Chapter 18

And so there were flapjacks again for breakfast, but no one seemed to mind. "Didn't get a bite, eh?" said Mae.

"No," said Miles, "nothing we wanted to keep."

That was true, anyway. And though Winnie blushed as he said it, she was grateful that he didn't explain.

"Never mind," said Mae. "You're likely out of practice. Tomorrow, maybe."

"Sure," said Miles. "Tomorrow."

But it was the thought of seeing Jesse again that kept Winnie's stomach fluttering. And at last he came down from the loft, yawning and rosy, rubbing his curls, just as Mae was piling the plates with flapjacks. "Well, slug-a-bed," she said to him fondly. "You come near to missing breakfast. Miles and Winnie been up for hours, out fishing and back already."

"Oh?" said Jesse, his eyes on Miles. "Where's the fish, then? How come we got nothing but flapjacks?"

"No luck," said Mae. "They wasn't biting, for some reason."

"Reason is, Miles don't know how to fish," said Jesse. He grinned at Winnie and she lowered her eyes, her heart thumping.

"It don't matter," said Mae. "We got plenty without. Come and get your plates, everybody."

They sat about in the parlor, as they had the night before. The ceiling swam with bright reflections, and sunlight streamed across the dusty, chip-strewn floor. Mae surveyed it all and sighed contentedly. "Now, this is real nice," she said, her fork poised above her plate. "Everyone sitting down together. And having Winnie here—why, it's just like a party."

"That's the truth," said Jesse and Miles both together, and Winnie felt a rush of happiness.

"Still, we got things to discuss," Tuck reminded them. "There's the business of the horse getting stole. And we got to get Winnie home where she belongs. How we going to do that without the horse?"

"After breakfast, Tuck," said Mae firmly. "Don't spoil a good meal with a lot of talk. We'll get to it soon enough."

So they were silent, eating, and this time Winnie licked the syrup from her fingers without pausing to think about it first. Her fears at last night's supper seemed silly to her now. Perhaps they *were* crazy, but they weren't criminals. She loved them. They belonged to her.

Tuck said, "How'd you sleep, child?"

And she answered, "Just fine," and wished, for a fleeting moment, that she could stay with them forever in that sunny, untidy little house by the pond. Grow up with them and perhaps, if it was true about the spring—then perhaps, when she was seventeen . . . She glanced at Jesse, where he sat on the floor, his curly head bent over his plate. Then she looked at Miles. And then her eyes went to Tuck and lingered on his sad, creased face. It occurred to her that he was the dearest of them all, though she couldn't have explained why she felt that way.

However, there wasn't time to wonder, for at that moment someone knocked at the door.

It was such an alien sound, so sudden and surprising, that Mae dropped her fork, and everyone looked up, startled. "Who's that?" said Tuck.

"I can't imagine," whispered Mae. "We

ain't never had callers in all the years we been here."

The knock came again.

"I'll go, Ma," said Miles.

"No, stay where you are," she said. *"I'll go."* She put her plate down carefully on the floor and stood up, straightening her skirts. Then she went to the kitchen and opened the door.

Winnie recognized the voice at once. It was a rich and pleasant voice. The man in the yellow suit. And he was saying, "Good morning, Mrs. Tuck. It *is* Mrs. Tuck, isn't it. May I come in?"

Chapter 19

The man in the yellow suit came into the sunlit parlor. He stood for a moment, looking around at them all, Mae and Miles and Jesse and Tuck, and Winnie, too. His face was without expression, but there was something unpleasant behind it that Winnie sensed at once, something that made her instantly suspicious. And yet his voice was mild when he said, "You're safe now, Winifred. I've come to take you home."

"We was going to bring her back directly, ourself," said Tuck, standing up slowly. "She ain't been in no danger."

"You're Mr. Tuck, I suppose," said the man in the yellow suit.

"I am," said Tuck formally, his back straighter than usual.

"Well, you may as well sit down again. You, too, Mrs. Tuck. I have a great deal to say and very little time for saying it."

Mae sat down on the edge of the rocker, and Tuck sat, too, but his eyes were narrowed.

Jesse said, uneasily, "Who in tarnation do you think you—"

But Tuck interrupted. "Hush, boy. Let him speak his piece."

"That's wise," said the man in the yellow suit. "I'll be as brief as possible." He took off his hat and laid it on the mantel, and then he stood tapping his foot on the littered hearth, facing them. His face was smooth and empty. "I was born west of here," he began, "and all the time I was growing up, my grandmother told me stories. They were wild, unbelievable stories, but *I* believed them. They involved a dear friend of my grandmother's who married into a very odd family. Married the older of two sons, and they had two children. It was after the children were born that she began to see that the family was odd. This friend of my grandmother's, she lived with her husband for twenty years, and strange to say, he never got any older. *She* did, but he didn't. And neither did his mother or his father or his brother. People began to wonder about that family, and my grandmother's friend decided at last that they were witches, or worse. She left her husband and came with her children to live at my grandmother's house for a short while. Then she moved west. I don't know what became of her. But my mother still remembers playing with the children. They were all about the same age. There was a son, and a daughter."

"Anna!" whispered Miles.

Mae burst out, "You got no call to come and bring us pain!"

And Tuck added roughly, "You got something to say, you better come to the point and say it."

"There, there, now," said the man in the yellow suit. He spread his long, white fingers in a soothing gesture. "Hear me out. As I've told you, I was fascinated by my grand-

COUNTRY ROAD
Alfred Morang
Collection of Mr. and Mrs. Graeme Gilfillan

mother's stories. People who never grew older! It was fantastic. It took possession of me. I decided to devote my life to finding out if it could be true, and if so, how and why. I went to school, I went to a university, I studied philosophy,[2] metaphysics,[3] even a little medicine. None of it did me any good. Oh, there were ancient legends, but nothing more. I nearly gave it up. It began to seem ridiculous, and a waste of time. I went home. My grandmother was very old by then. I took her a present one day, a music box. And when I gave it to her, it reminded her of something: the woman, the mother of the family that didn't grow old, *she* had had a music box."

Mae's hand went to the pocket of her skirt. Her mouth opened, and then she shut it again with a snap.

"That music box played a very particular tune," the man in the yellow suit went on. "My grandmother's friend and her children—Anna? Was that the daughter's name?—they'd heard it so often that they knew it by heart. They'd taught it to my mother during the short time they lived in the house. We talked about it then, all those years afterward, my mother, my grandmother, and I. My mother was able to remember the melody, finally. She taught it to me. That was nearly twenty years ago now, but I kept it in my head. It was a clue."

The man in the yellow suit folded his arms and rocked a little. His voice was easy, almost friendly. "During those twenty years," he said, "I worked at other things. But I couldn't forget the tune or the family that

---

2. philosophy (fi läs′ ə fē) *n.*: The study of thought, knowledge, existence, and reality.

3. metaphysics (met′ ə fiz′ iks) *n.*: A branch of philosophy that seeks to explain the nature of being and the nature of the origin and structure of the world.

didn't grow older. They haunted my dreams. So a few months ago I left my home and I started out to look for them, following the route they were said to have taken when they left their farm. No one I asked along the way knew anything. No one had heard of them, no one recognized their name. But two evenings ago, I heard that music box, I heard that very tune, and it was coming from the Fosters' wood. And next morning early, I saw the family at last, taking Winifred away. I followed, and I heard their story, every word."

Mae's face drained of color. Her mouth hung open. And Tuck said hoarsely, "What you going to do?"

The man in the yellow suit smiled. "The Fosters have given me the wood," he said. "In exchange for bringing Winifred home. I was the only one who knew where she was, you see. So it was a trade. Yes, I followed you, Mrs. Tuck, and then I took your horse and went directly back."

The tension in the parlor was immense. Winnie found that she could scarcely breathe. It *was* true, then! Or was the man who stood there crazy, too?

"Horse thief!" cried Tuck. "Get to the point! What you going to do?"

"It's very simple," said the man in the yellow suit. And, as he said this, the smoothness of his face began to loosen a little. A faint flush crept up his neck, and the pitch of his voice lifted, became a fraction higher. "Like all magnificent things, it's very simple. The wood—and the spring—belong to me now." He patted his breast pocket. "I have a paper here, all signed and legal, to prove it. I'm going to sell the water, you see."

"You can't do that!" roared Tuck. "You got to be out of your mind!"

The man in the yellow suit frowned. "But I'm not going to sell it to just anybody," he protested. "Only to certain people, people who deserve it. And it will be very, very expensive. But who wouldn't give a fortune to live forever?"

"I wouldn't," said Tuck grimly.

"Exactly," said the man in the yellow suit. His eyes glowed. "Ignorant people like you should never have the opportunity. It should be kept for . . . certain others. And for me. However, since it's already too late to keep you out, you may as well join me in what I'm going to do. You can show me where the spring is and help me to advertise. We'll set up demonstrations. You know—things that would be fatal to anybody else, but won't affect you in the least. I'll pay for your assistance, of course. It won't take long for the word to spread. And then you can go your way. Well, what do you say?"

Jesse said dully, "Freaks. You want us to be freaks. In a patent-medicine show."[4]

The man in the yellow suit raised his eyebrows and a nervous petulance came into his voice. "Of course, if the idea doesn't appeal to you," he said, blinking rapidly, "you needn't be in on it. I can find the spring and manage just as well without you. But it seemed the gentlemanly thing to make the offer. After all," he added, looking round at the cluttered room, "it would mean you could afford to live like people again, instead of pigs."

And that was when the tension burst. All four Tucks sprang to their feet at once, while Winnie, very frightened, shrank back in her chair. Tuck cried, "You're a madman! A loony! You can't let *no* one know about the water. Don't you see what would *happen?*"

---

4. patent-medicine show: A traveling show, popular in the United States during the 1800's, that offered a variety of entertainment. Between the acts of the show, medicines were peddled to the crowd.

"I've given you your chance," shrilled the man in the yellow suit, "and you've refused it." He seized Winnie roughly by the arm and dragged her up out of her chair. "I'll take the child, and be on about my business."

Tuck began to rave now, his face stretched with horror. "Madman!" he shouted. And Miles and Jesse began to shout, too. They crowded after as the man in the yellow suit dragged Winnie through the kitchen to the door.

"No!" she was screaming, for now at last she hated him. "I won't go with you! I won't!"

But he opened the door and pushed her out in front of him. His eyes were like blind firepoints, his face was twisted.

Then the shouting behind them stopped abruptly, and in the midst of the sudden silence came Mae's voice, flat and cold. "You leave that child be," she said.

Winnie stared. Mae was standing just outside the doorway. She held Tuck's long-forgotten shotgun by the barrel, like a club.

The man in the yellow suit smiled a ghastly smile. "I can't think why you're so upset. Did you really believe you could keep that water for yourselves? Your selfishness is really quite extraordinary, and worse than that, you're stupid. You could have done what I'm about to do, long ago. Now it's too late. Once Winifred drinks some of the water, she'll do just as well for my demonstrations. Even better. Children are much more appealing, anyway. So you may as well relax. There's nothing you can do to stop me."

But he was wrong. Mae lifted the shotgun. Behind her, Miles gasped, "Ma! *No!*"

But Mae's face was dark red. "Not Winnie!" she said between clenched teeth. "You ain't going to do a thing like that to Winnie. And you ain't going to give out the secret." Her strong arms swung the shotgun round her head, like a wheel. The man in the yellow suit jerked away, but it was too late. With a dull cracking sound, the stock of the shotgun smashed into the back of his skull. He dropped like a tree, his face surprised, his eyes wide open. And at that very moment, riding through the pine trees just in time to see it all, came the Treegap constable.

Reader's Response

If you were Mae, what would you have done? Why?

MULTICULTURAL CONNECTION

The Search for Immortality

"People who never grew older! It was fantastic," says the man in the yellow suit. The quest for eternal youth has fascinated people throughout time. Spanish explorer Ponce de León, for example, ventured to Florida in 1513 in search of a fountain of youth. Of course, no one has yet found the key to immortality. As the man in the yellow suit says, "Oh, there were ancient legends, but nothing more."

One ancient Greek myth, for example, tells of Tithonus, who was granted immortality but forgot to ask for youth. He grew older and older. Finally, helpless and shriveled by age, he was changed into a grasshopper.

Why does living forever continue to appeal to people?

Responding to the Selection

Your Response

1. Explain how you would have felt if you had witnessed the last scene in Chapter 19.

Recalling

2. What does the man in the yellow suit plan to do with the Fosters' wood?

Interpreting

3. How do Winnie's feelings about the Tucks change?
4. What do you learn about the man in the yellow suit from his offer of exchange?
5. Why does Winnie ask Miles to throw back the fish?
6. When he hears the man's plans Angus says, "You can't do that! You got to be out of your mind!" What does Angus think will happen?

Applying

7. Mae takes a desperate action to protect Winnie and the secret. Is the desire to protect others an instinct or do we learn it? Explain.

Analyzing Literature

Identifying Motives

Motives are the reasons or causes for a character's actions. Emotions, desires, even impulses can be strong motives.

1. What is Jesse's motive for asking Winnie to drink the water at age seventeen?
2. What is the man in the yellow suit's motive for tracking down the Tucks?
3. What are Mae's two motives for striking the man in the yellow suit with the rifle?

Critical Thinking and Reading

Recognizing Conflicting Motives

When two or more characters have different motives, a conflict may arise. If you recognize conflicting motives, you can understand why certain incidents occur, or you can predict what might happen.

1. What motivates the Tucks to keep their knowledge of the spring a secret?
2. What motive does the man in the yellow suit have for finding the spring?
3. The motives of the Tucks and the man in the yellow suit are in conflict. What problems are caused by their differing motives? What events in the plot take place because of their differing motives?

Thinking and Writing

Predicting Future Events

Think about the possible consequences of Mae's hitting the stranger. What if she has killed him? What will happen to Winnie? To Mae? Freewrite, considering these questions and any others you might have. From your freewriting, make a list of possible consequences. Use this list as the basis of a paragraph in which you predict the consequences of her action. Defend your point of view with details from the story. As you revise, make sure the details adequately support your predictions.

Learning Options

1. **Writing.** Pretend that you are a reporter for the *Treegap Times.* Write a news story about the kidnapping of Winnie Foster. Your article should answer the questions who, what, why, when, and where. You may wish to illustrate your article.
2. **Art.** Suppose that you have acquired control of the spring of water in the wood. You want to make money selling the water, but you do not want to be dishonest. Write an advertisement for the water. In your ad, list the disadvantages as well as the advantages of being immortal.

GUIDE FOR READING

Tuck Everlasting, Chapter 20–Epilogue

Theme

A **theme** is the underlying idea or important message about life presented through the characters and actions in a story. In this novel you have read about the experiences and emotions of Winnie in her dealings with the Tucks. She has learned about the consequences of living forever and about how fragile and complex life can be. What the Tucks attempt to tell Winnie and what she eventually must decide convey the major theme of *Tuck Everlasting.*

Focus

At the end of Chapter 19, you know that the constable has witnessed the murder of the man in the yellow suit. Using the model below, make a cause-and-effect chart. Begin when the man in the yellow suit grabbed Winnie. In the next box, write what happened as a result of this. Then, write what the next result was. Finally, make a prediction about what will happen next. As you read, see if your prediction was on target.

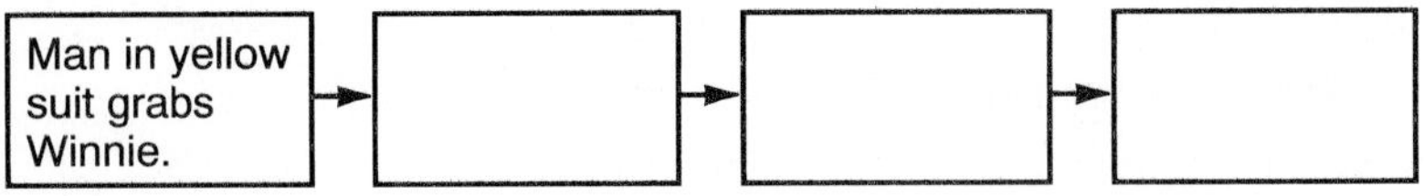
Man in yellow suit grabs Winnie.

Vocabulary

Knowing the following words will help you as you read the last chapters of *Tuck Everlasting.*

entranced (in transt′) *adj.*: Enchanted; fascinated (p. 723)

insistent (in sis′ tənt) *adj.*: Demanding (p. 725)

plaintive (plān′ tiv) *adj.*: Sad (p. 729)

prostrate (präs′ trāt) *adj.*: Exhausted (p. 730)

exultant (ig zult′ ’nt) *adj.*: Triumphant (p. 733)

sedately (si dāt′ lē) *adv.*: Calmly (p. 734)

apprehension (ap′ rə hen′ shən) *n.*: A feeling of uneasiness about the future (p. 734)

accomplice (ə käm′ plis) *n.*: A person who knowingly helps another in an unlawful act (p. 734)

wistful (wist′ fəl) *adj.*: Showing longing or sadness (p. 735)

revulsion (ri vul′ shən) *n.*: Extreme disgust (p. 735)

"For the second time in three short days . . . she was about to do something which she knew would be forbidden."

Chapter 20

Winnie was standing with her cheek pressed into Tuck's chest, her arms flung tight around him. She trembled, and kept her eyes squeezed shut. She could feel Tuck's breath come and go in little gasps. It was very quiet.

The Treegap constable knelt over the sprawled body of a man in the yellow suit, and then he said, "He ain't dead. Leastways, not yet."

Winnie opened her eyes a crack. She could see the shotgun lying on the grass where Mae had dropped it. She could see Mae's hands, too, hanging limp, clenching, then hanging limp again. The sun was scorching hot, and near her ear a gnat whined.

The constable stood up. "What did you hit him for?" he wheezed resentfully.

"He was taking the child away," said Mae. Her voice was dull and exhausted. "He was taking the child against her will."

At this the constable exploded. "Ding-dang it, woman, what you trying to say? Taking that child against her will? That's what *you* done. You *kidnapped* that child."

Winnie let go of Tuck's waist and turned around. Her trembling had stopped. "They didn't kidnap me," she said. "I came because I wanted to."

Behind her, Tuck drew his breath in sharply.

"You wanted to?" echoed the constable, his eyes wide with disbelief. "You *wanted* to?"

"That's right," said Winnie unflinchingly. "They're my friends."

The constable stared at her. He scratched his chin, eyebrows high, and eased his own shotgun to the ground. Then he shrugged and looked down at the man in the yellow suit, who lay motionless on the grass, the blazing sun white on his face and hands. His eyes were closed now, but except for that, he looked more than ever like a marionette, a marionette flung carelessly into a corner, arms and legs every which way midst tangled strings.

The one glance she gave him fixed his appearance forever in Winnie's mind. She turned her eyes away quickly, looking to Tuck for relief. But Tuck was not looking back at her. Instead, he was gazing at the body on the ground, leaning forward slightly, his brows drawn down, his mouth a little open. It was as if he were entranced and—yes, envious—like a starving man looking through a window at a banquet. Winnie could not bear to see him like that. She reached out a hand and touched him, and it broke the spell. He blinked and took her hand, squeezing it.

"Well, anyway," said the constable at last, turning businesslike, "I got to take charge here. Get this feller into the house before he fries. I'm telling you now: if he don't make it, you're in a pickle, you people. Now, here's what we'll do. You," he said, pointing at Mae, "you got to come with me, you and the little girl. You got to be locked up right away; and the little girl, I got to get her home. The rest of you, you stay here with him. Look after him. I'll get back with a doctor quick as I can. Should have brought a deputy, but I didn't expect nothing like this to happen. Well, it's too late now. All right, let's get moving."

Miles said softly, "Ma. We'll get you out right away."

"Sure, Ma," said Jesse.

"Don't worry about me none," and Mae in the same exhausted voice. "I'll make out."

"Make out?" exclaimed the constable. "You people beat all. If this feller dies, you'll get the gallows, that's what you'll get, if that's what you mean by make out."

Tuck's face crumpled. "The gallows?" he whispered. "Hanging?"

"That's it," said the constable. "That's the law. Now, let's get going."

Miles and Jesse lifted the man in the yellow suit and carried him carefully into the house, but Tuck stood staring, and Winnie could guess what he was thinking. The constable swung her up onto his horse and directed Mae to her own saddle. But Winnie kept her eyes on Tuck. His face was very pale, the creases deeper than ever, and his eyes looked blank and sunken. She heard him whisper again, "The gallows!"

And then Winnie said something she had never said before, but the words were words she had sometimes heard, and often longed to hear. They sounded strange on her own lips and made her sit up straighter. "Mr. Tuck," she said, "don't worry. Everything's going to be all right."

The constable glanced heavenward and shook his head. Then, clutching his shotgun, he climbed up behind Winnie and turned the horse toward the path. "You first," he barked at Mae. "I got to keep an eye on you. And as for you," he added grimly, speaking to Tuck, "you better hope that feller don't die on you. I'll be back soon as I can."

"Everything'll be all right," Tuck repeated slowly. Mae, slumped on the back of the fat old horse, did not respond. But Winnie leaned round the constable and looked back at Tuck. "You'll see," she said. And then she faced forward, sitting very straight. She was going home, but the thought of that was far from her mind. She watched the rump of the horse ahead, the swish of coarse, dusty hairs as he moved his tail. And she watched the swaying, sagging back of the woman who rode him.

Up through the dim pine trees they went, the constable's breath wheezing in her ears, and emerging from the coolness and the green, Winnie saw again the wide world spread before her, shimmering with light and possibility. But the possibilities were different now. They did not point to what might happen to her but to what she herself might keep from happening. For the only thing she could think of was the clear and terrible necessity: Mae Tuck must never go to the gallows. Whatever happened to the man in the yellow suit, Mae Tuck must not be hanged. Because if all they had said was true, then Mae, even if she were the cruelest of murderers and deserved to be put to death—Mae Tuck would not be able to die.

Chapter 21

Winnie pulled her little rocking chair up to her bedroom window and sat down. The rocking chair had been given to her when she was very small, but she still squeezed into it sometimes, when no one was looking, because the rocking made her almost remember something pleasant, something soothing, that would never quite come up to the surface of her mind. And tonight she wanted to be soothed.

The constable had brought her home. They had seized her at once, flinging the gate open and swooping down on her, her mother weeping, her father speechless, hugging her to him, her grandmother babbling with excitement. There was a painful pause when the constable told them she had gone away of her own free will, but it only lasted for a moment. They did not, would not believe it, and her grandmother said, "It was the elves. We heard them. They must have bewitched her."

And so they had borne her into the house, and after she had taken the bath they insisted upon, they fed and petted her and refused, with little laughs and murmurs, to accept her answers to their questions: She had gone away with the Tucks because—well, she just wanted to. The Tucks had been very kind to her, had given her flapjacks, taken her fishing. The Tucks were good and gentle people. All this would have been swept away in any case, however, this good impression of her friends which she was trying to create, when she told them what had happened to the man in the yellow suit. Had they really given him the wood in exchange for finding her? They had. Well, perhaps he wouldn't want it now. Mae had hit him with the shotgun. He was very sick. They received this news with mingled hope and horror, and her father said, "I suppose the wood will be ours again if that man should . . . that is, if he doesn't . . ."

"You mean, if he dies," Winnie had said, flatly, and they had sat back, shocked. Soon after, they put her to bed, with many kisses. But they peered at her anxiously over their shoulders as they tiptoed out of her bedroom, as if they sensed that she was different now from what she had been before. As if some part of her had slipped away.

Well, thought Winnie, crossing her arms on the windowsill, she *was* different. Things had happened to her that were hers alone, and had nothing to do with them. It was the first time. And no amount of telling about it could help them understand or share what she felt. It was satisfying and lonely, both at once. She rocked, gazing out at the twilight, and the soothing feeling came reliably into her bones. That feeling—it tied her to them, to her mother, her father, her grandmother, with strong threads too ancient and precious to be broken. But there were new threads now, tugging and insistent, which tied her just as firmly to the Tucks.

Winnie watched the sky slide into blackness over the wood outside her window. There was not the least hint of a breeze to soften the heavy August night. And then, over the treetops, on the faraway horizon, there was a flash of white. Heat lightning. Again and again it throbbed, without a sound. It was like a pain, she thought. And suddenly she longed for a thunderstorm.

She cradled her head in her arms and closed her eyes. At once the image of the man in the yellow suit rose up. She could see him again, sprawled motionless on the sun-blanched grass. "He can't die," she whispered, thinking of Mae. "He mustn't." And then she considered his plans for the water in the spring, and Tuck's voice saying,

LANDSCAPE—SUNSET ON LONG ISLAND
William Hart
National Academy of Design, New York City

"They'd all come running like pigs to slops." And she found herself thinking, "If it's true about the spring, then he has to die. He must. And that's why she did it."

Then she heard hoofbeats on the road below, a horse hurrying into the village, and not long after, there were footsteps and a knocking on the door. Winnie crept out of her room and crouched in the shadows at the top of the stairs. It was the constable. She heard him saying, "So that's that, Mr. Foster. We can't press no kidnapping charges, since your little girl claims there *wasn't* no kidnapping. But it don't matter now, anyway. The doc just got back a few minutes ago. That feller—the one you sold your land to? He's dead." There was a pause, and the murmur of other voices; then a match striking, the acrid smell of fresh cigar smoke. "Yep, she got him a good one, all right. He never even come to. So it's an open-and-shut case, since I seen her do it. Eyewitness. No question about it. They'll hang her for sure."

Winnie went back to her room and climbed into bed. She lay in the dark, propped up on the pillows, and stared at the lighter square of her window, at the heat lightning throbbing. It was like pain, she thought again, a dull pain on the fringes of the sky. Mae had killed the man in the yellow suit. And she had meant to kill him.

Winnie had killed a wasp once, in fear and anger, just in time to spare herself a stinging. She had slammed at the wasp with a heavy book, and killed it. And then, seeing its body broken, the thin wings stilled, she had wished it were alive again. She had wept for that wasp. Was Mae weeping now for the man in the yellow suit? In spite of her wish to spare the world, did she wish he were alive again? There was no way of knowing. But Mae had done what she thought she had to do. Winnie closed her eyes to shut out the silent pulsing of the lightning. Now *she* would have to do something. She had no idea what, but something. Mae Tuck must not go to the gallows.

Chapter 22

Next morning Winnie went out to the fence directly after breakfast. It was the hottest day yet, so heavy that the slightest exertion brought on a flood of perspiration, an exhaustion in the joints. Two days before, they would have insisted that she stay indoors, but now, this morning, they were careful with her, a little gingerly, as if she were an egg. She had said, "I'm going outside now," and they had said, "All right, but come in if it gets too hot, won't you, dear?" And she had answered, "Yes."

The earth, where it was worn bald under the gate, was cracked, and hard as rock, a lifeless tan color; and the road was an aisle of brilliant velvet dust. Winnie leaned against the fence, her hands gripping the warm metal of the bars, and thought about Mae behind another set of bars in the jailhouse. And then, lifting her head, she saw the toad. It was squatting where she had seen it first, across the road. "Hello!" she said, very glad to see it.

The toad did not so much as flick a muscle or blink an eye. It looked dried out today, parched. "It's thirsty," said Winnie to herself. "No wonder, on a day like this." She left the fence and went back into the cottage. "Granny, can I have some water in a dish? There's a toad out front that looks as if he's just about to die of thirst."

"A toad?" said her grandmother, wrinkling her nose in disgust. "Nasty things, toads."

"Not this one," said Winnie. "This one is always out there, and I like him. Can I give him a drink of water?"

"Toads don't drink water, Winifred. It wouldn't do him any good."

"They don't drink water at all?"

"No. They take it in through their skins, like a sponge. When it rains."

"But it hasn't rained forever!" said Winnie, alarmed. "I could sprinkle some water on him, couldn't I? That would help, wouldn't it?"

"Well, I suppose so," said her grandmother. "Where is he? In the yard?"

"No," said Winnie. "He's across the road."

"I'll come with you, then. I don't want you leaving the yard alone."

But when they came out to the fence, Winnie balancing a small bowl of water with enormous care, the toad was gone.

"Well, he must be all right," said her grandmother. "If he could hop off."

With mingled disappointment and relief, Winnie tipped the water onto the cracked earth at the gate. It was sucked in immediately, and the wet brown stain it left behind paled and vanished almost as quickly.

"I never saw such heat in all my life," said Winnie's grandmother, dabbing uselessly at her neck with a handkerchief. "Don't stay out here much longer."

"I won't," said Winnie, and was left alone once more. She sat down on the grass and sighed. Mae! What could she do to set Mae free? She closed her eyes against the glaring light, and watched, a little dizzily, as brilliant patterns of red and orange danced inside her eyelids.

And then miraculously, Jesse was there, crouching just on the other side of the fence. "Winnie!" he hissed. "You sleeping?"

"Oh, Jesse!" Her eyes flew open and she reached through the fence to grasp his hand. "I'm so glad to see you! What can we do? We have to get her out!"

ON THE FENCE
Winslow Homer

"Miles's got a plan, but I don't see how it can work," said Jesse, speaking quickly, his voice almost a whisper. "He knows a lot about carpentering. He says he can take Ma's window frame right straight out of the wall, bars and all, and she can climb through. We're going to try it tonight when it gets dark. Only trouble is, that constable keeps watching her every minute, he's so durned proud of having a prisoner in that new jail of his. We been down to see her. She's all right. But even if she can climb through the window, he'll come after her soon's he sees she's gone. Seems to me he'll notice right off. That don't give us much time to get away. But we got to try it. There ain't no other way. Anyhow, I come to say goodbye. We won't be able to come back here for a long, long time, Winnie, if we get away. I mean, they'll be looking for Ma. Winnie, listen—I won't see you again, not for ages. Look now—here's a bottle of water from the spring. You keep it. And then, no matter where you are, when you're seventeen, Winnie, you can drink it, and then come find us. We'll leave directions somehow. Winnie, please say you will!"

He pressed the little bottle into her hands and Winnie took it, closing her fingers over it. "Jesse, wait!" she whispered breathlessly, for all at once she had the answer. "I can help! When your mother climbs out the window, I'll climb in and take her place. I can wrap myself up in her blanket, and when the constable looks in, he won't be able to tell the difference. Not in the dark. I can hump up and look a lot bigger. Miles can even put the window back. That would give you time to get away! You'd have at least till morning!"

Jesse squinted at her, and then he said, "Yep—you know, it might work. It might just make the difference. But I don't know as Pa's going to want you taking any risk. I mean, what'll they say to you after, when they find out?"

"I don't know," said Winnie, "but it doesn't matter. Tell your father I want to help. I *have* to help. If it wasn't for me, there wouldn't have been any trouble in the first place. Tell him I have to."

"Well . . . all right. Can you get out after dark?"

"Yes," said Winnie.

"Then—at midnight, Winnie. I'll be waiting for you right here at midnight."

"Winifred!" an anxious voice called from the cottage. "Who's that you're talking to?"

Winnie stood up and turned to answer. "It's just a boy, Granny. I'll be in in a minute." When she turned around again, Jesse was gone. Winnie clutched the little bottle in her hands and tried to control the rising excitement that made her breath catch. At midnight she would make a difference in the world.

Chapter 23

It was the longest day: mindlessly hot, unspeakably hot, too hot to move or even think. The countryside, the village of Treegap, the wood—all lay defeated. Nothing stirred. The sun was a ponderous circle without edges, a roar without a sound, a blazing glare so thorough and remorseless that even in the Fosters' parlor, with curtains drawn, it seemed an actual presence. You could not shut it out.

Winnie's mother and grandmother sat plaintive all afternoon in the parlor, fanning themselves and sipping lemonade, their hair unsettled and their knees loose. It was totally unlike them, this lapse from gentility, and it made them much more interesting. But Winnie didn't stay with them. Instead, she took her own brimming glass to her room and sat in her little rocker by the window. Once she had hidden Jesse's bottle in a bureau drawer, there was nothing to do but wait. In the hall outside her room, the grandfather's clock ticked deliberately, unimpressed with anyone's impatience, and Winnie found herself rocking to its rhythm—forward, back, forward, back, tick, tock, tick, tock. She tried to read, but it was so quiet that she could not concentrate, and so she was glad when at last it was time for supper. It was something to do, though none of them could manage more than a nibble.

But later, when Winnie went out again to the fence, she saw that the sky was changing. It was not so much clouding up as thickening, somehow, from every direction at once, the blank blue gone to haze. And then, as the sun sank reluctantly behind the treetops, the haze hardened to a brilliant brownish-yellow. In the wood, the leaves turned underside-up, giving the trees a silvery cast.

The air was noticeably heavier. It pressed on Winnie's chest and made her breathing difficult. She turned and went back into the cottage. "It's going to rain, I think," she told the prostrate group in the parlor, and the news was received with little moans of gratitude.

Everyone went to bed early, closing windows firmly on their way. For outside, though it was almost dark, shreds of the hard brown-yellow light lingered on the rims of things, and there was a wind beginning, small gusts that rattled the fence gate and set the trees to rustling. The smell of rain hung sweet in the air. "What a week *this* has been!" said Winnie's grandmother. "Well, thank the Lord, it's almost over." And Winnie thought to herself: Yes, it's almost over.

There were three hours to wait before midnight and nothing whatever to do. Winnie wandered restlessly about her room, sat in her rocker, lay on her bed, counted the ticks of the hall clock. Beneath her excitement, she was thick with guilt. For the second time in three short days—though they seemed many more than that—she was about to do something which she knew would be forbidden. She didn't have to ask.

Winnie had her own strong sense of rightness. She knew that she could always say, afterward, "Well, you never told me *not* to!" But how silly that would be! Of course it would never occur to them to include such a thing on their list of don'ts. She could hear them saying it, and almost smiled: "Now, remember, Winifred—don't bite your fingernails, don't interrupt when someone else is speaking, and don't go down to the jailhouse at midnight to change places with prisoners."

Still, it wasn't really funny. What would happen in the morning, when the constable found her in the cell and had to bring her home for the second time? What would they say? Would they ever trust her again? Winnie squirmed, sitting in the rocker, and swallowed uncomfortably. Well, she would have to make them understand, somehow, without explaining.

The hall clock chimed eleven. Outside, the wind had stopped. Everything, it seemed, was waiting. Winnie lay down and closed her eyes. Thinking of Tuck and Mae, of Miles and Jesse, her heart softened. They needed her. To take care of them. For in the funny sort of way that had struck her at the first they were helpless. Or too trusting. Well, *something* like that. Anyway, they needed her. She would not disappoint them. Mae would go free. No one would have to find out—Winnie would not have to find out—that Mae could not . . . but Winnie blocked the picture from her mind, the horror that would prove the secret. Instead, she turned her thoughts to Jesse. When she was seventeen—would she? If it was true, would she? And if she did, would she be sorry afterwards? Tuck had said, "It's something you don't find out how you feel until afterwards." But no—it wasn't true. She knew that, now, here in her own bedroom. They were probably crazy after all. But she loved them anyway. They needed her. And, thinking this, Winnie fell asleep.

She woke with a jerk sometime later, and sat up, alarmed. The clock was ticking steadily, the darkness was complete. Outside, the night seemed poised on tiptoe, waiting, waiting, holding its breath for the storm. Winnie stole out to the hall and frowned at the clock face in the shadows. And at last she could make it out, for the black Roman numerals were just barely visible against their white ground, the brass hands glowed faintly. As she peered at them, the long hand snapped forward one more notch, with a loud click. She had not missed her moment—it was five minutes to midnight.

Chapter 24

Leaving the house was so easy that Winnie felt faintly shocked. She had half expected that the instant she put a foot on the stairs they would leap from their beds and surround her with accusations. But no one stirred. And she was struck by the realization that, if she chose, she could slip out night after night without their knowing. The thought made her feel more guilty than ever that she should once more take advantage of their trust. But tonight, this one last time, she had to. There was no other way. She opened the door and slipped out into the heavy August night.

Leaving the cottage was like leaving something real and moving into dream. Her body felt weightless, and she seemed to float down the path to the gate. Jesse was there, waiting. Neither of them spoke. He took her hand and they ran together, lightly, down the road, past other sleeping cottages, into the dim and empty center of the village. The big glass windows here were lidded eyes that didn't care—that barely saw them, barely gave them back reflections. The blacksmith's shop, the mill, the church, the stores, so busy and alive in daylight, were hunched, deserted now, dark piles and shapes without a purpose or a meaning. And then, ahead, Winnie saw the jailhouse, its new wood still unpainted, lamplight spilling through a window at the front. And there, in the cleared yard behind it, like a great L upside down, was the gallows.

The sky flashed white. But this time it wasn't heat lightning, for a few moments later a low mumble, still far away, announced at last the coming storm. A fresh breeze lifted Winnie's hair, and from somewhere in the village behind them a dog barked.

Two shadows detached themselves from the gloom as Winnie and Jesse came up. Tuck pulled her to him and hugged her hard, and Miles squeezed her hand. No one said a word. Then the four of them crept to the back of the building. Here, too high for Winnie to see into, was a barred window

MOONLIGHT
George Inness
Mildred Anna Williams Collection
The Fine Arts Museum of San Fran

through which, from the room in front, light glowed faintly. Winnie peered up at it, at the blackness of the bars with the dim gold of the light between. Into her head came lines from an old poem:

> *Stone walls do not a prison make,*
> *Nor iron bars a cage.*[1]

Over and over the lines repeated themselves in her head till they were altogether meaningless. Another roll of thunder sounded. The storm was moving nearer.

Then Miles was standing on a box. He was pouring oil around the frame of the window. A swirl of wind brought the thick, rich smell of it down to Winnie's nostrils. Tuck handed up a tool and Miles began to pry at the nails securing the window frame. Miles knew carpentering. Miles could do the job. Winnie shivered and held tight to Jesse's hand. One nail was free. Another. Tuck reached up to receive them as they came out one by one. A fourth nail screeched as it was pried up, and Miles poured on more oil.

From the front of the jailhouse, the constable yawned noisily and began to whistle. The whistling came nearer. Miles dropped down. They heard the constable's footsteps coming up to Mae's cell. The barred door clanked. Then the footsteps receded, the whistling grew fainter. An inner door shut, and the lamp glow disappeared.

At once Miles was up again and prying at the nails. An eighth was out, a ninth, a

1. **Stone walls . . . bars a cage:** Two lines from the poem "To Althea: from Prison," by English poet Richard Lovelace (1618–1657).

tenth. Winnie counted carefully, while behind her counting, her mind sang, "Stone walls do not a prison make."

Miles handed down the prying tool. He grasped the bars of the window firmly, ready to pull, and stood poised. "What is he waiting for?" thought Winnie. "Why doesn't he . . ." Then—a flash of lightning and, soon after, a crack of thunder. In the midst of the noise, Miles gave a mighty heave. But the window did not budge.

The thunder ebbed. Winnie's heart sank. What if it was all impossible? What if the window would never come out? What if . . . She looked over her shoulder at the dark shape of the gallows, and shuddered.

Again a flash of lightning, and this time a crashing burst of noise from the swirling sky. Miles yanked. The window frame sprang free, and still grasping it by the bars, he tumbled backward off the box. The job was done.

Two arms appeared in the hole left by the missing frame. Mae! Her head appeared. It was too dark to see her face. The window—what if it was to small for her to squeeze through? What if . . . But now her shoulders were out. She groaned softly. Another flash of lightning lit her face for an instant and Winnie saw an expression there of deep concentration, tip of tongue protruding, brows furrowed.

Now Tuck was on the box, helping her, giving her his own shoulders to pull on, Miles and Jesse close at his sides, arms upstretched, eager to receive her bulk. Her hips were free—now, look out!—here she came, her skirts tearing on the rough edges of the the boards, arms flailing—and they were all in a heap on the ground. Another crash of thunder muffled Jesse's bursting, exultant laugh. Mae was free.

Winnie clasped her trembling hands thankfully. And then the first drop of rain plopped precisely on the tip of her nose. The Tucks untangled themselves and turned to her. One by one, as the rain began, they drew her to them and kissed her. One by one she kissed them back. Was it rain on Mae's face? On Tuck's? Or was it tears? Jesse was last. He put his arms around her and hugged her tight, and whispered the single word, "Remember!"

Then Miles was on the box again, lifting her. Her hands grasped the edges of the window. This time she waited with him. When the thunder came, it tore the sky apart with its roar, and as it came, she pulled herself through, and dropped to the cot inside, unharmed. She looked up at the open square and saw the frame with Miles's hands holding it. The next obliging roll of thunder saw it wedged once more into place. And then—would Miles put back the nails? She waited.

Rain came in sheets now, riding the wind, flung crosswise through the night. Lightning crackled, a brilliant, jagged streak, and thunder rattled the little building. The tension in the parched earth eased and vanished. Winnie felt it go. The muscles of her stomach loosened, and all at once she was exhausted.

Still she waited. Would Miles put back the nails? At last, standing tiptoe on the cot, she grasped the bars of the window, pulling herself up till she could just see through. Rain blew into her face, but at the next flash of lightning, looking down, she saw that the yard was empty. And before the thunder followed, in a pause while wind and rain held back for one brief moment, she thought she heard, fading in the distance, the tinkling little melody of the music box. The Tucks—her darling Tucks—were gone.

Chapter 25

The first week of August was long over. And now, though autumn was still some weeks away, there was a feeling that the year had begun its downward arc, that the wheel was turning again, slowly now, but soon to go faster, turning once more in its changeless sweep of change. Winnie, standing at the fence in front of the touch-me-not cottage, could hear the new note in the voices of the birds. Whole clouds of them lifted, chattering, into the sky above the wood, and then settled, only to lift again. Across the road, goldenrod was coming into bloom. And an early-drying milkweed had opened its rough pod, exposing a host of downy-headed seeds. As she watched, one of these detached itself into a sudden breeze and sailed sedately off, while others leaned from the pod as if to observe its departure.

Winnie dropped down cross-legged on the grass. Two weeks had gone by since the night of the storm, the night of Mae Tuck's escape. And Mae had not been found. There was no trace of her at all, or of Tuck or Miles or Jesse. Winnie was profoundly grateful for that. But she was also profoundly tired. It had been a trying two weeks.

For the hundredth time she reviewed it all: how the constable had come into the cell soon after she had settled herself on the cot; how he had let down a shutter over the window to keep out the rain; how, then, he had stood over her as she hunched under the blanket, her breath heavy, trying to look as large as possible; how, finally, he had gone away and not come back till morning.

But she had not dared to sleep, for fear she would kick off the blanket and give herself away—give the Tucks away—unwittingly. So she had lain there, pulse thudding, eyes wide open. She would never forget the rattle of the rain on the jailhouse roof, or the smell of wet wood, or the darkness that had saved them all; or how difficult it was not to cough. She had wanted to cough as soon as it occurred to her that she mustn't, and she passed a long hour trying to swallow away the tickle that perversely constricted her throat. And she would never forget the crash outside that made her heart race, that she could not investigate, and did not understand till morning, when on the way home she saw that the gallows had blown over in the wind.

But oh!—it made her tremble still to remember the constable's face when he found her. She had heard first a bustling in the front of the jail, and smelled fresh coffee, and had sat up, stiff with apprehension. Then the inner door opened—the door, she now saw, which separated the office from the pair of cells—and in the light that streamed before him, the constable appeared, carrying a breakfast tray. He was whistling cheerfully. He came up to the barred door of her cell and looked in. And his whistling died on his lips as if it had run down and needed to be wound up again. But this comical astonishment lasted for a moment only. And then his face flushed red with anger.

Winnie had sat on the cot, eyes downcast, feeling very small—and very like a criminal. In fact, he was soon shouting that if she were older, he'd have to keep her there—that it *was* a crime, what she had done. She was . . . an accomplice. She had helped a murderer escape. She was, in fact, a criminal. But too young to be punished by the law. Worse luck, he told her, for she badly needed punishing.

She was released, then, into the custody of her mother and father. And these new words, "accomplice" and "custody," chilled her blood. Over and over they asked her, shocked at first and then wistful: why had she *done* such a thing? *Why?* She was their daughter. They had trusted her. They had tried to bring her up properly, with a true sense of right and wrong. They did not understand. And finally she had sobbed the only truth there was into her mother's shoulder, the only explanation: the Tucks were her friends. She had done it because—in spite of everything, she loved them.

This of all things her family understood, and afterward they drew together staunchly around her. It was hard for them in the village, Winnie knew it was, and the knowledge gave her pain. For they were proud. And she had shamed them. Still, this side of the affair was not without its benefits, at least for Winnie. Though she was confined to the yard indefinitely and could go nowhere, not even with her mother or her grandmother, the other children wandered by to look at her, to talk to her through the fence. They were impressed by what she had done. She was a figure of romance to them now, where before she had been too neat, too prissy; almost, somehow, too *clean* to be a real friend.

Winnie sighed and plucked at the grass around her ankles. School would open soon. It wouldn't be so bad. In fact, she thought as her spirits lifted, this year it might be rather nice.

And then two things happened. First of all, the toad appeared out of the weeds, on her side of the road this time. It bounced out of a cover of old dandelion leaves and landed—plop!—just beyond the fence. If she had reached her hand through the bars, she could have touched it. And next, a large brown dog, with easy gait and dangling tongue, came loping down the road toward them. He stopped opposite the fence and looked at Winnie with a friendly swish of his tail, and then he saw the toad. At once he began to bark, his eyes bright. He pranced up, his hind quarters leaping independently from side to side, nose close to the toad, his voice shrill with enthusiasm.

"Don't!" cried Winnie, leaping to her feet and flapping her arms. "Go away, dog! Stop that! Go away—shoo!"

The dog paused. He looked up at Winnie's frantic dancing and then he looked at the toad, who had pressed down close to the dirt, eyes tight shut. It was too much for him. He began to bark again, and reached out a long paw.

"Oh!" cried Winnie. "Oh—*don't* do that! Leave my toad *alone!*" And before she had time to realize what she was doing, she bent, reached through the bars, and snatched the toad up and away from harm, dropping it on the grass inside the fence.

A feeling of revulsion swept through her. While the dog whined, pawing uselessly at the fence, she stood rigid, staring at the toad, wiping her hand again and again on the skirt of her dress. Then she remembered the actual feel of the toad, and the revulsion passed. She knelt and touched the skin of its back. It was rough and soft, both at once. And cool.

Winnie stood up and looked at the dog. He was waiting outside the fence, his head on one side, peering at her longingly. "It's *my* toad," Winnie told him. "So you'd better leave it alone." And then, on an impulse, she turned and ran into the cottage, up to her room, to the bureau drawer where she had hidden Jesse's bottle—the bottle of water from the spring. In a moment she was back again. The toad still squatted where she had dropped it, the dog still waited at the fence. Winnie pulled out the cork from the mouth of the bottle, and kneeling, she poured the precious water, very slowly and carefully, over the toad.

The dog watched this operation, and then, yawning, he was suddenly bored. He turned and loped away, back down the road to the village. Winnie picked up the toad and held it for a long time, without the least disgust, in the palm of her hand. It sat calmly, blinking, and the water glistened on its back.

The little bottle was empty now. It lay on the grass at Winnie's feet. But if all of it was true, there was more water in the wood. There was plenty more. Just in case. When she was seventeen. If she should decide, there was more water in the wood. Winnie smiled. Then she stooped and put her hand through the fence and set the toad free. "There!" she said "You're safe. Forever."

Epilogue

The sign said WELCOME TO TREEGAP, but it was hard to believe that this was really Treegap. The main street hadn't changed so very much, but there were many other streets now, crossing the main street. The road itself was blacktopped. There was a white line painted down its center.

Mae and Tuck, on the seat of a clattering wooden wagon, bumped slowly into Treegap behind the fat old horse. They had seen continuous change and were accustomed to it, but here it seemed shocking and sad. "Look," said Tuck. "Look, Mae. Ain't that where the wood used to be? It's gone! Not a stick or a stump left! And her cottage—that's gone, too."

It was very hard to recognize anything, but from the little hill, which had once lain outside the village and was now very much a part of it, they thought they could figure things out. "Yes," said Mae, "that's where it was, I do believe. 'Course, it's been so long since we was here, I can't tell for certain."

There was a gas station there now. A young man in greasy coveralls was polishing the windshield of a wide and rusty Hudson automobile. As Mae and Tuck rolled past, the young man grinned and said to the driver of the Hudson, who lounged at the wheel, "Looky there. In from the country for a big time." And they chuckled together.

Mae and Tuck clattered on into the village proper, past a catholic[2] mixture of

2. catholic (kath′ ə lik) *adj.*: Including many; all kinds.

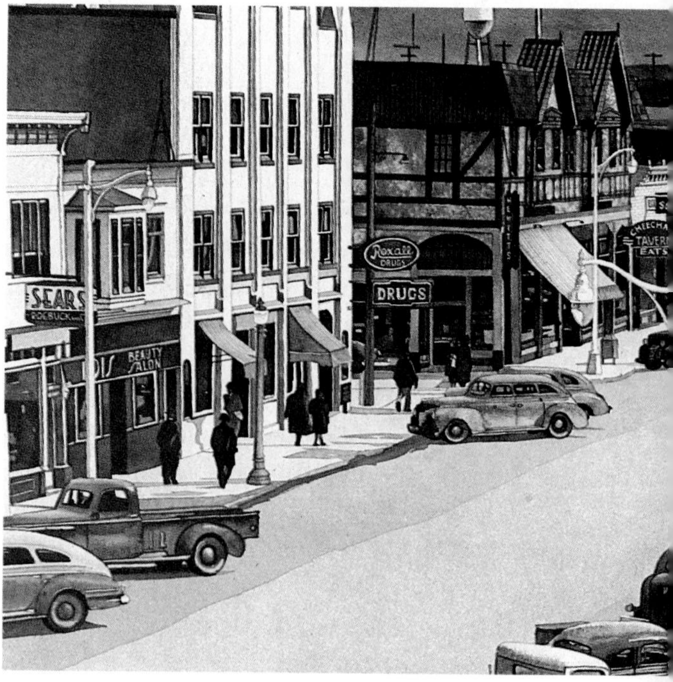

houses which soon gave way to shops and other places of business: a hotdog stand; a dry cleaner; a pharmacy; a five-and-ten; another gas station; a tall, white frame building with a pleasant verandah, The Treegap Hotel—Family Dining, Easy Rates. The post office. Beyond that, the jailhouse, but a larger jailhouse now, painted brown, with an office for the county clerk. A black and white police car was parked in front, with a red glass searchlight on its roof and a radio antenna, like a buggy whip, fastened to the windshield.

Mae glanced at the jailhouse, but looked away quickly. "See beyond there?" she said, pointing. "That diner? Let's stop there and get a cup of coffee. All right?"

"All right," said Tuck. "Maybe they'll know something."

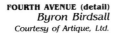

FOURTH AVENUE (detail)
Byron Birdsall
Courtesy of Artique, Ltd.

Inside, the diner gleamed with chrome and smelled like linoleum and ketchup. Mae and Tuck took seats on rumbling swivel stools at the long counter. The counterman emerged from the kitchen at the rear and sized them up expertly. They looked all right. A little queer, maybe—their clothes, especially—but honest. He slapped a cardboard menu down in front of them and leaned on the foaming orangeade cooler. "You folks from off?" he asked.

"Yep," said Tuck. "Just passing through."

"Sure," said the counterman.

"Say," said Tuck cautiously, fingering the menu. "Didn't there used to be a wood once, down the other side of town?"

"Sure," said the counterman. "Had a big electrical storm, though, about three years ago now or thereabouts. Big tree got hit by lightning, split right down the middle. Caught fire and everything. Tore up the ground, too. Had to bulldoze her all out."

"Oh," said Tuck. He and Mae exchanged glances.

"Coffee, please," said Mae. "Black. For both of us."

"Sure," said the counterman. He took the menu away, poured coffee into thick pottery mugs, and leaned again on the orangeade cooler.

"Used to be a fresh-water spring in that wood," said Tuck boldly, sipping his coffee.

"Don't know nothing about that," said the counterman. "Had to bulldoze her all out, like I say."

"Oh," said Tuck.

Afterward, while Mae was shopping for supplies, Tuck went back through the town on foot—back the way they had come—out to the little hill. There were houses there now, and a feed-and-grain store, but on the far side of the hill, inside a rambling iron fence, was a cemetery.

Tuck's heart quickened. He had noticed the cemetery on the way in. Mae had seen it, too. They had not spoken about it. But both knew it might hold other answers. Tuck straightened his old jacket. He passed through an archway of wrought-iron curlicues, and paused, squinting at the weedy rows of gravestones. And then, far over to the right, he saw a tall monument, once no doubt imposing but now tipped slightly sidewise. On it was carved one name: Foster.

Slowly, Tuck turned his footsteps toward the monument. And saw, as he approached, that there were other, small markers all around it. A family plot. And then his throat closed. For it was there. He had wanted it to be there, but now that he saw it, he was overcome with sadness. He knelt and read the inscription:

In Loving Memory
Winifred Foster Jackson
Dear Wife
Dear Mother
1870–1948

"So," said Tuck to himself. "Two years. She's been gone two years." He stood up and looked around, embarrassed, trying to clear the lump from his throat. But there was no one to see him. The cemetery was very quiet. In the branches of a willow behind him, a red-winged blackbird chirped. Tuck wiped his eyes hastily. Then he straightened his jacket again and drew up his hand in a brief salute. "Good girl," he said aloud. And then he turned and left the cemetery, walking quickly.

Later, as he and Mae rolled out of Treegap, Mae said softly, without looking at him, "She's gone?"

Tuck nodded. "She's gone," he answered.

There was a long moment of silence between them, and then Mae said, "Poor Jesse."

"He knowed it, though," said Tuck. "At least, he knowed she wasn't coming. We all knowed that, long time ago."

"Just the same," said Mae. She sighed. And then she sat up a little straighter. "Well, where to now, Tuck? No need to come back here no more."

"That's so," said Tuck. "Let's just head on out this way. We'll locate something."

"All right," said Mae. And then she put a hand on his arm and pointed. "Look out for that toad."

Tuck had seen it, too. He reined in the horse and climbed down from the wagon. The toad was squatting in the middle of the road, quite unconcerned. In the other lane, a pickup truck rattled by, and against the breeze it made, the toad shut its eyes tightly. But it did not move. Tuck waited till the truck had passed, and then he picked up the toad and carried it to the weeds along the road's edge. "Durn fool thing must think it's going to live forever," he said to Mae.

And soon they were rolling on again, leaving Treegap behind, and as they went, the tinkling little melody of a music box drifted out behind them and was lost at last far down the road.

Reader's Response

Do you think that Winnie made the right decision about the water? Why or why not?

RESPONDING TO THE SELECTION

Your Response

1. Do you feel sorry for Jesse? Explain your answer.
2. Do you think the Tucks could make better use of their immortality? How?

Recalling

3. Why would it be a disaster if Mae Tuck went to the gallows?
4. Describe how Treegap looks when Mae and Tuck return at the end of the novel.

Interpreting

5. Why does Tuck look at the unconscious stranger with envy?
6. When Winnie returns, her family believes that some part of her has "slipped away." What part of Winnie has "slipped away"?
7. Think about how the storm develops from the time of Winnie's homecoming to the escape of Mae. How does the weather match the events in the story?
8. Winnie thinks that "she would make a difference in the world" by helping the Tucks. What difference is she thinking about?
9. Why is Angus both happy and sad at the cemetery?

Applying

10. Sometimes a person must do something that seems wrong in order to prevent a greater wrong. Can you think of situations where this might be justified? Explain.

ANALYZING LITERATURE

Understanding Theme

A **theme** is a general idea that is expressed through the characters and the events in a novel. *Tuck Everlasting* explores ideas about a person's place within the natural world and the responsibilities of being a person. In the final chapters of the novel, Winnie makes several important decisions regarding these ideas.

1. Winnie decides not to drink the water. How does this decision relate to Tuck's comparison of life to a wheel?
2. When Tuck mutters, "Good girl," at Winnie's grave, for what is he praising Winnie?
3. In your own words, what do you think is the theme of *Tuck Everlasting*?

CRITICAL THINKING AND READING

Evaluating a Novel

Evaluating a novel means making judgments about its quality or value. A good novel has realistic characters who grow as people. It has a conflict that holds your interest, and it contains ideas that are interesting and thought-provoking.

Answer the following questions about *Tuck Everlasting,* using details from the novel to support your answers.

1. Does Winnie seem like a real person in the way she acts? Does she change and grow?
2. Does the central conflict hold your interest throughout the novel?
3. Are the ideas expressed in the theme interesting and thought-provoking?

THINKING AND WRITING

Writing an Evaluation

Write a letter to a friend who has not read *Tuck Everlasting*, telling him or her whether or not you think it is worth reading. Begin by deciding whether you liked or disliked the novel. Then brainstorm for the strengths or the weaknesses or both. Use your answers to the Critical Thinking and Reading section as an aid. Look over your notes and choose the best reasons to support your evaluation. As you draft your letter, make sure you are not simply retelling the plot. Check that you included details from the novel to support your evaluation as you revise.

ONE WRITER'S PROCESS

Natalie Babbitt and Tuck Everlasting

Living Forever Before you read *Tuck Everlasting,* had you ever thought what would it be like to live forever? Novelist Natalie Babbitt, author of *Tuck,* says that living forever is something she has thought about since she was very young. "*Tuck*" she says, "was mostly a way of finding out what my true feelings were." To this end, she gave each member of the Tuck family "a different idea of the value of everlasting life."

PREWRITING

The Importance of Planning Babbitt reports that she plans all her stories very carefully. "I have to know how a story will end," she says, "before I know how to begin it." After figuring out the beginning and end, she works on the plot. Babbitt reports that "the hardest thing about writing *Tuck* was figuring out the plot."

Developing Characters One of the most important parts of Babbitt's planning is getting the characters right. The characters mostly come "from bits and pieces of people I've known," she says. Babbitt wanted the members of the Tuck family to be "very ordinary people—innocent, kind, warm. . . ." The heroine of *Tuck Everlasting,* however, is based on the person Babbitt knows best. "Winnie Foster is very much like me as I was at her age—and still am, in many respects," Babbitt admits.

DRAFTING

A Movie in Your Head Because Babbitt plans her novels carefully, the actual writing comes fairly easily. She reports that describing "the places, the weather, the characters" was the easiest part of writing *Tuck.* "By the time I begin to write," Babbitt says, "the scenes are very vivid in my mind. Writing them is almost like describing a movie as it plays in your head."

Thinking of a Title Babbitt came up with the title for *Tuck Everlasting* early in the writing process. "That's usually the way," she says. "But when a title doesn't come early, it can be very, very hard to think of one."

A Place to Write Babbitt has certain writing habits. For example, she always writes her stories "on white legal pads and in pen, while sitting in a corner of the living room sofa." As she finishes each chapter, she types it out on a typewriter.

REVISING

A Constant Process Revision is an ongoing process for Natalie Babbitt. She revises each sentence, even each phrase, as she goes along. "Some writers," she points out, "prefer to write the story from beginning to end, and then go back and revise from the beginning. I have always fussed over each little bit until I'm satisfied with it before I go on to the next little bit."

Pleasing Yourself Babbitt says that the most important person a writer has to please is himself or herself. After all, as she points out, different people have different opinions about what should be changed and how to change it. "And," she says, "since all readers are different, young *and* old, there isn't any one reader to please, so you'd better please yourself."

PUBLISHING

The Fifth Grade Natalie Babbitt has a very specific audience in mind when she writes—the fifth grade. "My fifth-grade year was just about perfect in every way—I remember it clearly. People are special at the age of 10 or 11—open-minded, curious, articulate, not afraid to talk about *anything,*" she says. "Fifth grade is the last, best year of childhood and one of the great times of life."

Letters From Readers Fifth-graders and other young readers have written to Natalie Babbitt to tell her what they think of her books and to ask her questions. The most common criticism she hears about *Tuck Everlasting* is that the first three chapters are a bit slow.

Babbitt sometimes rereads these chapters to see if she should have begun the book differently. "But," she says, "I am a member of another generation—I like slow beginnings to stories—and so I always decide that I like *Tuck* best beginning just the way it does." Besides, she adds, "most readers get into the story soon after that and seem to enjoy it."

The Ash Tree The question most people ask about *Tuck Everlasting* concerns the ash tree. Readers want to know how it could possibly be destroyed, since it's watered by the magic spring. "There is a very logical answer to this question, but I didn't put it into the story because it would have slowed things down," explains Babbitt. "I have written it all out, and when a reader writes to me asking the question, I just mail off the explanation," she says.

The reason why lightning can destroy the tree is based on a myth about where lightning comes from. If you're curious, just write to Babbitt and she'll send you the whole explanation.

Advice to Young Writers Some young people complain that they have a hard time writing stories in school because they can't think of things to write about or don't know how to do it right. "Writing is *very hard work*" says Babbitt, "and the only thing that makes it possible is a huge amount of enthusiasm—passion, really—for what you're writing about. . . . In addition," she continues, "I think the only way to learn how to write stories is to read stories."

Although a career in writing may not be for everyone, Babbitt maintains that "words *are* for everyone. Words are the tools everyone uses to communicate with each other. And words can be a lot of fun."

THINKING ABOUT THE PROCESS

1. Natalie Babbitt says that "self-doubt is always present" when writing. What techniques have you learned to help you fight against self-doubt when you begin a new writing project?
2. What are the two revision methods mentioned in this article? Name some advantages and disadvantages of each.
3. **Individual Exploration** Natalie Babbitt wrote *Tuck Everlasting* as a way of finding out her true feelings about immortality. List some of the questions you have about life. How could writing help you find out the answers to these questions?

Making Generalizations

We often hear people say things like, "Many young people enjoy sports." This is a **generalization**—a general statement or conclusion that applies to many different situations. For example, when we make statements about the theme of a poem or novel, we make generalizations. After all, a theme is a general idea or insight about life. We gain meaning by making generalizations that apply to our own lives. You should also be able to evaluate generalizations, that is, judge whether they are sound or faulty.

Sound Generalizations

When you hear or read a generalization, think about it carefully. Is it sound, or correct? Or is it faulty, or incorrect? A **sound generalization** is based on many different facts and it must be true for many cases or situations. For example, "People are often suspicious of strangers" is a generalization; it is a broad statement about a group—strangers. But is it a sound generalization based on many different facts, examples, or situations? You can support the statement with many examples and situations: In *Tuck Everlasting,* Grandmother Foster is suspicious of the stranger when he first arrives at their front gate, and Winnie is suspicious of the Tucks when they are strangers to her. Also, in real life people tend to be suspicious of strangers. Can you find any exceptions to the statement? You probably can. However, by saying *often,* instead of *always,* the statement allows for exceptions. Therefore, "People are often suspicious of strangers" is a sound generalization.

Faulty Generalizations

When a generalization is not sound, it is a **faulty generalization**. Most faulty generalizations are overgeneralizations. An **overgeneralization** is so broad that you can find exceptions to it. For example, in the novel the stranger makes the generalization that people would pay a fortune to live forever. However, it is an overgeneralization because you can find exceptions to it: The Tucks and Winnie would not pay a fortune to drink from the spring. Overgeneralizations usually have words like *all, must,* or *always* that are clues because they indicate there can be no exceptions.

A **hasty generalization** is another type of faulty generalization. It is not sound because it is based on only a few facts. For example, you might make the following generalization based on the incidents in *Tuck Everlasting*: "Most strangers are greedy and up to no good." This is a hasty generalization because it is based on only one case. In reality, it is possible to meet strangers who are kind and generous.

Guidelines for Evaluating Generalizations

- Make sure the generalization is a broad statement or conclusion.
- Make sure the generalization allows for exceptions.
- If the generalization does not allow for exceptions, check to see if you can find any.
- Make sure the generalization can be supported by many different examples and facts.

Activity 1

Read each of the following statements based on the characters and events in *Tuck Everlasting*. Identify whether each is a sound generalization or a faulty generalization.

1. All mothers and grandmothers are overprotective of their children.
2. Young girls should not wander alone in the woods.
3. Many older people have more wisdom and a better understanding of the world than do younger people.
4. People who live off by themselves are different from people who live in towns.
5. Kidnappers are kind and loving people.

Activity 2

Choose two selections from this textbook and make a sound generalization about the theme of each. Provide evidence from the selections and from your own experience to support each generalization.

Writing About a Novel

How many times has someone asked you, "What did you think of the movie?" or "Did you like the book?" It's easy to say "I liked it," or "I didn't like it." But when you are asked "Why?" it is more difficult to answer.

Answering the question "Why?" means giving an evaluation, or judgment. This involves far more than recounting the part of the book that you liked best. Instead, you must come up with reasons or evidence to support your judgment. An evaluation of this kind can lead to increased understanding about a book.

One way you can take a closer look at what a novel means to you is to focus on one episode or scene and examine how it relates to the entire work.

Your Turn

Select a scene from *Tuck Everlasting* that you think is important to the rest of the novel. The scene should have an impact on the characters, the plot, or the theme of the novel, and should be a scene that you found meaningful. You will write an evaluation, or explanation, of its importance.

Prewriting

1. Choose a Scene. Skim through *Tuck Everlasting* and choose the scene that is most meaningful to you. Then, discuss the reasons for your choice with two other students. The discussion will help you clarify the scene's importance to you.

2. Choose a Format. You may do your evaluation in one of the following ways.

a. Write a one- or two-page monologue from the point of view of a minor character watching the scene you have chosen. Relate just enough background information for your audience to know what's going on. Discuss the scene's importance to the characters, including yourself, to the conflict, and to the theme of the book.
b. Write a one- or two-page essay about the scene you have chosen. In your essay evaluate the scene's importance to the characters, the conflict, and the theme of the book, and to you. You will support your judgment with reasons and evidence from the book.
c. Prepare a storyboard portraying and evaluating the scene you have chosen. A storyboard combines writing with illustration to graphically depict a scene or scenes. Using drawings and writing, convey the necessary background information regarding the setting, characters, and theme of the novel. Draw or describe the scene you are evaluating. Then, in writing, explain why the scene is important to the book and to you.

3. Take Notes. After you have chosen your format, reread the scene you have chosen. Keep in mind that no matter what format you've chosen, you need to focus on the scene's importance to you and to the rest of the novel. Jot down answers to the following questions:

- What happens in the scene you have chosen?
- What's important about what happens?
- Does something of consequence happen later in the plot because of this scene, or does it resolve any conflicts between characters or within characters?
- Why is your scene important to the theme?
- How does what happens to the characters involved relate to the theme?

Think about and write down the reasons and evidence from the book to support your evaluation.

Finally, write about the scene's importance to you. Here, you may want to take notes showing the connections between the scene, the characters, the theme, and your response to the novel.

Drafting

Using your notes, write a first draft. Organize your evidence and examples to justify your evaluation of the scene's importance. One student, who chose the essay format, wrote the following opening paragraph:

```
    The scene in Chapter 4,
where Winnie meets the stranger
for the first time, is a very
important scene. I enjoyed this
scene because it was suspenseful.
It gave hints and raised
questions that made me want to
read on and find out what would
happen next. The scene was also
meaningful because it introduced
an important character, the
stranger, and hinted at the
conflict between the stranger and
the Tucks and Winnie. This scene
led to many more important events
in the novel.
```

As you write your own draft, be thoughtful, reflective, and original.

Revising

In a writing conference with a peer or teacher, concentrate on making clear the connections you have made in your writing.

- Can you eliminate any unnecessary details?
- Do your examples and details support your evaluation?
- Can you add thoughts or feelings that make your judgment clearer to the reader?

If you've chosen the storyboard as your project, you'll need to share your sketches and talk about the connections you want to make between your art work and the text you write. Make sure that the two work together to make clear your ideas.

Proofreading

Use the checklist for proofreading on page 753. Be sure you've made clear the scene's significance to the rest of the novel and to you.

BOOKSHELF

If you enjoyed *Tuck Everlasting,* and you're searching for some other novels to read, try some of these. In each of the novels, you'll meet interesting and exciting characters and explore new worlds.

THE INCREDIBLE JOURNEY, Sheila Burnford. Bantam Books. Three house pets, a Siamese cat, a bull terrier, and a labrador retriever, set out through the Canadian wilderness in search of their home. Together they face starvation, exposure, and wild animals, but their love for their owners drives them instinctively toward their goal.

ISLAND OF THE BLUE DOLPHINS, Scott O'Dell. A Dell Yearling Book, 1960. A tale of adventure and natural beauty, this is the story of Karana, an Indian girl who was left behind when her people were moved from the Island of the Blue Dolphins. As she waits year after year for a ship to take her to her people, she learns the skills of survival and she learns some things about herself.

MRS. FRISBY AND THE RATS OF NIMH, Robert C. O'Brien. Aladdin Books, 1971. Mrs. Frisby is a widowed mouse with four children. Although this may sound strange, the rats of NIMH are a highly intelligent group of rats—and they have a secret plan. They are also the only creatures who can help Mrs. Frisby save her son from almost certain death. In return, Mrs. Frisby is able to help them with their plan.

STRAWBERRY GIRL, Lois Lenski. A Yearling Book, 1945, 1973. Birdie Boyer's hopes are high when she and her family move to the Florida backwoods, where they plan to grow sugar cane, oranges, and even strawberries. But heat waves, cold snaps, drought, and even unfriendly neighbors don't make things so easy. Will Birdie ever become a "strawberry girl"?

THE WESTING GAME, Ellen Raskin. Avon Books, 1978. Sam Westing has sixteen possible heirs, one of whom has murdered him. All take part in trying to solve the crime, for whoever solves it inherits Westing's entire fortune! This is a murder-mystery in which only you have all the clues. Can you solve the crime before one of the characters does?

UNIT ACTIVITIES

Writing

1. Write a narrative describing where the Tucks go and what they do immediately after Mae has broken out of jail. To begin, reread the chapter that describes their escape; then freewrite about where they might have gone and what they might have done. Choose the best ideas from your freewriting to develop into a narrative. Make sure that the actions and statements of each of the Tucks match what you know about them.

Writing

2. Imagine that you are one of the Tucks and twenty years have passed since you last saw Winnie. Write Winnie a letter. Briefly explain where you have been and what you have been doing. Write down your hopes for what Winnie has decided to do regarding the spring. As you write, keep your character's traits in mind.

Speaking and Listening

3. Research and report on one aspect of the age-old fascination human beings have with immortality. Narrow your topic to one aspect such as myths about immortality, contemporary literature or films about immortality, or historical quests for immortality. Prepare an oral report on your findings and present it to the class. If you wish, use audiovisual aids to enhance your presentation.

Cooperative Learning

4. Imagine that the spring has been destroyed, and the Tucks have let their immortality be known to the world. Working in groups of five, prepare an interview between the Tuck family and a television reporter of today. Work up a set of questions and answers for the interview. When you are ready, present your interview to the class, with one person taking the part of the reporter, and the other four taking the parts of the Tucks.

Creative Response

5. Working alone or in a group, create a map showing the locations for all of the scenes from *Tuck Everlasting*. Include the Fosters' cottage, the wood, the Tucks' cottage and pond, and the village. Look back through the novel to get an idea about the location of each place relative to the others. As you create your map, label the location of significant events from the book. You might want to color your map, add small illustrations, or include a scale of miles.

HANDBOOK OF THE WRITING PROCESS

Lesson 1: Prewriting

Writing is a process that involves the following stages:

1. *Prewriting:* All the research, thinking, and organizing you do before you begin to write
2. *Drafting:* Putting your ideas down on paper and creating a first version, or draft, of your writing
3. *Revising:* Making improvements in your first draft. This stage might include sharing your work with others, who can respond to and give you suggestions
4. *Proofreading:* Checking your work for errors in grammar and usage, spelling, punctuation, and capitalization
5. *Publishing:* Sharing your work with others

These stages may overlap.

You may return to any of the stages at any time during the writing process. For example, in the revising or proofreading stage, you may find that your work is disorganized and is lacking some important information. To improve your work, you may return to the prewriting stage before you continue on to the final product.

Prewriting is getting ready to write. You plan how to get ideas for your topic, if one is assigned, or you choose a topic for your assignment. Then you gather the information you need. The prewriting phase of the writing process can be broken down into the following steps.

STEP 1: LIMITING A TOPIC

Once you have your assignment, you must limit your topic to one that can be easily handled. The following are a few ways of generating ideas, which will help you narrow your topic:

1. *Brainstorming:* Brainstorming is a process of gathering ideas from a group of people. As a class or in a small group, discuss possible topics for your assignment. First generate as many general ideas as possible and list them on the chalkboard or overhead projector. Then select one topic you are interested in and brainstorm for specific ideas and details about it. At this point do not pause to think about or evaluate your ideas.
2. *Freewriting:* Write down everything that comes to your mind about the topic. Don't worry about spelling or about writing complete, grammatical sentences. Simply write nonstop for a few minutes. Then read your freewriting and look for ideas or topics you can use.
3. *Clustering:* Write your topic in the middle of a piece of paper and circle it. Then write all the ideas you can think of that relate to your topic in circles around the main topic. Connect your circles with lines that show how your ideas, or subtopics, branch out from your main topic. You may even think of some ideas that branch off from your subtopics. If you need to narrow your topic further, you might select one of your subtopics as a new main topic and repeat the process.

   For example, Neil wanted to write about baseball, but baseball is too broad a topic to cover in a short assignment. So Neil began a clustering diagram, shown on the next page, with baseball as the main topic.

Brainstorming, freewriting, and clustering all generate many ideas about a large topic, from which a limited topic can be chosen. Neil chose one of his subtopics—collecting baseball cards—as the final topic for his paper.

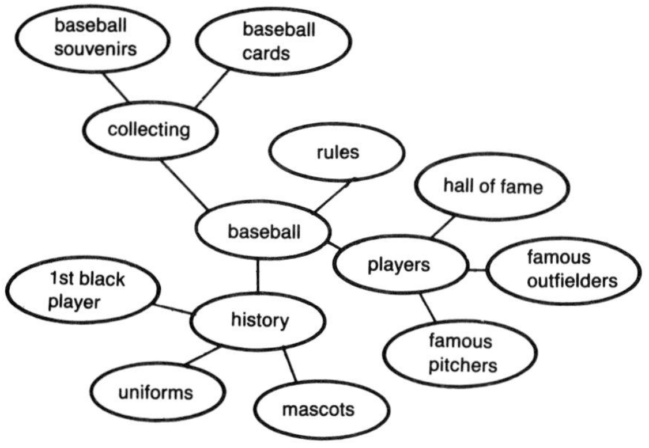

STEP 2: DECIDING ON YOUR PURPOSE

Your assignment will often determine the purpose and the kind of paper you will write. If not, you must decide on whether the purpose of your paper will be to entertain, to inform, or to give your opinion about your topic. What is the point you want to make? You must also decide if a comparison and contrast, description, or narrative will best suit your purpose.

STEP 3: DETERMINING YOUR AUDIENCE

When determining your audience, think about who will most likely enjoy or benefit from reading your work. Writing for your selected audience involves using vocabulary, details, and examples that best suit your intended audience.

STEP 4: GATHERING INFORMATION

There are many ways to gather information. The techniques covered in Step 1 give several possible ways to come up with ideas. In addition, you might try the following ways:

1. *Questioning:* Make a list of questions about the topic. Begin your questions with words like *who, what, where, when, why,* and *how.* Then find the answers to the questions in an encyclopedia, dictionary, almanac, and so on.
2. *Using Outside Sources:* Talk to other people about your topic. You might want to conduct a formal interview with someone who is an expert on your topic. You can also read relevant books, pamphlets, newspapers, magazines, and reference works. You might also try watching movies or television shows or listening to radio programs that deal with your topic. Take accurate notes that you can refer to when writing your first draft.
3. *Making Charts or Lists:* Make a list or chart of important information that is appropriate for your topic. Possibilities include a time line, an ordered list of events, a pros-and-cons chart, a list of reasons, and a list of parts.

Any of these methods for finding information can also be used to identify a topic in Step 1.

STEP 5: ORGANIZING YOUR NOTES

Once you have gathered enough information, you will have to organize it. Careful organization will make your writing easy to read and understand. Ways to organize your paper include numbering notes in order, making an outline, and putting notes in time or place order. For example, if you were describing an event, you might use time order, or chronological order. For a description of a scene or object, you might organize your work in the order you see it, such as from left to right or from top to bottom. When writing an opinion paper, you might organize your ideas according to their order of importance, for instance, or from worst to best.

When you have gathered the information you need and organized it, you are ready to begin writing the first draft of your work. In Lesson 2, you will find the information you need for the next two stages of the writing process—drafting and revising.

Lesson 2: Drafting and Revising

WRITING A DRAFT

Drafting is the second stage in the writing process. When you write your first draft, you simply write down ideas and information in sentence form. The following are important points to remember about drafting:

1. Write your first draft slowly or quickly—whichever way works for you. Some writers like to work from detailed, thorough outlines and to write very slowly, correcting and polishing as they go. Other writers prefer to jot down brief outlines, write their rough drafts very quickly, and then go back to make corrections and revisions. Each of these methods is perfectly fine. Only you can decide which approach works best for you.
2. Do not try to make your rough draft a finished product. The main point of a draft is to get your ideas down on paper. Once this is done, you can go back and make improvements. Save concern over spelling, punctuation, and so on, for the revising and proofreading stages of the writing process.
3. Refer to your prewriting notes as you draft. Do not ramble on about unrelated subjects—stick to your main topic.
4. Keep your audience and purpose in mind as you write.
5. Be flexible. Don't be afraid to set aside earlier ideas if later ones work better. If you have already written part of a draft and a more interesting aspect of your topic comes to mind, use it! Remember, too, that you can always do more prewriting activities to gather more information or to focus your thinking.
6. Write as many drafts as you need. After you have written one draft, you might review it and realize that you need to add more information, to change your purpose, or to narrow your focus. If this happens, try more prewriting activities and then write another draft. When you have a draft you are satisfied with, you are ready to go on to the next stage of the writing process—revising

REVISING YOUR DRAFT

Revising is the process of reworking what you have written to make it as good as it can be. As you revise, use the Checklist for Revision on the next page. If you answer "no" to any of the questions on the checklist, then you will have to change, or revise, your draft accordingly.

One way to get ideas for revising is to give your paper to a peer to read and respond to. In peer editing or responding, a writing partner reviews your work and gives you hints on what you can make clearer, where your strong and weak spots are, and what he or she likes most about your work. Incorporate your partner's comments into your paper when you write another draft.

EDITING SYMBOLS

When you revise a rough draft, use the standard editing symbols in the chart on the next page.

CHECKLIST FOR REVISION

Topic and Purpose

- ☐ Is my topic clear?
- ☐ Is my topic narrow enough to be fully covered in my paper?
- ☐ Does my writing have a purpose?
- ☐ Do I achieve my purpose?

Audience

- ☐ Will everything that I have written be clear to my audience?
- ☐ Do I use appropriate language for my audience?
- ☐ Will my audience find my writing interesting?
- ☐ Will my audience respond in the way I would like?

Information

- ☐ Did I use the best resources for gathering information for my paper?
- ☐ Is all my information important to the topic, or can I eliminate some of it?
- ☐ Have I supported all the points I have made?

Organization

- ☐ Have I organized my paper in the best way?
- ☐ Does my work have a clear beginning, middle, and end?
- ☐ Are my ideas connected with transitions?

EDITING SYMBOLS

SYMBOL	MEANING	EXAMPLE
	move text	She wants to go also
ℓ or —	delete	Meghan is ~~quite~~ very happy.
^	insert	of that book
	close up; no space	dish washer
⊙	insert period	was free.
^,	insert comma	pencils, books, and pens
~	transpose	to quickly run
¶	begin paragraph	book. ¶ If
/	make lower case	the President
≡	capitalize	president Adams

Following is a portion of one student's revision on the first draft of the Thinking and Writing assignment for "The Wise Old Woman," on page 577.

"Oh, my goodness!" the mother thought to herself. "This year I will turn seventy-one. I will have to obey the lords demand and go to the mountain to die ~~and~~ somehow make my leaving easier on my son, but how?

As the days passed and the time for her leaving grew near the mother noticed her son's troubles ~~and~~ noticed him begin to say something ~~and~~ but then turn away.

Then one day the mother spoke of the lord's decree. "Well, my son" she said, "the time has come for you to take me to the mountains. We must hurry before the lord sends his soldiers for you." Although she spoke with confidence and did not seem worried on the outside, on the inside she was scared and angry with the lord.

"This lord," the mother thought to herself, "Does not understand the wisdom old people have when he turns seventy-one I wonder if he will feel useless and will banish himself to the mountains. these foolish young people are throwing away years of knowledge and experience."

As she and her son began the climb up the mountain the mother looked at her son with pity and pride. "I have a fine son," she told ~~her~~ ~~son~~ him. "I know you do not want to perform this task, but you know duty bounds you and I am proud of you for that. I also ~~no~~ know that it is killing you to have to take me up this mountain to leave me ~~their~~ there to die."

Lesson 3: Proofreading and Publishing

PROOFREADING YOUR FINAL DRAFT

Once you have finished revising your rough draft, the next step is to make a clean copy and then proofread it. When you *proofread,* you check for errors in grammar and usage, spelling, capitalization, and punctuation. Use editing symbols when proofreading your paper.

If your answer to any of the questions in the checklist is "no," use editing symbols to make the necessary corrections on your final draft. Refer to a dictionary or language arts textbook as necessary.

PUBLISHING, OR SHARING YOUR WORK

After proofreading your final, revised draft, you are ready for the final stage in the writing process—sharing your work with others. Much of the writing that you do for school will be handed in to your teachers. However, you can share your writing with other people as well. These are some of the many ways in which you can share your work:

1. Share your writing in a small group by reading it aloud or by passing it around for others to read.
2. Read your work aloud to the class.
3. Make copies of your writing for members of your family or for your friends.
4. Display your work on a classroom bulletin board.
5. Save your writing in a folder for later publication. At the end of the year, choose the best pieces from your folder and bind them together. Share the collection with your relatives and friends.
6. Submit your writing to the school literary magazine, or start a literary magazine for your school or for your class.
7. Submit your writing to your school or community newspaper.

CHECKLIST FOR PROOFREADING

Grammar and Usage

☐ Are all of my sentences complete?
☐ Do all of my sentences express only one complete thought?
☐ Do the verbs I have used agree with their subjects?
☐ Have all the words in my paper been used correctly? Am I sure about the meanings of all of these words?
☐ Have I used adjectives and adverbs correctly?

Punctuation

☐ Does every sentence end with a punctuation mark?
☐ Have I used commas, quotation marks, and apostrophes correctly?

Spelling

☐ Am I sure that each word is spelled correctly?
☐ Did I look up questionable words for their spellings and meanings?

Capitalization

☐ Have I capitalized any words that should not be capitalized?
☐ Should I capitalize any words that I have not capitalized?

HANDBOOK OF GRAMMAR AND REVISING STRATEGIES

STRATEGIES FOR REVISING PROBLEMS IN GRAMMAR AND STANDARD USAGE

Problems of Sentence Structure

■ Run-on Sentences

GUIDE FOR REVISING: A run-on sentence results when no punctuation or coordinating conjunction separates two or more independent clauses. A run-on sentence also occurs when only a comma is used to join two or more independent clauses.

Strategy 1: **Create two sentences by using a period to separate independent clauses.**

First Draft Norman dressed in old clothes, he pulled on boots to protect his feet from the rocks.

Revision Norman dressed in old clothes. He pulled on boots to protect his feet from the rocks.

Model From Literature Ages seemed to him to have passed. On Sunday the bird was still hanging on the lofty powerline, fluttering feebly.

—*Cope, p. 174*

Strategy 2: **Use a comma and then a coordinating conjunction (*and, but, or, for, yet, so*)** to join the two sentences.

First Draft The two girls were nearly the same size, Meg was shorter and thinner than average.

Revision The two girls were nearly the same size, but Meg was shorter and thinner than average.

Model From Literature It was evening time, but sunshine was still big patches in yards and on housetops. —*Berry, p. 48*

■ Fragments

GUIDE FOR REVISING: A fragment is a group of words that does not express a complete thought. Although a fragment may begin with a capital letter and end with a period, it is only part of a sentence because it lacks a subject, a verb, or both.

Strategy 1: **Add a subject when necessary.**

First Draft Isaac Asimov was born and raised in Brooklyn. Wrote his first story when he was eleven years old.

Revision Isaac Asimov was born and raised in Brooklyn. He wrote his first story when he was eleven years old.

Strategy 2: **Add a predicate when necessary.**

First Draft In Myron Levoy's story "Aaron's Gift," Aaron's experience with the gang.

Revision In Myron Levoy's story "Aaron's Gift," Aaron's experience with the gang teaches him the value of standing up for his rights.

Strategy 3: **Correct a sentence fragment by connecting it to a complete sentence.**

First Draft By mentioning the time of day, the temperature, and the hills in the first sentence of "Mowgli's Brothers."

Revision By mentioning the time of day, the temperature, and the hills in the first sentence of "Mowgli's Brothers," Kipling gives the setting of the story.

Model From Literature Remembering the courage of the ancient young men who had struggled in this same place to gain the summit and seek their visions, he was determined not to go back. —*Sneve, p. 122*

Problems of Clarity and Coherence

■ Effective Transitions

GUIDE FOR REVISING: You can help your readers by using transition words and phrases to signal connections and relationships between words, sentences, and paragraphs.

Strategy 1: **Use transitions to indicate chronological order.**

First Draft Maibon saw something bouncing beside a fallen tree. He hurried across the field.

Revision When Maibon saw something bouncing beside a fallen tree, he hurried across the field.

Model From Literature He tried to carve another sapling and broke that one. It was so dark by now that he could not see at all. He had to find the next sapling by feel. —*Yep, p. 138*

Strategy 2: **Use transitions to indicate relationships in space.**

First Draft The girl in "Eleven" moved the red sweater.

Revision The girl in "Eleven" moved the red sweater to the corner of her desk.

Model From Literature When we got there, Mamá walked *up* to the house. She went through a white gate, past a row of rose bushes, up the stairs to the front door. —*Jiménez, p. 145*

Strategy 3: **Use transitions to indicate comparison or contrast.**

First Draft The emperor ordered Breaker to build a bridge. He did not say how long it was supposed to last.

Revision The emperor ordered Breaker to build a bridge. On the other hand, he did not say how long it was supposed to last.

Model From Literature I glanced at the other diners, but the ones at the nearby tables were not on their soup course, while the more distant ones were invisible in the darkness. —*Namioka, p. 163*

Strategy 4: **Use transitions to signal other logical relationships, such as introducing another item in a series, an illustration or an example, a result or a cause, a restatement, a conclusion or a summary, or an opposing point.**

First Draft Bimbo was determined to help Tito escape. He drove the boy on, snapping at his heels.

Revision Because Bimbo was determined to help Tito escape, he drove the boy on, snapping at his heels.

■ Vivid Modifiers

GUIDE FOR REVISING: Modifiers such as adjectives, adverbs, and prepositional phrases describe subjects, verbs, objects, or other modifiers. Try to make your modifiers as vivid and specific as possible.

Strategy 1: **Replace vague or abstract modifiers with specific, concrete ones.**

First Draft Mama had bought the pot in some store.

Revision Mama had bought the old, large, dented pot in an army surplus store in Santa Maria.

Model From Literature Raw celery has a slight sparkle, a zingy taste that you don't get in cooked celery. —*Namioka, p. 159*

Strategy 2: **Try to use fresh, original modifiers instead of stale, trite ones.**

First Draft With a loud cry, the starlings flew toward the butcher-bird.

Revision With a screaming cry, the starlings flew in a menacing bunch toward the butcher-bird.

Model From Literature When she came out of the bedroom tying her robe, she yawned a hat-sized yawn and blinked red eyes at the weak brew of coffee I had fixed for her. —*Soto, p. 255*

■ Pronoun-Antecedent Agreement

GUIDE FOR REVISING: Personal pronouns must agree with their antecedents in number (singular or plural), person (first, second, or third), and gender (masculine, feminine, or neuter).

Strategy 1: **Avoid shifts in person. Guard especially against using the second-person pronoun *you* to refer to a third-person antecedent.**

First Draft Francisco Jiménez grew up in a family of migrant workers. They traveled around the West, where you picked whatever crop was ripe.

Revision Francisco Jiménez grew up in a family of migrant workers. They traveled around the West, where they picked whatever crop was ripe.

Strategy 2: **Be sure to use a singular personal pronoun when its antecedent is a singular indefinite pronoun.**

First Draft Andy Rooney and Bill Cosby are popular television personalities; each has written about reading in their essay.

Revision Andy Rooney and Bill Cosby are popular television personalities; each has written about reading in his essay.

Model From Literature Everyone had a different explanation—and everyone's explanation was louder and sillier than his neighbor's. —*Untermeyer, p. 114*

Problems of Consistency

■ Subject-Verb Agreement

GUIDE FOR REVISING: Subject and verb must agree in number. A singular subject needs a singular verb form, and a plural subject needs a plural verb form.

Strategy 1: **If the subject is singular (it names only one thing), then the verb form must also be singular. If the subject is plural (it names two or more things), then the verb form must be plural.**

First Draft San Diego have an outstanding zoo.

Revision San Diego has an outstanding zoo.

Model From Literature His smiles were rare though, and most of the time his face was expressionless. —*Johnston, p. 302*

Strategy 2: **Use a singular verb form with two or more singular subjects joined by *or* or *nor.* When singular and plural subjects are joined by *or* or *nor,* the verb must agree with the subject closer to it.**

First Draft Neither the setting nor the characters in *The Phantom Tollbooth is* realistic.

Revision Neither the setting nor the characters in *The Phantom Tollbooth are* realistic.

Model From Literature Anyone can read a newspaper any way he or she wants to. —*Rooney, p. 269*

Strategy 3: **A compound subject joined by *and* is usually plural and requires a plural verb.**

First Draft Esono the elephant and Gyata the lion is characters in "Osebo's Drum."

Revision Esono the elephant and Gyata the lion are characters in "Osebo's Drum."

Model From Literature Even where he was, Shere Khan's shoulders and forepaws were cramped for want of room, . . . —*Kipling, p. 98*

Strategy 4: **Make sure that when a subject follows the verb, the subject and verb still agree with each other in number.**

First Draft There is many trickster tales in folk literature all over the world.

Revision There are many trickster tales in folk literature all over the world.

Model From Literature Around the steelwork itself were more screens of barbed wire, . . . —*Cope, p. 169*

■ Confusion of Adjectives and Adverbs

GUIDE FOR REVISING: Adjectives modify nouns and pronouns. Adverbs modify verbs, adjectives, or other adverbs.

Strategy 1: **Use an adjective to modify a noun or pronoun.**

First Draft "The All-American Slurp" is a humorously story.

Revision "The All-American Slurp" is a humorous story.

Model From Literature Crestfallen and sheepish, Maibon began thinking his wife was right, and the dwarf had indeed given him no more than a common field stone. —*Alexander, p. 153*

Strategy 2: **Use an adverb to modify a verb, adjective, or other adverb.**

First Draft Mr. Lema said that Panchito was reading nice now.

Revision Mr. Lema said that Panchito was reading nicely now.

Model From Literature Norman stepped warily over the many cracks and holes that pitted the surface. —*Sneve, p. 123*

Strategy 3: **Be careful to make the correct use of troublesome adjective and adverb pairs such as *bad/badly, fewer/less,* and *good/well.***

First Draft In "The Riddling Youngster," the chief and his attendants treat their opponents bad.

Revision In "The Riddling Youngster," the chief and his attendants treat their opponents badly.

Model From Literature There's nothing I do so much of that I do so badly. —*Rooney, p. 269*

First Draft T. S. Eliot says that a cat should have no less than three names.

Revision T. S. Eliot says that a cat should have no fewer than three names.

Model From Literature The more you want, the less you get, and the less you get, the more you have. —*Nanus, p. 230*

■ Inconsistencies in Verb Tense

GUIDE FOR REVISING: Check to see that you maintain consistent verb tenses from sentence to sentence. Verb tenses should not shift unnecessarily.

Strategy 1: **Be sure that the main verbs in a single sentence or in a group of related sentences are in the same tense.**

First Draft Auntie left the house and set out on her errand. She hurries toward the letter box.

Revision Auntie left the house and set out on her errand. She hurried toward the letter box.

Model From Literature With great effort he dug his way through the snow. He was a village boy and knew what to do. —*Singer, p. 7*

Strategy 2: **When you want to describe the earlier of two actions that occurred at different times in the past, use a verb in the past perfect tense. This tense is formed with the helping verb *had* and the past participle of the main verb.**

First Draft Until Noah Webster created his dictionary, many American words were not in a dictionary.

Revision Until Noah Webster created his dictionary, many American words *had* never been in a dictionary.

Model From Literature Nobody ever again *thought* of selling Zlateh, and now that the cold weather *had* finally set in, the villagers needed the services of Reuven the furrier once more. —*Singer, p. 11*

Problems With Incorrect Words or Phrases

■ Nonstandard Pronoun Case

GUIDE FOR REVISING: Use the nominative case for a personal pronoun that is either the subject of a sentence or a predicate nominative. Use the objective case for a personal pronoun when it is a direct object, an indirect object, or an object of a preposition.

Strategy: **Be sure to identify the case of a personal pronoun correctly when the pronoun is part of a compound subject or a compound object. It is often helpful to reword the sentence in your mind.**

First Draft Len and me enjoyed reading Brenda Johnston's story about James Forten.

Revision Len and I enjoyed reading Brenda Johnston's story about James Forten. [Could be reworded as: I enjoyed reading Brenda Johnston's story about James Forten.]

Models From Literature

You and I may not pick up exactly the same words when we skim the same piece, but we'll both get a pretty similar idea of what it's all about. —*Cosby, p. 392*

After his mother died, his father and he came up on the river, step by step, from camp to camp, till now they are settled down on the Mazy May Creek in the Klondike country. —*London, p. 25*

■ Double Negatives

GUIDE FOR REVISING: A double negative is the use of two or more negative words in one clause to express a negative meaning.

Strategy: **Use only one negative word to give a clause or sentence a negative meaning.**

First Draft The poet says that no sun cannot probe the underground dungeons.

Revision The poet says that the sun cannot probe the underground dungeons.

Model From Literature We need to write, otherwise nobody will know who we are. —*Keillor, p. 343*

Problems of Readability

■ Sentence Variety

GUIDE FOR REVISING: Varying the length and structure of your sentences will improve your writing and help you to hold your readers' attention.

Strategy 1: **Add details to the subject, verb, or complement of short simple sentences.**

First Draft Villages sold dragon bones.

Revision Until 1927, villages in China raised money by digging and selling dragon bones.

Model From Literature Geological study now proved that the sarsen stones of gray sandstone must have been brought from the Marlborough Downs 24 miles away. —*Shippen, p. 374*

Strategy 2: **Combine two or more short simple sentences to make a longer simple sentence, a compound sentence, or a complex sentence.**

First Draft Susy Clemens was thirteen years old. She wrote "My Papa, Mark Twain" in her journal.

Revision Susy Clemens was thirteen years old when she wrote "My Papa, Mark Twain" in her journal.

Model From Literature Nevertheless, James was still able to volunteer for extra jobs , and in his usual manner he picked the ones that kept him on deck and out of the stinking hole as much as possible.

—Johnston, p. 308

Strategy 3: **Separate rambling compound or complex sentences into two or more shorter sentences.**

First Draft Born in New York City, Louis Untermeyer spent the first part of his career designing jewelry in a family company, but in 1923 he resigned this job and became a full-time writer.

Revision Born in New York City, Louis Untermeyer spent the first part of his career designing jewelry in a family company. In 1923, he resigned this job and became a full-time writer.

Model From Literature We had been invited to dinner by our neighbors, the Gleasons. After arriving at the house, we shook hands with our hosts and packed ourselves into a sofa. *—Namioka, p. 159*

Strategy 4: **Begin your sentences with different openers: subjects, adjectives and adverbs, phrases, and clauses.**

First Draft A fisherman and his wife live by the seaside. The fisherman leaves their hut each morning to catch fish. He and his wife are sad because they have no children.

Revision A fisherman and his wife live by the seaside. Each morning, the fisherman leaves their hut to catch fish. Because they have no children, he and his wife are sad.

Model From Literature Defeated as a politician, he decided to try his luck as a frontier merchant. With a fellow named William Berry as his partner, Lincoln operated a general store that sold everything from axes to beeswax. But the two men showed little aptitude for business, and their store finally "winked out," as Lincoln put it.

—Freedman, p. 297

SUMMARY OF GRAMMAR

Nouns A **noun** is the name of a person, place, or thing. A **common noun** names any one of a class of people, places, or things. A **proper noun** names a specific person, place, or thing.

Common nouns	**Proper nouns**
poet	Eve Merriam, Nikki Giovanni
river	Missouri, Congo, Rio Grande

Pronouns **Pronouns** are words that stand for nouns or for words that take the place of nouns. **Personal pronouns** refer to (1) the person speaking, (2) the person spoken to, or (3) the person, place, or thing spoken about.

	Singular	**Plural**
First person	I, me, my, mine	we, us, our, ours
Second person	you, your, yours	you, your, yours
Third person	he, him, his, she, her, hers, it, its	they, them, their, theirs

I know *her* as being bubbly and bouncy, . . .
—*Hopkins, p. 281*

A flea and a fly in a flue
Were caught, so what could *they* do?
—*Anonymous Limerick, p. 501*

How can *you* buy or sell the sky, the warmth of the land? The idea is strange to *us.*
—*Chief Seattle, p. 332*

Demonstrative pronouns point out people, places, or things.

this is John   *this* is larger than *that*
that tastes good   *those* who know

Indefinite pronouns refer to people, places, or things, often without specifying which ones.

They did *much* of the work yesterday.
Several of our guests are at the door.
All of these apples are ripe.

Verbs A **verb** is a word that expresses the condition of a person, place, or thing. An **action verb** indicates the action of a person or thing. The action can be physical or mental.

The tiger's roar *filled* the cave with thunder.
—*Kipling, p. 98*

Tilted umbrellas *nod* in soft sand.
—*Livingston, p. 512*

". . . I *understand* your concern, but you mustn't come along." —*Babbitt, p. 710*

A **linking verb** joins a noun or pronoun at or near the beginning of a sentence with a word at or near the end. The word at the end identifies or describes the noun or pronoun.

The Lakeview *was* an expensive restaurant, . . .
—*Namioka, p. 163*

Arithmetic *is* numbers you squeeze from your head. . . . —*Sandburg, p. 474*

Suddenly it *seemed* too late for Tito.
—*Untermeyer, p. 117*

Helping verbs are verbs that come before the main verb and add to its meaning.

We *had invited* Chinese friends to eat with us before, but this dinner *was going* to be different.
—*Namioka, p. 164*

Adjectives An **adjective** is a word that describes something. Adjectives answer these questions:

What kind?	*silver* tray, *large* can
Which one?	*that* bus, *those* flowers
How many?	*eight* minutes, *many* people
How much?	*no* clouds, *much* traffic

The articles *the, a,* and *an* are adjectives. *An* is used before a word beginning with a vowel sound.

Adverbs An **adverb** is a word that modifies a verb, an adjective, or another adverb. Adverbs answer the questions

Where? When? In what way? To what extent?

She *often* sang. (modifies verb *sang*)
We swim *regularly.* (modifies verb *swim*)
Shut the door *gently.* (modifies verb *shut*)
He was *very* happy. (modifies adjective *happy*)
You read *rather* well. (modifies adverb *well*)

Prepositions A **preposition** relates a noun or pronoun to another word in the sentence. Prepositions are almost always followed by nouns or pronouns.

before the end   *in* my room   *except* them
at sunset   *without* us   *behind* that car

Conjunctions A **conjunction** connects words, groups of words, and whole sentences. **Coordinating conjunctions** connect similar kinds or groups of words.

trees *and* flowers   faint *but* visible

Correlative conjunctions are used in pairs to connect words or word groups.

both Dad *and* Mom   *either* she *or* I

Interjections An **interjection** is a word that expresses sudden excitement or strong feeling.

"*Psst,*" I said to each person who came in. —*Hunter, p. 74*

"*Ho! ho!*" said Mowgli. —*Kipling, p. 102*

Sentences A **sentence** is a group of words with two main parts: a complete subject and a complete predicate. Together these parts express a complete thought.

I worried more about making mistakes, . . . —*Namioka, p. 161*

Two flat rocks jutted up on either side of a narrow opening, . . . —*Sneve, p. 124*

The first eight were given to Felix on his ninth birthday. —*Clark, p. 382*

Near the edge of the Liberian rain forest, on a hill overlooking the Cavally River, was the village of Kundi. —*Courlander and Herzog, p. 611*

A **fragment** is a group of words that does not express a complete thought.

The Roman writers with whose work he was familiar —*Shippen, p. 371*

whirled with the angry words his parents had spoken —*Sneve, p. 129*

SUBJECT-VERB AGREEMENT

To make a subject and verb agree, make sure that both are *singular* or both are *plural.* Two or more singular subjects joined by *or* or *nor* must have a singular verb. When singular and plural subjects are joined by *or* or *nor,* the verb must agree with the closer subject.

They are here.	*She is making* sandwiches.
He or *I answers.*	Both *dogs are* gray.

Neither the *road* nor the *paths are marked* here.
Many of the houses *need* painting.

Phrases A **phrase** is a group of words, without a subject and verb, that functions in a sentence as one part of speech. A **prepositional phrase** is a group of words that includes a preposition and a noun or pronoun.

during the play	*inside* that drawer
to school	*in* the neighborhood

An **adjective phrase** is a prepositional phrase that modifies a noun or pronoun.

Kai felt a chill *of dread.* Had he mistaken the look *of sympathy in Kelii's face*? —*Thompson, p. 590*

An **adverb phrase** is a prepositional phrase that modifies a verb, adjective, or adverb.

He broke a cookie *into small crumbs* and tossed some *toward the pigeon.* —*Levoy, p. 83*

An **appositive phrase** renames, identifies, or explains the noun with which it appears.

I pulled [the stinger] out quickly, ran water over the sting and packed it with mud, *Grandmother's remedy.* —*Soto, p. 256*

A **participial phrase** is a participle modified by an adjective or adverb phrase or accompanied by a complement. The entire phrase acts as an adjective.

Looking at the fly on the pole, the boy said, "A fly is a good enough witness for me." —*Vo-Dinh, p. 544*

It was a fixed routine, a custom *understood between boy and dog since the beginning of their friendship,* and the way it worked was this: . . . —*Untermeyer, p. 112*

Clauses A **clause** is a group of words that contains both a subject and a verb. An **independent clause** has a subject and a verb and can stand by itself as a complete sentence.

Abraham passed his eighth birthday in the lean-to. —*Freedman, p. 292*

He has never seen a train of cars nor an elevator in his life, and for that matter *he has never once looked upon a cornfield, a plow, a cow, or even a chicken.* —*London, p. 25*

A **subordinate clause** has a subject and a verb but cannot stand on its own as a complete sentence.

The Law of the Jungle, *which never orders anything without a reason,* forbids every beast to eat Man . . . —*Kipling, p. 97*

Since I could not sleep, I decided to get up and join Papá and Roberto at breakfast. —*Jiménez, p. 147*

Breaker kept hold of the pellets *until he reached the inn.* —*Yep, p. 138*

SUMMARY OF CAPITALIZATION AND PUNCTUATION

CAPITALIZATION

Capitalize the first word of a sentence and the first word of a direct quotation when it is used as part of a longer sentence.

Once the snakes decided that they would give a costume ball; . . . —*Quiroga, p. 561*

After I asked, Mom looked kind of funny and said, "He was in the museum at the very time." —*Asimov, p. 42*

Capitalize all proper nouns and adjectives.

Myron Levoy	Jane Yolen	C. S. Lewis
Stonehenge	Liberia	April
Chinese	Kentucky	New Salem

Capitalize a person's title when it is followed by the person's name or when it is used in direct address.

Reverend   Chief Seattle   Miss Crawford

Capitalize titles showing family relationships when they refer to a specific person, unless they are preceded by a possessive noun or pronoun.

Daddy   Auntie   her niece

Capitalize the first word and all other key words in the titles of books, periodicals, poems, stories, plays, paintings, and other works of art.

Tuck Everlasting   "The King of Mazy May"
"The Sidewalk Racer"   "The Riddling Youngster"

Capitalize the first word and all nouns in letter salutations and the first word in letter closings.

Dear Mr. Cosby,   Sincerely yours,

PUNCTUATION

End Marks Use a **period** to end a declarative sentence, an imperative sentence, an indirect question, and most abbreviations.

The sun was just beginning to rise when John woke Norman the next morning. —*Sneve, p. 121*

"Don't get any ideas into your head, and don't go near that pylon." —*Cope, p. 173*

No one knew what caused these earthquakes. —*Untermeyer, p. 114*

Mr. Lema, the sixth-grade teacher, greeted me and assigned me a desk. —*Jiménez, p. 147*

Use a **question mark** after an interrogative sentence or after a word or phrase that asks a question.

How did you do that? —*Nanus, based on Juster, p. 230*

But if you did get up, what then? —*Cope, p. 173*

Use an **exclamation mark** after a statement showing strong emotion, an urgent imperative sentence, or an interjection expressing strong emotion.

"It's just beginning to rain*!*" —*Pearce, p. 65*

"Mush*!* Hi*!* Mush on*!*" —*London, p. 28*

"No, no*!*" cried Maibon. —*Alexander, p. 156*

Commas Use a comma before the conjunction to separate two independent clauses in a compound sentence.

He could just make out the pale, murky shape of a mound, but that was all. —*Yep, p. 139*

Use commas to separate three or more words, phrases, or clauses in a series.

During the struggle one of the men received a dislocated shoulder, two had bruised ribs, and three were momentarily blinded by dirt thrown by the snake. —*Nhuong, p. 412*

Every window, every dish, every stitch of clothing was totally destroyed, . . . —*Levoy, p. 87*

The next day, Miss Smith read my letter to the class, praised me for using my imagination, and said everyone else in the class had to try again. —*Cleary, p. 321*

Use a comma after an introductory word or phrase.

"*First,* I know just what you want to buy," said Mr. Sanderson. —*Bradbury, p. 186*

"*By the time I was seven,* I knew that life must be freedom; . . ." —*Hopkins, p. 282*

Use commas to set off interrupting words and phrases.

Well, as anyone knew, the hills around town were wild with friends putting cows to riot, . . . —*Bradbury, p. 185*

Use commas with places and dates made up of two or more parts.

Sandra Cisneros was born in Chicago, Illinois.

F. Scott Fitzgerald wrote to his daughter Scottie on August 8, 1933.

Use commas after items in addresses, after the salutation in a personal letter, after the closing in all letters, and in numbers of more than three digits.

The Kilns, Headington Quarry, Oxford —*Lewis, p. 336*

Dear Josh,   Yours truly,   4,589

Use a comma to set off a direct quotation.

"Besides," he added, "my father dreamed of this happening." —*Sneve, p. 121*

Semicolons Use a semicolon to connect two independent clauses that are closely connected in meaning.

Last year they and several others had spent much toil and time on the Mazy May, and endured great hardships; the creek, in turn, was just beginning to show up its richness and to reward them for their heavy labor. —*London, p. 25*

Colons Use a colon after an independent clause in order to introduce a list of items.

Mrs. Gleason exclaimed at the beautifully arranged dishes of food: the colorful candied fruit in the sweet-and-sour pork dish, the noodle-thin shreds of chicken meat stir-fried with tiny peas, and the glistening pink prawns in a ginger sauce. —*Namioka, p. 166*

Use a colon in numbers giving the time, in salutations in business letters, and in labels used to signal important ideas.

From 9:00 to 9:30 we take our early midmorning nap . . . —*Nanus, p. 210*

Dear Chairperson Rawls: Danger: Forest Fire Zone

Quotation Marks A direct quotation represents a person's exact speech or thoughts and is enclosed in quotation marks.

Commenting on her childhood, she states: "I was born in a miserable corner of southern Ohio and dutifully raised there, . . ." —*Hopkins, p. 281*

An indirect quotation reports only the general meaning of what a person said or thought and does not require quotation marks.

They said that no man sentenced to the *Jersey* survived unless he was removed in a short time, but then, James thought, most prisoners were white. —*Johnson, p. 308*

Always place a comma or a period inside the final quotation mark.

"Louder," said Miss Harrington. "I can't hear you." —*Cleary, p. 323*

Place a question mark or exclamation mark inside the final quotation mark if the end mark is part of the quotation; if it is not part of the quotation, place it outside the final quotation mark.

She looked back at him questioningly, as if to say, "Where are you taking me?" —*Singer, p. 5*

Did Lynette write her report on Carl Sandburg's "Arithmetic"?

Underline the titles of long written works, movies, television and radio series, paintings, sculptures, and specific vehicles.

Dandelion Wine *The Phantom Tollbooth*
The Return of the Jedi *Star Trek*
Magnolia *Man Walking*
the *Enterprise*

Use quotation marks around the titles of short written works and other short artistic works.

"Aaron's Gift" "Letter to Joan" "The Shark"
"Daydreamers" "Jingle Bells" "Arachne"

Hyphens Use a hyphen with certain numbers, after certain prefixes, and with some compound nouns.

eighty-nine mid-March
six-year-old son-in-law

Apostrophes Add an apostrophe and *-s* to show the possessive case of most singular nouns.

Clemens's stories a mother's prayer

Add an apostrophe to show the possessive case of plural nouns ending in *-s* and *-es*.

the spectators' cheers the Martinezes' car

Add an apostrophe and *-s* to show the possessive case of plural nouns that do not end in *-s* or *-es*.

the men's store the deer's tails

Use an apostrophe in a contraction to indicate the position of the missing letter or letters.

It's as crunchy as a bone. —*Nanus, p. 214*

"Where do they go when *they're* away?" asked Winnie. —*Babbitt, p. 698*

GLOSSARY OF COMMON USAGE

accept, except

Accept is a verb that means "to receive" or "to agree to." *Except* is a preposition that means "other than" or "leaving out." Do not confuse these two words.

Aaron sadly *accepted* his father's decision to sell Zlateh.

Everyone *except* the fisherman and his wife had children.

affect, effect

Affect is normally a verb meaning "to influence" or "to bring about a change in." *Effect* is usually a noun, meaning "result."

The sight of the pigeon with a broken wing *affected* the boy, and he broke the cookie into small crumbs to feed the bird.

The wizard's spell had an immediate *effect* on the queen. She turned into a rosebush.

ain't

Ain't was originally a contraction of *am not.* It is not considered standard English. Avoid it in all writing and speaking.

"I *am not* impressed by Father's advice," said the eldest son to himself.

among, between

Among is always used with three or more items. *Between* is generally used with only two items.

"Arithmetic" was *among* the poems Jill liked best.

The conversation *between* Larry and his father shows that Larry must think for himself.

amount, number

Amount refers to quantity or a unit, while *number* refers to individual items that can be counted. Therefore, *amount* generally appears with a singular noun, and *number* appears with a plural noun.

You don't need a large *amount* of mathematical knowledge to appreciate *The Phantom Tollbooth.*

Auntie has a *number* of special character traits.

any, all

Any should not be used in place of *any other* or *all.*

Santos thought "The All-American Slurp" was funnier than *any other* story he had read this year.

Of *all* the characters in "Mowgli's Brothers," I like Bagheera best.

around

In formal writing, *around* should not be used to mean *approximately* or *about.* These usages are allowable, however, in informal writing or in colloquial dialogue.

The turtle laid *approximately* a dozen eggs.

The rural community, *about* sixty miles north of the Ohio River, is the home of Antioch College.

as, because, like

The word *as* has several meanings and can function as several parts of speech. To avoid confusion, use *because* rather than *as* when you want to indicate cause and effect.

Because the excavator noticed a pattern on the stone, he looked more closely.

Do not use the preposition *like* to introduce a clause that requires the conjunction *as.*

C. S. Lewis advises Joan to write *as* an educated person would speak.

at

Do not use *at* after *where.*

Where is Stonehenge?

bad, badly

Use the predicate adjective *bad* after linking verbs such as *feel, look,* and *seem.* Use *badly* whenever an adverb is required.

Mouse does not feel *bad* about tricking Coyote.

In the myth, Athene treats Arachne *badly.*

because

Do not use *because* after *the reason.* Eliminate one or the other.

The reason I began to hurry was that my arms were hurting and my stung foot looked like a water balloon.

I began to hurry *because* my arms were hurting and my stung foot looked like a water balloon.

because of, due to

Use *due to* if it can logically replace the phrase *caused by.* In introductory phrases, however, *because of* is better usage than *due to.*

The huge migration of fortune hunters was *due to* the discovery of gold in Alaska.

Because of the mayor's demonstration, Heyerdahl concluded that the statues had been carved with crude stone tools.

beside, besides

Do not confuse these two prepositions, which have different meanings. *Beside* means "at the side of" or "close to." *Besides* means "in addition to."

Sitting *beside* his parents, Greyling sings songs of the wonders that lie beneath the sea.

Besides "Alone in the Nets," what other poems did you like this year?

bring, take
Bring means to carry something from a distant place to a nearer one. *Take* means the reverse: to carry something from a near place to a more distant place.

The emperor commanded his servants to *bring* the clever builder to him.

Panchito's father *takes* his family to Fresno in search of work.

can, may
The verb *can* generally refers to the ability to do something. The verb *may* generally refers to permission to do something.

Maibon replies that he *can* still see the dwarf.

In Jack Cope's story, the officials tell Andre that they *may* not cut off the power, even for a minute.

compare, contrast
The verb *compare* can involve both similarities and differences. The verb *contrast* always involves differences. Use *to* or *with* after *compare.* Use *with* after *contrast.*

Rena *compared* Lewis's "Letter to Joan" *to* Fitzgerald's "Letter to Scottie."

In many works of science fiction, elements of fantasy *contrast with* the reality of the everyday world.

different from, different than
Different from is generally preferred over *different than.*

Fables are *different from* myths because fables usually involve animal characters.

done
Done is the past participle of *do.* It should always follow a helping verb.

The director and his assistant felt that the dog *had done* something strange.

don't
Use *doesn't,* not *don't,* with third-person singular pronoun subjects and singular noun subjects.

Norman *doesn't* agree with his grandfather about the cause of the thunder and lightning.

fewer, less
Use *fewer* for things that can be counted. Use *less* for amounts or quantities that cannot be counted.

Which poem has *fewer* rhyming lines: "April Rain Song" or "Ankylosaurus"?

Because Walt had to harness the team quickly, he had *less* time than he needed to choose a good lead dog.

gone, went
Gone is the past participle of *go.* It should be used as a verb only with a helping verb. *Went* is the past of *go* and is never used with a helping verb.

Her family thought that Auntie *had gone* to mail a letter.

When James *went* down to the docks, he took only his mother's Bible and a bag of marbles.

good, well
Use the predicate adjective *good* after linking verbs such as *feel, look, smell, taste,* and *seem.* Use *well* whenever you need an adverb.

Most people feel *good* when they receive letters from friends.

In "The Dog of Pompeii," Louis Untermeyer describes the eruption of the volcano especially *well.*

hopefully
You should not loosely attach this adverb to a sentence, as in "Hopefully, the rain will stop by noon." Rewrite the sentence so that *hopefully* modifies a specific verb. Other possible ways of revising such sentences include using the adjective *hopeful* or a phrase like *everyone hopes that.*

Bill Cosby writes *hopefully* about three ways to help people read faster.

When I read "The Circuit," I was not *hopeful* about Panchito's future happiness.

in, into
In refers to position and means "within" or "inside." *Into* suggests motion from outside to inside.

"Sarah Tops" takes place *in* New York City.

The swallow became caught when it flew *into* the pylon.

its, it's
Do not confuse the possessive pronoun *its* with the contraction *it's,* standing for "it is" or "it has."

The village of Kundi was well known for *its* rice and cassava fields.

The mathemagician says that *it's* numbers that count.

kind of, sort of
Do not use *kind of* and *sort of* to mean "rather" or "somewhat."

Sandra thought that the fate of Orpheus was *rather* cruel.

In "Thunder Butte," the atmosphere at dinner is *somewhat* strained.

lay, lie
Do not confuse these verbs. *Lay* is a transitive verb meaning "to set or put something down." Its principal parts are *lay, laying, laid, laid. Lie* is an intransitive verb meaning "to recline." Its principal parts are *lie, lying, lay, lain.*

Aaron *lays* some popcorn on the floor for Pidge.

The boy makes a pillow out of some hay and *lies* down to sleep.

learn, teach
Be careful not to use *learn* (meaning "to acquire knowledge") when your context requires *teach* (meaning "to give knowledge").

Did you *learn* a lot about hatching turtles from Jean Craighead George's essay?

For fifteen years, Carrol Alice Stout *taught* in a rural Colorado school.

leave, let
Be careful not to confuse these verbs. *Leave* means "to go away" or "to allow to remain." *Let* means "to permit."

When the volcano erupted, Bimbo did not want to *leave* Tito's side.

At playtime she opened the tin and *let* the cockroach fly into my blouse.

like
Like is a preposition that usually means "similar to" or "in the same way as." *Like* should always be followed by an object. Do not use *like* before a subject and a verb. Use *as* or *that* instead.

Myths *like* "Arachne" explain the origins of things in nature.

Tuck Everlasting did not end *as* Alicia expected.

loose, lose
Loose can be either an adjective (meaning "unattached") or a verb (meaning "to untie"). *Lose* is always a verb (meaning "to fail to keep, have, or win").

Chief Seattle believes that the links between human beings and the land should be strong, not *loose.*

Auntie realized that to save Billy's life she would have to *lose* her own.

may be, maybe
Be careful not to confuse the verb phrase *may be* with the adverb *maybe* (meaning "perhaps").

Conflicts *may be* external or internal.

Maybe the cobbler's first son would have succeeded, if he had paid attention to his father's advice.

of, have
Do not use *of* in place of *have* after auxiliary verbs like *would, could, should, may, might,* or *must.*

Maibon realizes that he *should have* destroyed the stone.

raise, rise
Raise is a transitive verb that usually takes a direct object. *Rise* is intransitive and never takes a direct object.

During the whole time they *raised* Greyling, the fisherman and his wife never allowed the child to go into the sea.

When the bell rings for lunch and the other children *rise* to leave the classroom, Rachel sees Phyllis Lopez.

set, sit
Do not confuse these verbs. *Set* is a transitive verb meaning "to put (something) in a certain place." Its principal parts are *set, setting, set, set. Sit* is an intransitive verb meaning "to be seated." Its principal parts are *sit, sitting, sat, sat.*

The Walrus *sets* a loaf of bread and some pepper and vinegar on the rocks.

I would like to read "Sea Songs" while I *sit* on a beautiful beach.

so, so that
Be careful not to use the coordinating conjunction *so* when your context requires *so that. So* means "accordingly" or "therefore" and expresses a cause-and-effect relationship. *So that* expresses purpose.

In "Dragon, Dragon," John Gardner includes many elements from fairy tales, *so* the story has a broad appeal to young readers.

Stonehenge was designed *so that* an observer behind the Altar Stone on Midsummer Day could look straight through the great horseshoe and see the sun come up behind the Hele Stone.

than, then
The conjunction *than* is used to connect the two parts of a comparison. Do not confuse *than* with the adverb *then,* which usually refers to time.

Rudyard Kipling lived longer *than* Jack London.

The water in the public fountains boils, and *then* the streets of Pompeii start to crumble.

that, which, who
Use the relative pronoun *that* to refer to things or people. Use *which* only for things and *who* only for people.

The ancient coup stick *that* Norman finds might have been buried with a dead warrior.

The theme, *which* is the central message of a literary work, is often not directly stated.

Robert Frost is a poet *who* writes vividly about nature.

their, there, they're

Do not confuse the spelling of these three words. *Their* is a possessive adjective and always modifies a noun. *There* is usually used either at the beginning of a sentence or as an adverb. *They're* is a contraction for *they are.*

In Thurber's fable, some of the beasts did not even know what *their* fight was about.

There was nothing that could frighten Isabel in Ogden Nash's poem.

Limericks are short. *They're* usually also humorous.

to, too, two

Do not confuse the spelling of these words. *To* is a preposition that begins a prepositional phrase or an infinitive. *Too,* with two *o*'s, is an adverb and modifies adjectives and other adverbs. *Two* is a number.

Mr. Lema spoke *to* Panchito about learning to play the trumpet.

The weather was *too* cold for Old Ben, so he holed up for the winter in the hayloft.

Bruh Bear and Bruh Rabbit are *two* characters with strength and experience.

unique

Since *unique* means "one of a kind," you should not use it carelessly instead of the words *interesting* or *unusual.* Avoid such illogical expressions as "most unique," "very unique," and "extremely unique."

Billy gradually realized that Auntie was *unique,* and he never forgot her.

use to, used to

In formal writing, do not replace *used to* with the nonstandard phrase *use to,* which sounds very similar in speech.

According to Russell Freedman in "A Backwoods Boy," Abraham Lincoln never *used to* talk much about his early life.

when, where, why

Do not use *when, where,* or *why* directly after a linking verb such as *is.* Reword the sentence.

An argument is a set of reasons that lead to a conclusion. (Rewording of: An argument is *when* a set of reasons lead to a conclusion.)

In a biography, a writer tells the life story of another person. (Rewording of: A biography is *where* a writer tells the life story of another person.)

The author wrote this essay to persuade the reader. (Rewording of: To persuade the reader is *why* the author wrote this essay.)

who, whom

In formal writing, remember to use *who* only as a subject in clauses and sentences and *whom* only as an object.

Nikki Giovanni, *who* wrote "Winter Poem," often expresses her concern for the black community.

One poet *whom* Cesar especially liked was Juan Ramón Jiménez.

HANDBOOK OF LITERARY TERMS AND TECHNIQUES

ALLITERATION *Alliteration* is the repetition of initial consonant sounds. Writers use alliteration to create musical effects and to draw attention to certain words or ideas. Paul Fleischman uses alliteration in his poem "Fireflies," on page 466. In the following lines from "Great Farm," Philip Booth uses alliteration to imitate the sound of buzzing bees:

> The orchard is loud: bees
> and blossoms claim the bough;
> a meadow of frogs, a sky
> of swallows, flood the air now.

ANECDOTE An *anecdote* is a brief story about an interesting, amusing, or strange event. Writers tell anecdotes for specific reasons. For example, in "The Drive-In Movies," on page 255, Gary Soto tells several anecdotes about his Saturday activities. He tells these anecdotes to create a feeling of anticipation for his ending.

ARTICLE An *article* is a nonfiction selection that is complete in itself. Articles appear in magazines, newspapers, and books. "Space Stations of the Mind," on page 275, by Neil McAleer, is an article.

ATMOSPHERE *Atmosphere,* or mood, is the feeling created in the reader by a literary work or passage. Writers use many devices to create mood, including images, dialogue, setting, and plot. Often a writer creates a mood at the beginning of a work and then sustains this mood throughout. For example, from the very beginning, the atmosphere in "Thunder Butte," on page 121, is one of uncertainty and danger.

AUTOBIOGRAPHY *Autobiography* is a form of nonfiction in which a person tells his or her own life story. "The Platoon System," on page 319, is an excerpt from the autobiography *A Girl from Yamhill* by Beverly Cleary.

Although autobiographies are a form of nonfiction, the best autobiographies contain many elements of short stories, including plots, settings, and characters. Most autobiographies, including *A Girl from Yamhill,* are written in the first person. However, a few autobiographies are written in the third person.
See *Biography* and *Nonfiction.*

BIOGRAPHY *Biography* is a form of nonfiction in which a writer tells the life story of another person. Biographies deal with real people and real events. Examples from the text include "A Backwoods Boy," on page 291, and the excerpt from *Between the Devil and the Sea,* on page 301.
See *Autobiography* and *Nonfiction.*

CHARACTER A *character* is a person or animal who takes part in the action of a literary work. A major, or main, character is one on whom the story focuses. He or she is the most important character in a story, poem, or play. A minor character is one who takes part in the action but who is not the focus of attention. In Virginia Driving Hawk Sneve's "Thunder Butte," on page 121, Norman is the major character. His grandfather, mother, and father are minor characters. You learn more about the qualities that make up Norman's personality than you do about the qualities of the minor characters.
See *Character Traits, Characterization, Hero/Heroine,* and *Motivation.*

CHARACTER TRAITS *Character traits* are the qualities that make up a person's personality. For example, in the story "Auntie," on page 61, Auntie possesses the character traits of having wonderful eyesight, being able to see into the future, caring deeply about her family, never being discontented, being busy at sewing and mending for the family, and so on.

CHARACTERIZATION *Characterization* is the act of creating and developing a character. Writers use two major methods of characterization—direct and indirect.

When describing a character directly, a writer simply states the character's traits, or characteristics. Auntie in the story "Auntie," on page 61, is described directly in the following paragraph:

> Auntie's real interest—all her care—was for her family. She never married; but, by the time of her retirement from work, she was a great-aunt—although she was never called that—and she liked being one. She baby-sat and took children to school and helped with family expeditions. She knitted and crocheted and sewed—above all, she sewed. She mended and patched and made clothes. . . .

When describing a character indirectly, a writer depends on the reader to draw conclusions about the character's traits. Sometimes the writer describes the character's appearance, actions, or speech. At other times the writer tells what other participants in the story say and think about the character. The reader then draws his or her own conclusions. In "Mowgli's Brothers," on page 95, the reader must draw his or her own conclusions about Mowgli from his actions and what other participants in the story say and think about him:

> Akela lifted his head again, and said: "He [Mowgli] has eaten our food. He has slept with us. He has driven game for us. He has broken no word of the Law of the Jungle."

See *Character, Character Traits,* and *Motivation.*

CLIMAX See *Plot.*

CONCRETE POEM A *concrete poem* is one with a shape that suggests its subject. The poet arranges the letters, punctuation, and lines to create an image, or picture, on the page. "The Sidewalk Racer," on page 477, is an example of a concrete poem.

CONFLICT A *conflict* is a struggle between opposing forces. Conflict is one of the most important elements of stories, novels, and plays because it causes the action.

There are two kinds of conflict: external and internal. An external conflict is one in which a character struggles against some outside force. For example, in "The King of Mazy May," on page 25, Walt Masters struggles against the weather and harsh terrain, as well as the claim jumpers.

An internal conflict is one that takes place within the mind of a character. The character struggles to make a decision, take an action, or overcome a feeling. For example, in "Eleven," by Sandra Cisneros, on page 77, Rachel struggles with her own thoughts and feelings.
See *Plot.*

DESCRIPTION A *description* is a portrait, in words, of a person, place, or object. Descriptive writing uses images that appeal to the five senses—sight, hearing, touch, taste, and smell. In "The Hatchling Turtles," on page 397, the writer presents details that appeal particularly to sight and touch.
See *Image.*

DEVELOPMENT See *Plot.*

DIALECT A *dialect* is the form of a language spoken by people in a particular region or group. The English language contains many dialects. British English differs from American English. The English spoken in Boston differs from that spoken in Charleston, Chicago, Houston, or San Francisco. This variety adds richness to the language. Dialects differ in pronunciation, grammar, and word choice.

In *Tuck Everlasting,* on page 675, Natalie Babbitt uses dialect to make the Tucks seem more realistic.

> "He landed plum on his head," said Mae with a shudder. "We thought for sure he'd broke his neck. But come to find out, it didn't hurt him a bit!"

DIALOGUE A *dialogue* is a conversation between characters. In poems, novels, and short stories, dialogue is usually set off by quotation marks:

In "The Sound of Summer Running," on page 183, the following dialogue appears.

> "Dad!" He blurted it out. "Back there in that window, those Cream-Sponge Para Litefoot Shoes . . . "
>
> His father didn't even turn. "Suppose you tell me why you need a new pair of sneakers. Can you do that?"
>
> "Well . . . "

In a play, dialogue follows the names of the characters, and no quotation marks are used, as in this example from *The Phantom Tollbooth,* on page 205:

> MILO. I didn't know I was going to have to eat my words.
>
> AZAZ. Of course, of course, everybody here does. Your speech should have been in better taste.

See *Drama.*

DRAMA A *drama* is a story written to be performed by actors. Although a drama is meant to be performed, one can also read the script, or written version, and imagine the action. The script of a drama is made up of dialogue and stage directions. The dialogue is the words spoken by the actors. The stage directions, usually printed in italics, tell how the actors should look, move, and speak. They also describe the setting and effects of sound and lighting.

Dramas are often divided into parts called acts. The acts are often divided into smaller parts called scenes. *The Phantom Tollbooth,* on page 205, is a two-act drama. The first act has two scenes, and the second act has one scene.

ESSAY An *essay* is a short, nonfiction work about a particular subject. Most essays have a single major focus and a clear introduction, body, and conclusion.

There are many types of essays. A narrative essay, like "Old Ben," on page 363, tells a story about a real-life experience. An explanatory essay, like "The Truth About Dragons," on page 351, relates information or provides explanations. A persuasive essay, like "How to Write a Letter," on page 343, presents and supports an opinion. "The Strange Geometry of Stonehenge," on page 369, contains passages that describe Stonehenge. Most essays contain passages that describe people, places, or objects. However, there are very few purely descriptive essays. See *Description, Narration,* and *Persuasion.*

EXPLANATION *Explanation,* or explanatory writing, is writing or speech that informs or presents information. This kind of writing is also called exposition. This Handbook of Literary Terms is an example of explanation.

FABLE A *fable* is a brief story, usually with animal characters, that teaches a lesson, or moral. The moral is usually stated at the end of the fable.

The fable is an ancient literary form found in many cultures. The fables written by Aesop, a Greek slave who lived in the sixth century B.C., are still popular with children today. Many familiar expressions, such as "crying wolf," "sour grapes," and "crying over spilt milk," come from Aesop's fables. Other famous writers of fables include La Fontaine, the seventeenth-century French poet, and James Thurber, the twentieth-century American humorist. Thurber called his works fables for our time. Many of Thurber's fables have surprise endings. "The Tiger Who Would Be King," on page 617, is a Thurber fable. See *Irony* and *Moral.*

FANTASY *Fantasy* is highly imaginative writing that contains elements not found in real life. John Gardner's "Dragon, Dragon," on page 15, is a fantasy. The story contains such unreal, fantastic elements as a talking dragon and a queen who turns into a rose bush. Many science-fiction stories contain elements of fantasy.
See *Science Fiction.*

FICTION *Fiction* is prose writing that tells about imaginary characters and events. Short stories and novels are works of fiction. Some writers base their fiction on actual events and people, to which they add invented characters, dialogue, settings, and plots. Other writers of fiction rely on imagination alone to provide their materials.
See *Narration, Nonfiction,* and *Prose.*

FIGURATIVE LANGUAGE *Figurative language* is writing or speech that is not meant to be taken literally. The many types of figurative language are known as figures of speech. Common figures of speech include simile, metaphor, and personification.

Writers use figurative language to state ideas in vivid and imaginative ways. You will find examples of figurative language in the poem "Ankylosaurus," on page 454.
See *Metaphor, Personification, Simile,* and *Symbol.*

FIGURE OF SPEECH See *Figurative Language.*

FOLK TALE A *folk tale* is a story composed orally and then passed from person to person by word of mouth. Folk tales originated among people who could neither read nor write. These people entertained one another by telling stories aloud, often ones dealing with heroes, adventure, magic, or romance. Eventually, modern scholars like Wilhelm and Jakob Grimm began collecting these stories and writing them down. In this way folk tales have survived into the present day. The Brothers Grimm collected many European folk tales and published these as *Grimm's Fairy Tales.* The Grimms' tales include such famous stories as "Cinderella," "Rapunzel," and "The Bremen Town Musicians." In the United States, scholars have also collected folk tales. These tales deal with such fanciful heroes as Pecos Bill, Paul Bunyan, and Davy Crockett. "The Fly," on page 543, is a retelling of a Vietnamese folk tale.
See *Fable, Legend, Myth,* and *Oral Tradition.*

FORESHADOWING *Foreshadowing* is the use, in a literary work, of clues that suggest events that have yet to occur. Writers use foreshadowing to build their readers' expectations and to create suspense. An example of foreshadowing appears in *Tuck Everlasting,* on page 675:

> . . . Mae Tuck didn't need a mirror, though she had one propped up on the washstand. She knew very well what she would see in it; her reflection had long since ceased to interest her. For Mae Tuck, and her husband, and Miles and Jesse, too, had all looked exactly the same for eighty-seven years.

By using this foreshadowing, the author creates suspense about why people would look the same for eighty-seven years.

FREE VERSE *Free verse* is a type of poetry. In a poem written in free verse, the poet is free to write lines of any length or with any number of strong stresses or beats. "Winter Poem" by Nikki Giovanni, on page 463, is an example of free verse.
See *Meter.*

HAIKU *Haiku* is a three-line Japanese verse form. The first and third lines of a haiku have five syllables. The second line has seven syllables. A writer of haiku uses images to create a single, vivid picture, generally of a scene from nature. See the examples of haiku on page 503.

HERO/HEROINE A *hero* or *heroine* is a character of great courage and nobility. The actions of a hero or heroine are inspiring. Often heroes and heroines struggle mightily to overcome foes or to escape difficulties. This is true, for example, of Perseus in "The Gorgon's Head," on page 633.

Note that the term *hero* was originally used only for male characters and the term *heroine* for female characters. However, it is now acceptable to use *hero* to refer to females as well as to males.

HUMOR *Humor* is a comic quality in situations or incidents that causes amusement and laughter. When the wizard in "Dragon, Dragon," on page 15, turns the queen into a rose bush by mistake because he has forgotten his spells, it is an example of humor.

IMAGE An *image* is a word or phrase that appeals to one or more of the five senses. Writers use images to describe how their subjects look, sound, feel, taste, and smell. In "The Worker," Richard W. Thomas uses images that appeal to your sight, hearing, and touch:

My father lies black and hushed
Beneath white hospital sheets
He collapsed at work
His iron left him
Slow and quiet he sank

Meeting the wet concrete floor on his way
The wheels were still turning—they couldn't stop
Red and yellow lights flashing
Gloved hands twisting knobs—they couldn't stop
And as they carried him out
The whirling and buzzing and humming
machines
Applauded him
Lapping up his dripping iron
They couldn't stop

INTERVIEW An *interview* is a meeting in which a person is asked about opinions, activities, and so on. Interviews are often conducted by newspaper or television reporters. The published, taped, or filmed account of the meeting is also called an interview. "Virginia Hamilton," on page 281, is an example of an interview.

IRONY *Irony* is the general name given to literary techniques that involve surprising, interesting, or amusing contradictions. In verbal irony, words are used to suggest the opposite of their usual meaning. In dramatic irony, there is a contradiction between what a character thinks and what the reader or audience knows to be true. In "The Stone," on page 151, the reader knows that having the stone will cause Maibon trouble, but he only expects his wish to be fulfilled. In irony of situation, an event occurs that directly contradicts the expectations of the characters, the reader, or the audience.

LEGEND A *legend* is a widely told story about the past, one that may or may not have a foundation in fact. Every culture has its own legends—its familiar, traditional stories. Stories about King Arthur are examples of legends.
See *Oral Tradition.*

LETTER A *letter* is a communication in writing between friends, relatives, business persons, and so on. "Letter to the U.S. Government," on page 332, "Letter to Joan," on page 336, and "Letter to Scottie," on page 338, are examples of letters.

LIMERICK A *limerick* is a humorous, rhyming, five-line poem with a specific meter and rhyme scheme. Most limericks have three strong stresses in lines 1, 2, and 5 and two strong stresses in lines 3 and 4. Most follow the rhyme scheme *aabba.* See the limericks on page 501.

LYRIC POEM A *lyric poem* is a highly musical verse that expresses the observations and feelings of a single speaker. Examples of lyric poems in the text include "Sun" by Valerie Worth, on page 451, "Change" by Charlotte Zolotow, on page 520, and "Daydreamers" by Eloise Greenfield, on page 521.

MAJOR CHARACTER See *Character.*

METAPHOR A *metaphor* is a figure of speech in which something is described as though it were something else. A metaphor, like a simile, works by pointing out a similarity between two unlike things. In the riddle by Ian Serraillier, on page 479, a motorcycle is compared with an animal. In the poem "Mosquitoes," José Emilio Pacheco uses metaphors to describe mosquitoes:

> They are born in the swamps of sleeplessness.
> They are a viscous blackness which wings about.
> Little frail vampires,
> miniature dragonflies,
> small picadors
> with the devil's own sting.

Mosquitoes are compared to vampires, dragonflies, and picadors, who ride on horses and prick the bull with lances during a bullfight.
See *Simile.*

METER The *meter* of a poem is its rhythmical pattern. This pattern is determined by the number and types of stresses, or beats, in each line. To describe the meter of a poem, read it emphasizing the beats in each line. Then mark the stressed and unstressed syllables, as follows:

My̆ fáth/er̆ wás / thĕ fírst / tŏ heár/

As you can see, each strong stress is marked with a slanted line (ˊ) and each weak stress with a horseshoe symbol (˘). The weak and strong stresses are then divided by vertical lines (/) into groups called feet.
See *Free Verse.*

MINOR CHARACTER See *Character.*

MOOD See *Atmosphere.*

MORAL A *moral* is a statement telling what is generally considered to be good or right. A fable usually ends with a moral. For example, in Aesop's fable, "The Miller, His Son and Their Donkey," the following moral is stated:

> "When you try to please everyone, you end up by pleasing no one."

See *Fable.*

MOTIVATION *Motivation* refers to the reasons that explain or partially explain a character's thoughts, feelings, actions, or speech. Writers try to make their characters' motives as clear as possible. If the motives of a main character are not clear, then the character will not be believable.

Characters are often motivated by needs such as hunger or comfort. They are also motivated by feelings such as fear, love, and pride. In "Aaron's Gift," on page 83, Aaron is motivated by concern for the injured pigeon, desire to belong to a gang, and love for his grandmother.

MYTH A *myth* is a fictional tale that explains the actions of gods or heroes or the origins of elements of nature. Myths are part of the oral tradition. They are composed orally and then passed from generation to generation by word of mouth. Every ancient culture has its own mythology, or collection of myths. The stories "Arachne" (page 623), "Orpheus" (page 629), and "The Gorgon's Head" (page 633) are retellings, in writing, of myths from ancient Greece. These myths, known collectively as classical mythology, tell about such gods and heroes as Athene, Zeus, and Perseus. "Iduna and the Magic Apples," on page 641, is the retelling, in writing, of an ancient Norse myth. It tells about such Norse gods as Odin and Loki.
See *Oral Tradition.*

NARRATION *Narration* is writing that tells a story. The act of telling a story is also called narration. Fictional works such as novels and short

stories are examples of narration. So are poems that tell stories. Narration can also be found in many kinds of nonfiction, including autobiographies, biographies, newspaper reports, and magazine articles.
See *Narrative Poem* and *Narrator.*

NARRATIVE POEM A *narrative poem* is a story told in verse. Narrative poems often have all the elements of short stories, including characters, setting, conflict, and plot. Examples of narrative poems include "The Walrus and the Carpenter," on page 483, and "Alone In The Nets," on page 489.

NARRATOR A *narrator* is a speaker or character who tells a story. A third-person narrator is one who stands outside the action and speaks about it. A first-person narrator is one who tells a story and participates in its action. "Zlateh the Goat," on page 3, has a third-person narrator, while "Eleven," on page 77, has a first-person narrator.
See *Point of View.*

NONFICTION *Nonfiction* is prose writing that presents and explains ideas or that tells about real people, places, objects, or events. Autobiographies, biographies, essays, reports, letters, memos, magazine and newspaper articles, such as those in the Nonfiction unit, are all types of nonfiction.
See *Fiction.*

NOVEL A *novel* is a long work of fiction. Novels contain all the elements of short stories, including characters, plot, conflict, and setting; however, novels are much longer than short stories. The writer of novels, or novelist, can therefore develop these elements more fully than a writer of short stories can. In addition to its main plot, a novel may contain one or more subplots, or independent, related stories. A novel may also have several themes. This textbook contains one full-length novel, *Tuck Everlasting,* by Natalie Babbitt, on page 675.
See *Fiction.*

ONOMATOPOEIA *Onomatopoeia* is the use of words that imitate sounds. *Crash, hiss, neigh, jingle,* and *cluck* are examples of onomatopoeia. In the poem "hist whist" by E. E. Cummings, on page 470, the words *scuttling, rustling,* and *whisk* are onomatopoeic words used to describe the actions of mice.

ORAL TRADITION The *oral tradition* is the passing of songs, stories, and poems from generation to generation by word of mouth. Folk songs, folk tales, legends, and myths all come from the oral tradition. No one knows who first created these stories and poems. They are anonymous. "How Coyote Stole Fire," on page 551, is an example of a story from the Native American oral tradition.
See *Folk Tale, Legend, Myth,* and *Origin Tale.*

ORIGIN TALE An *origin tale* is a story from the oral tradition that seeks to explain the beginnings of certain natural events, such as how the seasons began, how the world began, why the sun travels across the sky, and why animals act as they do. "How Coyote Stole Fire," on page 551, and "How the Flamingoes Got Their Stockings," on page 561, are examples of origin tales.

PERSONIFICATION *Personification* is a type of figurative language in which a nonhuman subject is given human characteristics. In "He Lion, Bruh Bear, and Bruh Rabbit," on page 605, the animals have the human abilities to speak and to reason.

PERSUASION *Persuasion* is writing or speech that attempts to convince the reader to adopt a particular opinion or course of action. Advertisements and campaign speeches given by political candidates are examples of persuasion. Newspaper editorials and letters to the editor sometimes are examples of persuasion. In "Letter to Scottie," on page 338, F. Scott Fitzgerald attempts to persuade his daughter to be virtuous and to fulfill her duties.

PLOT *Plot* is the sequence of events in a literary work. In most novels, dramas, short stories, and narrative poems, the plot involves both characters and a conflict. The plot usually begins with a problem situation, or the conflict. The conflict then increases during the development until it reaches a high point of interest or suspense, the climax, or turning point. The climax is followed by the conclusion, called the resolution, in which the conflict is resolved.
See *Conflict.*

POETRY Poetry uses a more concentrated style than other forms of literature. Traditionally rhythmic, poetry is often divided into lines and stanzas. However, some poems are written in free verse, which does not place strict constraints on the length or rhythm of lines. Most poems use imagery, figurative language, and precise words. Some incorporate rhythm and rhyme in the expression of thoughts, ideas, experiences, events, or emotions. Major types of poetry include lyric poetry, narrative poetry, and concrete poetry.
See *Concrete Poem, Haiku, Limericks, Lyric Poem, and Narrative Poetry.*

POINT OF VIEW *Point of view* is the perspective, or vantage point, from which a story is told. The commonly used points of view are first person and third person.

In first-person point of view, the story is told by one of its characters, who refers to himself or herself with *I* and *me.* First-person point of view is used in "Becky and the Wheels-and-Brake Boys" by James Berry, on page 47.

In stories told from the third-person point of view, the person telling the story narrates the action but does not participate in it. Third-person point of view is used in "Power" by Jack Cope, on page 169.
See *Narrator.*

PROSE *Prose* is the ordinary form of written language. Most writing that is not poetry, drama, or song is considered prose. Prose is one of the major genres of literature and occurs in two forms: fiction and nonfiction.
See *Fiction* and *Nonfiction.*

REFRAIN A *refrain* is a regularly repeated line or group of lines in a poem or song. In the poem "The Fairies' Lullaby" by William Shakespeare, on page 468, the lines labeled "Chorus" are the refrain. "If I Were in Charge of the World" by Judith Viorst, on page 518, contains the repetition of the title as the first line in each stanza as a refrain.

REPETITION *Repetition* is the use, more than once, of any element of language—a sound, word, phrase, clause, or sentence. Repetition is used in both prose and poetry. In prose a situation may be repeated with some variations. Poets make use of many varieties of repetition. Rhyme, alliteration, and rhythm are all repetitions of sounds or sound patterns. A refrain is a repeated line. Patterns of rhythm and rhyme may be repeated throughout a long poem, as occurs in "Adventures of Isabel" by Ogden Nash, on page 435.
See *Alliteration, Meter, Plot, Rhyme,* and *Rhyme Scheme.*

RESOLUTION The *resolution* is part of the sequence of events of a story's plot. The resolution is the conclusion, or end, in which the conflict is resolved.

RHYME *Rhyme* is the repetition of sounds at the end of words. Poets use rhyme to lend a songlike quality to their verses and to emphasize certain words and ideas. Many traditional poems contain end rhymes, or rhyming words at the ends of lines. See, for example, the end rhymes in "The Geese" by Richard Peck, on page 433.

Another common device is the use of internal rhymes, or rhyming words within lines. Notice, for example, the internal rhymes in the following passage from "The Raven" by Edgar Allan Poe:

> Once upon a midnight dreary, while I pondered, weak and weary,
> Over many a quaint and curious volume of forgotten lore—
> While I nodded, nearly napping, suddenly there came a tapping,
> As of someone gently rapping, rapping at my chamber door.

See *Rhyme Scheme.*

RHYME SCHEME A *rhyme scheme* is a regular pattern of rhyming words in a poem. To indicate the rhyme scheme of a poem, one uses lowercase letters. Each rhyme is assigned a different letter, as is shown in the following stanza from "The Tropics in New York" by Claude McKay:

> Bananas ripe and green, and gingerroot, *a*
> Cocoa in pods and alligator pears, *b*
> And tangerines and mangoes and grapefruit, *a*
> Fit for the highest prize at parish fairs, *b*

The rhyme scheme of these lines is thus *abab.*

RHYTHM *Rhythm* is the pattern of beats, or stresses, in spoken or written language. Just as you can determine the rhythm of music by noting the number of beats in a measure, so you can determine the rhythmical pattern of poetry by counting the number of beats per line.
See *Meter.*

SCENE See *Drama.*

SCIENCE FICTION *Science fiction* is writing that tells about imaginary events that involve science or technology. Many science-fiction stories are set in the future. In "Space Stations of the Mind," on page 275, some science-fiction movies mentioned are *Star Wars* and the movies based on the television series *Star Trek.*

SENSORY LANGUAGE *Sensory language* is writing or speech that appeals to one or more of the five senses. Lesle Marmon Silko's poem, "How to Write a Poem About the Sky," on page 456, uses imagery to describe the Landscape of the Alaskan tundra.
See *Image.*

SETTING The *setting* of a literary work is the time and place of the action. The time includes not only the historical period—the past, present, or future—but also the year, the season, the time of day, and even the weather. The place may be a specific country, state, region, community, neighborhood, building, institution, or home. Details such as dialects, clothing, customs, and modes of transportation are often used to establish setting.

In most stories the setting serves as a backdrop—a context in which the characters interact. In some stories the setting is crucial to the plot. For example, the setting in the city of Pompeii is central to the plot of Louis Untermeyer's story "The Dog of Pompeii," on page 111. Setting can also help to create an atmosphere, or feeling. In "Thunder Butte," on page 121, Virginia Driving Hawk Sneve's description of the butte, as Norman begins his climb, creates an atmosphere of danger and uncertainty.
See *Atmosphere.*

SHORT STORY A *short story* is a brief work of fiction. Like a novel, a short story presents a sequence of events, or plot. The plot usually deals with a conflict faced by a main character. The events in a short story usually communicate a message about life or human nature. This message, or central idea, is the story's theme.
See *Conflict, Plot,* and *Theme.*

SIMILE A *simile* is a figure of speech that makes a direct comparison between two unlike subjects using either "like" or "as." Everyday speech often contains similes such as, "dry as toast," "fought like a tiger," "ran like the wind."

Writers use similes to describe people, places, and things vividly. Poets, especially, create similes to point out new and interesting ways of viewing the world. In the poem "A Parrot," by May Sarton, the parrot's murmurs are compared with someone talking in his or her sleep:

> But he murmurs some muffled words
> (Like someone who talks through a dream)
> when he sits in the window and sees
> The to-and-fro wings of wild birds
> in the leafless improbable trees.

SPEAKER The *speaker* is the imaginary voice assumed by the writer of a poem. In other words, the speaker is the character who tells the poem. This character, or voice, often is not identified by name. The following lines from "Alone In The Nets" by poet Arnold Adoff, on page 489, help you identify the speaker as a soccer goalie.

> That grinning forward gets her shot away too
> soon,
> and I am there, on my own time, in the air,
> to meet the ball,
> and fall on it
> for the save.

See *Narrator.*

STAGE DIRECTIONS *Stage directions* are notes included in a drama to describe how the work is to be performed or staged. Stage directions are usually printed in italics and enclosed within parentheses or brackets. Some stage directions describe the movements, costumes, emotional states, and ways of speaking of the characters.
See *Drama.*

STAGING *Staging* includes the setting, the lighting, the costumes, special effects, music, dance, and so on that go into putting on a stage performance of a drama.
See *Drama.*

STANZA A *stanza* is a group of lines in a poem, considered as a unit. Many poems are divided into stanzas that are separated by spaces. Stanzas often function like paragraphs in prose. Each stanza states and develops a single main idea.

Stanzas are commonly named according to the number of lines found in them, as follows: a couplet has a two-line stanza, a tercet has a three-line stanza, a quatrain has a four-line stanza, and so on.

SURPRISE ENDING A *surprise ending* is a conclusion that is unexpected. Sometimes, a reader thinks that the conflict has already been resolved but then is confronted with a new twist that changes the outcome of the plot. Often a surprise ending is foreshadowed, or subtly hinted at, in the course of the work. "Becky and the Wheels-and-Brakes Boys," on page 47, has a surprise ending.
See *Foreshadowing* and *Plot.*

SUSPENSE *Suspense* is a feeling of anxious uncertainty about the outcome of events in a literary work. Writers create suspense by raising questions in the minds of their readers. For example, in "Zlateh the Goat," on page 3, Isaac Bashevis Singer raises questions about whether Aaron and Zlateh will be able to survive in the storm. In "Mowgli's Brothers," on page 95, Rudyard Kipling makes you wonder whether Mowgli will survive Shere Khan's hatred.

SYMBOL A *symbol* is anything that stands for or represents something else. Symbols are common in everyday life. A dove with an olive branch in its mouth is a symbol of peace. A blindfolded woman holding a balanced scale is a symbol of justice. A crown is a symbol of a king's status and authority.

In the story "Power," by Jack Cope, on page 169, the power line and birds are symbols of the outside world. The trapped bird is a symbol of André, a child dependent on his parents and living a restricted life. By taking responsibility for seeing that the bird is free, a symbolic act, André assumes power over his own life and actions.

THEME A *theme* is a central message, concern, or purpose in a literary work. A theme can usually be expressed as a general statement about human beings or about life. The theme of a work is not a summary of its plot. The theme is the central idea that the writer communicates.

A theme may be stated directly by the writer, although this is unusual. In "Zlateh the Goat," on page 3, Isaac Bashevis Singer writes: "We must accept all that God gives us—heat, cold, hunger, satisfaction, light, and darkness." This interpretation of what Zlateh means by her "Maaaa," is a general statement about life Singer believes applies to everyone. He shows in the story how Zlateh's acceptance of her lot helps save Aaron's life.

Most themes are not directly stated but are implied. When the theme is implied, the reader must figure out what the theme is by looking carefully at what the work reveals about people or about life.

TRICKSTER The *trickster* is a character in a folk tale who relies on wit and intelligence, instead of strength, to outsmart bigger or more powerful opponents. The trickster is often an animal. "Señor Coyote and the Tricked Trickster," on page 599, is a tale in which one trickster tricks another.

TURNING POINT The *turning point* in a plot is the high point of interest or suspense. The turning point is also called the climax.
See *Plot.*

VERSE A *verse* is a single line of poetry. It may be a complete sentence, but most of the time it is only part of a sentence. The word *verse* also refers to poetry in general.

GLOSSARY

READING THE GLOSSARY ENTRIES

The words in this glossary are from selections appearing in your textbook. Each entry in the glossary contains the following parts:

1. Entry Word. This word appears at the beginning of the entry, in boldface type.

2. Pronunciation. The symbols in parentheses tell how the entry word is pronounced. If a word has more than one possible pronunciation, the most common of these pronunciations is given first.

3. Part of Speech. Appearing after the pronunciation, in italics, is an abbreviation that tells the part of speech of the entry word. The following abbreviations have been used:

n. noun **p.** pronoun **v.** verb
adj. adjective **adv.** adverb **conj.** conjunction

4. Definition. This part of the entry follows the parts-of-speech abbreviation and gives the meaning of the entry word as used in the selection in which it appears.

KEY TO PRONUNCIATION SYMBOLS USED IN THE GLOSSARY

The following symbols are used in the pronunciations that follow the entry words:

Symbol	*Key Words*	*Symbol*	*Key Words*
a	asp, fat, parrot	**b**	bed, fable, dub
ā	ape, date, play	**d**	dip, beadle, had
ä	ah, car, father	**f**	fall, after, off
		g	get, haggle, dog
e	elf, ten, berry	**h**	he, ahead, hotel
ē	even, meet, money	**j**	joy, agile, badge
		k	kill, tackle, bake
i	is, hit, mirror	**l**	let, yellow, ball
ī	ice, bite, high	**m**	met, camel, trim
		n	not, flannel, ton
ō	open, tone, go	**p**	put, apple, tap
ô	all, horn, law	**r**	red, port, dear
o͞o	ooze, tool, crew	**s**	sell, castle, pass
o͝o	look, pull, moor	**t**	top, cattle, hat
yo͞o	use, cute, few	**v**	vat, hovel, have
yo͝o	united, cure, globule	**w**	will, always, swear
oi	oil, point, toy	**y**	yet, onion, yard
ou	out, crowd, plow	**z**	zebra, dazzle, haze
u	up, cut, color	**ch**	chin, catcher, arch
ʉr	urn, fur, deter	**sh**	she, cushion, dash
		th	thin, nothing, truth
ə	**a** in ago	***th***	then, father, lathe
	e in agent	**zh**	azure, leisure
	i in sanity	**ŋ**	ring, anger, drink
	o in comply	**’**	[indicates that an **l** or **n** following the symbol is a syllabic consonant, as in *able* (ā′ b'l)]
	u in focus		
ər	perhaps, murder		

A

abashed (ə basht′) *adj.* Ashamed

abolish (ə bäl′ ish) *v.* To put an end to

abstract (ab strakt′) *adj.* Referring to qualities, not objects

abuse (ə byo͞oz′) *v.* To mistreat or to misuse

accommodate (ə käm′ ə dāt′) *v.* To help; to do a favor for

accommodation (əkäm′ ə dā′ shən) *n.* Lodging

accomplice (a käm′ plis) *n.* A person who knowingly helps another in an unlawful act

adamant (ad′ ə mənt) *adj.* Not giving in

admire (ad mīr′) *v.* To regard highly

admonish (ad män′ ish) *v.* To disapprove, in a warm fashion

agate (ag′ it) *n.* Hard, semiprecious stone with striped or clouded coloring

alternate (ôl′ tər nit) *adj.* First one and then the other; succeeding each other

ambition (am bish′ ən) *n.* Strong desire

amiable (ā′ mē ə bəl) *adj.* Friendly

ancestral (an ses′ trəl) *adj.* Inherited from ancestors

anonymity (an′ ə nim′ ə tē) *n.* The condition of being unknown

anthropology (an′ thrō päl′ ə jē) *n.* The scientific study of the physical and cultural development of human beings

antiquarian (an′ ti kwer′ ē ən) *n.* A person who studies ancient works of art

anxious (aŋk′ shəs) *adj.* Uneasy in mind; worried

appease (ə pēz′) *v.* To satisfy; gratify; please

apprehension (ap′ rə hen′ shən) *n.* A feeling of uneasiness about the future; worry

aptitude (ap′ tə to͞od′) *n.* Natural ability

archeologist (är′ kē äl′ ə jist) *n.* A scientist who studies evidence of the life and culture of ancient peoples

arrest (ə rest′) *v.* To catch and keep one's attention

arrogant (ar′ ə gənt) *adj.* Proud, overbearing

assassinate (ə sas′ ən āt′) *v.* To murder by surprise attack

atrocious (ə trō′ shəs) *adj.* Very bad, unpleasant, inferior

avenge (ə venj′) *v.* To take revenge on behalf of, as for a wrong

B

banish (ban′ ish) *v.* To send away; get rid of

barometer (bə räm′ ət ər) *n.* An instrument used to forecast changes in weather

belligerent (bə lij′ ər ənt) *adj.* Showing readiness to fight or quarrel

beseech (bē sēch′) *v.* To beg for
betray (bē trā′) *v.* To be a traitor to; help the enemy
bewilderment (bē wil′ dər mənt) *n.* Confusion; puzzlement
billiards (bil′ yərdz) *n.* The game of pool
billow (bil′ ō) *n.* Large, swelling masses, like waves
boon (bo͞on) *n.* A welcome benefit
buffet (buf′ it) *v.* To thrust or toss about
burly (bʉr′ lē) *adj.* Big and strong
butte (byo͞ot) *n.* A steep hill standing alone in a plain

C

calamity (kə lam′ ə tē) *n.* Disaster
calligrapher (kə lig′ rə fʉr) *n.* Person who uses artistic handwriting
cater (kā′ tər) *v.* To try hard to supply what another needs
cavernous (kav′ ər nəs) *adj.* Deep and empty
ceremony (ser′ ə mō′ nē) *n.* A formal ritual or occasion
circumvent (sʉr′ kəm vent′) *v.* To go around
clamor (klam′ ər) *n.* A loud demand or complaint; outcry or shouting
clan (klan) *n.* A group composed of several families, all claiming descent from the same ancestor
cleat (klēt) *n.* Piece of wood, plastic, or metal fastened to the underside of a shoe to prevent slipping
coax (kōks) *v.* To try to persuade
colander (kul′ ən dər) *n.* A bowl-shaped pan with many small holes in the bottom to drain off liquids
colossal (kə läs′ əl) *adj.* Huge; gigantic
columnist (käl′ əm nist′) *n.* Person who writes newspaper or magazine columns
commend (kə mend′) *v.* To praise
companionable (kəm pan′ yən ə bəl) *adj.* Friendly
compelling (kəm pel′ iŋ) *adj.* Irresistible; forceful
complex (käm pleks′) *adj.* Not simple; complicated
compound (käm′ pound′) *adj.* Made of two or more separate parts
comprehension (käm′ prē hen′ shen) *n.* Understanding; knowledge
concocter (kən käkt′ ər) *n.* Inventor
concrete (kän krēt′) *adj.* Real; in material form
condemn (kən dem′) *v.* To doom
conformity (kən fôrm′ ə tē) *n.* Action that follows customs, rules, popular opinion, and so on
conquer (käŋ′ kər) *v.* To take control over
conscience (kän′ shəns) *n.* Knowledge of right and wrong
console (kən sōl′) *v.* To comfort
consternation (kän′ stər nā′ shən) *n.* Confusion or bewilderment; frustration
consumption (kən sump′ shən) *n.* Eating; drinking; using up
contemplative (kən tem′ plə tiv′) *adj.* Thoughtful
contemporary (kən tem′ pə rer′ ē) *n.* Person of about the same age
contempt (kən tempt′) *n.* Feeling one has toward something considered worthless
corncrib (kôrn′ krib′) *n.* A structure used for storing corn
correspondence (kôr′ ə spän′ dəns) *n.* Letters
crane (krān) *v.* To stretch the neck for a better view
crest (krest) *n.* A tuft on the head of some animals or birds
crescents (kres′ ənts) *n.* Any things that have one edge curved like the outside of a ball and one edge curved like the inside of a ball
crestfallen (krest′ fôl′ ən) *adj.* Made sad or humble; disheartened
crimson (krim′ zən) *n.* Deep red
cudgel (kuj′ əl) *n.* A short, thick stick or club

D

deceive (dē sēv′) *v.* To mislead; to make a person believe something that is not true
decisive (dē sī′ siv) *adj.* Unwavering; determined
decline (dē klīn′) *v.* To refuse
decree (dē krē′) *v.* To issue an official order or decision
defiance (dē fī′ əns) *n.* Bold behavior intended to challenge
defy (dē fī′) *v.* To resist openly
delve (delv) *v.* To dig
delver (delv′ ər) *n.* Investigator
destitute (des′ tə to͞ot′) *adj.* Extremely poor
detain (dē tān′) *v.* To hold back
deteriorate (dē tir′ ē ə rāt′) *v.* To become worse
determined (dē tʉr′ mənd) *adj.* Having one's mind made up
devour (di vour′) *v.* To swallow greedily; destroy
dialects (dī′ ə lekts′) *n.* Forms of speech that are peculiar to a region or community
dignified (dig′ nə fīd′) *adj.* Noble
diminutive (də min′ yo͞o tiv) *adj.* Very small
disciplined (dis′ ə plind) *adj.* Self-controlled; trained
discontent (dis′ kən tent′) *adj.* Wanting something more or different
dismal (diz′ məl) *adj.* Depressing; miserable
dismay (dis mā′) *n.* A loss of courage when faced with trouble or danger
dispute (di spyo͞ot′) *n.* An argument; debate; quarrel
dissonance (dis′ ə nəns) *n.* A harsh or disagreeable combination of sounds
documentation (däk′ yo͞o mən tā′ shən) *n.* Supporting evidence
dote (dōt) *v.* To be excessively fond
dowry (dou′ rē) *n.* Property that a woman brings to her husband at marriage
drab (drab) *adj.* Dull; dreary
drone (drōn) *n.* A continuous humming sound
dwindle (dwin′ dəl) *v.* To shrink; become less

E

earnestly (ʉr′ nist lē) *adv.* Seriously
editor (ed′ it ər) *n.* The head of a newspaper department
efficient (e fish′ ənt) *adj.* A way producing the best result with least effort
elation (ē lā′ shən) *n.* High spirits
elevate (el′ ə vāt′) *v.* To lift up
embers (em′ berz) *n.* Smoldering or burning remains of a fire
emigrate (em′ ə grāt′) *v.* To leave one country to settle in another
encroach (en krōch′) *adj.* Extend in a gradual way beyond limits
endure (en door′) *v.* To hold up under
engulf (en gulf′) *v.* To overwhelm
entrance (en trans′) *v.* To charm; put into a trance
entranced (en trans′d) *v.* Enchanted; fascinated
envious (en′ vē əs) *adj.* Feeling jealousy toward someone who possesses something that one desires for oneself
episode (ep′ ə sōd′) *n.* A series of related events
etiquette (et′ i kit) *n.* Acceptable social manners
evade (e vād′) *v.* To avoid; escape
evaporate (ē vap′ ə rāt′) *v.* To disappear like vapor; vanish
exasperated (eg zas′ pə rāt′ əd) *adj.* Irritated; annoyed
expedition (eks′ pə dish′ ən) *n.* Trip
expense (ek spens′) *n.* Cost or sacrifice
extraordinary (ek strôd′′n er′ ē) *adj.* Very unusual
extravagant (ek strav′ ə gənt) *adj.* Excessive; beyond reasonable limits

F

fallow (fal′ ō) *adj.* Inactive; underproductive; unplanted
feat (fēt) *n.* An act showing unusual daring or skill
fertile (fʉrt′′l) *adj.* Rich in resources or invention
fevered (fē′ vərd) *adj.* Brightly illuminated
flabbergasted (flab′ ər gast′ əd) *adj.* Speechless; surprised or astonished
flaw (flô) *n.* Break; crack
flit (flit) *v.* To fly lightly and rapidly
flue (floo) *n.* A tube for the passage of smoke, as in a chimney
foresight (fôr′ sīt′) *n.* The power to look forward; seeing into the future
forlorn (fôr lôrn′) *adj.* Pitiful
foster (fôs′ tər) *v.* To take care of; to rear
frenzy (fren′ zē) *adj.* Wild; frantic
frothy (frôth′ ē) *adj.* Foamy
furrow (fʉr′ ō) *n.* Narrow groove

G

gait (gāt) *n.* Manner of walking or running
galleon (gal′ ē ən) *n.* Large Spanish warship from the fifteenth and sixteenth centuries
galling (gôl′ iŋ′) *adj.* Causing extreme irritation
gauze (gôz) *n.* A very thin, transparent, loosely woven material
geometry (jē äm′ ə trē) *n.* The branch of mathematics that deals with shapes
gibbous (gib′ əs) *adj.* Half or partially illuminated
glimmer (glim′ ər) *v.* To give a faint, flickering light
glint (glint) *v.* To gleam or flash
graffiti (grə fēt′ ē) *n.* A scribbled drawing on a public surface
grimace (grim′ əs) *v.* To twist the face in fun or in a look of pain or disgust
gristle (gris′ əl) *n.* Cartilage; tough, elastic tissue that is part of the skeleton
gutter (gut′ ər) *n.* A narrow channel along the side of a road or street, to carry off water

H

hanker (haŋ′ kər) *v.* To crave; long
hatchling (hach′ liŋ) *adj.* Recently brought forth from an egg
haughty (hôt′ ē) *adj.* Proud, arrogant
hayloft (hā′ lôft′) *n.* An upper story in a barn or stable used for storing hay
heathen (hē′ thən) *adj.* Uncivilized
heaving (hēv′ iŋ) *adj.* Rising and falling rhythmically
hideous (hid′ ē əs) *adj.* Very ugly; horrible
hindsight (hīnd′ sīt′) *n.* The understanding of an event after it has already occurred
hoard (hôrd) *v.* To store away
hover (huv′ ər) *v.* To hang over, linger
hysterical (his ter′ i kəl) *adj.* Emotionally uncontrolled; wild

I

ignorance (ig′ nər əns) *n.* Lacking knowledge, education, or experience
illiterate (i lit′ ər it) *n.* A person who does not know how to read or write
immemorial (im′ me môr′ ē əl) *adj.* Ancient; extending back before memory
immortal (i môr′ t′l) *adj.* Living forever.—*n.* A being who does not die; who lives forever
immunization (im′ myoo nīz ā′ shən) *n.* Protection from disease by getting a vaccine, or shot
impassively (im pas′ iv lē) *adv.* Calmly
implement (im′ plə mənt′) *n.* Carry out
implore (im plôr′) *v.* To beg
impudence (im′ pyoo dəns) *n.* Disrespectful behavior; rudeness
impudently (im′ pyoo dənt lē) *adv.* Shamelessly; disrespectfully
in cahoots (kə hoots′) *n.* In partnership, usually in doing something dishonest
in earnest (ʉr′ nist) *adv.* Seriously and sincerely

inadvertently (in′ ad vurt′′nt lē) *adv.* Unintentionally, not purposefully
incandescent (in′ kən des′ ənt) *adj.* Glowing; bright
incessantly (in ses′ ənt lē) *adv.* Constantly
indignantly (in dig′ nənt lē) *adv.* Done with anger about something that seems unfair
indomitable (in däm′ i tə bəl) *adj.* Not easily discouraged or defeated
inedible (in ed′ ə bəl) *adj.* Not fit to be eaten
inevitable (in ev′ i tə bəl) *adj.* Certain to happen
innovation (in′ ə vā′ shən) *n.* A change; new idea
inquire (in kwīr′) *v.* To ask
inscrutable (in skrōōt′ ə bəl) *adj.* Mysterious
insistent (in sis′ tənt) *adj.* Demanding
inspiration (in′ spə rā′ shən) *n.* Something that brings on creative activity; motivation
instinct (in′ stiŋkt′) *n.* Inborn knowledge
instinctively (in stiŋk′ tiv lē) *adv.* Done by instinct, without thinking
intent (in tent′) *adj.* Firmly directed
intimidate (in tim′ ə dāt′) *v.* To make afraid
intrigue (in trēg′) *v.* To fascinate
iridescent (ir′ i des′ ənt) *adj.* Showing changes in color when seen from different angles

J
jubilation (jōō′ bə lā′ shən) *n.* Great joy; triumph

K
kaleidoscopes (kə lī′ də skōps) *n.* Constantly changing sets of color
kin (kin) *n.* Relatives; family

L
laborious (lə bôr′ ē əs) *adj.* A manner requiring much hard work
lair (ler) *n.* The resting or dwelling place of a wild or imaginary animal
lash (lash) *v.* To whip; strike
lattice (lat′ is) *n.* A structure of crossed strips of wood or metal, used as a support or a screen
liable (lī′ ə bəl) *adj.* Likely
loathsome (lōth′ səm) *adj.* Disgusting
logic (läj′ ik) *n.* Correct reasoning
loiter (loit′ er) *v.* To linger or hang around
lure (lōōr) *n.* Anything that attracts or tempts
lyre (līr) *n.* A small stringed instrument, similar to a harp

M
maim (mām) *v.* Cripple; disable
makeshift (māk′ shift′) *adj.* Used for a while as a substitute
malice (mal′ is) *n.* Desire to do harm to others
malicious (mə lish′ əs) *adj.* Showing evil intentions
mammoth (mam′ əth) *adj.* Huge
marrow (mar′ ō) *n.* The soft tissue that fills most bones
mascot (mas′ kät′) *n.* Any person, animal, or thing adopted by a group that is meant to bring good luck
meander (mē an′ dər) *v.* To wander aimlessly; ramble
meandering (mē an′ dər iŋ) *n.* Aimless wandering
meditate (med′ ə tāt) *v.* To think quietly, often about mysterious or religious events
membranes (mem′ brānz′) *n.* Thin, flexible layers, especially of animal or plant tissue
menace (men′ is) *n.* A threat; troublesome or annoying person
menacing (men′ is iŋ) *adj.* Threatening; sinister
mentor (men′ tər) *n.* Advisor; teacher or coach
migrated (mī′ grāt′ id) *v.* Settled in another region
mimic (mim′ ik) *v.* To imitate or copy
minuscule (min′ ə skyōōl′) *adj.* Tiny
mirage (mi räzh′) *n.* Something that seems real but is not
misapprehension (mis′ ap rə hen′ shən) *n.* Misunderstanding
mocking (mäk′ iŋ) *adj.* Imitating
monarch (män′ ərk) *n.* Supreme ruler
monitor (män′ i tər) *v.* To watch or check on
monotonous (mə nät′′n əs) *adj.* Tiresome because it does not vary
mortal (môr′ təl) *adj.* Referring to humans, who must eventually die
mortar (môr′ tər) *n.* Hard bowl in which grain is pounded
mortified (môrt′ ə fīd′) *adj.* Ashamed; extremely embarrassed
motivated (mōt′ ə vāt′ əd) *adj.* Driven to move forward or to progress
mourning (môrn′ iŋ) *n.* Sorrowing for the dead

O
obligatory (əb lig′ ə tôr′ ē) *adj.* Required
obliterate (ə blit′ ər āt′) *v.* To blot out
obscure (əb skyoor′) *adj.* Unknown; hidden
obstinacy (äb′ stə nə sē) *n.* Stubbornness
offense (ə fens′) *n.* Crime; hurtful act
ominous (äm′ ə nəs) *adj.* Threatening; frightful
opposition (äp′ ə zish′ ən) *n.* The other team
ordeal (ôr dēl′) *n.* A severely difficult experience

P
pantomime (pan′ tə mīm′) *v.* To act out silently with gestures
parchment (pärch′ mənt) *n.* The skin of an animal prepared as a surface on which to write
parson (pär′ sən) *n.* Clergyman
partition (pär tish′ ən) *n.* Something that separates or divides, such as an interior wall that separates one room from another
pauper (pô′ pər) *n.* An extremely poor person

peculiar (pē kyo͞ol′ yər) *adj.* Odd
pellet (pel′ it) *n.* Little ball
perceive (pər sēv′) *v.* To observe; become aware
perch (pu̇rch) *n.* A resting place, especially a high one or insecure one
perilous (per′ ə ləs) *adj.* Dangerous
perjure (pu̇r′ jər) *v.* Willfully tell a lie while expected to tell the truth or under oath to tell the truth
pessimistic (pes′ ə mis′ tik) *adj.* Seeing the gloomy or negative side of things
petulance (pech′ ə ləns) *n.* Unreasonable irritability
phantom (fan′ təm) *adj.* Unreal; ghostlike
phosphorescent (fäs′ fə res′ ənt) *adj.* Giving off light
physicist (fiz′ i sist) *n.* A scientist who deals with the relationships of energy and matter
pier (pir) *n.* Heavy structure supporting the sections of a bridge
pirouette (pir′ o͞o et′) *v.* To spin around on one foot
pitifully (pit′ i fəl lē) *adv.* Sorrowfully; regretfully
plagiarism (plā′ jə riz′ əm) *n.* The taking of ideas or writing from another and passing them off as one's own
plague (plāg) *n.* Deadly disease that spreads rapidly—*v.* To torment
plaintive (plān′ tiv) *adj.* Sad
platoon (plə to͞on′) *n.* A small military unit; any small group like this
plight (plīt) *n.* An awkward, sad, or dangerous situation
plunge (plunj) *v.* To dive or rush
poise (poiz) *v.* To balance
ponder (pän′ dər) *v.* To think deeply about; consider carefully
pondering (pän′ dər iŋ) *n.* Deep thought; careful consideration
prance (prans) *v.* To move gaily and with confidence
precautionary (prē kô′ shən er′ ē) *adj.* Taking care beforehand to prevent danger
precinct (prē′ siŋkt′) *n.* An election district
prevail (prē vāl′) *v.* To take advantage of
primitive (prim′ i tiv) *adj.* Having simplicity suggesting the earliest times
prodigy (präd′ ə jē) *n.* A child of highly unusual talent or genius
profile (prō′ fīl′) *n.* A side view of the face
promenade (präm′ ə nād′) *v.* To parade; march
prospective (prō spek′ tiv) *adj.* Expected
prospector (präs′ pək′ tər) *n.* Person who searches for valuable ores, such as gold
prostrate (präs′ trāt) *adj.* Exhausted
protest (prō test′) *v.* To object to strongly
proverb (präv′ u̇rb′) *n.* A short saying that expresses an obvious truth or familiar experience
prowl (proul) *v.* To crawl quietly and secretly
pulsating (pul′ sāt′ iŋ) *v.* Beating or throbbing rhythmically
pursue (pər so͞o′) *v.* To chase
pylon (pī′ län′) *n.* Towerlike structure

Q
quarry (kwôr′ e) *n.* Anything being hunted or pursued
quiver (kwiv′ ər) *v.* To shake; tremble

R
rabbi (rab′ ī) *n.* A scholar and teacher of Jewish law
ragged (rag′ id) *adj.* Tattered; old and worn
rancor (raŋ′ kər) *n.* Bitter hate or ill will
ravage (rav′ ij) *v.* To violently destroy; run
ravenous (rav′ ə nəs) *adj.* Greedily hungry
recumbent (ri kum′ bənt) *adj.* Lying down; leaning
reflect (ri flekt′) *v.* To think seriously about something
refuge (ref′ yo͞oj) *n.* Shelter; safe retreat
relic (rel′ ik) *n.* An object, custom, and so on that has survived from the past
reluctance (ri luk′ təns) *n.* Unwillingness; hesitation
reproachfully (ri prōch′ fəl lē) *adv.* With blame
repulse (ri puls′) *v.* To drive back; to repel an attack
resort (ri zôrt′) *v.* To turn to for help
respective (ri spek′ tiv) *adj.* Relating separately to each of two or more
revulsion (ri vul′ shən) *n.* Extreme disgust
rite (rīt) *n.* Formal ceremony or act carried out according to fixed rules
rivulet (riv′ yoo lit) *n.* Little stream
roiling (roil′ iŋ) *adj.* Unsettled, agitated
roust (roust) *v.* Stir or drive out; bring out of sleep
rudimentary (ro͞o′ də men′ tər ē) *adj.* Incompletely developed
rue (ro͞o) *v.* To regret
rueful (ro͞o′ fəl) *adj.* Regretful or sorrowful
rustle (rus′ əl) *v.* To make soft sounds

S
sacred (sā′ krid) *adj.* Religious; respected
sacrifice (sak′ rə fīs′) *v.* To give up on; surrender
saga (sä′ gə) *n.* A long story of adventure or heroic deeds
satellite (sat′′l īt′) *n.* An object that orbits another, larger object; in this case, a space station that orbits the earth
savor (sā′ vər) *v.* To dwell on with delight
scheme (skēm) *n.* A carefully arranged plan for doing something
scorch (skôrch) *v.* To burn slightly
scour (skour) *v.* To clean by hard rubbing with something rough
scribe (skrīb) *n.* Person employed to write letters, fill in documents and applications, and so on
scurry (sku̇r′ ē) *v.* To run hastily
scuttle (skut′′l) *v.* To scurry; scamper
scuttling (skut′′l iŋ) *adj.* Quickly moving
sedately (si dāt′ lē) *adv.* Calmly
seep (sēp) *v.* Gradually pass through openings
self-deprecation (self′ dep rə kā′ shən) *n.* Expressing lack of importance of oneself
sham (sham) *adj.* Make-believe; pretended

shear (shir) *v.* To cut off sharply
shimmer (shim′ ər) *v.* To shine with an unsteady light
sibling (sib′ liŋ) *n.* Brother or sister
sinew (sin′ yo͞o) *n.* Tendon that gives power and strength to muscles
skein (skān) *n.* Coil of thread or yarn
skulk (skulk) *v.* To sneak around or hide in
sleek (slēk) *adj.* Smooth and shiny
slough (sluf) *v.* To come off
smugly (smug′ lē) *adv.* With self-satisfaction
soothingly (so͞o*th*′ iŋ lē) *adv.* To calm or compose
sown (sōn) *v.* Planted for growing
span (span) *v.* To reach or extend over or from one side to another
spectacle (spek′ tə kəl) *n.* Foolish or unusual behavior
sphere (sfir) *n.* Ball; globe
splay (splā) *v.* To spread out
stock (stäk) *n.* Paper
stout (stout) *adj.* Strong
streaming (strēm′ iŋ) *v.* Floating; flying
stupefy (sto͞o′ pə fī′) *adj.* Stunned; astounded
substantiate (səb stan′ shē āt′) *v.* To show to be true; prove
successive (sək ses′ iv) *adj.* Following one after another in order
sulkily (sulk′ ə lē) *adv.* Gloomily; poutingly
summit (sum′ it) *n.* The highest point; the top
summon (sum′ ən) *v.* To send for; call forth
survey (sər vā′) *v.* To see; look at
systematic (sis′ tə mat′ ik) *adj.* Orderly

T
tangent (tan′ jənt) *n.* A sudden change of course
techniques (tek nēks′) *v.* Systematic methods or ways of doing something
tentacle (ten′ tə kəl) *n.* Flexible, slender growths about the head or mouth, used like arms to grasp and hold
terrestrial (tə res′ trē əl) *adj.* Having a worldly or commonplace quality
thrash (thrash) *v.* To move violently
thrive (thrīv) *v.* To grow successfully and strong
thwart (thwôrt) *v.* To prevent from happening
tingling (tiŋ′ gliŋ) *adj.* Stinging, as from excitement
toil (toil) *n.* Hard exhausting work and effort
treacherous (trech′ ər əs) *adj.* Dangerous
trowel (trou′ əl) *n.* A scooplike tool for loosening soil
tweed (twēd) *n.* Clothes made of a rough, multicolored fabric
tyrant (tī′ rənt) *n.* A cruel, unjust ruler

U
unfaltering (un fôl′ tər iŋ lē) *adv.* With certainty and steadiness
ungrateful (un grāt′ fəl) *adj.* Not thankful

V
valorous (val′ ər əs) *adj.* Brave
velvet (vel′ vit) *adj.* Smooth or soft like velvet fabric
vanish (van′ ish) *v.* To disappear
vanity (van′ ə tē) *n.* Too much concern for one's appearance
vapor (vā′ pər) *n.* Visible moisture floating in air; fumes
variegated (ver′ ē ə gāt′ id) *adj.* Marked with different colors in spots, streaks, and so forth
venomous (ven′ əm əs) *adj.* Poisonous
venture (ven′chər) *v.* Do or go at some risk
veranda (və ran′ də) *n.* An open porch, usually with a roof, along the outside of a building
veteran (vet′ ər ən) *n.* Person having experience
vigil (vij′ əl) *n.* Watch
villa (vil′ ə) *n.* A large estate
virtue (vʉr′ cho͞o) *n.* The quality of goodness
visionary (vizh′ ən er′ ē) *adj.* Being able to imagine the future

W
wallow (wäl′ ō) *v.* To roll and pitch
welfare (wel′ fer′) *n.* Well-being
wheeze (hwēz) *v.* To breathe hard with a whistling sound
wherewithal (hwer′ wi*th* ôl′) *n.* Necessary means to do something
winced (winst) *v.* Shrank or drew back slightly, usually with a grimace, as if in pain
wistful (wist′ fəl) *adj.* Showing longing or sadness
writhe (rī*th*) *v.* To make twisting or turning movements; squirm

INDEX OF FINE ART

INDEX OF SKILLS

ANALYZING LITERATURE

CRITICAL THINKING AND READING

LEARNING OPTIONS

READING IN THE CONTENT AREAS

THINKING AND WRITING

INDEX OF TITLES BY THEMES

Selections are listed here according to the theme shown on the selection page as well as under other themes that apply.

RITES OF PASSAGE

CONFLICTS AND CHALLENGES

OUR LIVING EARTH

CHOICES AND CONSEQUENCES

EXPLORING THE UNKNOWN

THE SEARCH FOR SELF

TURNING POINTS

OUT OF THE ORDINARY

LIVING AND LEARNING

DOING WHAT'S RIGHT

APPRECIATING OTHERS

INDEX OF AUTHORS AND TITLES

Page numbers in italics refer to biographical information.

ACKNOWLEDGMENTS

Susan Bergholz Literary Services
"Eleven" by Sandra Cisneros, copyright Sandra Cisneros 1989, from the forthcoming collection tentatively titled *The Sky Has Little Eyes,* Random House. From "Straw Into Gold" by Sandra Cisneros, first published under the title "A Writer's Voyage" in The Texas Observer, September 1987. Copyright 1987 by Sandra Cisneros. Reprinted by permission of Susan Bergholz, agent for Sandra Cisneros.

Georges Borchardt, Inc. for John Gardner
"Dragon, Dragon" from *Dragon, Dragon and Other Tales* by John Gardner. Copyright © 1975 by Boskydell Artists Ltd. Reprinted by permission.

Clarion Books, a Houghton Mifflin Company
"The Living Kuan-yin" from *Sweet and Sour Tales from China* by Carol Kendall and Yao-wen Li. Copyright © 1980 by Carol Kendall and Yao-wen Li. Copyright 1980 by Shirley Felt. "A Backwoods Boy" from *Lincoln: A Photobiography* by Russell Freedman. Copyright © 1987 by Russell Freedman. Reprinted by permission of Clarion Books, a Houghton Mifflin Company.

Don Congdon Associates, Inc.
"The Sound of Summer Running" by Ray Bradbury, published in *Saturday Evening Post,* 1956. Copyright © 1956, renewed 1984 by Ray Bradbury. "The Scribe" by Kristin Hunter, published in *Directions 3,* 1972. Copyright 1972, Kristin E. Hunter. Reprinted by permission of Don Congdon Associates, Inc.

Jack Cope
"Power" from *The Man Who Doubted and Other Stories* by Jack Cope. First published in 1967 by William Heinemann Ltd., London. Reprinted by permission of the author.

Harold Courlander
"Osebo's Drum" from *The Hat Shaking Dance and Other Ashanti Tales From Ghana* by Harold Courlander. Published by Harcourt Brace and World, Inc. Copyright 1957, 1985 by Harold Courlander. Reprinted by permission of the author.

Dell Books, a Division of Bantam Doubleday Dell Publishing Group, Inc.
"The Geese" by Richard Peck from *Sounds and Silences: Poetry for Now,* edited by Richard Peck. Copyright © 1970, 1990 by Richard Peck. Used by permission of Dell Books, a Division of Bantam Doubleday Dell Publishing Group, Inc.

Dial Books for Young Readers
Daydreamers by Eloise Greenfield. Text copyright © 1981 by Eloise Greenfield. "The Strange Geometry of Stonehenge" from *Portals to the Past* by Katherine B. Shippen. Copyright 1963 by Katherine B. Shippen. Reprinted by permission of the publisher, Dial Books for Young Readers.

Doubleday, a Division of Bantam Doubleday Dell Publishing Group, Inc.
"Mowgli's Brothers" from *The Jungle Books* by Rudyard Kipling. "The Giants of Easter Island" by Carrol Alice Stout from *Mysteries from the Past,* edited by Thomas G. Aylesworth. Copyright © 1971 by Doubleday, a division of Bantam Doubleday Dell Publishing Group, Inc. Used by permission of the publisher.

Paul S. Eriksson, Publisher
"My Papa, Mark Twain" by Susy Clemens from *Small Voices* by Josef and Dorothy Berger. © Copyright 1966 by Josef and Dorothy Berger. Published by Paul S. Eriksson. Reprinted by permission of the publisher.

Faber and Faber Limited
"Letter to the U.S. Government" by Chief Seattle from *The Faber Book of Letters,* edited by Felix Pryor. This collection © Faber and Faber Limited, 1988.

Farrar, Straus & Giroux, Inc.
Tuck Everlasting by Natalie Babbitt. Copyright © 1975 by Natalie Babbitt. "Light and Water" from *Selected Writings of Juan Ramón Jiménez* translated by H. R. Hays. Copyright © 1957 by Juan Ramón Jiménez. Renewal copyright © 1985 by Farrar, Straus & Giroux, Inc. "Sun" from *Small Poems* by Valerie Worth. Copyright © 1972 by Valerie Worth. Reprinted by permission of Farrar, Straus & Giroux, Inc.

Four Winds Press, an Imprint of Macmillan Publishing Company
Excerpts from *The Truth About Dragons* by Rhoda Blumberg. Copyright © 1980 by Rhoda Blumberg. Reprinted by permission.

Samuel French, Inc.
The Phantom Tollbooth by Susan Nanus, based on the book by Norton Juster. Copyright © 1977 by Susan Nanus and Norton Juster. Reprinted by permission of Samuel French, Inc. Caution: Professionals and amateurs are hereby warned that *The Phantom Tollbooth,* being fully protected under the copyright laws of the United States of America, the British Commonwealth countries, including Canada, and the other countries of the Copyright Union, is subject to a royalty. All rights, including professional, amateur, motion picture, recitation, public reading, radio, television and cablevision broadcasting, and the rights of translation into foreign languages, are strictly reserved. *The Phantom Tollbooth* may be given stage presentation by amateurs in theaters seating less than 500 upon payment of a royalty of thirty-five dollars for the first performance and twenty-five dollars for each additional performance. For amateur productions in theaters seating over 500, write for special royalty quotation, giving details as to ticket price, number of performances, and exact number of seats in your theater. Royalties are payable one week before the opening performance of the play, to Samuel French, Inc., at 45 West 25th Street, New York, N.Y. 10010, or at 7623 Sunset Blvd., Hollywood, Calif. 90046, or to Samuel French

(Canada) Ltd., 80 Richmond Street East, Toronto, Ontario, Canada M5C 1P1.

Greenwillow Books (A Division of William Morrow & Co.)
"Ankylosaurus" from *Tyrannosaurus Was a Beast* by Jack Prelutsky. Copyright 1988 by Jack Prelutsky. "Door Number Four" from *If I Had a Paka* by Charlotte Pomerantz. Copyright © 1982 by Charlotte Pomerantz. Reprinted by permission of Greenwillow Books, A Division of William Morrow & Co.

Greenwillow Books (A Division of William Morrow & Co.) and Laura Cecil
"Auntie" from *Who's Afraid? and Other Strange Stories* by Philippa Pearce. © 1978 Philippa Pearce from *Who's Afraid,* Puffin Books. Copyright © 1981, 1982, 1983, 1984, 1985, 1986 by Philippa Pearce. Reprinted by permission.

Harcourt Brace & Company
"Noah Webster's Dictionary," excerpt from *Dateline America* by Charles Kuralt. Copyright © 1979 by CBS, Inc. "Arithmetic" from *The Complete Poems of Carl Sandburg,* copyright 1950 by Carl Sandburg and renewed 1978 by Margaret Sandburg, Helga Sandburg Crile, and Janet Sandburg. "The Fairies' Lullaby" from *Shakespeare: Major Plays and the Sonnets,* by G. B. Harrison, copyright 1948, 1952 by Harcourt Brace Jovanovich, Inc. Excerpt from "The Harbor" in *Chicago Poems* by Carl Sandburg, copyright 1916 by Holt, Rinehart and Winston, Inc., and renewed 1944 by Carl Sandburg. Reprinted by permission of Harcourt Brace & Company.

Harcourt Brace & Company, and Faber and Faber Limited
"The Naming of Cats" from *Old Possum's Book of Practical Cats* by T. S. Eliot. Copyright © 1939 by T. S. Eliot; copyright © 1967 by Esme Valerie Eliot. Reprinted by permission of Harcourt Brace & Company, and Faber and Faber Limited.

Harcourt Brace & Company and Peters Fraser & Dunlop Group Ltd.
"One" from *When I Dance* by James Berry. Text copyright © 1991, 1988 by James Berry. Reprinted by permission.

HarperCollins Publishers Inc. and Arnold Adoff
"Alone In The Nets" from *Sports Pages* by Arnold Adoff. Copyright 1986 by Arnold Adoff. Reprinted by permission of the publisher and the author.

HarperCollins Publishers Inc.
"Aaron's Gift" from *The Witch of Fourth Street and Other Stories* by Myron Levoy. Copyright © 1972 by Myron Levoy. "Fireflies" from *Joyful Noise* by Paul Fleischman. Text copyright © 1988 by Paul Fleischman. "Whatif" from *A Light in the Attic* by Shel Silverstein. Copyright © 1981 by Evil Eye Music, Inc. "Change" from *River Winding* by Charlotte Zolotow. Text copyright © 1970 by Charlotte Zolotow. "Breaker's Bridge" from *The Rainbow People* by Laurence Yep. Text copyright © 1989 by Laurence Yep. "Señor Coyote and the Tricked Trickster" from *Trickster Tales* by I. G. Edmonds. Copyright © 1966 by I. G. Edmonds. "Zlateh the Goat" text only from *Zlateh the Goat and Other Stories* by Isaac Bashevis Singer, illustrated by Maurice Sendak. Text copyright © 1966 by Isaac Bashevis Singer. Illustrations copyright © 1966 by Maurice Sendak. "The Hatchling Turtles" from *Spring Comes to the Ocean* by Jean Craighead George. Copyright © 1965 by Jean Craighead George. Two limericks: "A flea and a fly in a flue" and "There was a young fellow named Hall" from *Laughable Limericks* compiled by Sara and John E. Brewton. Copyright © 1965 by Sara and John E. Brewton. "The Horse Snake" from *The Land I Lost* by Huynh Quang Nhuong. Text copyright © 1982 by Huynh Quang Nhuong. Reprinted by permission of HarperCollins Publishers Inc.

Highlights for Children, Inc.
"Paul Klee" by Hattie Clark from *Highlights for Children,* January 1986. Copyright © 1986. Used by permission of Highlights for Children, Inc., Columbus, Ohio.

Henry Holt and Company, Inc.
From *The Walrus and the Carpenter* by Lewis Carroll. "The Cow-Tail Switch" from *The Cow-Tail Switch and Other West African Stories* by Harold Courlander and George Herzog. Copyright 1947, © 1975 by Harold Courlander. "The Stone" from *The Foundling and Other Tales of Prydain* by Lloyd Alexander. Copyright 1973 by Lloyd Alexander. "Dust of Snow" by Robert Frost from *The Poetry of Robert Frost* edited by Edward Connery Lathem. Copyright 1923, © 1969 by Holt, Rinehart and Winston. Copyright 1951 by Robert Frost. Reprinted by permission of Henry Holt and Company, Inc.

Houghton Mifflin Company
"Arachne" from *Greek Myths* by Olivia E. Coolidge. Copyright © 1949 and renewed 1977 by Olivia E. Coolidge. "Rhyming Riddle I (Snow)" from *The Children Sing in the Far West* by Mary Austin. Copyright 1928 by Mary Austin, © renewed 1956 by Kenneth M. Chapman and Mary C. Wheelwright. All rights reserved. "The Shark" from *Fast and Slow* by John Ciardi. Copyright © 1975 by John Ciardi. Reprinted by permission of Houghton Mifflin Company.

International Paper Company
"How to Read Faster" by Bill Cosby. Copyright © 1987 by International Paper Company. Reprinted by permission of International Paper Company.

International Paper, Garrison Keillor, and Penguin Books Canada Ltd.
"How to Write a Letter" from *We Are Still Married* by Garrison Keillor. Copyright © 1987 by International Paper Company, copyright © Garrison Keillor 1989. Reprinted by permission.

Francisco Jiménez
"The Circuit" by Francisco Jiménez, *The Arizona Quarterly* (Autumn 1973). Reprinted by permission of the author.

Francisco H. Pinzon Jiménez for the Estate of Juan Ramón Jiménez
"Luz y Agua" by Juan Ramón Jiménez from *Selected Writings of Juan Ramón Jiménez.* Reprinted by permission.

Brenda A. Johnston
From *Between the Devil and the Sea* by Brenda A. Johnston. Copyright © 1974 by Brenda A. Johnston. Reprinted by permission of the author.

Alfred A. Knopf, Inc.
"April Rain Song" by Langston Hughes. Copyright 1932 by Alfred A. Knopf, Inc. and renewed 1960 by Langston Hughes. Reprinted from *The Dream Keeper and Other Poems* by Langston Hughes, by permission of Alfred A. Knopf, Inc. "He Lion, Bruh Bear, and Bruh Rabbit" from *The People Could Fly: American Black Folktales* by Virginia Hamilton. Text copyright © 1985 by Virginia Hamilton. Reprinted by permission of Alfred A. Knopf, Inc.

Little, Brown and Company
"Adventures of Isabel" from *The Bad Parents' Garden of Verse* by Ogden Nash. Copyright 1936 by Ogden Nash. "Books Fall Open" from *One at a Time* by David McCord. Copyright © 1965, 1966 by David McCord. Reprinted by permission of Little, Brown and Company.

Liveright Publishing Corporation
"hist whist" is reprinted from *Hist Whist and other poems for children,* by E. E. Cummings, edited by George J. Firmage, by permission of Liveright Publishing Corporation. Copyright © 1923, 1944, 1949, 1950, 1951, 1953, 1956, 1958, 1961 by E. E. Cummings. Copyright © 1963 by Marion M. Cummings. Copyright © 1972, 1976, 1977, 1978, 1979, 1981, 1983 by the Trustees for the E. E. Cummings Trust.

Lothrop, Lee & Shepard Books, a Division of William Morrow & Company
Mufaro's Beautiful Daughters by John Steptoe. Copyright © 1987 by John Steptoe. Reprinted by permission of Lothrop, Lee & Shepard Books, a Division of William Morrow & Company, Inc., with the approval of the Estate of John Steptoe.

Macmillan Publishing Company
"Orpheus" from *The Macmillan Book of Greek Gods and Heroes* by Alice Low. Copyright © 1985 by Macmillan Publishing Company. *Iduna and the Magic Apples* by Marianna Mayer. Text, Copyright © 1988 by Marianna Mayer. Excerpt from "Letter to Joan" from *C. S. Lewis Letters to Children,* Lyle W. Dorsett and Marjorie Lamp Mead, Editors. Copyright © 1985 by C. S. Lewis PTE Ltd. Reprinted by permission of Macmillan Publishing Company.

Mai Studio
"The Fly," from *The Toad Is the Emperor's Uncle* by Vo-Dinh. Copyright 1970 by Mai Vo-Dinh. Reprinted by permission of Mai Studio.

Margaret K. McElderry Books, an Imprint of Macmillan Publishing Company
"Lighting a Fire" from *The Forgetful Wishing Well* by X. J. Kennedy. Copyright © 1985 by X. J. Kennedy. Reprinted by permission.

Neil McAleer and Scott Meredith Literary Agency, Inc.
"Space Stations of the Mind" by Neil McAleer from *Boys' Life,* September 1989. Reprinted by permission of the author and the author's agents, Scott Meredith Literary Agency, Inc., 845 Third Avenue, New York, New York 10022.

Modern Curriculum Press, Inc.
"A Modern Dragon" from *Songs From Around a Toadstool Table* by Rowena Bastin Bennett. Copyright © 1930, 1968 by Rowena Bastin Bennett. Reprinted by permission of Modern Curriculum Press.

Lillian Morrison
"The Sidewalk Racer" from *The Sidewalk Racer and Other Poems of Sports and Motion* by Lillian Morrison. Copyright © 1977 by Lillian Morrison. Reprinted by permission of the author.

William Morrow & Company
"Winter Poem" from *My House* by Nikki Giovanni. Copyright © 1972 by Nikki Giovanni. "Beauty" from *I Am a Pueblo Indian Girl* by E-Yeh-Shure. Copyright © 1939 by William Morrow & Company, Inc. Renewed 1967 by Louise Abeita Chiwiwi. Reprinted by permission of William Morrow & Company.

Morrow Junior Books, a Division of William Morrow & Company
"The Platoon System" from *A Girl From Yamhill* by Beverly Cleary. Copyright © 1988 by Beverly Cleary. Reprinted by permission of Morrow Junior Books.

Lensey Namioka
"The All-American Slurp" by Lensey Namioka from *Visions,* edited by Donald R. Gallo. Copyright © 1987 by Lensey Namioka. Reprinted by permission of Lensey Namioka. All rights reserved.

Orchard Books, a Division of Franklin Watts, Inc. and Dieter Klein Associates
"Becky and the Wheels-and-Brake Boys" from *A Thief in the Village and Other Stories* by James Berry. Copyright © 1987 by James Berry. All rights reserved. Reprinted by permission.

Philomel Books
Greyling by Jane Yolen, text copyright © 1968 by Jane Yolen. Reprinted by permission of Philomel Books.

Random House, Inc.
"How to Read a Newspaper" from *Not That You Asked* by Andrew A. Rooney. Copyright © 1989 by Essay Productions, Inc. Reprinted by permission of Random House, Inc.

Marian Reiner
Haiku by Bashō and Soseki from *Cricket Songs: Japanese Haiku translated by Harry Behn.* © 1964 by Harry Behn. All rights reserved. Reprinted by permission of Marian Reiner.

Marian Reiner for Myra Cohn Livingston
Sea Songs by Myra Cohn Livingston. Holiday House. Copyright © 1986 by Myra Cohn Livingston. Reprinted by permission of Marian Reiner for the author.

Marian Reiner for Eve Merriam
Lines from "On Our Way" from *Catch a Little Rhyme* by Eve Merriam. Copyright © 1966 by Eve Merriam. All rights reserved. "Simile: Willow and Ginkgo" from *A Sky Full of Poems* by Eve Merriam. Copyright © 1964, 1970, 1973 by Eve Merriam. All rights reserved. Reprinted by permission of Marian Reiner for the author.

Charles Scribner's Sons, an Imprint of Macmillan Publishing Company
"Letter to Scottie" by F. Scott Fitzgerald, from *The Letters of F. Scott Fitzgerald,* edited by Andrew Turnbull. Copyright © 1963 by Frances Scott Fitzgerald Lanahan. Reprinted with permission of Charles Scribner's Sons, an Imprint of Macmillan Publishing Company.

Ian Serraillier
"Riddle" from *I'll Tell You a Tale* by Ian Serraillier. Copyright 1973, 1976 by Ian Seraillier. Reprinted by permission of the author.

Virginia Driving Hawk Sneve
"Thunder Butte" from *When Thunders Spoke* by Virginia Driving Hawk Sneve. Copyright 1974 by Virginia Driving Hawk Sneve. Reprinted by permission of the author.

Jesse Stuart Foundation
"Old Ben" from *Dawn of Remembered Spring* by Jesse Stuart. Copyright 1955, 1972 by Jesse Stuart. All rights reserved. Reprinted by permission of the Jesse Stuart Foundation, P.O. Box 391, Ashland, Kentucky 41114.

Third Woman Press
"Abuelito Who," by Sandra Cisneros from *My Wicked Wicked Ways.* Copyright 1987 by Sandra Cisneros, published by Third Woman Press, Berkeley, California. Reprinted by permission of Third Woman Press.

Rosemary A. Thurber
"The Tiger Who Would Be King" by James Thurber. Copyright © 1956 James Thurber. Copyright © 1984 Helen Thurber. From *Further Fables for Our Time,* published by Simon & Schuster. Reprinted by permission.

The Estate of Yoshiko Uchida
"The Wise Old Woman" by Yoshiko Uchida, from *The Sea of Gold and Other Tales From Japan,* adapted by Yoshiko Uchida. Copyright 1965 by Yoshiko Uchida. Reprinted by permission of the author's estate.

University of Hawaii
"The Riddling Youngster" is reprinted by permission of University of Hawaii Press, from *Hawaiian Legends of Tricksters and Riddlers* by Vivian L. Thompson. © 1969 by Vivian L. Thompson.

University Press of New England
"The Drive-In Movies" from *A Summer Life* by Gary Soto. Copyright 1990 by University Press of New England. Reprinted by permission of University Press of New England.

The Estate of Louis Untermeyer
"The Dog of Pompeii" from *Donkey of God* by Louis Untermeyer. Copyright 1932 by Harcourt Brace Jovanovich, Inc., and renewed 1960 by Louis Untermeyer. Reprinted by express permission of Laurence Starr Untermeyer for the estate.

Walker and Company
"Sarah Tops" from *The Key Word and Other Mysteries* by Isaac Asimov. Copyright © 1977 by Isaac Asimov. Reprinted by permission of Walker and Company.

Western Publishing Company, Inc.
"The Gorgon's Head" adapted from *The Gold Treasury of Myths and Legends* by Anne Terry White. © 1959 Western Publishing Company, Inc. Used by permission.

Wylie, Aitken and Stone
"How to Write a Poem About the Sky" from *Storyteller* by Leslie Marmon Silko. Copyright © 1981 by Leslie Marmon Silko. Reprinted by permission of Wylie, Aitken and Stone.

Yale University Press
"Days" from *Blue Smoke* by Karle Wilson Baker. Yale University Press, New Haven, 1919. Reprinted by permission of Yale University Press.

Note: Every effort has been made to locate the copyright owner of material reprinted in this book. Omissions brought to our attention will be corrected in subsequent printings.

ART CREDITS

Boldface numbers refer to the page on which the art is found.

Cover and Title Page: *Red Gate,* 1983, Elena Borstein, Collection of Glenn C. Janss; **v:** (top) *Portrait* (detail), Eloy Blanco, El Museo del Barrio; (bottom) *Mother, I Love to Ride,* 1992, Carlton Murrell, Courtesy of the artist, Photo by John Lei/Omni-Photo Communications, Inc.; **vi:** (top) *The Immortal* (detail), Chi-Fong Lei, Courtesy of the artist; **vii:** *Homework* (detail), 1946, Milton Avery, Thyssen-Bornemisza Collection; **viii:** (top) *Ezra Davenport* (detail), 1929, Oil on canvas, Clarence Holbrook Carter, Courtesy of the artist; (bottom) *Voices of the Clouds* (detail), Jessie Lee Geiszler, Courtesy of the artist; **ix:** *Double Dutch Series: Keeping Time* (detail), 1986, Tina Dunkley, Courtesy of the artist; **x:** (top) *Taketori Monogatari (The Bamboo Cutter or The Tale of the Shining Princess)* (detail), c. 1800, Japanese, The Metropolitan Museum of Art, Copyright © 1979 by The Metropolitan Museum of Art, Rogers Fund, 1921; (bottom) *Coyote,* Rufino Tamayo, Gift of the Print and Drawing Club, 1952.232, photograph © 1993 Art Institute of Chicago, All Rights Reserved; **xi:** (top) *Corn Kachina,* Clifford Brycelea, 21st Century Art Investment; (bottom) *Mandy's Sunhat* (detail), Robert Duncan, Courtesy of the artist; **xii:** *Bareback Riders,* W. H. Brown, National Gallery, Washington, D.C., Superstock Inc.; **4, 6, 9:** Illustrations from "Zlateh the Goat," 1966, Maurice Sendak, from *Zlateh the Goat and Other Stories* by Isaac Bashevis Singer, Harper & Row Publishers, Inc.; **13:** *Nuptial Dance,* Yaponi Araujo, Superstock; **29:** *Back Trail* (detail), 1988, Jon Van Zyle, © Copyright Jon Van Zyle, 1988, Courtesy of the artist; **31:** *Tommy* (detail), 1988, Bryan Moon, Courtesy of the artist; **49:** *Biking for Fun,* 1992, Carlton Murrell, Courtesy of the artist, Photo by John Lei/Omni-Photo Communications, Inc.; **50:** *Daddy's Girl,* 1992, Carlton Murrell, Courtesy of the artist, Photo by John Lei/Omni-Photo Communications, Inc.; **52:** *Mother, I Love to Ride,* 1992, Carlton Murrell, Courtesy of the artist, Photo by John Lei/Omni-Photo Communications, Inc.; **59:** *Women Reaching for the Moon,* 1946, Rufino Tamayo, The Cleveland Museum of Art, Gift of the Hanna Fund, 47.69; **62:** *The Dressmakers,* 1892, Edouard Vuillard, Josefowitz Collection; **67:** *Grandmother Reading to the Children,* Mary Cassatt, Superstock; **78:** *Portrait,* Eloy Blanco, El Museo del Barrio; **85:** *Pigeons,* John Sloan, American, 1871–1951, Oil on canvas, 26 × 32 in. (66 × 81.2 cm), The Hayden Collection, Courtesy, Museum of Fine Arts, Boston; **87:** *The Ice Eater,* Kathleen Cook, Courtesy of the artist; **93:** *The Water Lily Pond,* Claude Monet, National Gallery, London, Superstock; **94:** *Rudyard Kipling* (detail), 1899, P. Burne-Jones, By courtesy of the National Portrait Gallery, London; **95:** *Mates,* Al Agnew, Courtesy of the artist; **99:** *Akela the Lone Wolf,* 1913, Illustration by Maurice and Edward Detmold from *The Jungle Book* by Rudyard Kipling, The Century Company, The Central Children's Room, Donnell Library Center, The New York Public Library; **100:** *The Council Rock,* 1913, Illustration by Maurice and Edward Detmold from *The Jungle Book* by Rudyard Kipling, The Century Company, The Central Children's Room, Donnell Library Center, The New York Public Library; **103:** *Mowgli and Bagheera,* 1913, Illustration by Maurice and Edward Detmold from *The Jungle Book* by Rudyard Kipling, The Century Company, The Central Children's Room, Donnell Library Center, The New York Public Library; **106:** *Tiger Searching for His Prey,* Antoine Louis Barye, Cabinets des Dessins, Louvre, Giraudon/Art Resource; **118:** Mosaic of Dog, Naples, National Museum, Pompeii, Italy, Scala/Art Resource, New York; **128:** Indian *Coup* Stick, Shelburne Museum, Shelburne, Vermont; **133:** *Heliotropes,* Marc Chagall, Superstock © 1993 ARS, New York/ADAGP, Paris; **136:** *The Grotto of Chang Tao-ling (Chang kung tung),* left side (detail #2), Shih-t'ao, Ch'ing Dynasty, Handscroll, The Metropolitan Museum of Art, Copyright © by The Metropolitan Museum of Art, Purchase, The Dillon Fund Gift, 1982; **139:** *The Immortal,* 1990, Chi-Fong Lei, Courtesy of the artist; **144:** *My Brother,* 1942, Guayasamin (Oswaldo Guayasamin Calero), Oil on wood, $15\frac{7}{8} \times 12\frac{3}{4}$ in., Collection, The Museum of Modern Art, New York, Inter-American Fund; **152:** *Walk in the Country,* Javran, Superstock; **155:** *Harvesting the Fruit Crop,* Javran, Superstock; **174:** *Birds in the Sky,* 1978, Joseph Raffael, Collection of Mrs. Glenn C. Janss; **187:** *New Shoes for H,* 1973–1974, Don Eddy, The Cleveland Museum of Art, Purchased with a grant from the National Endowment for the Arts and matched by gifts from members of The Cleveland Society for Contemporary Art, 74.53; **200:** *Evening at the Met,* 1980, David Hockney, ESM, Art Resource, New York; **252:** *Bathers on a Beach,* 1915, Walt Kuhn, Thyssen-Bornemisza Collection, Art Resource, New York; **257:** *El Auto Cinema,* 1985, Roberto Gil de Montes, Oil on wood, Courtesy of Jan Baum Gallery, Collection of Patricia Storace; **263:** Noah Webster writing his dictionary: engraved title page of a 19th-century edition of *Webster's Dictionary of the English Language,* The Granger Collection, New York; **264:** Title page of the first known edition of Noah Webster's speller, *The American Spelling Book,* published in 1788, The Granger Collection, New York; **267:** *Map,* 1961, Jasper Johns, Oil on canvas, 6 ft 6 in. × 10 ft $3\frac{1}{8}$ in. (198.2 × 314.7 cm), Collection, The Museum of Modern Art, New York, Gift of Mr. and Mrs. Robert C. Scull, Photograph © 1992, The Museum of Modern Art; **270:** *Thomas Raeburn White,* 1940, Franklin Watkins, Collection of White and Williams, Philadelphia, Photo by Will Brown; **289:** *The Young Routy at Celeyran,* 1882, Henri Toulouse-Lautrec, Musée Toulouse-Lautrec, Giraudon/Art Resource, New York; **293:** *Nancy H. Lincoln,* Lloyd Ostendorf, Lincoln Boyhood National Memorial; **296:** *Peculiarsome Abe,* N. C. Wyeth, Free Library of Philadelphia; **303:** *Arch Street Ferry, Philadelphia,* 1800, William and Thomas Birch, Rare Book Department, Free Library of Philadelphia; **305:** *H. M. Brig* Observer *and American Privateer* Jack *off Halifax Harbour,* N.S., 29th of May, 1782, MacPherson Collection, Culver Pictures, Inc.; **307:** *Interior of the British Prison Ship* Jersey, 19th-century colored engraving, The Granger Collection, New York; **309:** *The Prison Ship* Jersey, Culver Pictures, Inc.; **310:** *James Forten,* Historical Society of Pennsylvania; **322:** *Homework,* 1946, Milton Avery, Thyssen-Bornemisza Collection, Art Resource, New York; **329:** *The Window,* Pierre Bonnard, The Tate Gallery, London, Art Resource, New York; **330:** *F. Scott Fitzgerald* (detail), David Silvette, The National Portrait Gallery, Smithsonian Institution, Washington, D.C., Art Resource, New York; **334:** *The Ever-Changing Color of the Seven Yei's* (detail), 1986, Baje Whitethorne, Sr., Courtesy of the artist, Photo by Wanda A. Green; **345:** *Laurence Typing,* Fairfield Porter, Parrish Art Museum, Southampton, New York, Photo by Richard P. Meyer, Gift of the Estate of Fairfield Porter; **349:** *The Anglers,* 1908, Henri Rousseau, Musée de l'Orangerie, Paris, Superstock; **362:** Detail from *The Thread that Runs So True* by Jesse Stuart, © Copyrighted by the Jesse Stuart Foundation, 1986; **365:** *Black Rat Snake,* Sy Barlowe, Courtesy of the artist; **379:** *The Artist's Daughter,* 1927, Frederick Carl Frieseke, The Brooklyn Museum, Gift of Mrs. Cornelius Zabriskie; **381:** *Puppet,* Paul Klee, Photo by Adriano Heitmann; **382:** *Cat and Bird,* 1928, Paul Klee, Oil and ink on gessoed canvas, Mounted on wood, 15 × 21 in., Collection, The Museum of Modern Art, New York, Sidney and Harriet Janis Collection Fund and gift of Suzy Prudden and Joan H. Meijer in memory of F. H. Hirschland; **393:** *The Critic,* After the original Japanese, *The Inland Printer,* Free Library of Philadelphia, Scala/Art Resource, New York; **415:** *Fugitive Slaves Escaping from Eastern Shore of Maryland before the Civil War,* 1872, Colored engraving, The Granger Collection, New York; **422:** *The Legend of the White Deer,* Tamas Galambos, Private Collection, Bridgeman Art Library, London, Superstock Inc.; **427:** *Ezra Davenport* (detail), 1929, Clarence Holbrook Carter, Oil on canvas, Courtesy of the artist; **429:** *Laurence at the Piano,* 1953, Fairfield Porter, Courtesy of Hirschl & Adler Modern, New York, Photo by © Zindman/Fremont; **432:** *Geese in Flight,* Roy Mason, From the collection of the John L. Wehle Gallery of Sporting Art, Genesee Country Museum, Mumford, New York, Photo by John Danicic; **434:** *Before the Wind,* 1983, Sheila Gardner, Collection of Mrs. Glenn C. Janss; **443:** "Esbjorn," 1918 illustration by Carl Larsson, reprinted by permission of G. P. Putnam's Sons, from *A Family* by Carl Larsson and Lennart Rudstrom, Copyright © 1979 by Bonnier Juniorforlag AB; **445:** *Dream Safari,* Marcy Cook, Student, Highlands Ranch, Colorado, From the 1991–1992 Crayola Dream-Makers Collection, Property of Binney & Smith, Inc., Reprinted with permission; **451:** *At Least for Now,* Illustration from *The Third Story Cat,* Leslie Baker, Courtesy of the artist; **457:** *Voices of the Clouds,* Jessie Lee Geiszler, Courtesy of the artist; **458:** *Langston Hughes* (detail), c. 1925, Winold Reiss, The National Portrait Gallery, Smithsonian Institution, Gift of W. Tjark Reiss, in memory of his father, Winold Reiss, Art Resource, New York; **460:** *Rainy Night,* 1930, Charles Burchfield, San Diego Museum of Art; **464:** *William Shakespeare* (detail), Artist unknown, By courtesy of the National Portrait Gallery, London; *Self-Portrait* (detail), 1958, E. E. Cummings, The National Portrait Gallery, Smithsonian Institution, Washington, D.C., Art Resource, New York; **470:** *Witch and Goblins,* from *The Legend of Sleepy Hollow* by Washington Irving, Arthur Rackham, David McKay Company, The New York Public Library; **472:** *Carl Sandburg* (detail), 1951, Emerson C. Burkhart, The National Portrait Gallery, Smithsonian Institution, Washington, D.C., Art Resource, New York; **481:** *Forest Scene,* Marck Frueh, Sal Barracca and Associates; **483, 485, 486:** Illustrations from *Alice Through the Looking Glass* by Lewis Carroll, John Tenniel, Photos by John Lei/Omni-Photo Communications, Inc.; **494:** *Emily Dickinson,* The Granger Collection, New York; **497:** *Reflets de Soleil sur L'eau (Reflections of Sun on the Water),* 1906, André Derain, Musée de l'Annonciade, Saint-Tropez, France; **502:** *Frog* (detail), 1814, Meika Gafu, Reproduced by Courtesy of the Trustees of the British Museum; **503:** *Frog,* 1814, Meika Gafu, Reproduced by Courtesy of the Trustees of the British Museum; **505:** *After the Shower,* John Atkinson Grimshaw, Christopher Wood Gallery, Bridgeman Art Library, London, Superstock Inc.; **509:** *Little Willie,* Raymond Lark, Serigraph, Courtesy of Edward Smith & Company; **510:** *The Wave,* Marsden Hartley, Worchester Art Museum, Worchester, Massachusetts; **512:** *The Calm After the Storm;* Edward Moran, Private Collection, Superstock; **513:** *Good Sailing,* Montague Dawson, Superstock; **522:** *Double Dutch Series: Keeping Time,* 1986, Tina Dunkley, Courtesy of the artist; **527:** *Chuck and Louise,* Mary Lake-Thompson, Courtesy of the artist; **538:** *Ta Matete,* 1892, Paul Gauguin, Musée Bale, Giraudon/Art Resource, New York; **549:** *Corn Kachina,* Clifford Brycelea, 21st Century Art Investment; **550, 552:** *Coyote* (detail), Rufino Tamayo, Gift of the Print and Drawing Club, 1952.232, photograph © 1993 Art Institute of Chicago, All Rights Reserved; **556:** *Turtle and Rocks* (detail), from *Mojave* by Diane Siebert, 1988, Wendell Minor, Artwork copyright 1988 by Wendell Minor, HarperCollins, Publisher; **558:** *Turtle and Rocks,* from *Mojave* by Diane Siebert, 1988, Wendell Minor, Artwork copyright 1988 by Wendell Minor, HarperCollins, Publisher; **562:** *Jungle Scene,* Painting by Robert Giusti; **564:** *Caribbean Scene with Flamingo,* © Wilson McLean; **569:** *The Indigo Snake,* 1976, Romare Bearden, Freedom Place Collection, Photo by Alex Jamison; Courtesy of the Estate of Romare Bearden; **572:** *Mountainous Landscape with Sailboat,* Chi-Fong Lei, Courtesy of the artist; **574:** *Two Buddhist Saints* (detail), Unknown artist, Lizzadro Museum of Lapidary Art, Elmhurst, Illinois; **579:** *The Road to Shu,* c. 1780–1781, Matsumura Goshun (Gekkei), Japanese, Edo period, 1752–1811, Ink and color on silk, Hanging scroll, $50\frac{5}{8} \times 19\frac{3}{4}$ in. (128.6 × 50.2 cm), The University of Michigan Museum of Art, Margaret Watson Parker Art Collection, 1970/2.152; **581:** *Taketori Monogatari, The Bamboo Cutter or The Tale of the Shining Princess,* c. 1800, Japanese, The Metropolitan Museum of Art, Rogers Fund, 1921, Copyright © 1979 by The Metropolitan Museum of Art (21.174.1); **586:** *Mahana Mao,* 1898, Paul Gauguin, Art Museum of Ateneum, Helsinki, Bridgeman Art Library, London, Superstock Inc.; **589:** *Matamoe,* Paul Gauguin, The Pushkin Museum of Fine Arts, Moscow, Photo by John Lei/Omni-Photo Communications, Inc.; **591:** *Tahitian Landscape,* 1891, Paul Gauguin, The Minneapolis Institute of Arts, The Julius C. Eliel Memorial Fund (49.10); **597:** *The Turtle,* Alain Thomas, Superstock; **600:** *Coyote and Moon,* from *Mojave* by Diane Siebert, Wendell Minor, 1988, Artwork copyright © 1988 by Wendell Minor, HarperCollins, Publisher; **602:** *Mouse,* from *Mojave* by Diane Siebert, Wendell Minor, 1988, Artwork copyright © 1988 by Wendell Minor, HarperCollins, Publisher; **606:** *Lion with Landscape,* 1855, A. J. Taylor, Shelburne Museum, Shelburne, Vermont; **610:** Staff with seated male figure atop (detail), Dogon or Bozo (African, Mali), Bronze metalwork, The Metropolitan Museum of Art, Edith Perry Chapman Fund, 1975, Copyright © 1985 by The Metropolitan Museum of Art (1975.306); **612, 613:** Staff with seated male figure atop, Dogon or Bozo (African, Mali), Bronze metalwork, The Metropolitan Museum of Art, Edith Perry Chapman Fund, 1975, Copyright © 1985 by The Metropolitan Museum of Art (1975.306); **617:** *Tiger,* 1940, Morris Hirshfield, Oil on canvas, $28 \times 39\frac{7}{8}$ in., Collection, Museum of Modern Art, New York, Abby Aldrich Rockefeller Fund; **621:** *The Chariot of Apollo,* Odilon Redon, Louvre, Paris, Giraudon/Art Resource, New York; **622:** *Arachne* (detail), Arvis Stewart, Reprinted with the permission of Macmillan Publishing Company from *The Macmillan Book of Greek Gods and Heroes* by Alice Low, illustrated by Arvis Stewart. Copyright © 1985 by Macmillan Publishing Company; **624:** *Arachne,* Arvis Stewart, Reprinted with the permission of Macmillan Publishing Company from *The Macmillan Book of Greek Gods and Heroes* by Alice Low, illustrated by Arvis Stewart. Copyright © 1985 by Macmillan Publishing Company; **628:** *Orpheus* (detail), Arvis Stewart, Reprinted with permission of Macmillan Publishing Company from *The Macmillan Book of Greek Gods and Heroes* by Alice

Low, illustrated by Arvis Stewart. Copyright © 1985 by Macmillan Publishing Company; **630:** *Orpheus,* Arvis Stewart, Reprinted with permission of Macmillan Publishing Company from *The Macmillan Book of Greek Gods and Heroes* by Alice Low, illustrated by Arvis Stewart. Copyright © 1985 by Macmillan Publishing Company; **640:** Illustration from *Iduna and the Magic Apples* (detail) by Marianna Mayer, Illustration copyright 1988 by Laszlo Gal, Reprinted by permission of Macmillan Publishing Company, Photo by John Lei/Omni-Photo Communications, Inc.; **642, 644, 648:** Illustrations from *Iduna and the Magic Apples* by Marianna Mayer, Illustration copyright 1988 by Laszlo Gal, Reprinted by permission of Macmillan Publishing Company, Photo by John Lei/Omni-Photo Communications, Inc.; **655, 658:** Illustrations from *Mufaro's Beautiful Daughters* by John Steptoe, Copyright © 1987 by John Steptoe, Copyright © by permission of Lothrop, Lee & Shepard Books, a Division of William Morrow & Company, Inc., with the approval of the Estate of John Steptoe; **663:** *The Procession of the Trojan Horse into Troy,* G. D. Tiepolo, The Granger Collection, New York; **670:** *Sun, Manana, Monhegan,* Rockwell Kent, Bowdoin College Museum of Art, Brunswick, Maine, Museum Purchase, Anonymous Gift, Courtesy of the Rockwell Kent Legacies; **673:** *Scene at Houghton,* Winslow Homer, c. 1878, Hirshhorn Museum and Sculpture Garden, Washington, D.C., Art Resource, New York; **676:** *Victor's Pride* (detail), JoAnn Wold, Courtesy of Artique, Ltd.; **680:** *Mandy's Sunhat,* Robert Duncan, Courtesy of the artist; **684:** *In the Woods,* 1860, William Trost Richards, Bowdoin College Museum of Art, Brunswick, Maine, Gift of the Misses Mary T. and Jane Masch; **694:** *Path in the Woods in Summer,* 1877, Camille Pissarro, Musée d'Orsay, Paris, © photo R. M. N.; **696:** *Making Pea Trellises,* 1887, Camille Pissarro, Musée de Faure, Aix-les-Bains, France, Photo by John Lei/Omni-Photo Communications, Inc.; **699:** *The Reaper,* Winslow Homer, Art Resource, New York; **703:** *Summer Night,* 1886, Eilif Peterssen, 133 × 151 cm., Nasjonalgalleriet, Oslo, Norway; **711:** *Green and Gold,* Ogden M. Pleissner, Shelburne Museum, Shelburne, Vermont; **713:** *The Boatman,* 1891, Winslow Homer, The Brooklyn Museum, Bequest of Mrs. Charles S. Homer, 38.68; **718:** *Country Road,* Alfred Morang, Collection of Mr. and Mrs. Graeme Gilfillan; **726:** *Landscape—Sunset on Long Island,* c. 1856, William Hart, National Academy of Design, New York City; **728:** *On the Fence,* WInslow Homer, Superstock; **732:** *Moonlight,* 1893, George Innes, The Fine Arts Museums of San Francisco, Mildred Anna Williams Collection (1942.22); **736:** *Fourth Avenue* (detail), 1943, Byron Birdsall, Courtesy of Artique, Ltd.

PHOTOGRAPH CREDITS

2: Courtesy of Elizabeth Thompson; **11:** Thomas Victor; **14:** UPI/Bettmann Newsphotos; **24:** The Bettmann Archive; **34:** Jason Stemple; **40:** Thomas Victor; **41:** R. Sheridan, Neg. #K13056, Courtesy Department of Library Services, American Museum of Natural History; **43:** Catherine Ursillo/Photo Researchers, Inc.; **46:** Camera Press/Globe Photos; **60:** Viking Kestrel; **76:** Ruben Guzman; **110:** Franklin Wing/New York Public Library; **113, 116:** Scala/Art Resource, New York; **123:** Jack Parsons/Omni-Photo Communications, Inc.; **126:** Bob Shaw/The Stock Market; **134:** Rick Browne; **142:** Charles Barry; **150:** Alexander Limonte; **158:** George August; **168:** Michael Cope; **170:** Jack Parsons/Omni-Photo Communications, Inc.; **173:** Roy Morsch/The Stock Market; **182:** Courtesy of Kristen Currise; **190:** Thomas Victor; **192:** Rex Joseph; **193:** David Pollack/The Stock Market; **198:** Rex Joseph; **204:** Sonya Friedman; **244:** Rex Joseph; **245:** James Phillips; **250:** Rex Joseph; **254:** Courtesy of Nicole Dietz; **258:** Dianne Trejo; **262:** Sygma Photo News; **268:** AP/Wide World Photos; **272:** Andree Abecassis/The Stock Market; **273:** Rex Joseph; **274:** Pat Hill; **283:** Ohioana Library Association; **290:** *Russell Freedman,* Photograph by Charles Osgood, Copyrighted May 23, 1988, Chicago Tribune Company, All rights reserved, Used with permission; **293:** (center) Lincoln Boyhood National Memorial; (right) Lincoln Boyhood National Memorial, Photo by John Lei/Omni-Photo Communications, Inc.; **312:** Mark Twain Memorial, Hartford, Connecticut, 96#1; **314:** Mark Twain Memorial, Hartford, Connecticut, (SLC and FanGos #5); **318:** Margaret Miller; **330:** (top) Culver Pictures, Inc.; (center) Religious News Service; **336:** Rex Joseph; **339:** Culver Pictures, Inc.; **342:** Jonette Novak; **368:** New York Public Library Picture Collection; **371:** Lawrence Migdale/Photo Researchers, Inc.; **373:** Lawrence Migdale/Photo Researchers, Inc.; **387:** Lloyd Pearson/DPI; **390:** AP/Wide World Photos; **396:** Ellan Young Photography; **397:** Carol Hughes/Bruce Coleman, Inc.; **398:** X. Gillett/Animals Animals/Earth Scenes; **400:** Jeff Simon/Bruce Coleman, Inc.; **402:** Wil Blanche/Omni-Photo Communications, Inc.; **403:** Ken Karp/Omni-Photo Communications, Inc.; **406:** Courtesy of Justin Vafa Williams; **408:** Guido Alberto Rossi/The Image Bank; **411:** Edmund Appel/Photo Researchers, Inc.; **412:** Photo by Carole Patterson; **414, 420:** Rex Joseph; **424:** Courtesy of Charles Smith; **426:** Ruben Guzman; **430:** (top) Don Lewis Photography; (center) Dmitri Kessel/*Life* Magazine, © Time Warner, Inc.; (bottom) AP/Wide World Photos; **438:** (top) Thomas Victor; (center) Courtesy of Charlotte Pomerantz; (bottom) Thomas Garland Tinsley/Fay Foto Service, Inc.; **441:** JAWS, © By Universal City Studios, Inc., Courtesy of MCA Publishing Rights, A division of MCA, Inc.; **446:** (top) James Salzano; (bottom) Temple Studio; **448:** Debra P. Hershkowitz/Bruce Coleman, Inc.; **449:** S. Dasher/Animals Animals/Earth Scenes; **452:** (bottom) Thomas Victor; **467:** Dr. Ivan Polunin/Bruce Coleman, Inc.; **472:** Isidro Rodriguez; **476:** Janeart, LTD/The Image Bank; **478:** (bottom) Courtesy of The Huntington Library, San Marino, California; **482:** New York Public Library Picture Collection; **488:** Virginia Hamilton; **494:** (top) New York Public Library Picture Collection; **498:** Jen & Des Bartlett/Bruce Coleman Inc.; **506:** (top) Camera Press/Globe Photos; (bottom) Marilyn Sanders; **516:** (top) AP/Wide World Photos; (center) Gregory Robertson; (bottom) AP/Wide World Photos; **526:** Courtesy of Markus Putnam; **529:** The Granger Collection, New York; **530:** Rex Joseph; **531:** Stan Tess/The Stock Market; **536:** Rex Joseph; **542:** Courtesy of Adine Le; **616:** UPI/Bettmann Newsphotos; **652:** Courtesy of Dorothulia Davis; **660:** James Ropiequet Schmidt; **662, 668:** Rex Joseph; **674:** Thomas Victor; **746:** Rex Joseph.